A STATE AT ANY COST

A STATE AT ANY COST

THE LIFE OF DAVID BEN-GURION

❖

TOM SEGEV

Translated from the Hebrew by Haim Watzman

B
BEN-GURION
SEG

FARRAR, STRAUS AND GIROUX | NEW YORK

Farrar, Straus and Giroux
120 Broadway, New York 10271

Grateful acknowledgment is made for permission to reprint the following material:
Cartoon on page 15: Illustration by the cartoonist Yosef Bass, courtesy of the heirs of his estate:
Yona Spiegelman, Yael Chen, Rafael Bass.
Cartoon on page 363: Illustration by the cartoonist Dosh (Kariel Gardosh), originally
published in *Ma'ariv*, November 13, 1964, courtesy of the Gardosh family.

Library of Congress Cataloging-in-Publication Data
Names: Segev, Tom, 1945– author. | Watzman, Haim, translator.
Title: A state at any cost : the life of David Ben-Gurion / Tom Segev ; translated from the
  Hebrew by Haim Watzman.
Other titles: Medinah be-khol meòhir. English
Description: First American edition. | New York : Farrar, Straus and Giroux, 2019. | "Originally
  published in Hebrew in 2018 by Keter Books, Israel." | Includes bibliographical
  references and index.
Identifiers: LCCN 2019000371 | ISBN 9780374112646 (hardcover)
Subjects: LCSH: Ben-Gurion, David, 1886–1973. | Prime ministers—Israel—Biography. |
  Israel—History.
Classification: LCC DS125.3.B37 S4413 2019 | DDC 956.9405/2092 [B]—dc23
LC record available at https://lccn.loc.gov/2019000371

Designed by Richard Oriolo

Our books may be purchased in bulk for promotional, educational, or business use.
Please contact your local bookseller or the Macmillan Corporate and Premium
Sales Department at 1-800-221-7945, extension 5442, or by e-mail at
MacmillanSpecialMarkets@macmillan.com.

www.fsgbooks.com
www.twitter.com/fsgbooks • www.facebook.com/fsgbooks

1 3 5 7 9 10 8 6 4 2

For my grandchildren, Liya, Ben, Lior, and Amit
And their parents, Shira and Itay

C O N T E N T S

A STATE AT ANY COST

INTRODUCTION:
IN THE FOOTSTEPS
OF HISTORY

On a cold January day in 1940, David Ben-Gurion rode down to the Kalia Hotel by the Dead Sea, where, at the lowest land point on the globe, he devoted some thought to the way he would appear in the book that some future biographer would eventually write about him and his colleagues, founders of the State of Israel. He imagined a "young, intelligent, and good biographer." Obviously, that biographer would discern the founders' "weaknesses, flaws, and shortcomings": none of them had been "ministering angels and seraphs and cherubs," Ben-Gurion wrote. But would he be able also to respect them and grasp the historic significance of their achievements? Would he perhaps even realize how much he'd missed by coming to know them only after their deaths?[1] Ben-Gurion was often preoccupied with death.

Like national leaders in other countries, Ben-Gurion worked diligently to shape the historical narrative of his time and of himself. When Israel was ten years old, he imagined an archaeologist excavating the country's artifacts three thousand years hence. The archaeologist might uncover a chronicle of the War of Independence of 1948 and learn from it about Israel's victory. But what if he instead found scraps of newspapers from Egypt, Syria, Jordan, and Iraq, telling of an Arab victory? Who would the archaeologist of the year 4958 believe, Ben-Gurion wondered?[2]

Ben-Gurion's diaries, articles, books, letters, and speeches comprise millions of words; he spent many hours writing nearly every day. "Sometimes I'm amazed by how much I have written," he once remarked.[3] Much of what he wrote was aimed at gaining the sympathy of future generations. He also tried to influence what others would write. When Israel's Ministry of Defense decided to publish an official history of the 1948 war, Ben-Gurion demanded that the book underline his efforts to obtain the arms that made victory possible. "Guns didn't fall from heaven," he told the author. Of another book, written and edited by Israel Defense Forces (IDF) officers who were no great admirers of his, he wrote: "The editors desecrated the War of Independence and thousands of the fallen."[4]

An avid reader of biographies, he often tried to piece together the motives of their authors. "Plutarch apparently did not like Marius," Ben-Gurion wrote regarding one of the books he took with him to Kalia, "and did not stint at humiliating and vilifying him, but for all that was unable to obscure his admirable manly character."[5] Gaius Marius was a Roman general and statesman who could have aroused Ben-Gurion's interests because of the inner contradictions of his character, with its frequent and sudden upswings and downturns.

On a few occasions he cooperated with biographers who acclaimed him as the founder of Israel. But there were others as well. At the beginning of 1967, a controversy broke out over the entry devoted to him in the *Hebrew Encyclopedia*. The author was the work's editor in chief, Yeshayahu Leibowitz, a professor at the Hebrew University and an old adversary. "I think that [Ben-Gurion] is the biggest catastrophe that ever happened to the Jewish people and the State of Israel," Leibowitz told the daily newspaper *Ma'ariv*; the entry he wrote took this view. Ben-Gurion put on a show of equanimity. "I don't care what Professor Leibowitz wrote," he responded, "but I care what I do, whether it's good or bad." But, in fact, he was furious. "Leibowitz is consumed by hatred," he wrote to the encyclopedia's publisher; he was Gaius Marius and Leibowitz Plutarch. He was quite naturally pleased when, a few years later, a sculptor told him about plans to erect a "Pantheon" in Haifa that would display busts of the great men of the nation: statesmen, writers, artists, military leaders, scientists, athletes, and others. "I told him that I liked the idea," Ben-Gurion wrote. "But I'll say no more than that."[6]

According to Golda Meir: "It was our heartfelt prayer that this man enter history in all his splendor, and it is painful that that is not coming to pass. Sad for him and sad for us."[7] Biographers of Ben-Gurion find themselves confronted with a huge amount of archival material that can affect their evaluation of the man, for good and for bad. As a whole this material demonstrates Ben-Gurion's forcefulness, merits, and achievements, but also his limitations, weaknesses, and failures.

"Ben-Gurion was a man who did not change," said one of his acquaintances. From the start, he exhibited ideological devotion and awed those around him.[8] The Zionist dream was the quintessence of his identity and the core of his personality, and its fulfillment his greatest desire. "The revival demands human sacrifices of us," he wrote in Hebrew when he was eighteen years old. "And if we, the young people who suffer the pain of our nation's ruin, are not swift to sacrifice ourselves, we are lost."[9] He believed that to the end of his life. He saw himself, and was seen by others, as an incarnation of history. His thinking was systematic and methodical, and even when he contradicted himself, the impression was that his pronouncements reflected extended, profound, consistent, unwavering, and considered judgment. He presumed to know what to do in almost every situation.

He very much wanted to be a leader and aspired to everything that leadership offers: the realization of a dream that was for him self-fulfillment, responsibility, power, and a place in history. He frequently evoked the Bible and Jewish destiny, but realized that achieving the dream of a Jewish state required exhausting labor and tiny, often exasperating steps forward. Many shared his vision, but few of his colleagues were as addicted to politics as he was, and from such a young age. Few of them were as diligent as he, or as able to grasp details. These characteristics made him an indispensable leader, although not an omnipotent one.

The drama of his life included threatening Jewish capitalists in his Polish hometown with a pistol, spending hours in the basement of a bookstore in Oxford, herding sheep in the desert, imbibing the scent of power in the White House, and waiting for Lenin to appear in Moscow's Red Square. He engaged in politics, made fateful decisions, sent people into war, stood over the bodies of fallen paratroopers, was captivated by the magic of Niagara Falls, and sought peace under the oldest oak tree in Palestine. He wrote fine accounts of all these episodes, often revealing a poetic emotionalism that few associate with him.

But of all the thousands of images that record his life, none captures its essence and gives better expression to his personality than that filmed on Rothschild Boulevard in Tel Aviv on the afternoon of Friday, May 14, 1948. It shows a short man with a mane of white hair bounding out of an official-looking black Lincoln. His wife, Paula, who had gotten out of the car before him, precedes him toward the stairs leading up to the municipal art museum. A crowd surrounds the building. Ben-Gurion wears a dark suit and a tie held in place with a silver pin. In his left hand he bears a homburg and a thin briefcase is under his arm. He looks more like a seasoned attorney than a daring revolutionary. Upon exiting the car he slams its door shut. An anonymous young man in the uniform of a country that does not yet exist stands by the car, but seems to have trouble deciding what he ought to do. Ben-Gurion halts in front of the young man and suddenly arches his back and shoots his right hand to his forehead in an energetic and stately salute. For a second he seems to identify the confused boy with the heroes of Jewish history.

Sixty-two years old at the time, he looks older, and a bit roly-poly. A few minutes later, he would proclaim the establishment of the State of Israel and oversee the signing of its Declaration of Independence. He was soon to become the new country's first prime minister and to lead it through the challenges of its initial period, for close to fifteen years. He runs up the stairs as if to make sure that the historic moment would not slip away from him.

❖

The week before the declaration of the state had been a busy one. He'd worked hard, worried much, and slept little. He'd spent most of his time in the company of army commanders. Some of them were dissatisfied and even voiced political rebellion. The ongoing war for Palestine had begun half a year previously and taken a heavy toll. Jerusalem had long been under siege, with its approaches blocked; several Jewish settlements had been compelled to surrender to Arab forces. Some military operations had failed; there were already fifteen hundred Jewish dead, most of them soldiers.[10] Ben-Gurion jotted down a long list of questions that awaited his decision, among which was "Should the Arabs be expelled?"[11]

By this time, tens of thousands of Arabs from all over the country had become homeless. Many Arab houses in a number of cities, among them Haifa and Jaffa, stood empty. It was the first stage of the Nakba. Ben-Gurion had never been closer to achieving his life's goal—a Jewish majority in an independent state in Palestine.

The previous night he had worked on the final version of the Declaration of Independence. There had been several drafts. Moshe Sharett (then still Shertok), Israel's foreign minister–designate, had collated them into a single version. "I composed a perfect draft," Sharett later related. "I cast the Declaration in the form 'whereas this and whereas that and whereas the other thing,' and then came the conclusion: therefore!" He thought that such a structure created "inner suspense." But Ben-Gurion didn't want a rental contract—he wanted an impressive and powerful historical declaration that would ring for generations to come. He took it home and pretty much completely rewrote it. Sharett never forgave him.[12]

Ben-Gurion's version put an emphasis on the Zionist narrative of Jewish history. The first two sentences diminished the contribution of Diaspora Jewry: "The Land of Israel was the birthplace of the Jewish people. Here their spiritual, religious and political identity was shaped." Sharett's version had begun with the Jewish exile; Ben-Gurion's rewrite stressed the independence that had preceded the destruction. He underlined the identity of the Jews who had settled in Palestine at the beginning of the twentieth century, himself among them: "pioneers and *ma'apilim* [immigrants who entered Palestine in defiance of restrictive British legislation]." This closely tied the Zionist enterprise to the labor movement. Sharett had cited the United Nations resolution on Palestine of November 29, 1947, which called for the creation of Jewish and Arab states in Palestine. Ben-Gurion suppressed the fact that the resolution stipulated a partition of Palestine between the two peoples. The Declaration promised equal rights for all and a constitution. The new country was to be a "Jewish state," but no one really knew what that meant, Ben-Gurion included.

The ceremony was organized hastily, so that it could end before the Sabbath began. The whole thing was almost canceled at the last minute because of a disagreement over whether God should be mentioned in the text. The representatives of the religious parties insisted on it; several members of the left opposed it. Ben-Gurion persuaded everyone to agree to the words "Rock of Israel." The calligraphy could not be done in time for the ceremony, so the signatories inscribed their names on the bottom of a blank piece of parchment.[13] Ben-Gurion viewed the declaration as a step toward a time two thousand years in the past, reestablishing Hebrew independence. He had good reason for optimism in signing the document, but in his diary he wrote that he felt like a mourner among celebrants—the state had not yet been assured. "States are not served to peoples on golden platters," he said, using a Talmudic expression. Ben-Gurion could also put it in simpler words: "The State of Israel will be no picnic."[14] His pessimism was a defense against illusion. "I have discerned the worst case that can happen," he once said. "I have done that all these years. If it doesn't happen, that's fine, but you need to be prepared for the worst. A human being is not a rational creature; you don't know what forces are impelling him, what might arise at certain moments."[15] He expected the armies of the surrounding Arab countries to invade Israel in order to destroy it. He believed that the Israelis could win; he also believed in his ability to lead them to victory. And he believed that the cost would be worth it. He termed the establishment of the state "recompense for the slaughter of the millions" in the Holocaust.[16]

After the ceremony, he returned to the Red House, as military headquarters were called, not far from the beach. He was handed disturbing bulletins from several fronts. During the night he was woken twice, once to be told that President Harry Truman had recognized the state and once to be taken to a radio studio so that he could broadcast a speech to the United States. Egyptian planes appeared in Tel Aviv's skies during the broadcast and explosions could be heard. "At this moment they are bombing Tel Aviv," Ben-Gurion told America. When he went home, he wrote this in his diary: "People in pajamas and nightgowns peered out of every house, but there was no evidence of disproportional fear." He recalled his time in London during the Blitz, and seems to have expected that Tel Aviv would also live through its finest hour. Cognizant of the power of words to make history, he sought twenty years later to correct the impression that Tel Aviv's inhabitants were not sufficiently brave by inserting into the original diary entry the words "I felt: they will endure."[17]

He did not take credit for founding the state, justifiably so. Israel came into existence at the end of a process that had begun thirty years previously, when the British resolved to assist the Zionist movement in establishing a Jewish national home in Palestine. Ben-Gurion led this process for a generation, in particular during the decade preceding independence. He had been in politics for forty years, beginning at almost the moment that he arrived in Palestine. He was involved in nearly every aspect of its Jewish community's life. His first political article, published when he was twenty-four years old, placed him in the ranks of the struggle. From that point he strove to achieve and maintain a position of national leadership. Those who were his seniors, first and foremost Berl Katznelson, in addition to several possible rivals, died one after the other. The death of Ze'ev Jabotinsky, his great nemesis on the right, and the decline of Chaim Weizmann, president of the Zionist Organization, whose mantle as the senior Jewish statesman Ben-Gurion sought to inherit, left him almost unopposed in the worldwide Zionist movement as well.

He generally respected the basic rules of Israeli politics and tended to position himself in the center of the spectrum. His willingness to pay nearly any price to realize the Zionist vision was on occasion coupled with tactical concessions and pragmatic compromises. He was frequently criticized by colleagues, both those in the opposition and in the governing coalition; sometimes his demands were ignored and his proposals rejected. But, in general, they accepted his leadership. His party saw him as a political and national asset; sometimes his colleagues acted like schoolchildren bad-mouthing a teacher behind his back: "I speak against, but vote in favor, because I trust Ben-Gurion and don't want to take responsibility," one of his Cabinet ministers once said.[18]

Ben-Gurion made many public appearances, answered letters he received, and made himself available to many of those who sought him out, eccentrics and gadflies among them.[19] He generally wrote his speeches in advance, but was adept at delivering them in a way that made it look as if he were speaking extemporaneously. Many of his speeches went on for hours; his sentences were long and complex, more fitting for the eye than the ear. His shrill voice and small stature were detrimental to the impression he made. But the whiter his mane, the more Ben-Gurion became a symbol of proper and achievable Zionism.

"When I approach a concrete question—what to do today, tomorrow, I turn into a computing machine," he once said; at another opportunity he explained: "I approach all Zionist matters scientifically. I always ask in a rational way what can be done."[20] He likened himself to an engineer preparing to build a house. The motivation for building is "aesthetic, religious, and transcendental," he said, but when it is time to build, "you have to weigh and measure . . . The same is true with statecraft."[21] In practice, he was often swept up by powerful emotions that steered his actions and dictated his decisions. At times he astounded others with self-righteous eruptions and impulsive obstinacy.[22] Such outbursts could be spurred by mental distress that might cause him to lose control of himself. At other times he planned such outbursts in advance. He often took attempts to challenge his leadership as not just a personal insult but an attack on the national interest. In Ben-Gurion, Zionism and ego blended into a single entity. It was not easy to live in the country he led; Israelis were expected to place the needs of the collective before their individual expectations and desires. Every citizen was a soldier in the service of history, and Ben-Gurion was history's commander.

❖

Those who knew him, including his wife, Paula, generally agreed that "he doesn't understand people"; this may have been a tactful way of referring to his self-important egocentrism and his habit of irritably insulting and humiliating others. At times he was a vindictive, deceptive quibbler; on occasion he lied. He had no sense of humor. He was a bad loser and only rarely apologized. One acquaintance said that Ben-Gurion had no real interest in people themselves, only in how he could use them.[23]

His writings give the impression that he had little interest in the frivolous pursuits of everyday life, but, as often happens, that was not actually the case. Rachel Yanait Ben-Zvi, who also numbered among Israel's founders, left to posterity a heavily shrouded secret that she kept to herself for many years. It was unearthed only after her death by researchers at the Ben-Gurion Heritage Institute. Yanait was also staying at the Kalia Hotel that day in 1940, and she saw Ben-Gurion in the company of a young woman. Yanait knew him well; he frequently fell in love, she remarked.[24] It often seemed that he was more in love with love itself than with any specific woman.

Likewise, he was in love with his dream and feared parting from it. "The messianic era is more important than the Messiah," he said. "The minute the Messiah arrives he will cease to be the Messiah. When you can find the Messiah's address in the phone book, he's no longer the Messiah." At times Ben-Gurion seemed to want his dream to come true and to fear that it would with almost the same intensity. He wanted to achieve Zionism's goal and feared waking up into the routine life of the future.[25] He shared this rumination on the Messiah with a group of writers he summoned for a meeting. He had a tendency to think that his personal dream was one of the great existential questions faced by mankind.

One day, in September 1948, he took a break from directing the war to make a defense of Plato. It came in response to an article by Yechiel Halperin, a writer and journalist for the daily newspaper *Davar*. Halperin had claimed that Plato "saw nothing unjust in perpetuating slavery." In a letter, Ben-Gurion corrected him: Plato makes no mention of slavery in his *Republic*. "Yes, Plato was an aristocrat," he wrote, "and his political views were aristocratic, but his intention was an aristocracy in the simple and correct sense of the word, that is the rule of the superior and the good, or as he himself put it, the rule of philosophers, meaning people of absolute truth and absolute justice, who derive no benefit and no advantage from government, who do not even have a desire to govern, but must do so as a human duty."

Three weeks later, with the war's final battles still to be fought, he sent Halperin another letter, this one regarding Plato's *Laws*. He had always wanted to believe that this dialogue was a forgery, and was sorry when he learned that it was indeed by Plato. In contrast with the humanist spirit that infused the *Republic*, he felt, the Plato of the *Laws* viewed life almost like an inquisitor. He tried to explain to himself how that might have happened. "The two books were written at different stages of life," he wrote. "The *Republic* was written when Plato was about fifty years old, at the height of his literary and intellectual powers, and it is his best book, philosophically and artistically. The *Laws* was written in old age, when Plato was already eighty years old and his heart grown hard, his soul ruthless, and his mind angry." The same thing would happen to Ben-Gurion himself. In his eagerness to defend Plato he added, however: "I am not sure that slavery was the most abominable injustice of those times—it seems to me that wars were worse than slavery (and were also a cause of it), and this injustice remains today." That was also Plato's view, he added; he should be appreciated.[26] Ben-Gurion was incorrect—slavery is indeed mentioned in the *Republic*. But Plato's dialogue served him as a guidebook for state building. He placed a bust of Plato in his study, alongside busts of the Buddha and Moses.[27]

He sponsored a Bible study class in his home and promoted two concepts to characterize the State of Israel's moral character and its destiny and duty to itself and the world: the first was "chosen people," a term coming from the covenant between God and the people of Israel (Exodus 19:5–6); the second was the Jewish people's commitment to the principles of justice and peace that make it a "light to the nations," in the spirit of the prophets (Isaiah 49:6). He frequently spoke and wrote about these concepts. He largely saw them in terms of a title he chose for one of his articles on the subject: "Noblesse Oblige."[28] Behaving in a manner that would make Israel a "light to the nations" reflected the country's vulnerability and dependency on its supporters around the world. But he also made statements to the contrary. "What the gentiles say is less important than what the Jews do," he declared.[29] In practice, he generally gave considerable weight to the regard of other nations. Like most of his countrymen, he was a man of contradictions. He liked to characterize the Israelis with a quote from the Babylonian Talmud: "This nation is likened to dust and likened to the stars. When they decline, they decline to the dust, and when they rise, they rise to the stars."[30] It was a psychic structure that he largely shared, as he was very much aware. "If you were to peruse my diary using the methods of critical biblical scholarship . . . ," he wrote to Sharett, "you could prove that this diary was actually written by two different people living in two different periods." He had a capacity for sensitive and courageous self-examination and a willingness to undertake it; this, too, is part of what makes him so fascinating a figure.[31]

❖

Many people assisted me in the writing of this book; their names appear in the acknowledgments. It took more than five years to write, and during that time hardly a week went by when Ben-Gurion was not mentioned at least once in the Israeli media. On top of that, four other biographies of him appeared in Israel, along with a shelf of other books in which he is at the center.[32] A documentary film based on a previously unknown interview with Ben-Gurion drew large audiences. That is testimony to how much Israelis long for leadership with integrity—as well as the power and drama of Ben-Gurion's life, and the widespread urge to understand this enigmatic man.

PART I

THE ROAD TO POWER

❖

BEN-GURION: When I was a boy of three I knew that I would not live in the place I had been born. Neither did I want to learn the language of that country.

JOURNALIST: Mr. Ben-Gurion, at the age of three you already knew that?!

BEN-GURION: At the age of three I knew that I would not live in that country! From the time I was three! . . . And that is how all the Jews were. We knew that our land would not be the place we were living, but in the Land of Israel.[1]

"On the Road" (1947), as seen by Joseph Bass

· 1 ·

THE VOW

About forty-five miles west of Warsaw flows a small and picturesque river, the Płonka; it also runs through the town of Płońsk. On one of the last days of summer in 1903, three friends went to swim there. The oldest of them, Shmuel Fuchs, was almost nineteen years old. Shlomo Zemach had just celebrated his seventeenth birthday; he was a few months older than David Yosef Gruen, who would later take the name Ben-Gurion. The three of them spent a lot of time together, bound in an intimate friendship that began in their early adolescence. "We'd swim and speak Hebrew," Ben-Gurion related many years later.[1] Sometimes they were accompanied by another young man, older than they were, Shlomo Levkowitz.

Like many members of their generation, Jews and non-Jews, they were given to gloom and overcome with existential doubts, and they were all in love. Shlomo Levkowitz and Ben-Gurion were in love with the same girl; Shmuel Fuchs was in love with Shlomo Zemach's sister, and Zemach was in love with Fuchs's sister. Zemach and Ben-Gurion were also in love with Shmuel Fuchs. It was a tormented camaraderie, but it endured throughout their lives; Fuchs and Levkowitz, who in the meantime changed his name to Lavi, died before Ben-Gurion; Zemach died a year after him. For seventy years, Ben-Gurion and Zemach remained joined by bonds of love and envy, just as they were on that late summer day in 1903, on the banks of the Płonka.

They had taken along the latest issue of *Hatzefirah*, a Hebrew-language newspaper published in Warsaw. Reading it on the riverbank, they learned that the Zionist movement was seriously considering the establishment of a Jewish state in East Africa, instead of in Palestine. The idea of establishing at least a temporary shelter there for European Jewry was known as the Uganda plan. Theodor Herzl, the venerated founder of the world Zionist movement and its first leader, refused to reject the idea out of hand; after a bitter debate, the Zionist Congress, the movement's supreme body, decided by majority vote to send an exploratory delegation to the area. Dozens of Jews had been slaughtered a few months earlier in the city of Kishinev, then part of the Russian Empire. The willingness of many Zionists to consider the Uganda proposal grew out of their sense that the Jews of Russia urgently needed a refuge, even if it meant one in Africa. The three boys from Płońsk had closely followed the news from Kishinev. They felt humiliated and helpless, Lavi later wrote, "disheartened in both body and spirit."[2] But the three of them were shocked by the Uganda plan. Zionism, they felt, was betraying itself; they broke into tears. On the spot, their emotions rising and their bodies wet with river water, they took an oath to leave Poland and settle in Palestine. It was a seminal moment in their lives.

❖

It is almost certain that most of the people that Ben-Gurion and his youthful friends knew at that time identified themselves first as Jews rather than Poles. In the eight hundred years since Jews had settled in Poland, they had suffered from discrimination and persecution, but their numbers rose into the millions and they became one of the world's most important Jewish communities. They had solid economic and cultural foundations there, self-governing bodies, and a lively political discourse.[3] Jews first settled in Płońsk about four centuries before Ben-Gurion and his friends were born. In 1815 the town came under Russian imperial rule. All government officials, including policemen and judges, served the czar; some of these were Russians themselves. Children were required to learn Russian, and young men were drafted into the Imperial Army. But just as the town's Jews did not see themselves as Poles, neither did they see themselves as Russians.

When Ben-Gurion was ten years old, Płońsk had eight thousand inhabitants, more than half of them Jews. According to Ben-Gurion, he never encountered outright anti-Semitism there, and he saw no reason to fear a pogrom.[4] Years later, long after leaving, some of its former Jewish inhabitants remained proud of being Płońskers, but they were first and foremost Jews; they felt no need to define their Jewishness beyond that. It was a small and fairly insular community. Everyone knew everyone else, and about everyone else. Most of them engaged in trades and crafts; a few were wealthy.

Zemach was the son of a businessman; his family had numbered among the community's aristocracy for several generations. Fuchs's family was also well-off. But many of Płońsk's Jews lived in poverty and hardship. Levkowitz grew up in a dark alley where sewage flowed, among stinking muddy pits. When he was twelve, a cholera epidemic raged through the town. His father worked for the Zemach family, and he himself was an apprentice in a bakery. He had little schooling and Ben-Gurion described him as a "savage."[5] Levkowitz's low station seems not to have bothered Shlomo Zemach's father; he did not try to interfere with the friendship between the two. He did, however, forbid his son to visit David Gruen's home, and when the boy disobeyed, his father slapped him. "The Gruen family did not have a good name in Płońsk," Zemach wrote, and another Płońsker said that "their name was not spoken in the city, neither for good nor for ill. As if they had been condemned to oblivion."[6]

Ben-Gurion's father, Victor (Avigdor) Gruen, made a living providing a range of paralegal services. Most of his clients were Poles, many of them illiterate. He filled out forms, wrote requests, and arranged affairs with the authorities. He sometimes engaged in brokerage, arbitration, and conflict resolution. Zemach wrote that the Gruen family's income was low and unstable.

Not well-off, neither were they poor. They had a two-story wood-frame home in Goat Alley, which later became Wspolna Street; it led to the market square. Ben-Gurion's eldest brother and his family lived in an adjacent house; the two homes were separated by a small, fenced-in garden containing apple, pear, plum, and cherry trees. The complex had been the dowry of Ben-Gurion's mother, Sheindel; it lay just next to the Catholic church and the priest's garden.

Coming and going among inspectors and policemen, bureaucrats and judges, Gruen befriended them, sent them felicitations on their holidays, and consoled them when they mourned. He presumably also bribed them. Quite naturally, his own community looked askance. Gruen was not the only Jew in Płońsk who worked and traded with Christians, but unlike the others he did not "dress Jewish." Flaunting convention, he wore a short jacket, as opposed to the traditional long coat; he sometimes sported a top hat, which the Jews of Płońsk simply did not do. In the eyes of his neighbors, he was frivolous and clownish, and the gossip was that cards were played in the house. He had a hand in local politics, and sometimes got into fights.[7]

❖

Dubche, or Dovidel, as the boy was called at home, was born on October 16, 1886, the third of three sons; he had an older and a younger sister. The family's language was Yiddish, but they also heard a lot of Polish and Russian. A government school for Jews was established in the town a few years before Ben-Gurion's birth, but most of the town's Jews preferred to give their children a Jewish education. They thus sent their sons to a heder, a one-room school in the home of an instructor who kept the boys under his charge in his house throughout most of the day, teaching them to read and write in Hebrew and Yiddish, and, even more important, to study Torah and Talmud. Some children in Płońsk began school at the age of three; Ben-Gurion began when he was five. He attended several such schools, one of them a modern version where Hebrew was taught by a new immersion technique, "Hebrew in Hebrew." He also spent a few hours each day in the government school, as the law required.[8]

Shlomo Zemach had other teachers, with better pedigrees and higher tuition fees. He also studied history, geography, and Greek mythology. He remembered Ben-Gurion as a skinny kid, short and a bit sickly looking. Ben-Gurion himself recalled that he suffered frequent fainting spells. The doctor recommended spending the summer with his mother's family in one of the nearby villages, and it was there, he related, that he first came into contact with agriculture. Zemach and Levkowitz also spent time in these villages.[9]

"IN EVERY SENSE AN ADULT"

A few months after Ben-Gurion turned eleven, his mother again went into labor. The child was stillborn, and a few days later she died of blood poisoning. It was a terrible blow. "For many, many nights I saw my mother in my dreams and I asked her, Mother, why don't we see you? And she did not answer," he wrote when he was more than eighty. "There is no barrier at all between a child and his mother . . . ," he continued. "A son is always his mother's son, and when his mother dies, there is no replacement. It is not closeness, and more than love. It is identification. And something more than that. Because there is nothing like a mother's love. There can be only one mother, and she is everything. Moreover, if she dies, no person, no friend, no acquaintance, no lover can take her place. A void remains, an empty void, full of sorrow, longing, unending sorrow and longing. Who can take her place? Orphanhood, orphanhood . . ." Ben-Gurion frequently spoke and wrote of his mother in later years; on more than one occasion he remarked that her death had never ceased to anguish him, in his dreams as well, even though he had no memory of her face and no photograph of her remained. "The loss has not left my heart," he wrote many years after her death. Even though she gave birth eleven times, she cared for him as if he were her only child, he wrote. She was "a wellspring of love difficult for me to describe." He identified her with his Zionist faith: "The nation's foundation is the mother," he declared at a Cabinet meeting.[10] He may also have seen her image in the Land of Israel itself: "I suckled the dream of the Land of Israel along with my mother's milk," he wrote. When he demanded that Palestine be handed over to the Jews, he said: "The care of a child cannot be given to any woman, even an upright and fitting one. But every child can be placed in the hands of his mother."[11] Apparently he saw her before him once or twice while making decisions about the status of women in Israel. When he sought to appoint Golda Meir to his first government, he said: "Each of us owes a bit of thanks to his mother."[12] He said that his father had been both father and mother to him. "It is hard for me to forget being an orphan as a child," he wrote, "although I was blessed with a beloved father to whom I owe much for my education and learning, and he lived to the age of eighty-six, but there is nothing like a mother."

About two years after being widowed, Avigdor Gruen remarried. Ben-Gurion called his stepmother "aunt," *momeh* in Yiddish, just as other orphans did. When he mentioned her in his letters to his father, he took care to do so with all due respect. But when he opposed handing over children who had survived the Holocaust to adoption in Israel, he wrote: "Only exceptional people are capable of adoption; we all know what a stepmother is." As his biographer, Shabtai Teveth, wrote, he seems here to have been thinking back on his own life.[13] In any case, his mother's death shattered his childhood. Sometimes he seemingly sought to heighten the devastation of losing his mother by saying that she died when he was only ten.[14] He usually recalled a brief childhood and early maturation, without joy and without games, "except chess."

Some boys who did not have to work or learn a trade would spend their post–bar mitzvah days in a *beit midrash*, a religious seminary, where they studied with the help of teachers and on their own for several years until they married and had families, or even beyond that. Others were sent out of town to a gymnasium, as academic high schools were called in Central and Eastern Europe, and then on to higher studies. Ben-Gurion studied for a time at a *beit midrash* with Shlomo Zemach, where, Zemach claimed, he did not excel. "His brain did not grasp the abstract logical paths in those studies," Zemach wrote, adding that he himself had excelled at Talmud.[15] So Ben-Gurion was a boy orphaned of his mother, a stepson, shorter than his fellows, less gifted at his studies, who heard everywhere that his father was a dubious character. He coped with his childhood trauma as many do—he tweaked it. He often referred to his father as an "attorney," and termed him a "recognized leader of the town's Jews." He claimed never to have felt any inadequacy because of his short stature—his mother had been short as well, he noted. Ben-Gurion also liked to say that a doctor who examined him when he was five years old noted that his head was relatively large and that there was a bump on the back. The doctor deduced from this that the boy had been endowed with tremendous abilities and had a great future before him. That was another reason to leave his melancholy childhood behind him, as soon as he possibly could. "At the age of fourteen I felt myself in every sense an adult," he later said.[16]

As a matter of fact, by that time he was idle. He did not attend school and was not working. A biographer suggested that Ben-Gurion helped his father out, learning how to write requests, milling with the crowds along with him on the steps of courthouses, trying to rope in new clients. He read books and began keeping a diary. On Hanukah in 1900, he, Zemach, and Fuchs founded an organization they called Ezra, after the biblical scribe. Their goal was to promote the use of Hebrew in everyday life. At its height, Ezra numbered several dozen members; it lasted for about six years. It was Ben-Gurion's first public initiative.[17]

Ben-Gurion later recounted that his Zionist views took form when he was a toddler of three or five; once he claimed, "I was born a Zionist." He presumably was more accurate when he wrote that "when I still could not understand the substance of discussions and debates, I absorbed the hope of Zion that filled our house."[18] His father was one of the first Zionist activists in Płońsk, one of those who identified with a cluster of initiatives referred to collectively as Hovevei Zion. The movement's older followers had lived through the Spring of Nations, the national and political revolutions that swept through Europe in 1848. Hovevei Zion was the Jewish answer to the upsurge in national identity and hopes for national independence that swirled around the Jews of Europe. Its adherents identified themselves not just as believers in the Jewish religion, but as members of a Jewish nation. The members of these different societies tried to form an international organization, but Hovevei Zion was fundamentally a romantic and even religious, rather than a political, movement. Many promoted it as a response to the discrimination and persecution of Jews. Socialism was also making its way into the Jewish communities of the Russian Empire at this time. Some of the socialist groups promoted agricultural settlement in Palestine, organizing settlers to found farming communities there, and supporting them thereafter. It was the beginning of what would later be called "practical Zionism."[19]

Zionism was a movement founded in Europe, inspired by its culture, and embedded in its history. Zionism's nationalism, romanticism, liberalism, and socialism all came from that continent. In this sense, the history of the Zionist presence in Palestine belongs to European history.

"A TALL, HANDSOME MAN"

Avigdor Gruen had not yet thought of settling in Zion. In fact, once he became active in Hovevei Zion, he had much less incentive to leave Poland. His social isolation, which might have driven him to emigrate, largely ended thanks to his Zionist activity, which brought him into contact with people who had previously done their best not to be seen in his company. He hosted them in his home once a week for a meeting where, among other things, they together read the Hebrew newspapers *Hatzefirah* and *Hamelitz*. Ben-Gurion could not remember whether his grandfather had also been a member of the group, but recalled sitting on his grandfather's lap and being taught Hebrew—first syllables, then words, and finally complete sentences.[20]

About four months before Ben-Gurion's tenth birthday, *Hamelitz* made its first mention of a man named Theodor Herzl, the author of a new book just published in Vienna, *The Jewish State*. The item was very positive.[21] Word of Herzl quickly spread. Rumors ran through Płońsk that the Messiah had arrived. Ben-Gurion recalled that they spoke of "a tall, handsome man" with a black beard.[22] Herzl was not, in fact, tall, nor did he promise divine redemption. Furthermore, as opposed to Hovevei Zion, he did not believe in the efficacy of the settlement of individual Jews in Palestine. His aim was a full-fledged nation-state; to that end he founded a global organization that would seek Jewish independence by negotiating an agreement with the Ottoman Empire and the European powers. In other words, his was political, rather than practical, Zionism. Avigdor Gruen immediately became an enthusiastic supporter of Herzl's. So did a local shopkeeper named Simcha Isaac. The two of them founded a society they named Bnei Zion—Children of Zion. They began to collect "shekels," as membership dues in the Zionist movement were called, and to send donations to Palestine. In September 1900, the organization reported having two hundred members.*

❖

The Zionist activity in Płońsk attracted outside attention. *Hamelitz* covered a meeting held in Gruen's home. A pamphlet in Yiddish, written by the famous author Shalom Aleichem, was read out loud. Its title was "Why Do the Jews Need Their Own Country?" After the reading, the assembled sang Zionist songs.[23] Ben-Gurion could certainly have imbibed Zionism in his childhood. Unlike several of his friends, his road to Zionism did not require him to rebel against his father. In that sense it was easier for him.

The newspaper report also indicates that a Zionist gathering in Płońsk was an exceptional event. In fact, most of Poland's Jews, including those of Ben-Gurion's age cohort, were not Zionists. Ben-Gurion and his friends were thus exceptional, on the verge of eccentric. He stood out among them because he could speak a bit of Hebrew; his friends had trouble keeping up with him on this score. Zemach related that his own Hebrew sounded ludicrous at first. Levkowitz found it even harder—at that time, he was barely able to read and almost never wrote, in any language. Rather than speak Hebrew, he would communicate with his friends by means of gestures and facial expressions.[24] Fuchs's Hebrew was that of his sacred studies and the synagogue liturgy; everyday Hebrew was a foreign language for him. For the first time in his life, Ben-Gurion had an advantage over his friends.

One seminary allowed them to organize an evening class that included Hebrew lessons and lectures on Zionist subjects; the teenage Ben-Gurion gave talks on Zionism and culture. Once or twice they circulated a mimeographed pamphlet. Ben-Gurion published poems there. One day he traveled

---

* Shlomo Zemach alleged that Gruen "was in no hurry" to deposit the dues he collected in the organization's coffers. He would use the money for his household expenses and had trouble paying it back when asked. As a result, the organization decided to stop collecting shekels. Ben-Gurion later related that he had wanted to collect shekels from his classmates, but that the adults did not allow it. (Zemach 1983, p. 19; Ben-Gurion 1974b, p. 31; *Hatzefirah*, Sept. 14, 1900.)

to Warsaw to ask for the support of *Hatzefirah*'s editor, Nahum Sokolow. It was Ben-Gurion's first public initiative outside his hometown. *Hatzefirah* did not write anything about Ezra. Sokolow might well not have seen anything new about it.[25]

It was certainly not Ben-Gurion and his friends who woke Hebrew from its long sleep. A hundred years before, Poland was already one of the centers of a new European Hebrew-language literary culture. Organizations to promote the Hebrew language were already in existence in any number of places; in Płońsk, Ezra was preceded by thirty years by another such group.[26]

Yiddish continued to be the principal language of the town's Jews, but the boys of Ezra became adept at Hebrew and used it as a kind of secret argot for themselves. They wrote their letters in modern Hebrew, generally correct, sometimes even rich; their penmanship is adept.

"I THOUGHT I HAD ASCENDED TO HEAVEN"

The letters that the four friends wrote to each other after they parted, and the memoirs they later published, exude tormented adolescent angst; they felt trapped between the outgoing century and the new one. "My soul is not at peace," Ben-Gurion wrote. "I do not know why I am sometimes so sad, so dejected, and I feel a deep emptiness, great and looming in my heart . . . I have intense longing for something, I know not what."[27] Levkowitz also recalled "youthful yearning for an unclear unknown" and for "all that is distant." He felt a "towering thirst" to do a "great deed," and suffered from intense depression and anxiety. He was sick of life. Zemach was tormented with similar thoughts. "We wondered about life as death and death as life, not understanding much of these, but nevertheless absorbing something into us," he wrote in his memoirs. He wrote to Fuchs: "It is impossible to die and I am unable to live."[28]

Zemach was tall and handsome, with curly hair and a black mustache; he was a proud, conceited gossip. Along with other boys, he made fun of Levkowitz for his ignorance and even publicly humiliated his father in synagogue. He mocked "Mr. Avigdor," as he called Ben-Gurion's father, for making spelling mistakes in Russian.[29] According to Zemach, Fuchs was an "emotional," "delicate," and somewhat "passive" boy. "His character was overdelicate and there was something feminine in every mood of his, but this tenderness was pleasant and very attractive," he wrote.[30]

Fuchs did not make himself out to be as depressed as his friends, but he seems to have shared Levkowitz's longing for "all that is distant." In 1904 he went to London, leaving behind in Płońsk Zemach's sister, whom he loved. Zemach wrote to tell him that she sometimes asked about him. But mostly he wrote about his own love for Fuchs's sister, and his feelings for Fuchs himself. "I so miss you, so very much desire and crave to see you, my beloved friend. O, if I only had shaken your hand before you left, if I could only embrace you and bestow kisses on you." He once signed a letter with the parting phrase "Your brother embraces you with fierce love and kisses you."[31] Sometimes he patronized him. In London, Fuchs intended to study at a rabbinical college, but had trouble supporting himself. Zemach admonished him: "You have just crossed the threshold and now I'm already hearing dissatisfaction, resentment, and grievances . . . What did you think, that they would roll out a band to welcome you upon your arrival in London?" Zemach described his relations with Ben-Gurion at that time as close friendship. The two met daily, and according to Zemach, there were no secrets between them save one—he did not speak of his love for Fuchs's sister. He may well not have spoken of his love for Fuchs, either.

Ben-Gurion told Fuchs that he first fell in love at the age of twelve. "My love then was as soft as the buds of spring," he recounted poetically when he was eighteen, "and it grew in time and ignited like a flame—and last summer I learned that she loves me . . . I thought I had ascended to heaven."[32] When he first saw her, she was about ten years old, a student at the government school that he attended. Her name was Rachel Nelkin and she had black braids. This may well be the same girl who "very much captured" Levkowitz's heart as well.

Levkowitz was a tall, slender youth with a long nose and small eyes. "He's not handsome," Zemach wrote.[33] He was also very shy. He first caught sight of Rachel at the home of her stepfather, Simcha Isaac, who regularly convened Zionist meetings for young people in the back room of his store. "Sometimes I thought that those boys were not enthralled so much by Simcha Isaac as by his beautiful daughter," Levkowitz wrote.[34] For a long time, he lacked the courage to speak to her. He only spoke with her father, with great gravity. He secretly envied his friends, who were more successful than he, but he put on a pretense of insouciance. Yet he thought of her incessantly, day and night. In the end, he fashioned a scheme to encounter Rachel alone, but after lying in wait, when he found himself face-to-face with her, he blushed, turned his face away, and pretended he had not even noticed her presence. Afterward, he cursed himself and his idiocy. Levkowitz seems to have found life a heavier burden than his friends did. His bashfulness might have killed him had Zionism not taken his mind off his plight, he later wrote.[35]

He sometimes went to the Gruens' house, which he also described as "a center of Zionism." Coming from a poor neighborhood, he saw the Gruens as wealthy. He was drawn there by "a magic that he did not understand," but something also repelled him—specifically, Ben-Gurion's two sisters. Paralyzed in their presence, there too he put on a show of having come to talk about the Zionist future.[36] It was a particularly tough time to be a teenager. In Płońsk, social interactions between the sexes were still subject to very strict rules. When a boy and a girl were in love, Ben-Gurion related, a matchmaker could generally be called in to arrange things. As Levkowitz put it, "We boys sat over our pages of Talmud, studied, fantasized, and waited for a good match."[37] When it seemed to him that Ben-Gurion was winning Nelkin's love, Levkowitz was crushed.[38]

Zemach did not have that problem. One night, when he was eighteen, he had trouble falling asleep. He turned from side to side, then got dressed and opened his bedroom window. Looking into the window of the house across the street, he saw his neighbors' daughter, Shoshana, Shmuel Fuchs's sister. For the next hour the two sat at their windows and gazed at each other, as dawn broke. Zemach felt "huge excitement," as he wrote afterward to Fuchs. "If I didn't go insane back then [it must be because] I am solid iron . . . David Gruen told me that I had the look of a lunatic."

In the months that followed, he continued to share his infatuation with Fuchs. "I am so much in love that I am sometimes ashamed of myself," he wrote. He promised that he had never even considered touching her, and again quoted their mutual friend: "D. Gruen tells me that I am overly idealistic and that he cannot understand how I can be that way."[39]

Zemach's Zionism was more than a national-ideological aspiration—it was also a fledgling's longing to flee the nest, to spread his wings, and to go where he wished. Life in Płońsk seemed "banal" to him; he wanted to go to Odessa, to study science and foreign languages, including Arabic and Turkish, the languages spoken in Palestine. Then he would return to Płońsk, not in order "to sink again into the bog" but to take Shoshana and to settle in the Land of Israel. He dreamed of being a Hebrew writer.[40] In the meanwhile, youth afflicted him. "I am not happy, my fate is evil and bitter," he lamented. "When will I finally stop being subject to my parents and become my own man?"[41]

Other adolescents felt the same way, deeply troubling their parents. They felt that they were losing their children. When the girls took their daily walk through town, Zemach and his companions did their best to impress them. They'd loiter on the sidewalk on the other side of the street and speak Hebrew to each other, as loudly as they could. Zemach smoked. In photographs from this period the boys are bareheaded, eschewing the traditional cap, and are in the company of girls.[42] Ben-Gurion swaggered, so as to impress the beautiful Rachel Nelkin. Once he went out for a walk with the daughter of family friends from Warsaw. "It was not long before the entire town was at our heels," he related.[43] Parents had a hard time accepting such scandalous behavior, and many of them attributed it to Zionism.

"A GREAT PASSION FOR A FREE AND NATURAL LIFE"

In its first article on *The Jewish State*, *Hamelitz* declared that Herzl "will not find a path into the hearts of the God-fearing," with just a few exceptions.[44] Longing for the Land of Israel had always been a part of the Jewish religion. It fostered a dream of a return to the Holy Land, of *aliyah*, literally "ascent," as the book of Genesis puts it in its account of Abraham's wanderings. Yet the Zionists angered the vast majority of Orthodox leaders, in particular the ultra-Orthodox ones who termed themselves Haredim.* Avraham Gruen,

---

* The religious argument against Zionism is based on a Talmudic passage that speaks of two prohibitions that God imposed on the Jews of the Exile: they were not to storm the wall (which was generally understood to mean taking the initiative or using force to regain the Holy Land), or to rebel against the nations. At the same time, the gentiles were enjoined not to overly oppress the Jews. Known as the "three oaths" to which God swore the Jews and the gentiles, they were traditionally understood as mandating Jewish passivity. They were to

Ben-Gurion's eldest brother, wrote of a "huge civil war," including persecution and boycotts, that also "made it difficult to earn a living." Some rabbis forbade their followers to marry into Zionist families.

Zionism required its supporters to reconsider their Jewish identities and to position themselves between the values of Jewish tradition and a new Jewish nationalism. It was a revolutionary challenge. At the founding assembly of Ezra, the organization that Ben-Gurion and his friends founded, blows were traded with Haredim who tried to disrupt the event. "The opponents of Zionism viewed us as Satan himself," Zemach wrote.[45] But the Zionist movement did not keep religious Jews out. Most Jews, including most *maskilim* (modernizing, "enlightened" Jews) and Zionists, continued to define their Jewish identities in religious terms.

Ben-Gurion described his father as being of "free opinions." Indeed, Gruen complained that religious education in Płońsk had created a "generation of ignoramuses."[46] He sent his son to a modernized heder, where secular subjects were also taught. But he remained on close terms with his religion. Most likely he was not sorry when his Dubche suddenly, at the age of seven, began strictly observing the commandments. Nor did he object, when the boy was a bit older, to his school's stress on Talmud as the main subject of study. He *was* upset when, at the age of fourteen, his son stopped putting on tefillin, the phylacteries worn by Jews during the morning prayer service. Gruen himself attended services at the synagogue every morning, but appears bareheaded in photographs.[47] His Orthodox rivals branded him a *maskil*. The conflict between Płońsk's Haredim and early Zionists was in fact one among religious Jews who differed in the strictness of their observance and their lifestyles. To a large extent, it was a power struggle. Gruen complained that Haredi functionaries had taken over the community leadership and said that some of them had informed on him to the police, charging him with smuggling money out of the country. Ben-Gurion's relations with his father were generally good. His friends had to deal with greater challenges.

Shlomo Levkowitz and his father went through an extended confrontation that was extremely painful to both. Zemach knew fathers who declared their

---

await help from heaven rather than take matters into their own hands. (Salmon 1990, p. 51; Bacon 2001, 2, p. 453ff.; Zemach 1963a, p. 42ff.)

sons dead and observed mourning rituals for them after the sons adopted a Zionist lifestyle. "You cannot imagine the pain," he wrote to Fuchs.[48] The Zionist faith of a number of Ben-Gurion's friends thus required much more fortitude, and sometimes more courage, than Ben-Gurion himself had to display.

❖

Zionist culture was easily accessible in Płońsk. The town had a library run by a man named Lipa Taub. He functioned as Ezra's secretary, but the library preceded the organization.[49] Apparently it was there that Ben-Gurion found the books he read, some of them in Hebrew—he later recalled being infatuated with Bialik's poetry, and reading other poets and writers. Avraham Mapu's *Love of Zion*, published in 1853 and considered the first Hebrew novel, intensified Ben-Gurion's longing for the Land of Israel. Avraham Zinger's translation of *Uncle Tom's Cabin*, published in 1896, impelled his revulsion at slavery, subjugation, and dependence; both books made a huge impression on him. He also read in Russian, adopting vegetarianism for a while after reading Tolstoy's *Resurrection*. Zemach also read a great deal, as did other young people. All of them were enthusiastic admirers of a Ukrainian-born Jew named Micha Josef Berdichevsky.

"In my youth, I recall," Ben-Gurion later wrote, "Berdichevsky's articles were the ones that most made an impression on the young people in my town." Berdichevsky had a much greater impact than Asher Ginsberg, who wrote under the pseudonym Ahad Ha'am; the two writers were on opposite sides of numerous literary and political controversies. To these young people, Ahad Ha'am sounded like the voice of tradition and narrow horizons, dry and severe; it was the voice of an old man. Berdichevsky sounded young, rebellious, masculine, exciting: "We have no room to move! . . . Our time has come to find our way out into the open spaces," he wrote in a public letter to Ahad Ha'am. Ben-Gurion and his companions heard in Berdichevsky's writing a call to take their fate into their own hands and to make history.

They did not always correctly comprehend Berdichevsky's position on Zionism, but his voice was an expression of what they felt churning inside them. Levkowitz found in his works "the mood of the thoughts rising from the heart into the brain and returning to pound on a restless heart." Ben-Gurion found in them "a great passion for a free and natural life in the land of our fathers."[50] In Berdichevsky's writing, the young people seem to have found a refuge from adolescent despondency and an answer to the life questions that tormented them.

❖

They felt more and more constricted in Płońsk. "The Jewish town is empty-ing of substance," Zemach wrote. "Life in Płońsk became tedious and I sought a new life."[51] The world outside called out not only to him and his friends but also to many others. In the fifteen years that preceded World War I, about 1.7 million Jews emigrated from Eastern Europe, mostly for the United States, Britain, and Argentina. It was not a new phenomenon, but it was surging and becoming a huge wave. A third of the region's Jews left dur-ing this period.[52] The emigrants sent letters home, and sometimes returned for visits. They told exciting and fantastic stories about their new lives in other lands, where the twentieth century was in full swing. It was an American dream, as Herzl wrote: "America must conquer Europe, in the same way as large landed possessions absorb small ones."[53]

From its inception, the Zionist movement had marketed itself as an agent of progress and had promised to bring modern technology to Palestine, in-cluding "roads and railroads, electric lines, the telephone, and water pipes."[54] Ben-Gurion and his friends could thus see Zionism as the doorway into the wonderful world that began to appear before their eyes at the beginning of the new century. In the spring of 1904, Gruen permitted his son to move to Warsaw. There Ben-Gurion could, for the first time, turn on an electric light, attend a moving picture show, and see an automobile for the first time in his life. There were telephones as well. "Technical science had given wings to the rhythm of life," Stefan Zweig wrote.[55] Coming of age alone in the big city could be exciting, but it could also be pretty depressing.

SCROLL OF FIRE

"I WILL BE AN EXCELLENT PHILOSOPHER"

Ben-Gurion left Płońsk before his friends did. But Fuchs, who left after him, was the first of the group to leave Poland. Before doing so, he and Ben-Gurion went to a photographer's studio in Warsaw. As was common practice at the time, the two dressed in dark suits and black bow ties to have their portraits taken. The photographer placed them on a set reminiscent of the salon of an aristocratic mansion, and of course they looked quite formal and festive. Fuchs, with his thick mustache, broad of shoulder and almost a full head higher than Ben-Gurion, looks dominant, decisive, and full of paternal confidence. His right hand is stuck in the pocket of his jacket, his left arm is joined with Ben-Gurion's right. It looks as if Fuchs is protecting and guiding him. Ben-Gurion looks slight, almost fragile. His left hand grips an elaborate tea table. His tense, boyish face radiates dependence and confidence in his older friend, and apparently also pride at having won the privilege of his friendship. To look into Fuchs's eyes he would have had to raise his head.[1]

Fuchs's move to London and later to New York pained him. "I feel so much alone, as if I have been left on a lonely and deserted island . . . ," Ben-Gurion wrote to him. "At night I dream that they have captured you and brought you back to Płońsk in chains."[2] Other than in the love letters he later wrote to his wife and a few other women, Ben-Gurion never bared his most intimate feelings toward another person, man or woman, the way he did in his youthful letters to Fuchs. "I miss you so much . . . Do you know that I am sometimes astounded by that and seek an answer, but for naught." When he read Fuchs's letters, he felt as if he were being "caressed," he once wrote to him. Twenty-four hours later, Ben-Gurion was even more self-effacing and apologized for his previous letter. "What a ridiculously sentimental style," he wrote. He called Fuchs "my big brother," "my precious and my beloved," and generally signed with his full formal name, David Yosef Gruen. Above his name he wrote "With the blessing of Zion."*

Ben-Gurion's memoirs create the impression that he went to Warsaw in keeping with his vow on the Płonka. "My plan was to train myself and to go to Palestine as an engineer," he wrote. "I thought: the land needs builders—I will be an engineer."[3] But he wrote to Fuchs that he "could no longer be in Płońsk." He explained that his love for Rachel Nelkin was "like a volcanic eruption" and that he imagined it blew him into the sky. But then he suddenly began having doubts about his feelings. "Am I truly in love?" he asked. The question had not let him sleep at night. Sometimes he was still amazed that such an idiotic question could even have come to mind, given the potency of his affection. Nevertheless, he slowly arrived at the awareness that he did not love her. "In my heart I continued to feel a strong emotion of love, but not for her," he went on. Perhaps he preferred someone else, or perhaps he had in fact never loved her, he pondered. "It was the middle of the winter. I

---

* Zemach, Fuchs, and Ben-Gurion once sent entries to a short-story contest sponsored by *Hatzefirah*. All three had literary ambitions. Zemach had translated a poem by Goethe into Hebrew at the age of thirteen. Ben-Gurion also tried his hand at poetry. Fuchs criticized the poems and Ben-Gurion immediately gave up. "Your severe criticism of my poems managed to excise my error before it took root in my heart," he wrote. (Ben-Gurion to Shmuel Fuchs, June 15, 1904, in Erez 1971, p. 15; Zemach 1983, pp. 17, 29ff.)

had been infinitely happy up to that time and miserable afterward . . . My heart pounded me so hard, remorse so troubled me, that I sometimes sat in bed for an entire night . . . and cried . . . That was one of the factors that impelled me to travel to Warsaw for the summer."[4]

He went home to Płońsk for the Shavuot holiday; the day after, he gave a lecture there at an Ezra meeting. He spoke about Baruch Spinoza. The central idea of the talk was that, rather than God choosing the Jews, the Jews had chosen God. Most of his listeners did not understand what he was saying; his remarks were not organized, he recalled, because the idea had come to him just the night before. When he returned to Warsaw, he had a hard time getting on his feet economically. He asked acquaintances for loans, not wanting to ask his father. He barely had enough money to buy bread. Fortunately, he was still vegetarian.[5]

His father wanted him to pursue academic studies and become learned and famous. He would have liked to send him to study outside Poland, and would have been pleased if his son enrolled at the rabbinical seminary in Vienna. Unfortunately, he did not have the money to fund such dreams. Being an expert on petitioning the rich and the powerful, Gruen wrote to Theodor Herzl, whom he'd never met, to ask for his support. "I do not have the wherewithal to support my son, of whom I am as fond as the apple of my eye," he wrote in flowery Hebrew replete with flattery. To bolster his request, he praised his son's acuity in Talmud, Russian, and mathematics. While his son desired to learn, all schools were closed to him because "he is a Hebrew." He cast this as a Jewish problem deserving of Herzl's attention. "What are we to do with our unfortunate children, whose superior talents are dissipating and going to waste?*[6]

Jews did indeed have a hard time enrolling in Polish institutions of higher education, but Warsaw was home to a technological college founded by and named for a Jewish philanthropist, Hipolit Wawelberg. Ben-Gurion applied. The entrance examination was rigorous; Ben-Gurion told Fuchs about mutual

---

* Some seventy years later, Prime Minister Ben-Gurion remarked, "I don't know if my father received a response from Herzl. I suppose he did not." He said that his father never told him about this letter. It was discovered in the Central Zionist Archives half a century after it was written. (Ben-Gurion to George Herlitz, Nov. 5, 1950, BGA; Ben-Gurion to his wife and children, May 14, 1942, BGA.)

acquaintances of theirs who did not pass. The college gave preference to candidates with professional experience of some sort. "I have no knowledge of any sort of work," Ben-Gurion noted. "You can no longer get in with a forged diploma, because they are very scrupulous about this now." It seems to have been the first time he ever considered engaging in fraud.

His financial tribulations did not last long. A young man from Płońsk who had decided to go to America handed over to Ben-Gurion his job as a teacher in a modern heder. Ben-Gurion began, for the first time in his life, to receive a salary. He took private lessons in Russian, mathematics, and physics, and believed that in a year's time he would be accepted at Wawelberg. "I can say that I am happy, as I am now totally independent," he wrote. He lived in a rented room that he shared with another young man, Ya'akov Bugato. He inventoried the room for Fuchs: two iron beds on either side of a window, a desk with books, "cooking machines," and teakettles. The walls were decorated with pictures and drawings, the floor was always swept, and everything was spic and span.

Once, he could not hold back, and despite Fuchs's low opinion of his poetic abilities, Ben-Gurion sent him a short lyric he had written: "Facing the coming future we rejoice; in the bosom of hope we play, because it will bring us only the good and the exalted." And one more thing, he added: "Recently, the thought that I have a great philosophical talent has given me no respite . . . It seems to me that in the future I will be an excellent philosopher." In fact, he didn't yet know what to do with himself. "I have wondered a great deal whether I have any talent, and for what," he wrote to Fuchs. If he only knew how to overcome that "profound lack" in his heart that he could not name, he wrote.

His landlord had two daughters, both in high school. One of them captured Ben-Gurion's heart; she was "innocent, spirited, and natural." He wrote that he had "a bit of a weakness for her," but it was more than that. "Mute longings whisper the intimations of hidden secrets in my ears and then I feel in my heart a sentiment of love that is so huge, as mighty as an autumn storm, and I yearn and wish and at times I long to weep on her bosom and pour out into her soul all the longings and hopes unknown even to myself."[7]

❖

Fuchs's letters from London were pessimistic in the extreme. At one point, the word in Płońsk was that he was wavering between two options—becoming a tailor or an ironer. Ben-Gurion responded with almost the same words that Zemach used: "Did you think that London would welcome you with roasted squabs?" Zemach told Fuchs not to send any more such letters. For his part, Ben-Gurion tried to buck up his spirits. "Melancholy is a natural sentiment, quite understandable," he told him patronizingly. He suggested that his friend write to him about everything that weighed on his heart. He also suggested that Fuchs learn English and get involved in Zionist groups. "What do you hear in London about Herzl's illness?" he asked.[8] Herzl died five days later. "We wept like children who had suddenly been orphaned of their father," Zemach wrote. Levkowitz was so upset that he completely lost control of himself, running through the streets of Płońsk like a madman, as startled passersby looked on. When he reached home, he began to wail. His frightened family could not calm him down; he wept all night.[9] Ben-Gurion went back to Płońsk and eulogized Herzl at his family's synagogue.[10]

He coupled Herzl's death with his personal predicament. A few days later, his roommate, Ya'akov Bugato, decided to leave. "I am left alone and forsaken," he lamented in a letter he sent to Fuchs the day after Herzl's death. "O, how great is my sorrow . . . and how terrible it is to suffer so much that, in my loneliness, my heart explodes into fragments." He promised Fuchs that he would send his response to Herzl's death in a long letter a few days hence, and he did so.

"O, horrible, scorching thought!" he began. He described Herzl as "the instrument of the gods," comparing him to a list of figures from Jewish history, among them Judah Maccabee and King David. "Only once in thousands of years is such an incredible man born," he wrote. But he asserted that he believed, "more than ever," in the victory of Zionism. "In the land of poetry and truth, of flowers and the visions of the prophets," he wrote, "a sacred river" flows under a wondrous, shining blue sky, and this river in ancient times heard the song of the shepherds and magical love, and in that land a new "poet of God" would arise who would play on the cords of the heart, singing a sublime song of a "small-large nation" that had been reborn.*

He had actually not intended to put all this down, Ben-Gurion told Fuchs, again in an apologetic tone. What he had wanted to do was say more about his loneliness, now that his roommate had gone. "Loneliness apparently affects the nerves and the imagination to the point that it is impossible to stop and get control of the tempestuous spirit . . . Yes, I will be alone all summer, because Ya'akov Bugato will certainly not come back before winter, and after that, who knows . . ." A few days later, he again bemoaned his loneliness. He sometimes told Fuchs about mutual acquaintances who were making preparations to immigrate to America.[11]

To get accepted to Wawelberg he had to study useless subjects that he found horribly boring, such as Russian history, Christianity, and elementary geography, he told Fuchs. It was a very heavy burden, and as a result, he had decided to apply to a private technological school, not as good as Wawelberg. The problem was that the private institution only accepted students up to the age of seventeen, and he was already almost eighteen. He had no compunctions about submitting false documents: "My father is trying to change my birth certificate." He assumed he would be accepted; his studies would take three years. The school offered three programs, in construction, technology, and chemistry; he intended to choose technology. His father seems to have managed to obtain a new birth certificate.[12]

"WHAT SHOULD I DO?"

In September 1904, Ben-Gurion wrote that he was despondent over any number of things that were troubling him. "Many possibilities and thoughts" were running through his head, he wrote three days later. One possibility was settling in Palestine. He estimated that it was the most likely possibility, largely for economic reasons: to live in a European country he would have to ask for assistance from his father, which he did not want to do. America was

---

* Asked, seventy years later, about this outburst of romantic sensibility, former prime minister Ben-Gurion sounded embarrassed. "I was young," he explained, and maintained that it was the last time he ever wrote anything of the sort.

also a possibility, but there he would probably have to go into commerce, and that was not an option. "I am not fit for that and I cannot bear business," he said. He did not want to remain in Poland. As such, he faced the "well-known question," as he wrote: "What should I do?"

For the time being, he intended to continue to do all he could to get into college. He was not sure he would succeed. "If I am not accepted . . . I don't know what I will do," he wrote. He tried to persuade himself that he wanted to settle in Palestine more than anything else, even if it meant being a teacher there. But for now he was not making a decision and saw no reason to rush—he had enough time to think about it. "I still have enough time to study for four years before being called up for military service," he wrote a friend in November 1904. In December, he took another tack: he wrote that, had he the money for his passage, he would go to Palestine that very winter. He presumed that he would not be accepted to the technical school and that he would then embark.[13]

Four days later, everything was clear to him. "Next summer I will certainly go to the Land of Israel," he declared, explaining that it was the only way to help the wretched nation that was approaching horrible destruction. "Let us not deceive ourselves with empty clichés! Our situation is so terrible, so horrible! And ours is perhaps the most dangerous era in our history!"[14] It was apparently a fairly sudden epiphany; just a day or two earlier, going to Palestine was at most one option among many, and not necessarily at the top of the list. Even now, he did not see himself as duty-bound to provide his wretched nation with concrete assistance in Palestine—not yet. "As for myself, I know nothing," he wrote in January 1905. "Some say that it will be easier to get into school this year, while others say the opposite."[15]

Fuchs could well have received the impression that his friend was casting about for excuses to evade a decision. "On the one hand I see the great urgency to work in the Land of Israel today," Ben-Gurion wrote. By this he apparently meant political work. "Organizing the national and vigorous forces and coordinating them." The future depended on that, he maintained. On the other hand, he wrote, he still hoped to obtain an education in technology and engineering. "I don't know today what to choose," he wrote. For the moment, it seemed as if it all depended on Fuchs: "If you were to go, then I would also make an effort to get there." It was important to him that

Fuchs not have any doubts about his Zionist commitment. He was determined to pursue his studies, he wrote ten days after his previous letter, but added: "Believe me, without the hope of the larger project of working in our land, I would have already cast aside the idea of finishing my education."[16] And so it was that Shlomo Zemach set out before he did.

❖

During that same period, and probably under the impact of Herzl's death, Zemach's desire to fulfill the oath at the Płonka surged. His first step was to send a letter to a man whose articles he sometimes read in *Hatzefirah*, a farmer and writer named Moshe Smilansky. Zemach asked him about finding work in Palestine; Smilansky replied that he should come to the country first and then seek work. Zionism offered an opening to get out, to flee, but he was waiting for the right time, Zemach wrote.[17]

Legally, he was still a minor. He had no documents that would enable him to leave Poland without his parents' consent, and he had no money, either. Neither did he want to abandon his beloved Shoshana, all the more so given that in their small town, where there were no secrets, everyone knew that the Fuchses were seeking a husband for her. The difficulties of emigrating were a central subject of discussion among the town's youth. One of them asked for Zemach's help—Shlomo Levkowitz. It was not easy for Levkowitz to do so. He had not forgotten Zemach's habit of disparaging him and his father. But he was very much alone. He had no friends to confide in. To his astonishment, Zemach did not scorn him. On the contrary, the two shook hands and, "from one friend's heart to another," as Levkowitz wrote, began to plan their departure.

The more they discussed the details, the clearer it became to them that it would be difficult for them to leave together. Then the rivalry began—each one wanted to be first. Levkowitz first tried the easy way. He asked his father's permission to settle in Palestine, along with a loan to cover the travel expenses, which he promised to pay back. If he were to fail to find work in agriculture, he could always revert to his profession as a baker, he assured his father. After all, people eat bread all over the world. His father refused. The Zionists, he contended, were bringing a huge catastrophe on themselves and on the Jewish people, and he would not allow his son to take part in such madness. The break between the two, which had opened when Levkowitz began to abandon religious observance and study, grew wider.[18]

In the midst of this, a salacious rumor began to run through the town— Zemach had stolen three hundred rubles from his father and absconded from the country. Zemach's father had begun to bring him into the business, he later related. One day he gave him three hundred rubles—a huge sum at the time—to deposit in the bank. "When I received those three hundred rubles and held them in my hands, it was instantly clear to me that the hour I had been waiting for had arrived." Zemach probably would not have "actually stolen" the money, he said, but when the rubles fell into his lap, he could not resist the temptation. On the way to catch the carriage out of Płońsk, he by chance encountered Lipa Taub, to whom he gave a letter to convey to his father. A few hours later, he was in Ben-Gurion's room in Warsaw.

He disappeared without saying a word to Levkowitz, who was furious, and who later wrote that he was jealous, insulted, amazed, but also truly happy that Zemach had finally managed to make his dream come true.[19] The insult ran deep also because Zemach had not acted alone—Ben-Gurion had helped him.

As expected, Zemach's father tried to stop his son; a day later, he also appeared at Ben-Gurion's room in Warsaw. Ben-Gurion told him that Shlomo was already gone. That wasn't true, and Ben-Gurion was not even sure whether his friend's father believed him. Whatever the case, he turned on his heels and went back to Płońsk. Zemach reached Palestine. His getaway, and the letters he began to send from Palestine, caused a stir in the town. Ben-Gurion reckoned that they began to change people's minds, and people began to think of going to Palestine rather than America. "Our Shlomo is a star!!!" he wrote to Fuchs.

❖

In the end, Ben-Gurion did not matriculate. Not because he was a Hebrew, as his father wrote to Herzl, but because he, like other Jewish candidates, did not meet the requirements for the technical college.[20] He tried to adjust to his failure and not lose hope, and continued to study, and to read Goethe,

Shakespeare, and Tolstoy. From time to time he went home for a visit, but Płońsk bored him as well.[21]

Zemach wrote that all of Ben-Gurion's talk about wanting to study was meaningless, because Ben-Gurion lacked the patience, diligence, orderliness, and systematic approach that a course of study required. As compensation to himself, Zemach maintained, Ben-Gurion got involved in socialist Zionist political activity.[22] Ben-Gurion himself wrote to Fuchs: "It's as they say—if I don't succeed in being a woodcutter, I'll be . . . a Cabinet minister." In the paragraph that followed, he added: "I have been called to take part in founding an organization for the dissemination of Zionism."

"COLD DESPAIR, AS AWFUL AS DEATH"

Following Herzl's death in the summer of 1904, the Zionist Congress shelved the Uganda proposal. But the controversy surrounding it continued, including among the people who invited Ben-Gurion to take part in founding the new organization in Warsaw. It was his first brush with politics. They called a general meeting, chose a leadership committee, and began to draft a manifesto. Everything seemed promising at the start. The manifesto proclaimed the organization's goal of spreading Zionism and expanding the use of the Hebrew language. The committee decided to establish a library and to collect books for it. That happened on Rosh Hashanah. But just two weeks later, when the Sukkot holiday arrived, the whole thing had "dissipated like froth on water," as Ben-Gurion wrote to Fuchs.

His disappointment ran deep; it was very emotional and personal. For a moment he had doubts about Zionism, and as was his habit he expressed this by pulling out all linguistic and lexical stops: "Doubts and uncertainty are sucking my seething blood and sapping my fortitude, and sometimes they infuse my soul with cold despair, as awful as death."[23] As usual, he sought encouragement from Fuchs. "Brother!" he wrote. "Maybe you can restore my simple, intense, and flawless faith whenever I have a doubt or a thought of despair?"[24]

He needed something to divert his thoughts, and knew what that should be. "I am thirsty for work," he wrote, "work that I can put my whole soul into, work that will rob me of all my senses, all my thoughts, that will obliterate all my strident emotions, make me forget all the vexing, cursed questions." In the meantime, he read a lot of newspapers and shared the things that interested him with Fuchs. He also followed political developments in the Zionist Organization, including the upcoming election of Herzl's successor.*[25]

One candidate, Max Nordau, believed that the new president of the United States, Theodore Roosevelt, would further Zionist goals. Ben-Gurion asked Fuchs how America's Jews had voted, the first time he took an interest in this subject. He sent Fuchs regular reports on the state of Zionism in Warsaw. Then revolution broke out there.[26]

❖

The uprising took the form of a groundswell of strikes and riots that swept through the Russian Empire, reaching to Warsaw. The czar's military forces put down the uprising with overwhelming force. Ben-Gurion turned out to have natural journalistic talent; his letters expertly interweave opinionated factual accounts of events, personal experience, and colorful observations, all written in flowing and clear Hebrew. He described the bodies of demonstrators lying in the streets; no one collected them.

Ben-Gurion would later say that he had supported the uprising. "I was a revolutionary," he related, "but when the uprising broke out, an empty spot remained in my heart. Because I knew that, while the revolution might liberate Russia, it would not do so for the Jewish people." Using more measured language, *Hatzefirah* expressed similar disappointment. The uprising was followed by a wave of hundreds of pogroms, which continued the following year, directed against Jews, in particular in Ukraine. Thousands were killed.[27]

❖

In March 1905, Ben-Gurion sent a letter to Menachem Ussishkin, one of the leaders of the Zionist movement, to ask his advice. He said he was

---

* Membership in the organization was open to all Jews of the world. There was a membership fee collected from the sale of the so-called Zionist shekel. National delegations at the Zionist Congress elected the organization's executive bodies, which were headed by the president. The organization would later come to be known as the World Zionist Organization.

writing in the name of a group of young single men who wanted to immigrate to Palestine.

Ussishkin had led the fight against the Uganda plan, and also maintained that Zionist activism should not be limited to diplomatic contacts. He demanded Jewish settlement in Palestine even before international agreement on a Jewish state could be obtained. Ben-Gurion's letter might possibly have been aimed at making it easier for him to get to Palestine, perhaps with his expenses paid by the Zionist Organization. Young Jews, friends of his included, had gone to Palestine of their own volition. But Ben-Gurion wrote: "We do not want, and are not free, to make a move of such great importance at our own initiative."

Ben-Gurion sent Ussishkin's political program to Fuchs. The Seventh Zionist Congress was scheduled to convene four months hence in Basel. Ben-Gurion wanted to be there, making his first-ever trip outside Poland. It was an opportunity to reunite with Fuchs. "Try to be a delegate to the Congress," Ben-Gurion told him two weeks after writing to Ussishkin. "It could be that I will be in Switzerland in the summer and then we can see each other."

That did not happen, and within a few months Ben-Gurion was displaying an almost suicidal frame of mind. "I can't find any interest in living anymore," he wrote. In the past he had been full of confidence in life and in other people, full of a strong faith in the victory of his ideals, in the rule of truth and justice. But there were moments, "and they are many and frequent," in which everything seemed insipid, tedious, dismal, and futile. On such days he tended to associate his personal plight with that of the Jewish people and to see Zionism as the solution for both. Sometimes it raised him to the heights of euphoria, but when he plunged into the abyss of depression, Zionism was not always enough. "Sometimes bitter, horrible doubts rise in my heart and a horrible despair gnaws like a mosquito at my brain and sucks my blood like a leech until the bile pours out and terror overcomes me," he wrote to Fuchs. "I ask for nothing of life, I want neither pleasures nor education, not honor and not love, I'll give it all up, all I want is one thing—hope!!! I ask for the ability to hope and believe and then I am prepared to bear the hardest labor and the heaviest yoke!" He apologized again for burdening Fuchs with his mental agonies. "Forgive me, my love," he asked.[28]

Zemach also missed Fuchs and needed him, as he wrote over and over again from Palestine. He dreamed of the three of them living together in the Land of Israel and marshaled his best skills to persuade Fuchs to come. He appealed to his Zionist duty and tried to coax his friend with a shared memory that was dear to both of them—had they not wept together when they heard of the Uganda plan?[29] Fuchs had trouble understanding what had brought Zemach to become a farmhand in Palestine. "It seems to me that you can have been even more useful to your people and the land in a higher and more spiritual calling than working the land," he wrote to his friend. "Because labor is something anyone can do. A person with a sharp mind is more beneficial in public, intellectual, or general work."[30] Zemach replied with a long exposition about the virtue of working the land. The longing to return to nature indeed stood at the center of the ethos and myth fostered by the Zionist movement.[31]

But it was an entirely hypothetical argument. Fuchs had chosen a different path from his friends, seeking his fortune in New York, where he planned to study dentistry. In doing so, he took the advice of his friend, who had himself not yet decided whether to settle in Palestine. Of course you should go to America, Ben-Gurion wrote to him, especially since your parents have now changed their position and have offered their consent. In the meantime, soon after his arrival in New York, Fuchs began publishing articles in a Hebrew-language weekly, *Hadegel*. Ben-Gurion wrote to him in a humoristic tone that is evident almost exclusively in his youthful letters to Fuchs: "The article's style is so fine that I have my doubts about whether you wrote it," he joked with his friend. If Fuchs were to indeed make his home permanently in New York, he ought to put out a Hebrew newspaper there, Ben-Gurion wrote, offering himself as the new publication's Polish correspondent.[32]

From Zemach, Fuchs heard the opposite: "Don't take David Gruen's advice." Zemach pleaded with him as a friend, brother, and beloved; in one final effort he tried to buy his company, offering to send him the money for his passage to Palestine.[33] Fuchs remained in America. That was the historical choice that Zionism offered to the world's Jews; most of them preferred not to settle in Palestine. Ben-Gurion was still unsure.

❖

In the meantime, Ben-Gurion made his way into the Zionist labor movement in Warsaw—a conglomerate of dozens of groupings, many of which never achieved prominence, though some would later gain significant political power in Israel.

One of the groups Ben-Gurion encountered was the Bund, which offered a socialist alternative to Zionism. Like the Zionists, the Bund also maintained that the Jews constituted a nation, but the Bundists did not see the Jews as a nation in exile. Instead, they maintained, the homelands of Jewish communities were the countries in which they resided. As part of this, the movement fostered the Yiddish language. In 1906 the Bund had tens of thousands of supporters in Poland, making it a bitter rival of the Zionists. The Bund also organized the Jews for self-defense.[34] Seeking to combine his Zionist faith with the rising tide of Jewish socialism, Ben-Gurion found his way to a young man of his age who conducted an ideological-political discussion group in his mother's house. The youth's name was Yitzhak Tabenkin; he was handsome and charismatic, with a talent for persuasion. Like Ben-Gurion, he had not had much formal schooling; neither did he generally work. He read a lot of books. The members of the group called themselves Po'alei Zion, the Workers of Zion.

Po'alei Zion belonged to the plethora of circles, cells, organizations, clubs, parties, and factions that appeared in Jewish Warsaw, as the old order began to collapse. Like Hovevei Zion before them, Po'alei Zion made its first appearance in the form of independent societies that operated at first without any central coordination. The members engaged in fiery ideological debates day and night, using concepts borrowed in part from socialist discourse, for which the Hebrew language did not yet have words.

Still, Ben-Gurion, whose work as a teacher and preparatory studies left him with a fair amount of free time, jumped into the fray with all his heart. The participants in these deliberations frequently resigned from associations and returned to them and left again; factions split into fragments, which united and split again.[35]

In December 1905, Po'alei Zion held a convention of the party's Polish branch, which Ben-Gurion attended as the delegate from Płońsk. Everyone else there was more senior in the movement than he, a marginal figure. But he learned much political craft there and found his place in the party.

❖

Ben-Gurion's final months in Warsaw seem to have been pretty wild. Sometimes the police arrested him and he spent several weeks in prison. He was arrested the first time, he said, because he had let his hair grow, leading the police to think he was a revolutionary.

The second arrest had to do with his attempt to mediate a conflict in the small-town Jewish community of Racionz over the choice of a new rabbi. He seems to have gone into his father's line of work, seeking to resolve disputes through arbitration, mediation, and compromise. In both cases he seems to have been released thanks to his father's connections. According to one source, he also worked as a member of a Po'alei Zion tribunal. A few weeks later, his doctor ordered him to set his studies aside, he related, and his father brought him back to Płońsk. The town was also safer than Warsaw, where violence was still raging.[36]

"WE'D GO AROUND WITH PISTOLS"

A short time after his return home, Ben-Gurion told Fuchs that Zionism was doing much better in Płońsk. He told of the establishment of a Central Committee that was meant to take responsibility for "the general management and oversight of community affairs."

He had decided to return to Płońsk, he said, because the Bund had sent its people there to enlist craftsmen's apprentices; in Ben-Gurion's words, the Bund was "attacking" Płońsk. "I hastened to Płońsk to uproot this affliction from our town," he wrote.[37] He brought with him the methods of political action that he had learned in Warsaw. Like other organizations, Po'alei Zion needed money to fund its work, which included purchasing arms, establishing strike funds, and organizing rallies, as well as to cover travel expenses, publicity, and publications. The same was true in Płońsk. "We'd go around with pistols," Ben-Gurion later recalled. He organized strapping young men who imposed a reign of terror in town. "We would go to rich householders, place the pistol on the table, and start talking about money." One of his compatriots, Yehezkel Blatnik-Yosifon, recalled: "The arms in the organization's possession made it possible to put pressure on employers to improve the living conditions of Jewish workers."

Płońsk was a center of the garment industry. The working conditions were harsh. Ben-Gurion commenced negotiations with the employers. He demanded a twelve-hour workday. The talks failed and the workers went on strike. The strike turned violent and the police had to intervene. Some of the strikers were put on trial, but in the end Po'alei Zion went down in Płońsk history: it won the battle.

With pogroms prevalent, Ben-Gurion hid a stash of weapons in his father's house, in case the Jews of Płońsk needed to defend themselves.[38] He and his brother Avraham were both members of the committee, along with Shlomo Levkowitz and two others.[39] In June 1905, Levkowitz left for Palestine as well.

❖

Levkowitz described his departure as a traumatic experience. He also stole money from his father to pay for his trip, but his father discovered the crime before he left, raged at him, and forced him to return the money. "Here are two people who love each other purely, each is capable of sacrificing himself for the other, and they stand like two enemies who cannot be reconciled," Levkowitz later wrote of himself and his father. He sank into depression and isolation. In the end he fled. He reached the carriage at the last minute, hoping to get away without being seen, but then his mother appeared, called out his name, grabbed his coat, and tried to pull him out. The carriage set off.[40]

All three of Ben-Gurion's boyhood friends had now left. At the branch of Po'alei Zion that he had founded, he was the person who called the shots, for the first time in his life. Zemach taunted him. Zemach himself was living in the land of Judea, gazing at the rising moon, he wrote to Fuchs, while Ben-Gurion was playing at politics in Płońsk: "David is surely setting up some association in Płońsk and speaking with terrible zeal about 'the people and the land,' 'freedom and slavery,' 'the strong and the weak,' 'assimilation and self-awareness,' 'cosmopolitanism and nationalism,' and other such issues." In another letter from the same period, Zemach wrote of Ben-Gurion: "He seems to have attained his goal, more than any of us."[41] He was right.

Ben-Gurion took the members of Ezra, the organization he had founded with his friends at the age of fourteen, and the Po'alei Zion cell he established in Płońsk at the age of nineteen, and combined them into a single force. "I added socialism to my Zionism" was how he later put it.

From time to time the Bund and Po'alei Zion held public debates in the town's main synagogue. Ben-Gurion was not a charismatic orator—he had a squeaky voice. He supposed, however, that he had a "local-patriotic" advantage by virtue of the fact that he was a native. The Bundist was an outsider. The debates were often tense; Ben-Gurion took a bodyguard with him. "Both sides came armed with pistols, as was common practice in those times," he wrote. The debates were attended by many of the town's inhabitants; some even closed up their stores.

Ben-Gurion received a lot of attention and his name appeared in a newspaper, apparently for the first time. A Bund publication wrote that Ben-Gurion began to shout during one of the debates, "We have weapons and we will kill you all like dogs." It called him a hooligan. "And I beat the Bund," Ben-Gurion boasted. "I ejected the Bund from Płońsk." The short boy who had never been happy, who as a youth failed in every endeavor and was on the verge of suicidal depression, was now a thuggish labor boss in a small town. And he still wasn't happy.[42]

❖

Shlomo Zemach had in the meantime tried his hand at farm labor in Palestine; it was very difficult. Nothing had prepared him for such work. His initial period there was profoundly disappointing. He encountered too many Arabs, too many Jews who employed Arabs and Haredim who opposed Zionism, and too many eccentrics of all kinds. He wrote that, at the time, he was a "gentle, naïve, and virtuous boy." When he saw the land in all its ugliness, he was shaken to the bottom of his soul. In his misery, he did what Ben-Gurion had done in Warsaw—he sent heartbreaking letters to Fuchs and joined the founders of a new labor party—in his case Hapo'el Hatza'ir, the Young Worker.

A few months after leaving Płońsk, in the summer of 1906, Zemach received a letter that bucked up his spirits. His father forgave him, invited him to come home, and sent him money for the journey. Something else also drew him to Płońsk; he had fallen out of love with Shoshana Fuchs. "I had to notify the girl that there was no longer any love between us, and I did not want to do that in writing, but rather to explain everything to her face-to-face."

Upon his arrival, an argument broke out between him and Ben-Gurion over their two parties—which was the correct ideology, that of Po'alei Zion or that of Hapo'el Hatza'ir? Ben-Gurion proposed uniting the two. Zemach said that, unlike Po'alei Zion, his movement refused to "recognize Yiddish" and did not accept Marxism. As such, their differences could not be papered over. Six weeks later, Zemach decided to return to Palestine, and Ben-Gurion resolved to go with him. Rachel Nelkin joined them.

She was now eighteen; Ben-Gurion was almost twenty. She enlisted in his party. Two of her brothers immigrated to America. One of them sent her fervid Zionist letters and told her that they had founded a Zionist association called Halutzei Zion, the Pioneers of Zion. Shmuel Fuchs joined them. They also founded a new newspaper together, *Der Yiddisher Kempfer*, meaning "The Jewish Fighter."[43] "They all shared the dream of going to Palestine, but they did not have the strength, because American life blinded them," Rachel Nelkin wrote.[44]

"THE SOLE, LAST RECOURSE"

There is no way of knowing if Ben-Gurion would have settled in Palestine without Rachel; Zionist ideology was not his only motivation. In any case, her decision made his easier. In his memoirs he explained that he delayed only because of Zemach's visit, planning to return with him. Avigdor Gruen was not happy. "This decision of mine was a deep disappointment for him," Ben-Gurion wrote; his father had not given up his dream that his David would be learned and famous.[45] Nevertheless, he gave his son his blessing. Before his departure, everybody gathered in the yard of the Gruen home and had their picture taken under the Zionist flag. As one might expect, in the photograph they look festive, but none of them looks happy. Ben-Gurion sits between two girls, Rachel and another.[46] "The mood was fraught," she later recalled. There was also a party, where farewell speeches were made. "Everyone shed tears and tried to be happy and enjoy themselves," she wrote. Before the party broke up, they sang the Po'alei Zion anthem, in Yiddish. Her brother Elazar wrote from New York: "You are firm of mind and prepared to give your soul for our people and our land." She hadn't a clue what she would do in Palestine, just that she wanted to live there and help make the desert bloom.[47] Ben-Gurion wrote to Berdyczewski's son that he was going to Palestine "as a Zionist, pioneer, and socialist."*[48]

But his Rachel knew the truth. Neither of them left Płońsk as a pioneer. "I came in despair, or more correctly out of despair," he once wrote to her.[49] He later wrote something similar to Shlomo Levkowitz. It was not a sense of calling or a pioneering imperative that motivated him—he sought and found a way to redeem himself, to bring about a change in a life he had grown disgusted with. He did it all for himself. It was, as he put it, "the normal selfishness" of a young person who felt that the ground was being pulled out from under him, and it was the only way out he could find.[50] Ben-Gurion had a sense of national despair, alongside the disappointment he often felt about his personal life. It was, he wrote, "complete and utter despair of the Exile, as well as of Zionism and socialism as they were in those days." The failure of the 1905 revolution in Russia also depressed him. "And out of this fourfold despair I immigrated to Palestine," he related. "I believed that here was the sole, last recourse."†[51]

There is one reason to believe that she might have taken this step even if Ben-Gurion had decided to remain in Płońsk. A few months before they

---

* The term "pioneer" (*halutz*) was taken from the Bible, where it appears in a military context. The literal translation of the word's biblical root reached French and from there entered many languages: "avant-garde," the advance force that precedes or leads the main force. Ben-Gurion referred to the pioneers as "the army of Zionist realization." (Ben-Gurion 1971a, p. 336.)

† Ben-Gurion's account of the despair that brought him to Palestine was included in the biography that Bracha Habas published in the weekly *Dvar Hashavua*, but was omitted in the book version that came out two years later. (*Dvar Hashavua*, March 9, 1950; Habas 1952, p. 61; see also Ben-Gurion at assembly with recruits, April 20, 1943, in Ben-Gurion 1949, 3, p. 140.)

set out, a young man who was passing through town on his way to Palestine visited her stepfather's home. His name was Yehezkel Halbovski, who would change his name to Beit Halahmi. She described him as a handsome boy with a delicate face, blue eyes, and curls. "I can now reveal that he attracted me," she wrote many years later. He recalled her as a tall, fair girl with black eyes.[52] Ben-Gurion could have known about Rachel's new love.

❖

On one of their last days in Płońsk, Ben-Gurion copied into a square-ruled notebook an epic love poem that Hayim Nahman Bialik had published a few months earlier, "The Scroll of Fire." It is a very long mythological work whose heroes are the last survivors of the destruction of the Temple in Jerusalem—two hundred young men and two hundred young women who find their way to an uninhabited island. All of them are naked. At the center of the poem are two boys "equal in stature and strength."[53] One is a gentle boy with fair eyes who looks to the skies, searching for his star. The second is intimidating and angry-browed, and he looks to the earth, "seeking his lost soul."

Later in the poem, the fair-eyed boy encounters one of the girls, which leads to a long monologue spoken by him. He relates that he has lost his father, that he is "young and alone and dreaming." The girl teaches him the pain of silence and the tortures of love. "My eyes devoured her bared white flesh and my soul tremblingly groped her virgin breasts," he says, "and in my tossings at night I sought you in my place of rest." He laments losing his youth, which he likens to losing a friend: "And I still chase and cling to him like a child, hugging and kissing his legs, catching the hem of his robe, and squirm and roar 'Don't leave me!'" He feels like a dog, and a slave. He searches for his beloved, but she, too, has disappeared. In his pain he shouts: "Fire, fire, fire!" In the end, he finds the fire in his heart and sets out to bring it to his exiled brethren and cries out for them, and no one can withstand his piercing gaze. He is alien, an enigma to all of them.

Bialik's "Scroll of Fire" has been termed by some a Zionist epic and a lyric of forbidden love, replete with erotic symbols, composed under the influence of Polish romanticism.[54] Ben-Gurion copied out the poem in a fine hand, word for word, taking special care with the punctuation. It covered thirty pages in the notebook. And he sent it to Shmuel Fuchs.

· **3** ·

BIRDS

"AND I THOUGHT I WAS DREAMING"

The depression that spurred Ben-Gurion to make his decision to go to Palestine, and the melancholy that he felt when he left, were quickly replaced by high spirits. The closer he came to his destination, the more elated he became, almost uncontrollably so. His letters home again demonstrated his sharp journalistic eye and poetic exultation. The travelers went by train to Odessa, where they met several Zionist leaders, Menachem Ussishkin among them. Ussishkin had never replied to the message Ben-Gurion had sent him a year earlier; along with Zemach, Ben-Gurion now tried to persuade him to give them money to put out a newspaper. Ussishkin was not receptive, and Ben-Gurion remarked that he was no longer surprised that his letter had been left unanswered.*[1]

---

* Levkowitz also paid his respects to Ussishkin on his way to Palestine, and was given the same cold treatment. (Lavi 1957, p. 121.)

Ben-Gurion then obtained a passport. To circumvent bureaucracy and regulations, he applied under an assumed name, using the passport of someone from another family, a practice often resorted to by Russian subjects who sought to travel.[2] Just before his ship set sail, he waxed poetic and declared: "In a few hours I will have gone from the vale of the dark Exile, and I will send you my greetings from the free realm of the sea, on the way to the land of rebirth. May we see each other soon on the hills of Zion!"[3]

❖

It was his first trip outside Russia, and his first time on a boat. The sea was inspiring. "The waves rise and break with wild defiance, chasing each other furiously, shooting myriad tiny shards of glowing water up to heaven—and then, under this spray rising to heaven, a multicolored rainbow shines in the depths."[4] His first encounter with the Orient came in the Turkish port of Izmir. When his boat left the port and made its way out to sea, he had a view of Izmir as a mountain strewn with stars, sapphires, and pearls. "From the ship's hold I gazed on this sight and I thought I was dreaming . . ." Among the passengers were Turks and Arabs, who made "a very good impression." As he wrote: "Almost all of them are goodhearted and friendly . . . You could say that they are big children." They sang and told jokes and "in general tried to entertain us whenever they could."[5]

On Friday, September 7, 1906, nine days after setting out from Odessa, the ship approached Jaffa. Ben-Gurion went up to the deck, his heart pounding. "A fresh breeze blew on our faces, and the call of a bird, the first of our entire journey, reached our ears," he wrote.[6]

Palestine was then a backwater of the Ottoman Empire, which had ruled it almost continuously since the sixteenth century. Many years before Ben-Gurion's arrival a legend arose there. Like other legends of the Holy Land, it has more than one version. According to the version preserved in the Ben-Gurion Archives, the heroes are three Jewish entrepreneurs on horseback. One morning, apparently in 1878, they set out from Jerusalem to Jaffa, and from there to an Arab village called Um Malabes, where they intended to buy a plot of land on which to found a farming colony. They brought a doctor with them, whom for some reason they believed to be an expert on environmental conditions. The doctor ascended to the roof of a house—or, some say, to the top of a hill—and stood there silently. He gazed all around, north and south, east and west. The entrepreneurs watched him expectantly from below. Finally the doctor descended and told them that, unfortunately, he had not seen a single bird, not in the sky and not on the tree branches. And everyone knows, he told them, that where birds do not live, neither can humans.

The three riders were very disappointed. They had had such great hopes for the project, and some time before had already arrived at a name for the new village: Petah Tikvah, meaning "Gate of Hope." In the end, one of them blurted out "Nonetheless!" And the second cried: "We'll try!" The third embraced his partners and they all broke out in tears of joy.[7]

It was not easy to settle Palestine, because the conditions were not fit for habitation, and they were entrepreneurs, adventurers, and dreamers, not farmers. The longing to till the soil of the Holy Land also attracted others, Jews and Christians alike; generally they were new to the country and unfamiliar with the conditions.

The country that Ben-Gurion and his friends found when they arrived in 1906 was awakening into the twentieth century after a long slumber. It was a frantic and charming jumble of colorful idealistic initiatives and religious delirium, of bold breakthroughs and hesitant beginnings and myriad fantasies. It wasn't always easy to tell which was which.

"A GREAT MIRACLE"

The country's population was rising steadily. By the 1880s, it reached close to four hundred thousand. Approximately four-fifths were Arabs, mostly Muslims, including thousands of nomads who did not number among the country's permanent population.[8] The accepted estimate is that at this time there were about thirty thousand Jews in the country, less than 8 percent of the population, and less than one-half of 1 percent of the world's Jews. There was a roughly equal number of Christians.

The religious awakenings that swept through Europe and the United States had sent a stream of visionaries, adventurers, romantics, and seekers of redemption to the Holy Land. Many of them believed that the Messiah was about to arrive. A number of the new arrivals were religious outsiders—such as the German Templers, and a group from Chicago who founded Jerusalem's American Colony—and had as such been persecuted in their home countries. They often arrived after a sudden epiphany, catastrophe, or inexplicable experience. Such was the case with a farmer from Russia whose task it had been to ring the bell of his village's church. One day, as he ascended to the bell tower, his eyes went dark and he lost his sense of direction. He sat down on the stairs and his sight came back to him, but when he tried again to ascend to the bell chamber, once more he saw only black. Then the man realized that it was no accident. The finger of God had shown him that he must abandon his Christian faith and return to the Jewish religion. When he arrived in the Galilee, he discovered there a community of Sabbath-observant Russians, the Subbotniks, some of whom had converted to Judaism.[9] It was the age of eccentricity in Palestine.

Most of the country's Jews also came from elsewhere. The majority were Sephardim, a term that literally means "Spanish," but which had already for some generations been used to designate all Jews with roots in the Islamic world. Most of the Jews who settled in Palestine from the mid-nineteenth century on came from Christian Europe and were called Ashkenazim. In the 1860s, this group grew to become the majority. In contrast with the Arabs, most Jews lived in the country's cities; a majority lived in Jerusalem and were pious scions of European Jewish communities, in whose name they were meant to engage in religious study and prayer. For their livelihood, most of them depended on funds that their home communities sent to support them.[10] European Jewish philanthropists also lent a hand to the settlement of Jews outside the cities.

In the twenty-five years that preceded the arrival of Ben-Gurion and his friends, some thirty thousand Jews settled in Palestine, and it is estimated that they doubled the number of Jews in the country. Most of them were refugees from Eastern Europe. This wave of immigration later came to be called the First Aliyah. Many of them were victims of pogroms and various other forms of persecution and discrimination.

❖

Many of the pogroms' victims were already needy Jews. The persecutions and attacks they suffered served as catalysts to immigrate to the United States or elsewhere, as tens of millions of other Europeans did in these years. The escape route to Palestine was shorter than to America and cost less; and those who hoped to return to Russia someday reckoned that it would be easier to do so from Palestine than America. This incentive was supplemented by the traditional longing to return to Zion. But most Jews fled Russia in panic. In many cases they suffered greatly when they left. According to one source, "Poverty disfigures them and leads the older girls among the many families wallowing in the city's streets into bad company." For the most part, the new arrivals landed in Jaffa and many stayed in that city.[11]

The difficulties faced by the newcomers spurred local entrepreneurs and wealthy Jews overseas to provide assistance. The result was the founding of new Jewish towns, called *moshavot*, or in the singular, *moshavah*. Their inhabitants were meant to make their livelihoods primarily by farming. Among the Jewish settlers were any number of oddballs and idealists. Here and there they benefited from the experience of the Christians, and formed groups and sects that shared similar dreams.[12]

Some of the students at the University of Kharkov's veterinary institute, in Ukraine, resolved in 1882 to head for Palestine and work there to "heal the nation" in idyllic moshavot. The group, which called itself Bilu, dreamed big: they planned to bring over between three and four thousand settlers. In the end, they brought no more than fifty young men and women. The group soon split, and some left the country; only about a dozen stayed behind. They did not achieve their goal and left the Zionist movement with nothing but a glorious legend.

In 1890 a small band of a few dozen farmworkers who lived as a commune in the moshavah of Rehovot formed a covert society, divided into cells. Each cell consisted of ten "brothers," led by a "big brother" who was given the title "captain of ten." New members were allowed in only after being carefully vetted and undergoing a secret initiation ceremony. It was called the Society of Brothers, changed soon afterward to the Society of

Tens. Its spiritual leader was a preacher and visionary from Russia named Michael Halperin, who had urged Russian Jews to organize in self-defense. He was one of the first to dream of the establishment of a Jewish army in the Land of Israel. The official *Haganah History Book* credits him with being the "herald" of Jewish self-defense in Palestine, but it also compares him to Don Quixote. One of his acquaintances described him as a stunningly handsome man, like a mythical hero. His fair curls reached down to his shoulders, imbuing him with prophetic majesty. He believed himself to be a descendant of King David; once, when a traveling circus arrived in Jaffa, he went into the lion cage and sang the Zionist anthem, "Hatikvah," to prove that Jews are brave. Many were captivated by him; after finishing the day's labors, they would gather for paramilitary training under a sycamore tree. The radicals among them demanded a death penalty for "brothers" who deviated from the right path.[13] Meanwhile, at a commune founded on the southern shore of Lake Kinneret lived a man named Noah Naftulksy, who wanted to make the Land of Israel into a world center for vegetarians and vegans.[14]

By the time Ben-Gurion arrived, twenty-five moshavot had been founded, home to some six thousand Jews. Petah Tikvah was one of them; the lack of birds had only delayed its establishment by a few years.[15] Prime Minister Ben-Gurion later said that Petah Tikvah was "a great miracle," the first step toward the renewal of Jewish sovereignty.[16] When he first got there, Petah Tikvah reminded him of a Jewish town in Poland. Ben-Gurion despised it.

"WAVES OF JOY"

Arriving in Palestine could be a traumatic experience. Ships anchored outside the port; Arab porters loaded the passengers and their luggage onto boats and rowed them to shore, for a price. "The Arabs clambered up our ship with their hands and feet," Ben-Gurion related. "A huge commotion and great anxiety broke out on the ship . . . It took a great effort to keep our belongings with us . . . It seemed as if the boat might flip over any moment, to be swallowed up by the waves that attacked us from all sides."

Levkowitz and Zemach also had harrowing memories of their arrival in Jaffa. Levkowitz, who arrived a few months before Ben-Gurion, described the Arab rowers as "human beasts" with "predatory eyes and entirely feral visages." They demanded an exorbitant fee, and raised it while the boat made its way to the shore, all in shouts and threats. "And as they shouted, they formed their fingers into the talons of birds of prey," Levkowitz wrote, "and held them out to the young passengers, as if they would at any moment plunge their black claws into their eyes."

Zemach termed the Arab porters "pirates." The fact that he had to enter the land of his fathers on an Arab boat left him with a sense of being "orphaned and affronted." To him, the Arabs looked like proud men in control of their fate; their muscular arms terrified him. At that moment, he felt like a prisoner of war going into exile, he wrote.

Ben-Gurion seems not to have been cognizant of the symbolic irony of his return to the land of his fathers, borne on the broad shoulders of Arab porters. "I felt waves of joy rising up from the depths of my soul and breaking on my heart," he wrote.*[17]

Shlomo Levkowitz was waiting for him at the dock. Yehezkel Halbovski had come to meet Rachel Nelkin.[18] Ben-Gurion did not like Jaffa. "Like in every Oriental city, the streets are narrow and crooked. Horrible dust always pervades the market, because there are no paving stones," he wrote to his father. He had no desire to stay in the grimy port city. "When I saw Jaffa I hated it," he said many years later. "I saw it's worse than Płońsk."[19] His reaction to Jaffa may have had something to do with the sight of Halbovski.

Whatever the case, on Friday afternoon he joined a small band that set out for Petah Tikvah. He enjoyed the journey. The air was wonderful, "full of fine scents, like the air of paradise, clear and transparent as pure glass," he wrote, adding, "I rode on a donkey." He later added that it was the first donkey he had ever seen. It was all new—the croaking frogs in the ponds, the shadows of citrus groves in the dark, the wonder of stars in the deep blue sky

---

* He later wrote that when he arrived in the country he felt as if he had been "born again." That suggests that, psychologically, he may have viewed the Land of Israel as a new mother. In his old age he numbered the years of his life from the day of his arrival; the date is engraved on his tombstone. (Ben-Gurion to Shazar, Nov. 11, 1969; Falk 1987, p. 45ff; Neumann 2009, p. 61ff.)

at dusk. In his memoirs he revisited his feelings that night. "I was awash with joy . . . as if I were hovering in a mythical kingdom. My soul was turbulent and a single sensation, 'Here I am in the Land of Israel,' overcame me, even as I wondered: Can it be?" They reached Petah Tikvah at ten at night. At the entrance to the moshavah they suddenly heard children wailing horribly. Ben-Gurion was alarmed. His friends explained to him that he was hearing the screams of foxes, not children. That night he stayed in the home of acquaintances from Płońsk; they spoke until dawn.[20]

❖

About thirty-five thousand Jews settled in Palestine in the ten years preceding World War I; this wave of immigration would later come to be called the Second Aliyah. Their socioeconomic profile was much like that of the Jews who immigrated to the United States during these same years. Most were married, many had children. Four out of every ten were women. Only three out of ten were young people, of the age of Ben-Gurion and his companions.[21] Most were indigents seeking a higher quality of life. Jewish newspapers described them as hungry, poverty-stricken migrants, "wretched as shadows." Many remained destitute in Palestine.

Zemach, Levkowitz, and others again and again encountered people who asked them, half in derision and half in pity, why they had come. At least half of those who arrived in the Second Aliyah ended up leaving the country. It may have been many more—Ben-Gurion himself estimated that nine out of every ten left. Many of those who left were young people of his own age. Rachel Yanait, who came two years after Ben-Gurion, commented that the people who left did not understand, nor did they really have a sense of, the historical tie between the Jewish people and the land of its fathers. "They remained lost children of the Exile, just as they had been before, so they abandoned the land," she wrote. Some of them, she insisted, had come to Palestine only to evade service in the Russian army. To stay in Palestine one needed a "huge will," Ben-Gurion wrote.[22] His Zionism was exceptional even in Palestine, just as it had been in Płońsk. There were only a few hundred ideological workers like him, men and women. Their numbers did not reach even half that of the Templers.[23] They also differed from one another, identifying with opposing groups and subgroups; some were rebels seeking a new life for themselves. They wanted equality, a simple life close to nature, collectivism, and self-fulfillment achieved by means of agricultural labor. Each one stood alone, with his own troubles and view of the world.[24] Ben-Gurion wrote that he came to identify himself as a pioneer only after his arrival.

❖

The day after reaching Petah Tikvah, Ben-Gurion moved into Shlomo Zemach's rented room. He and his companions had arrived at the moshavah on Saturday, and on Sunday morning at the latest Ben-Gurion must have seen what Zemach described as "droves of Arabs" who had come to work for the farmers.[25] That was not what he had aspired to, but at least he was not surprised, nor did he have to manage on his own; he thought he was able to identify some of the residents of the moshavah from Zemach's stories.[26] Petah Tikvah was then the largest moshavah in the country, home to more than a thousand people, about half of them farmers. Many of them were Haredim and spoke Yiddish.[27] They ate at a dining hall that Rachel Yanait would later celebrate in her memoirs: "Along the grimy walls stood rough wooden benches, by wooden tables that were filthy with oil stains and blotches of food . . . The air was heavy and stifling, full of tormenting flies and stinking kitchen smells."[28]

"MY PROPOSAL IS NOT A FANTASY"

Ben-Gurion's initial letters to his father continued to convey great happiness, offering picturesque descriptions of the landscape. "The wheel of the sun, red as blood, descends-sinks into the sea, which glitters with rays of gold," he wrote. Only in the Land of Israel could one see such a sunset, he insisted, saying that he was "thrilled and moved." Winter was approaching, but Ben-Gurion thought he could "sense" the spring flowers, and described "the sights of rebirth": a small Hebrew boy galloped confidently on a horse, a Hebrew girl of eight rode a donkey. "My health and looks are very good!" he proclaimed.[29]

Two weeks later that joy had dissipated. As in Warsaw, he sank suddenly into severe melancholy. Again he confided in Shmuel Fuchs. Four months had not yet gone by since his arrival, but Ben-Gurion wrote: "I have been in the Land of Israel for five months already and sometimes I feel all alone, without anyone close and friendly, without a companion who understands and feels my soul—and sharp longings burn and overcome me." When that happens, he continued, he takes up the letters he received from Fuchs and reads them hungrily, "and sorrow pierces me over what was, the past surfaces and rises up from the depths of my heart."

It seemed, he wrote, that he lacked nothing, that life was giving him everything he wanted, but his "psychological solitude" tormented him. "I cannot find, among all my acquaintances, a single one, or more precisely that one, a dear friend and brother, close and spiritually connected, in heart and soul." It might very well be, he thought, that such a relationship could form only in "the spring of youth"; perhaps it was only an accident that he was alone. Either way, "I cannot find by any means even a single lover, a friend as we understood the word, who will be part of my life, my heart." For a moment he again clutched at the illusion that Fuchs could come to Palestine: "May we see each other soon on the shores of the Mediterranean," he wrote. Ten years later, he recounted "nights of profound secrets, infused with mystery . . . everything was laden with enigma, intimations of longing, enigmatic turmoil, and an impassioned craving for what was not present."[30] He did not have a girlfriend. The only person he could talk to in the way he wished, he wrote, was Shlomo Zemach, but Zemach soon left Petah Tikvah for the Galilee, and Ben-Gurion remained "alone, with many companions and friends."[31]

❖

His day-to-day life was far from ideal. "More than I labored, I burned with fever and went hungry," he wrote. Only a few Jewish farmhands had steady jobs, and he was not one of them. He told of a kind of slave market. "The Jewish workers had to stand by the synagogue," he recounted, "until the Jewish farmers came to look for a laborer; they'd feel the workers' muscles and take them for work or, mostly, leave them standing there." A few days after arriving at the moshavah, Ben-Gurion found work in an orange grove. "I have work that is nice and clean," he told his father sarcastically, "manuring." He'd first load the manure on a pallet, carry it for a distance as long as that of the marketplace in Płońsk, and lay the dung in pits in the grove. Then, for a few days, he worked under an Arab. When he told his father about this, he placed an ellipsis before the word "Arab," so as to emphasize the grotesquery of the situation. It was, he said, "dirty work." His job was to convey to the Arab spades full of clay and cement.

But there were days when he did not find work, and then he did not have money to buy food. He suffered from hunger. "During the day I tried to evade it in all sorts of ways, or at least to distract myself from it," he wrote. "But at night, at night when sleep evaded me, the feeling of hunger grew stronger, it pinched my heart, darkened my mind, sucked the marrow from my bones, demanding and torturing, and then left at dawn, when I would fall asleep, shattered and broken." Later, he found in Knut Hamsun's *Hunger* a depiction of the nighttime hallucinations he experienced. "I thought I was going insane from the images of bread and butter and meat," he recalled.

Hunger weakened his body. Once every two weeks he suffered a malarial episode. "At first bitter cold would shake my body violently," he wrote, "but then, immediately, after half an hour, the cold would be replaced by a searing heat that lasted for three or four hours." Each such attack lasted for five or six days, meaning he was sick for two weeks out of every month. The more he was sick the less he could work, and the less he worked the more hungry he was. In the morning, when he washed himself, he saw that his hair was coming out. The doctor who treated him recommended that he go home.[32] The radical shifts of mood are typical of his memoirs. "We were exuberant, blissful, enthusiastic, and without worries," he wrote a few lines after describing his nights of hunger: "And in the night, after a day of work or fever, we would gather in the workers' kitchens, on the sandy paths between the vineyards and orchards, and dance and sing, holding hands, shoulder to shoulder, in a circle—we danced and sang." Everything was new there: nature, work, life itself. Together they found their redemption, he wrote.[33] Like everyone else, he wished for the rains to come, and when harvesttime arrived he was full of satisfaction—here he was, inhaling the wonderful air of the orange grove into his chest, and eating as many oranges as he wanted. Ten years later, he added with a farmer's pride: "And they are ours . . . we are workers of the soil and the soil is that of our homeland."[34] One of the moshavah's old-timers later remembered seeing Ben-Gurion driving a wagon drawn by two horses and loaded with hay.[35]

But Ben-Gurion was not good at farmwork and didn't like it. Philip (Pinhas) Cruso, who worked with him in the orange grove, described how they plodded together between the rows of trees, lugging heavy crates of fruit. It was hard work, especially on rainy days; they had to tread carefully, and coordinate their moves, to keep the crates from dropping and falling to pieces. Ben-Gurion's mind tended to be on other things. "It was not easy to work with him in harmony," Cruso later recounted. "I would not recommend him to anyone whose requirement was to have a good, efficient worker." He was one of those guys, Zemach said, who, instead of wielding a hoe, was wielded by it, getting pulled down to the ground. He got the reputation of being "a consummate idler." He wrote that the work bored him; the monotonous pounding of the picks maddened him.[36]

He often sat alone, reading and writing, but, as he had done in Warsaw and Płońsk, he made himself stand out among his fellow workers in Palestine. A former worker named Ya'akov Katzman, with whom Ben-Gurion lodged in a storeroom at one point, recalled a party for workers and farmers. Spirits were high and there was good food and wine. Then came the moment "to say a few words," but no one wanted to speak—not the foreman, or any of the workers. One of them, known for his socialist ideas, volunteered, but his fellows were afraid that he'd again give a lecture on Marx, which would not be to the liking of the farmers. Then another worker, one who was not very popular, stepped forward. His name was David Gruen. He said: "I'll speak." As best as Katzman could recall, he spoke well, and everyone was pleased.[37]

❖

Like many immigrants, Ben-Gurion had trouble separating from his home. "There are times when longings flare up and the heart hurts to bursting," he wrote. Later, he explained that he was "like a prisoner who has been freed, leaving all his companions and close friends in jail, walking free but drawn between the enclosing walls."[38] Each of his letters began with bitter disappointment: why were they not writing him more often? Also, he almost always complained about the mail service. He asked for news, as detailed as possible, about events in Płońsk—how was work going, what were his brothers and sisters doing, had his brother Avraham won the lottery?[39]

Someone from Płońsk brought him a package from home, but he was not entirely pleased. The boots were too small. He asked his father to send larger ones. The socks were superfluous, the sausage was spoiled, but the cakes were good. He repeatedly asked for his farewell photograph from Płońsk and a subscription to a Russian political journal. Sometimes he asked whether acquaintances of his had married, and what had happened in the elections in Płońsk and what was the state of Zionism there?[40] In a letter to Shmuel Fuchs he asked about people from Płońsk who had gone to New York.[41] Once he wrote to his small nephew: "Binyamin, my love, do you have anyone to play with?" If he came to Palestine, Ben-Gurion promised, he'd take him to gallop on an Arabian horse and to handle a rifle, so that he could be a Hebrew hero; he also promised sweets—grapes and almonds, peaches and oranges: "Just be a Hebrew mischief-maker!" He suggested to his brother's young daughter that she learn Hebrew, so that she could eventually be a teacher in one of the moshavot.[42] About a year after his arrival, he suggested to his father that he come to Palestine.

❖

The idea was that his father should bring the whole family, buy a plot of land, and become a farmer. "This time I am writing a purely practical letter, a proposal for settlement, colonization," Ben-Gurion wrote in 1907. "As befits a purely practical matter, I will endeavor to write concisely, dryly, commercially." With great confidence he laid out the future that awaited the family. Everything was clear to him, in the greatest detail. His father would plant an almond grove on his plot, which would be of such and such dimensions, costing such and such a sum; he listed the costs of cultivating it. There would be losses for the first three years; in the fourth year outlays and income would be equal, and in the fifth year profits would start coming in. He computed the sums to the first decimal place and laid out the payment schedule. He seems to have been thinking of a specific project, located not far from the town of Ramla. "My proposal is not a fantasy," he promised. The working assumption in his letters was that, when his family arrived, he too would become a farmer. Four or five years hence they would all be living tranquil, pleasant, and happy lives of labor on the soil of their homeland. "There is no risk of loss," he asserted, insisting that they reply "immediately," preferably by wire.[43]

His conceit about bringing his family to Palestine may have expressed an aspiration to place himself at its head and shape its future. Most of all, he just wanted to be with them. It was an unworkable idea that indicated how little he understood his family. He expected them to follow the path he set out for them, but at that point none of them had any intention of suddenly leaving behind his life in Płońsk to become a farmer. Avigdor Gruen played with the idea at his leisure, posing more and more questions to his son. It was not a serious plan of action but a product of the adjustment difficulties and pining for home of a lonely boy in a distant land.

"I NOW LIVE ALONE"

Loneliness also afflicted Shlomo Zemach, especially in the evenings. Before Ben-Gurion moved in with him, he also yearned for a friend of his, but the young man whose company he sought liked to travel all over the country. "Like a migrating bird, he wanders between different places," Zemach complained. For a time he'd lived in a rented room in Rishon Letzion, where he fantasized about a liaison with an Arab servant girl named Fatma who worked for his landlord. He thought she had the character of a cat. "This mournful sitting in a dim room was nothing less than madness," he wrote.[44]

Shlomo Levkowitz, who had found it hard to find love in Płońsk, described how he once walked the streets of Petah Tikvah in the late afternoon, watching pairs of lovers, tortured by his loneliness. "Who can now give me a warm bed and something beloved, warm, to press to my chest?" he thought.[45] Sexual abstention was often the norm. It sometimes served as an expression of their images of themselves as revolutionaries devoted to their cause, as well as the transition from a culture where young people were matched up by their parents to one typified by individual choice, including a reconsidering of life in a family. In some workers' communes there were many more men than women. It was a subject they spoke of quite a bit, Ben-Gurion later related.*

❖

Ben-Gurion never forgot his first love for Rachel Nelkin, but she soon chose his rival. Work among the fruit trees was hard, Nelkin later recalled. Her hands got cut and bloody. The farmer who employed them observed her from a distance, and in the evening, the foreman told her that with hands like hers she should sit at a piano, not work in a citrus grove. "I was dismissed and ashamed," she wrote, "and would not accept any of my friends' support." She was most likely hoping for a good word from Ben-Gurion. She got it instead from Yehezkel Halbovski, who was "good and gentle, always knowing how to provide encouragement and implant faith and hope," she wrote.[46] The two became a couple. On October 16, 1906, Ben-Gurion wrote to his father: "I am living alone today." It was his twentieth birthday.[47] His loneliness was his greatest problem. He dealt with it in two ways: writing and politics.

---

* The pioneers had their own local philosopher, a man three decades older than most of them. His name was Aharon David Gordon. The small community of Zionist laborers looked to him as a guide, spiritual mentor, and moral authority. Along with politics and ideology, they received guidance from him on sex and family life as well. (Zemach 1983, p. 61; Muki Tsur 1998, p. 112ff.; Ben-Gurion interview with Hayerushalmi, Feb. 28, 1972, BGA.)

· 4 ·

FOREIGN LABOR

"A NORMAL PERSON"

He wrote reams, with almost compulsive intensity, in a Hebrew that grew ever more erudite, as if he were a journalist on assignment or a member of some sort of fact-finding commission. Within six weeks of the day he began to send his father nearly daily reports about his new life, he asked him to preserve his letters. "It will be important for me some years from now to know what I thought about the Land of Israel at each moment and every stage," he explained. At the same time, he did his best to lend his reports an objective, reliable cast, and did not try to paper over difficulties he occasionally encountered. Wages were lower than in Russia, he related, but food also cost less. He offered a list of prices: so much for a cup of tea, so much for a loaf of dark bread, so much for sugar. Milk was expensive and hard to get in the summer. A full meal—borscht, lentil soup, and meat, without bread, cost such and such. He quoted the prices in Turkish currency and computed the equivalent in rubles. The wine was excellent, the honey better than in Russia. Oranges and lemons were to be had for the taking. A laborer who worked every day could live off a sum that was less than the going wage, the equivalent of six and a half Russian kopeks. But, he noted, most workers did not have work every day.[1]

He estimated that Petah Tikvah could provide employment for some three hundred Jewish workers each year, and that these workers could form "a healthy and strong working class . . . the hope of every free, normal nation." It was neither an illusion nor a dream, he assured his father again and again. "In Exile we had dreams," he wrote. "Here, in the land of our rebirth, we understand what they meant." This was his Zionist philosophy in a nutshell. "Zionism is not a future ideal," he wrote to Fuchs, "but rather a real state of affairs in the present, which is improving before my eyes as a natural imperative."[2] He mentioned that he had malaria but did his best to minimize its seriousness. Once he told his father that his temperature had gone up to 41.4 degrees Celsius (106.5 Fahrenheit). "Were that to happen in Russia I would have been in mortal danger," he wrote, "but here in Palestine *it is not at all dangerous!*" A doctor prescribed him medicine and before he even filled the prescription he had entirely recovered. "'Malaria is not a disease,'" he wrote, quoting a local saying. In general it passed in one to three days; if it lasted for weeks, it was a sign that a person had not kept himself fit. Lipa Taub, the librarian from Płońsk, had not yet had an episode and was healthy as a horse, Ben-Gurion related.

He informed his father about the political situation in the same spirit. He marveled at the autonomous freedoms that the Turkish authorities granted the Jews of Palestine. The government collected taxes, but other than that it did not interfere with their lives. The moshavot were "tiny Hebrew republics," he wrote. "Each moshavah is 'a tiny Jewish state.'"* The moshavah's elected council conducted its affairs with almost total independence.

---

* Petah Tikvah printed its own postage stamps and banknotes. Most of the country's Jews were citizens of other countries and thus enjoyed rights and protections guaranteed by foreign powers. (Ben-Gurion to his father, Nov. 13, 1906, Jan. 27, 1907, in Erez 1971, pp. 86ff., 99.)

That was not the whole story. Most newcomers entered the country as tourists and usually stayed on illegally. However, from time to time the authorities issued regulations that made it more difficult for Jews to enter the country, to remain there, and to buy land. Ben-Gurion also exaggerated in his descriptions of the development of Hebrew culture, which was still taking its first steps. Most of the Jews living in Palestine at the time did not speak Hebrew.

His letters were passed around in Płońsk, and Ben-Gurion knew it. He also knew about the "base slanders" that some Płońskers who had spent time in Palestine were disseminating. He termed them "the new spies," a reference to the Israelite spies who, after being sent to scout out the Promised Land by Moses, returned and spoke ill of it, frightening their compatriots. Such people, he wrote, were "mummified Jews who were sunk up to the neck in the swamps of the Exile." They would not rouse themselves even if they were to hear that the streets of the Land of Israel were paved with gold. Ben-Gurion stood behind his reports. "You can see from my previous letters that I do not paper over all the bad conditions in Palestine, and I even told you about the malaria. But just as I would not tolerate inflated praise of the country, so I will not remain silent when it is unjustly libeled."[3]

The reports he sent to Płońsk required him to keep abreast of events in Palestine and thus facilitated his assimilation into the community there. The optimism of his letters might have encouraged him as well as his readers. "Twenty-five years from now," he wrote, "we will live in one of the most flourishing, beautiful, and happy of countries, and an ancient-new nation will blossom in the ancient-new land, and then we will relate how we had malaria and labored, shivered and dreamed."[4]

❖

He sometimes remarked on the decline in the quality of Jewish immigrants. He termed many of the new arrivals "undesirable elements," who harm the community in Palestine more than they strengthen it. A letter he sent to Fuchs four months after his arrival reflected a sudden and painful awakening from his illusions. Only three years had gone by since they parted, he pondered. "You could say that we were still children then . . . innocent, dreaming, fantasizing children—and we have now gone on into life, cruel, rude, real life." Others, too, were disenchanted.*[5]

One of the first lessons he learned in Palestine was that people who came only to realize an ideal generally could not survive—only in exceptional cases did they succeed. "A normal person," as he put it, first needs to see to his material needs.[6] Soon Ben-Gurion found himself reenacting what he had done in Poland. He left his town, Petah Tikvah, moved to the nearby city of Jaffa, and began to build a career based on the only experience he had brought with him from Poland—organizing workers. As in Warsaw, he began to seek his own personal redemption, just like a normal person.

"A DEEP ABYSS"

When Ben-Gurion came ashore at Jaffa, he arrived as a member of the Po'alei Zion party. That same morning he encountered an activist in the rival party that Zemach had helped found, Hapo'el Hatza'ir. Both parties were tiny and regarded themselves as part of the local labor movement, which was still devoid of influence. The activist tried to get Ben-Gurion into a debate over historical materialism. Ben-Gurion told him he could take his historical materialism and go to hell.[7] In October 1906, Ben-Gurion received an invitation to attend a Po'alei Zion convention in Jaffa. Hapo'el Hatza'ir had scheduled an assembly for the same date. Ben-Gurion and Zemach thus went to Jaffa together. It took them three hours to walk there, through citrus groves, vineyards, almond plantations, and olive orchards. "The sights around us so overwhelmed our senses that we did not feel the heat of the fierce sun over our heads or the fatigue in our legs," he later wrote.[8] Most likely they debated the ideologies of their parties along the way.† Ben-Gurion would have reasserted his view that the differences were negligible, with Zemach stressing his own party's unique outlook. Both parties competed for the same public, and for

---

* Zemach wrote: "Bitter reality came and scratched our souls and spoiled something of the dream that I brought with me from overseas." (Zemach 1965, p. 65.)
† Ben-Gurion claimed that the members of Hapo'el Hatza'ir demanded that Zemach explain his friendship with a member of Po'alei Zion, and why he shared a room with him. Zemach might well have been reminded of the slap he received from his father for visiting the Gruen house. (Ben-Gurion 1971a, p. 23.)

the same sources of political support and funding overseas, making for much animosity between them. They parted in Jaffa, each to his party.

Ben-Gurion encountered an acquaintance in Jaffa, Israel Shohat, a young man his own age who had left Russia for Palestine a couple of years before he had. Shohat had also been a Po'alei Zion supporter in the old country. Ben-Gurion had heard of him in Płońsk; when he first met him, in Palestine, he discovered that Shohat had what Ben-Gurion termed "independent thoughts," of which he said "some were valid and others not."[9] Shohat had organized the Jaffa conference in a modest hotel, the Spector. He seems also to have managed to raise the necessary funds, probably from overseas supporters. He was the force behind the gathering and took Ben-Gurion under his wing.

Po'alei Zion had only about 150 sympathizers in Palestine. The meeting in Jaffa was aimed at setting up an organized political party.[10] Most of those who participated apparently had never taken part in such an event before. That gave Ben-Gurion an advantage—at the party congress that had been held in Warsaw the previous year, the delegate from Płońsk had become acquainted with the movement's dynamics and rhetoric; in Jaffa he displayed his skills and energy. Shohat preferred to remain behind the scenes, engineering Ben-Gurion's election as chairman of the meeting. It was the first time he had presided over such an assembly. He stuck to the agenda and the schedule. Discussions were conducted in Yiddish and Russian, but Ben-Gurion insisted on speaking Hebrew himself. Many of those present probably did not understand him. Like their counterparts in Warsaw, they spent a lot of time debating the fine points of socialist doctrine. Ben-Gurion introduced a practical resolution, the establishment of a labor union, what would eventually become the Histadrut. No one objected. But Ben-Gurion proposed that union membership be open only to Jews.[11]

❖

At that time, Palestine's Jewish farmers lived mostly in the moshavot and preferred to hire Arab laborers, who were cheaper, more experienced, less demanding, and more obedient than Jews were. The average wage of an Arab worker was some 40 percent of a Jewish worker's wages, and unlike the young

Jews who had just recently arrived, the Arabs did not preach historical materialism to their employers.[12] Ben-Gurion and his friends were resentful
about the farmers' "petty accounting"; the farmers responded with barely restrained hatred and overt scorn. "A deep abyss opened between the established farmers and the new workers," Ben-Gurion wrote. He later described
the Jewish farmers and Jewish workers as two different and hostile nations.[13]

Many of the Jewish workers viewed the cheap labor offered by the Arabs
as unfair competition. Some young Jews left the country because they were
unable to support themselves as they had hoped. But one of Ben-Gurion's
boyhood friends said that "whoever wanted to work and was able to work,
found work. The idlers did not find work."[14] The abyss Ben-Gurion referred
to was not caused merely by work problems. "They didn't give us civil rights,"
Ben-Gurion said many years later. He explained: "They didn't want us to
consort with the farmers' daughters."[15] His war against the farmers, whom
he hated from the day he arrived in Palestine, laid the foundation for the political rivalry between his leftist movement and its opponents. The farmers
saw things the same way—they claimed that he was not battling for "Hebrew labor" but rather organized labor. That is, he wanted to control the
labor market.[16] That was true, but Ben-Gurion and his comrades demanded
"Hebrew labor" mainly because they thought this was the best way to build
a powerful and secure Jewish presence in Palestine.

❖

Shlomo Zemach and Shlomo Levkowitz saw Arab laborers every day, and
did not like what they saw. Levkowitz once left Rishon Letzion for Rehovot.
He had intended to go by foot, leaving before sunrise. But on the main road
he encountered a large mass of workers heading toward Rishon Letzion, some
riding donkeys and others walking—hundreds of men, women, and children,
all Arabs. Levkowitz was worried about the danger to the moshavah's Jewish
laborers. "I shudder to think what might happen if the smallest gust of rebellion blows among these workers; they might well exterminate the few Jewish
men and women in an instant." But this sort of anxiety was not the main
thing that troubled him. He felt humiliated. "You see so few Jews in work

clothes, most of them are well-groomed and dressed in light suits, with Panama hats on their heads," he wrote. He went on his way, against the flow.[17]

Levkowitz recounted protest actions against Arab labor, among them some aimed at projects run by the Zionist Organization and funded by the Anglo-Palestine Bank. Levkowitz and another young man set out for Jaffa to search for the bank's director, Zalman David Levontin. By the time they arrived, night had fallen. Levkowitz had taken a dagger with him, and they also had sticks, but he and his companion were quite frightened as they walked alone in Jaffa's dark and convoluted alleys. Neither did they know Levontin's address. In the end, they encountered two Jewish night watchmen, who led them to the banker's home. His wife refused to open the door, saying that her husband was already asleep. They needled her to wake him.

Levontin appeared in a nightshirt and demanded that they leave their sticks and dagger at the gate. He was impatient, but listened to them. They said that they would not give up until the jobs on the plot near Lydda were given to Jews, threatening a scandal that would have repercussions overseas as well. Levontin said that he believed in their Zionist idealism, he just didn't believe that they were capable of labor. Nevertheless, he promised to suspend work at the site until he received instructions from the bank management in London.[18] In his letters he claimed that Jewish workers always went around armed with sticks and knives and that they treated the Arabs with arrogance, condescension, and hostility in their struggle for Hebrew labor.[19]

"THE MOST OBSCENE ARABIC WORDS"

When Ben-Gurion found himself in the company of Arab passengers on the boat he took to Palestine—Arabs who he said looked to him like large children—he must have realized, had he not known so already, that there were hundreds of thousands of Arabs in the country. Some Christian Zionists liked to think then that Palestine was a land without a people meant for a people without a land. The same proposition was voiced by some Jews, Zionists included; Ben-Gurion called that position "naïve Zionism." He believed that the Land of Israel belonged to the Jews and that they deserved to receive it despite the fact that it was populated by Arabs. Moshe Sharett later wrote: "We are not coming to a desolate land to inherit it; rather, we are coming to conquer the land from the nation that resides there."[20]

❖

Ben-Gurion could have read, at the age of fifteen, a dispatch from Palestine published in *Hatzefirah* by a journalist and Zionist activist. Among other things, the account told of his encounters with Arabs during his journey. He had felt threatened, and shared with his readers advice he had received about how to relate to them: "Show them an enraged face, and don't react to them or anything they say."[21] There were frequent scuffles, fights, attacks, and murders of Jews by Arabs, not necessarily for political reasons. *Hatzefirah* reported on any number of occasions about violence between Jewish farmers and Arabs, resulting from, for example, conflicts over grazing areas.[22]

The Arabs were often compared to the hostile Christian majority that had violated the rights of the Jews and persecuted them in their countries of origin. Many of the Jews who came to Palestine had lived through pogroms.[23] Though they may have preferred Arabs to Jews as workers, Jewish farmers often treated their Arab laborers condescendingly and contemptuously. Traveling through Palestine at the end of the 1880s, Ahad Ha'am wrote: "They behave toward the Arabs with hostility and cruelty, commit unwarranted trespass, beat them shamefully without any good reason, and brag about doing so." In another article, he wrote that the Jewish farmers treated their Arab tenants just as they treated their farm animals. "They do not think of the *fellahin* [peasants] as human," a resident of Jaffa, Israel Rokach, wrote to Levontin, the banker.[24] The Jewish farmers of Hadera printed up special identity cards for their Arab laborers. "The intention is not to impose on them, but to keep their mouths shut," the moshavah's governing council maintained.[25]

Far off in Russia, a Jewish revolutionary named Ilya Rubinowicz had asked in 1886: "But what is to be done with the Arabs? Will the Jews consent to being aliens among the Arabs, or will they want to turn the Arabs into aliens among them?"[26] About a year after Ben-Gurion settled in Palestine, a Jewish teacher there, Yitzhak Epstein, wrote an article questioning the way

Jewish immigrants were treating Arabs that set off a major debate on the Arab question.[27]

❖

The purchase of land for Jewish settlements sometimes involved the ejection of Arabs from land that they had cultivated as tenant farmers. Sometimes they were paid compensation and sometimes they were not. The farmer and writer Moshe Smilansky, whose articles Ben-Gurion and his friends read back in Płońsk, recounted seeing fellah women weeping and lamenting the lands and homes they had lost, without compensation. Jewish settlers had chased them off with sticks and then taken pride in doing so, "with shocking cynicism," he wrote.[28] He demanded that special caution be taken in the choice of lands that Jews purchased from Arabs, maintaining that inhabited land should not be bought. "The fellahin are closely bound to their land and will not easily leave it," he declared. "They have put down roots on it, built their homes and yards there, and buried there their loved ones and saints." They see the new settlers as a danger and virulently hate them, Smilansky added. No one should be surprised at that, he explained: "The land is dear to the fellahin and it is increasingly being taken by [Jewish] settlers . . . We should not take the hatred of the fellahin lightly."[29]

Smilansky was a regular participant in a long-running debate in the local press over Jewish-Arab relations. It dated back to before Ben-Gurion's birth and the founding of the Zionist Organization by Herzl. As Arab public leaders began to voice their opposition to Zionism and to call for restrictions on Jewish immigration, the issue became more urgent. To a large extent it was an ideological and political debate between "doves" who believed in the possibility of Zionist-Arab coexistence and "hawks" who maintained that realization of the Zionist dream would require a solid Jewish majority and deterrent force, and perhaps even violent confrontation. One of the questions on the table was whether the behavior of the Jews, including their treatment of Arab workers, really made any difference to the nature of relations between the two peoples.

It was also a cultural debate among intellectuals. Some preached complete integration into Arab culture. Others maintained that Jewish culture was superior to Arab culture, and that it had the potential to make the Jews the masters of the land. According to Herzl, the Jewish state would be "a rampart of Europe against Asia, an outpost of civilization as opposed to barbarism."[30] Many of the country's Arabs did indeed live in conditions of backwardness, illiteracy, filth, and disease.

The encounter between the two peoples produced not only a range of negative stereotypes, but also trepidation that the Jews would adopt Arab culture.[31] Sometimes Arab laborers lived, alone or with their families, in the yards of Jewish farmers. Sometimes they slept in the barns. Ben-Gurion related that when he worked at Zichron Ya'akov, a community on the southern spur of Mount Carmel, he found two Arab families living in the yard of almost every farmer, day and night. It worried him, in part because Jewish children were learning from Arab children "the most obscene Arabic words," which they used without understanding what they meant.[32]

Most of the Jewish immigrants arrived with a clear sense of having come to a land that belonged to them, the land that God had promised to Abraham. The Jewish settlers of the Second Aliyah, the vast majority of whom came from Eastern Europe, spoke of the Arabs as "foreigners" and "aliens."[33]

As he began his career in local labor organizing, Ben-Gurion's primary interest remained replacing Arab laborers with Jewish ones. As part of that he studied the history of the workers' union of Rehovot, the charter of which had stated, fifteen years before his own arrival in Palestine, that the country's Hebrew workers are "what blood is for the body of a healthy man; they give him life and preserve him from decay and death."[34]

Taking control of the labor market in Palestine would help Jews turn themselves back to a "normal people," he maintained. The socialist ideology that he and his friends brought with them from Russia sanctified manual labor and the working of the land as a supreme virtue. The backwardness of the Arabs and the patronizing attitude toward them in the moshavot only reinforced their view that it was essential to establish a separate Jewish economy, free of prejudice and exploitation.[35]

Smilansky also rejected Arab labor, on economic grounds. Every Jewish farmer provided a livelihood for three Arab families, he reckoned. Without Hebrew laborers, he found, the land would not return to "Israel"—that is, to the Jewish people.[36] Prior to this, Smilansky had praised the Boers in South

Africa for working, he claimed, with their own hands, and held them up as exemplars for the Jewish settlement of Palestine.[37] It was against this background that Ben-Gurion placed himself at the head of the fight for Hebrew labor. He saw it as "a fundamental question that will determine the fate of Zionism as a whole."[38] It was the logical extension of the thesis he had brought with him from Warsaw: the worker's interest and the national interest were identical. Since Jews were exploiting Arabs, better for them not to employ them at all. "Like every worker, the Arab laborer hates his taskmaster and exploiter," he wrote. "But, since alongside the class opposition here there is also a national difference between the workers and the farmers, this hatred takes the form of national hatred, and in fact the national element overwhelms the class element, and a powerful hatred of Jews is lit in the hearts of the masses of Arab workers."[39]

The campaign to eject the Arabs from their places of work and replace them with Jews was called "the conquest of labor." That term was coined by Shlomo Zemach.[40] Ben-Gurion and others labeled Arab labor with a term pregnant with biblical and religious connotations: *avodah zara*, literally "foreign labor," but it has its origin in Jewish religious texts, where it means "idolatry," forbidden to the Jewish people. And when Ben-Gurion and his associates spoke of "the conquest of labor," they meant the conquest of the country.[41]

"ALL MY FREE TIME"

He had opposed the employment of Arabs while he was still in Warsaw. Ussishkin's Zionist program, which Ben-Gurion sent to Fuchs, termed the employment of Arabs a "cancerous leprosy." Ussishkin feared that Arab workers would someday open their eyes and demand a share of the moshavot that they built with the sweat of their brows. "When the horse becomes aware of his strength," he warned, "it throws its rider to the ground." And he added that the employment of Arabs was also liable to raise them up economically such that they would no longer agree to sell their land to Jews.[42] He proposed establishing an "all-Palestine workers' organization" of single young people who would commit themselves to remaining in Palestine for three years "and perform their military duty to the Jewish people, not with a sword or rifle but with the spade and plow." Sound of mind and body, they would go to the moshavot and offer themselves as workers for the same wage received by Arabs.

Private letters and diary entries written by Jews of that time were much more explicit. Some of them were set down many years before Ben-Gurion came to the country, and even before he was born. In 1882, Vladimir (Ze'ev) Dubnow wrote to his brother, the historian Simon Dubnow, regarding what he termed the ultimate goal: "taking control of Palestine over time and restore to the Jews the political independence that has been denied them this two thousand years." To achieve this goal, he proposed "to try to ensure that the land and all production be in Jewish hands." He did not rule out the possibility that the Jews would seize control of the country by force. "The Jews will then rise up and, with arms in hand (if need be), they will declare themselves in a loud voice the masters of their ancient homeland.[43] Ben-Gurion quoted his letters in full in his memoirs and lauded him for his open-eyed view of the Zionist vision.[44]

At the Po'alei Zion convention in Jaffa, some of the leftists objected to Ben-Gurion's proposal that the new labor organization accept only Jews as members. He defended his position on patriotic grounds and it was eventually accepted.

The convention in Jaffa chose a Central Committee; Ben-Gurion was named one of its five members. The first task was to draft a party manifesto. To this end, they convened in an Arab inn in Ramla.[45] "We are very busy," Ben-Gurion wrote to his father from the secret meeting, which is why he only had time for a short evening stroll around Ramla. Typically, he sat down afterward and composed a detailed report about what he saw. He ascended 127 steps to the White Tower, from which he viewed one of those sunsets that always made him tremble, firing up his imagination. "Who knows," he wondered. "Maybe our heroes fought here thousands of years ago with those who took their land."[46] In later years, Rachel Yanait dismissed the importance of the event. A few nice young guys with tousled hair having a philosophical disputation was all it was, she wrote, but they still had no concept of the needs of the country's Jewish workers.[47]

Po'alei Zion's members reconvened in Jaffa in January 1907 to ratify what was called the Ramla Manifesto. Ben-Gurion was one of the central speakers. He declared that the proletariat's mission was to establish an independent Jewish state, reiterating an idea then current in Russia, where socialists proclaimed that what was good for the workers was good for the entire Russian nation.[48]

Ben-Gurion had begun to find himself, and his political destiny.

"I spend all my free time on public affairs," he wrote to his father, explaining why he did not write more often. It was the first time he placed public affairs above family duty.[49] In the meantime, he moved to Jaffa. The Arab city he hated, in part because of the masses of Jewish immigrants who congregated in its narrow streets, offered Ben-Gurion more than Petah Tikvah could, just as Warsaw had offered more than Płońsk.

❖

Politics still did not provide him with a livelihood, so as in Warsaw, he supported himself in Jaffa as a teacher. From time to time he visited Petah Tikvah, where he established a workers' organization, just as he had returned from Warsaw to Płońsk for the same reason. "In Petah Tikvah we founded the first trade union," he later wrote, echoing Herzl's famous declaration "In Basel I founded the Jewish state."[50]

He tried to establish similar organizations for tailors, carpenters, and cobblers. Dispatching reports of his activities to the American branch of Po'alei Zion, he solicited financial support, to be sent to his private address. He had no objection if the New York comrades wanted to disseminate his letter, he added; they did so. Written in Yiddish, it was his first published work.[51]

In early January 1907, a strike broke out among Jewish workers in the Rishon Letzion winery. It turned violent, and shots were fired. Ben-Gurion succeeded in brokering a settlement. No one came out victorious, no one was defeated, and no one was pleased. Between one meeting and another, almost everyone accused Ben-Gurion of causing the party damage. His political ascent ground to a halt. As he attempted to defend himself, a new figure appeared on the scene—Yitzhak Shimshelevich, a well-known senior Po'alei Zion leader from Russia, a high school graduate about two years older than Ben-Gurion. In Palestine he called himself Ben-Zvi. In the meantime, Ben-Gurion's partnership with his original Po'alei Zion comrade Shohat had come to an end. The Central Committee the two of them had put together fell apart and now Ben-Zvi reorganized the party. Its third convention was convened in September 1907, at a girls' school in Jaffa.

"IF WE MARRY, THERE WILL BE CHILDREN"

Ben-Zvi had met Shohat during a previous visit to Palestine; his impression was that the secrecy-loving young man was open to receiving political guidance from the party in Russia. Ben-Gurion was new to him, but Ben-Zvi quickly understood that this was a person with an inclination to act without instructions. The delegates to the Po'alei Zion convention voted to send Ben-Zvi and Shohat to the next Zionist Congress to be held in The Hague. Ben-Gurion was not chosen as one of the two members of the Central Committee, but Ben-Zvi arranged a position for him as a third member. In the terms of the political environment he lived in, that was a demotion.

In the meantime, Shohat fantasized about forming an underground militia. He gathered a secret cabal around himself, inspired by the Cossacks and Hebrew legends of heroism. The group intended to take the place of the Arab guards employed by Jewish settlements. Shohat's followers worshipped and obeyed him.

At the end of the Jaffa convention's third day of discussions, Ben-Zvi invited Shohat and about half a dozen of his people to his room. According to Ben-Zvi, it was "a special council with a special goal that must be discussed among a small circle of selected members." According to the *Haganah History Book*, the atmosphere at the meeting was thick with "the mystery and romanticism of underground action." Shohat was the main speaker. Everyone was impressed by his fiery personality; they resolved to found a secret military order, to be called Bar Giora, the name of one of the leaders of the Jewish revolt against the Romans of A.D. 66–70. Ben-Zvi proposed a motto: "In blood and fire Judea fell; in blood and fire Judea will rise." For the people at the meeting, it was a feeling of being present at the Creation, Ben-Zvi wrote.[52] Israel Shohat was named commander. Ben-Gurion was not invited. Although he was not one of Shohat's confidants, he was profoundly hurt. The new organization was meant to develop into his party's military wing, but had been established behind his back. Bracha Habas, Ben-Gurion's semiofficial biographer, asked Shohat why Ben-Gurion had been excluded. It was 1952; Ben-Gurion was prime minister and Shohat was a senior official in the Ministry of Police. Shohat spoke very carefully. "In terms of his nature and his approach to life in Palestine, he was fit to be one of us," he explained, but they had already found their spiritual leader, their "socialist rabbi," who would tell them what was permitted and what was forbidden, in Ben-Zvi. "We were concerned about having an additional spiritual leader," he said.[53] In other words, Ben-Gurion would not have accepted the leadership of Shohat and Ben-Zvi. And there may well have been another reason.

At the beginning of 1904, a twenty-five-year-old woman appeared in Palestine. Her name was Manya Wilbushewitz, and she bore on her young shoulders the consequences of radicalism and violence. She was a Russian revolutionary and self-confessed murderer. Obsessive and suicidal, she seems to have been more than a little out of her mind.[54] In Palestine she met Israel Shohat and, a short time after Bar Giora was founded, they married. She was seven years older than he. Ben-Gurion later recounted a fundamental debate among the workers of his youth. "We would meet, members of the Second Aliyah, and speak among ourselves about whether marriage was ideologically permissible," he wrote. The question arose, he said, because at the time they did not have the means to raise children properly and, after all, "if we marry, there will be children." At the time he did not have a girlfriend; in the conversations with his friends he was one of the opponents of marriage. The ideal home he imagined was composed of two working brothers and a sister who took care of the cooking and cleaning. "And the truth is that not many married then," he remarked. "The first one to get married, against our position, was Israel Shohat."[55] Shohat thus had more than one reason to exclude Ben-Gurion from his group of confidants. In Ben-Gurion's memoirs, Bar Giora gets only a single mention, and that in parentheses.*[56]

---

* In a letter Manya Shohat later wrote to Prime Minister Ben-Gurion, she said she remembered him as a "nice boy." (Reinharz et al. 2005, pp. 34, 579.)

❖

Alongside his political activity, Ben-Gurion continued to work in the moshavot. His letters to his father remained optimistic. The first rains came, then the winter rains, then the final showers of spring. The skies were clear, the air pure and healthy, and work in the citrus groves easy and pleasant.[57] He worked in the moshavot of Kfar Saba and Rehovot and Rishon Letzion, and once even tried his hand at a job that he did not write home about—he spent thirty-six hours straight inside a barrel, nearly naked, trampling grapes. "For several months after that I could not stand the smell of wine," he later related.[58] It was a good reason to look for a different way of living.

· **5** ·

SEJERA

"ZERO HOUR"

Soon after dawn on a wintry morning in 1908, in one of the fields of Sejera, Ben-Gurion trod the furrows behind a plow and a team of oxen, deep in thought, feeling as if he were in a dream. Sejera was a picturesque Arab village nestled in a serene landscape in the Lower Galilee; a European traveler who had visited there in the nineteenth century admired the purple summer blooms of the artichoke thistles that surrounded the village. Archaeological remains show that Christians, and perhaps Jews as well, once lived in the area, and it may be that one or the other garbled the original name, Shajar, which means "tree" in Arabic. The Jewish Colonization Association purchased a large part of the land in and around the village at the end of the 1890s and erected, on the top of a low hill, a farm for training Jewish agriculturalists.[1]

Like the letters he wrote during his first days in Petah Tikvah, Ben-Gurion's initial letters from Sejera were full of enthusiasm and inspiration, as if sent from a Galilean El Dorado. From afar he could see the southern end of Lake Kinneret. It was the color of the sky, and the sky was the color of the lake, Ben-Gurion told his father, "a deep and dreamy blue." When its waves crashed, it turned dark: "The curls of white foam add a special allure to the water's blackness and you stand astounded by the sight and ask: how did a rebellious wind find this baby sea?" Perhaps the Galilean lake was angry at being trapped between highlands, he suggested. To the north rose snowy Mount Hermon, the "elder among the mountains," he wrote, "its white locks gazing down on all the land of the Galilee." To the south, "rising in loneliness," was Mount Tabor. One could hardly help dreaming while plowing the soil of the Land of Israel, he asserted. Its magic, and the magnificence of its hues, he maintained, could hardly be anything but a dream.[2]

At the bottom of the hill, some of the graduates of the training farm founded a moshavah called Ilaniya, but everyone called it Sejera. Ben-Gurion distinguished between the moshavah and the Arab village by referring to the former as "our Sejera." He also saw it as quite different from Petah Tikvah. In his Sejera there were no shopkeepers or speculators, no "foreign" wage laborers. The mountainous and rocky Galilee emerges from his letters as having deeper roots than Judea, as the pioneers called the area in the southwest of Palestine. It was manlier also, but the principal difference between the two areas was that in the Galilee there were no Arab laborers. He thus felt as if he were more "at home."[3]

In fact, Jewish settlers in the Galilee also employed Arab laborers, and that was the case in Sejera as well. But Ben-Gurion preferred to see only Jewish workers.[4] Sejera was to Petah Tikvah as Petah Tikvah was to Płońsk, he wrote. Unlike the farmers of Petah Tikvah, the people of Sejera did not treat their workers with condescension but rather as partners in production. They all cultivated their land, enjoyed their work, and were happy doing manual labor, he wrote—the men plowed, the women milked the cows. He seems to have seen them as the new, proud, fighting Jews whom he described at about that time in a letter to his father, in the spirit of what he had read in Berdichevsky in his youth, and later in others. "Abandon the culture of your fathers," Shlomo Levkowitz wrote, and changed his name to Lavi, meaning "lion."[5]

❖

Once again, Ben-Gurion marveled in particular at the children, those "visions of the rebirth" who had captured his imagination during his first days in Palestine. "They ride on horses to their fathers in the field. They are country boys; they exude the scent of ripe grain and manure and their faces are burnt by the sun," he wrote. It intoxicated him to hear them speaking Hebrew, and tears welled up in his eyes. It was "zero hour," he said. "You are like a partner in the act of creation."[6] At Sejera he found the essence of the Zionist dream; a few weeks before his death, he said that it had been the most profound experience of his life: "I will always remember those days with love and wistfulness." It was a small and isolated community—in 1909 the population was about two hundred.[7]

Sejera did not attract Ben-Gurion because he wanted to work the land, but rather because it was so far distant from the places where he had endured disappointments during his first eighteen months in Palestine. It gave him a second chance. The person who had summoned him to the Galilee was Shlomo Zemach; Shlomo Lavi later joined them. Zemach, as Ben-Gurion put it, "discovered" Sejera a year before, just as he had settled in Petah Tikvah a year before Ben-Gurion. Zemach was among the founders, at his new home, of a team of workers called Hahoresh, meaning "The Plower," and had begun to publish stories in *Ha'olam*, a weekly put out by the Zionist Organization. And he did not abandon his friend in Petah Tikvah. "He returned," Prime Minister Ben-Gurion related many years later, as if he were still overwhelmed by this affirmation of their friendship. "He came back and said to me: there is a place where you will find the homeland. Come with me. We'll go to Sejera. And he led me to Sejera on foot." It took them three days. When they got there, they were nearly dead with exhaustion.[8]

❖

Ben-Gurion would later say that he spent three years at Sejera. In fact, he lived there for only thirteen months and they were not all happy.[9] The reason was that, just a few days after his arrival in October 1908, a Bar Giora posse led by Israel Shohat and Manya Wilbushewitz arrived to work at the training farm. The Collective, as it was known, had twenty members, including six women. They knew how to work and were able to finish the year with a profit. As a close-knit group, they commandeered the communal kitchen and laundry and took control of the social life of the Jewish day laborers. They also dominated the song-and-dance parties that they organized, which lasted well into the night. Zemach loathed them from the first moment. They were weird, loud, and arrogant, he said, and had come to take over the training farm, behaving like conquerors. He soon left Sejera because, he said, he did not want to take orders from Manya Wilbushewitz. But he may have left because of a girl from Rostov who worked in the granary and with whom all the boys flirted. It had seemed to him that she wanted him, but she chose another. Ben-Gurion, again without Zemach, claimed that Wilbushewitz maligned other workers to the farm manager.[10]

The members of the Collective, who were his age, knew about his activity in Po'alei Zion. But they were types who revered power and victory, and at that point Ben-Gurion's party activity had not yet made a leader out of him. They lived as they viewed themselves, as an insular band, an almost secret cult, as they plotted their next adventure. In all of Sejera they could not have found a more enthusiastic supporter than Ben-Gurion, but, once again, they did not include him.

"THE CIRCASSIAN WAS GONE"

A few days after arriving at Sejera, Ben-Gurion realized that the farm's security was provided by hired Arab and Circassian guards, a violation of the principle of Hebrew labor. There were reasons for this. The leaders of the Jewish Colonization Association had cautioned their representatives in Palestine to maintain good relations with the Arabs of Sejera, some of whom had been compelled to evacuate the lands that the company had purchased.[11] The local guards knew the surrounding area and its inhabitants; serving as guards imbued them with pride, and provided them with a livelihood. There was thus good reason to believe that they would do their job well. But the members of Bar Giora schemed to get rid of the "foreigners" and install themselves as the settlement's protectors.

The justification was not that Bar Giora guards would provide better security, but that they were Jews. "We could not accept the aliens guarding Jewish colonies," Israel Shohat wrote. The idea excited Ben-Gurion as well. Jews in their land should defend themselves, he wrote. It was a matter of national honor, and critical to the Jewish people's rebirth in its homeland, he declared.

That was Bar Giora's formative idea, forging it into an organization of great cohesion. They also expected to be paid more as guards than as farmworkers. On top of that, guarding appealed to their youthful macho spirit of adventure, which sometimes took the form of thuggery. Ironically, they always kept one eye on the Arabs—as models. They appropriated a number of badges of native Arab identity—they sported the kaffiyeh, the Arab headdress; they made Arab coffee in long-handled Arab coffeepots, peppered their speech with Arabic words, and staged demonstrations of their riding skills in honor of distinguished guests. Paradoxically, they were seeking to rid themselves of the immigrant culture they had brought with them from their countries of origin. They wanted to be "new Jews" and to demonstrate that they belonged in Palestine and that it belonged to them.*[12]

Ben-Gurion later proudly recounted the dismissal of the local guards in great detail, always using the first-person singular. The farm employed a Circassian guard named Hasan. The members of the Collective demanded that the manager of the training farm replace Hasan with a Jewish guard. The manager, Eliyahu Krause, refused. "The Arab guards, who know every hiding place in the moshavah, every way in and out, will be the first to attack and rob," he warned. "There will be blood." Ben-Gurion realized that defense of the community would not be handed over to them on the spot. "It was necessary to go to war," he wrote, "to fight step by step against each and every guard." They decided to begin with Hasan the Circassian. One night they led Krause's favorite horse to a hiding place and woke the manager to tell him that his horse had disappeared. Krause tried to summon Hasan, but to no avail. "The Circassian was gone," Ben-Gurion recounted. Some of the workers whom Krause had sent to the Arab village in search of Hasan found

---

* Theodor Herzl was treated to a colorful show of this sort when he visited Rehovot. The sight of these Jewish riders brought him to tears. Jews who once sold trousers are now like Wild West cowboys, he marveled. (Herzl, Diary, Oct. 29, 1898, in Herzl 1960, 2, p. 74.)

him in a "deathly stupor" after "a drinking party with friends." Krause dismissed him and appointed in his place a member of the Collective, Zvi Becker. "The first battle has been won," Ben-Gurion wrote, once again as if he had been among the victors. In January 1908, Bar Giora was put in charge of night pasturing. Ben-Gurion told the story frequently, and in later days said that had Krause not enabled the victory of the Hebrew guards, the State of Israel would not have come into being.[13] The Circassians responded as expected—they fired on the farm, night after night, for several weeks. The risk that hostilities would erupt increased.

The campaign Bar Giora launched against the non-Jewish guards required ratcheting up preparedness. The Jewish laborers, Ben-Gurion among them, took turns patrolling the farm. He told of a rainy winter night when he could not see even one step in front of him. "I and my partner had to hold each other's hands," he recounted. They couldn't even speak because "our voices were lost in the storm." They were ecstatic when Krause procured simple double-barreled hunting rifles for their use. "We played with the rifles like small children and did not put them down even for a minute," Ben-Gurion wrote. "We ate, walked, showered, read, and talked with the rifle in our hands or on our shoulders." They looked, he said, like a band of thieves, "about a score of boys sitting on their beds, each one with a rifle in hand! One cleaning the barrel and one doing target practice, one loading and unloading bullets and one filling his ammunition belt—comparing their rifles, listing the pros and cons of each one, hanging them on the wall and taking them down again, hoisting them over the shoulder and then taking them off until it was time to sleep."

But Bar Giora, the local "elite unit," remained closed to Ben-Gurion. Once again deeply insulted, he left the training farm and offered his services as a laborer to one of the farmers in the moshavah.

❖

The settlement's homes stood on the slope of the hill that was crowned by the training farm. When the security of the training farm was handed over to Bar Giora, the farmers also began hiring Jewish guards. "It was the first

moshavah to deploy Hebrew guards," Ben-Gurion later wrote; it was important for him to claim that he had been "the first night guard" there.[14]

His employer, Avraham Rogachevsky, took him into his home as a member of the family, and Ben-Gurion felt good there. "How pleasant and easy
is the plowing!" he rhapsodized. From time to time the oxen disturbed his
thoughts, straying from the path and requiring him to spur them back into
place. "When they return to the straight path, I return to my dreams," he
wrote. He kept a warm place in his heart for the man as long as he lived.[15] In
the evening he had fun with his friends; Rogachevsky's grandson wrote that
Ben-Gurion made out in the granary with the moshavah girls.[16] He read a
great deal and sometimes went down to Tiberias for a good time. But the
warm treatment of his employer and his relatively comfortable life did not
extricate him from his loneliness. On May 5, 1908, he sent his father one of
his heartrending letters of longing, a cry for help. A few months before, his
father had sent him ten rubles and suggested that he come home. Ben-Gurion
was insulted and returned the money. Rachel Beit Halahmi later recalled
that many other young people did the same. In the meantime, however, his
pride had eroded. He asked his father for money and set off for Płońsk.[17]

"WE KNEW THAT ONE OF US WOULD PAY WITH HIS LIFE"

He had many doubts before his trip—his friend Rachel was about to marry
Yehezkel Beit Halahmi. Ben-Gurion seems to have tried to draw encouragement from the story of another man who had also lost his Rachel: "Did
Jacob the Patriarch not suffer the heat of the day and the chill of the night
for his love?" he wrote to his father, explaining that if the love of a woman
was worth such suffering, all the more so the love for the Land of Israel.[18]
On the day they married, Ben-Gurion was already in Płońsk. The practical
reason for his trip had to do with his mandatory service in the Russian army,
to which he was now subject. Had he remained in Palestine, he would have
been listed as a fugitive and his father would have had to pay a large fine.
Ironically, the Russians did not impose a fine on citizens whose sons had
enlisted and then deserted. That is exactly what Ben-Gurion did, making use
of forged documents and bribes, just as others did at that time. Shlomo

Zemach also went back to Płońsk to put the issue of his military duty behind him.[19]

❖

While home, Ben-Gurion continued his efforts to persuade his father to settle in Palestine, perhaps at Sejera. He failed, but did not give up. After his visit—six months of idleness, he wrote—he continued to pressure his family to come. Finally, two and a half years after Ben-Gurion first arrived in Palestine, it seemed like his father might send his other children there as well. Ben-Gurion was on edge—he had promised in advance that if they came he would join the family farm, but he actually had no desire to do so. "I detest the ownership of land, which ties down and enchains its owners, and I love freedom with all my being, the freedom of body and soul," he wrote after returning to Palestine. He weighed studying law in Istanbul; he could hardly have chosen a more "Jewish" profession, or one further away from working the land. "I have one goal: to work for the sake of the Hebrew laborer in Palestine. That is the substance of my life and I will give myself over to that under all conditions," he wrote. In other words, politics. It was a "sacred labor" for him, adding that he took joy in it.[20]

Upon his return, late in 1908, he drifted from place to place rather than going back immediately to Sejera. He was seeking himself and lacked a definite plan. He worked here and there and a bit in Po'alei Zion affairs. "Everything was untamed, abandoned, and empty," he later wrote. As Pesach 1909 approached, he went to Sejera to take part in the general assembly of his party's membership in the Galilee. The members of Bar Giora had left Sejera the previous summer, as part of an effort to placate the Circassians.[21]

In preparation for the Pesach Seder, the workers evacuated the large room they slept in and decorated the walks with eucalyptus and pepper tree branches, as well as with hoes and pitchforks, rifles and swords. In lieu of tables, they placed boards on crates and covered them with white tablecloths. They wanted to have a Seder "like at home," with wine and matzah. Ben-Zvi recited the Haggadah. Those who participated later offered contradictory versions of the event, but they agreed on one point—it wasn't like home. In the middle of the ceremony a latecomer appeared—Moshe Pachter, who had been asked to photograph the Seder. He told them that he and a companion had been waylaid not far from the farm by several Arabs from the village of Kufr Kana, who had taken all their belongings, including his camera gear. Pachter had shot one of the robbers with his pistol. "We immediately grabbed our weapons and rushed out," Ben-Gurion wrote. "We spent a long time looking for the robbers' tracks, but to no avail. But we found bloodstains at the place of the incident. A long red stripe zigzagged down the road and then vanished." The next day, the people at the farm learned that a wounded Arab from Kufr Kana had been admitted to the hospital in Nazareth. According to his fellow villagers, he had had an accident with his gun and wounded himself.

The Po'alei Zion Assembly that opened the day after the Seder was a tense one. It was still a tiny party—most members knew one another. "The members looked older than their years," Rachel Yanait recalled. Her gaze lingered on one of them, who sat in a corner and seemed withdrawn. "He has something that sets him apart and makes him stand out among the rest," she wrote much later. He stood out because "his eyebrows were squeezed close together, completely concealing his eyes; only his forehead spoke for him. It was a broad and high forehead and curls crowned his unusually large head." It was David Gruen. She caught his eye for a minute and noted that "his gaze is distant." He seemed serene on the outside, but his penetrating glance showed, so she claimed, that a storm raged deep inside. He had a mustache at the time.

One of the organizers of the Assembly, Israel Korngold, introduced the two of them. He nominated Ben-Gurion to chair the meeting and Yanait as one of two members of the secretariat. Yitzhak Ben-Zvi offered the central address. Ben-Gurion listened only intermittently. "My hand did not move from the leather holster of my Browning," he would later recall. During the session, word arrived that Arabs had stolen several head of cattle from the training farm. The members halted the meeting and most of them left. Yanait and Ben-Zvi set out for Mes'ha, also called Kfar Tavor.

Two days later, the Arab robber who had been shot by the photographer Moshe Pachter while attacking him died of his wounds. On his deathbed, he revealed that he had not wounded himself accidentally, as he had told his family; he had been shot by a Jew from Sejera. His confession ratcheted up tensions. "We knew that the custom of vendetta was still practiced among the Arabs, and we knew that one of us would pay with his life," Ben-Gurion wrote.[22]

On the last day of Pesach, on April 12, 1909, at two in the afternoon, Korngold showed up, armed with a rifle and pistol. He said that he had encountered two unfamiliar Arab youths sitting on the hill past the cemetery. They had asked him something, but he did not understand them and had come to find someone who could speak to them in Arabic. The person chosen was one of the farmers, by the name of Adler. "Now," he said to his comrades, "we'll drag them here by the ears." Half an hour later, shots were heard, and a few minutes later, Adler returned and said that Korngold had been shot.

"We grabbed our weapons and ran," Ben-Gurion recalled; in the background a bell rang to sound the alarm. They found Korngold behind the hill, in his death throes. Ben-Gurion noticed a small dark-red mark on his chest—a bullet had cut through the dying man's heart and come out his back, he wrote. His rifle had been stolen. Two men remained with Korngold while the others set out in search of the murderers. According to Ben-Gurion, he was among the latter. They found nothing. "There are many hiding places among the boulders and caves of the Galilean hills," he explained. They returned "despondent and full of helpless anger and bitter despair."

As evening fell, they all gathered on the hill next to the training farm. One of them was Shimon Melamed. Ben-Gurion wrote that there was no happier man in the moshavah than Melamed, who had realized his dream of becoming a successful farmer. Ben-Gurion extolled his courage. He had rushed up to the training farm when he heard the gunshots. Always a collector and recorder of small details, Ben-Gurion noted that Melamed had, in his haste, forgotten to take his hat and his gun. "His young wife took down the rifle and rushed after him to give him the weapon. She went home to watch their child, and her husband went up to the farm."

At this point in his story, Ben-Gurion recounted a series of events whose details were obscure. The most salient part involved three Arabs running toward the Arab village of Sejera, pursued by two men from the training farm. Ben-Gurion, Melamed, and a third man went out to block the path of the fleeing Arabs. They approached the Arabs and shot at them, so the Arabs found themselves trapped from in front and behind. The Arabs of Sejera now came out to help their friends. But Ben-Gurion and his companions did not see them. The men who remained at the training farm saw the villagers and rang the bell in alarm. Ben-Gurion and his companions realized they were in danger and fell back. "And suddenly I heard Shimon's voice: 'They shot me!'" Ben-Gurion wrote. "He fell to the ground. I hurried over to him—he was already dead." According to Ben-Gurion, an Arab concealed behind a hedge of prickly pear cactuses had put a bullet through the farmer's heart. The bodies of Korngold and Melamed were wrapped in white sheets and laid in one of the rooms in preparation for a joint funeral the next day. "In the large room, where we held the Seder," Ben-Gurion noted. There are at least two more eyewitness accounts of this incident. Neither of them mentions Ben-Gurion.[23]

It was Ben-Gurion's first involvement in a gunfight with Arabs. As all this was happening, at Kfar Tavor he was being dealt one of the most painful blows to his political career that he ever endured, perhaps the worst ever.

"WHY DIDN'T YOU WANT ME?"

Kfar Tavor was a moshavah that lay about six miles south of Sejera. As emissaries of Po'alei Zion, Yanait and Ben-Zvi were warmly welcomed there. She wrote that they were greeted with "unbridled joy and thrilled faces, but it seemed, nevertheless, that they evinced a deep secret." They had come to found an organization of guards that would operate openly, in place of the secret Bar Giora organization, which was to be disbanded. But the discussions about the new group, Hashomer ("The Guard"), also took place "in inner rooms and deep secrecy." She was nervous. Among other things, she asked herself what roles the women would be assigned.

A meeting was held the next day, on the seventh day of Pesach, in a small house at the end of the moshavah. Yanait and the other participants did not yet know about the events at Sejera that day. Most of them sat on the floor, the rest on narrow benches along the walls. The atmosphere was one of "open and furtive whispers." As they saw it, the founding of Hashomer was a "bold and liberating" act.[24] According to Yanait, it was all meant for "our best people." The organization they established functioned for about ten years and, at its height, had about one hundred members, among them twenty-three women. They served as guards, labored, and established settlements. As with Bilu pioneers a few decades before, Hashomer's importance lay mostly in the myth that it bequeathed to subsequent generations. It is considered one of the cornerstones of the Israel Defense Forces. And Ben-Gurion was, once again, not invited to join.

❖

The clash at Sejera that claimed the lives of Korngold and Melamed took his mind off Hashomer's founding, but not for long. "The insult burned in Ben-Gurion to his last day," said Shaul Avigur, one of his closest associates. "He couldn't hold back when he spoke about it with me—how could such a thing have happened?" For years afterward he would ask Yanait, who had in the meantime married Ben-Zvi: "Why didn't you want me?"

Yanait Ben-Zvi did her best to explain that for posterity. For the most part, it was much like the explanation for excluding him from Bar Giora. Hashomer imposed iron discipline on its members, she explained; Ben-Gurion would have been unable to endure it. He thought too much and talked too much—he could not be restrained. His thoughts could not be mastered, she maintained.[25]

Avigur proposed a more direct explanation. There was one chief, his name was Israel Shohat, and he didn't want a second chief, especially not Ben-Gurion, a rebel who never accepted authority and argued with everyone. Under no circumstances Ben-Gurion. Avigur added that he had never understood why Shohat, of all people, had headed the organization. There were better candidates. He attributed it to "mass psychology," by which he apparently meant the mystical hold that Shohat had over some of the members.[*26]

Ben-Gurion's insult left clear tracks. He produced one of the most dramatic paragraphs he ever wrote to describe what he and the other people at

---

* The editors of Manya Shohat's letters believed that she and her husband felt at this time that they stood on the verge of becoming the future leaders of Palestine's Jews. A large portion of Hashomer's members belonged to a relatively small number of families, which reinforced the group's insularity and gave it the character of a clan. (Sinai 2013, p. 160ff.; Reinharz et al. 2005, p. 34.)

Sejera underwent after the members of Bar Giora left for the secret Hashomer meeting. "A black shadow spread around us," he wrote, "the shadow of death lying in wait. No one said it straight out, but each of us knew it inside and read it in the eyes of his friends—the sword of vengeance hung over us and would fall on the head of one of us. Fate would choose its victim. We were all prepared, and we waited." He offered this account of the funeral of Korngold and Melamed: "Instead of going out to work in the field, we stood in the cemetery and dug one grave for the two fallen men, one grave for our two comrades. Mutely we removed them from the workers' room, mutely we bore them on our shoulders to the Sejera cemetery, and mutely, without eulogies, we lowered them into their common grave."

❖

Ben-Gurion viewed the attack on Sejera as an allegory for Palestine as a whole. He said that it brought home to him, for the first time, "the huge might of Arab hostility." In a letter to his father he explained the fundamentals of his view of the "Arab question," as they said then. The problem was Jewish weakness. "The situation here was serious and a cause for concern for the future because all the Arabs around, upon sensing our weakness, began provocations and other actions and to taunt and vex us, and this spread a bit to the other moshavot." He shared his thoughts on Melamed's death with his friends: "I knew that I could be killed just like him, and that it was only a matter of chance that he was the one who was killed . . . Since then I have known—there is no way of escaping death."[27] At Sejera he learned the lesson that this was the price to be paid for achieving the Zionist dream.

❖

Israel Shohat later did much to memorialize Hashomer and foster its myth, including searching for the organization's lost archive. He needed financial support to do so. As with Bar Giora, the writing of Hashomer's history required great caution. In 1956 he sent Prime Minister Ben-Gurion a draft of his memoirs for approval. Ben-Gurion sent back a number of corrections. In 1957 Shohat hoped that Ben-Gurion would attend the organization's jubilee celebration. Shohat and two other members wrote to invite him, saying, "Even if you were not a member in practice, we are aware that that was a matter of chance and no more." Ben-Gurion did not attend, but sent a perfunctory greeting.[28]

About a year and a half before his death, Shohat dictated an article for publication in *Davar* in which he related that many people still asked him why one or another person had not been accepted into the organization. The time had come to explain, he said. "We chose the people who in our view were the most fit to serve as guards," he related. "We chose them with great care, after they had passed—without knowing it—a variety of tests." He made a cynical reference to the friendship between Ben-Zvi and Ben-Gurion: "If we accepted someone into our ranks, and his good friend in as well, who would remain in the party?"[29] Six decades after his sojourn there, almost one decade after resigning as prime minister, Ben-Gurion still felt a need to shore up his standing in history by copying into his memoirs an encomium that Israel Shohat wrote about him: "A young man full of energy, devotion, and a profound faith in the restitution of the nation . . . ready for all pioneering labor."

❖

He remained at Sejera until the summer of 1909. From time to time he made another attempt to persuade his sisters to join him. They did not come, disappointing and angering him—he had expected them all year, he wrote to his father, and when they did not write, he almost went mad with worry. He feared that something horrible had happened that they were not telling him about. Now it turned out that it was all just words. They had no will and no character. He was left with only one small request, he wrote to them—that they stop playing games with him.[30] He still did not know what to do with himself. "With regard to my goal," he wrote in August 1909, "whether I remain a farmworker or study law, I cannot at this moment decide anything." Prior to this he had again failed to get elected to represent his party at the Zionist Congress.

He left Sejera prior to the High Holidays, in protest, he claimed, over what he maintained was the unjust dismissal of one of the workers. The rest of the workers had gone on strike but then returned to work, contrary to the position of the three who left, among them Shlomo Lavi. Ben-Gurion packed his belongings into a small basket and set out for Yavne'el, a moshavah a few miles to the southeast. On the way, an Arab shepherd approached him, grabbed the basket, and ran off. When he reached Yavne'el, Ben-Gurion reported the theft to the Turkish police, who went to interrogate the chief of the neighboring Arab village. The chief claimed to know nothing. The police beat him with a riding crop, in Ben-Gurion's presence, once and then again, until he got up and brought the shepherd with the basket. The shepherd was tried in Acre and sentenced to two years in prison. But the basket was never returned to Ben-Gurion.[31]

His sisters' decision not to come, for the time being at least, helped persuade him to go to law school. In the months that followed he worked at Zichron Ya'akov, the town on Mount Carmel, overlooking the Mediterranean. He studied Arabic and French, and again found himself in euphoria. "If the Garden of Eden is even a bit like Zichron, that proves that it's the real Garden of Eden," he wrote to his father, going all out to describe the moshavah's beauty. There was the blue sea, gardens and vineyards, almond orchards, olive groves, orange groves, and meadows that were carpeted with lilies. He made good money and the farmers' daughters were friendly with the workers.[32]

But Sejera remained fixed in his memory as the high point of his life. The further distant it grew in time, the more its formative importance to him increased. "We are not workers—we are conquerors. Conquerors of the land. We are a camp of conquerors . . . We worked and conquered and we were joyful with victory," he wrote a few years after he left the moshavah. Were he given the opportunity to start his life over again, he would choose to be a farmworker, he wrote. "Here I found the Land of Israel that I dreamed of," he wrote. American donors must have been moved when they heard that.[33] Whatever the case, the road to his true destiny now led him to three fascinating cities: Jerusalem, Salonica, and Istanbul.

DEPORTATION

"A NIGHTMARISH HALLUCINATION"

Jerusalem did not attract him. The city was a maze of stinking alleyways and a mosaic of faiths, hallucinations and primal urges, fanaticism, corruption and decay. Everyone there skirmished with everyone else, and most of the city's inhabitants, both Arabs and Haredim, abhorred Zionism. During his first two years in Palestine, Ben-Gurion had traveled around the country, but without ever going to Jerusalem. The Arabs and devout Jews he encountered in Jaffa and Petah Tikvah seem to have been quite enough. His first visit to the city did not occur until soon after his return from his visit in Płońsk. At the end of 1908, he went there to prepare, along with Ben-Zvi, for the impending Po'alei Zion convention in Sejera. Unlike Lake Kinneret, whose beauty he recounted in vivid colors, Jerusalem did not inspire him. In his next letter he provided his father with his impressions of an uplifting encounter with Hayim Nahman Bialik in Jaffa, but offered not a word about his visit to Jerusalem.[1] In the meantime, Palestine had changed dramatically.

At the beginning of 1908, the Zionist Organization had opened an official bureau in Palestine, naming Arthur Ruppin, a German economist and jurist, to head it. The appointment reflected a growing awareness of the need to take practical measures to promote the Zionist dream. Up to this point, the movement had put most of its efforts into diplomacy. The well-funded Palestine Office operated in Jaffa and soon became a central player in the country. Ruppin eventually came to be seen as the father of the new Jewish settlements. Among his achievements was the establishment of Jewish training farms and labor details, one of which settled in 1909 on the southern shore of Lake Kinneret. Its members lived as a commune, called Degania, "the mother of the kibbutzim."[2]

On one of the days of the terrible week that Ben-Gurion and his comrades endured in Sejera in April 1909, several dozen Jews from Jaffa assembled on the beach just north of the city to participate in a lottery for plots of land on which they planned to build a new neighborhood, Ahuzat Bayit.[3] It was the embryo of Tel Aviv, the first Hebrew city. Ben-Gurion followed these events, but his own practical work did not yet extend beyond the bounds of his tiny political party.

On Pesach, the Po'alei Zion convention resolved to publish a Hebrew-language periodical in Jerusalem, to be called *Ha'ahdut* (The Unity). Several of the people whom Ben-Zvi invited to join the staff turned down his offer, so he suggested to Ben-Gurion that he come to Jerusalem. Ben-Gurion toyed with the idea of refusing. He claimed that he did not know how to write and that he had been solicited only because Ben-Zvi wanted a bona fide worker on the staff. But it didn't take much to persuade him. Ben-Zvi offered him his first opportunity to do something he was good at and liked—he was a proficient writer, and the future of the Jewish people interested him more than the cows and chickens of the moshavot. Working on the newspaper would help him achieve his goals. He was twenty-four years old. City life might also cure his loneliness.

❖

He was not involved in founding the journal; by the time he reached Jerusalem nearly everything was ready. Another party leader would soon arrive from Russia, from the same town as Ben-Zvi. Ya'akov Vitkin, who soon changed his last name to Zerubavel, became *Ha'ahdut*'s editor in chief. Ben-Gurion referred to himself as an editor, but he actually worked as a proofreader and translator. His salary was only a bit higher than what he had earned as a laborer in Zichron Ya'akov, but it was more expensive to live in Jerusalem. He handed over most of the money to a woman who was also a party member, in exchange for which she cooked his dinners. Sometimes he went hungry, he later related.[4]

His first home in Jerusalem was the Floyd House, built by one of those Christians who had come to Jerusalem from America in the hopes of finding his God. Nonreligious Jews had trouble finding housing in the city because most Haredi Jews refused to have them as tenants. Ben-Gurion had a dim room in the house; in lieu of a bed he laid some boards on two crates. All the house's tenants shared a single bathroom.[5]

For Ben-Gurion, it was a gamble. Ben-Zvi was the party's leader; when he arrived, he blocked Ben-Gurion's advancement. Now he was giving him work. Ben-Zvi was a warmhearted type. Ben-Gurion accepted his authority and the two became friendly. As long as Ben-Gurion did not try to shunt Ben-Zvi aside, Yanait could also handle him. She recalled his tone of voice, always clipped and emphatic.[6] He used that same clear-cut and incisive style in an article he wrote for the first issue. It was a fierce personal attack on the chief rabbi of the Ottoman Empire. Rabbi Haim Nahum, located in Istanbul, was not only the empire's top Jewish religious authority, but also served as the Jewish community's senior representative before the Ottoman authorities. He was visiting Palestine at the time the article appeared, filling what was clearly a political role. Ben-Gurion demanded that Nahum, "the religious official," as he called him, restrict his activities to purely religious matters. Contradicting his advocacy of strict separation between religion and the state, he also attacked Nahum for not furthering Jewish national interests, as other nations were doing in the wake of the Young Turk revolution.

The shortage of manpower required each member of *Ha'ahdut*'s staff to write multiple articles for each issue, so they also wrote unsigned pieces or used pseudonyms. Another piece by Ben-Gurion in the same issue railed against the fact that several of Petah Tikvah's leading citizens had not permitted a few of the workers to welcome Rabbi Nahum with a Zionist flag. As was customary in journalistic writing at that time, and as he had done previously in some of his letters, Ben-Gurion used some of the most charged words he knew in depicting the incident: "A nightmarish hallucination during a night of horror . . . terrifying . . . shameful treason . . . national provocation."

Ben-Gurion's third contribution to the first issue was a report from the field, based on his personal experience as a laborer in Zichron Ya'akov. He provided a more-or-less balanced account and signed the piece "Tzofeh," meaning "Observer."[7] Once, while in Haifa, Ben-Gurion caught the newshound bug—when he learned of an attack on the farmers of Yavne'el, he wired his office: "I'm going to the Galilee."[8] But he generally wrote opinionated analytical articles.

"MENTAL ADVANTAGE"

The first radical Hebrew-language socialist periodical appeared initially as a forty-four-page monthly and then as a weekly. Its print run was 450 copies.[9] Its masthead stated that it was published by the social-democratic Hebrew workers' party of Palestine. These words were carefully chosen, as Yanait later related; they showed that the party no longer saw itself as Marxist. They did not repudiate socialism, but as Ben-Zvi put it, "At this time the immediate task is the most important thing, creating a Jewish society in Palestine and organizing workers to defend their interests."[10]

It was in this context that the Zionist movement discovered the Jews of Yemen, some of whom had arrived in Palestine at the end of the nineteenth century, arguing that they could and should replace Arab laborers. "This is the simple, natural worker, able to work at anything, with no shame, no philosophy, and no poetry, either," one newspaper wrote. "And Mr. Marx certainly not to be found either in his pocket or his brain."[11] Arthur Ruppin, chief of the Palestine Office, also advocated employing Jewish workers instead of Arabs. He searched for "Jewish Arabs" who would make do with the conditions and wages that Arabs accepted, and the Yemenites fit the bill. While they were paid better than Arabs, they took less than European-born workers. He resolved to bring more Yemenite Jews to Palestine. It was not an easy decision for him, because they were dark-skinned. Ruppin maintained that there was no such thing as a dark-skinned Jew, but hoped that he could also find fairer Jews in Yemen.[12]

It was the first time that the Zionist movement took the initiative in bringing Jews to Palestine, not because it was ostensibly offering them refuge or redemption, but simply because they were needed to achieve Zionist objectives. The need to import labor from Yemen became more acute because of a mass exodus of European Jewish immigrants who had arrived in the Second Aliyah. It was in this context that one of Ben-Gurion's friends, Shmuel Warschawski, was sent to Yemen. At the time, he was the secretary of the new neighborhood that would become Tel Aviv. He and Ben-Gurion had first met in Yavne'el; Warschawski later changed his name to Yavnieli. Disguised as a rabbi seeking answers to halachic questions, he located able-bodied Jews in Yemen and gave them money for their passage to Palestine.[13]

Ben-Gurion was not involved in this operation, but he supported it enthusiastically. "Ashkenazi workers are certainly superior to Yemenites," he maintained, as they were "cultured" and had a "mental advantage," but, he acknowledged, only a small number of them had adapted themselves to conditions in Palestine. The Yemenites were a different sort of "human material." They were accustomed from childhood to labor and they did not have many needs. "From these elements a class of workers connected to the soil can be created," he said. He supported bringing them also because the Yemenites were Ottoman citizens. "The entry of the Yemenite laborers bolsters our political position," he wrote. The "Yavnieli immigrants" numbered more than twelve hundred. Many of them encountered prejudice and humiliation in the country. Ben-Gurion came to their defense, demanding "total equality, with no exceptions, nowhere and in no way."[14]

At the paper, Ben-Gurion focused from the outset on Zionism's political goals, a niche he carved out for himself that writers more senior than him generally did not write about. His work on *Ha'ahdut* enabled him to consolidate some initial thoughts on several of the fundamental questions presented by the prospect of life in a Jewish state. He believed that he knew how to solve the Jewish question in Palestine and prepared himself to take part in addressing it.

He still did not know how to lead. His party lacked influence and he did not carry much weight within it. At this point, he had not said anything very original. His aptitude was not for framing new ideas but for carrying them out politically.[15] But his political analysis now suddenly provided him with the standing of a pundit worthy of attention. When he later needed the help of the American consulate, they already knew of him there. In this context, Ben-Gurion made one of the most important decisions of his life—he shed his original family name and chose himself a Hebrew name that he used to sign his writing from this moment onward. At the time, it served only as a pen name.

❖

Yosef Ben-Gurion had been a Hebrew statesman of the first century A.D. He had assumed leadership of Jerusalem, in tandem with the high priest. It was then that Jewish rebels had begun to organize to oppose Roman rule. Bloody conflict broke out among the Jews. The contemporary historian Yosef ben Matityahu, better known as Josephus, praised Ben-Gurion for belonging to a noble family, but also because of his free speaking "for democracy"; he had "as great boldness and freedom of spirit as . . . any of the Jews." He devoted himself to fortifying Jerusalem. He was murdered during one of the waves of fanatic madness that swept through the city. According to Josephus, Ben-Gurion found his end not only because of his high pedigree but also because of his "free speaking." The impression is that he lost his life in an attempt to save his fractured people from themselves. Josephus enumerates only his noble characteristics as a statesman, as if he were a man without a past who was born a hero, just as Ben-Gurion liked to believe that he was born a Zionist. Changing one's name was an accepted practice at the time. It was meant to disconnect the person from life in exile and create a new Hebrew identity in Palestine. The historical Yosef Ben-Gurion's first name also sat well on David Yosef Gruen. He might have read Josephus long before, or he might have first encountered the historian in Jerusalem. Rachel Yanait, whose former name had been Golda Lishansky, was an avid reader of Josephus and taught his books at Jerusalem's Hebrew Gymnasium high school. Ben-Gurion may also have known that Micha Josef Berdichevsky, the author he so admired, had adopted the name Ben-Gurion in 1899. There was something else as well—the great opponent of the historical Ben-Gurion had been Shimon Bar Giora. Josephus portrays the latter as the thuggish leader of a brutal gang of terrorists who sought to make himself dictator of Palestine. Apparently Ben-Gurion's murderer was one of Bar Giora's henchmen. In taking his new name, David Yosef Gruen made his hostility to Bar Giora and Hashomer part of his new identity.[16]

"PURIFYING THE FILTH"

Ha'ahdut's printing press and editorial offices were located for a time in the Ezrat Israel neighborhood, north of Jaffa Road. This was not by chance, apparently, as it was a relatively inexpensive and liberal area. A number of members of the staff also lived there. Ya'akov Yehoshua, a longtime resident, recalled that they looked like Russian revolutionaries, dressed in embroidered Russian shirts and patched trousers, with a cap flattened on their heads and sandals with no socks. The local barbershop and pharmacy were their meeting places; they drank a lot of tea, debated into the small hours of the night, and at least once a week, on Saturday nights, partied by singing songs in Hebrew and Russian.

Aharon Reuveni, Ben-Zvi's brother, wrote a roman-à-clef about them, in which he changed *Ha'ahdut*'s name to *Haderech* (The Road) and Ben-Gurion to Givoni, a glum sort "with his face frozen in a barely controlled subversive obstinacy." The other writers for the journal talk about him when he is not around and laugh at him behind his back. He likes very sweet tea, they gossip—he fills half the cup with sugar. One character says that a passion for sweet food is shared by all those who advocate sublime ideals; everyone laughs. He is different from them—he is interested in abstract ideas. They refer to him as a fanatic and compare him to Savonarola, the Dominican friar and doomsday preacher who for a time became a power in fifteenth-century Florence. When he disagreed with someone, he gave him a disdainful look. They didn't like him. "He lacks any living feeling for living people," the novel's protagonist says.[17]

Ben-Gurion once wrote a short story praising Jerusalem's stonecutters over the generations. He was trying to be funny. It was a childish piece worthy of mention only because his colleagues did not stop him from publishing it. A month later, he wrote a short drama in honor of May Day with the title "The Labor Holiday." It, too, was unworthy of publication, but no one prevented him from making a fool of himself. No one said, "David, not this one." Both these works were bylined with the pen name "Ba'al Hahalomot," meaning "The Dreamer." On at least one occasion he went to the theater and published a scathing critique under the name of Dan. The story, direction, and acting of the "lovers of the Hebrew theater" who staged the show was "soulless," lacking psychology, he maintained.[18]

Shortly after Ben-Gurion made his home in Jerusalem, Shlomo Zemach followed. They met often, sometimes together with Ben-Zvi. Zemach published stories in another journal, *Hapo'el Hatza'ir* (The Young Proletariat). Once a week the two of them would take a walk along the Old City walls, visit the Western Wall and a Turkish bathhouse, returning home before dawn.[19] Zemach had a girlfriend, who would soon become his wife. Ben-Gurion had no one. He sometimes attempted to contact Rachel Beit Halahmi, who already had a baby girl. In a postcard he sent her, also signed by Shlomo and Hemda Zemach, he invited her to spend a few days in Jerusalem. She didn't come.[20]

❖

At the end of 1910, Ben-Gurion issued a call to found a "national political organization" that would represent the Jews of the Ottoman Empire and lobby the government and parliament to attain Jewish rights. Up to that time, there had been no such central institution. It was his first political article. It would have been hard to guess that he was a novice—he wrote like an experienced commentator. Alongside his praise for the empire's treatment of the Jews throughout its history, he complained of the suspicion with which the Young Turk government viewed Zionist settlement. He described at length Arab attacks on Jewish settlers: "The moshavot are in a state of war," he declared, and risked a bold assertion: "The local government almost abets the murderers and robbers, who will continue their deeds with no fear of the government." He stressed in particular the hatred of Christian Arabs. In this context he mentioned Naguib Azoury, an early Arab nationalist who declared in 1905 that the Jewish and Arab national movements were fated to battle each other until one defeated the other. Azoury's followers, Ben-Gurion wrote, were sowing hatred of Jews throughout the Arab nation.[21]

At the beginning of 1911, the Jewish world and Ben-Gurion himself were scandalized by an article the Hebrew novelist Yosef Haim Brenner published in the newspaper *Hapo'el Hatza'ir*. The subject was Jews who had converted to Christianity.[22] Brenner maintained that there was a Jewish national identity independent of religion and that this identity had no need of the precepts and observances of the Jewish religion. Supporters of *Hapo'el Hatza'ir* in Odessa, among them Ahad Ha'am, demanded Brenner's dismissal from the publication; if not, they threatened, they would cut off the financial support they had provided to the journal.

Hapo'el Hatza'ir was a competitor to *Ha'ahdut*, but Ben-Gurion took the side of Brenner. He stressed in particular the violation of Brenner's freedom of speech. "Who puts limits on what is in the heart?" he asked. He kept himself outside the real point at dispute, stating only that religion and politics should not be mixed. "Religion alone and nation alone," he asserted. But he could not keep himself from referring to the Haredim as "the blacks."[23]

Ben-Gurion and his colleagues at *Ha'ahdut* lived in a secular enclave, but they did not divest themselves of all religious observances. Rachel Yanait later related what one Yom Kippur eve looked like. "We went up to synagogues and peeked inside through their shuttered windows," she wrote. "For whatever reason, we didn't dare go inside, perhaps because of our secular garb, perhaps because since becoming Zionist workers of Po'alei Zion we were cured of going to synagogue."[24]

At that time, Jerusalem had a population of about seventy thousand, of whom forty-five thousand were Jews. Ben-Gurion had never before been part of such a large Jewish majority. He wanted to turn it into a unified force and to make the Haredim partners in the government of Jerusalem as a whole. But in this context he spoke of "the conquest of those communities," meaning a revolution in the Haredi way of life, and advocated for yeshivot, the religious seminaries where most Haredi men studied, to provide general and professional education as well. But the Haredi way of life was too strong to allow such changes; Ben-Gurion did not yet understand that.

The article in which he made this proposal was not antireligious—in it, he also condemned those of his colleagues who treated the Haredim with contempt. But the language was, as was his wont, very blunt. He called for "purifying the filth" and replacing it with "healthy elements."[25] He did not reject the practice of Jews in Palestine seeking financial support from Jews overseas. The New Yishuv, as the non-Haredi recent immigrants were called, were no less dependent on Jewish philanthropists in other countries than were the Haredim, who were called the Old Yishuv. He himself solicited donations for Po'alei Zion.[26] The argument was over control of the money. That was the main subject that interested him when he finally managed to get elected as one of the local party's delegates to the World Union of Po'alei Zion, which convened in Vienna in July 1911. He was delighted to make the trip. That summer he had again been overcome by a longing for home.

He made his second visit to the country of his birth in the five years since his move to Palestine. Shlomo Zemach happened to be in Płońsk at the time, as was Rachel Beit Halahmi; she had gone there to give birth to her second daughter. Ben-Gurion did not dare go into town, because he was officially a deserter and had left Poland on a passport that was not his. In Warsaw he was more anonymous. He asked Rachel to meet him there. She did not.[27] But his sister Rivka had in the meantime married a well-off businessman from Łódź and they gave him a warm welcome. Ben-Gurion had long since stopped pressing his family to settle in Palestine; his sister Feigele wanted to study in Berlin, and Ben-Gurion asked his father to support her.[28]

❖

Brenner soon left *Hapo'el Hatza'ir* for *Ha'ahdut*. It was an important acquisition and Ben-Gurion did not miss the opportunity to impress his father. "The famous author Y. H. Brenner has taken my place on the staff," he wrote. "He will be literary editor."[29]

At the age of twenty-five, with a pretty firm conception of who he was, Ben-Gurion played with the idea of representing the Jews of Palestine in the Turkish parliament; maybe he could even be the government's minister for Jewish affairs.[30] In the meantime, he intended to study in Istanbul like some of his friends. But first he had to spend some time in Salonica, which was also under Ottoman rule.

"THE SHADOW OF WAR"

A few days after he arrived in Salonica, Ben-Gurion received a piece of advice: under no circumstances should he reveal to his Jewish landlady that he was Ashkenazi. There were many Jews in the city, and nearly all of them were Sephardim. Young Ashkenazi men like Ben-Gurion were thought to be involved in trafficking women.[31] From time to time he had to explain why he did not speak Ladino, the principal language of Salonica's Jews. For the most part he did not understand them and they did not understand him. "All around me is that world of the Sephardi Jews, so alien and distant from me in its customs and language," he wrote to his father.[32] He lived in a small room; the mattress lay on the floor, a kerosene lamp beside it, with books and papers strewn around it. He stayed up until the lamp went out.[33]

He did not go to Salonica happily. As he lacked a high school diploma, Istanbul University insisted that he complete his secondary studies. He preferred to do that in a different city, before joining the students Ben-Zvi and Israel Shohat, who had diplomas and had gone straight to Istanbul. Salonica was less expensive to live in than the capital city. In his memoirs, Ben-Gurion wrote that he chose Salonica because it was "the most Jewish city in the world." He marveled in particular at the large number of Jewish laborers. And there was also "that matter," as he insinuated to his father—the university was not content with the classes he took in Salonica and demanded to see his high school records from Poland, which he did not have. Ben-Gurion dealt with that problem in the same way that people back then managed with such bureaucratic annoyances—Ben-Zvi obtained a forged diploma for Ben-Gurion, from the gymnasium high school he had attended in Russia. Ben-Gurion asked his father to pay for the forgery and to destroy his letter forthwith.[34]

❖

His father was also paying his costs in Salonica. His paralegal business was going well at the time, and he expanded into offering parabanking services.[35] Ben-Gurion apprised him of his progress. "The Turkish language isn't as hard as I thought," he wrote.[36] Four weeks later, he felt that he knew the language well enough to assert that Turkish was not yet worthy of being called a language. "You can't express a single modern idea properly in it," he maintained.[37] He began taking French lessons as well.

His Turkish language teacher was another student, Yosef Stroumsa, three years younger than he was. The two became friends, and three months later Stroumsa stopped charging for the lessons. They would go for walks along the beach each day and talk, in Turkish, about everything. It seems to have been another very intense friendship. The two needed each other. "Those were my happiest moments that year," Stroumsa later recalled. "All of me, I owe everything to him." Ben-Gurion wrote: "He was my Turkish teacher, and I was his guide in life."

But the impression is that he hated every day of his nine months in Salonica. He frequently wrote of his loneliness. Stroumsa's first impulse was to deny that his companion had been lonely. "Ben-Gurion didn't need people," he said. But on reflection he confirmed that Ben-Gurion missed his family and friends very badly and wrote to them once a week.[38]

Like his previous letters, the ones he sent from Salonica display extreme swings between happiness and depression. As he matured, he became more aware of his psychological dynamics. "Here, I began in joy and ended in sorrow," he once wrote. "Is that the result of the circumstances of my life or a fundamental characteristic? Even in my happiest moments I just cannot shake free that profound melancholy that has penetrated my entire being."[39]

He sent several articles to *Ha'ahdut*, one of them in Turkish, and kept tabs on his party.[40] In the meantime, he tried his hand a bit at local politics. On one occasion, he broke into a rally where a Jewish member of parliament was speaking and protested that the speaker had said nothing about Palestine. Stroumsa recalled: "All the Jews there were astounded—what did he want of us? What is he saying?" Ben-Gurion tried to set up a branch of Po'alei Zion in the city, hoping to enlist Jewish sailors who could serve as the kernel of a Hebrew fleet in Palestine. The city's socialists, almost all of whom were Jews, were hostile. Most were not Zionists. It was another conflict between Zionists and socialists, reminiscent of his contention with the Bund in Płońsk.[41]

Politics already ran in his veins, and he missed home badly. His landlord was religious, and everything was "kosher," Ben-Gurion wrote, putting the word in quotation marks, "but the Haggadah does not speak to me and the soup dumplings are tasteless." In his father's home there had been "secret moans . . . that wove fine threads and webs of woe and longing . . . My entire soul is drawn there." He had also experienced such moments in Palestine, generally on holidays, he added. God willing, he wrote in Turkish, *Mashallah*, they would all be reunited in Palestine.[42]

❖

While he was in Salonica, Turkey fought a war with Italy. It was his first war. The Turks issued an expulsion order against Italian nationals; in Salonica nearly all the deportees were Jews. Ben-Gurion reported this tragedy matter-of-factly, blaming the deportees themselves for their tragedy. They were Jews who had lived in the city for centuries, but had never accepted Ottoman citizenship. Ben-Gurion remarked that "Jews like to remain obstinate even when it hurts them and never think of their future." His father noted that Ben-Gurion himself had not accepted Ottoman citizenship. Ben-Gurion explained that he first had to be accepted to the university, because otherwise he would be drafted into the Ottoman army. Students were exempt from military service.[43]

He was indeed accepted, and moved to Istanbul, but then war broke out between the Ottoman Empire and a coalition of Balkan countries. Ben-Gurion's letters read like dispatches from a war correspondent. "The shadow of war stretches over the entire city," he reported.[44] He saw lots of soldiers, some of them mounted on horses; the rail terminal was closed because all the trains had been placed in the army's service. It was his second war.

"I TRIED AND I MADE IT"

On the first day of his studies, at the end of his second class, the university rector came into the room and demanded that the students volunteer for the army. The university enrolled seven thousand students, but only twenty-nine had enlisted. The rector said he was ashamed of them and walked out; the students went home. Turkey was fighting to retain its control over the Balkans. It was the empire's darkest era, Ben-Gurion thought, comparing its predicament to that of the Jews just prior to the destruction of the Second

Temple. He viewed the war as a clash between Islam and Christianity and maintained that even if Turkey won the war, Europe would not allow it to savor its victory. "We may be on the verge of a European war," he suggested. "In any case, it is clear that we are on the verge of huge historical events that will send Europe's politics on an entirely new path."[45]

It was a prediction that could have been made only by a person living on the margins of the European theater, looking at it from the outside. From the inside, everything still looked stable and hopeful. Forty years of peace had granted the world a wonderful complacency, wrote Stefan Zweig, who lived in Theodor Herzl's Vienna. "Never had Europe been stronger, richer, more beautiful, or more confident of an even better future."[46]

The university's lecture halls filled with wounded soldiers; studies were halted. Ben-Gurion and Ben-Zvi returned to Palestine. Ben-Gurion was not sure he could return. He considered going to Damascus to learn Arabic. He thought that, as an attorney in Palestine, he would find Arabic more useful than Turkish.[47] But in the months that followed he did little. He returned to *Ha'ahdut*, met with other members of Po'alei Zion, and joined a medical mission that went to Tiberias when a cholera epidemic broke out there. "If I die in Tiberias I name you trustee of my legacy," he wrote to an acquaintance.[48] Four months later, he was back in Istanbul.

❖

His father continued to send him money. The bank transfers from Płońsk were often delayed, apparently because of the war. The same thing had happened in Salonica. Ben-Gurion griped about this in reproachful impatience in almost every letter. Of course, he appreciated the help he was receiving. "I will never be able to repay you even a small part of all the sacrifices you are making for my studies," he wrote. But he reminded his father that this was a compact of sorts they had made—he would study, and his father would pay.[49]

Some of his letters home seem to have been meant to make his father feel guilty. Once he wrote that his lack of money had almost killed him. He came down with scurvy, the result of a severe lack of vitamin C in his diet. The doctor attributed the condition to "chronic non-eating." Ben-Gurion told his father that he suffered from agonizing pain in his mouth: "I couldn't sleep or eat." Sometimes he took a loan. "I have already had a number of bad experiences, but I never in my life had times like these," he wrote toward the end of his second year of studies. His health was deteriorating "and like always," at the toughest moments he remained penniless. It was time to take stock. "Apparently both of us made a terrible mistake," he wrote to his father. "You took on something that was beyond your means and I agreed to live in conditions that are liable to ruin all my physical and moral fortitude."[50] In January 1914, he became so ill that he spent several weeks in the hospital.[51]

Ben-Zvi shared a room with Ben-Gurion in a small boardinghouse. Yosef Stroumsa of Salonica had come to Istanbul to complete his studies and Ben-Gurion invited him to join them. It was a crowded bachelor student room, not clean, but apparently, contrary to what Ben-Gurion had written, none of them went hungry at any stage. Ben-Zvi worked as a teacher to pay for his studies; Ben-Gurion lived off his father and did not work. "They were like two brothers," Stroumsa later recalled. "More than two brothers—they were always together." Ben-Zvi had his Rachel, and others had girlfriends as well; some were already married. According to Ben-Gurion, he also had Turkish and Arab friends, but they never spoke about Jewish affairs.[52]

Sometimes he apologized for his impatience. Waiting for money drove him insane, he explained. "It seems to me that I am not the irate type at all, but when you live in Istanbul in conditions like mine and you get into a mood like mine, even iron nerves can burst and crack." But he had no reason to fear that he would be left without means. Stroumsa testified years later that Avigdor Gruen sent his son's monthly allowance. He didn't send a lot, but he was never late, Stroumsa claimed. If so, money coming late could not on its own have plunged Ben-Gurion into a profound crisis of the type he described. He complained of "nervous anger and depression" and "distress and pain," adding that "I cannot bear my mental distress—it is an internal hell for me." A few days later, he wrote: "There are moments when I would be happy if I could at least weep like a small child—perhaps the tears would take on some of the oppressive psychological suffering that has no outlet." Again he apologized: "Sometimes a heavy sigh breaks through my imprisoned emotions without my even being aware of it."[53]

His father and his sister Rivka suggested that he return home, as his father already had before. Ben-Gurion was furious. The goal he had set himself was "a question of life," he wrote, and only death would prevent him from achieving it. Suggesting that he give up on his goal was tantamount, "morally and spiritually," to suggesting that he commit suicide. He therefore wondered whether his father was even willing to assist him anymore. Rivka also often sent him money. He told her to stop—if she persisted, he would send it back. In any case, she sent more to their sister Feigele in Berlin, he noted resentfully: "Do whatever she wants with her money, but leave me alone."*[54]

He excelled at his studies, receiving a ten, the highest grade, on most of his exams. Once he sent a postcard to Rachel Beit Halahmi telling her about his high grades—he made a point of noting that Ben-Zvi had gotten only a six on a test that he had received a ten on, and on which Israel Shohat, also in town, had earned only an eight. In his reports to his father he also frequently noted that most of his friends got lower grades than he did.[55] "I tried and I made it," he reported to his father at the end of exam period. At first he tended to disparage the quality of the university, just as he had the Turkish language and Oriental culture as a whole. When he advanced and excelled at his studies, he stopped making such comments. In fact, the faculty was a fairly good one.[56]

❖

They were a band of young people from Palestine who were drawn to Istanbul by the revolutionary spirit of the Young Turks; so were many Arabs. Some of them later worked in the legal system in Palestine; three were appointed judges, and one served on the Supreme Court. Others found their way into the political elite. Israel and Manya Shohat were also there. Yosef Stroumsa recalled that, from time to time, Shohat would visit Ben-Zvi, his close friend from Hashomer. If Ben-Gurion was in the room, he and Shohat would have arguments and soon start shouting at each other.[57]

Shohat postured as if he were the leader of a nation, the head of a

---

* His eldest brother, Avraham, was in the meantime planning to set up a lottery in Palestine. Ben-Gurion wrote him that he was mistaken if he thought that "the filth and sordidness" of the ghetto would gain him redemption in Palestine. (Ben-Gurion to his father, April 3, 1913, in Erez 1971, p. 264.)

government-in-exile. When the Balkan Wars broke out, he claimed to have persuaded the Turkish war minister to establish a Jewish regiment in the Turkish army that would defend Palestine. When nothing came of that, Shohat offered the Turks fifty mounted volunteers that he would enlist from among the students from Palestine and members of Hashomer. He claimed that he had been appointed commander of the unit, with officer rank. Nothing came of that scheme, either. Ben-Zvi, for his part, tried unsuccessfully to persuade Jewish sailors from Salonica to move to Palestine.[58] He and Ben-Gurion were active in the Jewish student association in Istanbul and attended the Po'alei Zion convention in Kraców and the Zionist Congress in Vienna. It was Ben-Gurion's first Zionist Congress; most of the delegates outranked him. He seemed by this time to have made up with Rivka; he went to Łódź for Pesach and his father was there as well. It was Ben-Gurion's third visit to Poland since leaving.

❖

With their exams behind them, Ben-Gurion and Ben-Zvi boarded a Russian passenger ship in Istanbul on July 28, 1914. They were scheduled to arrive in Jaffa ten days later. The Austro-Hungarian crown prince had been assassinated a month before and the winds of war had begun to blow in Europe. On Saturday, August 1, soon after they set sail after a stop in Izmir, word reached the ship that Russia had declared war on Germany. Ben-Gurion and Ben-Zvi found themselves facing their third war. Among the dreams that were shattered at that moment nearly everywhere on the globe was Ben-Gurion's hope of achievement his father had never enjoyed—being a real lawyer.

A few months later, he was already thinking about the war's implications for Zionism's future. "One doesn't receive a country, one conquers it," he declared a few weeks after the outbreak of the Great War. "We will conquer Palestine by developing it," he wrote. This was the essence of practical Zionism, which had come to the fore after Herzl's death and the failure of his efforts to obtain Palestine by diplomatic means. But the central idea in the article could have come from Herzl himself: the Jewish people's principal task was to prepare for the peace conference that would be convened after the war. The world had to grant the Jewish people an autonomous homeland in Palestine to which Jews could immigrate without restrictions. Cautiously, and choosing his words with great care, he stated that "Palestine belongs to Turkey" and stressed that the Jewish public in Palestine remained, "as always," loyal to the Ottoman Empire.[59]

"I'D PUT THE COUNTRY UNDER LOCK AND KEY"

On the afternoon of Thursday, December 17, 1914, soon before it was time to light the candles on the fifth night of Hanukah, Turkish police forces surrounded the Jewish neighborhoods on the edge of Jaffa—Tel Aviv, Neveh Tzedek, and Neveh Shalom—and imposed a curfew. They broke into houses, dragged out their inhabitants, and brought them to a nearby police compound. A few hours later, the police put the Jews on Italian ships that left Jaffa that same night. The ships took them to Egypt, which the British had proclaimed a protectorate the month before.

An eyewitness described heartbreaking scenes: "A six-month-old baby was left in his cradle because his mother was captured on the street and put on a ship without giving her the opportunity to take her child . . . Children were sent on ships without their parents . . . Many fell into the sea and were saved only thanks to miracles, while what happened to others remains unknown to this day." Prior to this the authorities had issued an order expelling all citizens of enemy countries, including fifty thousand of the eighty-five thousand Jews who were living in Palestine at the time. Almost all of these were Russian subjects. On Saturday another mass expulsion took place.[60]

A furious debate broke out at the *Ha'ahdut* offices in Jerusalem. During the three months since Ben-Gurion and Ben-Zvi had returned from Istanbul, they had tried to persuade the Jews in Palestine to renounce their Russian citizenship and apply for Ottoman citizenship instead. The immediate goal had been to avert the prospect of thousands of Jews having to leave the country, whether by choice or expulsion. Ben-Gurion's political thinking on this point was a bit outlandish—Turkey was an unlikely ally for the Jews. He was well acquainted with the internal rot that plagued "the sick man of Europe," and his attitude toward Turkish culture was manifestly Orientalist. Furthermore, he had witnessed the empire's fiasco in the Balkan Wars. Despite this, he did not think it impossible that Turkey would win.

He considered himself an Ottoman patriot and cheered when the Turks abrogated the superior rights that foreign subjects enjoyed in Palestine. "Turkey is leaving slavery for freedom," he declared. He called the Ottoman Empire "our country." Thousands of Jews were now left without the protection of the consulates of the countries they had come from, but Ben-Gurion believed that loyalty to the Ottoman regime would, after the war, promote Zionist interests. He thought of a Jewish national district within the Ottoman state. Nor did he give up his dream of representing the Jewish public as a Turkish Cabinet minister.[61] Along with Ben-Zvi, he revived the proposal to establish a Jewish volunteer militia to defend Jerusalem. In the meantime, he went each morning to the offices of the chief rabbi, where he sat at a desk covered with a green cloth and registered the Jews who had decided to take Ottoman citizenship. He and Ben-Zvi sported red fezzes. "Real Turkish officials!" was how Aharon Reuveni described them in his novel.

It was not an easy decision to forgo Russian citizenship, in particular for young men who had evaded service in the czar's military. It would make them liable for conscription into the Turkish army. Both Zionist workers' parties called on Jews to remain in Palestine, but there were also other opinions, including on the *Ha'ahdut* staff. Several members confessed to their colleagues that they had no desire to die in defense of the Ottoman homeland.

Givoni, the Ben-Gurion character in Reuveni's novel, declares that he is willing to pay a very high price in human lives in order to achieve his people's historic destiny. Anyone who leaves the country is a traitor, he declares, adding, "If I had authorization to do so, I'd put the country under lock and key and not let a single soul leave." The explanation that Reuveni has Givoni offer is this: "Five thousand Jews who fall in Palestine are more important for us, for our future, than ten thousand who flee and save their lives in Egypt." His colleagues remark sarcastically that he seems to have no compunctions about taking responsibility for so much bloodshed; one thanks God for putting the Jews at the mercy of Djemal Pasha rather than Givoni.[62]

Djemal Pasha was one of the leaders of the Young Turks and the commander of the Syrian and Palestinian front. He would play a leading role in the Armenian genocide and was an outspoken opponent of Zionism.[63] The editors of *Ha'ahdut* were unsure whether to write about the deportations from Jaffa. It was a difficult decision, especially for Ben-Gurion as a supporter of the Ottomans. He reluctantly supported publication of an agonizing account that maintained that the deportation was not, in fact, aimed at foreign nationals but was directly aimed at Jews, including those who were Ottoman citizens. A few days later, the authorities shut down the periodical, confiscated the last 127 copies of the recent issue that they found in its offices, and locked the printing press.[64]

❖

A few weeks later, Ben-Zvi and Ben-Gurion were arrested and taken to the grandiose government house in the Muslim Quarter of the Old City. According to Ben-Gurion, they were arrested because their names appeared on a list of participants in the Zionist Congress of 1913. They were treated reasonably well. Ben-Gurion wrote that his interrogator was a coarse man, "but not overly aggressive in his coarseness." He wanted to know everything about Po'alei Zion and Hashomer, and seemed not to know the difference between them. Both, as far as he was concerned, were secret subversive organizations. Ben-Zvi recalled that they made friends with their guards, to the point that they were allowed to come and go as they pleased.

To avert deportation, the two of them penned, in Turkish, a heartfelt patriotic letter to Djemal Pasha. Ben-Zvi went so far as to seek Djemal out in person at his headquarters in the Augusta Victoria mansion on the Mount of Olives. Rachel Yanait went with him and watched from a distance, hiding among the cypresses. Ben-Zvi managed to address the Turkish commander in person; Djemal knew who he and Ben-Gurion were, but said there was nothing to talk about. The two were plotting to establish a Jewish state in Palestine and they would be deported to Egypt. Ben-Zvi and Ben-Gurion plunged into deep depression. Their friends organized a farewell party at a local hotel, but Ben-Gurion preferred to be alone. It was not easy for him to come to terms with the collapse of his conviction regarding Zionism's Turkish future. Ordered by the authorities to report for deportation in Jaffa, the next day they rented a horse-drawn carriage, at their own expense, for the trip. When they arrived, they were incarcerated for several days. Yanait was given permission to make farewells. A candle burned on the table. When it went out, Ben-Zvi and his girlfriend went out into the corridor. He bent over and kissed her. Ben-Gurion remained in the room.[65]

The deportation was meant to be permanent; they had also been expelled from Istanbul University. They arrived in Cairo without documents, only a letter of recommendation they had received from the American consul in Jerusalem, Otis Glazebrook. Henry Morgenthau, the United States envoy in Istanbul, also kept tabs on the two. Meanwhile they traveled, went to the museum, climbed pyramids, and waited to receive Egyptian laissez-passer papers. On Pesach eve Ben-Gurion wrote in his diary: "We are going to tell the story of the Exodus from Egypt and to conduct a Seder by the tombs of Pharaoh."[66]

In the weeks that followed, the two friends took an interest in the fate of thousands of refugees from Palestine and followed the activity of two Russian Jews who were already famous. One was an officer, Joseph Trumpeldor, a dentist who had fought heroically and lost his left arm in the Russo-Japanese War. He had come to Palestine in 1912 with several companions. They had originally joined a communal farm on the shores of Lake Kinneret, but then went to work at Degania.

The second was a well-known Odessa-born Zionist journalist, author, and translator who signed his articles with the pseudonym "Altalena," meaning "swing" in Italian. His real name was Ze'ev (Vladimir) Jabotinsky. In his hometown he had advocated establishing a Jewish self-defense militia. Trumpeldor had managed to flee Palestine before being threatened with deportation; Jabotinsky had arrived in Egypt as a roving correspondent. As Egypt was a British client, the two men proposed to the British that they enlist Jewish refugees into a volunteer military unit; the idea was approved. The result was the Zion Mule Corps, which took part in the Gallipoli campaign. The working assumption was that the Turks would be defeated and that it would thus be wise to help the British.[67]

Ben-Gurion and Ben-Zvi rejected the initiative for two reasons—they feared, with good reason, that providing military aid to an enemy of Turkey could have catastrophic consequences for the Jewish community in Palestine. They also continued to believe that Turkey might well remain in control of Palestine after the war, when it might grant the Jews autonomy. Turkey was, after all, on Germany's side, and many people believed that Germany would emerge victorious. Ben-Gurion's support of Turkey was in keeping with long Jewish tradition, which had a Zionist version as well, according to which it was best to obey whoever was in charge, everywhere and always. Beyond that, the two friends were peeved that Jabotinsky and Trumpeldor had carried out an idea that they, Ben-Gurion and Ben-Zvi, had failed at when they proposed it to the Turks. It was another Jewish armed force initiative in which Ben-Gurion had not been involved.

From a Zionist point of view, it was logical to prevent Jews from leaving Palestine. There was also logic in advocating that Jews should take out Ottoman citizenship so as to avoid deportation. Indeed, some Jews enlisted in the Turkish army.

But for many, the decision to remain in Palestine cost them their lives, whether they did so out of Zionist patriotism or for other reasons. As the war went on, conditions in Palestine worsened and thousands died of hunger. Ben-Gurion saw this, too, as one of the prices to be paid for Zionism.*[68]

He himself had not yet received Ottoman citizenship. He later claimed that he and Ben-Zvi applied for it and even paid the required fee; perhaps they were deported before the process was completed. When he entered the United States, his documents identified him as a Russian citizen. In early 1917, he also declared himself to be a Russian citizen.[69] In later years, Ben-Gurion found it difficult to acknowledge that he had erred when he encouraged the Jews in Palestine to take Ottoman citizenship. "It may have been a mistake on my part," he wrote, "but under those conditions I would again oppose leaving the country."[70]

❖

Had he wanted to, it seems that he could have remained in Egypt, but he wanted to go to the New World. At the age of twenty-nine, without a profession, he

---

* Historians estimate that about fifteen thousand Jews applied for Ottoman citizenship, while about eighteen thousand left Palestine or were deported. During the war, Palestine's Jewish population fell by about thirty-five thousand, from eighty-five thousand to fifty thousand. (Giladi and Naor 2002, p. 457.)

knew that he would never be a lawyer and, most likely, not a Turkish Cabinet minister, either. He no longer did manual labor and depended for his livelihood on money sent from overseas, in part from his father. But he had one big advantage over many others his age—he knew what he wanted to achieve and that he was capable of learning. His next stop was America.

On passage to the United States he marveled at the expanses of the Atlantic Ocean. He penned poetic depictions of the waves and the play of the light, just as he had done when he first sailed from Płońsk to Palestine.[71] His friends and acquaintances, who generally saw him as a glum introvert, would have had trouble believing that such romantic passages could have been written by him.

❖

On May 16, 1915, the first skyscrapers appeared in the distance. Ben-Gurion was stunned. From the moment he had settled in one of the third-class berths on the Greek ship *Patris* with Ben-Zvi, he had been carried away by the American dream that he had carried with him since childhood at the beginning of what everyone called the American Century. America sparked his imagination; he was almost as excited about going there as he had been about going to Palestine. The pulse of life in the most modern and democratic country in the world fascinated him, he wrote. When gulls began to circle the *Patris*, he stopped thinking about the awful food served on the ship; he suddenly identified with the myth of America's Founding Fathers. In his diary he wrote: "We, who want to build a new land in a wilderness out of ruins, need to learn how the deportees and persecuted people from England founded a huge, rich country with unparalleled treasures and creative power." In later years, he would compare the conquest of the American West with the conquest of Palestine. During the trip he began to study English.

His diary records a fantasy that he had from time to time—he travels to New York and surprises his friends there, not having informed them of his arrival. Shmuel Fuchs is not mentioned by name, but the "friends" he writes of are reduced, by the next page, to a single one. In anticipation of their meeting, Ben-Gurion again gave himself over to nostalgia, harking back to their "innocent and dreamy boyhood" when they were still "imbued with an illusion that was both naïve and pure." When they met again, they would be able to consider which of the two of them had made the right choice—the dreamer who had gone to Palestine and into politics, or his beloved friend, who sought his fortune as a dentist in Brooklyn. Either way, Ben-Gurion noted, "since I have been flung to America, I need to do some things there for Palestine." He was overjoyed when he realized that he would arrive in New York in time to celebrate the Shavuot holiday there.[72]

· 7 ·

NEW WORLD

⌒

"IT'S A BIT RIDICULOUS"

America gave him a warm welcome; the immigration procedures were simple and brief. "The Americans know the secret of speed," he said in awe. The mandatory medical examination was also less humiliating than he had feared. He declared his intention of becoming a citizen and in the meantime received a visa allowing him to live and work in the country. "Hooray!" he wrote in his diary, just as he had when he first came ashore in Jaffa. Waiting for him outside Ellis Island, the immigration center on the southern tip of Manhattan, were several members of the local chapter of Po'alei Zion. They conveyed to him awful news from Płońsk—a German bomb had hit a synagogue, killing some eighty people, among them Shlomo Zemach's father. The battles raging around Płońsk at the time were covered closely by *The New York Times*. Ben-Gurion's father and the rest of his family were safe and whole.[1]

Ben-Gurion was not immune to the fabled culture shock that often strikes people making their first visit to New York. It hit him like a "driving rain," with a force that he did not forget as long as he lived. During his first days in the city, he wandered Manhattan's avenues, dizzy and with no clear destination. On the third day he felt like he had already been there for weeks. His diary conveys enthusiasm—and here and there a bit of sarcasm—about the multistoried buildings, huge stores, endless streets, carriage and automobile traffic, masses of pedestrians, the whirlwind of colors and voices, the constant rushing, the uncontrollable desire of everyone to advertise something.

America presented him with two major challenges that required him to reexamine his most fundamental beliefs. As a self-proclaimed socialist, he had to cope with the recognition that America's power was the power of capitalism—there was no great demand for socialism. As a Zionist, he sought to enter into conversation with the more than two million Jews who, finding a new homeland in the United States, had begun to feel at home there. There was not much demand for Zionism, either. America's Jews reminded him of his father: "They claim to be Zionists, but they don't come to Palestine."[2] Only a small number of them understood Hebrew; he still lacked fluency in English. For the most part he spoke Yiddish. It was not the best way to get to know America.

❖

When they arrived in the United States, Ben-Gurion and Ben-Zvi made a point of presenting themselves as emissaries from Palestine, stressing that they had come for only a short time. When he had to cite his profession on some official form, Ben-Gurion wrote "journalist." That placed him in the ranks of other writers who sought to further the Zionist cause, among them Herzl and Jabotinsky. On his way over, Ben-Gurion had considered the possibility of publishing a Hebrew daily in the United States.[3]

His hosts took him at face value. They decided to send him and Ben-Zvi on a lecture tour to party branches, as emissaries from Palestine were more interesting than refugees and exiles. In the meantime, they organized a series of festive receptions, making long speeches in their honor and reporting their arrival to the Jewish press. "It's a bit ridiculous," Ben-Gurion remarked.[4]

Their hosts viewed Ben-Zvi as the senior of the two. They lived in a room they rented together in Brooklyn and, at first, lived hand to mouth—Ben-Zvi gave lessons, Ben-Gurion wrote articles. The party also supported them.

Po'alei Zion in America had been established as an extension of the party in Russia. Its activists, almost all immigrants, among them some relatives of Ben-Gurion's, brought with them the party's platform as well as the ideological differences that had preoccupied them in the Old Country, with all the intrigues and plots and the rivalries with other parties. There were chapters in several American cities, but only about three thousand members and sympathizers, constituting about half of the supporters of the Zionist labor movement in the United States. The movement put out a Yiddish newspaper in New York, *Der Yiddisher Kempfer*, with a print run of six thousand.*

Ben-Gurion had known some of the American Workers of Zion before his arrival, and they all had heard of him. Nahman Syrkin, the acknowledged intellectual leader of the party in America, related how he had tried, several years previously, to purchase Palestine from the Turkish sultan. He suggested enlisting tens of thousands of young people in the Hehalutz ("The Pioneer") movement, whose members were committed to settling as farmers in Palestine. Pinhas Rutenberg, a Russian revolutionary and terrorist, regaled Ben-Gurion with a plan to establish a Jewish army that would conquer Palestine.[5]

❖

For the most part, the Jews Ben-Gurion first encountered in America seemed to be in a pitiful state. He barely recognized his cousin. "His face had grown gaunt and his posture bent and he had aged entirely," he recorded, noting that his cousin's children spoke English and knew only a bit of Yiddish.[6] One of Rachel Beit Halahmi's brothers introduced him to the Association of Young Płońskers in America. He found them disagreeable. "Vacant, hollow, without any substance, lacking all aspiration," he wrote in his diary.[7]

---

* Mizrahi, the religious-Zionist movement, had three times the membership of Po'alei Zion. In 1918 all the Yiddish newspapers in the United States taken together had a print run of about half a million. (Raider 1998, pp. 33, 41; Teveth 1977, p. 312, note 30.)

Shmuel Fuchs was not one of them—he was not in town at the time. Ben-Gurion met his girlfriend, who was a Bundist. A few weeks went by, but Fuchs did not return. On Sunday, July 7, 1915, Ben-Gurion entered this in his diary: "Today there is a Po'alei Zion picnic. From what I've heard, S. Fuchs will come. We have not seen each other for twelve years . . . Tomorrow I leave." The next day, Ben-Gurion set out on a mission to the party chapter in Rochester, New York, the first stop in a lecture tour that included several other cities as well. His diary relates: "I was supposed to leave here at one, but I missed the train by a few minutes, wasting me the entire day, I'll arrive in Rochester only at eleven at night." There was not a word about Fuchs. Maybe he was at the picnic, maybe not. Maybe Fuchs was there and Ben-Gurion wasn't; maybe neither showed up. Or perhaps they both went and saw each other, and Ben-Gurion decided to repress that moment and not even mention it in his diary. Many years later, when he was prime minister, he remarked that he and Fuchs had met in New York. "I told him about our endeavors in Palestine and he slowly returned to Zionism," Ben-Gurion wrote. That was not entirely accurate.[8]

Fuchs belonged to Po'alei Zion when he first came to the United States, but he seems to have gradually lost interest in the party. He studied dentistry at New York University, married, enjoyed professional success, and bought an apartment building. He published poems and stories in Yiddish, some of them under the pseudonym "Emmanuel," a name he afterward gave to his son. He associated with other Yiddish writers and poets, gave them money, and supported the Yiddish theater.[9]

"HAD I BEEN A NEGRO"

Ben-Gurion's lectures to Po'alei Zion chapters around the country were aimed at seeking out young people who might possibly go to Palestine, and in the meantime to recruit them for Hehalutz, which was ostensibly devoted to promoting pioneering settlement in Palestine.[10] In conjunction with the tour, the party's Central Committee issued a call to its members to join that organization. But a close examination shows that Hehalutz's immigrants were also intended to serve as a military force. Its goals went through several formulations, at one point stating: "to organize a special group for self-defense in Palestine." In a discarded version preserved in the Ben-Gurion Archives, this passage, in Yiddish, is followed by two Hebrew words in parentheses, meaning "defense group."[11] The Hehalutz charter, quoted by Ben-Zvi in his memoirs, states that the organization will operate "physical fitness and military exercise clubs." The members were required to commit themselves to accepting the discipline imposed by the leadership.

❖

Ben-Gurion traveled alone, generally by train; he lodged with party activists. He did not always know if they would be waiting for him when he arrived; at times they weren't. Sometimes his hosts had forgotten to organize a lecture. "The comrades did not prepare anything," he complained at one point. That happened, "as expected," in Youngstown and Canton, just as it had previously in Pittsburgh. Canton was no great loss, he said; from the start it had not been worthwhile sending him there. But he was put out by the snafus in the larger Jewish communities of Youngstown and Pittsburgh.*

The party members in New York saw him as their emissary, and probably hoped that his appearances would help raise money for the party and subscribers for its newspaper. But he was not a great orator and did not attract big crowds; some who heard him later recalled that he spoke tediously and without imagination. Other speakers told stories; Ben-Gurion recited facts. Sometimes his speeches made a strong impression, but they were not lyrical. As a result, he was not very popular. Sometimes he spoke before an audience of barely twenty; forty was a good turnout. Once he canceled an event in Cincinnati because Justice Louis Brandeis was scheduled to speak elsewhere that same evening.[12]

---

* He carefully recorded his expenses down to the last cent during the trip, such as $1.91 for a train ticket, $0.50 surcharge for a sleeping car, $0.20 as a tip to the porter. (Ben-Gurion, Diary, July 26, 1915, Dec. 2, 1917, BGA; Ben-Gurion to Hirsch Ehrenreich, Dec. 29, 1915, Jan. 6, 7, 1916, in Erez 1971, pp. 330, 333, 334.)

❖

At the end of August 1916, Ben-Zvi and Ben-Gurion asked Brandeis to intervene with Ambassador Morgenthau in Istanbul and obtain for them permission to return to Palestine.[13] At the time, the two of them still believed
that Palestine might well remain under Ottoman suzerainty, although they
realized that another outcome was certainly possible. They thus had no way
of knowing whether the military force they wanted to put together would
operate on the side of the Turks or against them. In any case, Hehalutz was
presumably meant to operate against the Arabs. And it might have been
under Ben-Gurion's control. But that did not happen. "The response was not
massive," Ben-Gurion wrote; the American branch of Hehalutz numbered
only about a hundred members.[14] It was a failure. Ben-Gurion was a long
way from getting American Jews to move to Palestine.

He spent most of his time with other members of his party, but here and
there he stepped out of that narrow world and took a look around. He followed the presidential campaign and later recalled the suspense leading up to
Woodrow Wilson's election to a second term. "The fate of the World War
depended largely on the results of the election," he wrote. In Nashville he
saw, for the first time, what he called "the Negro Pale of Settlement," the
"Pale" being the term for the area the Russian authorities compelled Jews to
live in. When he boarded the trolley, he saw two signs indicating that the seats
in the front were for whites and in the back for "colored," as blacks were then
referred to in America. "When you enter the car, the whites sit in the front
seats," Ben-Gurion wrote to Ben-Zvi. "If any room is left the blacks are also
allowed to sit (but heaven forfend not on the same bench as the whites).
When people go out, the whites exit first, and then the blacks."* Ben-Gurion
also saw separate bathrooms for blacks and whites. Having grown up on

---

* Many years later, Prime Minister Ben-Gurion recalled how shocked he had been when he
first encountered discrimination against blacks in the United States. It especially troubled
him that there were Jews who supported it. "Had I been a Negro I would have been the ultimate anti-Semite," he remarked. (Ben-Gurion, Diary, Nov. 9, 1940, BGA; Ben-Gurion to
Ben-Zvi, Feb. 3, 1918, BGA, general chronological documentation; Ben-Gurion to the Cabinet,
Feb. 12, 1953, May 3, 1960, NA.)

Uncle Tom's Cabin, he was angry, hurt, and ashamed, he wrote, and told Ben-Zvi that when he went to see a movie he sat with the blacks. An usher immediately approached him and demanded that he sit apart from them.[15]

Here and there he took a break from politics. He was staggered by the sight of Niagara Falls, almost forgetting the convention he had traveled to Buffalo for, even though it had taken place in a large, packed hall. He often wrote about water, but the encounter with "the abyss upon abyss of magical miracle" brought on an almost religious experience. "Sit here mutely, son of Adam, and listen to this roar that has not ceased since the six days of creation," he wrote in his diary. "Sit here mutely and watch the sprays of foam that swathe this great sight—gaze mutely."[16]

Some of his letters and writings suggest that in America, too, Ben-Gurion suffered from sudden mood swings. His handwriting was generally even and legible, arranged in neat rows, with uniform margins and spacing, more or less. But there were times when his penmanship turned frantic, angular, hard to read, almost violent in appearance. The lines wended, there were no margins, they plunged down sharply toward the bottom left corner of the page.[17] In the months that followed, he would devote himself primarily to writing. It was a wise decision; thanks to his writing, he soon came to be recognized as more important a figure than Ben-Zvi.

"IN THE BEGINNING WAS THE DEED"

A while after founding *Ha'ahdut*, Ben-Zvi wrote an article in memory of one of the men murdered at Sejera, Ya'akov Plotkin. The article was printed in *Yizkor*, a memorial book issued in Jaffa in 1911; it would become a cornerstone of the heroic mythology of the labor movement in the Land of Israel. According to the book's cover, it was meant as a memorial to fallen Hebrew workers—they were not identified as members of Hashomer. It was devoted to eight men, six of whom fell at Sejera. Alongside eulogies, the book also included literary works, among them contributions by Shmuel Yosef Agnon and one by Shlomo Zemach. The book was a still-hesitant attempt to shape a secular culture of national memory. The words of the traditional *Yizkor* prayer, recited in synagogues on holidays, were revised; the opening words, "God will remember," were changed to "The Jewish people will remember."

An article on the value of giving one's life for a cause said that the thousands of religious Jews who had accepted martyrdom "in sanctification of God's name" had done so only to save their individual souls, whereas the workers memorialized in the book "set out to be killed in order to redeem the honor of their nation." The introduction included a political message in the form of a call to the Arabs to work together with the Jewish settlers to make "our barren land" bloom. The book came out in Hebrew; its editors were the elderly Y. Z. Rabinowitz and Yosef Haim Brenner. There were many typographical errors; Ben-Gurion did not contribute.[18]

A few months after their arrival in the United States, after they had begun to give lectures before party chapters, Ben-Zvi and Ben-Gurion realized that there was a shortage of written material on Po'alei Zion and Palestine in Yiddish. At their suggestion, the party decided to issue a Yiddish edition of *Yizkor*. It was an attempt to create a common mythology for the Jews of Palestine and America. The task of preparing the book was assigned to a number of veteran editors of *Ha'ahdut* who were then living in New York, among them Ben-Zvi. They took out the literary works, added the names of victims who had not been included in the Hebrew edition, and portrayed them as glorious heroes.

The book was also given a different introduction, written by Ya'akov Zerubavel. Printed in small, dense type over six pages, it was grueling to read. The main purpose was to extol secular Judaism and disparage the religious lifestyle. This could be seen in a contemptuous article written by Brenner that had not appeared in the original. The cover featured a drawing showing a mounted member of Hashomer. Similar drawings, in art nouveau style, appeared in the book itself. Its subtitle declared that the book memorialized "the guards and workers" of Palestine; in his introduction, Zerubavel referred to Shimon Bar Giora. Ben-Gurion wrote a fascinating autobiographical piece about his first years in Palestine. It was placed close to the end of the book.[19]

This publication was a huge success. Memorial evenings were held all across America, and Ben-Gurion became a sought-after guest. He finally had a story—how he had arrived in Palestine, shaken with malarial fevers, gone hungry, how he had felt.[20] Quite naturally, his mood soared. "Have you gotten together with Woodrow yet?" he asked Ben-Zvi, who was then in Washington, D.C.[21]

❖

Most of the response to the book was positive. But a Bund sympathizer who wrote under the name Moissaye, Joseph Olgin, published his "thoughts" on the book under the title "The Jewish Colonies in Palestine Were Founded on the Catastrophe of the Arabs." Its main point was that the Arabs were the ancient owners of Palestine and that their war against the Jewish settlers was a just one.

At this point, the Zionist movement was already often being asked to explain how it saw life with the Arabs. Ben-Gurion stressed that the country could be prepared for the absorption of four to five million Jews. He extolled their cultural and moral superiority and promised that the development would also bring about a renaissance of its Arab inhabitants. He cited Petah Tikvah as proof—it was home to five thousand inhabitants and another three thousand Arab laborers made their living there, he proudly related. There was not a word on his aspiration to replace them with Jewish laborers.[22] When the edition sold out and demand had not been satisfied, a second edition was decided on and this time the project was assigned to Ben-Gurion.

He showed himself to be a strong-minded editor. He maintained that Zerubavel's introduction was nothing more than "inflated polemics in an ostensibly poetic style." Ben-Gurion tossed it out and wrote a new one, half the length at only three pages. Unlike Zerubavel, he wrote in short, powerful sentences. The heroes he memorialized came out looking like gods: "They came not as beggars but as conquerors," Ben-Gurion began. That was followed by a period and then: "In the beginning was the deed." And so he went on. The message was nationalist and secular and related to the dead heroes themselves. They had created a "religion of labor" and shed their blood in defense of the land. And unlike Zerubavel, Ben-Gurion did not issue a call of peace to the Arabs. He said that they respected only those who knew how to defend themselves. He moved his autobiographical piece up to the start of the new edition, right after his introduction. Revising the order in which the fallen appeared, he gave the first two slots to the two men who had fallen in the incident he himself had been involved in back in Sejera. He deliberately wrote "workers and guards," in that order. Furthermore, he removed all mention of Bar Giora.

He did the editing job almost on his own, and also oversaw production. In the process, he had to learn a new profession and make endless decisions that required command of the tiniest details. These included what paper to use, what format to print the book in, and what graphics and illustrations to include. The result was a high-quality album in a silvery cloth binding, elegantly printed on high-quality stock. It made "a huge impression," Ben-Gurion wrote to his father.[23]

It looked as if Ben-Gurion had begun to realize who his target audience was. The book he edited provided readers with Jewish patriotism and much tear-jerking self-righteousness. This mix enabled them to adulate new heroes, Yiddish speakers like themselves, to identify with and be proud of them, without being expected, even by implication, to leave the good country that had taken them in in order to follow in the footsteps of their heroes. That was the main difference between the two editions—Ben-Gurion's *Yizkor* was more optimistic. He seems to have caught on to the role played by hope in the American ethos.

Nothing he had done in his life up to this point gave his reputation as much of a boost as editing this book. All the articles he wrote and all the lectures he gave taken together likely did not garner him as large an audience as *Yizkor*. Suddenly, he became one of the most prominent figures in his party. As he worked on the book, Ben-Gurion asked Ben-Zvi to return to New York from Washington to help him with the editing, making it clear that he would not be an equal partner. Ben-Zvi did not come. The massive editing job that Ben-Gurion planned, such a short time after the previous edition had come out, and no doubt the replacement of the introduction, were slaps in Ben-Zvi's face. Ben-Gurion even removed his friend's name from the list of editors; he could have been more forbearing. The book's dizzying success seems to have been one more provocation for Ben-Zvi. "There was a dispute between me and Ben-Gurion," he remarked in his memoirs.[24] But Ben-Gurion offered him a new project, a much more ambitious and challenging one that the two men would collaborate on—a comprehensive scholarly work, in Yiddish, on the geography and history of Palestine. Ben-Zvi consented. Ben-Gurion began spending each morning at the New York Public Library at Fifth Avenue and Forty-Second Street, passing the stone lions crouched at the bottom of the stairs, sitting at one of the wooden desks in the huge reading room. He very much liked the work. He focused largely on the books that had been written by survey delegations and Christian visitors to Palestine in the nineteenth century.

"A GREAT MARVEL"

The two divided the book's chapters between them. Ben-Zvi wrote mostly about the country's history and geography; Ben-Gurion wrote about its names, boundaries, and legal status, and in particular about its inhabitants. They traded drafts of the chapters they wrote and commented on each other's writing. They did some of their research at the Library of Congress in Washington and other libraries. "I neglected all my activity and entirely gave myself over to my research," Ben-Gurion told his father. He worked from nine in the morning to ten at night; he even restricted his daily newspaper reading to the trip from his home to the library. Ben-Zvi also devoted himself to the project. On one or two occasions the two resumed party activity. In April 1917, Ben-Gurion's name appeared in *The New York Times* for the first time, as one of the speakers at a large rally organized in the wake of the toppling of the Russian czar.[25]

One of his acquaintances in New York recalled that he also found time to have fun at Coney Island, see movies, and go out with women. One of them, Pauline Moonweis, agreed to accompany him to the library and copy out pages that he marked. The work lasted for a year and a half. On January 15, 1918, Ben-Gurion wrote in his diary that he had completed the last chapter.[26] In the meantime, one of the great dramas in Jewish history had taken place, as well as another drama in his personal life.

❖

About two years previously, after dinner, the British foreign minister, Arthur James Balfour, left his home in the company of Chaim Weizmann, a Russian-born chemist and Zionist activist who had settled in England. It was after midnight. Weizmann spoke most of the time as Balfour listened. Weizmann had presented the basic thesis in the past—that the interests of the Zionist movement were identical to those of the British Empire, and vice versa. It was therefore worthwhile for the British to conquer Palestine and to establish a Jewish protectorate there. Weizmann, a man of great personal charm, offered Balfour a great historic vision. He spoke the language of statecraft and politics, but also evinced a great religious awareness. Balfour's inclination was to accept Zionism as part of his Christian faith. It was a beautiful night; the moon stood in the sky. In March 1917, Balfour told the Cabinet: "I am a Zionist."

In April the United States entered the war alongside Britain; in November, Balfour issued a written declaration that recognized the right of the Jews to establish a "national home" in Palestine. General Edmund Allenby's army was advancing on Jerusalem. Ben-Gurion presumably followed its progress; it was one of the reasons he supported American entry into the war, unlike some of his friends.[27]

❖

Ben-Gurion almost certainly read about the Balfour Declaration in *The New York Times*; the headline was "Britain Favors Zionism." What that meant was that Great Britain recognized that the Zionist movement represented the Jewish people. Weizmann spoke of the declaration in biblical terms: "Since Cyrus the Great there was never, in all the records of the past, a manifestation inspired by a higher sense of political wisdom, far-sighted statesmanship, and national justice towards the Jewish people than this memorable declaration."[28] In the public eye, Weizmann was now the leader of the Jewish people. Ben-Gurion knew him, knew that he was working on the cause in London. Furthermore, the phrase "national home" was not foreign to him—it was the term the Zionist movement used to evade stating its real goal, a Jewish state. But the Balfour Declaration came as a total surprise. It apparently took him time to grasp its historic significance. He termed this public recognition of the right of the Jews to establish a national home in Palestine as "a great marvel" without parallel since Bar Kokhba's rebellion against the Romans, but he tended to play down its practical significance.

England could not return Palestine to the Jewish people, he wrote. Only the Jewish people could return it to themselves, through labor and settlement. In one of his speeches he illustrated this idea with an example: just as a woman cannot give birth to a baby in place of another woman, so one nation cannot create a national home for another nation.[29]

He had not been involved in obtaining the Balfour Declaration; presumably that bothered him. His initial dubiousness about it thus had a sour tang to it—Weizmann had made history while he was sitting on Fifth Avenue reading books. Most likely Weizmann would have reacted the same way had it been Herzl's achievement. Ben-Gurion would later copy into his memoirs an article he wrote in 1915 in which he called for, among other things, taking action so that the postwar peace conference would recognize the Jews' right to build their future in Palestine. The article appeared two years before the Balfour Declaration, he stressed, and when the declaration "materialized," he and his friends were already in touch with British representatives regarding the formation of a Jewish Legion that would fight in Palestine.[30]

"I WAS ALMOST BESIDE MYSELF"

The Balfour Declaration engendered a huge national awakening, while at the same time reigniting the debate over Zionism itself. *The New York Times* published a long piece by a well-known Reform rabbi denying that the Jews had a national identity. Their historic mission, he argued, was to disseminate their spiritual message. To that end, they needed to be scattered among the nations of the world. American Zionist leaders were not enthusiastic about Ben-Gurion's chilly reaction to the declaration, so he tried to walk back from his reservations in two further articles. The Balfour Declaration had brought Zionism in an instant, "as if by miracle," to the "verge of realization," he wrote, but the Hebrew homeland still had to be created, a "more important, serious, and more difficult task" than achieving the declaration.[31] The drama that accompanied the declaration also compelled him to abandon, once and for all, the hopes he had placed in Turkey since his arrival in Palestine. It wasn't an easy thing to do. It was no less difficult to admit that Jabotinsky had seen the Turkish defeat coming before he himself had.

A few weeks later, he had an almost instant epiphany, arriving at a new and unnerving realization—the Turkish age had ended and the Age of Britain had arrived. This took place in the celebrated Great Hall of the Cooper Union, where Abraham Lincoln once made a seminal address against the expansion of slavery. The room was filled to bursting; the audience had come to celebrate the Balfour Declaration and to announce the establishment of an action fund of $40,000. The crowd was enthusiastic, *The New York Times* reported. The newspaper named Ben-Gurion among the speakers. Another newspaper, Ben-Gurion reported to his father, called his speech "sublime and terrible." Ben-Gurion had been in a frenzy, he wrote: "I know only that I was almost beside myself when I spoke. I felt only the storm raging in my soul— and that storm fired words from my mouth."[32]

Five days later he married Pauline Moonweis.

❖

She worked as a nurse in the clinic of a gynecologist named Shmuel Elsberg, who liked to host young intellectuals of Po'alei Zion in his home. Ben-Gurion was sometimes among his guests, and it was there that he first set eyes on her. Four years younger than he, she had been born in Minsk, then a part of Russia, and came to New York as a teenager. Like many other immigrants who grew up using two languages, she was fluent in both Yiddish and English. When they met at the home of Dr. Elsberg, Ben-Gurion was still not fully articulate in English. They spoke Yiddish.

As one might expect of a young woman who had gone to nursing school, Moonweis was self-confident and candid and had an acerbic sense of humor. She had had another romantic relationship prior to Ben-Gurion. She was impressed by Ben-Gurion's idealism, or perhaps actually by his strong opinions. In photographs taken at the time he looks like a fairly good-looking boy—the aquiline nose that was his most prominent feature, along with his sensual lips, gave off an air of manliness and confidence. She looks intelligent and pleasant; he was probably happy to have found a woman shorter than himself. She wore round eyeglasses of the type favored by Emma Goldman, the American anarchist leader; according to Ben-Gurion, she admired Goldman and was herself an anarchist. She later confirmed this, by implication.*[33]

On top of that, she was not a Zionist. Until meeting Ben-Gurion, she had never dreamed of ever living outside the United States. When they fell in love, he told her that if she consented to marry him she would have to leave America and accompany him to a poor, small country where there was no electricity or gas. She agreed. So it was that on Wednesday morning, December 5, 1917, the two of them went to the Office of the City Clerk in Manhattan and officially became man and wife. He was thirty-one years old, she twenty-seven.[†]

It was 11:30 in the morning. Ben-Gurion recorded in his diary: "I have taken a wife"; he did not mention her name. They didn't invite anyone. From the clerk's office she went on with her day, while he went to party headquarters. Philip (Pinhas) Cruso, who knew them then, recalled that Ben-Gurion had disappeared for three days. We had meetings, but he never showed up, he related; Ben-Gurion appeared on the fourth day and said, "Say mazal tov to me, I got married." It was known that Paula was in love with another party member, even if he had not shown much interest in her. "That's why it was such a surprise," Cruso explained. Ben-Gurion went on to the offices of *Der Yiddisher Kempfer* and placed a wedding notice, in Hebrew. In doing so, he gave her a Hebrew name, Penina, putting "Paula" in parentheses. In Hebrew he spelled her last name like that of King Monobaz of Adiabene of the first century c.e., who according to legend converted to Judaism.

They did not throw a party and did not go on a honeymoon. According to Paula, her family opposed her marriage to Ben-Gurion because he was a

---

* Many years later, Shimon Peres related that Paula, as everyone had come to call her, had told him that, had she wished, she could have married Leon Trotsky, the Russian revolutionary who was living in New York at that time. Peres said that he asked Ben-Gurion if that was true. Ben-Gurion replied that Paula had once gone to hear Trotsky speak; when she returned, she said that he had fallen in love with her. "He didn't take his eye off me during the entire speech," she said. When he asked, she told him that her seat had been in the middle of the front row. (Peres and Landau 2011, pp. 30–31.)

† According to census records, she was born in 1890, but her Israeli identity card listed her year of birth as 1892. There is no reason to believe that she provided American census-takers with incorrect information. (1910 United States Federal Census, Pauline Moonvess, ancestry.com; identity card, Paula Ben-Gurion, BGA, personal documents.)

Zionist.* When, many years later, she was asked what had been the happiest day of her life, she said it had been the day she gave birth to her oldest daughter.[34]

"MUCH JEWISH BLOOD"

In the months that followed, Ben-Gurion worked with Ben-Zvi to complete their book. They could hardly have found a better time to put it out, immediately following the Balfour Declaration. By one estimate, twenty-five thousand copies were sold.[35] The cover named the authors as David Ben-Gurion and Yitzhak Ben-Zvi; Ben-Gurion was finally the first. "Two-thirds of the book is mine," he wrote to his father.[36] The central claim of the book was that most of the fellahin, the Arab peasant farmers in Palestine, were not of Arab descent. Rather, they were the descendants of Jews who had lived in Palestine before the Arab conquest. The only real Arabs, he argued, were the Bedouin tribes.[†]

The fundamental assumption was that Palestine had not emptied of Jews following the destruction of the Second Temple by the Romans in A.D. 70. They had continued to live there, primarily in the Galilee, and most of them were farmers. When the Arabs arrived at the beginning of the seventh century, most of these Jews adopted Islam and began to speak Arabic, and by doing so survived. The consequence was the creation of a variety of mixed identities, but most of the Muslim fellahin living between the Jordan River and the Mediterranean belonged to "a single racial type," Ben-Gurion asserted categorically. "Much Jewish blood flows in their veins, the blood of Jewish farmers who chose, in their time of distress, to repudiate their religion so as not to be uprooted from their land." He based this claim largely on anthropological

---

* Pauline Moonweis's name appears in American records in a number of spellings. Another member of the family was the Israeli writer Gabriel Moked, whose last name was Moonweis before he Hebraized it. He recalled that when he was a boy, Paula bragged to him about her aristocratic origins, as opposed to Ben-Gurion's proletarian family. The marriage certificate lists him as David G. Ben-Gurion. In other American documents he identified himself as David Gruen Ben-Gurion. (Gabriel Moked in conversation with the author; United States World War I Draft Registration Cards 1917–1918, FamilySearch https://familyserach.org.

† Ben-Zvi and Yanait had previously tried to find Bedouin of Jewish stock. (Yanait Ben-Zvi 1962, pp. 34, 58, 74ff.)

information he found in libraries. The fellahin, he wrote, had many traditions much like those described in the Bible as Jewish; they preserved biblical personal names and the names of biblical settlements, as well as Hebrew words.[37]

From a scientific standpoint, the thesis was highly controversial; its political significance was that the Jews had never left their land and continued to live there. It was solid proof that Zionism did not require clashing with the fellahin. It was also unequivocal proof that "Jewish blood" rather than religion determined Jewish identity. Ben-Gurion and Ben-Zvi did not go into all that; they simply presented their finding as if it represented proven scientific truth.

They also drew the map of the Land of Israel as if it were no more than a geographical issue. In doing so, they discarded the borders that, according to religious faith, God had promised to his people. They termed these "ideal borders," while themselves sufficing with "actual borders." In the north they included Mount Hermon, the headwaters of the Yarmouk River, the Litani River, and the city of Sidon. The eastern border was traced far beyond the Jordan, including the Hauran plateau. They did not mark a border in the eastern desert, because they presumed that the area of the land would expand or shrink in keeping with the national home's ability to exploit the wilderness. In the south the border extended from El Arish to Eilat. It was a Zionist compromise between what Ben-Gurion later described as Greater and Lesser Palestine. The land so bounded, Ben-Gurion and Ben-Zvi observed, had more than a million inhabitants. In other words, they did not claim that the land was empty. They did, however, assert that it was a "land without a nation" and that it "awaited a people." They grounded the Jewish right to settle the land not only in history; they offered ecological arguments as well. "The land of flowers and the sun," they wrote, "the consummately wonderful land without parallel on the globe," has become a wasteland, "innumerable thorns and thistles cover the beautiful valleys." The gardens and forests had vanished, the mountain slopes were lifeless. All this had occurred because it was a land without a nation. With the return of its people, its natural treasures would bloom again.[38]

They did their best to maintain an understated academic style; they presented claims and counterclaims, backed with lots of dates and tables of figures. The project turned out to be much more extensive than they had expected, requiring a number of volumes; for now, they had completed only the first. Ben-Gurion said he was not pleased. But after two years of work, sixteen hours a day, he had reached the conclusion that a book as comprehensive and thorough as he had hoped to write would require fifteen years of labor.*

In the meantime, events impelled him to put down the pen and take up the sword, he wrote. He was referring to the efforts to establish the Jewish Legion.[39]

❖

The story began with Trumpeldor's Zion Mule Corps and continued in London. Ze'ev Jabotinsky shared an apartment with Vera and Chaim Weizmann in Chelsea. He sought the establishment of a Jewish Legion that would participate in the conquest of Palestine, under the command of the British army. Weizmann did not oppose the idea; he understood its political value and its symbolic significance, but remained very cautious. His principal goal was to promote the Balfour Declaration, and he wanted nothing to stand in the way.

When Britain declared general conscription, the question arose of what to do with the about thirty thousand Jewish men of military age—the *schneiders* (meaning "tailors"), as they were called—who had emigrated from Russia. Most of them hoped to evade enlistment. The interior secretary, Herbert Samuel, searched for a way to go easy on them and kept deferring their mobilization. In the meantime, the number of British dead was rising, and as Ben-Gurion later related, "considerable justified anti-Semitic agitation began." In February 1917, the government demanded a decision—the Jewish immigrants should either enlist or return to Russia. Unwillingly, but with no other choice, Weizmann had to deal with the issue. He proposed acceptance of Jabotinsky's program for the establishment of a Jewish Legion.

---

* The book appeared in Hebrew in Israel only years after their deaths. It was a semiofficial edition; a few chapters were omitted, including the one on the descent of the fellahin. (Ben-Gurion to his father, July 1, 1919, BGA; Ben-Gurion to his father, Dec. 5, 1919, in Erez 1971, p. 445.)

When the United States entered the war, Weizmann proposed a similar arrangement for American Jews.

Pinhas Rutenberg, who had already spoken of this with Ben-Gurion, and Ben-Gurion himself went to see Justice Brandeis and proposed that a Jewish battalion be formed in the U.S. Army as well, and be deployed in the conquest of Palestine. Brandeis brought the idea before President Wilson. The president sent Brandeis to the British, reverting this initiative to London, to Weizmann and Jabotinsky. At the end of July 1917, the British War Office declared that enlistment could commence.[40]

Ben-Gurion spoke with the British ambassador to Washington and, during the months that went by before London approved the plan, he devoted himself to promoting Jewish enlistment. "Immigrating to Palestine in khaki uniform became a very popular slogan," wrote Ben-Zvi, who was also encouraging Jews to volunteer.[41] In the meantime, Ben-Gurion had become fed up with the intrigues and disputes in his party; he claimed to have been the victim of "personal attacks" and described "irritability and filth" that he attributed to the influence of American politics. They fought over, among other things, the allocation of party funds to activity in the United States and in Palestine. Ben-Gurion resigned from the party Central Committee.[42] At the end of April 1918, he reported to the British consul in New York, and a few weeks later he was sworn into His Majesty's army and set out for Windsor, Canada, where he began his training.[43] Paulichke, as he had begun to call his wife, was miserable when he left her, just half a year after they married. She felt hurt, frightened, and offended—and she was pregnant.

"I SEEK YOUR LIPS"

On the way to his training camp he passed through several cities. Members of their Jewish communities awaited him, pressed forward to shake his hand, asked him to make speeches, bore him on their shoulders, gave him and his companions flowers and chocolate. Six weeks of drills and rifle practice followed. From time to time the soldiers had to dismantle their tents and put them up again; they had kitchen and guard duty; from time to time they stood for inspection and were taken out for parades.

Nothing they did indicated that they were going to be deployed on a real front. "The military training we received is insufficient by any standard," Ben-Zvi wrote. Indeed, its main purpose was not military but rather political and symbolic. The Legion represented Zionist ideology, with its own flag and insignia; the soldiers formed a committee that represented them to their commanders. They made a variety of demands, such as the supply of kosher food. They had stationery printed, with a Hebrew logo. Ben-Gurion used the camp phone and received calls as well, organized a memorial rally for Herzl, and read *The New York Times*. The British commanders adapted themselves to the Legion's exceptional nature. As part of this, they engaged in extended negotiations before Private 3831, Ben-Gurion, David, as he was referred to on his military documents, agreed to accept the rank of corporal. He thought he would have greater authority as one of the soldiers, but in the end accepted. "I have a special job," he told his wife. "Anyone who has a complaint or thinks he was done an injustice comes to me. And if someone wants to know something, he comes to me. Add to this three meetings of the Committee and then you have my entire daily schedule."[44]

According to one document, twenty-seven hundred men enlisted in the Jewish Legion in the United States. These included soldiers who volunteered for Jewish and Zionist reasons, but there were others who were "uncouth types and criminals from birth," Ben-Gurion wrote. He was especially proud of how he handled a man who had been imprisoned at Sing Sing. The man was "a thief from Pennsylvania" who bragged about his wife being a whore. His encounter with this man strengthened his faith in humankind, he said: "I also believe in the sinner." The former convict had donated five dollars to help pay for the Herzl memorial event.[45]

❖

Ben-Gurion's letters to Paula read like those written by a boy to his mother from a summer camp. "I've become a pupil again," he wrote, and said that he looked like a boy of fourteen or fifteen. One would not guess that these were the letters of a soldier who had volunteered to fight in a war that had already claimed the lives of fifteen million. "I feel a little intoxicated by my new life," he told her. "It is very pleasant to wake up with the sun and it is pleasant to shower on the lawn in the fresh early morning air." It was probably not the right thing to write to a woman he had left to go through her pregnancy alone, but he frequently wrote to her about his love and described it as a little boy's love. For her part, Paula diligently took on the role of new mother. She reminded him again and again to brush his teeth. He promised her that he was doing as she said and that he was also laundering his handkerchiefs. Ben-Zvi wrote similar letters to Rachel Yanait.[46]

Paula wrote to her husband as often as three times a week, in English. Sometimes he received four or five letters at once. His letters to her, numbering in the dozens, were in Yiddish. "I want to hold you, not only in my heart but also in my arms and to my bosom," he wrote after several months of separation. "I want to gaze not only on your picture but on you yourself, to embrace you, to press you to my heart and kiss you, to kiss with love that has been held back and stifled for so long." A few months later, he wrote: "I feel as if I am in love with you for the first time, and I seek your lips, your arms, and I want to press you against me, to embrace you with burning hands, to stand by your bed, to lean over you and cling to you, to give myself over to your arms and to forget everything but you, like then, happy in your close love, together, arm in arm, lip to lip, heart to heart."

He recalled the magical night that lulled them to sleep after covering them "with a coverlet of rapture and bliss" and impelled them "to be together, together." He reminded her of the morning hours, when both of them were intoxicated with their love, "together in our arms, together in our hearts." Even then, he seems to have had trouble dividing his time between his work and his love; work came first, as if there were no real choice. "Do you recall the few moments in the morning when I set aside my work and came to you, and a few times, after sleepless nights of work, I found you sleeping and I woke you with kisses on the mouth and embraces of your bare arms, and your eyes pleaded with me to stay a little longer. And more than your eyes, my heart shouted: Remain, remain, and both of us counted those few moments that passed so quickly."[47]

But more than they portray a private love story, the letters put on display a role-playing game between two symbolic characters that took the place of the real David and Paula. At first she was just his "wife," as he wrote in his diary on their wedding day; that same day he invented a new name for her. She continued to sign her letters with her original name, Pauline. She called her husband "Ben-Gurion," and that is how he signed his letters to her. He loved her as a "wife," "mother," and "sister." In a will he wrote at this time, he divided custody of the baby between her and his father in Płońsk.*

In the role-playing, she was the injured, suffering, and accusing party; he was the transgressor, agonized by guilt feelings.

"THE REDEMPTION OF THE LAND IS COMPLETE"

Her letters conveyed severe, sometimes heartbreaking distress. She told him about annoying neighbors and pains in her legs, which had swollen during the pregnancy. She had trouble falling asleep and suffered toothaches, and the baby kicked her. The money he arranged for her had been delayed. But more than anything else she wrote of her loneliness. He was the only one she could share her troubles with and he was not around. She pleaded with him to allow her to join him in Canada; he replied that the trip was too expensive and that he might have to leave the camp any day. "You are a bad lover, husband, and father," she wrote to him, and again and again reminded him to keep his promise to her, which was apparently that he would not be unfaithful and would not be killed. "Everything is gloomy and dreary in my life," she wrote. "I feel so miserable . . . I read all your letters today and you could imagine how much I cried . . . and why shouldn't I cry, have I got anybody as near to me as you? You are my all [sic] life . . . and the rest seem to be dead to me . . . I never thought I could love so sublimely, but one (God) knows how much I love you . . . I picture, when I will come back from the hospital, nobody to welcome us . . . As nobody could take your place, you are so good, especially to me . . . I suppose I don't deserve anything better, and I have to suffer."[48]

His responses proceeded in stages. At first he answered her claim to have been hurt with his own: "You think, dear, that had I loved you more, I would

---

* Ben-Gurion, "a.k.a. David Gruen," as he wrote in his will, asked that the baby be given the name Yariv (meaning "fighter"); he expected a son. If it were to be a girl, he asked that she be named Geula ("redemption"). He wanted the child to be sent to school in Palestine and asked Paula to learn Hebrew, so that she could speak that language with his son. He bequeathed her $2,000, the proceeds of his life insurance, and $500 to his father, along with a request that he use the money to visit Palestine at least once a year. (Ben-Gurion, will, May 28, 1918, BGA, general chronological documentation, 1916–1918; Ben-Gurion 1971a, p. 104ff.)

not have volunteered for the Legion. Why do you know me so little!" He promised her that he was one of those people whose love was forever. After this, he sympathized with her and tried to take on himself, if he could, some of her suffering. "When I read your letters," he wrote, "I feel everything that you feel and suffer everything that you suffer." He said he missed her and desperately wanted to be with her. In the third stage, he sought atonement: "I want to fall at your feet and plead for your forgiveness." Then he promised her that her suffering would only enhance his love. "Now it is more than love," he wrote. "You are my saint, the suffering angel who hovers around me without my seeing, to which my soul is drawn, on which gaze my heaven-ward eyes, for I see you standing on high, above me; because what you have done is so great that I sometimes want to remove my hat and bow, bow down low to your valor, which I will not cease wondering at and adoring all my life." In the end, he depicted his service in the Legion as the essence of their love and happiness: "The greatest thing that I could do now for you is to part and volunteer for the Legion, to leave you with an unborn child and set out for the front, because that deed will sanctify our love and prepare the happiness of our lives."

When he fell in love with her and decided to unite their lives forever, he wrote, he did not want to give her "tiny, cheap, everyday happiness," but rather prepared for her "the greatest, most holy, most human happiness, acquired with suffering and agony." He was delighted to discover that she was capable of suffering together with him "for the sake of a great thing." There was an almost contractual element to his approach, like that which governed his relations with his father during his period of study. "We melded in our love and there is no longer 'I and you' between us," he wrote, "but instead my heart is your heart and your heart is my heart . . . and I still believe that I am not the only one who volunteered, but that both of us volunteered for the Legion."[49]

On display again here was a complete identity between the needs of the Zionist struggle and his personal feelings. Perhaps it was simply egotism on his part. Maybe he had been uneasy with the routine life of a married man; perhaps he viewed marriage as a division of roles between a warrior man and a woman whose duty was motherhood. Maybe he abandoned Paula as his mother had abandoned him. Perhaps he really believed that the Jewish Legion was worth the price that Paula had to pay, as if it were the judgment of history. Whatever the case, no one had compelled him to enlist; he did it of his own free will. It was probably the only way he could return to Palestine, and service in the Legion finally added a military chapter to his political biography. During the next world war, Ben-Gurion could comment, as if incidentally, "It is not easy and not pleasant to be a soldier. I remember well the days and nights of immense boredom, when my friends and I were in uniform." Those who heard him might have concluded that they were listening to a seasoned fighter.[50]

❖

By the end of the war, five thousand soldiers had served in the Jewish Legion. They came from England, the United States, Canada, Argentina, and Palestine. Some of them managed to take part in the final stages of the conquest of Palestine from the Turks. But the Jewish unit established in America was a Zionist illusion, of zero military value. Like Bilu and the American branches of Hehalutz, its principal contribution to the Zionist struggle was the myth it bequeathed to the movement.*

On the way from Canada to Scotland, Ben-Gurion imagined himself "at the head of the Hebrew battalion on its way to fight for the redemption of the land." The sea was a bit rough, he noted in his diary, and he was slightly nauseous. Corporal Ben-Gurion did not, of course, stand at the head of the battalion, and he would miss the "redemption of the land." By that time, the British had controlled Jerusalem for half a year, after taking it from the Turks. Chaim Weizmann had already ridden in a Rolls-Royce with General Edmund Allenby, the commander of the British forces in Palestine, to the peak of Mount Scopus. There he laid, "in the name of the Hebrew army," one of the cornerstones of the Hebrew University. About six thousand guests attended

---

* Many years later, an official publication of the Israel Defense Forces asserted: "The Legion had to be established simply in order to prove that the Jewish people were prepared to fight for the Land of Israel and spill its blood for it." (Elam 1984, p. 332.)

the ceremony; Lord Balfour sent his personal greetings. Ben-Gurion and his comrades-in-arms had landed on the shores of Britain two days previously. He immediately set out for London and the office of Po'alei Zion there, in Whitechapel.[51]

On August 12, 1918, Ben-Gurion received a rifle, and three days later set sail with the rest of his battalion for France; from there they continued on to Italy. On his way to the front, to deal the final blows to the Turks, he could tell himself that he owed them a lot. Thanks to the Turks, he'd gone to America, an introverted, clueless guy. He didn't want to be a laborer, and couldn't be a lawyer. During the three years he spent in New York, his youth came to an end; he married and acquired self-confidence. In the process, he came to understand the huge power of the capitalist United States, the advantages and disadvantages of its Constitution and governmental structure, and the good and bad aspects of the American melting pot.*[52]

London was still the center of Zionist activity, but Ben-Gurion already sensed that the future lay in America. His encounter with American Jews was disappointing, even if Palestine was not yet ready for mass immigration, as he told them.[53] He knew how to treat people like Shmuel Fuchs with forgiveness, but as a Zionist, he was frustrated by them. He knew that the future of Zionism depended to a large extent on the money of American Jews, which made him all the more frustrated.

But this first American episode in his life entirely changed his feelings about himself, and consolidated some of the fundamental elements of his personality: the ability to learn, the skill to express himself in writing, and his romantic sensibility. He gained fame as a journalist and an author. He gained a livelihood—not wealth, but enough to support his wife. He still did not look like a national leader, but his constant involvement in the Po'alei Zion's machine broadened his political experience. He had contact with people of influence, among them the Supreme Court justice Louis Brandeis. It was an acquaintanceship that enabled him to say that he was only one individual

---

* Leo Deutsch, a Russian revolutionary in exile who shared Ben-Gurion's table in the New York Public Library, recalled that Ben-Gurion read a great deal about the history of American political parties, as well as "practical guides in the techniques of swaying the masses." Soon after arriving at the library, Ben-Gurion recorded in his diary data on the high proportion of black soldiers in George Washington's army. (Grodzensky 1965.)

removed from the president of the United States. He sensed that a great historical responsibility lay on his party: "We must now grasp the greatness of our destiny; if we don't, we will cause a tragedy for generations to come," he wrote.[54]

❖

It took them almost three weeks to reach Egypt's Port Said. "I have returned to my land with my rifle in hand, under the Hebrew banner, a member of the Jewish Legion," he wrote to his sister.[55] In fact, his military career came to an end, for all intents and purposes, without him having heard a single shot in battle. Allenby was not enthusiastic about the members of the battalion coming to Palestine; most of them remained in Egypt. Ben-Gurion came down with dysentery and was again hospitalized for several weeks in a military hospital. There he followed the news from the front and wrote: "I fear that our battalion will not arrive in time to participate in the conquest of the land."[56] Meanwhile, Jabotinsky's battalion made it to Transjordan and participated in the fighting there.

On September 17, 1918, while Ben-Gurion was still in the hospital, he received, six days late, a telegram from New York informing him of the birth of his daughter, Geula. His first reply was restrained, almost formal. "I take part in your happiness and joy and partake of your pain and your concern and your suffering," he wrote to Paula. He added: "God has given us a precious, great, and beloved gift . . . a new world is revealed to you." He wanted to embrace and kiss her and the baby, he went on. Then he declared: "Our land is already free; the light of the great, free, and happy tomorrow of our people is now breaking on the mountains of Judea and the Galilee." After this, he asked how she was doing financially and how her Hebrew lessons were going, and he asked her to send him by mail his Hebrew–French dictionary. It had red covers, he added.

A week later, he found warmer and more personal words. It was his thirty-second birthday on the Hebrew calendar. "I am not capable of conveying to you in words what has come over me since I received the telegram . . . my heart trembled with joy. A few short words, but God, what great substance and what great happiness they brought me." He sent her "loving and blazing love to our precious baby and to you, Paulichke, my dear." Unusually, he even evinced a bit of humor: "Send me a picture of you and the baby and write to say if our girl is a little bit smart, even if only as much as her father, and full of charm, if only as much as her mother." Paula wrote to him: "Despite the fact that she looks like you, she is so pretty." In this letter, too, he noted that Geula came into the world at a tragic and sacred moment, toward a great future, and returned to his decision to abandon her at the time of her pregnancy and birth. "This awareness weighed on my heart like a heavy and terrible stone, but, Paulichke, that is what had to be," he wrote.

In his third letter he entirely set aside history. He told her for the first time of his illness and hospitalization, and how at the time of the birth he was plagued with fearful nightmares, and how much happiness he had received from her cable. His absence from New York only increased the intimacy between them, he promised. "There is intimacy that is truer and more real than physical closeness," he told her, "the intimacy of a great, immortal spirit, the eternal unity of souls." He sent her his impressions of a book he read in the hospital, Romain Rolland's *Jean-Christophe*. "The entire book breathes a great love of humankind," he told her, and recommended that she read all ten volumes, even if they bored her in some places.

On October 2, 1918, he wrote in his diary: "Yesterday morning the English entered Damascus. The redemption of the land is complete."[57] The world war lasted for about six weeks longer.

· **8** ·

AUTHORITY

"I WON"

On the morning of November 7, 1923, the sixth anniversary of the October Revolution, Ben-Gurion stood in Red Square in Moscow, waiting for Leon Trotsky. After returning from exile, Trotsky had become one of the most powerful men in the Soviet Union; only Lenin stood above him, and Lenin was on his deathbed. The square was awash with red flags and revolutionary slogans; masses of citizens and students in Communist youth shirts waved their own little flags. Ben-Gurion stood next to the speakers' platform, at the Kremlin wall, together with other overseas guests. They all wanted to see Lev Davidovich Trotsky, as David Ben-Gurion referred to him in his diary, to underline his Jewish origins.

The combination of the golden domes of the churches and the revolutionary slogans and images of Lenin on the Kremlin wall enthralled him.

"How spectacular is the irony of history, that this medieval Czarist Russian fortress is now the heart of world revolution," he wrote. A military band played "The Internationale," the Soviet anthem, and Ben-Gurion noticed that foreign diplomats were quick to rise to their feet and doff their hats, exposing their heads to the autumn chill. He thought it funny to see the world proletarian hymn honored with such bourgeois propriety. He had risen early that morning. On the way to Red Square he saw a picture of Lenin in almost every window; here and there Karl Marx also appeared. The streets were open only to those who bore invitations. He had one—he was in the Soviet Union as an official guest, in his capacity as secretary of the General Organization of Hebrew Workers in Palestine, better known simply as the Histadrut—the Organization.[1] Ben-Gurion was one of three members of the secretariat of the Histadrut, which was founded in Haifa at the end of 1920 and had quickly become the principal labor union in Palestine. As he was the person who called the shots, everyone in the organization referred to him as the secretary-general, and that was the title he used—in error—in his memoirs.[2] For the first time in his life he wielded political influence.

The union had its inception in the Egyptian desert, four years previously.

❖

While still under treatment at the military hospital, Ben-Gurion read a speech by the revered labor leader Berl Katznelson, a man who, according to his biographer, Anita Shapira, "was both more and less than a political leader." That made it hard for anyone who wanted to talk politics with him, but Ben-Gurion saw in the speech an opportunity to promote himself into a leadership position. When he recovered from his dysentery, he was sent to the Tel-el-Kebir military base, not far from Cairo. It was a large prison camp the British built toward the end of the war as a place to intern the thousands of Turkish soldiers who had been captured in Palestine. Ben-Gurion joined the force responsible for guarding the facility. "At the very least," he comforted himself, "we are doing necessary and useful work here." Some of the other members of the Jewish Legion's Palestinian battalion were also sent to the camp. They waited for their order to go home; in the meantime, they were bored. Katznelson was among them.[3]

The two had already known each other for some time. They might even have met in Warsaw, where both were friendly with the Po'alei Zion leader Yitzhak Tabenkin. Katznelson, just a few months younger than Ben-Gurion, was seen by his many admirers to be a mature and exemplary figure. He was admired as an educator and beloved as a spiritual counselor, and played the role of a big brother on whom others could depend. Everyone called him by his first name. His personal prestige was based on the common belief that he followed only his moral compass and was devoid of any aspiration for office or position. Before enlisting in the Legion, he had wandered from one agricultural work detail to another and between two women he loved. During the final years of the war, he had raised vegetables near the Tombs of the Kings in Jerusalem. His public activity was largely restricted to an organization of farmworkers. They called themselves the Independents, and Katznelson's ambition was to unite them with the two labor parties, Po'alei Zion and Hapo'el Hatza'ir, creating a single political force. That was the theme of the speech that Ben-Gurion read in the hospital. He was ready to act.[4]

While he had settled in his new homeland thirteen years before, nearly seven of the intervening years had been spent overseas. He had not been with his people during the terrible war years and had not been party to the euphoria that had accompanied Allenby's entry into Jerusalem. Neither was he in Palestine when life began to return to normal, which included the first glimmerings of local politics. The British occupation authorities began to rebuild the shambles left by the Turks in almost every area of life, including security and law. Operating alongside the military regime was a Zionist Commission that arrived from London in coordination with the British government. The commission's task was to lay the foundations of the Jewish national home. Chaim Weizmann headed it first, before turning the position over to a psychoanalyst, Montague David Eder. Jabotinsky also joined the commission, in the role of liaison officer–cum–spokesman. Its members also awaited the return of Arthur Ruppin, who had during the war gone into exile in Istanbul. The American Jewish community sent a welfare and medical team; Justice Brandeis arrived to see what could be done to help. A Provisional Committee, an embryonic parliament of the Jewish community, convened in Jaffa. So were the Jewish community's first self-governing institutions born, under the sponsorship of the British military government, the Zionist movement, and overseas Jewish philanthropists.[5]

Ben-Gurion did not like the fact that new governing institutions were taking form without him. He had brought with him from the United States an intense passion to acquire political influence and make history, but also understood that the scattered remnants of his party would not get him very far. Katznelson's fusion initiative offered an opportunity that he did not want to miss.

❖

Katznelson received Ben-Gurion in his tent in November 1918 and gave him a green light to proceed with uniting the two labor parties. They were still stuck in the Egyptian desert, but Ben-Gurion wrote to Paula and asked her to send him his good suit—he was already planning his next trip to Europe.[6] Not everyone in the labor movement favored the merger. As chairman of meetings that were convened to advance the unification scheme, he had a hard time. "I had to avert the commotion that everyone was sure would soon cause an explosion," he wrote to Paula. He had never in his life seen such furious meetings, he said.[7]

The principal opposition came from Hapo'el Hatza'ir. That party's leader, Yosef Sprinzak, refused, at least for the time being, to give up his party's independence. Ben-Gurion knew his reasoning from his old debates with Shlomo Zemach. Like Zemach, Sprinzak was deterred by Po'alei Zion's socialism, which he deemed too radical. Together, the three labor factions numbered only a few hundred members, but Ben-Gurion maintained that a fusion of the parties would determine the fate of the Jewish people: "A deep abyss yawns before our people and threatens its existence," he claimed, apparently in reference to the deadly pogroms that had decimated Jewish communities after the war, especially in the Ukraine. That was the reason it was vital to build a national home in Palestine, he explained. If Jewish workers did not unite into a single body that would enable them to serve as educators of the people, and that would give them power within the Zionist movement, they would never overcome the danger presented by cheap non-Jewish labor.[8] The purpose of unification, he stressed, was thus to further the Zionist project, not the aspirations of the proletariat. But Sprinzak and most of his colleagues were not persuaded. Only three of them favored unification and left the party; one of them was Shlomo Lavi, Ben-Gurion's friend from Płońsk.[9] At the end of February 1919, a general convention was called to celebrate the unification. The 81 delegates in attendance, Ben-Gurion wrote, represented 1,871 Jews.[10]

The new Zionist Social Union of the Workers of the Land of Israel, Ahdut Ha'avodah (meaning "Unity of Labor"), defined itself as "a branch of the world socialist labor movement." But it carefully avoided radical language. Its platform included a demand for the nationalization of land, the creation of public capital, and equal rights, but not a word about the class struggle or the dictatorship of the proletariat. On the other hand, the unifying convention demanded "international guarantees for the founding of a free Hebrew national state in Palestine." It was a bold departure from the accepted Zionist terminology of a "national home."[11]

Katznelson brought more people into the new party than Po'alei Zion did—the farmworkers' organization he represented had already begun to establish mutual aid organizations, among them Kupat Holim, a medical services provider, and a marketing cooperative, Hamashbir.[12] Ben-Gurion brought a list of addresses of wealthy Americans to ask for assistance, along with the political experience he had gained in what he called the "Jewish Tammany Hall," after New York City's Democratic Party machine. Po'alei Zion also benefited from the help, if limited, of a fund for workers in Palestine set up by the party's overseas branches. But the major asset Ben-Gurion could offer the new party was his indefatigable energy and his passion to put everything he had into politics. He was willing to engage in endless conversations to pressure and persuade others, cut backroom deals, and make and listen to interminable speeches. "I had to conduct a difficult and bitter struggle—and I won," he wrote to Paula. "Too bad you did not see it yourself. You would have been proud then, not only of your daughter but also of your husband." Like the previous year, when he abandoned her in New York, he promised her that her presence at the hour of his victory would have made up for everything she had endured.[13]

"EVERYTHING WILL BE FINE"

Geula the baby was now half a year old. Paula regaled her husband with reports of the girl's playful personality and the beauty of her eyes. "She will have plenty of lovers," Paula predicted. While he was in Jaffa, conducting the final votes on the establishment of the new party, Geula's first two teeth appeared. But these were rare happy moments in Paula's life. Loneliness continued to torment her. She had a woman living with her, and she also received help from Dr. Shmuel Elsberg, at whose home she had met Ben-Gurion. Shmuel Fuchs once came to visit her. But as the months passed, her longing for Ben-Gurion grew and deepened her depression. On a couple of occasions she told him about nightmarish premonitions of death. "I am afraid you will have nobody to take to Palestine except your daughter," she wrote. The Spanish flu epidemic frightened her; she knew some people who had succumbed and died. If she were to die as well, Geula would be left "all alone," she wrote to him a few months later. "I cannot lead a life like I lead now. Life becomes a burden to me. If not you and baby [sic] I would kill myself long ago. But you both keep me back."[14] What she really wanted was to stay in America. She had heard that there was not good milk for children in Palestine. But she would go despite it all were it possible to arrange her trip immediately, before the summer. "I can't suffer any longer," she declared. One day he received eight letters from her all at once.[15]

He did his best to reassure her. "Everything will be fine," he promised. "The war has already passed." They would soon meet. There was a chance that he would go to London, and if so, he would continue on to America and bring her back to Palestine—that was the only thing he was thinking about. He very much wanted her and Geula to visit Płońsk. He told her that he had made a down payment on a house in a new project in Tel Aviv. And, he stressed, there was no lack of milk in Palestine—when they arrived, he would give Geula a milk bath. When he told her that Ben-Zvi and Yanait had gotten married, he allowed himself a bit of husbandly acerbity. "See, I'm not the only one to fall for such foolishness," he wrote. "I think I'm a bit to blame for this celebration—a bad example can have an effect."*

---

* There seems to have been another reason for his high spirits on the day he wrote this letter—he had gone to visit his first love, Rachel Beit Halahmi, in Petah Tikvah. (Ben-Gurion

Paula didn't believe him. He would not go to London because no one there wanted him to come, she wrote. He was sought after in New York, but he was making no effort to go there. His letters made it very clear to her where his mind was. "There are so many meetings and assemblies in Jaffa and they last so long that I don't have a free moment for you," he wrote her. Two weeks later, she opened a letter he wrote stating: "I am using the few moments I have for you to write you a few words." Nevertheless, he on occasion set politics aside to write impassioned love letters, expressing heartfelt longing for the child he had not yet seen and offering poignant sympathy for Paula's plight. "When I read what you are going through alone and helpless, I felt as if a sharp knife has spiked a hidden wound," he wrote. He reveled in her great love, which had enabled her to allow him to leave her in New York. To his father he wrote: "I think no woman has ever made such a sacrifice."[16]

❖

He tried to arrange for her to come. "I live in constant expectation of your arrival," he wrote to her. "That is my Messiah." But at that time it was still not easy to obtain all the necessary permits. He thought up all sorts of schemes; as part of one of them, he instructed Paula to write, falsely, on her application for an immigration certificate that she was a refugee who was returning to Palestine after being deported by the Turks during the war.

It was another example of Ben-Gurion's tendency to try to get around whatever legal obstacles stood in his way, just as in the past he had obtained a forged birth certificate and high school diploma, traveled on someone else's passport, and wriggled out of his mandatory service in the Russian army. The end justified the means. Officially he was still in the army, but in November 1918 his commanding officer allowed him to go to Palestine on leave. Once he went AWOL for several days and was punished.[17]

Somehow he managed to scrape together $900 to buy Paula a first-class ticket on a passenger ship. She and Geula arrived in November 1919, and the

to Paula, Oct. 8, Nov. 18, Nov. 20, 1918, July 25, May 17, 1919, Dec. 28, 1918, in Erez 1971, pp. 398, 400, 493, 427, 420, 406; Ben-Gurion to his sister Tzipora, Dec. 29, 1918, in Erez 1971, p. 409.)

three of them soon moved into a rented room in Tel Aviv. Geula had celebrated her second birthday a few months earlier, and Ben-Gurion wrote to
his father that she was the nicest, warmest, cutest, prettiest, and smartest girl
he had ever seen. Unfortunately, at this point she only understood her
mother, who spoke to her in English, but Ben-Gurion was certain that she
would soon learn Hebrew. "She is still nursing, but we have just decided to
wean her," he reported. They were expecting another baby in a few months.[18]

"THERE IS NO SOLUTION"

Politically, it was an interregnum. Prior to July 1922, when the League of
Nations approved the legal instrument that awarded Great Britain the administration of Palestine, the country's future was the subject of long international debate. It was in this context that Chaim Weizmann reached his
pinnacle as a statesman. Much as with the efforts that had produced the Balfour Declaration, Zionist diplomacy was conducted far from Palestine and
over the heads of its inhabitants, Ben-Gurion among them. In tandem
with that diplomacy, a protest movement arose among Palestine's Arab
population.

The Provisional Committee convened in June 1919 to address the growing tensions. Some of the participants demanded a peace initiative, partly
against the background of the eviction of Arab tenant farmers from land purchased by the Zionist movement. Others believed that peace with the Arabs
was impossible. Ben-Gurion was one of them. He spoke briefly and bluntly.
"Everyone sees the difficulty of relations between Jews and Arabs," he began,
"but not everyone sees that there is no solution to that question. There is no
solution. There is an abyss and nothing can fill that abyss." Two nations were
facing off against each other. "We want Palestine to be ours as a nation," he
explained. "The Arabs want it to be theirs—as a nation . . . I don't know
what Arab would agree to Palestine belonging to the Jews." During the
debate, a proposal was made to encourage the Arabs to learn Hebrew and
the Jews to learn Arabic. Ben-Gurion, who knew a bit of Arabic, responded
cynically—he did not understand why he should learn Arabic and he had no
need for "Mustafa" to learn Hebrew, he said. In fact, he didn't care if the
Jewish farmer who was dispossessing the Arab laborer knew Arabic or

whether the Arab killing a Jew knew Hebrew. Either way, the Arabs would not agree to give Palestine to the Jews, even if the Jews learned Arabic.[19]

Many years later, Ben-Gurion spoke dismissively of the "easy solutions" that had characterized the Zionist approach to the Arab problem, which he termed "fuss and prattle" growing out of a refusal to recognize the facts. From his time in the United States to the end of his life he took pains to sound optimistic, but the two foundational experiences that shaped his real attitude toward the Arabs instilled in him realism devoid of hope—the murder of the farmer Shimon Melamed before his eyes at Sejera, and another incident he recounted to his father four years after it took place, shortly before his expulsion by the Turks: He ran into one of his university classmates. When Ben-Gurion told him that he was about to be expelled, the young man retorted that, as his friend, he was sorry for him, but as an Arab nationalist he was very happy. These words hurt him, so he said, even more than the death of his friends at Sejera. "That was the first time in my life that I heard an honest answer from an Arab intellectual," he said many years later. "It was etched into my heart, very, very deep."*

There was no subject that preoccupied him more. His archives preserve copies of English-language intelligence reports that confirmed his fundamental view—Arab leaders in a number of Palestine's cities had reached the conclusion that only the use of force could prevent the immigration of Jews and their takeover of the country.[20] Arab opposition would indeed soon turn into organized violence, and as violence grew, Ben-Gurion's conviction that the conflict could not be resolved grew stronger. At most, he believed, it could be managed. The insight that he had received in Sejera also became ensconced ever deeper within him—this was the price of Zionism.

❖

Within seven months the conflict had taken a heavy toll. On Monday morning, March 1, 1920, several hundred Arabs massed at the gate to an isolated

---

* He told this story time after time, into his old age. Later, he claimed, he tried, unsuccessfully, to locate the classmate. (Ben-Gurion to his father, Dec. 5, 1919, in Erez 1971, p. 443; Ben-Gurion 1971a, p. 71; Ben-Gurion interview with Dov Goldstein, Ma'ariv, Sept. 28, 1966.)

Jewish farm in the Upper Galilee, not far from the Lebanese border, Tel Hai Farm. As tensions increased in the region, the members of the Provisional Committee had been divided over whether defensive forces should be sent to the Upper Galilee, or whether the Jewish settlers there should be instructed to leave. It was one of those fundamental dilemmas that the Zionist project had to face from time to time. Jabotinsky believed that there was no way to defend the settlers. He insisted that they be told the bitter truth and be brought south. Part of the debate was over the question of whether the settlers at Tel Hai should be allowed to die so as to bestow their country with a heroic myth; Jabotinsky thought not. Since the world war, he wrote, the value of martyrdom had very much declined. Ben-Gurion believed that Jews had a duty toward Zionist history. "We need to defend every place where a Jewish laborer works," he declared. "If we flee bandits, we will have to leave not only the Upper Galilee but also Palestine." It was a dispute over existential fundamental values—patriots who were ostensibly for the Galilee and defeatists who were against it. The Provisional Committee decided to send a delegation to the Galilee, but by the time its members were able to get through the snow that blocked the roads, it was too late.

Exactly what happened at Tel Hai that morning remains unclear. The residents called in help from a nearby settlement, Kfar Giladi. Ten men arrived, led by Joseph Trumpeldor, the Jewish Legion hero who had returned after the war and gained admirers thanks to his efforts to unite the labor movement. He took command at Tel Hai. At some point, everyone seemed to be shooting at everyone. Trumpeldor was killed, as were three other men and two women. Tel Hai Farm was abandoned, but became a symbol. That was the importance of the battle: it produced a myth of Zionist heroism. Someone granted Trumpeldor stirring final words: "It is good to die for our country." The Jewish public and leadership needed the myth because they had failed to help the Galilean settlers; Tel Hai was their failure. Ben-Gurion often evoked it; it overshadowed the myth of Hashomer. A delegation representing the international Po'alei Zion movement that was visiting Palestine when the incident took place passed a series of resolutions that Ben-Gurion copied into his memoirs. Among them were: Palestine will not be partitioned; all of Palestine will be the territory on which the Jewish home will be established; all uninhabited land in Palestine is to be handed over to the Jewish people. A year later, Colonial Secretary Winston Churchill came to Palestine and severed Transjordan from the territory designated for the Jews.[21]

"WE ARE DEALING WITH A NATIONAL MOVEMENT"

Katznelson, Tabenkin, and Ben-Zvi were considered, and felt themselves to be, above managing the new united party's day-to-day affairs. They may sometimes have also been too lazy to do so. And they had more lofty affairs to attend to. Ben-Gurion discovered that his position as party secretary offered many opportunities. Politics was his sole occupation now. As there was no one else who wanted to do this job, Ben-Gurion became the most powerful person in the party apparatus, which was then still in an embryonic stage. During this entire period, he was still officially a British soldier; Weizmann arranged long leaves for him and made him a member of the Zionist Commission. It was a convenient arrangement, because he continued to receive his army salary.[22] From this point to the end of his life he made his living as a full-time politician. As far as he was concerned, the Zionist Commission was a foreign government.[23] The beginning was a big scandal. The Ahdut Ha'avodah secretary Ben-Gurion sued David Eder, chairman of the Zionist Commission, for libel, demanding that he submit to a proceeding in the Jaffa Magistrates Court or some other forum. This happened in the framework of Ben-Gurion's efforts to obtain immigration and work permits for some 250 of his battalion comrades who wanted to remain in Palestine. While they waited without employment, some of the soldiers got into trouble with their British commanders and were sentenced to prison for attempted mutiny. Eder maintained that they deserved their punishment, charging that they had been molesting Arab women. "He said horrible things," Ben-Gurion told his friend. "His libels and profanity were hair-raising." Eder rejected the suit haughtily and coldly, saying that he saw it as "subversion of the sacred and profound right of free speech." In the end, Ben-Gurion backed down and settled out of court.[24]

The clash with the Zionist Commission was a power struggle. Aggressive as an agile fencer, Ben-Gurion also scared away a woman named Nellie Strauss, who had brought money from America with the good intention of founding an agricultural settlement for veterans of the Jewish Legion in the

Jezreel Valley. She represented an organization named Kehilat Zion. Lord Balfour gave his permission for the settlement to be named after him—it was to be called Balfouria. Ben-Gurion wanted his battalion's soldiers' committee to take charge of the project—in other words, he wanted to control it himself. He treated Strauss as if she represented a malevolent enemy and demanded a quasilegal inquiry into the project—who said what, who spoke the truth, and who lied.[25]

At this point, he already seemed to have developed a flair for such inquiries; they could salve a hurt ego, but also restore his self-control and avert outbursts and new insults. In contrast, he ran the elections to the Assembly of Representatives with the expertise of an old warhorse.

❖

The Jewish Assembly of Representatives was a body meant to advance the establishment of a national home and to institutionalize separation between Jews and Arabs. It was the first parliamentary institution in Palestine to be elected by general and equal suffrage, by secret ballot. The right to vote was granted to every Jewish resident in Palestine, of either sex, of the age of twenty and above. The candidates were associated with party slates but were elected on a personal basis. Twenty parties participated.

As with the production of the *Yizkor* book and his composition, together with Ben-Zvi, of his book on Palestine's geography, Ben-Gurion proved in this campaign how good he was at learning an unfamiliar task and investing everything he had in carrying it out. He was a sought-after speaker himself, but he considered organization and the workings of the party apparatus to be more important than rhetoric. He wanted to know everything and not to neglect even the tiniest detail; he covered pages of his diary with quantitative data on every potential voter at the most remote polling stations. It brings to mind the dictator's centralization of information and the addiction of a collector. His obsession with details became one of the cornerstones of his political power.[26]

❖

Early on Sunday, April 4, 1920, during the week of Pesach, Ben-Gurion made a visit to the Ben-Zvis in Jerusalem. They talked about the need to establish a guard force manned by Jewish Legion veterans. The city was tense; Rachel Yanait, as everyone continued to call her even after her marriage to Ben-Zvi, was anxious. She was a member of the Defense Committee that Jerusalem's Jewish community had established following the battle of Tel Hai, a body headed by Jabotinsky. He was openly training several dozen young people and even marched them through town, although not through the Old City. "A pogrom is liable to break out any day," he wrote to Weizmann; the inhabitants of the Old City's Jewish Quarter remained unprotected.

Soon after noon, Ben-Gurion and Ben-Zvi heard that Arabs were attacking Jews in the Old City; they rushed there, still dressed in their British army uniforms. Yanait later spotted them in one of the alleys, bearing a wounded person on a stretcher. Scores of Arab thugs, armed with knives and iron rods, were breaking into Jewish homes, raping and looting. Some of the eyewitnesses later reported seeing feathers wafting out of the houses, one of the definitive signs of a pogrom. Jabotinsky managed to get some of his men into the Old City, but too late. In the end, five Jews were killed and two hundred and sixteen wounded, eighteen of them seriously. Four Arabs had been killed, among them a small girl, and twenty-three Arabs wounded, one of them seriously. Seven British soldiers were also injured, all of them apparently having been beaten by rioting Arabs.[27]

Ben-Gurion and Ben-Zvi went to the Zionist Commission offices on Jaffa Road. Yanait did as well. "It was bitter and difficult to see them dressed in uniforms and unable to act as Hebrew soldiers," she wrote. They must have felt likewise. Jabotinsky was sentenced by the British to fifteen years' imprisonment, along with other Jews and Arabs who had been involved in the clashes. "For a century there has been no fighting of this sort," Moshe Smilansky wrote in *Ha'aretz*. Ben-Gurion's thinking on the conflict with the Arabs was reinforced. "We are dealing with a national movement," he wrote some time later in his diary. "Other than redoubling Jewish immigration and fortifying our positions, we do not have any way of responding to this national conflict."[28]

❖

The polling in Jerusalem for the Assembly of Representatives was postponed because of the riots. But that was not the only reason; they were delayed time and again because of a dispute that took many months to resolve. The city's Haredi Jews declared that they would boycott the elections because they opposed allowing women to vote, even in separate polling stations. Without Haredi participation, there was almost no point in holding the elections, because they were the strongest force in the city. Ben-Gurion reviled and ridiculed them with his best rhetoric; he referred to them as "blacks," just as he had in one of his first published articles, a decade before. Now he also asserted that they were the forces of "destruction and rot." He took a tough line—as the Haredim saw this as a matter of principle, he argued, they should not be allowed to win. If they were given their way, "they will want to bury every part of our lives by means of all sorts of arcane religious laws."[29]

Even so, he did not place himself at the front of the fight for women's rights. He noted that women did not vote in many countries; Jerusalem did not need to be a leader on this issue, he said. In the end, he agreed to a consummately creative arrangement—women could vote and be elected to the Assembly, but in the Haredi neighborhoods, men would vote twice, once for themselves and once for their wives.[30] It was the first time Ben-Gurion had entered into such an agreement with the Haredim. The arrangement was incompatible with the principle of gender equality that his party proclaimed, but he and his friends believed that the Zionist cause required the broadest possible participation in the elections by the entire Jewish community in Palestine, so that they would constitute a display of power and national unity for the Arabs and British. In the process, women demanding equal rights for their sex were asked to compromise again and again, or at least to put off their rights until better days, all in the national interest.[31]

Voter participation was high. Ahdut Ha'avodah emerged as the largest force in the Assembly, but it did not win a majority—it received 70 of the body's 314 seats. Ben-Gurion had good reason to be proud of himself—he received the largest number of votes of all his party's candidates, more even than Berl Katznelson. In the meantime, he had been discharged from the army.[32]

"TO SPILL BLOOD AS WELL"

In June 1920, Ben-Gurion again packed his suitcase and set out for London. This time Paula went with him; in August their son Amos was born there. They were away almost a year. The principal purpose of the trip was to raise money for Ahdut Ha'avodah. Hashomer had been disbanded and defense of the Jewish community had been placed in the hands of a new body, the Haganah ("Defense"), operating under the sponsorship of Ahdut Ha'avodah and the Histadrut; in other words, it was largely under Ben-Gurion's control.[33]

He arrived in London in a combative spirit—soon after landing he caused a scandal by declaring at a Zionist convention that "most of the moshavot, as they are now constituted, belong to the Arabs," by which he meant that they did not accept Jewish laborers. The moshavot farmers also had a representative at the convention, who shouted, in Yiddish, that Jewish laborers were worthless. "A horrible ruckus" transpired in the hall. Labor delegates branded the farmers' representative "filthy" and called him a traitor. Ben-Gurion had his day. He also used the convention to denounce Weizmann, and not for the first time. A short time after returning to Palestine from his American exile, Ben-Gurion took Weizmann to task for accepting a promise to establish a Jewish national home in Palestine, rather than insisting on the promise of a Jewish state. Weizmann responded that he did not demand a state because he would not have received one. He believed in cautious gradualism.[34] Ben-Gurion now argued that Weizmann had not done enough to advance the Zionist project in Palestine. It was a continuation of his fight against the Zionist Commission.[35]

It was not easy to represent a small party in the shadow of Weizmann, who continued to make national history while Ben-Gurion managed only to raise a bit of money for his party. He did not have good contacts in England, and some of the donors he solicited seem not to have understood why they should give money to Ahdut Ha'avodah rather than to the Zionist Organization. On top of that, the New York branch of Po'alei Zion did not answer his letters.[36]

❖

His children brought him great joy. While Paula recuperated in the hospital from Amos's birth, he remained at home with Geula. "I just hope that Amos will be at her level," he wrote. Many years later, he wrote that he preferred boys, but while they were small he heaped a proud father's praises on both of them. Sometimes he also went to the British Museum library. His reader's card lists two books on the history of Lebanon's Druze, one of them in French, as well as works on the history of the Eastern Church and the Church of England.[37]

But his spirits frequently fell—England was cold and monotonous. His long hours in his office seemed like a prison term. The letters of distress he received from Palestine must have intensified his sense of failure, as did the news that Jabotinsky had received ten thousand pounds from a wealthy Jew named Alfred Mond, Lord Melchett. "The noose is tightening," Katznelson wrote to him. "And we, for our part, are heading for ruin." Lord Melchett's money was designated for defense needs. Ben-Gurion had tried in the meantime to sell "shekels" to Britain's Jews, which granted them the right to vote in elections to the Zionist Congress. But he was no more successful than he had been years ago, when he tried to do the same with his classmates in Poland.[38]

Eventually, he decided that there was no sense in his remaining in London. At the beginning of April 1921, he sent Paula and the children to his father's house in Płońsk. He joined them three weeks later; in the meantime, he dealt with the affairs of his party.[39]

❖

The devastation wreaked by the war was visible everywhere in Poland, especially in the east and south. Many towns had burned down. Hundreds of thousands of refugees had still not returned to normal life. Some of them were Jews. Many had survived thanks to assistance from the Joint Distribution Committee (popularly known simply as "the Joint"), a Jewish welfare organization based in New York.[40] One of the members of the first medical team the Joint sent to Eastern Europe after the war was Dr. Shmuel Fuchs; his mission was to care for the teeth of Polish Jews. He founded eight new clinics, handed out 21,576 toothbrushes, and distributed more than 25,000 units of a toothpaste manufactured according to his own special formula.

His work took him to many Jewish communities, Płońsk among them.[41] Two paths converged for a time there. Fuchs believed in the future of Jewish life in the Diaspora and had come to Poland to help Jews rehabilitate themselves there; Ben-Gurion had come to search for "appropriate material for our labor needs in Palestine," meaning immigrants, as he wrote.[42] Apparently they missed each other; Fuchs seems to have arrived in Poland a few weeks after Ben-Gurion left.

The family visit in Płońsk turned into a nightmare. The room the Gruen family put their American guest and her children in had a ceiling stained with mildew. The hosts did not put on the heat and the water was not clean. Both children got sick. Ben-Gurion portrayed the problem as a mutual misunderstanding. "It was a meeting between two worlds that were a bit foreign to each other," he wrote. He and his family were accustomed to the quality of the water in Płońsk, he said, but Paula could not grasp how normal people could drink "such turbid stuff." Paula was disgusted also by the Gruens' habits—the way they talked, their table manners, "all those details of daily life that ostensibly seem to be of no value or interest," as Ben-Gurion put it, "but are what actually govern relations between people." Paula thought that they detested her and were trying to humiliate her. She was miserable. Ben-Gurion tried to bring the two sides together but failed. One day he abandoned her in Płońsk and returned to Palestine.[43]

❖

The trigger was the headline in *Hatzefirah* on May 3, 1921: "Details on the Riots in Jaffa." The newspaper based its report on the official statements released by the high commissioner, according to which 30 Jews and about 10 Arabs had been killed. The Zionist Commission's statement: 27 Jews had been killed and 150 wounded. Under these two statements the newspaper printed an item from a Jewish news service noting that the much-admired author Y. H. Brenner had been found murdered. The next day, *Hatzefirah* was still marking the item on Brenner's death with a question mark, but it was correct. At the time of his death, Brenner had been editing the writings of his friend Joseph Trumpeldor. On the day of the murder Shlomo Zemach and Israel Shohat had intended to visit him. Along the way they heard gunfire and someone told them not to go to where Brenner was living, because Jews were being slaughtered there. Soon before his death, Brenner had written of the Arabs: "There is hatred between us, and it must be, and it will be." His body, mutilated by his murderers, became one of the icons of the Zionist struggle.[44]

The main thrust of the Arab attack that day was directed against a symbolic target—the immigrants' hostel in Jaffa run by the Zionist Commission. But the rioting quickly spread to other places. Dozens of witnesses—Jewish, Arab, and British—all told the same story. Arab men bearing sticks, knives, swords, and in some cases pistols attacked Jewish passersby and broke into Jewish homes and stores. They beat and killed them in their homes, children as well. In some cases they sliced through their victims' skulls. In the wake of the attackers, Arab women came and looted. Many witnesses related that, this time as well, pillows and comforters were torn open and the feathers were thrown into the streets, an image familiar from pogroms in Russia. A commission of inquiry later termed it "an orgy of pillage." Moshe Sharett wrote: "The holocaust came precipitously."[45]

It was the deadliest blow that the Zionist settlement of Palestine had received since it began. It brought home to the settlers themselves just how dependent they were on Jewish communities overseas. The daily newspaper *Ha'aretz* issued an emotional call to the Diaspora: "Do not leave us alone on the front lines. Do not disregard the blood of your pioneers, whom you sent before the nation. Bring your masses to us, bring your great leaders to us—to reinforce the Hebrew position, to augment it with working hands, hands for defense!" That was not the voice of a national avant-garde but of a Jewish community in distress. The National Council, the Jewish community in Palestine's executive body, called on the Jews of the world to donate more money for the Jews of Palestine, just as the pious Jews of Palestine had done since time immemorial.[46]

High Commissioner Herbert Samuel feared that Palestine was liable to turn into a second Ireland. He immediately forbade entry into its territory. That made it difficult for Ben-Gurion to get back. He left Płońsk almost as soon as he read about Brenner's murder, but three months passed before he arrived in Palestine. In the meantime, he attended a meeting in Prague and then returned to his wife and family in Płońsk. His position on Zionism grew even more adamant in the wake of Brenner's murder. "We have the right to Palestine as a nation, not as a minority. We have a right to Palestine, not the Arabs. We should and can, from a moral point of view, use all means to break the opposition of the Arabs . . . When they attack us, we have the right to defend ourselves and, if necessary, to spill blood as well," he declared. He demanded that the leaders of the Zionist movement establish a large self-defense organization in Palestine, a strong and highly disciplined force. On the way back he visited several Italian cities, among them Venice, Florence, and Rome, where he dealt with the publication of the Italian translation of his book on Palestine. The immigrant ship *Sicily*, on which Ben-Gurion returned, apparently also carried arms that he was responsible for transporting to Palestine. "We left the ship quietly and completely peacefully," he wrote to his father at the beginning of August 1921. "The faces of the Arab sailors," he wrote, "were as they have always been."[47]

"MY CRIME AGAINST YOU IS SO GREAT"

"The Histadrut was born out of nothing," said Berl Repetur, who would become one of the labor organization's senior officials. Ben-Gurion and one of his colleagues on the three-man secretariat, David Zakai, rented a small Arab house not far from Meah She'arim, a Haredi neighborhood in Jerusalem, and furnished it with several desks. It was the Histadrut's first office. For a time the two of them lived in the same room, and as there was only a single bed, they took turns sleeping on it, one night Ben-Gurion and one night Zakai. Ben-Gurion then moved to Yegia Kapayim, one of the new and relatively expensive neighborhoods being built in the western part of the city. His rent, five Egyptian pounds, amounted to between a quarter and a third of his wages. He had a good salary, twice as high as the going wage for a Jewish worker.[48]

He wrote down all his expenses, in great detail. He generally ate his breakfasts, lunches, and dinners at the workers' kitchen run by the Histadrut. Bread, sugar, eggs, fish, cocoa, coffee, soap, watch repair, kerosene, getting his shoes polished. He also spent money on newspapers, shaves, underwear, a raffle, and cigarettes. The raffle only appears once; cigarettes were a standard expense of his at that time.[49]

And books. He bought books all the time, in Palestine and overseas, far more than he could ever read. It was one of the largest items in his monthly budget. The vast majority were works of history and political science, with some Jewish studies thrown in; most were in foreign languages. It was not the library of a bookworm but of a collector with a special weakness for multivolume sets of complete works. He counted them in March 1922, a total of 775 volumes, which he broke down not by subject but by the language they were written in: 219 were in German, 340 in English, 13 in Arabic, 29 in French, 140 in Hebrew, 7 in Latin, 2 in Greek, 7 in Russian, 2 in Turkish, and 15 dictionaries of a variety of languages.*

❖

Soon after the Histadrut was founded in 1920, Ben-Gurion had proposed the organization of "a general commune, under military discipline, of all the workers of Palestine," which he termed a "labor army." In the first stage, he wanted his party to require all its members to enlist in this labor army and to work, without questioning, anywhere and in any profession that "the army directorate" would impose on them. It was an idea he had read about in his youth, in Menachem Ussishkin's Zionist program. Ben-Gurion spoke of it as a "general and common labor economy for the country's entire working public," but it sounded rather authoritarian. "Instead of anarchy—order and discipline," he declared. Among other things, he meant that at least part of the workers' wages would not be paid to them in currency but rather in chits in exchange for which they would receive food and other provisions.[50] "My plan is the dictatorship of the Hebrew laborer," he explained. "The most important thing for us is a Hebrew Palestine." He restated the principle he wrote of in his early articles that the Hebrew proletariat would be "the nation's agent and the originator of its national initiatives." If that meant a "Zionist dictatorship," so be it, and if necessary, "even a dictatorship of the Zionist Organiza-

---

* These add up to 774. Ben-Gurion might have miscounted in his enthusiasm—that same day another 24 books arrived. In the summer of 1922 he bought, over the course of a few weeks, dozens of books in inflation-ravaged Berlin and Leipzig, taking advantage of the daily decline in the value of the German mark. (Ben-Gurion, Diary, March 20, Aug. 27, Sept. 3–Oct. 10, 1922, June 11, 1926, July 16, 1930, BGA.)

tion."[51] What he really meant was a dictatorship of his party and the Histadrut. His goal was to have the two take charge of all areas of life, including employment, housing, health, education, and culture.

His proposals caused an uproar and were met with hostility. His comrades were more realistic and more democratic. Ben-Gurion resigned. He wrote to his father that he had decided to take his legal exams. Then he came to his senses and revoked his resignation. In March 1922, he wrote: "I am now responsible for all the Histadrut's activities, and the responsibility is great and difficult." He was right.[52]

❖

In the meantime, throughout these events, over almost an entire year, Paula Ben-Gurion remained in Poland. It is not clear why she did not return to Palestine on her own. Whatever the case, it was a horrible year for her. The strain between her and the Gruen family became unbearable. "I cannot understand your attitude," she wrote to Ben-Gurion. "You know how much I hate to stay in Płońsk. My life is miserable I don't want to suffer I suffered enough in my life." She told him that the wife of his brother Michel had left him, and everyone was saying that she became a prostitute. Michel was furious and could not stand it when the children cried, while she, Paula, had to suffer. "If you have any love for me try to take me home."[53] She and the children soon moved in with other relatives of Ben-Gurion's, in a village named Rabiez. She endured the heavy Polish winter there, in conditions even more primitive than those in Płońsk.

Ben-Gurion claimed that he had not intended in advance to leave her in Płońsk for an entire year, and would not have agreed to do so. "But," he wrote, "as a result of events that no one could have anticipated, that is how it worked out." He did not indicate what "events" he was referring to. "I very much request, if Penina returns or is about to return from the village, that you clean the room well for her and hire her a maid," he asked his father, promising to cover all the expenses. The impression is that he did not go out of his way to bring her to Palestine. His father sent him a painful letter and Ben-Gurion quickly responded that it had been written by "the loving and fond hand of both a father and mother." The hostility between his wife and father required him to state his position; he came down on his father's side. He halfheartedly asked him to understand Paula—a devoted mother like her cannot overlook what she sees as substandard hygiene. His father's house had no bathtub, and the toilet was in the yard. But he did not defend her. "What you wrote very much saddens and pains me, and I will write to Penina about that in detail and I do not want to justify what she did because she was not right in doing it." The nature of the particular incident remains unspecified.

It was an emotional and submissive letter. "Even if you were to do an injustice to me or my wife or my children—if such a thing were possible— even then I would not be angry with you," he wrote. His interest was not in the tension between Paula and his father but rather his own relations with his father. He recalled the day he left Płońsk, evoking a child's sense of guilt. "I know how much you are aggrieved and angry at me and I know that you are in the right . . . My crime against you is so great that I cannot ask that you forgive me." He sent his father some money, so that his niece Sheindele could complete her studies.[54]

Paula returned to Palestine in early April 1922, looking thin and exhausted. "Geula is wonderful," Ben-Gurion wrote. He also marveled at Amos's lanky physique, but his complexion was not healthy. In honor of their return, Ben-Gurion bought a broom. Jerusalem was not Manhattan, but neither was it Płońsk. Paula recovered quickly.*

His diary reflects the division of labor in their home. "I gave Penina a weekly allowance of 2.50 Egyptian pounds" for household expenses, which had up until then been rather spartan, and to which meat, wine, and delicacies had now been added. Geula began attending a preschool. That same day he bought several books by Berdichevsky, and two months later a new bookcase. He and Paula did not go out much; he frequently went out on his own in the evening.[55]

---

* About four months after her return, Ben-Gurion still thought it necessary to write to his father to say, "It hurts me that you suspect Paula of hiding your letters from me. That is baseless. I assure you (and I plead with you to believe me) that Paula harbors no resentment against you." (Ben-Gurion to his father, Aug. 9, 1922, BGA.)

"IS THERE A HISTADRUT OR NOT?"

Six months after Joseph Trumpeldor was killed, a Labor Battalion bearing his name was founded. It was a national organization of communal teams whose members performed agricultural work and other kinds of labor, such as road paving and construction. Most of its members were young single people from Russia. For the most part, they were immigrants of the Third Aliyah, the name given to the wave of thirty-five thousand Jewish immigrants, largely from Eastern Europe, who settled in Palestine between the years 1919 and 1923. Many, perhaps most of them, considered themselves Zionist pioneers and intended to work in Palestine in farming, construction, and manufacturing.[56] Like the members of the Second Aliyah, they were described as "sensitive types, poets, who want to change the world . . . people of bold thoughts and rich imagination."[57]

Some of the pioneers of the Third Aliyah founded experimental communities similar to those that Jews and Christians had been founding since the end of the nineteenth century. In August 1920, twenty young men and four young women, members of a socialist-Zionist youth movement called Hashomer Hatza'ir, settled on a lonely hill overlooking Lake Kinneret. They paved roads and dug wells, and read Nietzsche and Freud. Some of them were also fascinated by Jesus of Nazareth. Even as they followed their dreams, they agonized over their loneliness and sexual frustration, and offered total obedience to a leader several years older than they were, who instructed them to extract intimate confessions from each other, deep into the night. The community was called Bitanya Ilit; its members later founded Beit Alfa, the first of dozens of kibbutzim established by Hashomer Hatza'ir in the years that followed.[58] The Histadrut also encouraged the establishment of kibbutzim. To a large extent, these communities laid out the borders of the national home, and were mistakenly identified as the elite of Jewish society throughout Palestine. In practice, they were exceptional communities that attracted only a small minority.

At its height, the Labor Battalion named for Trumpeldor had about eight hundred members, but through most of its existence it had many fewer. They worked hard for starvation wages. Some of its "companies," as the work teams were called, lived communally. At best they were able to obtain tents, but they often slept out in the open, at their work sites. Liberated and fervent, many of them fantasized about a Red future, in the spirit of the Russian Revolution. The Labor Battalion was supposed to follow the orders of the Histadrut, and as long as it did, Ben-Gurion liked it. But that did not last for long.[59] The battalion would soon threaten the standing of the Histadrut and Ben-Gurion himself, leading Ben-Gurion to act, for the first time in his life, with the brutality and ruthlessness of a leader. At the center of the story stood Shlomo Lavi.

❖

One morning at the beginning of June 1921, Lavi set out for the Jezreel Valley to scout out an area known by the name of a small Arab village at the valley's eastern end, Nuris. A few months later, the Zionist movement decided to purchase the so-called Nuris Block, the most important piece of property purchased up until then. Lavi was known as a simple young man who did not read books. "He drew his wisdom from the book of life," Ben-Gurion said.[60] He had been one of the first members of Hashomer, and unlike the other three friends of his youth, he remained a farmer.

"It seemed to me to be the Promised Land," Lavi wrote of his first visit, but the fields were full of Arab fellahin, as well as women and children—it was the end of the harvest season. "My greetings to the workers in the fields were met in some cases halfheartedly and in others by angry looks," he related. "I felt the hatred reaching down to the roots of each hair." There were also armed Bedouin, mounted on horses, "all of them with their faces covered, their fiery and piercing eyes visible." Then huge flocks of sheep and their herders blocked his way. They also gave him "fierce looks" and exchanged "murmurs" whose meanings he could guess. He almost forgot the purpose of his trip—the only thing on his mind was how to defend himself and get away without looking as if he were taking flight.

When he returned from what he called "the fields of my dreams," he had trouble falling asleep. "What a beautiful world we could build on that land," he said to himself. "We will drain the swamps, uproot the jujube trees, and slowly, slowly move out the Bedouin as well." He got out of bed, lit the lamp with a small flame, and began pacing his room. "My world has grown so large," he said to himself. "In an instant, this large tract, so appropriate for all my ideas. A society of many thousands can come into being there, a completely self-sufficient economy."[61]

What he was proposing was a large commune, rather than the small ones he had worked in up until that point. At the last of these, Kevutzat Kinneret, the members had gotten tangled in a painful web of animosity that led them to disband. Lavi attributed the crisis to the enforced intimacy of such a small commune. His idea was a cluster of settlements, each numbering at least 150 families. Anyone could join and work in any of a variety of areas—farming, construction, industry, even higher education. For efficiency and economy, the settlements would cooperate with one another.

The Labor Battalion agreed, as an experiment, to station several dozen of its members there, and Lavi went posthaste to Yehoshua Hankin, the Zionist Organization's land agent, to tell him to make the purchase. "How will we get rid of the Bedouin's tents?" Lavi asked Hankin, while demanding the evacuation of the Arab tenant farmers from their homes. They were compelled to move elsewhere. Some received compensation. Kibbutz Ein Harod was established on the spot, and next to it another kibbutz, Tel Yosef, where most of the inhabitants were members of the Labor Battalion. Lavi complained about the state of the houses left behind by the Arabs. There were no floor tiles, and almost no doors, he said.[62] The spring that supplied water to the settlers is mentioned in the Bible, in the book of Judges (7:5). It was there that Gideon, also known as Yeruba'al, tested his men and chose the three hundred who would fight the Midianites.

Lavi pitched his tent next to Tel Yosef's banana orchard, and as always, his loneliness tormented him. But one day he saw, among the eucalyptus saplings, a girl who stole his heart. Her name was Rachel. A very beautiful woman, Ben-Gurion said.[63] That same evening they went for a walk in the late autumn starlight. Their love blossomed, and they married and had two sons, Yeruba'al and Hillel. The casuarina trees took root, and in time the cucumbers also gave a good yield. Chicks peeped in the chicken coops and Berl Katznelson came for a visit. Lavi shed tears of joy. It could all have been so beautiful. But it wasn't. The members of Ein Harod and Tel Yosef, and of the Labor Battalion, were overcome by hatred—of each other.[64]

❖

Many years later, when he attempted to reconstruct what had happened, Lavi had trouble fathoming the divergence between their common faith in a better and more just world and the spite and extremism that shattered that idea. He could offer no real explanation, limiting himself to characterizing those who had been involved. "Coyotes in a single large cage. Friend to friend no longer spoke, rather despiser to despiser snarled." Lavi and most of his friends at Ein Harod were ten years older than most of the members of the Labor Battalion who had settled at Tel Yosef; many of them had learned the hard way that the ideals they had brought with them prior to the world war were impossible to realize. Most of the men and women of the Labor Battalions had not yet shed their ideological fervor, and condescended to their elders with youthful arrogance, professing to be better at grasping the pulse of life. Many had had exhilarating experiences during the Russian Revolution. Lavi could never put out of his mind his first encounter with them. They asked him if he had brought cigarettes; they showed no interest in the principles of his large commune.[65]

At some point, of course, the two groups found themselves at odds over money, but it was also a power struggle. The people of Ein Harod obtained more public funding than the Labor Battalion had, in part thanks to Lavi's unrelenting efforts, but also because a respected figure, Yitzhak Tabenkin, lived there. The Battalion demanded oversight of the common treasury. "One pocket for all," they chanted. Lavi retorted that their demand had nothing to do with ideology and made no sense economically. He demanded budgetary independence for Ein Harod. Eventually, he accused the Labor Battalion of theft and the Battalion demanded that he be sent packing. Lavi told of the gloom that descended on the two kibbutzim. No one sang or danced anymore. "Entering one of our two camps of an evening was like entering a house of mourning," he wrote.[66]

Ben-Gurion was drawn into this thicket only reluctantly. It looked to him like a distraction he could do without. "Elkind knows the score," he wrote of the Labor Battalion's leader. "He wants to compromise." But Ben-Gurion soon realized that the Battalion was seeking unwarranted independence. Menachem Elkind, whose mind was cold and analytic, called for the Labor Battalion to remake itself as a "national kibbutz." As that idea gradually took form, it came to sound more and more like the labor army that Ben-Gurion had proposed. The difference was that Ben-Gurion had wanted to use it as a means for strengthening the Histadrut, whereas Elkind wanted his national kibbutz to replace it.

Ben-Gurion received reports about the hostility to the Histadrut that was spreading through the Labor Battalion. Bolshevik tendencies occasionally surfaced. When Colonial Secretary Churchill entered the dining hall of a labor detail stationed in Lod, several workers lined up in front of him and sang "The Internationale," in a Hebrew translation done a year and a half before. It was an embarrassing provocation. After Churchill left, some Histadrut loyalists attacked the Bolsheviks and "broke their bones," as one of them wrote, putting that phrase in quotation marks. Once, Ben-Gurion and Katznelson paid a visit to one of the labor companies but were compelled to leave before they could speak.[67]

There was another problem as well. The Labor Battalion had taken the veterans of Hashomer into its ranks. Israel and Manya Shohat opposed the dismantling of the organization they had founded. They joined the Labor Battalion along with the last of their stalwarts and revived Hashomer as a secret militia called simply the Kibbutz. The militia stockpiled arms and trained fighters. A small paramilitary academy was established at Tel Yosef to train two groups of commanders. Some eighteen fighters were put through a course of physical fitness and academic studies.[68]

Ben-Gurion took resolute action.

At first most of the Histadrut leadership took the side of Ein Harod against the Battalion. "Ein Harod's failure will be a catastrophe so great that we will not be able to recover," he explained. He engaged in long nighttime conversations. "Last night there was a Battalion assembly here," he wrote in his diary, "and they came to blows."[69] When no compromise could be found, Ben-Gurion agreed, grudgingly, to partition. Tel Yosef would remain in the hands of the Labor Battalion. But then, as expected, the two sides could not agree which kibbutz would receive the single typewriter and sewing machine, which would get the hatchery, which the engine that powered the shower, and which Sharona the mare.

As the conflict deepened, Ben-Gurion inserted himself and exacerbated it. "The Histadrut might face a civil war," he warned, quoting a Labor Battalion member who, he claimed, had said that they were facing "a war of life or death." The real question was, "Is there a Histadrut or not?" he maintained.[70]

Several of his colleagues, Ben-Zvi among them, thought he was being carried away by his aggressive stance and proposed a softer line. At Ein Harod, Rachel Lavi also pressed her husband to moderate his extremism—peace is more important than justice, she tried to persuade him. Apparently it was too late, because the Histadrut's supporters at Tel Yosef had in the meantime moved to Ein Harod, and the Labor Battalion supporters at Ein Harod moved to Tel Yosef. Next, the Tel Yosef settlers raided Ein Harod and took various pieces of equipment, in violation of the arrangement brokered by the Histadrut. The Histadrut Executive decided to give them a choice: the stolen gear would be returned to Ein Harod within twenty-four hours or "they'll be out of the Histadrut."

That's what happened. Without further discussion, Ben-Gurion instructed the Histadrut and its subsidiary institutions to cut off all contact with Tel Yosef. It was tantamount to a death sentence, because the kibbutz received most of its food through Hamashbir, the Histadrut's buying and marketing cooperative. There was virtually no other supplier. Their health services were provided by Kupat Holim. The physician who cared for the members of both kibbutzim had already cautioned that their medical condition was very serious. Even before the crisis, they had suffered from malnourishment, malaria, and tuberculosis.[71]

Ben-Gurion was thirty-seven years old. There were people of higher standing in his political environment; the Ein Harod crisis gave him his first-ever opportunity to display leadership and exert authority. He tried to do so in a way that none of his associates had ever dared to do. None of them would have starved an entire settlement into submission and left it without a doctor. In fact, they had no intention of carrying out their threats and were dismayed when Ben-Gurion did so. "In my opinion it was mistaken and rash," Ben-Zvi said. Others spoke in the same vein. They decided to put off Tel Yosef's ejection from the Histadrut and make another attempt to reach a resolution. Ben-Gurion in the meantime set out for the Soviet Union.[72]

"A MAN OF IRON WILL"

The Bolshevik regime liked to put its successes on ostentatious display. In the summer of 1923, it held a huge fair to show off its agricultural accomplishments. The Soviet Union was still fighting for international recognition and to promote its image around the world, and it thus quite naturally sought to cast the fair as an international event.[73] Ben-Gurion, for his part, wanted to see the Soviet Union. It was an opportunity to make contact with Zionist activists there. The Jewish community in Palestine would have its own pavilion at the fair, so Histadrut officials packed up grains, olives, almonds, figs, citrons, and prickly pears, as well as canned goods, cigarettes, and chocolate manufactured by Palestine's Jewish economy. They prepared photographs and diagrams, and Ben-Gurion authored a special pamphlet, issued in Russian, on the growth of the Jewish population and the achievements of the Histadrut. He took another Histadrut official with him, and after numerous delays and adventures the exhibition reached Russia; a Jewish official was found who granted Ben-Gurion a permit to fly the blue-and-white Zionist flag alongside the Histadrut's red flag.[74]

His extended stay in the capital of the dictatorship of the proletariat required Ben-Gurion to examine, almost daily, his identification as a socialist, Jew, and Zionist. Prior to his visit, he told a World Union of Po'alei Zion delegation that he favored Bolshevism. "I believe in the dictatorship of the proletariat," he asserted.[75] It wasn't true. Ben-Gurion sometimes said things he didn't believe in, as a way of mollifying his opponents by seeming to meet them halfway. He continued to term himself a socialist his whole life, but after spending a while in Palestine he realized, so he related, that everything he had thought about socialism before his arrival was no more than a "miserable farce." He was right, because in Palestine his socialism was not an ideal to be sought after but a means to an end. In his memoirs he wrote: "Almost from the time I came to Palestine I grasped the simple and important truth that we, the youth . . . are not emissaries of the working class but rather of the entire nation."[76]

He spent a lot of time debating this issue, making hours of ideological speeches in countless forums, but he was never more than a conditional socialist. He sometimes claimed that there was no dividing line between his Zionism and his socialism, and that the more profound his Zionist faith became, so also became his faith in socialism.[77] In fact, he placed socialism in the service of nationalism. This led to the need for a transition "from class to nation," in words that Ben-Gurion would soon adopt, and which he used as the title of one of his books. It was an unambiguous choice—wherever a contradiction between Zionist and socialist interests arose, he always chose Zionism.[78]

In advance of his visit to the Soviet Union, he wanted to learn everything he could about the situation there. He assiduously followed the progress of the Russian Revolution during his time in the United States, marveling at the Bolshevik victory but mostly displaying an insatiable curiosity about it. Repetur's impression was that Ben-Gurion went to Moscow with great sympathy for the revolution and a respect for its pathos. Ben-Gurion himself would later say that it was a story of "faithful love." The fact that the revolution involved violence did not disturb him, he said, because the world war had shaken his faith in democracy.[79] He took a great interest in Trotsky; Repetur had told him of his electrifying effect as a speaker. Lenin was also a fascinating figure for him. He expected that the Soviets would see a resemblance between their revolution and the Zionist revolution, and would thus welcome a visitor from Palestine.[80]

❖

Moscow was a pleasant surprise—it was his first visit to the city, and he liked it. "The faces of the passersby display determination and vitality," he remarked. At the fairgrounds he was impressed by a display put out by a youth parade. They marched in threes, two boys in shorts and bare chests with a girl between them who also wore shorts. "Working youth. Healthy, energetic, and confident," Ben-Gurion wrote. He also liked a huge flower bed in which the blooms produced a portrait of Lenin.[81]

The festivities in Red Square lasted for a long time. In the meantime, Ben-Gurion read in *Izvestia* that Trotsky was ill and would not appear. "When I related the news to those around me, there was great disappointment," he wrote. "I also felt something like that. The main point of the celebration had been taken away." He stayed to watch the military parade, which included an air show.[82]

He remained in the Soviet Union until the end of December. About fifteen hundred young Jews were being trained there to farm in Palestine, and identified themselves as members of the Hehalutz movement. One of the training farms was named Tel Hai. "It is the most important and serious of all the things we have here," he wrote. He had long conversations with them, under the watchful eye of the secret police. It had been worth coming just for this, he wrote.[83] One of the young Jews he met took him to some bookstores; two other members walked the opposite sidewalk to guard him. This time he focused on military literature, including manuals explaining how to manufacture hand grenades and conduct guerrilla warfare; he bought about 150 of them.[84] He went twice to see *The Dybbuk* in Hebrew at Habima theater; Yevgeny Bagrationovich Vakhtangov's direction of the classic Yiddish play by S. Ansky moved him. In the theater, the labor leader from Palestine found himself again in a Jewish town and was overcome with nostalgia and longing for "the old soul of Judaism . . . the world of the study house and small synagogue . . . the spirit, the Torah, the devotion, the rapture." He bought the players a bottle of Muscat wine.[85]

He had a nice trip home; the sea was calm, the skies clear. On the deck of his passenger ship, off the coast of Greece, he relaxed and pondered his experience in Russia. He returned from there as a skeptical sympathizer. The fire of revolution sparked his imagination; until his death he maintained a special, ambiguous attitude toward the Soviet Union. But he was also aware of the revolution's tyranny and corruption. "The sublime hopes for liberation and justice and the ugly and poor reality—which will win out?" he wondered, but did not offer an answer. He presumed that the Communist regime would not be replaced anytime soon, and that the Zionist movement did not have much chance of success there. Nevertheless, he thought that it was important to maintain good relations with the government.[86]

❖

Lenin was still alive, but as Ben-Gurion wrote, "the light of his mind had been extinguished." When the Soviet leader died soon thereafter, Ben-Gurion eulogized him, the second time he had written such a text. But unlike when he was a confused and lonely eighteen-year-old who had lost his Herzl, Ben-Gurion did not suffer "horrible, scorching thoughts" at Lenin's death. Rather, it helped him to dispassionately evaluate the qualities of the ideal leader. He was, Ben-Gurion wrote,

"A man who disdains all obstacles, faithful to his goal, who knows no concessions or discounts, the extreme of extremes; who knows how to crawl on his belly in the utter depths in order to reach his goal; a man of iron will who does not spare human life and the blood of innocent children for the sake of the revolution; . . . he is not afraid of rejecting today what he required yesterday, and requiring tomorrow what he rejected today; he will not be caught in the net of platitude, or in the trap of dogma; for the naked reality, the cruel truth and the reality of power relations will be before his sharp and clear eyes . . . the single goal, burning with red flame—the goal of the great revolution."[87]

A single sentence of more than 130 Hebrew words, and the terms "Bolshevism" and "socialism" are nowhere to be seen. Neither is "Zionism." Because that was the model of leadership, dismantled into its component parts, almost instructions to national leaders. His visit to the Soviet Union was a seminal experience. He was emotionally attached to its achievements, but he did not return from his four-month stay there as a more enthusiastic socialist than he had been when he went, and he never became a Communist. What he admired was not Lenin's ideology, but his ability to reshape his people's destiny. In his political surroundings there was no one else who learned so systematically the structure of authoritarian leadership, and no one who so clearly laid out his life's goal. Ben-Gurion intended to be a Zionist Lenin.

9

SCANDALS

One night, in March 1926, Ben-Gurion had a nightmare about a lion; it was a few months before his fortieth birthday. His account of it, recorded in Berlin just a few days prior to another visit to Płońsk, makes for one of the most revealing entries in a diary full of color and feeling. In the dream, he wanted to go to a celebration that was being held on the other side of the garden belonging to the priest who lived next to his father's house, but he had been warned not to go. His enemies were lying in wait for him on the way and might kill him. He did not remember who they were, but, he wrote, "I think they might have been Arabs." He thus decided to go to a celebration closer by.

There were a lot of people there, but they "melted away," leaving only Aharon Eisenberg of Rehovot, one of the leaders of the farmers there and a close associate of Chaim Weizmann. He and Eisenberg sat in a large automobile that was hitched up to a lion, tall as a horse and blind. When Ben-Gurion tried to drive, the car skidded from side to side. He suddenly found himself outside the vehicle but close by it, and then the lion pounced on him. Ben-Gurion shouted as loudly as he could, telling Eisenberg to move the car, but Eisenberg did not hear him. "I barely escaped the lion's claws," he wrote. He woke up, but when he fell asleep again he was back in the same dream. It was a strange one, he wrote. He consulted his copy of Freud's *The Interpretation of Dreams* but found no explanation there.[1]

Four days before the night of that dream he had written: "My health has deteriorated to a great extent and my nerves are totally destroyed." Two months previously, he had needed to spend a few days in a sanatorium, but his condition seems not to have improved. "My nerves have been destroyed and my ability to work has been depleted," he wrote then.[2] He was working hard; the two and a half years that had gone by since his visit to Soviet Russia had been full of crises and struggles, some of them turbulent in the extreme, and there had been scandals and confrontations, some of them violent. At their height, Ben-Gurion uncovered a plot to murder him. It was now nearly two decades since he had settled in Palestine and gone into politics. He fell ill frequently, his nerves weakened; he endured many disappointments and was often away from home. But by the end of the 1920s, he had become one of the most powerful people in the Zionist labor movement, and thus in the entire Jewish community in Palestine; he endeavored to run the Histadrut as if it were the government of a state-in-the-making. At its height, the Histadrut was responsible for the armed defense of Palestine's Jews, the establishment of new settlements, and the provision of jobs, health services, and education to tens of thousands of workers.

❖

The Histadrut was the national home's first administrative institution; everyone wanted a piece of its power. Its leaders competed with one another, often hated and envied and thwarted one another. Some of them were salaried employees of the labor union, some activists in the two labor parties that were its principal components—Ahdut Ha'avodah and Hapo'el Hatza'ir. But Sprinzak and most of his colleagues were not persuaded. The

"Histadrut government" was notoriously wasteful, rife with irregularities and cronyism.[3]

The rejection of his proposal for a Labor Army did not put an end to Ben-Gurion's efforts to turn the Histadrut into the only workers' organization in Palestine's Jewish community and to gain it control of the community's entire labor market. People's willingness to join the Histadrut depended principally on its ability to provide them with employment through the Histadrut's Labor Bureau. To this end, the organization set up an Office of Public Works that functioned as a contracting company; in 1924 it was given the name Solel Boneh (Paver Builder). The company employed laborers to pave roads and put up buildings, mostly in the service of the British administration and the local representatives of the Zionist Organization who replaced the Zionist Commission. Another reason people joined the Histadrut was to enjoy the medical services provided by Kupat Holim, a Histadrut subsidiary. At the end of October 1922, Ben-Gurion marveled at the large number of workers—some sixteen thousand—who had joined. About half of them were already registered as dues-paying members, twice as many as there had been two years previously. "I never believed such a large number was possible," he wrote in his diary. "The Histadrut's great era is beginning."[4]

A short time after returning from Moscow, he proposed that the Histadrut expand its activities into industry. "The time has come to set up large factories belonging to and under the control of the workers," he declared. He envisioned "hundreds and thousands" of new jobs. He also raised the possibility that the Histadrut might seek private investors for these ventures. He seems to have been concerned that the leftists in his movement would raise ideological objections, and declared that cooperation between private capital and "workers' concerns" was accepted and successful practice in the Soviet Union.[5] In 1924 he demanded that the Zionist Executive provide funding to construct housing for urban workers, warning that if it was not done quickly, the result would be a catastrophe—people would leave the country.[6]

His opponents accused him of turning the Histadrut into his personal bailiwick, as if "the Histadrut *c'est moi*."[7] There was something to that, but it wasn't the whole story. No one else worked so assiduously, throughout the day and into the night. Ben-Gurion brought to his work for the Histadrut the same qualities that had been on display in his previous endeavors—passion and a capacity for learning, and unflagging, almost obsessive diligence. He boned up on issues that were to be discussed at meetings, where he generally did not speak much. When necessary, he lobbied for his position in advance of meetings to ensure that his proposals would pass.

During his first five years in the Histadrut, 158 strikes broke out, involving more than five thousand workers. He carefully categorized the strikes. Most of them, he claimed, succeeded; some ended in compromise; only a few failed.[8] He promoted the Histadrut's cultural activities, including its educational programs and its theater company. Soon there would also be a publishing house—he had strong opinions about which authors' books ought to be translated into Hebrew.[9] He edited *Kontres*, Ahdut Ha'avodah's political and literary journal, himself.[10] In February 1922, he hosted a visit to Palestine by Ramsay MacDonald, leader of the British Labour Party. "We have gained ourselves a friend," he wrote. "He is full of admiration." Not long after that it was important for him to drag Albert Einstein to a session of the Histadrut Convention, so as to offer brief greetings, apparently in German.[11] But translating the works of thinkers, and gaining the approbation of foreign VIPs, did not help him maintain control of the Histadrut. He had never been responsible for an organization of such wide-ranging activities; there were too many interests, egos, intrigues, and deceptions, and too many fiefdoms whose chiefs did not accept his authority—Solel Boneh, Kupat Holim, Bank Hapoalim, to name a few. Ben-Gurion thus established his own power base, among the workers themselves. Once a week, sometimes daily, he visited workplaces in the cities, at agricultural settlements, and on the roads. The workers began to see the Histadrut in his image. To them, he was the Histadrut, said Berl Repetur, then a foreman at the Haifa port.[12]

"I RAN OVER TO BINYAMINI"

In Repetur's account of the visit, he described Ben-Gurion as a short man in a long leather coat and pants that looked like riding breeches, tucked into high boots. He paused by a few workers, asked them questions, and recorded their answers in a small notebook—who they were, where they were from, when they had arrived and in what framework. He took interest in their jobs—their crates, iron, wood—how many hours they worked, how much they earned. Most of the workers knew only Russian and Yiddish. Then Ben-Gurion asked to speak to the foreman. Repetur was eighteen years old and had come to Palestine from Russia about a year and a half previously. Ben-Gurion asked to be shown around the facility. He was disappointed; there were too many Arab workers, he complained. He then asked Repetur whether the Jewish workers were armed, and Repetur told him that there were four pistols, in case they were attacked. Ben-Gurion asked about the mood of the workers, how many of them would stay in Palestine, how many would return to Russia, and what their political inclinations were. He then sat himself down in a dry rowboat and the workers gathered around them. He let them talk, and listened carefully. "He sometimes liked to go into such detail that it drove you crazy," Repetur related.[13] He also went to kibbutzim to get updated, recording facts about the goats, eucalyptuses, and lentil crops.[14]

Sometimes he sat in a circle with the comrades; sometimes he got up on a crate to address them. His short stature did not keep him from radiating determination. He would throw his head back, his chin pointing forward, one hand closed into a fist, the other shoved into his pants pocket.[15] His speech was decisive, his words incisive, sometimes blunt. When he could not promise work, he offered hope and faith in Zionism, one who had heard him speak then later related.[16] His grassroots work was simply a continuation of the way he had campaigned prior to the elections for the Assembly of Representatives in 1920.

❖

His close connection to what was happening in the field, the same proclivity that was on display during his youth in Płońsk, made him a popular and authentic labor leader. He was unable to tame the horde of politicians and bureaucrats who walked the corridors of the Histadrut's offices, but his standing in Ahdut Ha'avodah grew as he gained ever more support among the workers.[17] He also sought out power struggles outside the labor movement, the noisier the better. Such was the fight over the home of one of Tel Aviv's founders, Shmuel David.

In June 1923, about a dozen workers were employed in building the house. They belonged to the religious workers' organization, Hapo'el Hamizrahi. The

Histadrut demanded to be allotted some of the work and sent protestors to the site. Ben-Gurion made it into a cause célèbre, depicting it as a matter of life or death. There were also private contractors who competed with the Histadrut's Labor Bureau and Solel Boneh. It was a struggle between the "labor left" and the "bourgeois right"; many of the latter supported Jabotinsky's Revisionist movement.

The struggle needed a recognizable enemy, which Ben-Gurion found in a businessman named David Izmozhik, deputy mayor of Tel Aviv. When the battle over the construction of Shmuel David's house grew worse, Izmozhik called in the police. British policemen who had been transferred to Palestine from Ireland, supplemented by mounted Arabs, surrounded the Histadrut protestors and used clubs to disperse them. Some of the demonstrators were wounded and others arrested. A few were convicted and sentenced to prison terms. Ben-Gurion responded as if summoning the British police were an act of treason against the Jewish nation. As a Zionist elected official, Ben-Gurion maintained, Izmozhik should have referred the disagreement to internal arbitration, or taken it to the Jewish magistrate's court. He demanded, of course, an investigation.

The Histadrut called for a protest demonstration. Thousands participated. Ben-Gurion was the major speaker. He denounced Izmozhik as a villain, over and over again. Then the two men met and reached an agreement. Hapo'el Hamizrahi would carry on building Shmuel David's home, but 27 percent of the work hours would be allotted to the Histadrut. Politically, it was an effective compromise—a bit less than a year later, the religious labor union decided to become part of the Histadrut. It was another compromise with the religious camp in which Ben-Gurion gave way on a matter of principle in order to reduce tensions between religious and nonreligious Jews and maintain unity in the Jewish community.[18]

His personal standing as Histadrut secretary did not mean that he did not face the everyday tribulations of the average person. When his baby daughter Renana, one and a half years old, suddenly fell victim to a choking fit, he had to set off on a desperate search for a doctor, just like the most ordinary of citizens. He still did not have a telephone at home. His diary relates: "I ran over to [Dr. Aharon] Binyamini, but he wasn't home. I rushed to the Histadrut Executive's offices and telephoned Kupat Holim. No one answered. I went to Eliyahu [Golomb] and found [his wife] Adah and with her ran to search for a doctor. We first got to [Dr. David] Deutsch. But he did not want to come. I said, the girl is dying—but he had to go somewhere else and recommended going to a different doctor. In a rage, I ran with Adah to Dr. [Moshe] Cohen, he also refused at first, but when he saw what a state I was in he came with me immediately." By the time they reached Ben-Gurion's home, the attack was over. "I wasn't sure I would still find her alive," Ben-Gurion confessed. The next day, Renana suffered another attack and developed a high fever. Her father again ran to find a doctor. "I was desperate," he wrote. Paula succeeded in lowering the fever with cold compresses.[19]

In December 1924, Ben-Gurion demanded to be given enhanced and more centralized powers, and a few months later again announced that he was resigning. It was part of the way the political game was played then, and according to the usual routine his resignation was not accepted. Bowing to his colleagues' demand that he rescind his resignation was an almost ritual part of the political culture of the time. He remained the man who called the shots.[20] At the same time, he hounded the Communists, the Labor Brigade, and especially the veterans of Hashomer and their secret Kibbutz, or the Circle, as it was also called. He saw them as a separatist military cabal. That wasn't far from the truth. His efforts to counter them amounted to a purge— this was Ben-Gurion as a non-Communist Zionist Bolshevik. That's what his entire generation was, Isser Harel, the all-powerful head of Israel's security services, later related. "I told them—when it comes down to it, you are Bolsheviks. Not in the Communist sense, but in the sense of the dictatorship of the party . . . you are Zionists, but in your outlook, that is, your mentality, you are Bolsheviks."[21]

"BETRAYAL AND DECEPTION"

In May 1923, a member of the Circle murdered an Arab policeman, Tewfiq Bey, whom many Jews held responsible for the attack on the immigrants' hostel in Jaffa two years previously. The *Haganah History Book* states that the Haganah's national coordinator, Yosef Hecht, had been briefed in advance about this "first political murder." The next victim was a Jew, Jacob Israël de Haan. He was one of the eccentric adventurers, dreamers, and zealots whom

Jerusalem has always attracted. A jurist, poet, and journalist, he had come to the Holy City from Holland. He made friends with Arab boys and wrote homosexual poetry. At first he was respected as a Zionist intellectual; he represented European newspapers and taught law. But he then grew closer to the Haredi community, adopted its opposition to Zionism, and became one of its spokesmen. The Zionist establishment condemned him as an anti-Semitic rogue; nearly everyone agreed he was insane. Ben-Gurion accused him of "betrayal and deception, talebearing and slander."

De Haan received death threats and meditated on the possibility that he would be murdered: "As a fledgling flies / take wing, my song / until the gun fires at my heart," he wrote. It happened on June 30, 1924. He set out for the evening service at a synagogue; three bullets hit him, one of them piercing his heart. The murderer was twenty-one-year-old Avraham Zilberg, who later changed his name to Tehomi. Born in Odessa, he arrived in Palestine in 1923 and took part in some of the Haganah's first operations in Jerusalem. There seem to have been several people plotting to murder de Haan; Tehomi later claimed he had been given the go-ahead by Yitzhak Ben-Zvi.*

Ben-Gurion went to watch the funeral. He estimated that there were about two hundred people in attendance. "I did not see among the mourners any profound anger," he reported. "Apparently most of the Jews accepted it without getting much exercised about it." The question of whether Ben-Gurion had been involved in the murder would soon arise; in other words, the question was whether Ben-Zvi would have taken upon himself to approve such a deed without informing Ben-Gurion. Perhaps he would have. It was a Jerusalem story, with all the delirium and extremism that Jerusalem can offer. And Jerusalem was Ben-Zvi's fiefdom; he was the senior public authority with regard to the Haganah's activity in the city. Probably nothing irked him more than having to recognize Ben-Gurion's seniority. There is no reason to believe that Ben-Gurion saw any need to liquidate de Haan.

Ben-Zvi maintained contact with Hashomer's veterans, among them Israel and Manya Shohat. She was arrested after the murder, but was released

---

* According to the Haganah's official version, the order came from the Haganah's commander, Yosef Hecht, who himself confirmed giving it.

without being charged. The question of who gave the order continues to be debated by historians to this day.[22]

❖

De Haan's death left Ben-Gurion unmoved, but he likely saw the assassination as just one more in a series of subversive acts carried out without the authority of the Histadrut, and that was intolerable.

A few months prior to the murder, several Hashomer veterans from Kfar Giladi attacked a gang of cash smugglers who had come from Lebanon and robbed them of fifteen thousand pounds sterling, in gold coins. The money had apparently been set aside to fund the purchase of arms to be used in attacks on Arabs. Ben-Gurion suspected that the arms would be used not just for defense of the kibbutz but also by a Communist underground militia that was plotting to take control of the Galilee and maybe all of Palestine.[23]

Hashomer's veterans were not a real danger to the Histadrut. Their sedition was mostly that of nostalgia and fantasy, longing for their impetuous youthful days in the Galilee. It seems unlikely that they could have carried out even a small putsch, especially given that they were embroiled in internal conflicts in which they accused one another of transgressions that no outsider could possibly understand; the cords of pioneering camaraderie of past years were severed and replaced by insults and blows. Many tears were shed. Against this background, Ben-Gurion had no trouble breaking up the Circle and the Labor Battalion. He related that, as he was involved in this, Ben-Zvi relayed to him a threat on his life; Ben-Zvi confirmed doing so. In April 1924, the Communists would have a similar fate. The Workers' Faction of the Communist Party was a loud and sometimes violent opposition, but, given that its members were a tiny minority, they were no threat to the parties that controlled the Histadrut. Ben-Gurion fought them as if they were a clear and present threat to the future of Zionism; among other things, he accused them of inciting Arab workers against Jews.[24] The Histadrut Council branded the Workers' Faction "the enemy of the Hebrew nation and the working class in Palestine." A few months later, Ben-Gurion explained: "The Faction betrayed the working class and as such the Council decided to expel them from the Histadrut as traitors."[25] Once expelled from the Histadrut as such, the Communists faced many hardships in finding employment and were not able to receive medical care from Kupat Holim.

As in the first round of the Ein Harod conflict, Ben-Gurion's conduct was roundly criticized by Yosef Sprinzak, the Hapo'el Hatza'ir leader. "It was hard for me to listen to Ben-Gurion's tone when he spoke of the members of the Faction," he said. "It was an incendiary speech against all those who are not members of Ahdut Ha'avodah." He censured Ben-Gurion for stirring up hatred and accused him of imposing a "spiritual inquisition." Ben-Gurion responded that he was not one of the bleeding hearts who knew how the Faction needed to be dealt with but balked at doing so with a display of "Christian patience," as Sprinzak was. "We have to fight them," he declared. He humbly suggested that he be tried by his comrades—if they found that he had not spoken the truth, he would accept any sanction they imposed on him.[26]

❖

Ben-Gurion did not oppose the use of force in principle. He eventually instructed Yosef Hecht to establish, alongside the Haganah, a Histadrut militia that would later become known as Plugot Hapo'el, the Workers' Squads, which engaged in fistfights with opponents of the labor movement. Yet there were many times when he opposed acts of violence, especially when he was afraid that his men would lose their self-control. His principle was that the Histadrut had to maintain a monopoly on the use of force.[27]

Ben-Gurion could have filed a lawsuit to dissolve the Circle, but he preferred a surer method that had proven itself in the past—a commission of inquiry. He appointed its members and drafted five simple questions for it to answer, ostensibly with a simple yes or no: Was there a clandestine society within the Labor Battalion? Had its members stolen weapons? Had they stolen gold? Had they operated outside the Haganah command? Had they had contact with the Soviet Union?

The whole sensational story was supposed to be kept top secret, as it involved arms smuggling and robbery. But, as usual, there were leaks and rumors and half-truths spread by word of mouth, in agitated whispers. When Manya Shohat heard what Ben-Gurion was saying, she wrote to him: "I never thought you would be capable of using such means to harm the Labor Battalion. I had too much personal respect for you. The path you have chosen will destroy us and you. I have no forgiveness in my heart. And I am severing all personal relations between us." Ben-Gurion sent her a chilly response, saying that her letter had not changed anything in his attitude toward her.[28] His suspicions grew when Israel Shohat made a trip to the Soviet Union along with the Labor Battalion chief Menachem Elkind. Shohat seems to have been checking out the possibility of establishing a new political axis with Moscow. The Soviet Union would issue a new "Balfour Declaration" stating that it viewed with favor the establishment of a Communist Jewish state in Palestine. He hoped to receive arms and asked the Soviets to give flight training to young men from Palestine so that the Jewish state could have an air force.[29]

As expected, the committee found that the Circle of Hashomer veterans had operated as an armed underground. Ben-Gurion came out looking like the person who had saved the authority of the Labor movement.[30] But by the time the committee submitted its findings, the incident had lost almost all its importance, as the Labor Battalion had already been dissolved.[31] Elkind and a few other members moved back to the Soviet Union.*

In the meantime, the country had changed.

"BIRDS FLY UNDER US"

In the spring of 1924, the United States instituted a new immigration policy that, among other things, made it more difficult for Jews to enter the country.[32] Zionism had not had such an opportunity since the Balfour Declaration. At the same time the new American policy went into force, Poland was hit by an economic crisis, of which the country's Jews were also victims. With America no longer an option, tens of thousands of Polish Jews settled in Palestine; in 1924 more than thirteen thousand arrived and in 1925 more than thirty-four thousand.[33] They made up the bulk of the Fourth Aliyah. To enter Palestine they needed permits from the British authority; quotas for Jewish immigration were set from time to time, in keeping with availability

---

* Elkind founded a farming commune in the Soviet Union. He was executed during Stalin's purges. (Tzachor 1990, p. 128ff; Tzachor 1994, p. 57ff; Kantrovitz 2007, p. 217ff.)

of employment in the country. While the Zionists never stopped protesting the quotas, the Jewish national leadership largely acceded to them. That was the deliberate and cautious aspect of Zionist messianism. In general the authorities approved the immigration requests submitted through the Zionist movement.*

As secretary of the Histadrut, Ben-Gurion abhorred this wave of immigration of "kiosk owners," as he termed the new residents of Tel Aviv, even though there were also manual laborers who arrived during this period. The kiosk owners, as small businessmen rather than workers, were liable to align with the opponents of his movement and thus weaken it. "Promotion of the immigration of workers is now a central and vital need of our movement," he declared.[34] It was one of the tasks he set for the Histadrut, even though it had practically no influence over the decisions of Jews to settle in Palestine.

In April 1924, the Mandate authorities issued twenty-four hundred immigration certificates, including three hundred for young women. The Histadrut informed several Jewish communities, most of them in Eastern Europe. Ben-Gurion hoped to bring in at least two thousand workers on the grounds that they were needed for a new venture, the cultivation of tobacco. But "Palestine called for workers, and they did not come," he said. He assumed that Jews might come from the Soviet Union, but the Soviet government severely restricted all emigration. Ben-Gurion wanted to go there to address the problem, but this time a visa was denied.[35] His failure irked him; his inability to extricate Jews from the "destruction, fear of death, and terror" they suffered in the Soviet Union humiliated him as a Zionist and was detrimental to his standing as Histadrut secretary.[36]

❖

The initial immigrants of the Fourth Aliyah belonged to the middle class.[37] They brought with them their urban culture and expected to carry on living

---

* The authorities generally refused to allow in the mentally ill and tubercular, or prostitutes and sex offenders. The law also provided for refusing immigration permits for political reasons. Britain feared the massive immigration of Communist Jews. Weizmann promised to do all he could to keep such undesirables from coming. (Ben-Gurion, Diary, June 4, 1929, July 30, 1924, BGA; Avraham Tarshish, interview transcript, BGA.; Segev 2000, p. 228.)

as they had lived in Poland. One out of every two of these settled in Tel Aviv; the city's population doubled in the space of a year. At the end of 1925, it had a population of forty thousand. Kiosks selling *gazoz*, a blend of fruit juice and soda water, sprouted on every corner. *Gazoz*, and the kiosks that sold them, became emblematic of Tel Aviv's middle-class culture, the antithesis of the pioneer ethos.[38]

Ben-Gurion sometimes liked to equate agricultural settlement with Zionism and to proclaim that working the land was the ultimate consummation of its ideals. The movement from city to country was unique to Zionism and had not been done in almost any other country, he asserted: "The return to the land is first of all a return to the soil."[39] He also depicted his move to Palestine as a result of his desire to work the land. But other than his brief experience as a farmhand, Ben-Gurion was a man of the city who lived a manifestly bourgeois lifestyle and had middle-class tastes. He wrote to his sister Tzipora, who had considered joining a kibbutz, that the members of the commune in question "are not our element," as they came from Transylvania. Better, he advised, to make your home in the city.[40]

Rents were rising in Tel Aviv, he complained in 1921. Nevertheless, its expansion excited him. It would soon be a large Jewish metropolis, he wrote to his father, and a Jewish port would be built there as well.[41] He paid ten pounds a month in rent, the equivalent of a month's wages for close to 40 percent of the Histadrut's membership in Tel Aviv. The family bought a piano and the children took lessons. Geula did well at the Herzliya Hebrew Gymnasium high school. An entire room in their apartment was set aside for the library. A photograph from 1927 shows Ben-Gurion in his apartment wearing a tie and jacket.[42]

Yigael Yadin, the son of a well-known professor and later a well-known archaeologist in his own right, suggested that Ben-Gurion's passion for books grew out of a "very strong sense of inferiority toward people with college educations." One such was Chaim Weizmann, the chemist whose contribution to the British war effort helped him obtain the Balfour Declaration. Arthur Ruppin and Haim Arlosoroff had doctorates in economics. Berl Katznelson and Ze'ev Jabotinsky were men of letters. The thousands of books with which Ben-Gurion surrounded himself, those he read and those he merely collected, may have been intended to raise himself up, at least in his own eyes, to the

level of better-educated Zionist leaders.[43] The books could also take the place
of the friends he did not have and satisfy his urge for power, standing erect
on his shelves in exemplary order, like soldiers. He always expected to find
each one in its place, just like the columns of statistical data in his diary. He
read the Bible and the ancient Greeks largely as political documents, almost
as guidebooks for rulers.[44]

He appreciated the power of the written word. Even though he did not
read much fiction, he was well aware that its authors wielded political influence. From time to time he summoned novelists and poets for what might be
called national guidance talks, as a philosopher-king might do. His broad-
mindedness was limited to the bounds of the Zionist discourse, as he once
demonstrated when Martin Buber skeptically remarked: "We said we would
redeem the land, and we meant to make it Jewish land. Why does it have to
be Jewish land?" Ben-Gurion interrupted. "To bring forth bread from the
earth!" Buber retorted: "Why?" "To eat!" Ben-Gurion replied. "Why?" Buber
insisted. "That's enough," said Ben-Gurion. He thought that the question
"Why?" was out of place. The correct question was "How?"[45]

As a member of the first generation of the twentieth century, he believed
that humankind was destined to "dominate the forces of nature," as he put
it, including the desert and the sea. "There in particular, faced with these
turbulent expanses, man divines his full power and ability, his great capacity
to smooth a path through the sea and cut a safe way through great waters, as
much as the fearless human spirit desires."[46] With childlike excitement, he
decided to take his first passenger flight, in September 1924.

He wanted to fly from Danzig to Berlin, but was only able to get a seat to
a town along the way. The journalist in him compelled him to write it up—he
told how he arrived at the airport, was searched, had to pay for excess baggage;
the ticket cost eleven marks. "We ascended very slowly . . . I saw the sun in
front of me, in front of my face. As if it and the airplane were both hung in the
firmament . . . Birds fly under us . . . and on the road a horse-drawn carriage
sways—little children's toys . . . and the plane slowly proceeds through the atmosphere; it is actually flying at a speed of 130 kilometers per hour. We are at
an altitude of 300 meters . . . and here we touch earth again, it rolls a bit more
on the ground—whistling, creaking, roaring—and falls silent. We flew for
half an hour." Ben-Gurion recorded the plane's make and model: Elberfeld

D-24. As it happened, the plane crashed seven weeks later, killing its three passengers and the same pilot from his flight, he reported.[47] When he returned, he threw himself into a new controversy, or as they said then, a "scandal."

"VENOMOUS TALEBEARING"

Mordechai Mottel Makov was one of the well-off citrus farmers of Rehovot and one of the founders of the Kupat Am bank. In 1925 he hired Arab workers to build his home. Jewish workers tried to disperse the Arabs and Makov called the police. It came to blows, and the conflict extended far beyond the moshavah. Makov received the backing of the Farmers' Association, which was headed by Moshe Smilansky. The Histadrut supported the Jewish workers.

It was a political dispute, grounded in the traditional rivalry between farmers and workers. As an opponent of the employment of Arabs, Ben-Gurion not only came off looking like a workers' advocate but also as the greater Zionist patriot. In practice, the campaign against Arab labor had not achieved much, but it was still the banner he raised.

In December 1925, the British governor of Jaffa brought together representatives of both sides, including Ben-Gurion and Smilansky. A farmers' representative read for the governor a memorandum that Ben-Gurion described as "venomous talebearing." Smilansky expressed no reservations.[48] Speaking in the Assembly of Representatives, Smilansky criticized Makov, but also roundly condemned what he called the "terror" committed by Jewish workers. In a private letter he complained about Ben-Gurion's "demagogic politics."[49] Incensed by Makov's appeal to the British authorities rather than to the Jewish autonomous leadership, Ben-Gurion called Makov an informer and Smilansky filed a libel suit against Ben-Gurion in the Tel Aviv Magistrates Court. A leading figure in the Histadrut tried to mediate between the two, employing Ben-Gurion's friend Shlomo Zemach, who was then married to a niece of Smilansky's.

❖

Five years after settling in Palestine, Zemach was also sick of being a laborer. In 1909 he went to France to study agronomy. Before doing that, he had married and gotten divorced. When he completed his studies, he went to visit his father in Płońsk. The day after he arrived, a German zeppelin passed over the town and the war broke out.

Over the next six years, Zemach and his partner, Hannah Smilansky, drifted from one city to another. He barely made a living by working as a teacher; he also published some stories. Sometimes he stayed with Bialik or with another famous Hebrew poet, Shaul Tchernikovsky. While they were in Odessa, Shlomo and Hannah married, and they soon had a daughter. The civil war between the Bolshevik Reds and the counterrevolutionary Whites raged around them. A mounted Cossack relented at the last minute after intending to run Zemach through with his sword. "Don't ask what we endured," Zemach wrote to Ben-Gurion. "The shadow of death is a constant companion in my life these seven years."

He accepted the revolution wholeheartedly, he wrote. His life had been saved when the Red forces entered his wife's hometown, where the family was hiding in her parents' house. After further vicissitudes, they finally made it to Jaffa. "Here I live," he informed "my cherished brother" Ben-Gurion. "How much I want to see you!" He assured his friend that the political differences that used to divide them had vanished. Ben-Gurion was in Vienna at the time. When he returned, he tried to persuade Zemach to switch to Ahdut Ha'avodah, but Zemach refused. In the meantime, he asked Ben-Gurion for a bit of money. Uncle Moshe Smilansky also helped. Zemach and Hannah were hired as teachers at the Mikveh Israel agricultural school, which paid a good salary and also provided an apartment for them to live in. He wrote and published and began to realize the dream of his youth by becoming a Hebrew writer.[50]

❖

Zemach tried to mediate the dispute between Ben-Gurion and Smilansky, and as one might expect, he got into trouble. Ben-Gurion had no interest in resolution—he wanted a political trial, as public as possible, in which he would take the role of the shining knight defending the workers against the farmers, against Arab labor, against "informers." He got his way but lost the trial. The judges ruled that he had no grounds for calling Smilansky a tale-bearer.[51]

In the months that followed, Ben-Gurion sought publicity in a series of further fights of this sort. In one case he even joined the defense counsel for Jewish workers who had tried by force to prevent the entry of Arab laborers into a citrus grove owned by a farmer from Petah Tikvah. The trial was a citywide sensation, according to *Ha'aretz*. Large crowds massed around the courthouse, but only journalists were allowed to enter.[52]

The struggle against the employment of Arab laborers patently contradicted the Zionist claim that the movement would develop Palestine for the benefit of all its inhabitants. But Ben-Gurion continued to promise, as he had since he began writing articles, that the establishment of a Jewish national home would not hurt the Arabs. On the contrary, he insisted, Zionism did not claim that the Jews were a master race and did not seek to establish an aristocratic society. It was all about national and human values. He vowed again and again that "only an anti-Semite would see our war for our right to work in the moshavah as detrimental to the Arab laborer."[53] Sometimes Ben-Gurion even claimed that one of the goals of the campaign for Hebrew labor was to extricate the Arab laborer from his backwardness, as if it were a moral and socialist mission. Perhaps he was thinking in terms of the "white man's burden" that British colonialism claimed to take on its shoulders when he mentioned that the British refrained from bringing Indian laborers to England, so as to preserve their country's national character.[54]

He did not relent on his claim that the conflict in Palestine did not permit compromise with the Arabs, but in his search for the best way to manage the conflict, he considered the idea of a "compact" between Jewish and Arab labor organizations.[55] It seemed like an advantageous thesis. It accorded with the socialist thinking of the labor movement and spoke to Zionism's supporters in Palestine and overseas. Most Jews in Palestine had not lived there for a long time, and for them to stay they needed at least a smidgen of hope and a dash of belief in peace. "Every Jew who intends or will intend to move to Palestine must ask himself if his life and property are secure in this country," Ben-Gurion wrote. "The feeling that the Jews here sit atop a volcano is liable to subvert the foundation of the Zionist movement." Neither could wealthy Jews be expected to contribute their money to a national project that was doomed to eternal conflict. Advocating coexistence also furthered Zionist diplomacy as it sought to gain friends and public support.

❖

When the British began to employ Jews and Arabs in joint workplaces, the Zionist leadership was concerned that the wages and work conditions in services such as the trains and post office would not reflect Jewish needs and culture, but rather the lesser needs and inferior culture of the Arabs, as Ben-Gurion put it.[56] It thus became imperative to organize Arab workers as well and to demand that they receive wages and conditions equal to that of Jews. About a decade before, Ben-Zvi had explained this position—if Arab workers were not less expensive than Jews, the major incentive to hire them would end.[57] Ben-Gurion hoped to look after Arab workers without having them join the Histadrut, and firmly rejected the demand that the word "Hebrew" be stricken from the union's full name, the General Organization of Hebrew Workers in Palestine. In lieu of that, he tried to persuade the Arabs that it was in their interest to support Zionism.[58] According to a report he received, many Arabs were wrestling with the issue of whether to remain under the protection of the Histadrut or to reject it.[59] The attempts at cooperation were not successful; Ben-Gurion made a list in his diary of violent clashes between Jewish and Arab workers, some of them deadly.[60] Repetur noted another problem—some Jewish railway workers used their work facilities to manufacture bombs for the Haganah.[61]

"MY HEART BLEEDS"

Avigdor Gruen was now sixty-eight years old. The economic crisis in Poland destroyed the credit business he had built up before the war. In his memoirs he claimed that the authorities had revoked his license to work as a "private attorney" because he was a Jew, and that as a result he had no choice but to take the job of secretary of the Płońsk Jewish community.[62] Some ten years after Ben-Gurion sought to persuade his family to leave Płońsk, they were now prepared to go, but Ben-Gurion did not hurry to arrange for them to do so. He said he would help them only if they brought sufficient means to support themselves.[63] His sister Rivka, now a widow, sent him what he called a "heartbreaking" letter. She described the plight of the Jews of Płońsk and her own personal distress, asking whether her brother could expedite her arrival. "I feel with every bone of my body her horrible situation," Ben-Gurion wrote to his father, but he could not bring himself to advise her to come. Rivka wrote that she was prepared to perform any kind of work, and her brother believed she was sincere, as he wrote, "but I don't believe that she will be able to work or that work can be found that she is capable of." He cited how much of an income a family of two would require to live in Palestine— fifteen pounds a month—and asked whether "the sum you have will thus suffice for even a year?" He was traveling again and advised putting off the question until after his return. In the meantime, he sent her a copy of his book.[64]

Ben-Gurion's attitude infuriated his father. The son tried to apologize: "I am very sorry that you think it's my fault that you have not yet come to Palestine," he wrote. He had wanted to bring him over that very winter, but unfortunately he could not do so, he explained, because of his political work. As for Rivka, it was not sufficient for her to be able to support herself for a year—she needed enough money to be able to live off the interest, not her capital, meaning at least three thousand pounds.[65] Another year went by. Meanwhile, his sister Tzipora's husband also died, leaving her with two small children. "My heart bleeds, it is as if I had been struck by lightning," Ben-Gurion wrote to his father. The very next morning, he promised, he would try to obtain an immigration certificate for Tzipora and her children. "I will share my bread with her and I will adopt her children as my own and be a father to them," he promised.

Several months went by. His sister asked if he had forgotten her. Ben-Gurion quickly informed her that the subject disturbed him profoundly. "Is not your hope my hope, your plight my plight, your future my future, and your children mine?" he wrote. He said that the certificates had been delayed for so long because he did not know the name of one of her children and had thus not been able to apply for a certificate for him. Tzipora finally arrived in May 1923, a year and a half after he began, so he said, to make the arrangements.[66]

While he was dealing with Tzipora's immigration, Ben-Gurion again promised to bring his father, "perhaps at the middle of next year."⁶⁷ His brother Avraham also wanted to come; in the meantime, Ben-Gurion tried to obtain a certificate at least for his son Binyamin. That did not take long. In August 1923, Ben-Gurion reported to his father that his nephew Binyamin was working in Tel Aviv and that he was a fine young man. Avraham, for his part, lacked a profession; Ben-Gurion opposed his coming until he first sent his other children, son Israelik and daughter Sheindele. The daughter, he said, could come on condition that she had a mastery of Hebrew. She needed to learn typing before she arrived, and if possible bookkeeping as well. Only after the children came and were on their own feet economically would it be possible to talk about Avraham's arrival. He underlined the words: but not before that. If Rivka could obtain a sum of five hundred to six hundred pounds, she would be able to manage "one way or another," but he would send the necessary paperwork only when she notified him that she was ready for the trip. He then addressed the case of his father.

It sounds as if his father refused to believe that the secretary of the Histadrut could not arrange for the entire family to come. Ben-Gurion did not rush to respond. "I was overloaded with work," he explained, noting that, among his other duties, he had been conducting talks with Britain's Labour government. "I know that you are already treating me with a bit of suspicion," he wrote, promising again that his public activities were keeping him from dealing with the matter. He was also neglecting his duties to his wife and children, he noted. When he traveled overseas, he missed the children and longed to be with them again, but at this point in his life, clearly, his family, including his father and wife, and even his children, were less important to him than his work.

His father wrote that he could now sell his house and get between three hundred and four hundred pounds for it. Ben-Gurion agreed that he could come. He could manage even with a smaller sum, he assured him. "I hope that you will also be able to find work befitting your abilities and your knowledge," he wrote. But to avoid any further misunderstandings, he stated explicitly that he had no intention of helping his father find work. Yes, the doors of every one of the Palestinian Jewish community's institutions was open to him, and any of them would gladly agree to his request to employ someone, but precisely for that reason he would not help his father. "I would not want anyone in Palestine to think, when you are working for some institution, that you are working there not because you are qualified for the job, but rather because you received it thanks to me." The letter made no mention of the "aunt"—that is, his stepmother. In contrast with most of his letters to his father, in this one he did not even send her greetings. On the other hand, he suggested that "perhaps you might also be able to build a house together with Rivka."[68] Another year went by.

Gruen presumably could have settled in Palestine with his wife even without his son's connections, just as tens of thousands of other Jews did. But Gruen wanted to make use of that influence, and in the end he may well have been right to insist on it. Despite his advanced age, he immediately landed a job in the offices of Solel Boneh, the Histadrut construction company. He arrived without his wife. Ben-Gurion brought him to his house in Jerusalem; four days later, he set out on another overseas trip.[69] The job Gruen found was in Haifa, where he lived with Tzipora. He changed his name to Ben-Gurion. When he sold the house in Płońsk, his wife had no choice but to move in with relatives in Łódź. David Ben-Gurion went to visit her in 1926. "She is old and weak and bedridden," he noted in his diary. She arrived in Palestine a year later.*[70]

They arrived during one of the worst years of Ben-Gurion's life. The Histadrut faced the most serious crisis of its history; Ben-Gurion himself had never before faced such disconcerting accusations.

"EVERLASTING COLD, DEVASTATION, OBLIVION"

In the months that preceded his fortieth birthday, his mood was grim, almost suicidal. He gazed out from the deck of the boat that was taking him home after a long stay in Paris and jotted down a few lines about the meaninglessness of life. "It will all pass, end, everlasting cold, devastation, oblivion, endless nothingness. What is the meaning of our entire miserable, momentary,

---

* Ben-Gurion's two sisters, Rivka and Tzipora, both married opera singers in Palestine. His brother Michel was long the proprietor of a kiosk in Tel Aviv. His brother Avraham's daughter, Sheindele, remained in Poland. (Giladi 1973, p. 47; Hagani 2010, p. 174ff.)

pointless existence, which will leave nothing behind. Who can answer? Who can say? The one answer is the grave. The only endpoint."[71] Prior to his stay in Paris, he had participated in a convention of some sort in Germany and had also visited Płońsk. A few hours after he got home, he was already back at work. Then Solel Boneh collapsed and threatened to drag down the entire Histadrut.

❖

The immigrants of the Fourth Aliyah needed places to live. The result was that, in 1925, a full 64 percent of all Jewish investment in Palestine went into housing. The construction boom benefited a large range of factories and businesses. People also built homes to rent. The assumption was that the immigrants would continue to settle in Tel Aviv and that the city would continue to flourish. The immigrants flowed in, but then it looked like everything was going to crash. One reason was that the capital that many of the newcomers brought with them was in the form of Polish currency. As inflation rose in Poland, the value of the currency plummeted; people who had made down payments on new homes could not pay the remaining cost and stopped building. Construction companies and the associated industries collapsed one after another. Workers lost their jobs. In June 1924, Ben-Gurion wrote in his diary: "The job shortage is growing steadily. Yesterday people lost consciousness in the labor bureau." He often had to speak to angry jobless workers—because the Histadrut was not just a labor union but also owned a construction company, Solel Boneh, and other concerns, they saw him not only as their representative but also as their employer. As unemployment rose, each job seeker was allotted just a few days of work a week. Resentment grew. Repetur recalled that at one point it became necessary to assign Ben-Gurion a bodyguard.[72]

At the height of the crisis, the Jewish unemployment rate reached 35 percent of the labor force; one out of every two of the jobless lived in Tel Aviv.[73] Many left the country; in 1926 half as many emigrated as immigrated, and in 1927 there were more emigrants than immigrants.[74] The Histadrut was not prepared to handle such a major crisis. The British administration expanded its public works, but only reluctantly and in a limited way.

Politicians took the crisis as an opportunity to assail one another. Ben-

Gurion claimed that the blame for the crisis lay on members of the middle class, who had wanted to make their livelihoods in the same occupations that Jews in the Diaspora pursued. He depicted the bourgeoisie in almost anti-Semitic terms. They were, he said, "sellers of *gazoz* and land speculators and usurers and those who live off the labor of others." They were "*luft*-masses, eager to speculate, living in the air," as well as "dangling, sterile, and parasitic." In his memoirs he referred to them in the third-person male form, which is often used to label something sordid, such as "the Jew" and "the Arab."*

The Zionist movement had not reached such a low point in the last twenty years, he maintained. He quoted Hayim Nahman Bialik, who said that the crisis was the result of the great and horrible failure of the nation as a whole. Ben-Gurion translated the poet's words into political terms: "the nation as a whole" became the Zionist Executive, with its seat in London, where it obeyed Chaim Weizmann and "was estranged from the working class." What he meant was that it had not restricted middle-class immigration and not given enough certificates to workers. He demanded a much higher investment in developing Palestine and a huge wave of labor Zionist immigration that would revitalize the Zionist enterprise.[75]

His attacks on the Zionist movement received a lot of attention. The local and American press began to watch him. His stance, with his hands stuck in his pockets, intensified the sense of power he radiated, *Ha'aretz* wrote. "He feels always that he has a large party behind him . . . in his own words, there is weight." He copied into his diary a complimentary description of his strong personality and character published by the *Forverts* in New York.[76] He had supporters and opponents, admirers and haters—but very few friends.

"LIKE A DEAD MAN ROLLING DOWN A HILL"

Since the company's principal goal was not to earn a profit but rather to supply jobs for Jews, Solel Boneh offered its clients generous credit. It then took

---

* On another occasion, Ben-Gurion spoke in this way of the "sick mind of the ghetto Jew." (Ben-Gurion 1971a, pp. 546, 333, 334; Ben-Gurion to the Fourth Convention of Ahdut Ha'avodah, May 13, 1924, in Ben-Gurion 1971a, p. 275.)

loans and issued bonds to fund the projects in the interim. In 1926 it began to have trouble collecting its debts from its customers, and thus to meet its loan payments. In June 1927, the company shut down.[77] Like other companies, it was a victim of the economic crisis. But it seems to have been hit particularly hard as a result of poor management, including the high salaries it paid to its executives. Its ideological commitment to organized Jewish labor led it to disregard labor productivity. As secretary of the Histadrut, Ben-Gurion bore overall responsibility; as a devotee of details, he had intimate knowledge of the state of affairs at Solel Boneh.[78]

It was not just an economic story. First and foremost, it was a political and even more so a personal drama. The director of Solel Boneh was David Remez, one of Ahdut Ha'avodah's leaders. The party's rivals, most notably Hapo'el Hatza'ir, tried to use the company's collapse as a springboard for a reorganization of the Histadrut as a whole. They demanded Remez's dismissal, but it was Ben-Gurion who was really in their sights. Ben-Gurion backed Remez almost unreservedly, seeking to protect himself. In January 1927, his party passed a resolution demanding that the Zionist Executive provide, within two weeks, at least three thousand jobs; if not, the Histadrut would abdicate responsibility for labor, cease to assist the unemployed, and instruct its representatives on the Zionist Executive to resign. It would then organize a workers' struggle. "We are like a dead man rolling down a hill, with an abyss yawning underneath," he said. As in the past, his colleagues did not rush to line up behind his belligerent position. The Histadrut Council rejected his proposal to resign from the Zionist Executive.[79]

A rumor that had been going around Jerusalem for some time would soon be proven true. The Zionist Executive had signed contracts to build three large public buildings in Jerusalem. One of the agreements was made with a private contractor who submitted a bid lower than that proffered by Solel Boneh, but the contract did not require him to employ workers according to the conditions set by the Histadrut. The Zionist Executive also excused him from the obligation to employ only Jewish workers.

It was a scandal waiting to be exploited. Hundreds of unemployed workers surrounded the Zionist Executive offices, breaking down doors and shattering windows. Tensions rose by the day; a mother of three killed herself. The story spread that she was driven to it because she and her family were starving.

The Jerusalem Workers Council called on all members of the Histadrut to attend her funeral. Instead of taking her body to the cemetery, they took it to the offices of the Zionist Executive. Ostensibly it was not the Histadrut that had told the workers to take to the streets; technically the call came from the Workers Council. In fact, Ben-Gurion was behind it. In the end, the two sides agreed to new negotiations between the contractor and the Workers Council.[80] The outcome burnished Ben-Gurion's image as the workers' tribune. In the meantime, everyone was gossiping about what quickly turned into the next scandal.

❖

It was even more embarrassing than Solel Boneh. At its center was money that several senior Histadrut officials, Ben-Gurion among them, had taken from the Histadrut treasury. Ben-Gurion's regular income did not cover his lifestyle, in particular his book-buying addiction. He thus frequently took loans from acquaintances and from his movement's institutions.[81] His monthly salary as Histadrut secretary was at first nineteen and then reduced to seventeen pounds. A Histadrut census showed that nine out of every ten workers in the country earned less than he did.*

He was also one of the senior figures in the Histadrut's top tier who received advances and generous loans. According to his diary, he received a loan from Bank Hapoalim to pay off his debt to the Histadrut. His archives preserve documents that point to an ongoing debt equivalent to about two monthly salaries.[82] At one point, a Histadrut committee decided to wipe out the debts of its senior officials. The highest debt owed was that of Ben-Gurion, a full 283.50 Egyptian pounds, the equivalent of about sixteen monthly salaries.

There was no choice but to appoint an internal committee to investigate the Solel Boneh crisis; Ben-Gurion and his colleagues agreed to cancel the elimination of their debts. The only remaining question was whether the

---

* At the apex of the Histadrut pyramid, there were some who received more. The director-general of Bank Hapoalim, a Histadrut subsidiary, received thirty pounds. (Giladi 1971, p. 131ff; Ben-Gurion Diary, June 14, 1927, BGA.)

committee's findings should be published. Ben-Gurion was adamantly opposed, claiming that publication would be detrimental to the Histadrut. Everyone knew everything about it, and Ben-Gurion promised to take steps to rationalize and "purge" the Histadrut. He used the latter word twice, in Hebrew and in Russian. In the end, no one was held responsible. And there is no evidence that Ben-Gurion repaid all the money he had received.[83]

"THE BASEST LIBELS"

In Ben-Gurion's memory, this period remained a profound trauma. He spoke of panic, despair, ideological confusion, impotence, of people deserting the battlefield. For the first time in his life he voiced real doubts about the Zionist vision's chances of being realized, given that everything seemed to be on the verge of falling apart because of "internal infirmity." He claimed that "most" of the immigrants of the Fourth Aliyah had left Palestine. That was not true. Neither had this wave of immigration been a failure, as he claimed.[84] The economic crisis did not last long; soon the citrus industry would begin to flourish, primarily thanks to new export opportunities and industrial advances. The recovery was largely the result of private enterprise. A man named Simcha Whitman won a place in history by being the first to make ice cream in Tel Aviv. His kiosk became famous as a meeting place for people on their way to or from Brenner House, as the offices of the Tel Aviv Workers Council were called.[85]

❖

More than seventeen thousand voters took part in the elections to the Histadrut Convention at the end of 1926. Ben-Gurion was the big victor; for the first time, Ahdut Ha'avodah received an absolute majority, 53 percent of the vote.[86] But when the Convention met, the leadership found itself facing withering criticism. In his diary, Ben-Gurion wrote: "The working public is resentful. The anger is especially strong regarding the matter of salaries and advances and the lack of contact with the public."[87] That was an understatement, given the record of the proceedings. One of the delegates shouted:

"There is terror in the Histadrut and the workers are afraid to open their mouths."[88]

One Hapo'el Hatza'ir delegate angered Ben-Gurion in particular. He was a twenty-eight-year-old with a Ph.D. whose star was rising, named Haim Arlosoroff. He offered what he termed a merciless analysis of the fundamental mistakes Ben-Gurion had made, the first of them being haste. It was a debate over principles—Arlosoroff used the Solel Boneh scandal as a metaphor. "Had Solel Boneh known its limits and had not entered into fantasies of unrestricted growth, it would have expanded gradually, in a healthy way, and served its purpose," he said. Instead, "we leapt fifty years ahead." The damn advances kept coming up again and again; Berl Katznelson himself called them "a moral failing."*[89]

Ben-Gurion told the Convention that he felt like an accused man defending himself against "the basest libels." He did not have much to say regarding the substance of the criticism. He reverted to cliché, sounding almost pathetic. "Only a person who has done nothing can be unerringly wise; a person who manages something can be allowed to make mistakes." If he were to be in the same circumstances again, he would do exactly what he had done with Solel Boneh, he said. After all, the goal was to promote the Zionist cause. "If we don't milk the cow with Zionist intention, then the cow will be milked by Mustafa and not one of our cooperatives," he asserted. At this point, his tone turned sentimental, conciliatory, comforting, flattering, almost prophetic. "We are a small group of people who have great needs and a huge desire for redemption," he said. Sovereignty had not yet been achieved, but they were not like the Jews of the ghetto. "For the first time, we have a Jewish worker with national consciousness who sees before him, in the Land of Israel, a historic destiny—to be the ruler and builder who decides his people's fate."

---

* Remez termed the criticism of the advances "a miniature pogrom." The advances had been justified, he said, and had been given to only seven or eight of Solel Boneh's employees. "They could have earned their living elsewhere," he maintained. "But we rode these beasts of burden day and night. They did not hide the sums they owed and their debts were not canceled." (Ben-Gurion and Remez at the Third Histadrut Convention, July 10, 1927, Ben-Gurion, minutes, pp. 74ff., 72.)

From his vantage point at the heights of history, his critics looked like irritating quibblers. He did not mention the advances. And the Convention was his.

❖

After his speech, Ben-Gurion fell ill and stayed home. The Convention's final session stretched into the night and was adjourned only at dawn. At a quarter to six in the morning, the delegates sang "The Internationale" followed by "Hatikvah." Behind the scenes, contacts were already underway regarding a hitherto unlikely merger between Hapo'el Hatza'ir and Ahdut Ha'avodah. A united Party of the Workers of Palestine, or Mapai as it came to be called by its Hebrew acronym, began to look like a real possibility. The delegates formed circles and danced the hora to wake up, and then set out in procession to Ben-Gurion's home. He could not have wished himself a more enjoyable morning. In a conciliatory and unifying gesture, one of his opponents ascended to his apartment and pulled him out to the balcony, dressed in a bathrobe. At least one participant reported that he saw tears glistening in Ben-Gurion's eyes.[90]

10

UNIFICATION

"THE CATASTROPHE IS FAR GREATER THAN I THOUGHT"

In September 1930, Ben-Gurion returned to Berlin, where he observed with alarm the rise of the Nazis. He called them "German Revisionists," with reference to Jabotinsky's Revisionist Zionist movement. "I read Hitler's newspaper today and it was as if I were reading Jabotinsky in *Doar Hayom*," he wrote. "The same words, the same style, the same spirit." Jabotinsky spent most of his time in Europe, but a branch of the Revisionist movement he had founded operated in Palestine. In the latter part of the 1920s, he positioned himself as the leader of the Zionist opposition, rival of Chaim Weizmann and nemesis of the labor movement. As a popular journalist and much-admired poet, he excelled, unlike Ben-Gurion, at public speaking. In further contrast to Ben-Gurion, he exuded charisma and was considered an outstanding Jewish intellectual.

Since solidifying his control of the Histadrut, Ben-Gurion had come to realize that the political arena of Palestine's Jewish community had limited capacity for advancing Zionist goals. His routine work as Histadrut secretary no longer satisfied his ambitions. Weizmann, Katznelson, Tabenkin, and a number of other figures were more prominent and more admired. The older among them had worked personally with Herzl and had been Ben-Gurion's own mentors in his youth. Menachem Ussishkin, who headed Keren Kayemet (the Jewish National Fund), the Zionist movement's land-buying corporation, was a nearly legendary figure in right-wing circles. Ben-Gurion saw him as a nuisance, but treated him with respect. During this period, he also had dealings with Nahum Sokolow, who for a time replaced Weizmann as president of the Zionist Organization. "No one took him seriously," Ben-Gurion remarked. It was Sokolow who, as editor of *Hatzefirah* three decades previously, had rejected the sixteen-year-old Ben-Gurion's suggestion that the newspaper do a piece on his Ezra club.[1] Then there was Moshe Smilansky, whose articles Ben-Gurion had read while he was still a teenager in Płońsk; in comparison, Ben-Gurion was still almost a neophyte. Even in his own party he hardly reigned supreme—the road to power was still a long one, and he wanted to shorten it.

❖

The Shavuot holiday arrived on Friday, May 25, 1928. That morning Ben-Gurion met with the Jerusalem Workers Council's board. That afternoon he took Paula, Geula, and Renana to spend the weekend in Ben Shemen, a farming village on the coastal plain, home to a new agricultural boarding school. Berl Katznelson joined them. Ben-Gurion acknowledged Katznelson's preeminence and during his lifetime made no effort to take his place. He needed his backing and, often, his advice. In later years, he would say that he had had only three real friends his whole life; the names varied, but Katznelson was always one of them.*[2]

Katznelson was a politician, too, but in his own way. His speeches tended

---

* Among the others were Yitzhak Ben-Zvi, Shmuel Yavnieli, Shlomo Zemach, and Shlomo Lavi.

to be overly ideological, overly vague, and, especially, overly long. More than anything else, he needed to be loved. Ben-Gurion believed in power. Katznelson admired Ben-Gurion's political abilities and generally supported him; unlike Ben-Gurion, Katznelson had many friends. The two went to Ben Shemen to attend a youth assembly. At the time, the negotiations between Ahdut Ha'avodah and Hapo'el Hatza'ir over the formation of a unified party were still under way. The impetus for a merger intensified as the Revisionists and the middle-class forces of the Fourth Aliyah gained strength.

The car taking them to Ben Shemen was crowded. Ben-Gurion did not know how to drive, and the driver of the car brought his wife and two daughters along. "When we came to a bend in the road, the car was unable to make the turn properly and I saw we were about to fall off the road," Ben-Gurion wrote. "I felt my breathing stop for a moment, as if someone was choking me." When he came to, he found himself sprawled in a field with the other passengers strewn around him. Paula and Renana were covered with blood. Katznelson was sitting in a ditch. Ben-Gurion asked how he was and Berl responded with a wince, indicating that he could not move. "Apparently his bones are broken," Ben-Gurion thought to himself. He was wounded, too. "I felt pain in my foot and my head. Blood ran down from my forehead. All my clothes were full of blood," he recounted. They received medical care and were sent home. Katznelson suffered severe injuries and required a long hospital stay.[3]

❖

The accident delayed the unity negotiations, which had stretched on for a few years. The anguished discussions that both parties held gives today's reader the impression that each of them was called on to bridge a deep ideological abyss. As was their wont, the members of each group clashed vehemently and passionately over ideas and isms. The issue of class struggle was one point of contention, but the principal issues were the wording of the united party's manifesto and its name. Ben-Gurion employed all his political experience in the negotiations, and must have required nerves of steel to get through the logorrhea alive.

In the meantime, Arab terror once more loomed.

❖

The attack on the Jews of Jaffa in 1921 was followed by several relatively peaceful years. The number of Jews killed by Arabs each year reverted to an average of two a year; in 1928, apparently, none were killed at all.[4] This seemed to provide a foundation for the Jewish-Arab workers' alliance that Ben-Gurion spoke of. It was, however, an illusion that could last only for as long as the Arabs did not shatter it, which they did in September 1928. The trigger was a dispute over prayer arrangements at the Western Wall. On Yom Kippur eve a curtain was placed at the site, to separate women and men, as is customary in Orthodox synagogues. It was not the first time this had been done, but this time the Muslim religious authorities, who exercised control over the site, demanded that the curtain be removed. British policemen showed up on Yom Kippur morning and told the Jews to remove the curtain. Some of the worshippers refused and a fight broke out between them and the police. The incident made the Western Wall the focal point of tensions in the city. From time to time violent clashes between Jews and Arabs broke out there. Internal conflicts on each side also exacerbated tensions. Arab and Jewish leaders accused their political rivals of weakness and defeatism; people on both sides were swept along by nationalist demagoguery and religious fanaticism.

A few days after the curtain incident, Ussishkin spoke out at a meeting of the National Council, the executive board of the Assembly of Representatives. He said that the Jews should demand of the British administration that it expropriate the Western Wall from the Muslims who were in charge of it. *Doar Hayom* reported that the meeting was a stormy one, of "great fury." Ben-Gurion responded with restraint: every Jew, including nonreligious ones, had been shocked by what happened at the Wall, he said. He added that the Zionist movement had missed several opportunities to purchase the site. Those efforts should be continued, he maintained. Only if the "Arab nation" refused to sell, he said, should the Jews demand expropriation. "Redemption" of the Western Wall needed to proceed with caution and moderation, he advised. "If we don't succeed today," he said, "we'll do so half a year from now." He seems not to have been caught up in the rage the incident set off; he saw the Wall as an issue that did not require an immediate resolution. The problem was not who controlled the Wall, he maintained, but rather the fact that there were not enough Jews in Palestine.

Exceptionally, Jabotinsky himself took part in the discussions—he was a rare guest in Palestine and everyone waited in suspense for his speech. He had arrived in Jerusalem a few days before the confrontation, and would soon take over as editor of *Doar Hayom*, a daily newspaper that had for years conducted a strident campaign against the labor movement. Charging that the country's Jewish leadership was not standing up sufficiently to the British administration, he voiced his fear that it would not be long before the Arabs staged a "bloody onslaught" against the Jews. "We cannot dream of a willing agreement between us and the Arabs, not now and not in the foreseeable future," he declared, quoting words he had written in 1923. He reiterated his opinion that the Arabs needed to be told the truth: the Zionist movement aspired to a Jewish majority in Palestine. No fool would believe any attempt to conceal that. His speech evinced prudence and leadership; the Zionist project required time and patience, he said. He made no mention at all of the labor movement.

Ben-Gurion sounded angry. He did not believe that peace with the Arabs was possible, any more than Jabotinsky did, and could give no less grim a speech, as he had done ten years previously. He, too, had always insisted that the Arabs should be told the truth about Zionism's aims. But that was now a privilege available only to the opposition. As secretary of the Histadrut, Ben-Gurion bore a share of national responsibility, and he was also committed to the socialist value of the brotherhood of nations. He attacked Jabotinsky personally, recalling his opposition to the defense of Tel Hai.[5]

As the summer of 1929 approached, tensions in Jerusalem increased. Rumors once more spread among the Arabs that the Jews were plotting to destroy the Islamic shrines on al-Haram al-Sharif, and rebuild their Temple on the site, which for the Jews is the Temple Mount. At the same time, hostility was on the rise between the Revisionists and the members of the labor movement, including slanders, threats, fistfights, and stone throwing. It was mostly a struggle over power and control. A worker who did not join the Histadrut was virtually unable to find a job; furthermore, the labor movement controlled nearly all the funds that the Zionist Organization allocated to development in Palestine, and also the distribution of immigration certificates. The Revisionists fought to obtain a share of these. Jabotinsky encouraged his supporters to break strikes. The Revisionists carried out their campaign in part with the help of their paramilitary youth movement, Betar. The Histadrut deployed its Workers' Squads.[6]

In August 1929, on the eve of the fast of the Ninth of Av, which commemorates the destruction of the Jewish Temples, the police permitted three hundred young Jews to stage a procession to the Western Wall; the police also provided protection to the thousands of Jewish worshippers who went to pray there that night. On the following day, Friday, the Muslims celebrated the Prophet Muhammad's birthday. When the prayer service at the al-Aqsa mosque on the Temple Mount ended, thousands of Arabs streamed toward the Wall, drove away the Jews, and put several Torah scrolls to the torch. There were other incidents in the city as well, and over the next two days the entire country erupted in bloody clashes, and dozens of Jews were murdered in Hebron.

❖

At the time, Ben-Gurion was in Nice on the French Riviera, resting after his travails at a recent Zionist Congress. The reports he received from Palestine were fragmentary at first, among them a telegram from Paula telling him that she and the children had not been injured. Her message may well have helped him internalize the horrors of what had happened. "The catastrophe is far greater than I thought," he wrote in his diary. He quickly returned home. While still on board his ship, he formulated the central question: would the riots hinder or help the Zionist enterprise? He was not certain what the answer was. They might dishearten the public, cause despair, deter immigration, stymie capital investment, and destroy Zionism. But they might also reveal "hidden strengths" and bolster determination to succeed.

On board, Ben-Gurion met several members of his movement; they, too, were returning from the Zionist Congress. He convened them for a consultation. They made note of one of the fundamental characteristics that enabled him to establish his standing—he was able to respond to nearly every situation immediately, precisely, decisively, and with confidence that he was right. His practical approach, almost devoid of sentiment, reflected the fact, perhaps, that in 1929, as in 1921, he had not experienced the horrors himself.*

Shlomo Lavi, of Ein Harod, recalled sixty children suffering from whooping cough, three of his own among them, packed into one of the kibbutz's two barns. "The enemy lies in wait and you do not know where he will appear," he wrote. "There was no fear at all that one of the defenders would fall. But there was great fear that a bullet coming from afar would hit one of the youngsters." None of Ein Harod's children were hurt.[7] According to official figures, 130 Jews were killed and more than 300 wounded. More than 100 Arabs were killed and more than 200 wounded, most of them by British security forces.[8] It was the harshest blow dealt to the Jews of Palestine since World War I.

"IN POLITICAL TERMS IT IS A NATIONAL MOVEMENT"

The mass murder ostensibly corroborated the view of the Arabs that Ben-Gurion had always held—they were "primitive," he maintained. "We were faced with an outbreak of the worst instincts of savage masses—enflamed religious extremism, a compulsion for robbery and looting, and a thirst for blood," he said. He offered a psychological explanation for Arab hatred, attributing it to the envy of the "son of the desert" who viewed Tel Aviv from his "shack"; even the Jews' barns looked to him like royal mansions. An alliance of Jewish and Arab workers now seemed to him far off and less relevant than ever, but Ben-Gurion nevertheless tried to maintain the possibility, at least as a fiction.

He opposed any form of revenge, including a boycott of Arab merchandise. "Let us not forget even at this hour that we must live with the Arabs in this land," he declared. He also noted that there had been cases in Tel Aviv in which Jews attacked Arabs, and there were Arabs who had saved Jews.

---

* The most personal thing he said about the violence came nearly two years later. The disturbances of August 1929, he said, reminded him that Palestine was still the Jews' "stepmother," and that it was a "painful and tragic memory." In a letter to his father he wrote a few days after the disturbances, he refrained, exceptionally, from asking after his stepmother. (Ben-Gurion, "Hamediniyut Hahitzonit shel Ha'am Ha'ivri," Ben-Gurion 1931, p. 153; Ben-Gurion to his father, Oct. 1, 1930, in Erez 1974, p. 156.)

Saying this was important for the Zionist movement's public image. "We must stress the positive," he said. "It is not good for us to stand in the light of 'the whole world is against us.'"

But the riots of 1929 again reinforced, as the ones in 1921 had done, his appraisal that the conflict was not amenable to compromise. Huge numbers of Arabs had attacked Jews, he noted, and their purpose had been clear: "annihilation of the entire Jewish community and the destruction of our enterprise in Palestine." That being the case, there was no point in debating whether there was or was not an Arab national movement. "The movement is a mass movement and that is the principal fact. We do not see a national revival movement, and its moral value is questionable, but in political terms it is a national movement." As Ben-Gurion saw it, the Arabs were not interested in an agreement with the Zionists because they constituted a majority in the country. "They are fighting to preserve the status quo and to do that they have no need of an agreement of any sort," he wrote. He did not know whether the Arab masses answered the call to fight the Jews because that was what they wanted or because they were afraid not to. Either way, it seemed unlikely that they would respond with the same alacrity if their leaders were to call for peace. "The Arab worker, too, is not just a worker. He belongs to his people," he asserted, adding, "Every nation gets the national movement it deserves."[9]

❖

Against this backdrop, Ben-Gurion needed to engage in a measure of verbal acrobatics so as to distinguish his movement from its rivals to the right and left; he needed to sound no less patriotic than the Revisionists and no less peace-loving than Brit Shalom, a small organization that offered an alternative to Zionist policy. He feared that the Revisionists would grow stronger, and as such he accused them of feeding the flames of violence. They constituted the "black wing" of Zionism, he claimed, and depicted them as nationalist, chauvinist, and fascist fanatics.[10] Jabotinsky had previously published an article against the Histadrut's control of Palestine with the title "The Red Swastika." And he was not the most extreme figure on the right. A journalist, Abba Ahimeir, founded a tiny society called Brit Habiryonim (the word *biryonim* means "strongmen," or "thugs"), and put out a small newspaper called *Hazit Ha'am* (The People's Front). In April 1933, the paper carried an article with the headline "The Stalin–Ben-Gurion–Hitler pact."[11]

Brit Shalom had no more than a hundred members, and unlike the Revisionists, they were no threat to Ben-Gurion's political standing. As such, he treated them politely. Among them were a number of prominent intellectuals. They advocated a binational Jewish-Arab state. As a corollary of that position, they opposed the goal of creating a Jewish majority in Palestine and consented only to the creation of parity between the two communities.*

Judah Leon Magnes, chancellor of the Hebrew University, did not officially belong to Brit Shalom, but he worked to promote a peace plan that involved an Arab-Jewish agreement on a Jewish national home in Palestine, with the Jews giving up their demands for a Jewish majority and an independent state. Ben-Gurion apparently saw this simply as harmless and deluded naïveté, divorced from the political realities. He spent many hours in conversation with supporters of Brit Shalom. It bothered him that they believed that their Zionism was more just than his, so he spoke to them mostly about morality. "According to my moral outlook, we do not have the right to discriminate against even one Arab child, even if such discrimination would obtain for us all that we seek," he declared.[12]

At this point, no concrete decisions had to be made. The Arabs had not submitted a peace proposal. The choice between Zionism and peace was at best a theoretical issue, as was his debate with Magnes and Brit Shalom. But Ben-Gurion believed that the question required an answer. His choice was unambiguous—he gave Zionism preference over peace, just as he had given it preference over socialism. The Histadrut Executive was not prepared to sacrifice even 1 percent of it for "'peace,'" he wrote, putting the word between quotation marks.[13] Against this background, and in order to position

---

* Ten years previously, Yitzhak Tabenkin had estimated that it would be possible, within a decade or two, to settle nine million Jews in Palestine. Ben-Gurion spoke of far fewer. In fact, no one really knew how many Jews would settle in Palestine and when. "We need to prepare for the maximum," Ben-Gurion said. (Ben-Gurion to the Provisional Committee, June 9, 1919, CZA 1/8777; Ben-Gurion and Tabenkin to a Po'alei Zion delegation, March 7, 16, 1920, in Haim Golan 1989, pp. 189, 195.)

himself and his movement in the center of Zionist discourse, Ben-Gurion proposed a partition plan.

"COMMANDERS' REVOLT"

He worked hard and feverishly, and in November 1929, he had in hand a six-page plan for the establishment of two autonomous administrations under British suzerainty. His idea was a federation of cantons that would develop gradually, over a long period, after parity of the Jewish and Arab populations was achieved. It would separate Jews and Arabs and divide rule over the country. The plan included a precise scheme of governing and representative bodies; it gave the impression that all was ready to put into practice.[14] He also proposed two things for immediate implementation—the establishment of a Jewish military force and the immigration of forty-five thousand pioneers.[15]

Willingness to divide the country into Jewish and Arab cantons was meant to guarantee not only the security and livelihood of the Jews but also their fundamental values. If they were not a majority in Palestine, the Jews would fall into "the claws of the fate that pursues them in the lands of their Exile" and would assimilate among the gentiles, in this case the Arabs.[16]

He could not assume that the Arabs would accept his federal plan, and it hardly seems that he could have seen it as a final status arrangement. It was a staged plan—every achievement was, in his view, one more step along a long road.[17] But the plan provided a platform to stand on and to present to political rivals at home, on the right and the left, as well as to foreigners, including the Mandate administration.

❖

Ben-Gurion's stress on expediting Zionist activity saved him from a more vexed topic: the neglect of the Haganah. In August 1929, most Jews in Palestine had lacked any real defense against their Arab attackers. Ben-Gurion rightly condemned the British authorities' feeble response. They had not taken action against Arab incitement and had not taken the steps necessary to ensure the security of the country's Jews.[18] But since Hashomer had been dismantled, the Histadrut had taken responsibility for self-defense. And the Haganah was ill prepared. The organization had a few hundred members, nearly all of them young volunteers. They were too few, had not received proper training, and were not armed with the right weapons. The lack of arms was especially scandalous given that at this time it was not difficult to obtain them and smuggle them into the country. The Arab offensive of August 1929 came as a total surprise to the militia.[19]

Ben-Gurion knew that the Haganah was in a bad state; its national coordinator, Yosef Hecht, had alerted him to this from time to time, and he recorded the details in his diary. In doing so, he used coded language, as if the subject were farm equipment—instead of "rifles" he wrote "plows," instead of "pistols" he wrote "hoes," and he referred to machine guns as "tractors." Hecht told him that there was a shortage of all these. For the last six years the Haganah had not received funds from the Zionist Executive, he noted. Three months before the August disturbances, he told Ben-Gurion that even existing weapons were not being cared for properly. He needed an armorer to maintain them, he said. Ben-Gurion was more interested in the ties between the Haganah and the Histadrut. "We need to reinforce the Histadrut's influence and responsibility," he said, remarking that what really needed attention was the Workers' Squads. By the summer of 1928, the Haganah central command was but a fiction. Hecht asked the Histadrut Executive to release him from his position, but no one else was prepared to accept this thankless job.[20]

As secretary of the Histadrut, Ben-Gurion bore responsibility for the fiasco of the Haganah's lack of preparedness. But he evaded the blame, just as he had avoided accountability for Solel Boneh. At that time, he had stood by David Remez, the man in charge of the company; this time he stood by Eliyahu Golomb, who was a prominent activist in the Haganah, and regarded by many as its official commander. The two of them claimed that Hecht had not been loyal to the Histadrut and sought his dismissal.[21]

It was another struggle for the control of the Zionist movement's first security forces, with the same passions and some of the same antagonists. When Hecht sought to maintain control of the organization, he was accused of staging a "commanders' revolt." Investigation followed inquiry followed paralegal proceedings, among them a Committee of Five whose members were unable to resolve the dispute.[22] As it grew ever more convoluted, the

Jerusalem branch of the Haganah split, with Avraham Tehomi, the man who had admitted to murdering Jacob de Haan, founding, in 1931, a new militia tied to the Revisionist opposition. It was first called Haganah Bet and then Etzel, the acronym of its Hebrew name, Irgun Tzva'i Le'umi, meaning National Military Organization. Ben-Gurion wrote many years later about the "organizational deficiencies" of the Haganah in 1929. "Up to that point," he wrote, "the Haganah had been in practice headed by a single man, Yosef Hecht, who refused to accept the involvement of any public institution." As he depicted it, the problem was political and involved in part "hatred of the left."[23] The Hecht affair reflected Ben-Gurion's guiding instincts and the compulsion he had developed since the days of Bar Giora to destroy every armed force that he did not control. As the scandal grew, Ben-Gurion's role in it was forgotten. Hecht was dismissed.

"FEAR, O BRITISH EMPIRE!"

The events of August provided the final push for the unification talks between the two labor parties. The denouement finally came in January 1930, in Tel Aviv's Beit Ha'am hall, festooned with the red banners of socialism and the blue-and-white flags of Zionism, as well as portraits of the movement's spiritual progenitors, among them Karl Marx and Joseph Trumpeldor. At the end of three days of speeches, Ben-Gurion announced the new party's name: the Palestinian Workers' Party, soon known by its Hebrew acronym, Mapai.* And he led the crowd in singing the anthem of the first immigrants of the Second Aliyah, "God Will Build the Galilee."

At that point, according to *Davar*, "it was as if a blocked spring suddenly spurted forth, jets of enthusiasm and fraternal joy shot upward . . . the fire spread to all four corners of the hall and the entire assembly turned into a raucous brew . . . hand was extended to hand and shoulder to shoulder." They sang "The Internationale" and "Tehezaknah," the labor movement's unofficial anthem, also "Hatikvah." Then Ben-Gurion went home. But once again, as following the Histadrut's third convention, his comrades did not let him

---

* To quell any doubts the name might raise regarding the national nature of the party, *Davar* made it clear that its English name would be the Palestine Jewish Labor Party.

rest. According to *Davar*, this time, too, they marched to his house and, at almost three in the morning, in the rain, they sang, danced, and "cheered as one," with Ben-Gurion leading.[24] The establishment of Mapai was the most important political development in Palestine's Jewish community since the inception of the Zionist project. Ben-Gurion had been present at the birth of the idea of unification, in Berl Katznelson's tent in the Egyptian desert, after World War I, and he played a central role in establishing Mapai. It was, at that point, his major political achievement: Mapai would be the ruling party for decades, and it became the organizational embodiment of his power.

❖

In the meantime, a commission of inquiry arrived from London. Its report led, in 1930, to what the British call a White Paper, an official declaration of government policy. It reinterpreted the Balfour Declaration as a dual and equal commitment to both Jews and Arabs. From this point onward, Jews would be allowed to settle in Palestine only on condition that they did not cause Arab unemployment. The new policy also placed restrictions on the purchase of land for Jewish settlement.[25]

Up until this point, Ben-Gurion had taken care not to upset the British, and with good reason—the Zionist enterprise was advancing quickly under the sponsorship and with the assistance of the British authorities. During the first decade of British rule in Palestine, about one hundred thousand Jews had settled there and dozens of new settlements had been established.*

The commission's report roused a storm of protest among the Zionists. Ben-Gurion at first chided his colleagues: "A commission of inquiry comes out against us—and we are overcome by panic . . . An important newspaper publishes an article in our favor—we celebrate. Such hysterical mood swings are not to our credit and we need to fight them with all our strength." It was

---

* From the time of Ben-Gurion's arrival in 1906 and the end of the 1920s, the number of Jews in Palestine had doubled, reaching approximately 180,000. The Arab population rose by about 200,000 in the 1920s, reaching approximately 850,000. (Tomaszewski 2001, 1, p. 422; Ben-Avram and Nir 1995, pp. 107, 193; Lissak 1986; Lissak 1994, pp. 173ff., 215; Palestine Royal Commission 1937, p. 279; Anglo-American Committee of Inquiry 1946, 1, p. 141.)

an accurate depiction of the psychological dynamic that had frequently, since his youth, determined his own responses and positions. And indeed, he soon saw that the White Paper seemed to demolish his entire political worldview; the Devil himself could not invent crueler tricks, he said.[26] In October 1930, he proposed declaring war on the British Empire.

It was his wildest outburst up to that point. After accusing the Labour government of hostility, treason, anti-Semitism, murder, and theft, he suddenly shouted: "Fear, O British Empire!" And he demanded going to war against it. There is no boulder that cannot be blown up with a small amount of explosive powder, he promised. He knew that such a war would be, for the Jews, a catastrophe no less than that of the destruction of the Second Temple, but that was what needed to be done. At this point, his speech became even more hallucinatory. The Jews would not fight the empire alone, but rather in alliance with the Arabs of the Middle East, from Egypt to Iraq. "If we can make use of the demon, we will use the demon," he added.

The speech was to Mapai's governing Council; the members of his party were in shock. Some of them rose to protest his call for war. Ben-Gurion stood his ground but tried to reassure his colleagues. Before war with the British all political channels should be exhausted, he acknowledged. That would take at least twenty years. He did not repeat the idea of allying with the Arabs.[27]

❖

About half a year previously, Ben-Gurion visited a famous physician in Paris. He was experiencing, not for the first time, an attack of severe pain in his legs; he also noticed blue spots on his shins. He was forty-four years old. The doctor said that, physically, he was completely healthy, including his heart and kidneys, but that his nervous system was "fundamentally shaken" and "on the verge of collapse." He attributed this to tension and fatigue.

Ben-Gurion at times complained of exhaustion during these months. "All my strength is gone," he wrote to his father, "and I was not able to work." And in a letter to Golomb he said: "I have no strength, and contact with people is especially difficult, even a simple exchange." The doctor ordered him to go to a sanatorium outside the city and to disengage from his work "for at least" two months.[28] He thus made his "declaration of war" against the British Empire during a period in which his mental condition required him to receive extended treatment. Ben-Gurion thought that the doctor in Paris was correct, but did not obey him. His condition did not improve. "I am so weary that I can only with difficulty get my thoughts together," he wrote to Paula. Weizmann soon succeeded in getting the new White Paper policy revoked, and everyone forgot Ben-Gurion's outburst.[29]

❖

Ben-Gurion spent much time in Europe and the United States during this period; he traveled at least once a year and often more. Sometimes he spent more months outside Palestine than in it. Between 1927 and 1933, he was absent from Palestine for more than two years, cumulatively.[30] He always went for political reasons, but he enjoyed the travel—the tourist sites, views, city centers, museums, and bookstores. He also delighted in cuisines that Tel Aviv did not offer.[31] His expenses were paid by his movement or his hosts, and he generally traveled third or second class; on ships he would crowd into a berth with other travelers. He generally did not stay in the most expensive hotels, and at times had no choice but to make do with uncomfortable lodgings. He went without Paula; in the thirteen years since she gave birth to Amos in London, she did not leave the country. The long months he spent alone overseas gave him the chance to meet other women. Paula suspected, and in fact knew about it. "Your letters come more seldom. What is the matter, you have found new attractions?" she reproached him.[32]

❖

In August 1929, in Zurich, the world Zionist Organization signed an agreement with several non-Zionist Jewish organizations. Most of these organizations were American; Ben-Gurion was moved almost to tears, as if a time machine had taken him back to Herzl's First Zionist Congress. The compact was concluded during the Zionist Congress. Zurich's Tonhalle concert hall—Johannes Brahms had attended its opening—overflowed with elation; Albert Einstein was among the guests.

The negotiations had dragged on for years. In the end, they agreed on the establishment of a Jewish Agency, in which Zionists and non-Zionists would take part. The new body was meant to serve as the executive branch of the Zionist Organization. It was to replace the Zionist Executive that sat in London and Jerusalem, and to operate in parallel with the quasi-parliamentary bodies of the Jewish community in Palestine, the Assembly of Representatives and the National Council.

In ideological terms, the Zionists made a rather humiliating concession by accepting a partnership with non-Zionist organizations. Egos and mutual distaste made it difficult to establish a partnership. The non-Zionists also had to make difficult compromises. They did not like the term "national home," but agreed to the expansion of immigration, the purchase of more land, the encouragement of Hebrew labor, and the use of the Hebrew language.[33]

"I was moved deeply by the profound and staggering experience," Ben-Gurion wrote to Paula. Einstein was a genius and his face, shining like that of an angel, imbued the dais with majesty and splendor."[34] The Zionist coffers were empty; there were times when the Zionist Organization was unable to use all the immigration certificates that the British authorities issued. The assumption was that the American non-Zionists' money would save the Zionist enterprise in Palestine from catastrophe, just as it had saved the country from famine during World War I. He began to think about "the conquest of Zionism," meaning control of the Zionist Organization. That was the real center of power.

Jabotinsky and his followers claimed that the establishment of the Jewish Agency violated the principles of democratic representation. Some in the labor movement also had trouble overcoming their repugnance for partnering with American capitalists, whom they saw as the enemies of both Zionism and socialism. Ben-Gurion declared: "We are not completely at ease with the Jewish Agency . . . yet we accept [it] because we believe that Palestine will be built by cooperation among all Jewish forces. For us, democracy is not just an empty expression, but we have a principle more dear to us than democracy, and it is the building of Palestine by Jews."[35] Democracy thus became one with socialism and peace—in Ben-Gurion's thinking, it was, like the others, ranked under the goals of Zionism. At the next Zionist Congress, held in Basel in 1931, a huge drama took place. Chaim Weizmann deviated from the Zionist mainstream and was ousted from the presidency of the movement.

"GRATUITOUS FOOLISHNESS"

The wave of terror of 1929, the White Paper that followed it, and the Zionist movement's opening to non-Zionists all renewed the debate over what Zionism's ultimate goal was, and what it could realistically achieve. In advance of the Basel Congress, Weizmann said that there was no way to establish a Jewish majority in Palestine in the foreseeable future, and as such there was no point in demanding a Jewish state. "The propaganda which is carried out in certain Zionist circles, like the Revisionists, for a Jewish state, is foolish and harmful," he wrote, saying that demanding a Jewish state in Palestine was like demanding one in Manhattan. At the Congress, in an interview with the Jewish Telegraphic Agency, he was even blunter: he opposed seeking a Jewish majority in Palestine on the grounds that the world would see it as a plan to expel the Arabs. He maintained, however, that there was a chance of achieving an agreement on the basis of parity.[36]

He caused a scandal. The Revisionists made the most of it—they demanded a resolution explicitly stating that the Zionist movement sought a Jewish state. Weizmann, Ben-Gurion, and many others believed that such a declaration would be detrimental to the cause and that it would be best to maintain ambiguity. The labor movement again had trouble deciding where it stood. Ben-Gurion believed that Weizmann was spouting "gratuitous foolishness," but he could live, for the time being, with the parity principle, given that the Jews were still a minority in Palestine. Furthermore, were he to come out against Weizmann, it would benefit the Revisionists.[37]

Weizmann was short a few votes for reelection to the presidency. Ben-Gurion decided to help him. Weizmann phoned the British prime minister Ramsey MacDonald and asked him to receive Ben-Gurion that evening and grant him a statement supporting the parity principle. Ben-Gurion said he was surprised that Weizmann sent him and not Haim Arlosoroff, whom Weizmann had also consulted on the issue. Arlosoroff, who headed the Jewish Agency's Political Department, was close to the president, and his English was better. "My English was very bad then," Ben-Gurion observed. Weizmann seems to have been thinking of the labor solidarity that tied Ben-Gurion to Prime Minister MacDonald and his son Malcolm; Weizmann had one of his own close associates, the eminent historian Lewis Namier, accompany Ben-Gurion.

The two flew to London. But because of a mechanical malfunction they arrived late. The prime minister had waited for them, but when they did not arrive he set off for a weekend in Chequers, a grim estate outside London. Ben-Gurion and Namier were invited to come for breakfast the next morning.

It was the first time that Ben-Gurion had taken upon himself such a delicate political mission, on such a high level. The prime minister told them that he would never forget his visit to Palestine. He was referring to his trip of 1922, which Ben-Gurion had worked so hard to organize and at the end of which he wrote that Zionism had gained a friend. The statement of support he requested of MacDonald required negotiation, conducted in a positive atmosphere, and a telephone call to Weizmann. Ben-Gurion was pleased with the result. Then the question arose of how Ben-Gurion would return to Basel. There was no direct flight on Sunday, and they had missed the flight to Paris. The younger MacDonald telephoned his father's office. Downing Street had looked into several options, but they were all too expensive. Sending a plane especially was ruled out due to the concern that it would prompt a provocative parliamentary question. In the end, it was decided that Ben-Gurion would return to Switzerland by train. It was a wonderful idea, but it raised a problem of its own—Ben-Gurion did not have a transit visa allowing him to cross French territory. MacDonald disturbed the weekend repose of the French ambassador to make that arrangement. He accompanied Ben-Gurion to London. Ben-Gurion called him Malcolm.

The story demonstrates the ongoing special relation that British prime ministers had with Zionism, the same combination of awe and fear that produced the Balfour Declaration. Weizmann made an art out of exploiting this phenomenon—almost every door in London continued to be open to him; in the same manner, it went without saying that Ben-Gurion would be invited to breakfast with the prime minister on a day's notice. Ben-Gurion learned from his trip to Chequers that the Zionist movement needed its own airplane.[38]

Before he was able to return to Basel, a telegram arrived there from Tel Aviv. It was from Eliyahu Golomb and it warned that, were the Congress to pass a resolution declaring Zionism's ultimate goal to be a Jewish state, it would set off a new round of Arab terror. The Revisionist resolution was rejected. Jabotinsky climbed on a chair, tore up his accreditation as a delegate, and cast the scraps in the air. Several of his opponents tried to strike him, his supporters defended him, and one of them took Jabotinsky on his shoulders and took him out of the hall. Weizmann was ousted nevertheless.[39]

❖

The routine work that awaited Ben-Gurion when he returned from the Congress was dreary and wearying. The issues that required his involvement offered no challenge; among other things, he had to put considerable time into a school janitors' labor action. More and more people were coming to him with personal problems. He appeared as a prosecutor in the Histadrut's high court, in a proceeding regarding the struggle against the Communists and the employment of Arab workers. By this point, it was already clear that his campaign against the employment of Arab workers had failed, even if it was not his fault. The facts of life were stronger than ideology. "There are Jewish citrus groves that Jewish workers do not set foot in," he complained, offering a long list of Zionist projects that were carried out by Arab workers, among them the Herzl Forest and the laying of the cornerstone of Tel Aviv's first neighborhood.[40]

He looked after his family, which moved into a home in a new workers' neighborhood in north Tel Aviv. It had two floors, and 140 square meters (1,500 square feet) of floor space. For the construction, Ben-Gurion received a mortgage, loans, discounts, and various other considerations, all thanks to the generosity of the Histadrut Executive. The nearby homes also belonged to Histadrut leaders, but they had only one floor.[41]

Some three months after the family moved into its new home, Ben-Gurion recorded a grievance he had heard in one of his conversations with workers. "Histadrut officials receive high salaries," the worker had charged. "You all have houses, and received large advances from Solel Boneh and Kupat Holim." Overseas travel was another bone of contention. "If, instead of going from Paris to London and from London to New York, the leaders would come in a car to see what was going on here, it would be better," said another worker.[42] Ben-Gurion took the bus to the Histadrut offices when he was in Tel Aviv, but that seemed not to be enough. During those months, he recorded much such resentment from the public: "apathy," "negligence," "discrimination," "exploitation," "rot," "failure," "disgrace," and "despair" were just some of the words he heard. It all meant that the Histadrut was no longer on the side of justice, they told him. He also encountered ethical disappointment. In the Histadrut's ten years of existence, they told him, the ideals it had been dedicated to degenerated and disappeared, especially among young people. Ben-Gurion sadly recorded in his diary that, instead of reading books, they played soccer and danced the fox-trot. Workers spent too much money on clothes.[43]

Not only did this cast a pall over the Histadrut's achievements during its first decade; even more so it disheartened Ben-Gurion. His diary is full of disappointment and ennui. Soon thereafter he traveled to Vienna. "I will finally have time to be alone for a few days," he wrote in his diary. That was not correct; Vienna was home to a young woman named Rega Klapholz, whom Ben-Gurion desired to see. He informed her of his arrival and asked to keep it a secret.[44]

"VLADIMIR HITLER"

The Hebrew press in Palestine headlined the rise of the Nazis; there was no doubt that it was a horrifying development. From the start, *Davar* was unequivocally pessimistic. Hitler, the paper asserted the day after the takeover in Berlin, intended "to pull the Jews out by the roots." But these same writers had trouble comprehending and explaining Nazism as a phenomenon—its evil force was of a magnitude they had never encountered before. Likewise, Ben-Gurion's initial reaction was to focus only on the German election. A few days after Hitler came to power, on January 30, 1933, Ben-Gurion opened the Histadrut Convention with a long, data-replete, and optimistic speech. Toward the end he referred to developments in Germany. "The forces of obliteration and destruction are not restricted to a single country," he said. "The emissaries of Hitlerism," he asserted, were also active in the Zionist movement.

He meant the Revisionists.[45] At a public rally in Tel Aviv, he once called his nemesis "Vladimir Hitler."[46]

During those months, Ben-Gurion extricated himself from the dull work of the Histadrut and began preparing himself for what would be his greatest battle to date, for the leadership of the Zionist Organization, which he hoped to win at the next Zionist Congress. He intended to enlist his soldiers from among the masses of Jews who remained in Poland's cities. He seems not to have been aware of the irony; as far as he was concerned it was the natural thing to do. At first he made a preliminary trip to collect information about the mood and the power relations there, and about his chances of winning. It was a kind of self-taught seminar—part journalist, part intelligence agent, he went from political party to political party, from party official to party official, jotting down names and numbers and trying to penetrate the internal politics of every city and town. He found much resentment and petty jealousies; he was unable to unite all the left-wing factions into a single party. His only consolation was that the Revisionists had also split. In September 1933, he returned home, via Vienna, and the following April he went back to Poland. This time, too, he wrote to Rega Klapholz to tell her he was coming. "I'd like," he wrote to her, but did not complete the sentence. Instead of a period, he put down a portentous dash and added: "In Vienna I will tell you what I would like . . ." The mysterious ellipsis appears in the original.[47]

❖

He conducted the election campaign as a military operation in every way. He brought the strategy from home; the tactics he crafted only after he arrived. The first step was to register Polish Jews to vote—that is, to induce them to pay dues, *shekalim*, in exchange for which they would receive membership cards in the Zionist Organization. The assumption was that people who paid their dues through the representatives of a given party would vote for that party in the election. But before that happened, the people who had paid their dues needed to be convinced to go to the polls and vote. That was the second step.

Ben-Gurion headquartered himself in Warsaw in the offices of the

League for Labor Palestine, a coordinating body for the parties of the Zionist leftists in Poland. Soon after his arrival, he summoned an activist from Hehalutz, which had, by Ben-Gurion's estimation, some forty thousand members. Haim Fisch, twenty-five years old, worked in the organization's central office; he apparently had been recommended to Ben-Gurion. Ben-Gurion proposed to him that he coordinate the *shekalim* operation. The next day he asked Fisch what he proposed to do. That was the way Ben-Gurion worked— once he chose an assistant, generally one many years younger than he was, he gave the assistant freedom to accomplish his mission as he thought best. Fisch suggested conducting a survey of Jewish communities, so as to obtain an up-to-date picture of where they were politically; it was exactly what Ben-Gurion had thought to do. He drafted the questionnaire himself. It asked for figures on the local population, the number of Jews, the results of the previous Zionist election, the number of members of each party, and the number of *shekalim* that each party had sold. Respondents were asked to provide the names and addresses of relatives living in Palestine and information about election rallies, the distribution of leaflets, and, most important, a forecast of the outcome.[48]

The members of the staff at Ben-Gurion's headquarters later remembered him as a strict boss with a talent for instilling in them devotion to their mission. He preserved a businesslike distance from them. He generally wore a black overgarment, something between a shirt and jacket, like a Russian commissar's, with a stiff collar in Chinese fashion. Many of his colleagues were skeptical, but he persuaded them that they could win, on condition that the campaign be properly organized. "I believe in power," he said.[49] He used military metaphors, terming the Revisionists a "dangerous enemy" requiring "maximum mobilization of all our forces." These forces would be sent to "the combat front." He also engaged in political espionage. On one occasion he received information from a "more or less reliable" source regarding the Revisionists' bank account. The information indicated that, at the last minute, Jabotinsky's people were liable to distribute membership cards without requiring the payment of dues. At difficult moments he would say, "Our movement is just not organized for war," and once he also warned: "Our members will have rifles without bullets."[50] The questionnaires soon began to come in. Ben-Gurion studied them, eagerly copying out their columns of numbers. "We have business to do in six to seven hundred towns," he remarked, and embarked on his campaign.

❖

During the weeks that followed, he crisscrossed Poland by air, rail, and car. He held three or four events a day, many of them ending in the small hours of the night. His message was dramatic: "This is not an election battle, but a decisive battle for life, a battle for the fate of Zionism and for the Histadrut and pioneering immigration." A labor victory would strengthen the Zionist presence in Palestine, and enable an enlargement of pioneering immigration; defeat would be tantamount to the defeat of Zionism.[51]

But in many cases the message was less important to his audience than was the fact that he had come all the way from Palestine to visit the remotest villages so as to call their inhabitants to war. Everywhere he went, people congregated at the train station to greet him; some came from nearby, even more godforsaken places. Sometimes they came on foot, through rain and mud. He was very obedient, going where he was sent; only once did he rebel: "In the town of Bielsk we can obtain at most two hundred votes. Is it worth going there?"

He always began his speeches on time. He began one event before an almost empty hall. One of his helpers, Baruch Azanya, recalled that Ben-Gurion forbade him to send out invitations with the word "exactly" after the time. "Seven-thirty is seven-thirty exactly, there is no such thing as seven-thirty inexactly," he insisted. He displayed an interest in the makeup of local politics, and addressed people by name. "He had a card file in his head of people who could help him," one of his people later recalled.[52]

It was a work model that had proven itself in the past—direct contact with as many people as possible and close tracking of what was being done in each cell of the political hive he sought to conquer. That was how he had conducted the campaign for the Assembly of Representatives and taken control of the Histadrut. In the next elections to the Assembly (1931) and the Histadrut (1932), Mapai won major victories.[53]

"Sometimes I am overcome by fear," he wrote to Paula. "Everywhere I find young people studying my articles and speeches . . . I never expected that, I never wanted it, never aspired to it . . . I see what a great responsibility lies on me and I am overcome by fear." One member of his staff had a different impression: "After returning from his first rally, he literally sprouted wings," he wrote. "The difference, with him, between a relaxed and a tense mood was always huge . . . When he was tense, he was tense to the limit, and when he was relaxed he was unrecognizable because he was an entirely different person."[54] The small towns filled him with hope; in Warsaw and Łódź he had trouble winning support. "Our situation is very worrisome in the big cities," he wrote, but he still believed in the chance of receiving an absolute majority.[55]

Many urban Jews supported the Revisionists; the campaign was seen as a personal contest between Ben-Gurion and Jabotinsky; it was fierce and violent. Here and there Ben-Gurion's speeches were disrupted, and there were some brawls. In Warsaw, two stink bombs were discovered in a hall in which he was about to speak. During his speech, he called Jabotinsky a "maniac" whose goal in life was to be the dictator of the Zionist Organization. "When I finished that sentence, a heavy object fell at my feet and my pants were covered with yellow dust," he related. "The hall erupted . . . they thought a bomb had been thrown. But it was only a tin can full of sand and dust and bricks. The can was thrown from the balcony by a Betar girl, a young student, and it was aimed at my head and it was good it missed." The girl was arrested and Ben-Gurion went on with his speech. A brawl was under way outside. A few days later, eggs got thrown at him. The campaign provided him with bodyguards, who were told that his life was under threat."[56]

At this point, Ben-Gurion was once again close to collapse, both physical and mental. "I do not know if I will make it safely to Election Day," he wrote two months before the end of the campaign. Some of his traveling was indeed extremely fatiguing. He had trouble sleeping at night and lost his voice at one point. A doctor ordered total silence and Ben-Gurion had to cancel several events. He once went to Płońsk to rest. "I still haven't been at home," he explained. His family was no longer there; perhaps there were some matters that demanded his attention. Whatever the case, he didn't enjoy a respite there. Everyone wanted him to use his influence to obtain immigration certificates for them. Only a few members of the party traveled to Poland to help. Haim Arlosoroff came for two days.[57]

"WE WILL HOLD BACK ON OUR PAIN"

Ben-Gurion arrived in Vilna, the capital of Lithuania, in the evening hours of Saturday, June 17, 1933. An excited throng awaited him at the train station; many of them accompanied him to his hotel. Along the way, they began to ask him if he had already heard the news from Tel Aviv; they had a telegram for him but were uncertain whether to show it. Ben-Gurion understood that something had happened, and then they gave him the message. Arlosoroff had been assassinated. "My world went dark and I collapsed," he wrote to Paula.

When he recovered, they told him that Arlosoroff had gone out for a walk on the Tel Aviv beach the previous night, with his wife. Two young men approached the couple, and one of them shot him. He was rushed to the hospital, where he died. Researchers at the Ben-Gurion Archives put some effort into trying to find out how exactly and when Ben-Gurion learned of the event. The problem is that Ben-Gurion, who recorded so many superfluous details in his diary, was atypically vague in documenting this incident. This raised the question of whether he really fainted—no reference to that can be found in his diary entry of that day. It is not clear at what point he received the cable his party sent from Tel Aviv; it is thus not clear what he knew about it when he cabled his party that Arlosoroff "died at the hands of thugs thirsty for our blood." The word "thugs" hinted at the identity of the murderers—followers of the far-right Abba Ahimeir. The use of the first-person plural, "our blood," underlined the political nature of the murder. Ten days later, Ben-Gurion instructed his people in Tel Aviv to send someone to the library to collect incriminating articles by Ahimeir.[58] Ahimeir and two of his men were charged with the murder. One of them was sentenced to death, but in the end all three were acquitted on appeal. The question of who killed Arlosoroff remained an open wound.

As the head of the Jewish Agency's Political Department, Arlosoroff had been involved in negotiations with the Nazi authorities to allow tens of thousands of Jews to leave Germany and settle in Palestine, and to bring some of their property with them. The Haavara ("transfer") Agreement aroused much opposition, led by Ahimeir's *Hazit Ha'am*, principally on moral-national grounds. The claim was that there should be no negotiations with Hitler's government; the newspaper condemned Ben-Gurion as well as Arlosoroff. Between the lines was the message that both deserved to die.[59] The Vilna police provided a guard for Ben-Gurion, and when he returned to Warsaw, he moved his lodgings because the Revisionists had learned where he was staying.

Arlosoroff's murder naturally raised the question of how Ben-Gurion would be affected. Arlosoroff was considered a rising star. His death may well have removed an obstacle along Ben-Gurion's path to the top of the Zionist movement. The immediate concern was that the murder would lead to a postponement of the elections. At this point, Ben-Gurion's confidence was on the rise; at the beginning of July, he wrote in his diary, "If the elections are held, our victory is certain." He thus told his people not to attribute the murder to the Revisionists. "Jabotinsky wants to use the murder to build himself up, and right now he is succeeding!" he warned. He had earlier regretted accusing "thugs" of the murder. He sent another telegram to Tel Aviv: "We will hold back on our pain, God will avenge!"[60]

He had no clue of who the murderer or murderers were and what the motive had been. In the meantime, he focused on the election campaign.

❖

About two weeks before the election, Ben-Gurion wrote: "For a long time I have not felt such manifold strength in this war that I find myself in, but I believe the battle will be a decisive one and that victory will be ours."[61] He thus considered what needed to be done to "purge" the Zionist movement after the elections. The Revisionists needed to be punished, and the non-Zionists needed to be expelled from the Jewish Agency. The establishment of the Agency, about which he had been so enthusiastic in 1929, had been "a shameful criminal mistake," he now wrote. "We humbled the banner of Zionism and of the popular will." It was, he claimed, "the greatest catastrophe that had ever happened to the Zionist movement." He admitted to being partly responsible for the mistake, but castigated and cursed the non-Zionists in his best style. They were, he said, "a gaggle of presumptuous bourgeois eunuchs who still make themselves out to be the proxies for the people, but they are nothing but miserable and impotent bankrupts." The word "bankrupts" appeared twice, and revealed the real problem. The economic crisis that befell the United States in 1929 made it very difficult for America's wealthy Jews to meet the expectations that the Zionists had of them. Ben-Gurion did not forgive them for terming their money "charity." He treated them as if they carried a plague: "We can cut out this cancerous disease and purify the air around us," he threatened, suggesting that they go to hell.

The results were very good. The labor movement received 42 percent of the vote in Poland, some eighty thousand votes more than they had received in the previous elections. The Revisionists doubled their vote, receiving about fifty-three thousand votes, less than 25 percent of the total. The labor movement became the largest faction in the Congress, but did not enjoy an absolute majority.[62] Ben-Gurion did not vote; he spent Election Day in Płońsk. Two days later, still without the results in hand, he rushed off to Vienna.[63]

"HOW I WOULD LIKE TO"

Rega Klapholz was a medical student. Her father was a Polish-born businessman who opened his house to Zionist activists and visitors from Palestine. Apparently this was the background to his two daughters' decision to attend the 1929 Zionist Congress in Zurich. They mingled among the delegates, asked for autographs, and joined in the Zionist ruckus. A labor movement representative from Vienna introduced them briefly to Ben-Gurion. In 1931, Ben-Gurion visited Vienna, where he renewed the relationship Rega Klapholz.[64] She was twenty-four years old. In August 1932, she wrote to him that she would like them to meet in order to discuss several problems that were preoccupying her. As is customary in German, she addressed him in the third person. Ben-Gurion was in London at the time. He immediately responded, in the familiar second-person singular, that he very much wanted to see her and proposed several options. Perhaps it was childish on his part, he said, but he alone was not to blame for that—she was, too.[65]

Over the next three years he wrote her dozens of letters, first in Yiddish and then in Hebrew, which she had just begun to learn. They evince a paternal friendship that turned in time into a love that was disloyal to Paula and ultimately, as he would find out, impossible to sustain. His initial letters could be taken for a father's letters to his daughter. He wrote to her about his work, about his travel plans, and about how he longed to see her. Whenever he could, he traveled to Vienna to spend several days in her company. He stayed in a hotel.

About a year and a half after they began to correspond, Ben-Gurion sent her the most revealing letter he had written since his youthful correspondence with Shmuel Fuchs. His letters to Paula were never more intimate, and some of those he sent to Rega display more maturity and depth and less emotional blackmail. It was a letter congratulating her on her twenty-sixth birthday. He wished her "valuable work" to which she could devote herself and gain satisfaction from, and "great love," in that order. He philosophized about each wish. He did not know life's purpose and reason, he wrote, nor did he even know if there was purpose and reason to life and the world. "But we ourselves create the purpose of our existence," he wrote, "in the task to which we devote our lives. We set ourselves a goal and the goal grants content and meaning and reason to our lives, and all the good we have in us we put in the service of that goal." It was the most precise formulation so far of his profound identification with the Zionist vision—the national goal and his desire for self-fulfillment were one.

But that fact alone could not provide all that a person needed or complete satisfaction, he continued. He thus wished her "a man who will love you and whom you will love." Love is "a human weakness that nothing should be done to counter," he continued, referring to their own affection. "Dear Rega, I love you, I love you with my entire soul, but I cannot give you anything—the happiness a woman needs, a complete love and total devotion of a loving man—I pray that you will find in your life a man who is right for you."

Briefly he reverted to a paternal stance. "Study and work—never mind! There are difficulties in life, or troubles, there is sorrow and agony, but there is also something to live for, to suffer and to fight for, and there is also love in life, and even if love gives only suffering, it hardly matters." He then waxed romantic again: "I love you—what can I do? I want nothing and I cannot want anything, and it does me good to see you here and there, a bit, and when I am lonely and sad I recall our meetings, I see your face and your steady eyes, so precious to me, and my heart pounds from far away and I miss and yearn and I know, for naught, and I pray for your happiness. Don't worry, the difficult times you are having now will pass and other difficult times will come and good times as well. Your whole life is before you and I love you, my Rega, and I will be happy when I see you are happy, happy in work and with the love you will find in Palestine."

For a moment he had his doubts and he added: "You will not oppose my loving you, will you, Rega? Dear and beloved Rega, I am yours." He scribbled his full name on his initial letters, as he did on endless letters and documents. Then he started to sign DBG, but for this letter he was "David."[66]

That was the high point of the affair. In February 1934, he was still writing: "How I would like to embrace and kiss you now." But five months later, he pronounced himself a "bad boy," and Rega, who would soon be a physician, seemed to metamorphose into his mother, just as Paula the nurse had done. "Such a bad boy," he termed himself, "certainly much more than you think," because he had for so long not answered her letters. It was just like when he abandoned Paula during and after the war, perhaps just as his mother had left him all alone. In that same letter he shared with Rega the pain he felt upon the death of Bialik; the poet had died in Vienna. Ben-Gurion wrote that he had been "stolen from us." The pain he shared with Rega was similar in its force to the pain he had felt on Herzl's death, which he had shared then with Shmuel Fuchs. Just as he sent Fuchs Bialik's "The Scroll of Fire," he suggested to Rega that she devote herself now to his poetry, instead of to the lexicon of Hebrew medical terms he had sent her. He took at least partial comfort in Bialik's death. "Shall we resent the blind and cruel fate that stole Bialik from us?" he asked. "Must we not also thank fate for giving him to us?"[67] If Rega indeed resented him for leaving her, she, too, could have taken similar comfort.

At this point in his life, Ben-Gurion had already lost most of his ability to maintain a modicum of privacy. Apparently quite a few people knew about the affair, just as they knew that other Zionist leaders had cheated on their wives.

Rega and Ben-Gurion once had their picture taken at a café in Vienna. Her sister was also with them. Maybe he was trying to make his relations with her look merely social, the kind that required no secrecy. Maybe he thought there was nothing wrong with the affair. Whatever the case, at some point he crossed the fine line between a calculated risk and recklessness. He tried to deceive Paula, and she caught him in the act. It was a rather operatic scene. He told Paula to come to Warsaw and said he would wait for her there, but in the meantime he went to Vienna to visit Rega. Paula arrived in Warsaw earlier than expected. According to one version of the story, when she discovered that he was not in the hotel where they were to stay together, she swallowed a large quantity of sleeping pills, as if she were trying to kill herself. Ben-Gurion was summoned urgently back to Warsaw and arrived on the first train.[68] His relationship with Rega Klapholz did not last long. She settled in Palestine, working first as a doctor at a kibbutz, Ramat Hakovesh. When she had a crisis there, she appealed to Yosef Baratz, a public figure with some influence, but far less than Ben-Gurion. "Understand that you are my only hope," she wrote to him. "If you don't help me, I am lost." Her letter was part of a long correspondence she conducted with Baratz, at the same time as her relationship with Ben-Gurion.[69]

In July 1933, Ben-Gurion asked Rega to obtain for him Konrad Heiden's history of the Nazi Party. He had been told that it was the best book available on the Nazis, and it could no longer be purchased in Germany. A month later, he took a train that had a stop in Munich. He got off on the platform and bought a copy of Adolf Hitler's *Mein Kampf*.[70]

11

CONVERSATIONS

"TEARS AND HELPLESSNESS"

On one of the first days of spring in 1935, Ben-Gurion set out for "beyond the mountains and desert," as a famous Israeli song puts it, "a place from which no one has yet returned alive." The place was Petra, the remains of a Nabatean city that thrived some twenty-five hundred years ago to the north of the Gulf of Aqaba. Petra's mystery was the stuff of legend: "Great and terrible," as Berl Katznelson, who accompanied Ben-Gurion, recorded in his diary, "an enigma." The trip there from Jerusalem was still arduous and risky at the time. They joined a small convoy of black automobiles, through Transjordan. The wadi in which Petra is located is named after Moses; Ben-Gurion thought he saw water dripping from its rocks. The next evening, they conducted a Pesach Seder there.

Paula also came. A photograph shows her dressed in a button-down sweater, a skirt below the knees, low-heeled shoes, and with a kaffiyeh on her head. Ben-Gurion is standing next to her, in a gray office suit and leather shoes. He wears a kaffiyeh, too.

They look out of place and weary, with smiles that seem forced; most likely they're smiling at the request of the photographer. Some years later, Ben-Gurion recalled standing at the police station at Um Rashrash, a fishing village on the northern tip of the Red Sea, and saying to his friends, "Here we will establish our Eilat." He believed that this was the site of the city of that name mentioned in the biblical stories of King David. He wanted to settle Jews there, as well as in the Negev Desert and in Transjordan.[1] The local hotel treated them like official guests. In the elections of 1933, Ben-Gurion had been elected to the Zionist Executive, a two-headed body consisting of the Jewish Agency in Jerusalem and the Zionist office in London. At the time of his trip to Petra, the labor movement was in an uproar over the most dramatic political maneuver he had accomplished thus far.

❖

The transition from overseeing labor relations in Palestine to the political leadership of the global Zionist movement was a fairly smooth one. His "conquest of Zionism" elevated his standing and prestige within his own movement. He conditioned acceptance of the new post on retaining his post as secretary of the Histadrut, working in the Jewish Agency offices only twice a week, dealing there only with political matters, and receiving, for the first time, a telephone in his home, with an unlisted number.[2] Two years later, he claimed to have resolved to leave the Jewish Agency. "My most profound desires and aspirations, my psychological and human relations, my private and public lives, my real world as a human being, Jew, worker, and man of our era are all connected to the Histadrut, or more precisely to the labor movement." To Geula and Amos he wrote: "Separation from the Histadrut would be for me like leaving the country."

But the other members of the Jewish Agency Executive insisted that he remain and accept leadership of that body. "Comrade Tabenkin sat with me for six hours and brought me to the point of tears and helplessness," Ben-Gurion related. "I saw to my astonishment and apprehension that I may be the only person in the Zionist Organization who has the confidence of all the parties, even of the Revisionist leaders. That terrified me. To bear such responsibility in the Zionist movement is beyond the capacity of any human being, or at least beyond my own." His comrades were stronger than he was. "I never felt such brutal desolation and I could not do anything but give in," he wrote.[3]

Weizmann had returned to the presidency of the Zionist Organization, and the Jewish Agency needed a stronger chairman than Arthur Ruppin, who had run it up to this point. Following Arlosoroff's death, Ben-Gurion was practically the only candidate. "I was soaked with sweat, through my overcoat," he wrote at the end of a four-hour speech he gave, in Yiddish, at that year's Zionist Congress.[4] As his party lacked an absolute majority, he had to bring other parties into the Zionist Executive. Nor could he do as he wished in Mapai. As a statesman at the beginning of his career, his principal occupation was seeking appropriate responses to events over which he had no control—the rise of the Nazis, the Arab Revolt, and the Palestine partition plan.

❖

About a year after Hitler's rise to power, Ben-Gurion said that the German dictator was a danger to the entire Jewish people. As for many people in Europe, Ben-Gurion found the period following the Nazi ascension one of uncertainty and apprehensiveness. Like many other observers, he believed that Hitler was liable to send Europe into war. In his estimation, that would happen within five years. "For us here," he said, "the danger is severe sevenfold, and for us to stand fast when the holocaust comes, we must double our numbers during this period and maximally fortify ourselves internally."[5]

The sense that, in Palestine, Hitler was a sevenfold danger crystallized gradually. As it did, Ben-Gurion increasingly came to see the persecution of the Jews in Europe as part of a war against the Zionist enterprise. In December 1938, he asserted that "Hitler connives to do in Palestine what he is doing in Germany." He claimed that Nazi agents in Palestine were provoking the Arabs. "The homeland is in danger," he warned. "Zionism is in danger."[6] It was this intuition that led him to assert, as early as 1934, that if the Jewish population of Palestine did not double, to half a million, the country's Jews were liable to be "wiped out."[7]

Ben-Gurion belonged to a generation that had internalized the atrocities of the Kishinev pogrom of 1903. In his memoirs he quoted a sentence he had heard from Bialik in 1927: "Diaspora Judaism is rolling down into an abyss and perhaps only a few will survive."[8] That was the way he felt throughout his life, and as such he saw the rise of the Nazis as one more link in a long chain of historical catastrophes that had befallen the Jews. But millennia of survival and renewal also sustained the Jewish faith in the Messianic age and redemption. As a consequence, Ben-Gurion believed that the worse the plight of world Jewry became, the greater the chances that the Zionist project in Palestine would succeed. "Hitler gave the boost," he declared. "The issue of German Jewry can without a doubt serve as a huge political and economic boost for the Zionist enterprise." He spoke in such terms even before the rise of the Nazis; he would continue to do so in the months that followed.[9]

"MESSIANIC ERA"

Hitler's boost worked very well. More than thirty-five thousand Jews settled in Palestine in 1933, about three times as many as the previous year. In 1934 more than forty-five thousand came, and more than sixty-five thousand arrived in 1935, in a wave of immigration that came to be called the Fifth Aliyah. "I see these times as the 'messianic era,' not at all in the mystical, religious sense but in the very realistic and actual sense," Ben-Gurion wrote. "The Jewish people is being annihilated and strangled . . . This enormous persecution, which now weighs on Diaspora Jewry, is sending an abundance of opportunities to Palestine, of a kind unknown ever before. I see no obstacle to the mass immigration of tens and hundreds of thousands in the years to come."[10]

The wave of newcomers was made possible largely thanks to the Haavara Agreement between the Nazi regime and the Zionist movement in Germany, facilitated by Haim Arlosoroff. It proved, after the Holocaust, to have been the most significant rescue operation initiated by the Zionist movement. The agreement was beneficial to both sides. Germany rid itself of unwanted Jews and the Zionists received immigrants who arrived with some of their belongings, money, and professional skills. Theodor Herzl had suggested something of the sort in his book *The Jewish State*.[11]

The Haavara arrangements revived a controversy that had played a central role in the Zionist elections of 1933. Jabotinsky and his followers, as well as other circles in the Jewish world, demanded an economic and political boycott of Germany aimed at toppling Hitler's regime. The Revisionist newspaper *Hayarden* accused Jewish Agency officials of being degenerates acting as Hitler's agents.[12] Ben-Gurion defended the agreement in his usual way. "What's wrong with you, have you lost your minds?" he exclaimed. "We want Hitler to be destroyed, but as long as he lives, we have an interest in exploiting him for the benefit of the country."[13]

The Jewish Agency also had to grapple with a fantasy promoted by Jabotinsky, according to which a million and a half Jews would be sent to Palestine from Poland over a fifteen-year period. The Revisionists touted what they called the Evacuation Plan as an alternative to contacts with the Germans. With its fifteen-year horizon, it demonstrated just how far removed Jabotinsky was from a realistic assessment of the clear and present danger faced by the Jews of Europe. In fact, some Revisionists also had contacts with the Nazis, and Ben-Gurion himself continued to dream about extricating millions of Jews from Europe, "at least eight million," he once said.[14]

In the meantime, tens of thousands of Jewish refugees from Europe saved themselves by coming to Palestine. The Zionist movement wanted to speed up the rate of their arrival. Ben-Gurion told the British high commissioner about the still mostly economic plight of the Jews in Poland and the potential danger facing them in case of war, which he had seen with his own eyes, and stressed to him that "the only hope is Palestine."[15] As chairman of the Jewish Agency, Ben-Gurion announced the establishment of a committee on German Jewry. There was not much more he could do. "The debate over this is entirely theoretical, because we are helpless," he had said in 1935. From that point on, this was the story's central motif.[16]

"THE CHILDREN WILL BE BORN IN THIS COUNTRY"

For the most part, the Fifth Aliyah stayed within the basic rules of the game that the Mandate authorities and the Zionist movement had agreed on. The worsening plight of the Jews in Germany and Eastern Europe did not change the fundamental principle that Jews would be allowed to settle in Palestine in keeping with the country's economic capacity to absorb them. The immigration certificates allotted by the British did not meet the demand, and it was thus necessary to make difficult and cruel choices among those who were, as Ben-Gurion put it, "bursting to immigrate." The upshot was that it felt as if every Jew who received a certificate would live at the expense of another Jew who would not be rescued. He personally took part in some of these "selection" proceedings, as they were called. Eight months after the Nazis came to power, he again asserted that "Palestine today needs not just any immigrants but pioneers, and the difference between them is clear—the immigrant comes to take from the country, while the pioneer comes to give to the country." His views on this issue were well formed and solid.[17] He would choose young people, not old, he said. As in the past, neither would he give preference to children. "The children will be born in this country," he reiterated.[18] As in the days of the kiosk proprietors of the Fourth Aliyah, Ben-Gurion griped that too many immigrants were settling in the cities. "We cannot place all the Jews of Germany and Poland in high-rises built in Tel Aviv," he said.[19]

None of this differed from the principles that had guided the Jewish Agency's immigration policy prior to the Nazi threat.[20] The officials who handled immigration complained from time to time about "bad human material" or useless immigrants who had managed to evade the selection process.*

Three years after the Nazi ascension, the Histadrut established, along with the Tel Aviv municipality and others, a special fund to pay the cost of sending back to Europe immigrants "who had become a burden on the public and its social institutions," including the incurably ill. By the end of December 1936,

---

* The violinist Bronisław Huberman persuaded Arturo Toscanini to conduct the inaugural concert of the Palestine Symphony Orchestra, but had trouble obtaining immigration certificates for its fifty-three musicians, among them a dozen from Poland and thirty from Germany. A letter from Huberman to Ben-Gurion had no effect, so the famed violinist complained to Weizmann. In the end, the high commissioner provided the immigration certificates for the players, going beyond the quota given to the Jewish Agency. (Bronisław Huberman to Ben-Gurion, April 3, 1936, and Bronisław Huberman to Chaim Weizmann, July 22, 1936, Felicja Blumental Archives; Toeplitz 1992, p. 20ff.)

the fund had overseen the return of several dozen such people. The tendency to see European Jews as the "human material" needed for the establishment of a state was common wisdom in the labor movement, and thus hardly unique to Ben-Gurion. Katznelson also supported "selection of human material." As chairman of the Jewish Agency Executive, Ben-Gurion led this policy.[21]

But as the persecution of Europe's Jews worsened, Ben-Gurion came to worry that the inability to save them would deprive Zionism of its major historical justification. It was in this context that he waged a fierce battle against an initiative to enable Germany's Jews to save themselves outside Palestine. The Jews of the United States and England set up a Rescue Committee, but Ben-Gurion saw it as competing with the Zionist enterprise. "The German-Jewish question is a historical test case of Zionism," he maintained. "Whatever it be—victory or failure—it will be decisive."[22] The danger increased as oppression grew worse. "In normal years, immigration needs Zionism," he remarked. "Now Zionism needs immigration, or more precisely, it depends on immigration." Because if Palestine could not take in a "fair quantity" of refugees, it would lose the support of the Zionists themselves. "When tens and hundreds of thousands of Jews are being finished off and crushed in detention camps, even Zionists will not respond to the needs of Palestine," he said, meaning that it would be harder to raise money overseas.[23] The need to buttress the Zionist project, in the face of the Nazi threat as well, was one of the motives that led Ben-Gurion to reconcile with his greatest opponent.

"THE IRON WALL"

In the months following Arlosoroff's murder, hostility between the Revisionists and the labor movement intensified and the level of violence between them reached new heights. The Histadrut continued to deny jobs to Revisionists, and the Zionist Executive did not give them immigration certificates. The Revisionists established a rival labor union and tried to obtain immigration certificates of their own, directly from the British authorities.[24]

The violence on both sides helped the two movements distinguish themselves from each other, but it was in danger of going out of control, so their leaders sought to rein it in. The rise of the Nazis also strengthened the feeling that a moratorium and negotiation were needed. About a year before Ben-Gurion, Jabotinsky had written that if Hitler's regime remained in power, all of world Jewry would be doomed to destruction.[25] Ben-Gurion wanted the Revisionists to remain in the Zionist movement and place themselves under his authority, just as he wanted the Haredim in the Assembly of Representatives and Hapo'el Hatza'ir in Mapai. As the battle to "conquer Zionism" intensified, he evinced the generosity of the conqueror and commenced talks with Revisionist representatives in London.[26]

One day, in October 1934, he received a call from Pinhas Rutenberg, the colorful revolutionary whom Ben-Gurion knew from his period of exile in the United States. At the time of the call, both of them were in London. Rutenberg had in the meantime become a wealthy entrepreneur and considered himself to be the responsible adult of Zionist politics. He asked if Ben-Gurion would be willing to meet Jabotinsky face-to-face. Ben-Gurion agreed, on condition that Rutenberg issue the invitations to both of them.[27] As befits his journalistic vocation, Ben-Gurion set down a colorful account of the entire affair. One night, soon after midnight, he is sitting in a train on the northern line of London's Tube. He gets off at the third stop, Tottenham Court, with a feeling of relief that no one recognizes him or the passenger sitting next to him. For a moment he allows himself to imagine the scandal that would break out if a journalist were to chance on them and see them talking to each other, for his travel companion is Jabotinsky. The two rival leaders, each of whom had likened the other to Hitler, have spent the previous six hours in Rutenberg's lodgings, and are now heading home together. Before Ben-Gurion gets off the train, they agree to meet again the next day.[28] In the weeks that followed, they saw each other about a dozen times, sometimes in the apartment of a friend of Jabotinsky's in Golders Green, and sometimes in the offices of the Zionist Executive at Russell Square. They reached two points of agreement and began to work on a third.

It was a real earthquake, but in retrospect, the dialogue between them seems quite plausible. Ben-Gurion spent most of his time in Palestine and had played a larger role than Jabotinsky in the Zionist enterprise, among other things as secretary of the Histadrut. This had required great patience given that, as Weizmann had put it, achieving Zionism's goals was a matter of "adding one village to another, building home after home, purchasing one piece of land after the other, raising a goat and then another goat."[29] Politics was his sole occupation, one he lived at every hour and every moment. Jabotinsky, alongside his political work, had pursued a journalistic and literary career. From his perch at the head of the opposition, he argued that everything was happening too slowly, without momentum. But the chasm that separated them was largely a personal and political one; it was not hard to bridge it ideologically. Both of them were fervent Zionists and sought to establish a Jewish state in Palestine—that was a fundamental point of agreement. Both realized that most Jews were not Zionists and did not want to live in Palestine, which gave grounds for an alliance.

Each drew his view of the world from a different ideological source, but the differences between them were mostly tactical, sometimes strategic. The common ground was enough to make up for the differences. The state they sought to found was to extend over the entire territory of the Land of Israel, including Transjordan. "Our final goal—the Jewish people's independence in Palestine on both sides of the Jordan, not as a minority, but as a polity of many millions," Ben-Gurion said; three years earlier, he had heard these words from Jabotinsky.[30] Both of them believed in the "conquest of labor." Ben-Gurion was still living in Płońsk when Jabotinsky wrote that, first of all, the Arab workers must be "pushed out of the Hebrew colonies." Like Ben-Gurion, he viewed Jewish workers as the "kernel of the nation," and compared them to soldiers.[31]

And both of them believed that the Arabs would not agree, of their own volition, to compromise with the Zionists, and assumed that the Jewish state could survive only if it were strong and fortified enough that it could not be destroyed. Ben-Gurion said as much in 1919. Jabotinsky voiced the same thesis in a famous article he first published in 1923, entitled "The Iron Wall." Six years later, Ben-Gurion adopted this term, declaring that each city and town should be surrounded with an "iron wall" of labor settlements.[32] Both of them promised to respect the civil rights of the Arab minority in the Jewish state. Both believed that Zionism's future depended on Britain; both of them admired the English and their culture.

Jabotinsky was not a fascist any more than Ben-Gurion was a Marxist. Ben-Gurion was no less nationalist or militarist than Jabotinsky. The right-left divide in the Zionist movement was largely a matter of style and modes of operation, not of fundamental values. In the large picture, it was a fight over power more than it was over ideas. Jabotinsky identified with liberal democratic ideas, and the free market, but did not reject state-sponsored development and settlement projects; Ben-Gurion called himself a socialist but did not reject private enterprise. He was really a social democrat. Jabotinsky's movement attracted many workers, and many members of the middle class supported Ben-Gurion.

When he was not calling him a Nazi or an underworld criminal, Ben-Gurion tended to dismiss Jabotinsky. His Zionism, he said, was a "Zionism of words," centered on demagogy and national symbols. But Ben-Gurion spoke no less and wrote no less than Jabotinsky; he was no less appreciative of the importance of national symbols and the significance of words. They had a common language—in London they conversed in Hebrew.

The sense that they were together promoting the national interest brought them closer. In less than three weeks, Ben-Gurion was calling Jabotinsky a "friend," which Jabotinsky emotionally thanked him for. They spent many hours together. "The rapport and mutual cordiality surprises both of us," Jabotinsky wrote as their conversations were in progress. Their time together in Golders Green reminded him of his student days in Italy. Ben-Gurion made him an omelet, he related, and joked that when his party learned about that he would be lynched.[33] At one point, the two spoke of the possibility of a new Zionist Organization leadership, a triumvirate composed of the two of them and Rutenberg.[34]

"WHAT'S ALL THE EXCITEMENT ABOUT?"

The talks were not easy, but they were largely dispassionate. They led to a mutual commitment to refrain from violence and incitement, observing "Zionist morals and social decorum." Among other things, each promised not to turn members of the rival group over to the British authorities. Ben-Gurion consented to recognize the Revisionist labor union, while Jabotinsky recognized the right to strike. Their third agreement, on relations between the Revisionists and the Zionist Organization, was meant to require the Revisionists to accept the authority of the Zionist Congress; the Revisionists would receive a portion of the immigration certificates that the British issued to the Jewish Agency. Ben-Gurion acknowledged that withholding immigration certificates was a "heavy weapon" and that his movement had gone too far in denying them to the Revisionists. The issue remained open, however, because the storm set off by the first two agreements prevented the signing of the third.

Ben-Gurion knew that the agreements he had signed, under great secrecy and without his party's sanction, were likely to encounter opposition. He thus should have promoted the sudden peace with Jabotinsky with a great deal of sensitivity and political caution, but that is not what he did. The agreements landed on Mapai before any preparatory work had been done. It was a serious error. Katznelson heard of the talks only shortly before they were made public; he warned Ben-Gurion not to commit himself to anything and to return to Tel Aviv forthwith. Ben-Gurion was taken by surprise. "What's all the excitement about?" he asked when he returned.[35]

The opponents of the agreement peppered him with angry telegrams; Amos and Geula also demanded an explanation. Amos received an exposition that stressed, for the most part, the need to put an end to the internecine violence. He commended Amos for his sudden interest in politics; in fact, he suspected that someone in the party had dictated his son's letter.[36]

❖

Amos was fifteen years old. It was not easy to be Ben-Gurion's son; his children were not high on his list of priorities. His letters to Amos have a stilted feel to them. Most included abstruse reports of his meetings and work; they often had a reproachful tone. "If you want a child not to grab a burning ember, you need to let him grab an ember once," he said. "He'll get burned and learn that you shouldn't grab embers."[37] Amos was a problem at school, but when he was older, he could not recall his father ever going to meet his teachers. Only on one occasion did the father summon the son into his library on their home's second floor to discuss his performance. Amos was not often admitted to that sanctum. Half a century later, he could still remember the awe he felt and how his knees knocked. Friends of the family related that Ben-Gurion repeatedly asked his son how old he was and what grade he was in.[38]

Geula was sixteen. She, too, saw her father only rarely; Paula told her not to disturb him. Many years later, Geula claimed that her mother had kept her away from her father out of jealousy and because she wanted him for herself. That was also the impression received by Amos's wife, Mary—she related that Paula kept him away from his children. "I think she was envious of them," Mary said, adding that he really did not understand his children. She believed that he was ashamed of them.[39] His letters to his youngest daughter, "Renanele," as he called her, were paternal and warm; she was the only one of the children he called by a pet name.[40] Many years later, Renana Leshem Ben-Gurion described her father as a family man who always washed the dishes and loved to take walks with Boxer, the dog. "I remember that he used to wash my hair and feed me when I was little. I remember that he hugged, kissed, he was very much a warm father." She did not like it when he read Plato to her and the other children, but liked when he told stories. Of the three of them, she was the most talented.[41] At the time of the talks with Jabotinsky, Paula was in London.

❖

Opposition to the agreements with the Revisionists gathered steam, especially among the Histadrut's local chapters and in left-wing circles. The only way to back out of the agreements was to put them up for a vote by the Histadrut membership. Katznelson overcame his initial opposition and lent them his support. But some fifteen thousand of the twenty-five thousand who voted said no. It was a humiliating defeat for Ben-Gurion; he swallowed it and traveled to Petra with Katznelson.

Jabotinsky also encountered resistance in his camp. His ability and willingness to engage in talks with the person who had compared him to Hitler astonished his followers, and one of the youngest of them demanded that he explain how he could have shaken the hand of a person who had slandered him in such a horrible way. The young member's name was Menachem Begin. Jabotinsky responded that he had kept in mind Ben-Gurion's service in the Jewish Legion.[42]

A few months later, Jabotinsky founded the New Zionist Organization. Ben-Gurion reverted to seeing him as an enemy. "As I know him," he wrote, "he will ally himself with every adversary and enemy as long as . . . it will help him destroy the Zionist Organization." But he did not regret his agreements with Jabotinsky and did not admit to making any mistake in promoting them.[43] The Revisionists renewed their fight against any contact between the Zionist movement and the Nazis; Ben-Gurion maintained the ban on granting immigration certificates to Revisionists. "There is a Jewish Nazi Party," he declared.[44]

"THERE'S NO ADDRESS"

On April 19, 1936, Arabs attacked Jewish homes in Jaffa and on its border with Tel Aviv. Nine Jews were murdered and dozens injured. Ben-Gurion went to visit the wounded and then to the common funeral. He said that it was clear to him on that day that the decisive battle for Palestine had begun.[45] The Arab Revolt was under way.

Four weeks later, Ben-Gurion sat in his office in Jerusalem, working along with several of his people; it was Saturday night. As the chairman of the Jewish Agency, his position was equivalent to prime minister. The documents produced by his office address the great variety of issues that required his attention, from the tribulations of Ha'ohel Theater to those of Zionism in India. But most of his mental and physical energy went into politics and statecraft. That evening he and his staff composed a letter to the high commissioner.

Soon after nine in the evening, a member of the Haganah appeared and reported an attack in which three Jews had been killed. The victims had been on their way out of the Edison movie theater, a short walk from the Jewish Agency offices, after seeing a Russian movie entitled *Song of Happiness*. Two of them were in their twenties, the third was thirty years old. All—a doctor, baker, and student—had recently arrived from Poland. One left a pregnant wife, one had married six months previously, and the third was waiting for the arrival of his girlfriend from Poland. The gunman fled; he was reported to be an Arab, also in his twenties. The Haganah officer asked Ben-Gurion to approve a reprisal. He refused and demanded restraint. The officer continued to argue with Ben-Gurion into the night, and when Ben-Gurion had used up all his arguments, he threatened to resign. Only then, just before midnight, did the Haganah accept his decision.[46] The incident brought home the limits of his power during that period—his authority was acknowledged, but it was not beyond challenge.

The Haganah was still weak, and its small size was much criticized. Ben-Gurion was well aware of that. When he eulogized the Jaffa dead, he said that they were "the victims of an error." He explained: "We did not see to it that we would have sufficient force . . . We are all to blame for their loss, the entire Jewish people." In fact, it was not an error, but rather a continuation of the same failure that had been on display in 1929. During the seven intervening years, it would have been possible to establish "an entire army," as a member of the Revisionist opposition said. The lessons of 1929 had only been learned in part, and very slowly. With the Arab Revolt, the Haganah was once again taken by surprise, and found it insufficiently prepared. As the head of the Jewish Agency, Ben-Gurion bore ministerial responsibility for the Haganah. He did not suffice with saying that "we are all to blame." He also said the equivalent of "I told you so." The murders in Jaffa had been possible, he claimed, because Jews and Arabs continued to live among each other, and because Jews continued to employ Arab laborers. But at the end of the year, he received a status report on the Haganah: "There is no military spirit, there is no plan, and there is no thinking toward bad times, and in particular the outbreak of war."[47]

❖

Arab terror swelled and waned and became a part of life. Some of the attacks were directed against Jewish farmers, some of whom worked land that had previously been tilled by Arab tenant farmers.[48] The Arab national movement was led by the mufti of Jerusalem, Hajj Amin al-Hussayni. In 1935, a charismatic religious leader, Sheikh Izz a-Din al-Qassam, of Haifa, had led a band of fighters. His death in battle granted the movement a heroic myth. "It's a kind of Arab Tel Hai," Ben-Gurion said. "A way of educating Arab youth to sacrifice themselves."[49] The fact that most Arab attacks in the 1930s were directed against the British bolstered his view that the Arab Revolt was the product of an organized and disciplined national public acting with political maturity, dedication, idealism, and death-defying bravery. They were, he argued, "national liberation fighters facing off against a foreign government." This was tantamount to almost entirely abandoning the theory that the Jewish-Arab conflict grew out of the economic disparities between the two peoples. He also ceased to ascribe Arab terror to the inborn homicidal nature of its perpetrators. Were he a politically and nationally aware Arab, he would also enlist in the fight, he said.[50]

At this point, it was no longer possible for the Arabs to obliterate the national infrastructure that the Zionist movement had put into place; in the five preceding years, some two hundred thousand Jews had settled in Palestine. They doubled the number of Jews, making them 30 percent of the country's population.[51] For the Arabs, the revolt came too late, Ben-Gurion said. But, for the Jews, he continued, it came too early—they were still a minority in the country and not strong enough to defend themselves on their own. By the end of the year, the number of Jewish dead had risen to eighty. In the meantime, Ben-Gurion initiated a series of conversations with Arab leaders.[52]

❖

Musa al-Alami was a graduate of Cambridge, a Muslim jurist, and a senior official in the Mandate administration's public prosecutor's office. From one of Jerusalem's wealthiest families, he was not a popular leader, but he had close relations with both Mufti al-Hussayni and High Commissioner Sir Arthur Grenfell Wauchope. On a summer day in 1934, Alami hosted Ben-Gurion in his home in Sharafat, a small village to the south of Jerusalem. They sat in the shade of a magnificent oak; Alami told Ben-Gurion that there was no older tree of its kind in Palestine. It was not the first time they had met. The contacts had begun a few weeks earlier in Jerusalem, in the home of Moshe Sharett; as Arlosoroff's successor as head of the Jewish Agency's Political Department, Sharett devoted much of his time to relations with the Arabs.

Ben-Gurion presented Alami with an enhanced version of the program he had formulated a few years previously. It was based on two central ideas: Jewish and Arab participation in government on a temporary basis of equality (what Ben-Gurion termed "parity"), and the establishment of a regional federation of which Palestine would be a part. The Jews would eventually become a majority in Palestine and the Arabs a minority, but the federative link with neighboring states would grant them a regional majority. Alami agreed to convey Ben-Gurion's proposal to the mufti and suggested that the two might meet. According to Ben-Gurion, Alami later told him that the mufti had seen the idea as a "bombshell." He had not imagined that there were Jews who sincerely wanted to reach accommodation with the Arabs. Ben-Gurion continued to meet with Alami, as well as George Antonius, a Palestinian Christian theorist of Arab nationalism, also a Cambridge man. Both made good impressions on Ben-Gurion. Other Arabs made negative ones. Another participant in some of these meetings was Judah Leon Magnes, who was a Brit Shalom sympathizer. The talks went nowhere, confirming what Ben-Gurion had thought in advance. "Never in history has there been, nor I think will there be in history, a case of a nation giving up its land of its own volition," he said again. In an almost ritualistic way, nevertheless, it was important for him to stress that this opposition between the two nations was not "absolute and eternal." It would come to an end, he maintained, when the Arabs "despaired" of the possibility of getting rid of the Jews.[53]

❖

The Arab figures he met aroused his curiosity. He had not met many Arabs previously and had not been involved in diplomatic contacts with them. His interest had, as it so often did, a journalistic cast, as if he knew that someday he would write a book about these talks. His conversations with Alami produced a story: as usual he promised Alami that the Zionists had come to develop Palestine for all its inhabitants. In Ben-Gurion's telling, Alami responded that he preferred to leave the land poor and desolate for another century, until the Arabs could develop it themselves. Ben-Gurion told that story over and over in the years that followed, until his final days.

The story does not appear in the detailed notes that he put down on paper some six weeks after his first meeting with Alami, nor can it be found in the forty-one-page report that Ben-Gurion composed in April 1936. In 1941, he referred to a similar response from an unnamed Arab. Apparently, over the years, Ben-Gurion amplified Alami's response into a seminal experience of his life, much as he had when his Arab fellow student had said he was delighted that Ben-Gurion had been expelled from Palestine. The two stories were meant to provide that there was no basis for an agreement with the Arabs or, as he once said, "there's no address." In other words, no partner. He never met the mufti.*[54]

The Arab Revolt caused the Jewish Agency and the Mandate Administration to close ranks and to cooperate in suppressing the uprising. The British did so with a heavy hand, just as they did in some of their colonies; it included the wrecking of homes, the use of torture in interrogations, and targeted killings. Ben-Gurion viewed this cooperation as a cornerstone of the national home, and when one of his Arab interlocutors asked him whether there was any chance of pursuing a common struggle against the occupying power, he responded that the Jews would never fight the British and immediately reported the remark to the high commissioner.

Wauchope was the first high commissioner to recognize Ben-Gurion as the leader of Palestine's Jews. "He is the best high commissioner we have had," Ben-Gurion wrote, and Wauchope himself said that he had never felt that the Jews were more secure than under his own administration. They met frequently. Ben-Gurion called him "the old man." The Jewish Agency derived its authority from the Mandate, and its ability to function depended largely on cooperation with the British administration.[55] The British did not only assist the "state-in-the-making"; as Arab terror increased, they also lent a hand to the establishment of an "army-in-the-making." The words "Jewish army" can be found in Ben-Gurion's diary in 1936. Two years later, he told his party: "Over this period we have made gains in our defense system that it would have been hard to even dream of."[56]

❖

The Haganah National Command, founded in the wake of the 1929 riots, was still in the nature of an executive committee with members appointed on a political rather than a professional basis. It operated with the sanction of

---

* Alami's biographer quoted this story from Ben-Gurion's memoirs, without comment. Many years later, Alami said that he thought that Ben-Gurion and the mufti were much alike—neither of them concealed their national intentions. In a conversation with a Jewish friend, he courteously remarked that regretfully the Arabs had not produced their own Ben-Gurion. (Elath 1958, p. 22; Furlonge 1969, p. 231.)

the Jewish Agency Political Department, headed first by Arlosoroff and then by Sharett. At the time, Ben-Gurion did not do much in this area. Eventually, the Haganah became a mass organization, its hundreds of members becoming thousands. Many of them were trained in special courses, in which they learned, among other things, to operate on a coordinated regional basis rather than defend each settlement alone. Communications, intelligence, and medical services were developed gradually. Haganah emissaries in Europe purchased arms and military equipment and smuggled them into Palestine. Here and there small plants opened, producing bombs and grenades. At this point, finally, the Haganah also began to employ quartermasters and logistical personnel. But none of this was sufficient.[57] "There is need for immediate action, with the help of Wise," Ben-Gurion wrote in 1935, and he set off for the United States.

❖

Rabbi Stephen Wise was a Budapest-born attorney and Reform rabbi; he served as president of the Zionist Organization of America. Ben-Gurion was hoping he would help raise $100,000 to boost the Haganah's activities, by which he meant, as he wrote in his diary, "special operations." He also toyed with the hope of meeting President Franklin Roosevelt. This time, too, America raised his spirits. "As magical a sight I have never seen in my life," he wrote upon landing in Chicago after a night flight from New York. "Fiery squares . . . rectangles and diagonals and lit-up towers . . . they seem to have been taken out of some imaginary legend and magical song."*[58] Justice Louis Brandeis, almost eighty years old, remembered him, and again gave him sage advice, promising $25,000 to fund settlement in the Negev and on the Gulf of Aqaba. He then agreed that the money could be used for "other purposes." Someone gave Ben-Gurion $10,000 "for the Histadrut," but the hope for $100,000 did not materialize. Most American Zionists did not have a lot of money and most wealthy Jews were not Zionists; their priority at the time

---

* The jurist Felix Frankfurter advised him to give up all hope of being received at the White House. "Washington is deep in its own troubles," he told Ben-Gurion. (Ben-Gurion, Diary, June 1, 1935, Sept. 6, 1936, May 17, 1937, BGA.)

was to aid German Jewry. "It is a criminal, idiotic, and cowardly position," Ben-Gurion responded. He called them "sacks of gold."[59]

He managed to raise some money in London as well, but the shadowy term "special operations" did not always make the hoped-for impression. James de Rothschild gave him only a thousand pounds. Ben-Gurion disparaged him: "This Jimmy is cowardly, foolish, and resentful," he wrote. He claimed that Rothschild was opposed in principle to establishing a Jewish army.[60] At that stage, this fund-raising was Ben-Gurion's principal form of involvement in the Haganah.[61]

❖

As Arab resistance and terror increased, the British became fed up with Palestine. The worse the situation grew, the more they realized that the country had become a burden that they no longer had a good reason to bear. They began to seek a way out. Wauchope tried to form a Jewish-Arab legislative assembly, without success. No one wanted it. Both Jews and Arabs sought victory, not compromise.[62] Then the British did what they had done on more than one occasion throughout their empire—they sent a royal commission of inquiry. Ben-Gurion spent a lot of time in London. It was a difficult period in his life. "I have spent months in nervous distress like none I have ever known and which I do not have the ability to express in any way," he wrote. "I am frantic, as I sense that we stand on the verge of events that are liable to change the course of our history, events of a sort that have taken place only two or three times throughout our three millennia."[63] He made friends with a young woman named Doris May; Chaim Weizmann was getting on his nerves.

"AS IF MY NERVES HAD GONE TO PIECES"

During most of his time in London, Ben-Gurion tried to gain access to decision makers and other people of influence. There was something pathetic about it—to the extent that leading Londoners had any interest in Palestine, they preferred to speak with Weizmann and only with him. Weizmann, who had been reelected president of the Zionist Organization in 1935, was not excited about Ben-Gurion's arrival and viewed his activity as superfluous. When he managed to arrange a working dinner with the leaders of the parliamentary parties, Winston Churchill among them, he did not invite Ben-Gurion. Churchill heaped praises on Weizmann at the dinner, and Weizmann made a point of telling Ben-Gurion about it. He also revealed that Churchill had gotten stone drunk. Ben-Gurion had to find his way through official London almost entirely on his own.[64]

He had a certain advantage in Labour circles; when Malcolm MacDonald served as colonial secretary, his door was always open. Ben-Gurion looked down on him. "The guy is thirty-seven and still a bachelor," he wrote to his children. "I am doubtful whether he would have reached the rank of minister were he not the prime minister's son."[65] MacDonald really wanted to help, Ben-Gurion believed, but the problem was that he was weak—the high commissioner told him what to do, instead of the opposite.[66] In the spirit of socialist fraternalism, MacDonald seems also to have seen Ben-Gurion at his actual size, as an influential politician who was still gaining support, but not the leader of the Jewish people. That was Weizmann.

❖

One day, in June 1936, Ben-Gurion drove with Weizmann and his wife, Vera, to Churt, a village an hour and a half from London and the home of David Lloyd George. They wanted to prepare him for a coming parliamentary debate on Palestine. His hair had gone totally white, his face was full of life, and his eyes were young and warm, Ben-Gurion related; Lloyd George received them with great affability. He was seventy-three years old and full of Zionist spunk—he was astounded that British officials in Palestine did not understand that the situation would be much worse if the country fell into the hands of the Muslims. They are all anti-Semites, he said, asking if the Jews had sufficient arms to defend themselves. In any case, he declared, more army units should be sent. He knew that the Arabs were apprehensive that Palestine would become a Hebrew state, and said they were right—it will. He paused for a beat and then repeated, stressing the words: it will. They then spoke about the Bible and the geography of Palestine. He told them that he had known the names of the rivers, valleys, and mountains of Palestine before he knew a single geographical name in his own country.[67] There was no more enthusiastic supporter of Zionism in the entire British Empire, and Ben-Gurion delighted in the touch of history, but that day he was "terrified," because Weizmann raised the possibility that the Zionist movement would consent to a temporary suspension of immigration, as a goodwill gesture while the royal commission did its work. "This thing came down on me like an ax blow," Ben-Gurion said to the members of his party. He told Weizmann that he was "depressed and in despair" because of the idea. Weizmann responded coldly that a person had no control over his feelings. Ben-Gurion was not reassured, and through the weeks that followed agonized almost to the point of losing control of himself.[68]

Weizmann met—on his own—with Colonial Secretary William Ormsby-Gore, and then took Ben-Gurion with him for another meeting. The secretary proposed that the Zionist movement indeed not oppose a partial suspension of immigration, for the duration of the commission's work, and according to Ben-Gurion, Weizmann remained silent, which Ormsby-Gore took as consent. "I left there shattered, miserable, and depressed in a way I maybe never have been before," Ben-Gurion wrote to Sharett. "Chaim failed us in this battle." These words reflected his mood, not Weizmann's position.

According to a record of the conversation that Ben-Gurion himself made, Weizmann threatened the colonial secretary that if immigration were suspended, he and Ben-Gurion would boycott the royal commission. At Ben-Gurion's insistence, Weizmann also wrote a letter to the secretary clarifying that he had not agreed to a suspension, but Ben-Gurion's mood remained tumultuous. Three days later, he flew to Palestine for a four-day visit, an exceptional and dramatic gesture in those days; he came to salve his mental distress, he told members of his party.[69]

He brought a disturbing piece of news—suspension of immigration was expected to be announced in a week's time, and there was practically no way to prevent it. He blamed it on Weizmann. "He is an utterly dangerous person for Zionism," he declared, and shared his doubts with his party. "We are in a miserable situation, facing a war of life and death, and there cannot now be any commander other than Weizmann, but he can give us away out of irresponsibility and misunderstanding."[70]

❖

His four days in Palestine were extremely busy, and included a conversation with Wauchope. The high commissioner said that he opposed a suspension of immigration; that was a good sign. The British police inducted eighteen hundred Jewish men, a move that made the Jewish community feel more secure. Ben-Gurion said there was "the feeling of a Jewish state." Before his return to London, he visited the construction site for the Tel Aviv port. "Our boys, with tanned skin, work half-naked in the sea," he marveled, and he was suddenly overcome by great happiness. He had trouble remembering a time when he had ever been happier. "The sight of the pier is enough to raise my spirits and dispel sorrow and agony," he wrote in his diary. A passerby asked him in Yiddish whether there would really be a port there. "A port and a state," Ben-Gurion responded. He spoke a great deal about the importance of the sea and the port. "I want a Jewish sea," he once said to his party members. "We must expand our reach."[71] The port was necessary because the Arabs at Jaffa's port had gone on strike. They should be rewarded, Ben-Gurion wrote. A while later, he added that "the mufti did a great service to the Jewish people."[72]

He remembered Tel Aviv's beginnings and abruptly conjured up a vision of the destruction of Jaffa, the city he had hated from the moment he first set foot in it. "I never felt hatred of the Arabs," he wrote, "and none of their mischief ever elicited in me vengefulness. But the destruction of Jaffa, the city and the port, will come, and for the best. This city, which grew fat from Jewish immigration and settlement, deserves destruction when it raises an ax over the heads of its builders and providers." It was an idea that had previously fired his imagination: "The city itself has sentenced itself to destruction, and it would be a crime for us to save it."

The terrible dejection that had oppressed him vanished as if it had never been. "Four days made me into a new man," he wrote. Soon he was flying over the Italian Alps; he recounted the incredible view in a 224-word sentence that concluded with the words: "It seems to me that an eternal stillness pervades this majestic, awesome sight that passes under one like the notes of a magical song that are not heard but sound in the heart." None of the other passengers could have been as happy as he was.[73]

❖

During the subsequent year, his mental state deteriorated once again. This time it happened in the wake of Weizmann's testimony before the royal commission, in December 1936. To Ben-Gurion's dismay, Weizmann agreed to restrict immigration to forty thousand for each of the next twenty-five years. The colonial secretary had declared prior to this that there would be no halt to immigration, which Ben-Gurion considered Zionism's most important victory since the Balfour Declaration. He had been involved in the lobbying that produced the announcement. Weizmann's consent to limiting immigration to a million over a quarter century was, in his view, a "political disaster." He submitted his resignation.*[74]

In January 1937, he wrote, "I felt as if my nerves had gone to pieces." Six months later he had a panic attack. "It is hard for me to explain to you," he wrote to Paula, "the psychological tension and mental torment I have been living with during these weeks in London." Three weeks later, he wrote: "I have never been in such an awful state. Awful in every way, first of all psychologically and I am prepared least of all to speak about mental suffering and distress." Two months later, he sent Weizmann a letter replete with admiration and love. They had differed over an appointment to the Zionist Executive; Ben-Gurion had insulted Weizmann and felt a need to apologize. He had disagreed with him in the past and might well do so in the future, he wrote, "but even in the fury of war not an iota of my love and admiration for you dissipates . . . You are permeated with the spirit of the Jewish people . . . You are now the king of Israel . . . The royal crown of Israel shines on your head . . . I love you with all my heart and all my might."[75]

"COMPULSORY TRANSFER"

The royal commission headed by Lord Peel reached the conclusion that there was no possibility of Jewish-Arab coexistence, and it thus recommended

---

* During his visit to Palestine in June 1936, Ben-Gurion told his party that he would agree to limiting immigration to sixty thousand a year for five years. (Ben-Gurion, Diary, Nov. 5, 1936, BGA; Ben-Gurion to the Mapai Central Committee, June 18, 1936, in Ben-Gurion 1973, p. 278ff.)

partitioning Palestine into two independent states. During each of the following five years, only twelve thousand Jews would be permitted to settle in the country. In its report, the commission quoted an English proverb: "Half a loaf is better than no bread."[76]

That was also how Ben-Gurion viewed the situation. As a longtime supporter of separation between Jews and Arabs, he had submitted a partition proposal of his own to his party and believed that the state's borders were less important than its actual establishment. Over time, he maintained, it could enlarge its territory. "A partial Jewish state is not the end but the beginning," he explained to his son, Amos. He told his colleagues: "We presume that this is only a temporary situation. We will settle first in this place, become a major power, and then find a way to revoke the partition." It was one of the cornerstones of the staged program that had guided the Zionist movement from its inception. "Just as I do not see the proposed Jewish state as a final solution of the Jewish question, so I do not see partition as a final solution to the Palestine question," he said.[77]

When it first became clear that the Peel Commission would recommend partition, he was overcome by a "burning enthusiasm," he wrote. "I see the realization of this program as an almost decisive stage at the beginning of our full redemption," he wrote in his diary, "and the strongest possible impetus for the step-by-step conquest of Palestine as a whole . . . It is a greater redemption than the days of Ezra and Nehemiah . . . and I am prepared to give my life to realizing this program."[78] The proposal to limit immigration for the next five years hardly bothered him. But three days later, the British government announced that it would issue only eight thousand immigration certificates for the coming period; Ben-Gurion had hoped for more. "I was like a madman for a few days," he wrote, "as if I were being roasted alive in a fiery furnace with white-hot iron ingots burning my entire soul."[79]

When he received the report's summary from Sharett, he immediately realized that the commission was proposing to remove the Arabs from the territory of the proposed Jewish state, but he still did not dare believe what he saw.[80] Only when he read it a second time was he persuaded that this was indeed the plan. He reacted with two words: "compulsory transfer," underlining the words in his diary.[81] The commission estimated that 225,000 Arabs would be affected. The relevant passage was extremely brief and phrased with great caution, as part of an agreement and only as a last resort. While the authors used the charged word "transfer" itself, they did so only in reference to the transfer of populated land.[82]

He suffered sleepless nights. "I am tired and exhausted from the horrible tension of the last two months," he wrote to Amos, "and I am almost unable to do any work, and discussion and debate are especially difficult." But the Zionist Congress was scheduled to convene soon in Zurich, so he had to make one more great effort.[83]

❖

The partition plan compelled the Zionist movement to reexamine its real relation to Palestine. It required ideological, emotional, religious, and political soul-searching; every Zionist had to examine his or her beliefs. The sense was that this was a moment of truth and that a momentous decision had to be made. It was the most excruciating question the movement had faced since the Uganda plan.

The election campaign for the upcoming Congress was in full swing when the Peel Commission report came out; the issue of partition had been part of the debate even before. The Revisionists and the other factions of the right, as well as most of the religious factions and Palestine's chief rabbis, headed the fight for the "integrity of the land," but there were leftists who also opposed partition, and that was Mapai's position.[84] In contrast with the debate over the agreements Ben-Gurion had concluded with Jabotinsky, this time his party did not wait for him to return from London. A few days after the commission's proposal became public, the party took a clear position against it.*[85]

Ben-Gurion was not disturbed by the storm of protest against the

---

* Two of Jabotinsky's close aides later related that he had first favored partition but then backpedaled. On the Zionist left, partition was opposed by Hashomer Hatza'ir, which advocated a binational state. Magnes attacked partition in an article in *The New York Times*. (Benjamin Akzin, "Emdat HaZ.H.R. Legabei Tochnit HaHolukah," in Avizohar and Friedman 1984, p. 164; Binyamin Eliav 1990, p. 82ff.; Ben-Gurion, Diary, Aug. 12, 1937; Magnes, "Palestine Peace Seen in Arab-Jewish Agreements; Authority on Question Disagrees With Royal Commission's Finding That Partition Is Necessary Precedent to Future of the Country," *New York Times*, July 18, 1937.)

Peel Commission proposal. He actually welcomed it, on the grounds that approval of partition would be more likely if it looked as if it were being forced on the Zionists against their will.[86] Some of the Mapai opponents believed that any concession of any part of Palestine was a national sin and a betrayal of the Zionist ethos; that was Yitzhak Tabenkin's position. Ben-Gurion argued with them. Berl Katznelson's opposition bothered and pained him much more, however, precisely because Katznelson did not object to partition for ideological reasons. He argued rather that it would not be successful and that it would be worse than the continuation of the Mandate. His opposition was a challenge to Ben-Gurion's political wisdom.

When Ben-Gurion proposed accepting the Peel Commission's proposal in principle, Katznelson used even sharper language. "We have not stood in the breech, we have not erected a dike against the inundation of panic that is sweeping away our official policy," he balked, warning against "spiritual weakness and chaos without direction." Ben-Gurion, apparently deeply hurt, made his case in a long and emotional letter to his party. "We have never been 'inundated' by panic," he proclaimed, meaning him and Moshe Sharett. On the contrary, "we have not given in and we have not despaired," and as such "we do not need to confess a sin we have not committed."

In the letter's most important paragraph, he positioned himself alongside Katznelson, as if they were boyhood friends. "We all came to Palestine when we were still young men, and many of us have already grown old," he wrote, "but I believe that our faith has not declined. My faith today is much more deeply rooted and firmer than it was in my youth, but it is much more clearheaded and realistic." Katznelson, in contrast, had fallen behind the times. "Panic and weakness can be spoken of only as extravagant use of language or out of ignorance," Ben-Gurion needled him.[87]

It was a personal clash, and the members of his party were well aware of its significance. "The friendship between them was not always what Ben-Gurion said," Rachel Yanait noted.[88] It was, perhaps, the most important political result of the debate over the partition plan—Ben-Gurion claimed for himself a status equal to that of Katznelson.

"I MADE A LIST OF ARAB VILLAGES"

The exhaustion that had made Ben-Gurion a nervous wreck in London vanished and was forgotten when he appeared before the labor caucus at the Zionist Congress in Zurich. He was focused, concentrated, systematic, and clear. Probably no one knew the Peel Commission's recommendations better than he did. The major part of his presentation was devoted to the plan's bad points, including the narrow borders of the proposed Jewish state, which did not include the Negev and a number of Jewish settlements, including Degania. It also stipulated a British corridor running from Jaffa to Jerusalem, a British presence in the large cities for an unspecified period, the restriction of immigration to twelve thousand a year, and a further list of legal and political impositions. None of the plan's opponents set out its problems better than Ben-Gurion, who reiterated his emotional and political commitment to the integrity of the land. "Our right to Palestine, all of it, is unassailable and eternal," he declared at the Congress. A few months later, he went so far as to say, "I am an enthusiastic advocate of a Jewish state within the historical boundaries of the Land of Israel . . . I will not concede a single inch of our soil." He reiterated that the proposed partition map did not include Transjordan, and noted another concession that pained him in particular—the port of Tel Aviv. The commission's proposal "bitterly and brutally plays with the fate of the Jewish people," he declared. He promised to make every effort to improve it.

But he placed the fact of the establishment of a Jewish state on the same level as the Balfour Declaration, if not above it, "a new page in the annals of our liberation," and certainly not the last, as "borders are not forever." He wrote to his party, "I doubt whether there is a single border on the globe that has not changed." He would have considered the partition plan advantageous even if the state proposed consisted of Tel Aviv alone, he asserted. In any case, a day would come when the world would no longer be divided into countries. "I believe," he wrote, "that the future of humanity depends on the establishment of a single state for all humanity, that is the elimination of all states." A few months later, he again got carried away, in the opposite direction. "Our movement is maximalist. Even all of Palestine is not our final goal," he said.

He warned that a continuation of the current situation would turn Palestine into "a miserable ghetto in an Arab region," in which Jews would not want to settle and many would actually leave. The establishment of a state would, in contrast, make it possible to increase the Jewish population by 100,000 a year, 1.5 million over fifteen years, he said, just like Jabotinsky before him. There were two requirements, and both of them could be realized in the division of the country—full sovereignty and population transfer.[89]

❖

The hope of emptying Palestine of its Arab inhabitants had been a part of Zionist discourse from its first days. Its earliest incarnation appears in Herzl's diary. "We shall try to spirit the penniless populations across the border by procuring employment for them in the transit countries, while denying them employment in our own country," Herzl wrote in June 1895. He specified that this should be done "discreetly and circumspectly."[90] Over the next twenty-five years the question was not relevant, but when the British conquered Palestine, the evacuation of Arabs from their villages became an inseparable part of the establishment of the Jewish national home, another step in the program that began with the fight for Hebrew labor. "There were but a few locations of our new settlements in which we did not have to move the previous inhabitants," Ben-Gurion said. "For the most part, these transfers were arranged as part of an agreement freely entered into with the tenant farmers, and only in a small number of cases was forced transfer required."[91] In the ten years that followed, the Arab population of Palestine continued to grow.

The evacuation of the Arabs from the territory of the projected Jewish state came up for discussion again and again, in a variety of contexts. Specific plans for doing so were examined for feasibility by a special committee formed by the Jewish Agency and in other forums. "I made a list of Arab villages," Ben-Gurion wrote a few days after seeing the partition proposal. Alongside the name of each village, which he recorded in Arabic script, he listed how many inhabitants it had.[92]

Like Herzl, Ben-Gurion believed that the transfer of the natives out of the territory of the Jewish state needed to be done quietly; as such, he denied, over and over again, that it was one of Zionism's goals. "While the dispossession of large numbers of inhabitants by force is not impossible," he wrote in 1926, "and while we have just witnessed the dispossession of thousands of Greeks from Turkey and hundreds of thousands of Turks from Greece, only madmen or miscreants can attribute such a desire to the Jewish nation in Palestine." He meant Jabotinsky. He promised Brit Shalom that a Jewish majority would be created by means of immigration and natural increase, without reducing the number of Arabs.[93] When the Mandate authorities refused to permit the Zionist movement to settle Jews in Transjordan, east of the Jordan river, he proposed demanding that Arabs who lost their land in the partition plan be resettled only in there, not elsewhere in Palestine. It was the first indication of his willingness to cede Transjordan as part of the national home, if only as a practical necessity.[*94]

In November 1935, Ben-Gurion said again that the Arabs could not be expelled and that no one would do so. But when the high commissioner brought up the subject with Ben-Gurion and Sharett the following July, asking whether the Zionist movement would agree to fund the transfer of the Arabs to Transjordan, Sharett responded that the movement would do so happily.[95]

Jewish Agency officials distinguished between forced transfer and the removal of Arabs by consent, but by that they did not mean the consent of each and every individual fellah but rather an agreement between the Zionist movement and Arab rulers. Members of the labor caucus at the Zionist Congress of 1937 in Zurich also spoke of transfer. None of them opposed it for moral reasons; one, Aharon Zisling, conditioned it on a "real population exchange," by which he meant that the Jews of Iraq and other Arab countries would be brought to Palestine.

Ben-Gurion may well have heard moral doubts about the idea that did not make it into the record of the proceedings. "As before," he said, "I am aware of all the horrible difficulty of a foreign force uprooting some hundred thousand Arabs from the villages they have lived in for hundreds of years." But he reiter-

---

* A few years later, however, Ben-Gurion preferred to transfer Palestine's Arabs to Syria, not Transjordan, saying, "We'll need that for ourselves." (Ben-Gurion to Yosef Weitz, Diary, Nov. 23, 1943, BGA; Yosef Weitz, "Kavim Klali'im Letochnit shel Ha'avarat Uchlusin 1937," CZA S25.10060; Yossi Katz 1998, p. 347ff.)

ated to his colleagues that this was not dispossession but rather emigration. He did not, he insisted, have to explain the difference. But he also noted that the Peel Commission had stipulated that if the Arabs refused to evacuate their lands of their own volition, it would need to be done by force. In any case, the Arabs would not be moved into worse conditions than they had previously had, he promised.

Some said that transfer was not practical. "I would agree to the Arabs leaving the country," said Golda Meir, whose name was still Myerson, "and my conscience would be entirely clean. But is it really a possibility?" Katznelson spoke in the same vein—unfortunately, transfer was but a fantasy, he said.

The labor caucus had to decide between Ben-Gurion and Katznelson, but they tried their best to avoid doing so. At one point, Ben-Gurion threatened again to resign the leadership of the Jewish Agency Executive. Meir provided a way out when she moved that the Congress authorize the Jewish Agency to inquire of the British what precisely they were proposing, and to return to the Congress with further information. That was not the decision that Ben-Gurion hoped to achieve. Katznelson reported that Ben-Gurion was despondent. At moments he plunged into a state of "tottering limbs and bitter grief, to the point that he despaired even of himself." Katznelson added, "I had to bandage his wounds."[96] He chose his words with great care; the phrase "tottering limbs and bitter grief" is taken from Ezekiel 21:1, where it denotes a combination of physical destruction and mental debility.

❖

Among the delegates to the Zionist Congress were two of his boyhood friends, Shlomo Lavi and Shlomo Zemach. Lavi, now a widower, remained at Ein Harod with his three small children. "So was the canopy of my life cut down—so my world went dark," he wrote. Along with Tabenkin, he was one of the leaders of Hakibbutz Hameuchad, the largest kibbutz movement; unlike Tabenkin, he spoke in favor of the partition proposal. "It was a very difficult episode," he wrote to his sister. "The debate was between emotion and cold calculation. It was perhaps an inner debate for each of us, but in the public debate we heard emotion on the side of the opponents, and cold calculation on the side of the advocates."[97]

Zemach was the founder and headmaster of the Kadoorie Agricultural High School. It was a prestigious and very patriotic institution; Amos Ben-Gurion was among its students. It was run by the government, meaning that Zemach was sometimes torn between his Zionist loyalties and his duty to his employer, the Mandate administration. He opposed the partition of Palestine and thus also the Peel Commission proposal. Ben-Gurion approached him at a café and said: "I've heard that you oppose partition." Zemach said, "Yes," and Ben-Gurion turned and left. They met again the next day. "Listen, David, why didn't you argue with me?" Zemach asked. Ben-Gurion replied: "With you I don't argue. We're finished arguing. You stand your ground and I mine. We're finished."[98]

Zemach was hurt, but probably not surprised. A few years previously, he had published a story à clef about the relations between two mules. Atara, representing Ben-Gurion, is domineering, overbearing, and manipulative. She puts on a show of affection, but brings about the death of Rezeleh, the mule who represents Zemach. Atara drags Rezeleh's corpse into a field and abandons it to the jackals and buzzards. She remains alone, friendless and feeling orphaned and sorrowful.

The caucus's decision obligated Zemach and he submitted. He later regretted not listening to his conscience. He should have resigned, allowing his party to fill his seat, he later wrote, but he did not dare: "I knew I had acted with cowardice and afterward I distanced myself from all activity in Mapai." He devoted himself to raising bees.[99] Some 300 Congress delegates voted in favor of considering the plan, while about 150 voted against. Ben-Gurion's reaction was devastating—the Congress's debate, as opposed to that of the labor caucus, was replete with "cheap demagoguery." Ussishkin was the most prominent opponent. His speech, according to Ben-Gurion, was a "heap of bland banalities."[100] Paula attended the Congress but did not enjoy it. Ten months later, he wrote to Paula about his loneliness: "Maybe my nature is to blame, but I am a solitary and lonely man, and sometimes it is very, very difficult for me. There are moments in which my heart is boiling and torn, and bitter and difficult questions plague me and I have no one to turn to. I stand alone and a heavy burden weighs on me, an unbearable burden, sometimes."[101] That same November, Geula got married; she was nineteen years old. Her father seems to have had a hard time parting from her. "For me, at least, you are still my little girl, and it will be a long time before I get used to the idea that you are a woman who looks after herself and her livelihood." A few months later, Geula sank into despair and dejection. Ben-Gurion sent her a fatherly letter of encouragement. "You write as if you were already an old woman whose life has gone by without interest or purpose," he wrote, "and it is a little ridiculous that you are trying to sum up your life. It has barely begun!" He promised to pay for English lessons.[102]

"HOW TO FOUND A NEW COUNTRY"

In the meantime, the Jewish Agency set up committees to begin planning for the state. This was the principal benefit that the Jewish public in Palestine gained from the partition proposal. It gave the Zionist dream a very practical cast, and a visible horizon. Ben-Gurion asked to be briefed about "what the procedure is, how to found a new country." He later wrote that the question led him to the dialogues of Plato that addressed this question.[103]

The removal of the Arabs from the Jewish state continued to occupy his thoughts. "In my opinion the Peel proposal was a good one, had we carried out the transfer," he said a year later, adding, "I favor forced transfer. I do not see it as something immoral, but forced transfer is possible only by England and not by the Jews." Six months later, he suggested that the Zionist Organization offer Iraq ten million pounds for the absorption of one hundred thousand Palestinian Arab families, a total of half a million people. But he soon declared that the conditions "were not amenable" for it and that it was thus not a practical idea. The reason was that the British had backed off. The partition plan, transfer included, was not feasible, because neither the Jews nor the Arabs wanted it.[104] In April 1938, the British established a new commission charged with giving them a way of disregarding the findings of the previous one.

❖

Paula had been through a very difficult period that summer, ending up in the hospital. When Ben-Gurion heard of it, he wrote to her, "I hardly need tell you how much it hurt to read what you wrote to me." After her release, she joined Ben-Gurion in London for a few weeks. At the end of her stay, Ben-Gurion accompanied her to the train station, and when he returned to his hotel, he was again overcome with terrible loneliness. "The room emptied—it is as if everything has emptied, and I feel as if abandoned, alone, without support," he wrote to Renana, who was thirteen years old. "I don't know why loneliness troubles and depresses me, alone, without anyone, emptiness, profound sorrow. If I were a boy I would cry, maybe it would be easier. I don't cry, but it is suffocating." The next day, he sent the very same words to Paula. It might have been a continuation of the difficult exchange they had had before she left, or perhaps it was a preemptive response to a harsh letter he expected he would receive from her and which he sought to head off.[105]

When Paula got home, she wrote to him that she knew that he had another woman in London and hinted, once again, that she intended to kill herself. "I have no desire to live, eventually it will be so. Why, for what . . . I have no desire to be in somebody's way."[106] She was referring to Doris May, one of the two senior secretaries in the Zionist office. Miss May, as everyone called her, was youthfully cheerful and freely friendly with Ben-Gurion and his colleagues. He must have found her company pleasant. Her letters to him evince a profound commitment to the office's work and the Zionist vision, but apparently, at this stage in their acquaintance, there was no romance between them.[107]

· 12 ·

WINDS OF WAR

"WE NEED A FOREIGN, EXTERNAL REGIME"

On an autumn day in 1937, several Haganah leaders came to Ben-Gurion's home and proposed bringing several dozen members of Hehalutz from Poland. The idea was to transport them covertly by boat and put them down on one of Palestine's beaches under cover of night. Since Ben-Gurion entered Palestine on a passport that wasn't his, tens of thousands of Jews had made their way into the country without immigration certificates, coming over the Lebanese and Syrian borders, or entering on tourist visas but not leaving when they expired. In the summer of 1934, the first boat bearing illegal immigrants, whom the Zionists called *ma'apilim*, arrived. The ship's name was the *Vallos*, but became known in Hebrew as the *Hetz*, meaning "arrow." Several dozen immigrants had arrived illegally earlier in 1937, on a boat with a defiant Hebrew name meaning "nevertheless."

Ben-Gurion opposed bringing in immigrants in violation of the law. The numbers who could be brought in like this were small, he maintained, and the damage to cooperation with the British would be much greater than any benefit to be gained. The operation to transport immigrants outside the law, which received the name *ha'apalah*, was initiated by Hakibbutz Hameuchad, the kibbutz movement whose members accepted the authority of Yitzhak Tabenkin. Ben-Gurion wanted immigration to remain under the sole purview of the Jewish Agency. The Haganah men who came to ask his approval revealed to him that, in fact, the operation was already in motion. A boat, the *Poseidon*, had been purchased, and the passengers were ready to set sail. Ben-Gurion responded angrily and threatened to bring his guests up for disciplinary action. But when they left his study, he quickly ran down the stairs after them and asked them to wake him when the immigrants arrived. He would be the first to help them descend from the ship, he said—but in the future they were not to act without an order from him.

It is a story that has been told many times since. One of the participants reported to his colleagues that Ben-Gurion was "opposed and displeased," but did not forbid it. The report of the meeting referred to him as "the old man." A year later, Ben-Gurion again astonished his colleagues by suddenly proposing an "immigration rebellion" against the British. He advocated purchasing boats, loading them with thousands of Jews, and sailing them to Palestine, both covertly and openly, by day.

❖

Hakibbutz Hameuchad's illegal immigration operation may have grown out of something more than just concern for Hehalutz operatives in Poland. It may also have been a response to Tabenkin's humiliating defeat in the partition debate. Similarly, Ben-Gurion's sudden decision to declare an immigration rebellion might not have just been about "saving Zionism," as he put it; it may have come out of his recognition that opposition to the initiative was isolating him within his movement—Berl Katznelson favored it. In the meantime, the Revisionists began sending boatfuls of Jews to Palestine. Ben-Gurion could not permit them to present themselves as more enthusiastic patriots than the members of the labor movement. When the number of immigrants who arrived this way reached three thousand, he changed his position. Illegal immigration boats began to arrive at a rate of about one per month, as Ben-Gurion tightened his control over the Haganah.[1]

The Haganah was able to operate largely thanks to assistance from the authorities. "We need a foreign, external regime to defend us," Ben-Gurion declared in 1936, because the English were not just helping to found the state-in-the-making but also its army.[2] One way they did so was by recruiting and arming thousands of young Jews into the British security forces as guards and policemen. The guarding of settlements was broadened to include operations targeted against Arab villages. Ben-Gurion spoke of the need for "aggressive self-defense." Later, field units were formed, which augmented the Haganah's military character.[3] He told Brandeis in 1935 that the Haganah also needed aircraft. Three years later, he wrote in his diary: "We have planes with English motors"; he named three pilots. The planes came from Poland.[4] He also wanted a navy and formulated a list of strategic goals, such as control of the country's central highlands and the establishment of a military industry. "I am occupied almost exclusively with security matters," he said in 1937; he seems not only to have found security to be his calling but also to have derived great satisfaction from the work.[5]

As of April 1938, some twenty-one thousand volunteers were serving in the Haganah, including four thousand women. The vast majority were part-timers. By and large, they served as a guard force. At the end of that year, Ben-Gurion told the National Council that the authorities had enlisted fifteen thousand Jewish security personnel, of whom twelve thousand were stationed as guards in settlements; the force had eight thousand rifles. Dozens of new settlements were established in the Tower and Stockade (*Homah Umidgal*) project, a semilegal Haganah operation led by Moshe Sharett.

The settlement of the land thus became part of the security efforts. According to Ben-Gurion, tens of thousands of Arabs had been forced to flee the country when their farms were destroyed during the British suppression of the Arab Revolt. They were the aggressors, Ben-Gurion said, noting that Jaffa was "half-destroyed."[6] Once a year he traveled to the United States and spoke at fund-raising dinners. He hated that part of his job. "I don't wish on anyone to speak before an American audience sitting around dinner tables in evening dress," he wrote. At one such evening, he made his first speech entirely in English.[7] The Haganah, he told the diners, was "the first Jewish army since Bar Kokhba's defeat."[8]

The Haganah's almost complete dependence on funds from the Zionist Organization laid the foundation for an important tradition that was not self-evident. The security forces of the state-in-the-making were subordinate, at least in principle, to the elected civilian leadership. It made sense—the National Council soon instituted a sort of voluntary security tax and some-time later instituted "mandatory" service for men. It was meant to be the first test of whether the state-in-the-making could assert its authority, which Ben-Gurion was determined to assert. He warned against the worst. "Oblit-eration and destruction await us," he wrote early in 1936, and reiterated at the end of that what the Jewish community in Palestine faced was "not riots but obliteration." He feared that Italy and Germany would assist the Arabs, including Iraq and Saudi Arabia. "Mussolini has declared himself the pro-tector of Islam and in his Nuremberg speech Hitler shed crocodile tears over the plight of the Arabs," he wrote to Paula.[9] Cooperation with the British security services enhanced the Haganah's prestige, which in turn shored up Ben-Gurion's standing. At the time, the Haganah was at best an army-in-the-making, but it was the first one Ben-Gurion had ever controlled.

He was, for all intents and purposes, the minister of defense for the Jewish community in Palestine, and he held the post primarily because he wanted it. Katznelson did not want the job, nor did Tabenkin, and there were no other realistic candidates. Most of the Haganah's senior command-ers belonged to the labor movement. But as the Haganah turned into a pres-tigious power center and its maintenance required an ever-increasing proportion of the Zionist budget, members of the Jewish Agency Executive tried to im-pose a measure of oversight on Ben-Gurion. They agreed to hand security affairs over to him, but demanded the appointment of a "management com-mittee" that would operate alongside him. Ben-Gurion refused to work with a committee. In accepting the position, he demanded the authority to ap-point the person of his choice as commander of the Haganah. The Executive had no choice but to accede. Just as his colleagues in the Jewish Agency sought to constrain his power, there were those in the Haganah who opposed his political line.[10]

"I AM BRINGING MY PUBLIC LIFE TO AN END"

On a summer morning in 1939, a deafening explosion woke up the inhabitants of Jerusalem's pastoral Rehavia neighborhood. Ben-Gurion was one of them. He was living at the time in a room with a separate entrance that he rented from the Gravitzky family, a few steps away from his office. Yosef Gravitzky was the director of the Zionist Organization's news service, Palcor. His daughter, Shoshana Vardinon, later remembered Ben-Gurion as a nice man who fit in well with the family. Every day, after breakfast, two armed young men would arrive at the house and escort him to the Jewish Agency building; he would sometimes come back to the house for lunch and ask her how it had gone at school. It seems to have been the most pleasant family milieu that he had ever enjoyed; on weekends he went home to Tel Aviv.[11]

His diary records the hour of the attack: 5:25 a.m. Several people saw the "scoundrels," as Ben-Gurion called them, but no one thought it important to pursue them. They were two Jewish young men who had thrown a bomb at a car carrying Arab laborers. "Who knows what will happen if we do not mobilize in the war against these Jewish gangs," he wrote. He was referring to Etzel, the Revisionist's National Military Organization, whose members had split away from the Haganah in 1931. They believed in reprisals and refused to countenance Ben-Gurion's policy of restraint.[12] They threw bombs at Arab buses, stores, and cafés; some of their attacks were deadly. Rehavia's neighborhood committee issued a fierce condemnation. Ben-Gurion maintained that the Haganah should be made "available for action against Etzel, by which he meant it should cooperate with the Mandate authorities.[13]

In April 1938, three Etzel operatives attacked an Arab bus that was on its way from Safed to Rosh Pina. No one was hurt. It was a reprisal against the murder of four Jews, including a child and two women. The British captured the three assailants and brought them to trial. One of them, Shlomo Ben-Yosef, became the first Jewish terrorist to be executed. Someone unfurled a black flag on the Histadrut building. Ben-Gurion ordered it removed. "I am not shocked by the hanging of a Jew in the Land of Israel," he said. "I am ashamed of the act that led to the hanging." He saw the incident as a political danger. Jabotinsky was trying to make Ben-Yosef into a greater martyr than Trumpeldor, he said. "He hopes to use this cult to sow confusion and division among our youth," he charged.[14]

But, like illegal immigration, the war against Arab terror was seen as a test of national loyalty. Restraint was seen as weakness, and revenge as heroism and moral strength.[15]

Such grassroots pressure was not the only challenge to his authority. "The big difficulty is Eliyahu," he wrote, meaning the Haganah's Eliyahu Golomb. "He controls everything; he does as he pleases and presents me with an established fact, he does not take into account what others say, yet he has great power and when the wagon needs to be extricated from the mud, he is the man. But he's impossible to work with."[16] Golomb enjoyed public esteem much like Katznelson's; his reputation was due largely to his persona. While he held no official position, he called the shots in the Haganah. He was one of the first initiators of the illegal immigration operation. He conducted negotiations in an effort to unify the Haganah and Etzel. Ben-Gurion, in London at the time, forbade him to do so, but Golomb disobeyed.

Golomb's real crime was not seeking an agreement with Etzel; it was conducting negotiations without informing Ben-Gurion. "I see this act as a knife in the back of our political activity," he wrote, and responded with his doomsday weapon. "Upon my return to Palestine I am bringing my public life to an end," he wrote. "My mission on behalf of the movement," he added, "is over." He thanked Golomb for unburdening him of the yoke he had borne for five years. Golomb was forced to back down; Ben-Gurion sent him a humiliating reprimand.[17]

When he analyzed the dilemma between "Thou shalt not murder" and "an eye for an eye," Ben-Gurion agreed that the psychological needs of the members of the Haganah needed to be taken into account. He understood that pressure required an outlet, but maintained that psychological needs could not justify a military operation if it was not also morally or politically mandated, and could only be carried out under his authority and with his sanction.[18] And then he gave in to them again, just as he had done with illegal immigration.

In the summer of 1939, a revenge organization was established that, for all intents and purposes, was under his command in his capacity as chairman of the Jewish Agency Executive. These "Special Squads," as they were called, were considered an elite unit. Its members specialized in terror attacks against Arabs. "Pressure from the ranks has forced the top commanders to provide an outlet for the anger and desire for vengeance that filled their hearts," the Haganah's official history relates.*

"I WOULD CHOOSE THE SECOND"

In the summer of 1938, after Nazi Germany annexed Austria, the United States organized an international conference at the beautiful spa town of Évian in France. Dozens of countries were meant to offer immigration permits to save Jews. Two years previously, Ben-Gurion had said to High Commissioner Arthur Wauchope: "If there were a possibility of sending the Jews of Poland to America or Argentina, we would do so despite our Zionist ideology. But the entire world is closed to us, and if there is no place for us in Palestine, our people will be left with no recourse but to commit suicide."[19] In fact, he was very worried about the Évian conference. He thought it would cause Zionism "huge damage."

The invitations were sent out by President Roosevelt, who did not see Palestine as a solution to the Jewish problem. "We must see to it that this dangerous position does not find expression at the conference," Ben-Gurion maintained. "It would be best for us to minimize the conference's importance." He managed the issue as if it were another round in the debate over the Uganda proposal.

Three days later, he sounded even more pessimistic. "Just as Zionism began at a certain point, it can also come to an end, to end with defeat," he said.[20] Not everyone agreed with his approach. Ben-Gurion responded, "Like every Jew, I am interested in saving all Jews everywhere where that is possible, but nothing takes priority over saving the Hebrew nation in its land."[21] The Zionist movement's representatives at Évian demanded that Jews be saved by allowing them into Palestine, but they did not reject sending Jews to

---

* Following the murder of an Arab family in the village of Kfar Lubia, Ben-Gurion ordered a temporary suspension of all activities by the Special Squads. (Ben-Gurion, Diary, June 5, 22, 1939, BGA; Dinur 1954–1964, 2, p. 841; Segev 2000, p. 382ff.)

other countries.[22] A few weeks later, the Jews of Germany were terrorized on Kristallnacht. During this period, the Jewish Agency tried to persuade the British to grant immigration certificates to tens of thousands of German Jewish children.

❖

The royal commission meant to prove that the partition program was not practicable was slated to issue its findings in November 1938. Ben-Gurion had to reevaluate his political position and his personal stance toward the British government and Britain as a whole. He appreciated the role the British had played in building the Jewish national home and the fact that, up to this point, it had kept most of its promises to the Zionist movement. Unlike many other promises, the Balfour Declaration had not been forgotten. He sometimes felt that he needed to explain to his colleagues and the Jewish public the way the British thought and what their motivations were. It was not simple, and it became harder the more the change in their policy became evident. He said that he could almost feel with his fingers how the British were abandoning Zionism.[23]

Colonial Secretary MacDonald went out of his way to present the anticipated betrayal in the best possible light, and even went so far as to make a quick visit to Palestine, of less than forty-eight hours. He made a point of meeting frequently with Weizmann and Ben-Gurion, who saw Britain's new policy take form with surprising transparency, almost before their eyes. On September 20, 1938, Ben-Gurion wrote to Paula: "The situation seems more or less clear to me. The government has decided to hand us over to the Arabs. No state, no immigration." Weizmann hadn't yet gotten the message, he claimed. "He is being misled with soothing rhetoric, without discerning their bitter and dangerous meaning. I feel as if I can no longer bear joint responsibility with Chaim."[24] At this point, that no longer meant anything—neither of them could stop the inevitable deterioration of British support.

One of their meetings with MacDonald was postponed because Prime Minister Neville Chamberlain was spending the day with Hitler in Berchtesgaden, Bavaria. Ten days later, Weizmann asked MacDonald whether he had read *Mein Kampf*, and Ben-Gurion wrote to Paula: "The world is in a bad state if these are the people determining its fate."[25] Three days subsequently, Ben-Gurion heard Hitler speak on the radio. It was horrifying. "Hitler roared, bellowed, raged, cursed, and vilified, threatened and frightened, provoked and insulted. The crowd roared after him." He did not speak like the leader of a nation, Ben-Gurion said, "but like the leader of a gang of thugs and hangmen." He was in London at the time. The British began digging trenches in public parks and the citizenry received gas masks; the maid in his hotel told him about a plan to evacuate the city's children.[26]

Czechoslovakia was compelled to cede the Sudetenland, and on October 1, 1938, the German army entered the territory. On that same day, Weizmann hosted Ben-Gurion and Katznelson for dinner; when the meal was over, they were joined by Jan Masaryk, who would soon become the foreign minister of the Czechoslovakian government-in-exile. "We heard many instructive and shocking details about how the Czechs were misled and how much they had been deceived," Ben-Gurion wrote. "They were handed over to Hitler behind their backs." Weizmann remarked that there was no reason to hope that the British would give the Jews fairer treatment than they had given the Czechs.

Ben-Gurion sympathized with Czechoslovakia's fate. "Abandoned, the little nation was raped," he wrote to his children. But, like most observers at the time, he believed that the capitulation to Hitler had averted a war. "Hitler would have to be crazy" to go to war, after he had achieved nearly everything he wanted without it, Ben-Gurion said. He portrayed the horrors of the war that had been avoided—Europe destroyed, millions of civilians killed, among them millions of Jews. "It is impossible not to rejoice that a holocaust has been prevented," he declared. Nevertheless, he surmised that the peace would be but an interim period in which Germany would be able to grow stronger. The British were also preparing for war and seeking Arab support. "I fear that our turn is about to come, all the signs point to the worst," Ben-Gurion wrote, and headed home.[27]

❖

In December 1938, Ben-Gurion surveyed the situation for his party. He informed the members of Mapai about negotiations aimed at obtaining immigration certificates for ten thousand Jewish children from Germany. "If I knew that it was possible to save all the children in Germany by transporting them to England, but only half by transporting them to Palestine, I would choose the second, because we face not only the reckoning of these children but the historical reckoning of the Jewish people."[28]

He did not in fact face such a choice—it was all theoretical. He did not have the power to save all of Germany's Jewish children, or even half of them. But his willingness to pay such a horrible human price in order to achieve Zionism's goals was something he had voiced from the time he first arrived in Palestine. The words he chose when he spoke about leaving half these children to their fate so as to live up to his obligation to history is reminiscent of the position attributed to him twenty-five years previously, when he reportedly argued that the five thousand Jews who would fall in the ranks of the Turkish army in Palestine were more important to the Zionist movement and its future than the ten thousand who had taken refuge in Egypt.

With a new White Paper on Palestine taking form in London, Ben-Gurion proposed an immigration rebellion. "Without a major, daring, goal-directed deed . . . we will not be able to prevent the ruin of Zionism at this moment," he said. To succeed, boats needed to be purchased and a network of smugglers established in Germany, Austria, Poland, Greece, and Romania. As much of the operation as possible should be done publicly, and it should include a world Jewish convention in the United States. When Britain announced its new policy, the Jewish Agency Executive should publicly resign (while continuing to function in practice) and announce a policy of political noncooperation with the British. In the meantime, the Jews should augment their presence in Haifa, the most important port and industrial city in Palestine's north, where "we will announce the establishment of a Jewish state." He spoke of the "Judaization" of Haifa, by which he meant conquering it with a military force. He did not conceal what the consequences would be. "They will shoot at us!" A few days later, he said: "In the era of Hitler, we are compelled to resort to belligerent Zionism."

Massive *ha'apalah* was meant to force Britain to either shoot at Jewish refugees or send them back to where they came from. "That will outrage the world and rouse humanitarian scruples even in England," he predicted. Jewish refugees were, in his mind, soldiers in Zionism's struggle. Ben-Gurion seems to have presumed that his plan for an insurgency might spark endless debates. For that reason, he told his party that the first person he informed about it was Katznelson. "And this sworn skeptic told me, after much consideration, that perhaps this is the right thing to do."[29] It was the first time he presented a plan that was liable to cost lives, taking another step from politics toward national leadership.*

"WE DO NOT WANT TO BE THAT SORT OF JEW"

A few months after abandoning Czechoslovakia, Chamberlain received Weizmann and Ben-Gurion. "I saw him for the first time," Ben-Gurion wrote. "He gives the impression of being an honest person . . . uninspired, but not without human kindness . . . The sympathy he expressed was, without a doubt, sincere—but the question is how far it goes." Not far, as it turned out. With war approaching, the view taking shape in London was that it was essential to hold Palestine and Egypt and maintain relations with Iraq. In wartime, it was supposed, the Jews would have no other option—they could only support Britain. The Arabs, however, could easily throw their support behind Germany. To ensure their support, MacDonald proposed halting Jewish immigration entirely, for the entire duration of the war. "If we must offend one side," Chamberlain told his Cabinet, "let us offend the Jews rather than the Arabs."[30]

In March 1939, MacDonald convened a diplomatic farce at St. James's Palace, ostensibly meant to give the Jews and Arabs a final opportunity to reach an agreement. The British needed the conference in order to justify their policy reversal. Ben-Gurion continued to think that it was necessary to talk to the Arabs, "so that no one will be able to say later that we missed an opportunity." On another occasion he remarked that "in political life, fiction has a value."[31] When MacDonald heard that Ben-Gurion had come down with a cold, he sent flowers. Ben-Gurion thought that there was something to

---

* Unlike the fantastical "declaration of war" of 1930, the immigration rebellion produced dramatic results. In the ten months after it was declared, up until World War II broke out, more than eighteen thousand refugees were brought to Palestine's shores. Most were allowed to stay. (Ofer 1988, p. 474ff.; Ben-Gurion, Diary, June 5, 1939, BGA.)

be learned from the manners of British officials. "Even when they take you to the gallows, they remain gracious and smile," he said.[32]

❖

MacDonald's White Paper was issued on May 17, 1939. It stated that an independent, binational state would be established in Palestine within ten years. In the meantime, restrictions would be placed on the transfer of Arab land to Jewish ownership. The number of Jews permitted to settle in Palestine in the five years to come would not exceed seventy-five thousand. The intention was that the Jews constitute a third of the population. Any further Jewish immigration beyond this number would require Arab consent. Ben-Gurion proclaimed that Britain had, essentially, revoked the Balfour Declaration. "The Devil himself could not devise a more crushing and horrible nightmare," he wrote in his diary. He had reacted in just the same way to the White Paper that followed the wave of Arab terror in 1929.

MacDonald was now a swindler, liar, fraudster, dissembler, and traitor. "He is our archenemy, perhaps the most dangerous enemy of the Hebrew nation after Hitler," Ben-Gurion declared. He wondered how England could stand such a "deplorable fellow" in its midst. With the hypocrisy and intrigue of a cheap lawyer, MacDonald was fit to serve only gangsters and blackguards.

As a politician, however, Ben-Gurion marveled at MacDonald's tactics. With "his supplications, his manner of persuasion, his way of handing out promises, the caresses he offered us, his attempts to frighten us, his dialectics," MacDonald was undoubtedly one of England's greatest crooks.[33] Ben-Gurion was offended with good reason—MacDonald, of Mapai's sister Labour Party, had been one of Ben-Gurion's most senior friends in England.

❖

Reckoning that British public opinion was more sympathetic to the plight of the Jews than to Zionism's goals in Palestine, Ben-Gurion did his best to present the campaign against the new policy as a battle for all Jews, all over the world. He insinuated that Britain was liable to adopt Hitler's anti-Semitism.

"Political affinity with Hitler," he said, "can hardly avoid bringing in its wake sympathy for Nazi ideology."[34]

One summer day, Ben-Gurion copied W. H. Auden's poem "Refugee Blues" into his diary: "The consul banged the table and said: 'If you have got no passport, you're officially dead.'"[35] But at the Zionist Congress held in August 1939 in Geneva, he expressed little solidarity with the Jews in Europe. "Call me an anti-Semite, but I have to say it . . . We are choked with shame from what is going on in Germany, Poland, and America, that Jews do not dare fight back. Can we not be brave anywhere in the world? . . . We do not belong to that Jewish people. We do not want to be that sort of Jew." On the eve of the war he asserted that "the fate of Palestine hangs in the balance."[36] The delegates knew that they might never see one another again. The previous January they had read that Hitler himself had declared that if the Jews pushed Europe into war, Germany would destroy the entire Jewish people. The Hebrew press had reported it.[37] Ben-Gurion returned from the Congress just twenty-four hours after the German army invaded Poland.

"LIKE A MEMBER OF HITLER'S GANG"

Three weeks after the war began, Ben-Gurion told the members of the Jewish Agency Executive that protecting the Jewish people throughout the world was now "beyond human capacity," and as such they needed to focus in particular on local affairs. That was his thinking until the end of the war. He was now fifty-three years old; he had been in politics for three decades and was approaching the acme of his powers, but there were still some battles to be fought. In the dingy room in the Jewish Agency building, he saw before him eleven men sitting under a portrait of Herzl, projecting Zionist continuity. It was his national coalition. Only a few of them represented any real political power. Most were from Eastern Europe; all had been born in the previous century. Ussishkin and Ruppin were already almost mythological figures. Another man Ben-Gurion had known for many years was Yitzhak Gruenbaum, who had grown up in Płońsk. Never had such heavy responsibility ever been placed on such a helpless Jewish government. Gruenbaum, who had once served in the Polish parliament, was affiliated with the General Zionists, a free-market party representing the middle class. He wanted the

Executive to give him responsibility for bringing Poland's Jews to Palestine. None of the other members objected, but they warned him that there was not enough money to do much.[38]

When he told them that it was not within human power to save the Jews of Europe, Ben-Gurion meant that the Zionist movement was incapable of doing so. He had said this back in 1936, but the feeling intensified as the war proceeded. "Five or six million Jews are being crushed and we have no guarantee that Palestine will not be dragged into the war," he said in April 1941. "There are things over which we have no control. We cannot eject Hitler from Europe, we cannot prevent him from getting to Egypt."[39] From time to time he oversaw rescue operations even though he did not believe in them, just as he managed the conflict with the Arabs even though he did not believe in peace. Only a state that could not be destroyed could, he believed, lead the Arabs to recognize it. Likewise, he maintained that only the defeat of Nazi Germany could save whatever Jews remained alive. He was right.

He now spent much time pondering history, internalizing it as personal experience and making it part of his perception of reality. As the war approached, he read the memoirs of Ferdinand Foch, the supreme allied commander in World War I. "I learned some important things from it," he wrote to Paula. Eight days after the German army invaded Poland, he said: "The world war of 1914–1918 brought us the Balfour Declaration; now we must bring about the Jewish state."[40] The threat of eradication that he believed the Zionist enterprise faced impelled him to focus, in the meantime, on saving it. As such, he sounded more like a local leader than a man responsible for world Jewry. "For us as Zionists, defending and saving Palestine is our paramount duty," he wrote in a memorandum to the British authorities. If the worst were to happen and Palestine was lost, he wrote, "Jewish history and our own conscience will never forgive us."[41]

❖

The White Paper required Ben-Gurion to lead his people in a way that was very difficult for him to explain to them, because it seemed self-contradictory. "We will not fight England," he said. "The war is against the policy of the British government." It was a convoluted position. He found a catchier way of saying it: "We must aid the English in their war as if there were no White Paper, and we must stand against the White Paper as if there were no war." It was what later came to be called the "dual formula." He hoped that the war would postpone implementation of the White Paper.[42] He was wrong.

❖

A few months before the summer of 1939, the National Council and the Jewish Agency began conducting a census, in preparation for enlistment. About one hundred thousand Jews, half of them women, signed declarations of consent to volunteer for service. At the time, there were fewer than half a million Jews living in Palestine, meaning that one out of every three adults was prepared to sign up.[43]

Here and there people began joining the British army on their own. Ben-Gurion wanted them to go through the Jewish Agency, but no one there knew what to do with so many volunteers.[44] He hoped that the British would place them in Jewish battalions, as in World War I, and proposed establishing such units in other countries as well, like the American battalion he had served in. That way the Zionist movement would receive, at war's end, a trained army, and perhaps the standing of a belligerent at the peace talks. As during the previous war, Ben-Gurion ascribed great importance to the Jewish character of these units, which should have their own anthem, banner, and insignia, and use Hebrew as the language of operation and command. When the war broke out, the Haganah had a plan to organize the volunteers into four battalions. Ben-Gurion participated in the logistical planning and in computing the costs: "establishment of a training camp for 100 trainees will cost P£ [Palestine pounds] 632; 29 tents—P£ 261; two large tents—P£ 70; kitchen and storehouse P£ 100; showers and latrines—P£ 60, and tables, mattresses, kitchen equipment, and sundries a similar sum.[45] He also took part in determining the cultural programs to be conducted among the volunteers, including teaching them "a minimum of Hebrew" and translating books that constitute "an organic part of Jewish culture and that have great human importance." Among the authors he wanted translated into Hebrew were Philo of Alexandria, Benjamin Disraeli, Heinrich Heine, and Baruch Spinoza.[46]

But more than anything else he insisted that the Jewish battalions serve solely in Palestine and neighboring lands. The British immediately grasped the political intention behind this and rejected it. Relations deteriorated rapidly. More and more of the Haganah's operations violated the law.[47]

A few weeks after the war broke out, forty-three young members of the Haganah were arrested not far from Beit She'an. They were returning from training and bore illegal arms. One of them was Moshe Dayan, the son of one of the leaders of the labor movement. They were court-martialed; one was sentenced to life in prison, the rest to ten years. It was not easy to obtain their release. Ben-Gurion rushed to London. The city greeted him with a wartime blackout; it was only thanks to the headlights of buses that he was able to cross Oxford Street. His impression was that Weizmann and his associates were living in a fool's paradise. There had always been a gap between the reality in Jerusalem and the sense of things in London, he wrote, but this time it was not a gap but an abyss. Weizmann continued to meet with Mac-Donald; Ben-Gurion said that it was "psychologically impossible" for him to do so. "In my view, he is like a member of Hitler's gang, and our friends need to know that no Jew can meet with him." Weizmann said that a Jew needed to meet even with the Devil, and noted that Rabbi Leo Baeck goes almost every day to the Gestapo in Berlin. In any case, it was simply unthinkable that Ben-Gurion would be in London and not see MacDonald.*

Ben-Gurion gave in. As always, MacDonald received him graciously, with a smile, and even asked about the citrus crop. Ben-Gurion reported feeling as if he had been forced to swallow a frog. He was overwhelmed by memories of the better days he had spent with MacDonald in this same room. Dayan and the other Haganah men were released about three months later.[48]

"A JEWISH GHETTO HAS BEEN ESTABLISHED IN PALESTINE"

It was not easy to navigate between the two sides of the "dual formula," in part because Etzel had in the meantime resumed its operations with a series

---

* Moshe Sharett recounted debating the point with Ben-Gurion. Sharett argued that it was impossible to avoid contact with MacDonald, for example in the context of a particular initiative to save 2,900 German Jews. "Ben-Gurion has determined that our political future is more important than saving 2,900 Jews," Sharett claimed. "He was prepared to do without them." (Sharett, Diary, Nov. 13, 1939, in Sharett 1968–1974, p. 487.)

of deadly attacks against Arab civilians and sabotage of British facilities, such as telephone lines, electrical transformers, railroad tracks, and mailboxes. The Haganah brought in immigrant ships and acted against Arab citizens, but the Revisionists were again able to portray themselves as the Jewish people's true patriotic champions.[49] The land transfer regulations that severely limited the sale of Arab land to Jews, promulgated almost a year after the White Paper was issued, were taken to be a menace to the Zionist enterprise itself, and more immediately the standing of the Labor movement and of Ben-Gurion. He remembered how he had been compelled, during the debate over restraint and illegal immigration, to adopt a more belligerent line than he had then thought correct. This time he took a firmer line than his colleagues from the start.

On Saturday, March 2, 1940, tens of thousands gathered in the centers of Palestine's large cities to protest the land law. Three demonstrators were killed in clashes with the police, one in Jerusalem, one in Tel Aviv, and one in Haifa.[50] It was the first time that Ben-Gurion sent so many people into the streets; he had the Haganah get them out. The goal was to create, Ben-Gurion declared, "an atmosphere of unrest," greater than there had ever been before, and to pay the British back in kind, "penalty for penalty, punishment for punishment."[51] The demonstrations gave him, for the first time, the image of a leader of the masses.

Some members of the Jewish Agency Executive opposed his aggressive tactics. They thought that the danger the country faced from the Italians, Germans, and Arabs required tightening cooperation with the British.[52] They also seem to have been concerned about Ben-Gurion's growing power. One of them described Ben-Gurion's line in the struggle against the British as "national fascism."[53] Against this background, Ben-Gurion again found himself in the midst of a military-political scandal in which a quasilegal investigation sought to determine who had given an order.

A member of the National Council claimed that the Haganah command had received an order to equip the demonstrators with stones and Molotov cocktails. He claimed that the demonstrators intended to set fire to British army vehicles and that the order was rescinded only at the last minute, because it turned out to have been unauthorized. Ben-Gurion shouted at him that he was lying. A committee was established to investigate. As chairman of the

Jewish Agency Executive, Ben-Gurion could not be involved in a plan to sabotage government vehicles. But Ben-Gurion insisted during the inquiry that he was the only person with the authority to give the Haganah such an order. The investigation challenged his position as the supreme commander and gave him an opportunity to establish it even more firmly. In the end, the committee decided that he had not given the order, although he had instructed the demonstrators not to avoid clashes with the security forces.[54]

Among his opponents were several Mapai leaders, including Yitzhak Ben-Zvi. "The time has not yet come for a policy of force," he said. Neither did Katznelson stand by Ben-Gurion. He had been worried about the situation in his party for some time. "I confess my own sins," he said to the Mapai Central Committee a few weeks after Kristallnacht. "In these terrible times, at the beginning of the destruction that threatens European Jewry, and perhaps on the eve of the end of the Mandate, I am concerned about the elections to the party branch in Tel Aviv," where factional infighting was threatening to split the party. And in June 1939 he had said: "The party is not functioning. In my opinion, that is the central problem."[55]

So there were one hundred thousand volunteers whom the British government did not want, despite the dangers threatening Palestine; an adversarial Jewish Agency Executive; a growing and intractable opposition; and an adversarial and internally divided party. Ben-Gurion's diary indicates that he sometimes felt as if everything was falling apart. "I went to participate in a meeting of the workers' committees in Tel Aviv, convened by the Histadrut committee," he wrote, "and I heard about growing suffering and hunger and despair within the working public, with the Histadrut unable to help."[56]

The cumulative effect of all this seems to have been more than he could handle. His behavior evinced dejection. He was busy nearly every hour of the day, and in nearly every area of his activity there were people who supplied him with information. He trusted many of them, but, when push came to shove, he was nearly alone, without a personal staff, without a wise friend to consult, without any real friends at all, without any ability to save his people and realize his aspiration of leading them.

He did not confide in Paula. "He knew that Paula was distant and foreign and did not care," Rachel Yanait said in testimony she gave to the Ben-Gurion Heritage Institute. "She came to us once, to me and Ben-Zvi," she said, "and told us that she had decided to kill herself, because she could not live this way, she was alone at home, with just the children. He didn't tell her anything, he didn't talk to her." And sometimes he would fall in love, Yanait related. "He had an unusual temperament," she noted. "I saw that as a good thing."[57] In January 1940, he spent ten days at the Dead Sea. From time to time he went up to Jerusalem for meetings, but he seems to have spent most of his time with a pile of books he brought with him. He read them all in parallel and each day made note of how many pages he had gotten through in each one: Fritz Fischer, historian; Arthur Schopenhauer, philosopher; Basil Liddell Hart, British strategist.[58] That same January, in 1940, the first reports of the extermination of the Jews began to accumulate on his desk.

❖

Less than three weeks after the war began, a leader of the Zionist movement in Czechoslovakia came to Ben-Gurion and told him that the situation of the Jews there had grown much worse since the arrival in Prague of an SS officer named Adolf Eichmann. "I promised him that the Executive would do everything it could, as if we ourselves were sitting in hell," Ben-Gurion wrote in his diary. Reports he received about German actions in occupied Poland told him that "synagogues full of Jews were put to the torch . . . Hundreds of Jews were drowned in the river in the city of Radom." He heard from Łódź that masses of Jews were being deported from the city and sent to Warsaw. Thousands of Jews were loaded onto cattle cars, which were closed and locked. Because the tracks to Warsaw were blocked, the train was parked on a side rail and left there for three or four days. The Jews remained locked in the cars, without water or food. Some died of suffocation. It was a freezing December. Some of the deportees froze to death.[59]

The information confirmed his worst expectations, but did not change his belief that "danger is [more] severe sevenfold" in Palestine than in Europe. Over the years he had concocted an ideological explanation for this gut feeling, first put into words in 1934. "The Jews in Palestine as human beings are not in the same condition as the Jews of Germany, or even the Jews of Lvov or Warsaw," he said. "But from a Zionist point of view—and I know no other—we are worse off than the Jews in the darkest part of the Exile. The persecutions in each country affect only the Jews in that country. What happens here strikes at the heart of the nation, deals a blow to its soul . . . Palestine is a question of life or death for the Jewish people."[60] In February he resigned from his post at the Jewish Agency Executive.

The immediate trigger was the Land Transfers Regulations. "At five o'clock I ceased, together with every Jew in Palestine, to be a citizen with equal rights in my homeland," he wrote. "As of yesterday, a Jewish ghetto has been established in Palestine." He compared the land law to the Nuremberg laws. His colleagues, unsurprisingly, were aghast and told him that they would not allow him to leave. They refused to accept the resignation. Ben-Gurion said, as he always did, that his mind was made up and his decision final. He wrote to his party that, in parallel with his resignation from the Jewish Agency Executive, he was bowing out of "all political activity, official and unofficial, within the Executive and outside it."[61]

His colleagues apparently made note of the words "for the time being" that he included in his resignation letter. They took it to mean "until I return." They all tried to guess what he wanted—according to a rumor making the rounds, he had decided to settle on a kibbutz.[62] He apparently wanted some time out from the depressing malaise that had overcome him. Less than three weeks later, he again packed his bags and set off for London. Nearly ten months went by before he returned. Five months subsequently he went again, spending more than a year away from Palestine. He generally stayed alone in a hotel or in rented rooms.

"HOW BLESSED IS THIS NATION"

Saturday, September 7, 1940, was a horrible day in London. Close to the hour at which the British customarily take their afternoon tea, 350 German bombers and 600 warplanes appeared in the sky and began to drop hundreds of tons of bombs on the city. The attack lasted all night, and by Sunday morning there were nearly 900 dead and another 2,000 wounded.[63]

Ben-Gurion did not descend to a bomb shelter. He remained in bed and, so he claimed, did not even wake up. "I choose sleep and rest whenever I can," he told Paula. It was not the first air raid on London; Ben-Gurion frequently heard artillery and explosions. "As of now the attacks have not disturbed even one hour of my work or one night of sleep," he wrote. As he toiled over his letter another siren sounded, but he stayed put. "From the start I made it a rule not to heed warning sirens and not to make use of defense shelters," he wrote.[64]

The next day, on September 9, 1940, Italian planes bombed Tel Aviv's city center. More than a hundred people were killed. Ben-Gurion's response was terse. "What I feared has come to pass. The Italians have commenced operations to obliterate the Hebrew community." Not since 1929 had so many Jews been killed in Palestine all at once. Ben-Gurion had not been in the country then, either, and this time, too, he seems to have had trouble empathizing with the magnitude of the trauma. "I have no clue of what was going on during those months in Palestine," he said when he returned. In the meantime, he was appalled that the British press had not mentioned that Tel Aviv was a Jewish city, while making a point of reporting that five of the dead were Arabs. Sharett and Eliyahu Golomb cabled him that Paula and the children were fine.[65]

The Blitz first aroused his journalistic instincts. "Never has London been as interesting and as close to the heart as in these days," he wrote to Paula, "and I am dumbfounded by the levelheadedness and inner confidence of this wonderful nation. It is as if nothing can shock it and nothing undermines its faith and confidence that victory will come in the end." He soon became addicted to the thundering of Britain's antiaircraft cannons. "No concert by a choir in Palestine has ever given me as much enjoyment as the thunder of the artillery that shakes the four walls of my room for hours on end."[66] In the meantime, he moved from his hotel to Maida Vale in northwest London, where he resided in the home of Arthur Lourie, a Zionist movement diplomat who was in the United States at the time.

His refusal to take shelter during alerts was the insolence of a teenage boy defying death. Most of all, it was irresponsible. In the months that followed, some thirty thousand Londoners were killed in the bombings.[67] But there is competing testimony. Lourie's housemaid wrote to him from London that Ben-Gurion frequently did his writing on the kitchen table, and the kitchen was in the basement. Whatever the case, the addictive exhilaration took control of him and, paradoxically, soothed him and bolstered his confidence. In refusing to take refuge in a bomb shelter, he took part in the British nation's heroism, and when he recounted this again and again, he acquired some of its grandeur. "I spent only two months there during the Blitz," he told his colleagues when he returned from London, "but I have never had a more profound experience. I saw the glory of man at its most sublime zenith." By that he meant national glory in wartime. "I saw consummate heroism, physical and moral, not of individuals, not of pioneers, but of a nation, of millions of workers, merchants, shopkeepers, office workers, Cabinet ministers, journalists. I know of no more majestic and sublime sight in all of history." Nothing could be further from the helplessness he felt in Palestine. He was in euphoria again. London was now his Jerusalem, as Płońsk once had been. "For every Jew, Palestine is the sacred thing," he said, "but I have to say—I not only loved London, but London became sanctified for me. I felt holiness in that place." It was an epiphany that a man not gifted with Bialik's tongue, "or at the very least, with Churchill's," could not put into words, because he would only "defile it," Ben-Gurion said. He had a hard time restraining himself. "It was the utmost human vision of the greatness and moral beauty of which man is capable."

The English deserved all this because they had refused to surrender. France, in contrast, had turned Paris over to the enemy to keep it from being destroyed. As a result, Hitler was able to have his picture taken at the foot of the Eiffel Tower. The fall of France pained him, "as if my own nation and land had been devastated," he wrote to Paula. The French were unable to allow their Champs-Élysées to be razed; the Louvre also still stood. But nothing might well remain of the British Museum, he noted. "London will be destroyed, Liverpool will be destroyed, Manchester will be destroyed, but if the English nation remains free, it will build it all anew."* He claimed that he was not deciding which of these two responses was correct. "History will judge that," he said. But there could be no doubt as to which side he was on. England would win, and that would happen because of the path it had chosen.

---

* He included the Jews of Whitechapel in the glory he accorded to the British. "As a Jew, I did not need to be ashamed of their behavior," he later said. "They conducted themselves just like the English." In another context, he suggested that the fear that Britain would be overrun prompted the Zionist movement to send its archives to Canada. (Ben-Gurion to the Mapai Central Committee, Feb. 19, 1941, and to the Smaller Zionist Executive, Feb. 14, 1941, in Ben-Gurion 2008, pp. 202, 231.)

"The English nation will acquire a place in human history that no nation has yet had," he declared.[68]

❖

The Blitz also enlightened him on the issue of leadership. He had always believed that the people, not the leaders, were paramount, but he now learned that, in some crises, leadership can be decisive. A few days after he arrived in London in May 1940, Prime Minister Chamberlain was compelled to resign, to be replaced by Winston Churchill.

"How blessed is this nation, which was granted such a leader at a fateful hour," he wrote to Paula. He referred to Churchill as "the old man." He listened to all the new prime minister's speeches, and copied passages from them—in English—into his diary. It was, he said, the professional admiration of "a man who has purchase on this craft" and makes speeches.[69] He had not had such a seminal experience since his visit to Moscow, almost twenty years previously. He discerned in Churchill some of the ideal leadership traits he had attributed to the dying Lenin, among them determination to pay the price of victory. Lenin was "a man of iron will who does not spare human life and the blood of innocent children for the sake of the revolution." Churchill was doing the same for Britain, Ben-Gurion maintained; he incorporated their experiences into his own persona.

On Sundays he went to the Speakers' Corner in Hyde Park. Some of the orators there claimed that it was wrong to risk the lives of millions and all of London; better, they argued, to seek accommodation with Hitler. There were also two speakers who claimed that there was only one honest statesman in the world, Hitler. They were allowed to speak. That surprised Ben-Gurion more than what they actually said. "In America they would have been lynched," he said many years later. "In Israel, too, we would not allow someone to say that Nasser is the greatest of statesmen." His admiration for Britain's political culture grew even more profound.

"I think that a new democracy is being forged by the war," he said. Unlike in the previous war, now the entire nation was fighting. Every man and woman. And as bombs did not distinguish between rich and poor, laborer and aristocrat, the British faced a common fate that produced a sense of brotherhood, as if all of England were a single family fighting for its very life. "And Churchill, in the eyes of the English nation, is not just a leader, but the family's father, beloved and venerated." War, then, offered an uplifting expression of all that was good and sublime in the nation. Ben-Gurion soon found an ideological justification for his refusal to seek safety in a bomb shelter. "The English people needs to live, to eat, to dress, to build tanks and aircraft, and if a German plane comes and everyone runs for cover, Hitler has won."[70] It was his war with Hitler, too—he did not even think of surrender.

❖

In London, Ben-Gurion sought to promote the establishment of Jewish battalions. He was able to get meetings with various officials, as well as with the new colonial secretary, George Lloyd. The secretary complained to him that the Cabinet was overly "Zionist," and that Churchill kept asking him whether Ben-Gurion wanted more than just a conversation. Churchill was very busy, he explained, entirely preoccupied with matters that would determine the outcome of the war.

But Churchill was not too busy to see Weizmann. He invited him to lunch and, during the meal, authorized Weizmann to notify the chief of the imperial general staff that he consented to the conscription of Palestinian Jews to defend the country and its immediate environs. Churchill also agreed that some Palestinian Jews would be given officer training. Jews from other countries would be recruited into units that would be sent to all fronts, as needed, including the Near East. When Ben-Gurion notified the Jewish Agency Executive of the development, he presented it as the product of work in which he had been involved. "We made efforts to arrange a meeting between Dr. Weizmann and Churchill. The attempts failed for a long time, but in the end were successful." He also claimed to have been involved in drafting the proposals that Weizmann presented at the meeting.[71]

He was not overly busy in London. From time to time he took the train to Oxford, to browse at Blackwell's, his favorite bookstore. There, surrounded by the classics, he did his best to disregard the explosions outside. He began studying ancient Greek. He later told an acquaintance that he had seen that Plato offered guidelines for establishing a state, and thus wanted to read the *Republic* in the original. In his diary he wrote that he studied the language so as to "fill up my leisure time." He also read the writings of Marcus Aurelius, and those of Homer and other poets. With the help of a dictionary, he translated several poems into Hebrew. He read the book of Genesis in the Greek Septuagint translation.[72]

He seems not to have missed life with Paula. Blanche "Baffy" Dugdale, Weizmann's astute political adviser, was a pleasant person to spend time with. She was Balfour's niece. He also spent time with Doris May, the bubbly Catholic secretary who also worked at the Zionist Organization's offices. Baffy once took him to the Sunday service at the Scottish church that her father, an architect, had built. The minister read from the third chapter of the book of Exodus, in which God tells the shepherd Moses to tell Pharaoh, Let my people go. He then gave a sermon on the words "I am that I am," God's response when Moses asks what to tell the children of Israel when they ask the name of the God who has sent him. Ben-Gurion heard in the sermon a belief that there was always someone to turn to, even in wartime. Then came "the shocking shriek of the siren." Cannon thundered outside and explosions sounded. But the minister continued to speak, and the worshippers continued to sit in their pews, rising only to sing hymns. When Ben-Gurion went outside after the service, it turned out that a German plane had been shot down not far away.[73]

"Miss May" was forty-one years old, a graduate of Oxford, and unmarried. Her fiancé had been killed in the Royal Air Force. She frequently wrote to Arthur Lourie about her relations with Ben-Gurion. Her letters evince admiration but still, at this stage of their relationship, not romance. She wondered why he was not always surrounded by bevies of adoring females, and termed him a boy in need of protection. She found him "devastatingly appealing" in his helplessness, but the feelings he aroused in her, she wrote, were "maternal."

She told Lourie, in whose house Ben-Gurion was lodging, that she twice slept over there because she could not get home during air-raid alerts. "For the second time in a week," she informed Lourie, she got into "the inappropriate promiscuity of your bed and D's pyjamas."[74]

❖

At the beginning of November 1940, two ships that had set out from Romania came into Haifa's port. A third ship joined them at the end of the month.
Together they bore thirty-six hundred passengers, most of them Jews from
Germany and Austria. They had arrived without immigration certificates.
The authorities announced that the refugees would be deported to the island
of Mauritius in the Indian Ocean. In the meantime, some of the passengers
had been transferred to a detention camp at Atlit, just south of Haifa. In
preparation for their deportation, about seventeen hundred of them were put
on a ship named the *Patria*. Ben-Gurion learned about it from the press. Weizmann warned him that it was not the right time to embarrass the British—
the negotiations over the establishment of the Jewish battalions had reached a
critical juncture. Ben-Gurion agreed, and proposed a compromise. From this
point forward the British fleet would not allow boats carrying Jewish refugees
to reach Palestine's shores, but the refugees who had already arrived would
be allowed to stay. Weizmann did not succeed in acting on this suggestion,
because five days later the Haganah placed a bomb in the *Patria*. The explosion killed about 250 of the passengers, as well as several British servicemen.
Not all the bodies of the missing were found.[75]

No one knew for sure who had given the order; the question remains
unanswered to this day. It seems probable that Haganah officials, among
them Eliyahu Golomb, acted on their own volition; conceivably, Katznelson
and Sharett were in on the secret plan. Perhaps the original plan went awry
by mistake, or on purpose. The principal question was whether the Zionist
struggle justified putting the lives of the *ma'apilim* at risk. As at the time of
the battle of Tel Hai, it was a moral and ethical question that required a
choice between an honorable death and a shameful life. One outcome of the
debate was a sharp condemnation in *Hapo'el Hatza'ir*, the Mapai newspaper.
"A malicious hand" sank the ship, the newspaper declared. The article infuriated members of the Haganah. Two young men showed up at the editorial
offices and one of them, Amos Ben-Gurion, slapped the editor. His father
defended his deed, without mentioning him by name. He said that the whole
affair should be seen as the "greatest possible moral failing," because before

the sabotage, no one had risen up to prevent the deportation of the refugees by force.[76]

As he awaited a decision on the establishment of Jewish battalions in Palestine, Ben-Gurion hoped that Amos would stand out among the warriors defending the country; he sought to arrange for his son to serve under an officer named Orde Wingate, known by the Jews of Palestine simply as "the friend," for his actions in defense of the community during the Arab Revolt. Amos wanted to be a pilot; as a British subject by birth, he could join the Royal Air Force. Weizmann's son, Michael, served there. Ben-Gurion at first remained adamantly against the idea, but in the end, in part under the pressure of Paula's telegrams, he gave up. Apparently his troubled relationship with his son made it impossible for the two to communicate directly about the issue. Ben-Gurion sent his final recommendation to Moshe Sharett, as if it were an issue of national importance. Amos was not accepted into the RAF; he served as an army officer and was wounded in Italy.[77]

Naturally, Ben-Gurion was asked his opinion of the sabotage of the *Patria*. He was in favor—it was a "Zionist action," he maintained; had he been in Palestine at the time, he would not have prevented it. At the same time, he offered a reasonable version of what had happened. "No one expected so many victims," he said. "It was an act of God." His version became that of the history books.[78] The survivors of the *Patria* were permitted to remain in Palestine. Ben-Gurion was in the United States at the time.

"I WAS IN DESPAIR"

His stay in London had ended in another break with Weizmann. This time it happened when Foreign Secretary Anthony Eden and Colonial Secretary Lloyd thwarted Churchill's agreement to enlist Palestinian Jews to serve in the defense of their country. Ben-Gurion asked Weizmann how that had happened. Weizmann responded, as he often did, with sarcastic condescension. Was he under cross-examination, he asked? "I was in despair," Ben-Gurion related. He demanded to be present at any meeting Weizmann had on this matter, and gave him an ultimatum. "Either you don't move a hand or foot without me on matters of defense and the army, or you won't see my face again." He explained that he could not return to Palestine and tell people there that they should enlist in an army that was not designated to defend their own country. Weizmann rejected his demand. All the more disappointing was Baffy Dugdale's failure to support him. "Something new came to light this morning, which I had not suspected," he wrote three days after she took him to the church service. "This woman has ambitions to dominate Zionism through her domination of Chaim," he wrote.[79]

❖

When he reached America in October 1940, he found it caught up in a presidential election. Ben-Gurion was for Roosevelt. For some reason, he thought some of the rhetoric of the Republican candidate, Wendell Willkie, compared with the propaganda that put Hitler in power. As usual, he recorded the polls in his diary. It was the second time he had closely followed an American presidential election. "Then, too, there had been unusual tension before the election," he wrote to Paula, referring to Woodrow Wilson's reelection campaign. "The fate of the world depended to no small extent on the results of the election." As in Wilson's time, Ben-Gurion hoped to gain support for the establishment of a Jewish army. He managed to get a donation to fund the first Jewish pilots' course. But he summed up the effort with disappointment and arrogance. "The Jews of America live in fear," he wrote. "They are afraid of war and they are afraid of peace. In the elections, they were afraid that Willkie would be elected but also afraid to support Roosevelt openly. The Zionists fear the non-Zionists and the non-Zionists fear the non-Jews." He presumed, however, that the conscience of American Jewry would eventually wake up.[80]

He met with leaders, spoke at rallies, tried to interest journalists. His arrival in the United States was noted by *The New York Times*, along with the arrival of other personages. A reporter for that newspaper who heard him speak about the need to recruit a Jewish battalion responded: "But that is Jabotinsky's idea." Jabotinsky had died three months earlier, in August 1940. But Ben-Gurion noted that the Revisionists were adept at public relations and even received professional advice in that field. An acquaintance of Ben-Gurion's who had come to the United States from Palestine said that "the national spirit was depressed." Unlike the massive willingness the Jews of

Palestine had displayed to enlist in the British army before the war, at this point only four hundred had volunteered for a unit that would actually defend the country. Ben-Gurion thought that was horrible, and in January 1941 set out for home. Because of the war, the trip took a month—he had to journey via New Zealand, Australia, and India. He brought with him an inner, Churchillian drive to heighten the public's spirit. He was now a full-time "Zionist preacher," he declared. That is what he did during the months that followed. He had never felt as much a "Zionist soldier" as he felt following his return from the London of Churchill and the Blitz, he said.[81]

ZIONIST ALERTNESS

"WHAT HAVE WE COME TO?"

One evening, in February 1941, Ben-Gurion attended the Palestine Folk Opera. The show was Johann Strauss's *Die Fledermaus*. He did not often listen to music, but attended the theater from time to time. "I had a nice evening," he told the members of his party. "There was pleasant music and good acting and I enjoyed myself." It was not unusual—the newspapers of the time show that wartime Tel Aviv offered a wealth of cultural events and leisure activities. Advertisements invited the public to attend sports competitions and fashion shows, end-of-year sales, plays, concerts, and other entertainments. The city's cafés and bars, hotels and dance clubs, remained crowded and lively, as if there were no world war. Terror attacks were almost entirely a thing of the past.

The problem was that the operetta began late. The audience was already seated and the singers were waiting for the curtain to rise. Ten minutes passed. Ben-Gurion went to ask the manager what was going on. The manager explained that they were holding for a senior British official who had been invited and had confirmed that he would attend. Ben-Gurion saw it as a national insult.

Yes, it's a tiny matter, there are worse things, he admitted, but for him it was "very bad." True, he had never gone to the opera in London, he said, but he had never heard of a performance being held up because some dignitary was running late. "I was ashamed," he said. "What have we come to? Why are we spitting in our own faces? If that is how we are, why are we incensed when others insult us?" In his opinion, the tardy bureaucrat should have been told to wait for the intermission.

At this time, Ben-Gurion was going from one public assembly to another preaching "Zionist alertness." He demanded that Palestine's Jews "stand tall," including to the British regime. "I am not interested in whether they love or hate us, but I want them to respect us," he said in the wake of the incident at the opera. "We will act with honor and they will respect us."[1]

The term "Zionist alertness" (literally, "Zionist tension") thus also gave expression to patriotic anger against the British. Never had cooperation with the British been tighter and more vital than during the war. As part of this, the Jewish Agency's Political Department used the Haganah's intelligence service to ferret out German and Italian spies among Jews who reached Palestine. But Ben-Gurion said that the English had imposed a "half-Nazi regime" in the country.[2]

❖

While he was still in New York, Ben-Gurion had been cut off from Palestine. When he returned, he felt isolated. "I have no personal interest in delving into what happened here," he said. The leaders of the Jewish Agency and Mapai in Palestine did not frequently report to him about what was happening and generally did not consult him. That irked and troubled him, and from time to time he protested. Yitzhak Gruenbaum filled in for him at the Jewish Agency; Sharett, the Jewish Agency treasurer Eliezer Kaplan, and Golomb continued to coordinate ties with the British, the economy, and security, respectively. The sky did not fall. When they needed a leader to offer guidance, they asked Katznelson. Upon his return from the United States, Ben-Gurion was a private individual; following his resignation, he held no official post. "I sit before you at the moment as just an ordinary Jew," he said to his colleagues in the Jewish Agency. But the members of the Executive asked him to rejoin the body, and his resignation might as well have never happened. He did not immediately have much to do; in the meantime, he placed himself on the sidelines and waited.[3]

The country he had left was deep in an economic crisis that had its origins in the time of the Arab Revolt. The one he returned to ten months later was flourishing. Tens of thousands made their livings off the war, some of them by building defensive fortifications, mostly on the northern border. In total, the British security apparatus employed about 15 percent of the Jewish labor force. The British decision to make Palestine a supply depot was due in part to the lobbying Weizmann and Ben-Gurion had done in London. Military production in the service of the British also encouraged the Haganah's own military industry.[4]

The atmosphere of complacency that he encountered upon his return filled him with "fear and trepidation." He had the impression that the people in Palestine were not living the war, he said. In April 1940, Sharett reported to the Executive that, given the situation on the Balkan and North African fronts, a German invasion of Palestine could not be ruled out. It was very unlikely, he said, and did not shake his confidence that Britain would be victorious, but he felt duty-bound to inform his colleagues that he was under public pressure to work out a plan for a massive evacuation from Palestine. Ben-Gurion was present. A few days later, he was speaking of a Nazi invasion as if it were already under way and he was the only one to have noticed. "Palestine is already at the front, the conflagration has reached us but we don't see it. We are not preparing for it and are not living it . . . but the war has now reached the gates of Palestine, that is now a fact." He did not argue that more "Zionist alertness" could prevent a Nazi invasion. On the contrary, "it is a volcano that cannot be put out with a cup of tea," he said, "but we must see it. When will we see it? When the lava covers us?"[5]

As the German advance continued, the Jewish Agency considered whether some of its leaders should be sent overseas, where they perhaps should function as a kind of government-in-exile, just as other nations had done. The Executive asked Ben-Gurion to go to London, but he refused. It was precisely in such hard times, he said, that "each of us must become a Zionist preacher."[6]

❖

It was a traveling political awakening show and a personal journey to his roots. Over and over again he laid out the fundamental principles of Zionism for his listeners, as if he had just discovered them for the first time; again and again he shared some of his most profound experiences that had shaped him as a person, and he seemed to relive them each time. It was an ideological and indeed an ethical experience—"the Jews of Palestine needed to tell the Jews of the Exile: 'Zion, not as a lesson for the future, but for our own time.'" And it was a political campaign as well. Zionist patriotism fortified Ben-Gurion's power; he frequently intervened in his party's affairs and bolstered his hold over defense affairs. The term "Zionist alertness" thus dictated the proper attitude toward the war and the slaughter of the Jews of Europe.

He described this work as a life-or-death engagement. Hence the need to help the English destroy Hitler. All the nations participating in the war were interested in their collective victory, and each one wanted its own victory, he said, and the Jewish people were no different. He meant a victory for Palestine. He believed that Germany would be defeated, but took into account that after the war the British would not repay the Jews for the assistance they had given. That meant that the Jews of Palestine should lend assistance to the British as allies, "not as servants, not as nameless people." Therefore, a Jewish army was also needed to defend Palestine against the German army. It was also a matter of honor. "At the very least Jews will die as men and not as dogs," he said.[7]

"Zionist alertness" toward "the annihilation of European Jewry," as he already termed it then, in 1940, required at this point preparations for the absorption of those Jews who remained alive after the war. "Zionism is now one thing and only one thing: concern for saving five million Jews." When he said "now," he was referencing "concern." Rescue would come only after the war.[8] He presumed that there would be millions of Jewish refugees in

Europe at that time. He did not know precisely how many and cited estimates, between three and eight million. They would have no future in Europe, he asserted. Even if they were promised full and equal rights, it would be nothing but an "empty dream" that could undermine the Zionist enterprise in Palestine. That was why it was essential, even in this time of Jewish catastrophe, to fight "quack remedies," as he referred to plans for Jewish immigration to other countries. He termed it "greater Zionism." He believed in the power of "Zionist alertness" in Palestine to make an impression on American Jews and to reinforce their willingness to harness themselves to the promotion of Zionism.[9] He left some ends loose regarding the basics of Jewish identity. Despite that, the lectures were well organized and clear, among his best.

During those months, he was in a constant state of nostalgia; it sometimes seemed as if he were making farewell visits to stations along his life's road, beginning with Yitzhak Tabenkin's room in Warsaw and his early days in Palestine. "There was a different atmosphere then," he said wistfully about the Second Aliyah. The Jewish community was small and weak, half of it was starving to death, but there was "moral inspiration." He meant, among other things, the influence of the Russian Revolution. Everyone was affected by it, he said, even those who claimed not to be. "I may not believe in Karl Marx, but I am a socialist and I am a Zionist," he stressed.[10] Time and again in his speeches he harked back to Sejera, and as is often the case, his memories grew more and more embellished. The story of the Arab who almost killed him turned into a kind of Galilean legend.

He surveyed the terror waves of 1921, 1929, and 1936 and told of his conversations with Arabs "who still have not made peace with the fact that they are not the only masters of the land." He recounted the partition debate, the Blitz, and of course how he had come to admire the spiritual magnitude of the English nation.*[11]

---

* The historiosophical mood that overcame him during these months led him again, as in the past, to compare pioneering Zionism to Europe's colonial conquests, but following several days in India and Africa he again said: "For the first time I felt that I belonged to the white race . . . and one is ashamed of that. I in any case was ashamed of it, in particular in light of the war against the country that claims to be the master race." (Ben-Gurion to Hitahdut Bnei Hamoshavot, April 14, 1941, in Ben-Gurion 2008, p. 358; Ben-Gurion to the Jewish Agency Executive, Oct. 4, 1942, BGA.)

Many of the people who came to hear his speeches had settled in Palestine after the war began. He saw them as a problem, since they had come as refugees, rather than Zionists. "And they remained alien to our enterprise and our vision," he said. "They are different and can bring a holocaust upon us." He nevertheless sought to raise their Zionist alertness. He seems to have had German Jews in mind, as he spent more time meeting with them than with any other group.[12] In contrast, he sang the praises of native-born Palestinian Jews, who were tall and breathed the scent of the soil, "a young Hebrew generation that we should not be ashamed of," as opposed to Diaspora Jews, whose "cowardice" he condemned time and time again.

His thoughts ranged between redemption and hell. "We Jews have real power to help destroy Hitler," he said at the beginning of March 1941, praising the clout of the Zionist enterprise. "Jewish strength in Palestine consists of every Jewish child, every Jewish school, every Jewish tree, every Jewish goat," he declared. A few weeks later, he fantasized that Zionism's end was approaching. "Only a blind man can't see it," he said in early April 1941. "We are on a terrible decline. All of us. The great project of a generation is being destroyed." Six weeks later, he announced: "We now stand, once again, before a revolutionary period, the sea of life storms and roils, and we can again solve the problem of Palestine."[13]

He was a man in his midfifties who was already taking account of his past and shaping how he would be seen in history books. He had received his political education from the French and English, he said. From the French he took clarity and from the English simplicity. "I am nothing but a single craftsman, and at this moment I am working only on Zionism," he said. In one discussion from this time he suddenly declared: "I want our friends [in America] to know that I demanded this of them before my death, that they take care of Zionism at the end of the war."[14]

In general he lectured and spoke, rather than engaging in dialogue with his audience. He imbued everything he said with gravity—the art of humor was almost entirely foreign to him. If he said something funny, he would first make an excuse in the form of "I once said," as if the only legitimate witticism was one from the past, or quoted from others. "I once said that if the Histadrut Executive were to call on ten thousand workers to die, they would die, but if it demanded that they pay a penny more, no one could be sure they would," he related. He attributed to Herbert Samuel the epigram "The Jews are just like the gentiles, but more so."[15]

Some differed with him, but no one could dismiss what he said. His inner conviction made a great impression on those who heard him. With the exception of the elderly Ussishkin, perhaps, there was no other person who lived Zionism so profoundly as part of his personal identity.

"AS IF THE WORLD HAD RETURNED TO ITS PATH"

A few weeks after he began his preaching circuit, Ben-Gurion demanded that the Jewish Agency adopt a "Great Zionism" plan for after the war. It was a fairly long document. Ussishkin complained that it was too long, and Ben-Gurion responded that it could be summed up in a few words: Jewish state, the war against Hitler, Jewish army, war against the White Paper, and Zionist alertness. There was nothing new about it and it was not a pressing matter. The Zionist movement had always been committed to establishing a Jewish state in Palestine, and there was no way to establish one before the war ended. The demand that the Jewish Agency Executive accept his plan thus looked like a display of leadership, and probably grew out of his sense of isolation from Zionist affairs because of his lengthy sojourn overseas.

The members of the Jewish Agency Executive took up the plan. Their debates sound like a continuation of the dispute over the partition plan. To defuse their opposition, Ben-Gurion modified his position, as he often did. As part of this he promised that there would be no forced transfer of Arabs, and if they were to ask him, he thought that the Jewish state should be a British dominion, as Canada was.[16] But the liberalism of the German Jews exasperated him—some of them were demanding a binational state. "Does this man not see himself as a Jew?" he responded to an article by Martin Buber. "If not, he has no business intervening in what the Jews are doing. If he is a Jew, he should act like one." At another opportunity he said that Buber had the "psychology of a servant." He warned the advocates of binationalism that "if you reach an agreement with the Arabs, you will be in Hitler's camp."[17]

Menachem Ussishkin attacked his plan from the perspective of what he considered true Zionism. There was no point talking about an independent state as long as there was not a Jewish majority in Palestine, he said, warning against Zionist apartheid. "In South Africa," he noted, "the blacks are eighty percent and the rulers there are the twenty percent of whites; the eighty percent have no rights at all . . . do you want that the Jews who are twenty percent should rule in Palestine? If that's what you say, then the way you use the term 'Jewish state' is comprehensible. But you won't say that, because you can't say that, since there is no hope that anyone in the non-Jewish world would accept that concept, and also a large part of the Zionist movement would oppose that concept, justly or not." The Bible's laws of war teach, with regard to certain nations, that "you shall utterly destroy them" (Deuteronomy 20:17), Ussishkin pointed out, but times had changed. "Today, first, a Jewish state, and second, equal rights for the Arabs, and third, transfer of the Arabs only if they consent, as Mr. Ben-Gurion has written, that is squaring the circle, it is impossible." Nor was there any use in talking about a "Jewish state of Tel Aviv and its environs," Ussishkin said, as it would be impossible for such a state to take in five million Jews. He thus proposed limiting the Jewish Agency's goals in the years to come to large-scale immigration.

Ben-Gurion did his best to accommodate him, proposing that the question of borders be left vague at this point. "We won't say now what the borders should be. If they ask me what the Land of Israel is, I will say that it will be determined by our Zionist strength." That is what he had always said. "No one should ask me about borders," he told his colleagues in 1939. "It depends on our strength." But Ussishkin stood his ground. "Why fool ourselves?" he asked. "After all, every one of us knows that it will not happen during his lifetime." He died four months later.[18] Weizmann remained the last Zionist statesman whose career had begun during Herzl's lifetime.

❖

In June 1941, the British army employed several dozen members of the Haganah in reconnaissance, in advance of its incursion into Syria, which was controlled by the French Vichy government. A few days later, the Haganah reconnaissance detachment participated in the invasion itself. Among its members were two young men who were to play major roles in the military and politics—Moshe Dayan and Yigal Allon. Dayan lost his left eye in the operation. It was one of the first operations of the Palmach (Strike Forces), which the Haganah had recently set up in cooperation with the British. Ben-Gurion saw it as a step toward the establishment of a Jewish army. For him, the purpose of the Haganah's mission was not just security; it was also to "assemble around it" all Zionist Jewish youth and to prepare for the conquest of the Negev Desert. The long political struggle over control of the Haganah had not yet been decided; some of the Jewish Agency Executive were displeased with Ben-Gurion's militaristic attitude. Gruenbaum warned his colleagues to watch out for people with "a large, fiery, and impulsive temperament." Then, as usual, the Executive accepted Ben-Gurion's program.[19]

❖

Around that time, Ben-Gurion received a letter from Shlomo Zemach. After resigning from his post as headmaster of the Kadoorie Agricultural High School, he served as a Jewish Agency emissary in the United States, and then in South Africa. When he returned to Palestine, he made his home in Jerusalem. He didn't have a job. So he wrote to his friend David. "I know that you cannot and probably should not attend to individual cases at this time," he began, "but, believe me, were it not for the fact that my family depends on me, and if not for the shadow of literal hunger at the door to my home, I would hold back and wait patiently and not bother you today." He had had many failures in life, he wrote, but had succeeded as an agronomist. He worked for nine years at the Jewish Agency's Agricultural Experimental Station in Rehovot, furthering intensive farming, which at the time was but a dream. He had fought for water, for irrigation methods, for vegetables, for crop rotation, and, thank God, he wrote, his dream had become reality. He did not care where he worked, who would be his boss, how much he would earn—the main thing was that they take him back. He asked for Ben-Gurion's assistance in the name of the friendship of their youth, he wrote. "You know very well that my hands are not versed in writing about personal matters. I speak to almost no one about them, but I said, with you, David, I can speak as a friend. After all, there were days when I hid nothing from you."

Zemach did not just mail a letter—he went to see Ben-Gurion in his office. There he told Ben-Gurion why the Experimental Station had not taken him back. He had been blacklisted by a high Jewish Agency official who knew that Zemach knew that he, the official, was a thief. "All Ben-Gurion had to do was pick up the phone and say a word to [the treasurer] Kaplan and everything would have worked out," he later wrote in his memoirs. "But when I went to him and told him, so foolishly, speaking to an old friend, that I was down to my last loaf of bread, what I saw in his eyes was not sorrow over his friend's troubles, but a glint of joy, a spark of pleasure, as if he wanted to say, 'Look how things have worked out—I can finally see the son of Abba Zemach standing before me in the pangs of poverty, asking me to have mercy on him.' That was so transparent in his face that I ended the conversation and left the room." Not long thereafter, Zemach found a different job and began to write the book on humor that would become his favorite.[20]

❖

On June 22, 1941, Germany invaded the Soviet Union, and three days later, Ben-Gurion said that the war between the two could save the world "and our land as well." For the moment, it looked as if the attack on the Soviet Union had distanced the war from Palestine. He felt much better. Under the new circumstances, it was no longer as hard, psychologically, to leave Palestine. Five months after beginning his Zionist preaching campaign, he set off for the United States again. On the way he stopped over in London for several weeks, reliving "those good days," as he said. His beloved city, "abounding with and radiating confidence and bravery," had recovered. Here and there one could still see evidence of the bombings, and young people were dressed in khaki, but the bombardments had stopped and the sirens no longer wailed. It was hard to get a decent meal in a restaurant, but other than that the war was felt only in the newspaper headlines, "as if the world had returned to its path," he wrote. He got together with acquaintances—journalists, officials, and politicians, among them the new colonial secretary, Lord Moyne. Ben-Gurion told him that, after the war, Europe would have three million Jews who would need to be settled in Palestine. Lord Moyne suggested that, after the war, a Jewish state be established in East Prussia. Ben-Gurion made no progress with his main goal, the establishment of a Jewish army under British control. In contrast, he established close relations with the U.S. ambassador, John Winant, and received from him a promise to arrange a talk with President Roosevelt. Weizmann had first met with Roosevelt in February 1940.[21]

"JEWISH COMPLEX"

In July 1942, Ben-Gurion met in New York with a man named Francis Kettaneh, who confirmed reports that the Germans had put into operation a plan to methodically annihilate the entire Jewish population of Poland. Kettaneh was an Arab Catholic from Palestine living in America. At the time, Ben-Gurion knew that hundreds of thousands of Polish Jews had already been murdered, but the information provided by Kettaneh had a much greater impact than early reports on the slaughter of the Jews had had. "What he told me seems to be true," Ben-Gurion later informed the members of the Jewish Agency Executive.[22]

❖

When the war broke out, the American Zionist Organization established an Emergency Committee, headed by the Reform rabbi Stephen Wise, of whom Ben-Gurion wrote: "Personally, he is the person most esteemed and beloved and respected by the broad public, but because of much bother and many meetings and the search for funding and thousands of different goals, he is always tired and fatigued, dozing off at meetings and unable to focus when something vital is on the agenda." There was talk of replacing him, perhaps with another Reform rabbi, Abba Hillel Silver. Silver, according to Ben-Gurion, was "forceful in his opinions, a proud Jew who knows Hebrew and Palestine (more than other leaders), and is not fearful about displaying dual loyalty, but the Zionist public does not like him and he has no clue about Zionist policy."[23] With these two, and innumerable other activists who spent most of their time arguing with and intriguing against one another, Ben-Gurion did his best to heighten Zionist alertness among America's Jews. He knew everyone; twenty-five years had passed since he first came to them. In the large picture, nothing had changed—the same mentality, the same sensi-tivities. He knew exactly what he could expect from them, but hoped to get more. He tried to engage the non-Zionists. His contacts with administration officials were meant to persuade the American government to press Britain to form a Jewish army in Palestine.

He established himself in the Winthrop Hotel in New York, on Lexing-ton Avenue. This time, too, most of the people he saw were Jews. He spoke at rallies, went to meetings, had lunch with people. He did everything himself—made phone calls to set up meetings, wrote letters, took the train from place to place. When, two months later, he moved to Washington, he packed up his books himself.[24] He had not previously engaged in American political lobbying, and as was his common practice, he studied the craft, as he did every new subject. People he consulted advised him to gather a group of young people around him and to seek ties with progressive-radical forces in the government, including the agrarian circle around Vice President Henry Wallace.

He brought with him to Washington a very valuable phone number, that of the Supreme Court justice Felix Frankfurter, whose acquaintance he had made through the late justice Louis Brandeis. Ben-Gurion asked for an hour or two of his time, to get his advice. Frankfurter asked if it would be an hour or two hours, and invited Ben-Gurion to come to his home at 9:00 p.m.; he opened the door himself. Ben-Gurion seems to have done most of the talking. Among other things, he said that America's entry into the war improved the prospects of the Zionist struggle. Frankfurter, who was older than Ben-Gurion, treated him with paternal affection; according to Ben-Gurion, the justice lauded his intelligence and credibility, and revealed to him a state secret that would be made public only twenty-four hours hence—Winston Churchill was in town.

Frankfurter promised to do his best to help, and a week later invited Ben-Gurion to his chambers for a lunch with David Nyles, the son of a Jewish tailor who was an aide to President Roosevelt; one of his tasks was managing the White House's contacts with minority groups. A third guest was Ben Cohen, whom Ben-Gurion had met in London; Cohen was a close associate of the president's. Two of these three influential American Jews had heard Ben-Gurion in the past; Nyles was listening for the first time. Ben-Gurion opened, as usual, with the story of his early years in Palestine, how he had been one of the sowers and reapers, pavers and builders, and how the wasteland had become fertile. He said that the officials of the colonial administration in Palestine were hostile to the Zionist project. They knew that after the war there would be three million Jewish refugees who would need a home, but would do everything in their power to prevent the Jews from coming to Palestine. He had thus come to the conclusion that the future of Zionism depended on America, and when he said America, he meant Roosevelt. The president, he knew, did not live in a void. He was surrounded by advisers and friends. He, Ben-Gurion, had come to Washington to win the hearts of twenty or thirty people.

Cohen said that he needed to go and asked what plan Ben-Gurion was seeking support for. Ben-Gurion said a Jewish army, as well as a regime that would permit large-scale Jewish immigration. He did not say a Jewish state. Why a Jewish army, Cohen asked dubiously, why not simply volunteer for the British army? That was a question that many people asked; for Ben-Gurion, it was a "Jewish complex." Nyles, an introverted and quiet man, did not say much, but he also counseled caution, lest the Zionists give the impression that they were looking only after their own interests. He proposed that he and Ben-Gurion meet privately, "for a more serious discussion." When the two advisers left, Frankfurter told Ben-Gurion that he had made a good impression on Nyles.[25] It was the most important conversation Ben-Gurion had had up to that point in the United States. His hopes that he would get a meeting with Roosevelt grew.

But the request that the United States promote the establishment of a Jewish army in Palestine encountered opposition. *The New York Times* rejected the idea, since the British opposed it—with good reason, the *Times* thought—because of their concerns about how the Arabs would react. An editorial the paper published also voiced ideological opposition. Everyone knew, it said, that the ultimate purpose of a Zionist army would be to compel the United Nations to establish a Zionist state, an idea that many Jews opposed. In the new world that would rise after the war, "Jews along with other religious and national minorities may live peaceably and happily in every nation, enjoying the full rights of other citizens."[26] Ben-Gurion declared that it was a "vicious article," but he did not give up. "The chances of uniting American Jewry are not bad at all," he declared. Following a meeting with members of the Zionist youth group Habonim, he wrote that they were "alert, vigilant, perceptive, and of much promise."[27]

His work plan proceeded successfully. Secretary of the Treasury Henry Morgenthau Jr. was the son of the ambassador who had intervened on his behalf when he had been imprisoned under Turkish rule. By this point, Ben-Gurion had become an expert lobbyist. Before parting from Morgenthau, he made a point of asking for his phone number, and requested permission to call whenever he felt it necessary. He prepared himself well for meetings; a transcript of a long conversation he had with members of the research and analysis staff of the Office of Strategic Services, headed by the Harvard historian William L. Langer, shows that he spoke to them as equals.[28]

Frankfurter invited him to dinner at his home with William Bullitt, the first U.S. ambassador to the USSR and an intellectual who had coauthored a book with Sigmund Freud. Bullitt was about to set out for a visit to the Middle East at the president's behest. Ben-Gurion remarked that Billy and Felix, as they called each other, began the evening with a whiskey; he did not have a drink. During the subsequent conversation, Bullitt declared that all the Arabs should be expelled from Palestine and a Jewish state established there. Ben-Gurion responded, as always, very cautiously, that there was no need to deport the Arabs, because the country was economically capable of supporting them all. From this point forward, Ben-Gurion and Bullitt met frequently.[29]

The Emergency Committee in New York paid for his stay in Washington, and also agreed to send a secretary, Miriam Cohen, and pay for ten days of her work there. It was the beginning of a love story.[30]

"IS THAT NOT TRUE, DEAR LOVE?"

During those months, Ben-Gurion worked on organizing a large Jewish conference, in lieu of the Zionist Congress, which could not be convened during the war. He sought to gain as broad a consensus as possible for a program the Jewish Agency Executive had approved before he left Palestine, including the demand for the immediate establishment of a Jewish army and, after the war, of a Jewish state. As usual, he met opposition. America's non-Zionist Jews enjoyed great public prestige and economic power. Ben-Gurion tried to integrate them into the Zionist effort, and as part of that had to explain why he rejected Magnes's binational approach; it was not always easy. In contrast, he developed close ties with Hadassah, the American women's Zionist organization. Once he went so far as to force himself to go with the women and their husbands to a benefit performance of *The Marriage of Figaro*.[31] Even though he was well acquainted with American Jewish life, he felt alien among them. "I feel here altogether alone among so many people, but it is like a wasteland," he wrote to Doris May. "In lonely sleepless nights I am still with my Plato."*[32]

May had heard that Ben-Gurion was overcoming his loneliness. She continued to correspond with the Zionist diplomat Arthur Lourie, and Lourie knew that his secretary Miriam Cohen and Ben-Gurion had fallen in love. He passed this hot bit of gossip on to London, and May seems to have enjoyed it.[33]

❖

In April 1942, Ben-Gurion came down with back pains. At Miriam Cohen's suggestion he traveled, alone, to a resort in the Catskills, not far from Beaver Lake. The letters he sent her from there read much like the poetic outpourings that he sometimes wrote when he encountered the majesty of nature, at sea or in the air, whether at Niagara Falls or Trogen and Buergenstock in the Swiss Alps. The skies of upstate New York "declare the glory of God," and the sun was "a divinity." The frogs sang "wonderful symphonies" and he marveled at the cattle as well—it was all like in Palestine—so different from "that empty, forsaken desert called the city of New York." He thought wistfully of the protagonists of his beloved Greek mythology and fantasized about another companion, "much taller than any of the Athenians, very upright, poised, fresh-looking, always deep thoughts, sure of himself, unmoved although very sensible." He "never uses any of these long-winded, empty,

---

* His boyhood friend Shmuel Fuchs, who was now spelling his name Fox, did not mingle with Zionists, and the ties between the two men were tenuous. When Ben-Gurion needed urgent treatment, he went to a different dentist. (Ben-Gurion to Paula, Jan. 12, 1939, BGA.)

high-sounding words," and, Ben-Gurion added, "he never tells a lie!" He was an ideal friend. He told Ben-Gurion the story of his love and held forth on the meaning of life and love, and a "wonderful story of mysterious drops falling from the heavens, of refreshing, caressing breezes, of unspeakably beautiful and generous rays of light." He was a tree, "a true, living, evergreen tree, deeply in love with the earth, which he does not want to leave for a single moment. Is that not true, dear love?" he wrote to Cohen. They exchanged their thoughts about the world and words of longing.

As new lovers do, the two of them wove a web of romantic mystery around their letters and around themselves. They called the letters the "BL papers," after Beaver Lake. She referred to Ben-Gurion as Winthrop, after the name of the hotel he generally stayed at in New York. Ben-Gurion assured her that, while he could be unpleasant at times, he would always be a faithful friend on whom she could trust entirely. His word was sacred. In this sense, the letters evince a longing for friendship as much as promises of love. He was as heady as a teenage boy; the eroticism with which he imbued his natural surroundings recall Bialik's "Scroll of Fire," which Ben-Gurion had once sent to his beloved friend Fuchs.[34]

The secret of Ben-Gurion and Cohen's love quickly spread and soon it was the talk of the town in Jewish New York. From there it reached Tel Aviv; Paula took it hard. Beginning in early January, she sought to obtain, through Jewish Agency officials, including Moshe Sharett, a copy of her diploma from her nursing school in New York. She presumably intended to start providing for her own livelihood. A few months later, Ben-Gurion told her that there was no way to receive the document.[35]

Geula and Renana sided with their mother and severed contact with their father. Renana was preparing for her high school graduation exams at the time, and Ben-Gurion wrote to her saying that he understood her silence. After all, she had a lot of schoolwork and also needed to play, go to the movies, and spend time with friends. "The last thing that comes to your mind is a letter to me," he wrote, as if this were the only reason for her lack of communication. He sent her a long account of his activities in America, like those he had sent in the past to Paula, and asked that she write to him about what was going on at school and in the neighborhood. The most personal sentence he was able to write was "I bought nylon stockings for you and Mother and

Geula, but I don't know how to send them to you." Apparently Renana was not interested in stockings at the time. "I thought that betrayal is a horrible thing," she later said. "Mother was hysterical."[36]

"I WILL NEVER SEE HIM AGAIN"

In mid-April 1942, Chaim Weizmann arrived in the United States. He was not pleased to find Ben-Gurion there and Ben-Gurion was not happy about his arrival. At the time, he was ratcheting up his efforts to get a meeting with Roosevelt, and had wanted to see him before Weizmann came. He told Frankfurter that Ambassador Winant had promised to arrange an appointment; Frankfurter promised to speak with the White House. The president's emissary to the Middle East, William J. Donovan, promised to convey to the president a memorandum on the need for a Jewish army; nothing more than that happened.[37]

Ben-Gurion heard that Winant was in Washington and sought him out in the White House and State Department; he left him messages at the hotel where he was supposed to be lodging. The ambassador did not take his call; Ben-Gurion sent him a telegram and did not receive an answer. He met with another judge, Samuel Rosenman, whom he was told had been a close friend and confidant of the president's for the last twenty years, and a frequent visitor at his home. Rosenman told him that "everyone" in Washington was asking if he had already met Ben-Gurion. But Rosenman also offered only to convey a memorandum to the White House. Ben-Gurion said to himself that perhaps it was harder to get access to the "captain," as he called him, because of the war.[38]

❖

Weizmann represented only the Zionist Organization, but since the time of the Balfour Declaration he had conducted himself as if he were the king of the Jews. Aside from his prestige as a scientist and his appealing British-Jewish humor, he acted the role of the statesman, projecting optimistic melancholy and aristocratic grandeur. In New York he lodged at the luxurious St. Regis hotel. "Hotels are always optimistic," he once said.[39] In London he stayed at the Dorchester. He most likely never made a phone call himself to set up a meeting. Prior to his arrival he published a long article in *Foreign Affairs*, a prestigious forum for leaders of countries. He demanded a Jewish state in Palestine.[40] In the months that followed, he met three times with Vice President Wallace, mostly about his own scientific work; he was developing a chemical process that would begin with corn and end up, so he hoped, with rubber.

❖

The disagreements between Ben-Gurion and Weizmann were not fundamental. Ben-Gurion could easily have penned Weizmann's *Foreign Affairs* article, had he been asked. Weizmann also agreed that the fate of Zionism would be decided, in large measure, in Washington and New York. He was more apprehensive than Ben-Gurion was, however, about a break with Britain. With regard to bringing millions of Jewish refugees to Palestine within a short time after the war, he was skeptical. While not opposing a Jewish army in Palestine, he believed that the efforts to gain British consent had failed.

The surrogate Zionist Congress convened on May 9, 1942, in the historic Biltmore Hotel on Madison Avenue in New York. It was attended by several hundred delegates, most of them from the United States. As the representative of the Jewish Agency, Ben-Gurion positioned himself as an outside conciliator between self-aggrandizing activists who sought respect and were addicted to the joy of insulting one another. He was also deeply involved in the scheming behind the scenes that preceded the conference. He put most of his efforts into battling over the wording of the Zionist declaration that he wanted to take home with him. Nearly every word was the subject of debate and required compromise.

The Biltmore Program was perhaps the strongest possible declaration that could have been extracted at that time from America's Zionists, but it barely came close to the fundamental aspirations of Zionist ideology. It called only for making Palestine into a "Jewish Commonwealth integrated in the structure of the new democratic world." The word "state" does not appear. The conference called for the Jewish Agency to receive authority over immigration and development. According to the program, the White Paper regulations were to be revoked and a Jewish army established to defend Palestine. Ben-Gurion also held himself back—the boldest political statement he made was that "the Mandate must be entrusted to the Jewish people themselves," in the form of "governmental authority." It was still too early to say what would happen thereafter. Neither did the Zionist preacher call on America's Zionists to ready themselves or their children to return to their historical homeland. He spoke of immigration to Palestine only in connection with the persecution of the Jews of Nazi-occupied Europe and the plight of the refugees who would survive the war, not in terms of the Zionist dream of the redemption of the entire Jewish nation. He evoked the tragedy of the *Struma*, a ship carrying 760 Jewish refugees from Romania that had been sunk two months previously in the Black Sea.

Not long afterward, Ben-Gurion told his colleagues in the Jewish Agency Executive that the goal of the conference had been to bolster unity among American Zionists, to clarify Zionism's goals, and to put both the unity and the goals on public display. The event was an important one, he stressed, although he had hoped for a more explicit commitment to Jewish independence. He used the words "commonwealth" and "self-governing Jewish Palestine" at the Jewish Agency Executive meeting as well.[41] The Biltmore Conference would later come to be seen as a milestone in the struggle for the establishment of the State of Israel.*

❖

Two days after the conference, Ben-Gurion's father died in Tel Aviv at the age of eighty-six. During his final years, he split his time between the homes of his two daughters, Tzipora Ben-Gurion, who lived in Haifa, and Rivka

---

* According to *The New York Times*, the conference was a show of confidence in the leadership of Weizmann and Ben-Gurion. While Ben-Gurion must have been pleased by that formulation, he probably would not have liked hearing one delegate describe the dramatic climax of the event as the moment when Rabbi Stephen Wise, chairman of the Emergency Committee, placed on Chaim Weizmann's finger a signet ring he said he had received from Theodor Herzl at the end of the Second Zionist Conference. The significance of the gesture was not lost on the mesmerized audience—America's Zionists were designating Chaim Weizmann as Herzl's heir. ("Zionists in Accord at Meeting Here," *New York Times*, May 12, 1942; Louis Lowenthal, interview transcript, BGA, p. 6.)

Har-Melech, who lived in Tel Aviv. Aside from his son David, he was survived by two other sons: Avraham, a religious Histadrut official, and Michel, the kiosk proprietor. Avigdor Ben-Gurion received a Histadrut burial and was eulogized by David Remez and Moshe Sharett. The latter termed him "a veteran soldier of the Zionist movement." Ben-Gurion's absence was strongly felt; Sharett called him "the lion among us"; Shlomo Lavi said: "His spirit is with us." Geula sent her father an almost formal letter of condolence.

Ben-Gurion sent Paula a terse telegram in English and the next day sat down to write a long letter in Hebrew. He described his father as a man full of love, upright and good-hearted, a faithful Jew full of love of Zion. "He gave me a great deal," he wrote, mentioning also his mother's death. In many ways, the letter reads like notes for a political autobiography; the impression is that his father's major contribution to Zionism was not holding his young son back from becoming its leader: "When we, the boys of Płońsk, secretly founded a self-defense force and purchased weapons, and I stood at the head of the organization and hid the weapons in our house—Father knew of it and did not interfere." He recalled that his father had been deeply saddened when his son decided to go to Palestine, because he had hoped that David would become a celebrated scholar, but he came to understand the value of the letters he received from Palestine. "Everyone in town would come to read them," Ben-Gurion noted. He related how he had come down with malaria and gone hungry, and how he had worn tattered and ragged clothes. His father wanted him to come "home," as Ben-Gurion wrote, with quotation marks, and also "tried" to send him money, "but when I asked him to stop, he stopped." On one of the bottom corners of the page he wrote something in tiny, spidery letters that are very hard to make out. "When I return home, I will see him no more. I will never see him again."[42] Disappointed, frustrated, in love, and sad, following with trepidation the British efforts to halt the ongoing German advance toward Palestine, Ben-Gurion prepared to oust Chaim Weizmann; it was one of the most dramatic battles he ever fought. By this time, the conflict between the two had turned into profound personal antipathy, reflexive and seething. Ben-Gurion envied Weizmann; Weizmann sensed that Ben-Gurion was plotting to take his place.

"YOU'RE A TRAITOR!"

On June 10, 1942, Ben-Gurion told Weizmann by phone that he no longer saw himself as his partner. The next day, he sent him a long letter that had gone through a number of drafts. As in the past, his charge was that Weizmann was acting on his own. "You identify your personal position with that of Zionism," Ben-Gurion asserted. "You are here almost two months. You have talked in Washington and New York to many people on Zionism. I wasn't consulted. I wasn't told before or after." That last line seems to be saturated with Ben-Gurion's feeling that he had been insulted: in a previous conversation, Weizmann had told him matter-of-factly that Ambassador Winant had asked him to convey an apology to Ben-Gurion for not having yet kept his promise to arrange a meeting with Roosevelt, which he was still prepared to do. Weizmann passed on the message only weeks later.

Ben-Gurion's letter was largely couched in generalities rather than specifics. "You do not grasp political realities," he wrote. He quoted a number of statements by Weizmann that implicitly disparaged the importance of establishing a Jewish army. Unusually, he did not announce his resignation from the Jewish Agency. Instead, he made a veiled threat to oust Weizmann from his leadership of the Zionist Organization: "If I am asked whether you shall continue to act as you are acting here, or you should resign, my personal advice would be that you should resign."[43]

Weizmann coldly and haughtily rejected all the charges, just as he had when he received a similar ultimatum from Ben-Gurion in London. It was, Weizmann averred, "merely the result of a temporary mood, dictated not by calm judgment but rather by an imaginary grievance caused undoubtedly by the many heartbreaking disappointments which all of us must face in this crucial hour." Ben-Gurion responded, but Weizmann declared that there was no point in continuing the correspondence. The moment of truth had arrived.[44]

❖

On the afternoon of Saturday, June 27, 1942, six leaders of American Zionism convened at the home of Rabbi Stephen Wise, at Ben-Gurion's request.

Weizmann was summoned as well. The meeting had been coordinated by an exchange of written messages; the main points were set down in an official record. Ben-Gurion saw it as a kind of hearing, ending in conviction. He argued that Weizmann's activities in the United States were at this point endangering Zionism's goals. But before initiating the process of unseating Weizmann, he wished to bring the problem to the attention of the Zionist leadership.

Prior to the meeting, Weizmann wrote to Wise denying Ben-Gurion's charges. "I think the real cause of his unhappiness is the failure in persuading the British to agree to our plans for a Jewish fighting force," Weizmann maintained. "But nobody is more unhappy about it than I." He added sarcastically that he did not expect it to be a tribunal that would pass judgment. Actually, the clash between the two men bore a greater resemblance to a fight between two gladiators. With the exception of physical blows, they used all weapons at their disposal. One of those present, Nahum Goldmann, later recalled the following exchange, not recorded in the minutes:

Ben-Gurion: If we had a state, we would have to shoot you. You're a traitor!

Weizmann: And if we had a police force in the state, we would need to send you to a madhouse.

Both of them meant every word they said, and that wasn't Weizmann's worst invective. He maintained that Ben-Gurion was leveling "charges out of the void" of the type Hitler and Mussolini used before they liquidated enemies in purges.[45]

Ben-Gurion reiterated that Weizmann was acting alone, and chronicled their relations since 1935. Weizmann, he said, could never say "no" to an Englishman. He argued that Weizmann had for all intents and purposes set aside the demand for the establishment of a Jewish army, and had consented to counterproposals he had received in London, including a common Jewish-Arab army and a Jewish force that would be enlisted in England but not fight in Palestine. Only the United States could compel Britain to agree to a Jewish army, he claimed, but Weizmann had been dismissive of this demand, even after it had been adopted by the Biltmore Conference. "If Weizmann can do the work only the way he is doing it, it is better that he should resign," Ben-Gurion insisted. He mentioned Ambassador Winant's promise to arrange a meeting with Roosevelt and asked for the support of the assembled leaders.

Initially, Weizmann displayed regal condescension, as if it were below his station to bicker with Ben-Gurion. He said that he would leave it to others to decide whether there was a need for someone to certify that he was kosher. He argued that Ben-Gurion was plotting a "political assassination." With a mocking reference to Shakespeare's *Julius Caesar*, he compared Ben-Gurion to Brutus, implying that he himself was Caesar. But, he assured the others, "the future corpse is not worried." Only the Zionist Congress could force him to resign, he maintained. For the last two and a half years, he claimed, Ben-Gurion had seen the establishment of a Jewish army as the sole problem facing Zionism. "Everything else in comparison with that fades into insignificance," he said. "We may obtain Palestine without an army and we may obtain an army without Palestine." He did not think that the world began and ended with America. Everything had to be done to ensure American and British cooperation in advancing Zionism. The United States could not act without Britain. Zionism could not do anything without Britain. In this context, he remarked that it was not true that he did not know how to say "no" to the British. The word "no" appears in the minutes in Hebrew. He reminded the rest of the men of his deep roots in the Zionist movement, dating to "prior to the Balfour Declaration." Ben-Gurion had then been almost an unknown. The more Weizmann spoke, the more he found it difficult to hold back his anger; each sentence was harsher than the last.

At first he said that Ben-Gurion's chargers were "futile and unjustified," but afterward he referred to them as "misinterpretation, misunderstanding, and in many cases misstatements." By the time the meeting broke up, Weizmann was convinced that Ben-Gurion was out of touch with reality, hallucinating, and suffering from a "sick imagination."[46]

The six Zionist leaders recalled that battle of titans as one of the most tragic incidents in the history of Zionism. One of them, Hayim Greenberg, could not take it and ran out of the room in tears.[47] Ben-Gurion tried to do to Weizmann what the young Weizmann had done to Herzl—his Zionist career was also built, in part, on the demand for a more radical Zionist policy, as if radicalism was evidence of greater patriotic commitment. They competed for the trappings of power and honor; it also manifested the rivalry between the Jews of Palestine and the global Zionist movement, which dated back to the Zionist Commission's arrival in Palestine. Weizmann won this round—five of the six Americans supported him and gave him their confidence. Only one thought that Weizmann should resign.[48]

The next day, Weizmann recounted his efforts to persuade Ben-Gurion to go home. "But he seems to be taking his time over it," he wrote, perhaps with a wink at his affair with Miriam Cohen. "Besides, means of transport are difficult," Weizmann added, as if to stress that that was not the only thing keeping Ben-Gurion in New York.[49] He knew how to be wicked, petty, and vindictive. In the meantime, he continued to humiliate his rival. "We have battled against Revisionism for years under the leadership of Jabotinsky. It would be a calamity to have to fight a new and more dangerous brand of fascism under the leadership of Ben-Gurion," he said. He liberally spread worried insinuations about Ben-Gurion's mental state, and in a letter to the Jewish Agency Executive in Jerusalem—which he did not send in the end—he wrote: "His conduct and deportment were painfully reminiscent of the petty dictator, a type one meets with so often in public life now. They are all shaped on a definite pattern: they are humorless, thin-lipped, morally stunted, fanatical and stubborn, apparently frustrated in some ambition, and nothing is more dangerous than a small man nursing his grievances introspectively." He is obsessed by his mission in life, Weizmann went on. He alone knows what is right, and woe to anyone who disagrees. "Anybody who is unfortunate enough to question some of his statements is simply jumped upon and shouted down and he terrorizes his audience by interminable ranting speeches."[50]

The British embassy in Washington tensely tracked the struggle; its archives show that they knew almost everything. Among other things, they managed to obtain the exchange of letters between Ben-Gurion and Weizmann. Ben-Gurion feared that the British would not allow him to return. The ambassador, Lord Halifax, along with High Commissioner Harold Mac-Michael, and Colonial Secretary Lord Moyne, pondered where Ben-Gurion would do the least damage, in America or in Palestine. An intelligence dossier was prepared for them, covering the power relations between Weizmann and Ben-Gurion. "I doubt whether he will be an embarrassment to Dr. Weizmann in the U.S. Dr. Weizmann is after all a man of great distinction, not only in his own movement but in the world of science, whereas Mr. Ben-Gurion is a nonentity except in his own movement, and in that his reputation is more a local Palestinian one than a worldwide one," the report maintained. "It is rather the case of the elephant and the mosquito. If it comes to a showdown between Dr. Weizmann and Mr. Ben-Gurion, then I put my money on Dr. Weizmann every time." Weizmann asked the ambassador to act to have Ben-Gurion ejected from the United States.[51]

On July 1, 1942, Ben-Gurion arrived in Washington. Weizmann was also there. Ben-Gurion's plan was to visit Lord Halifax so as to discuss with him the state of the Middle Eastern front. They did not meet. "At noon Dr. Weizmann's secretary called to say that she had learned from his chauffeur that he had already been to see Lord Halifax," Ben-Gurion recorded in his diary, in English, as if to designate the entry as testimony against Weizmann. A short time later, Weizmann called to brief him on the talk with the ambassador. Later that day, Weizmann met with Under Secretary of State Sumner Welles. In the evening, Weizmann's secretary phoned again. He was very tired and had gone to bed, she informed Ben-Gurion, but had asked her to tell him that the interview with Mr. Welles had been very successful.[52]

Justice Frankfurter was scheduled to meet with Roosevelt on July 3. Ben-Gurion knew about it and asked, in writing, if there was a possibility that he could also be given an appointment with the president, even for only ten or fifteen minutes, so as to explain the need for a Jewish army. He attached a memorandum summarizing what he intended to tell the president. The forces of Field Marshall Erwin Rommel were approaching the borders of Palestine, he wanted to tell Roosevelt, and "to the Jewish people throughout the world this will mean more than the massacre of some six hundred thousand Jews; it will be the ruin of their Third Temple, the destruction of their Holy of Holies." He intended to tell him that in Palestine there were sixty thousand Jewish men who could be called up. "It may be that with all the Jews of Palestine fighting to the last, invasion and destruction cannot be avoided. But even then it will be a matter of supreme importance whether Jews of Palestine perish as soldiers and men fighting their enemies or are slaughtered like defenseless sheep." Furthermore, "it will deal a fatal blow to the prestige of the British government." Ben-Gurion wanted to impress on the president that "only the friendly intervention of the president of the United States with his British ally" could make it possible to mobilize all Jewish manpower and "avert the catastrophe threatening Palestine."[53]

Five days later, the president received Weizmann for a twenty-five-minute conversation. "Incredible," Ben-Gurion cabled Frankfurter.*[54]

Ben-Gurion returned to New York; it was a weekend, so no one was in the office. "Even with Rommel nearing Alexandria, everybody left for the country for the weekend," he noted scornfully.[55] The next day, he met with Francis Kettaneh, the Palestinian Arab who told him about the annihilation of the Jews of Poland.

"I WAS TERRIFIED"

During the months that Ben-Gurion spent in America, many people he did not know approached him, Jews and non-Jews, with all kinds of ideas and all sorts of plans to improve the world.[†]

He listened to them just as he hoped they would listen to him. He, too, operated largely as a lone lobbyist. Kettaneh, then forty-five years old, had been born in Jerusalem and studied engineering at the American University of Beirut. Together with his three brothers he founded a firm in Beirut that traded in automotive industry products; the business expanded to Damascus, Baghdad, and Tehran. During the 1930s, he was elected secretary of the Rotary Club, and then district governor of all the organization's chapters in the Middle East, including those in Palestine. He and his family settled in the United States in 1942, when he served as the director of Rotary International.[56] A few months prior to his first meeting with Ben-Gurion, he wrote an article in the organization's magazine lauding Jewish-Arab coexistence in Rotary Clubs in Palestine. "During the tragic years of 1936–1938, when Arab and Jew were murdering each other in the Holy Land," he wrote, "the

---

* Roosevelt was most interested in his guest's efforts to advance the production of synthetic rubber, but Weizmann was able to get a few words in about the need for a Jewish army. Lord Halifax had previously asked the White House whether the president would consent to receive Weizmann for a conversation "about the Jews." Roosevelt promised Weizmann a further meeting in two weeks. They next saw each other a year later. (Weizmann to Walter Laqueur, July 15, 1942, in Michael Cohen 1979, p. 330ff.; Lord Halifax request to the White House, BGA, general chronological documentation, June–Aug. 1942.)

† The editors of the official version of his papers frequently note that they have not been able to identify some of the people he mentions in his diary. (Ben-Gurion 2012, p. 225; Ben-Gurion 2008, p. 124, editor's note et al.)

only peaceful oasis were the Rotary Clubs of Jerusalem, Haifa, and Jaffa–Tel Aviv."[57] He may well have been introduced to Ben-Gurion by Aharon Rosenfeld, one of the first shipping agents in Palestine and an active member of Rotary in Haifa. Rosenfeld and Kettaneh knew each other both from Rotary and from the shipping business.*

Whatever the case, Kettaneh brought Ben-Gurion a peace plan based on the division of Palestine into cantons. He noted Arab sympathies for the Nazis and said that they would not believe a word of what they heard from the English. He thus proposed calling a convention under American sponsorship, and listed the senior Washington officials who he thought should participate in the discussions as observers. Ben-Gurion was acquainted with the names and knew some of the officials personally. Kettaneh told Ben-Gurion that he was a British agent, but Ben-Gurion suspected that he might have actually been sent by the State Department.[†]

Ben-Gurion told Kettaneh that Zionists were primarily interested in immigration, and asked for the names of Palestinian Arabs who were prepared to accept Kettaneh's plan. Kettaneh mentioned the mayor of Jaffa, Omar al-Bitar. He also said that Palestine could not absorb six million Jews. They would need to be settled elsewhere, most of them in the United States.[58]

Kettaneh told Ben-Gurion about talks he had recently held with members of the Polish government-in-exile in London. Ben-Gurion received the impression that he had perhaps met with its prime minister, Władysław Sikorski himself, even though Kettaneh did not mention him by name. The Poles told him, Kettaneh said, that they were counting on Hitler to solve Poland's Jewish problem; by the end of the war, he would exterminate them all. If he didn't, they would finish off the job themselves. No Jews would remain in

---

* Ben-Gurion claimed that they were introduced by a man named Rosensky, from Haifa, but he may well have been mistaken. (Ben-Gurion, Diary, July 7, 1942, BGA; Aharon Rosenfeld 1982; Haifa Rotary Club no. 3592 and Rotary Haifa 1932–1955, Haifa Municipal Archive, file 56910; Claim of F.A. Kettaneh Bros. Ltd. against Air Ministry, NA [UK] CO 733/472/7 [680796] 1945–1947.)

† Another acquaintance of Ben-Gurion's, Isaiah Berlin, then on the staff of the British embassy, mentioned in an internal document that Kettaneh worked with both British and American intelligence services. According to Berlin, Kettaneh sent him "a flood of letters." (Isaiah Berlin to Agnus Malcolm, Aug. 2, 1943, in Berlin 2004, p. 440.)

Poland. Kettaneh gave the impression of being honest and was not an anti-Semite, Ben-Gurion later related.*

It was the first time he had heard of the Nazi plan to exterminate Poland's Jews from a non-Jewish source. "I was terrified," he told the Jewish Agency Executive. He and Kettaneh agreed to remain in contact, and they met again three weeks later.[59]

Several researchers at the Ben-Gurion Institute later sought to learn from his acquaintances when, in their estimate, "he learned about the Holocaust." None of them could offer a definitive answer.[60] There seems to have been no clear dividing line before which Ben-Gurion did not know and after which he did know. Discrimination against and persecution of the Jews in Nazi Germany, and later in the occupied lands, were widely reported. They were seen, justifiably, as part of the same spectrum, a line leading, step by step, from Dachau to Auschwitz. When the war broke out, the Germans did their best to conceal the slaughter of the Jews, and in particular their plan of systematic extermination. They were successful only in part—reports leaked continuously, from several sources, and had no great difficulty reaching the West, almost in real time, by mail, telegraph, and telephone, as well as via reports from people who were able to get out of the occupied countries. Some of them were eyewitnesses—refugees, diplomats, businessmen, emissaries of various kinds, spies. In February 1940, the Jewish Agency Executive in Jerusalem received a fairly thorough report on the persecution of Poland's Jews that reached the conclusion that the entire Jewish population there was at risk of being eradicated. Some of these reports reached the general public.[61]

It was not possible to verify all the reports, but even a cautious and critical reading of them could leave no room for doubt—the Nazis were murdering the Jews systematically; news of extermination in gas chambers soon followed. The reports that reached Ben-Gurion's desk from time to time also seemed to confirm the inevitable fate of the Jews in Nazi Germany.

---

* Ben-Gurion did not tell his colleagues what Kettaneh had been doing with the exiled Poles in London. Perhaps he did not know. He may have offered to sell them vehicles for the army of General Władysław Anders, which was then deployed in the Middle East. Whatever the case, Ben-Gurion presumed that, as Kettaneh was a Catholic, the Poles spoke frankly with him.

While in the United States, he could have read about this from time to time in *The New York Times* and other newspapers. On March 1, 1942, the *Times* reported that the persecution of the Jews in Poland was proceeding in accordance with a systematic plan to eliminate them. The newspaper's source was Henry (Chaim) Shoskes, a well-informed economist and journalist from Poland who had served as a delegate to several Zionist Congresses. He warned that if the Nazis continued with their program, every Jew in Poland would be dead within five years.[62] For Ben-Gurion, these reports fit easily into the historical viewpoint that had produced the Zionist movement. "The persecution and destruction of Jews is not a new invention of Hitler's. It has been going on through the ages," he told a Jewish women's organization in Detroit in June 1942. "There is not a country, except, perhaps, in the New World, which has not persecuted and tortured Jews. They asked us for one little thing—that we should change our names and call ourselves not Jews but Christians." Even at this stage, he had yet to internalize the unique nature of Nazi racial anti-Semitism.[63]

That same month a quite detailed report on the extermination of the Jews was smuggled from Poland to London. It reached the press by a tortuous road; on July 2, 1942, it appeared in *The New York Times*. The report cited the number of Jews murdered thus far in several major Polish cities, and put their number at about seven hundred thousand. It also reported that Jews had been killed in gas chambers, at a rate of a thousand a day, and named two of the extermination sites: Chelmno and Majdanek.[64]

The *Times* attributed the report to Szmul Zygelbojm, a leader of the Bund, the anti-Zionist party that Ben-Gurion had battled in his youth in Płońsk. Zygelbojm lived in London and was close to the Polish government-in-exile; the report reached him from members of his party in Poland. When Ben-Gurion told the Jewish Agency Executive how he knew about the plan to exterminate Poland's Jews, he made no mention of the Bundist, only of the Arab Rotary officer.*

---

* In 1948, Kettaneh published a plan to resolve the Palestinian refugee problem, and in the 1950s he represented Yemen as a registered lobbyist in Congress. He was occasionally mentioned in *The New York Times* as attending social and cultural events. He died in 1976 at the age of seventy-nine. (Kettaneh 1949; Francis Kettaneh to Allen Dulles, April 20, 1955, CIA-RDP80R01731R000500540006-6.pdf.)

Between his two meetings with Kettaneh, a crowd of twenty thousand assembled in Madison Square Garden to protest the murder of the Jews of Poland. President Roosevelt and Prime Minister Churchill sent messages of support. In advance of the demonstration, Ben-Gurion published the memorandum on the need for a Jewish army that he had presented to Roosevelt. He did not speak at the event. Jewish organizations raised money and sent it to Palestine through him.[65]

❖

Weizmann scored another small victory before Ben-Gurion left the United States. On August 6, the British colonial secretary announced the establishment of a regiment for the defense of Palestine in which Jews and Arabs would both serve, not necessarily in equal numbers. The decision was understood to be an achievement of a sort and the product of the efforts Weizmann had made since the war began. He was pleased and wrote that he had always known it would happen. The Colonial Office's statement was made public three days after Ben-Gurion explained to the Zionist Executive in New York why the British were refusing to establish such a unit. "They do not want to have Jewish soldiers because after the war they may turn against them . . . They do not want to have Jews become a strong force in Palestine, because they will have a claim to Palestine. I see this very clearly."

He termed the establishment of the new regiment as "a slap in the face of the Jewish people." Its soldiers, he charged, would have "inferior standing; they have not the same training, the same equipment, or the same chances as other battalions." They would be, he claimed, "the stepchildren of the British army." Nevertheless, he promised to encourage enlistment, "not for the benefit of the British but for our own."[66]

❖

Ten months after he arrived in the United States, Ben-Gurion left for home. In the meantime, the United States entered the war. As when he returned after World War I, he felt that he had experienced the making of a new world, and brought with him an updated version of the American dream. It was a feeling that had incubated within him beforehand, while he was preaching Zionism in Palestine, but it grew during his stay in America. "This war, perhaps more than the previous one, will shake the foundations of the earth, make hearts and minds tremble, and impel a profound and exhaustive soul-searching," he prophesized. There would thus be a ready ear after the war for great and bold solutions, including the vision of "greater Zionism."[67] He dreamed that it would happen under U.S. protection. "The American army will be in every country. I hope that they will also come to Palestine. I pray that they will come to Palestine. They will have power. America can send ten million soldiers. And that's enough for peace. They will have economic power." The Soviet Union would also gain influence, he estimated, but the world would depend on America. "They will rule with the power of their army, food, and money," he predicted.

Zionism's faith in technological progress dated back to Herzl and had sparked Ben-Gurion's own imagination in his youth. Now it excited him in particular with regard to the transport and communications revolutions that the war had brought about. Time would no longer be what it had been, and in the new world there would no longer be a need for a Zionism of stages, as there had been for the last sixty years. Two million Jews would be moved into Palestine after the war, all at once. He did not know if it would take six or eight months, he said, or perhaps a year or two. The transfer of two million Greeks had taken a year and a half. As soon as he returned, he called on Ruppin to draft an appropriate plan.[68] His journey home lasted two weeks; he had to fly via Bermuda, South Africa, and Egypt. One of the passengers who sat next to him on one of the flights noticed the book he was reading and wrote him a note in ancient Greek: "Love the dialogues of Plato."[69]

· 14 ·

HOLOCAUST AND SCHISM

"HORRORS AND TORMENTS"

On a sun-drenched winter day in February 1943, some four months after his return from America, Ben-Gurion endured several of the most difficult hours of his life. They involved an encounter with a young girl, about sixteen years of age, who had just arrived from Poland. She told him what had happened to her during the war. "A story of horrors and torments that no Dante or Poe could possibly imagine," Ben-Gurion wrote to Miriam Cohen. The girl, Helena (Halinka) Goldblum, was one of fifteen Jews who had been exchanged for Germans residing in Palestine; about two hundred other Jews had already reached Palestine as a result of such exchanges. These first Holocaust survivors to arrive and say what was going on there, in the ghettoes and death camps, were debriefed by Jewish Agency officials.*

---

* Such exchanges of civilians were the result of extended negotiations between the British and the Germans. Most of the Jews were chosen from a list drawn up by the Jewish Agency. Halinka Goldblum's parents already lived in Palestine. (Porat 1986, p. 277ff.; Ben-Gurion, Diary, Nov. 11, 1942, BGA; Eliyahu Dobkin to the Jewish Agency Executive, Nov. 11, 1942, BGA.)

She told, in Yiddish, of abuse and torture and mass murder, and of deportations to Treblinka and Auschwitz. Ben-Gurion spent three hours with her—he wanted to know every detail. He later thought he remembered that Paula was also present. When Ben-Gurion took his leave, Halinka saw tears in his eyes; Ben-Gurion had wept. "And you feel totally helpless, you can't even get furious, and the sun is shining in all its glory," he wrote to Miriam Cohen. His words captured precisely the helplessness he felt during the war. His principal task was to wait for it to end. "It's not easy, believe me," he wrote. "But we must carry on with what we began here sixty years ago, and in doing so save perhaps a remnant." It was the only thing he could do, and, he told her, "it is my intention to do it, whatever I can and as long as I can." Later in the same letter he told Cohen how he was trying to resolve the crisis in the Tel Aviv Workers Council.[1] For the next eighteen months, partisan politics was his main preoccupation, including two election campaigns. He again proved that he had no real rivals in that field. Saving the Jews was not the center of his activity.

❖

A few weeks after he returned to Palestine, at the beginning of October 1942, the armies of Germany and Britain fought their third battle near the Egyptian town of El Alamein. Ben-Gurion was able to get a sense of the fear that had swept in waves through Palestine while he was gone. It seemed quite possible that the Nazis could conquer Palestine, and at times it seemed a near and immediate certainty. The records of the discussions held then in the Jewish Agency Executive, Histadrut, and Haganah testify to disarray and even more to a lack of leadership. No one knew what would happen, everyone agreed that something had to be done, but everyone also agreed that there was no way to stop the Germans. Hitler's army would only need a hundred paratroopers to conquer Tel Aviv, they said to one another. They thus debated what was best, to stay there or flee, to fight or surrender. They deluded themselves that their decision would make a difference. In fact, they were entirely dependent on the power of the British army to stop the Germans.

Ben-Gurion took part only in the end of this collective trauma. As during the days of terror in 1929 and the bombardment of Tel Aviv and Haifa in 1940, he experienced his nation's dread largely through newspapers he read overseas. As far back as the days of Tel Hai, he had generally associated himself with those who preferred death with honor to life with dishonor, as he wrote in his memorandum to President Roosevelt. In the end, the choice did not have to be made. On November 5, 1942, *Davar*'s banner headline read "Enemy Forces in Flight in the Western Desert." And so, thanks to the British army, the Jews of Palestine were saved from Nazi conquest.[2]

❖

The ruptures in Mapai that Ben-Gurion tried to patch up prior to his trip widened during his absence. He recalled previous attempts to undermine his position and lamented "the Faction," as his opponents called themselves, made up of the Labor Battalion and the underground cell, the Circle, that the veterans of Hashomer had established.[3] The Faction was loyal to Tabenkin. The local conflict in the Tel Aviv party branch thus became one of the greatest political crises he had to address. Petty disputes over posts and honors produced, in time, political blocs and ideological differences. "What business do we have with ideology-shmideology? The Jewish nation is being destroyed!" declared Ben-Gurion, but the Holocaust did nothing to restrain political passions. For Ben-Gurion, it was an opportunity to place himself at the head of his party like a white knight and make everyone forget how little he had accomplished in America. "We are all at fault for what has happened," he said, as he always did, and summoned the chairmen of all of Mapai's branches.

Katznelson, in decline, supported him, and so did Remez, Sharett, Kaplan, Golomb, and Golda Meir. He stressed the value of comradeship and tried to persuade Tabenkin to accept the party line, as he called it. "I have no appetite for a break," he proclaimed. "I have been with you since 1904." They sat all night, parting at 4:00 a.m. without having reached an agreement. Apparently they spent most of their time arguing about factional infighting, but each held fast to his position. They also touched on some matters of principle.[4]

"THEY DID NOT WANT TO LISTEN TO US"

Ben-Gurion brought with him from America the decision made by the Zionist assembly that convened at the Biltmore Hotel. Prior to his return, no one had seen it as a program to be implemented, only as yet another Zionist manifesto that was no more binding than any of its predecessors. The Biltmore Conference had not accomplished anything new, Ben-Gurion acknowledged, but he presented its decisions as the Zionist movement's plan of action for the postwar period. He thus brought it before the Jewish Agency Executive for approval. Everyone understood that the practical implication of the Biltmore Program was independence at the earliest possible moment, with the best borders that could be achieved at that time, which presumably meant a partition of Palestine.[5]

Those who rejected partition had not changed their minds since the great debate of 1937. Shlomo Zemach was one of them. He was one of a small group of Mapai members with whom Ben-Gurion shared his plan before he went to America. In his memoirs, Zemach related how he had confronted Ben-Gurion. "What you actually want is partition," Zemach told him, "and my understanding is that you want to conceal your real intentions from the world. But here, with us, you need to speak openly." Ben-Gurion was furious. He returned from the convention with a sense of deep remorse about the debate. "Had a Jewish state been established seven years ago, we would have brought hundreds of thousands, perhaps millions of Jews from Poland and Romania to that tiny Jewish state, and they would be here," he declared. "We will not be able to bring them here, not because we don't have a state, but because those Jews are no longer alive." He claimed that in 1937 he had not known that catastrophe was so close and that it would be so horrible, but as early as twenty-five years previously, with his sense of Jewish fatalism, he had agreed to divide the land. "I did not give up on the whole land; rather, I thought that bringing two million Jews was worth more than fine rhetoric about the integrity of Palestine," he said.[6]

The connection between the partition plan of 1937 and the Holocaust grew ever stronger in his mind. It became a standard claim of his and he stated it more and more starkly as the years went by. Once he said that hundreds of thousands of Jews could have been saved had a state been established according to the Peel Commission's partition proposal, and on another occasion he put the number at five million. Twenty years after that debate, he declared that had a Jewish state come into being in 1937, "the six million Jews of Europe would not have been annihilated; instead, most of them would be in Palestine."[7] The claim was unfounded—Ben-Gurion had no factual basis for claiming that it would have been possible, by the end of the war, for Palestine to absorb a majority of the millions murdered in the Holocaust. Most of the European Jews who escaped extermination were those who had immigrated to the United States and other countries before the killings began. He blamed the Holocaust on those Jews who had remained. In the background was the Zionist ideological negation of the Exile that presented the Jews of the Diaspora as passive and weak and thus as contemptible. It was a common claim—instead of coming to Palestine, the Jews of Europe let the Nazis murder them, and thus undermined the Zionist project. "They did not want to listen to us," Ben-Gurion said.[8]

The appropriation of the Holocaust as an argument for Zionism intensified the internal debate over the future of Palestine, as Shlomo Zemach came to realize. "I wanted Palestine to remain under the British Mandate for another twenty years," he later recalled. And "I believed that after the war we needed to obtain from international institutions sanction to take in enough immigrants to bring our numbers in Palestine up to those of the Arabs." He hoped that, over time, Jews and Arabs would come to relate to each other in a new way, and that cooperation between them would make it possible to bring more Jews, presumably leading to the establishment of a state with a Jewish majority. "In any case, I became dubious about my loyalty to Mapai," he wrote. The public discourse no longer permitted a nonpolarized position like his.[9] Ben-Gurion tended to identify his own party with the state. The party was the "instrument of implementation," he told his colleagues. The party thus needed greater control of its members than a state needs over its citizens, even stronger than a military commander requires over his army. A military commander has unlimited control over life and death, but the party, he maintained, needed "control of the soul."[10] The ideological debate, replete with fanatical passion, bisected the labor movement. Hashomer Hatza'ir, a Marxist rival to Mapai that had a large constituency in its kibbutzim, opposed the establishment of a Jewish state and advocated a binational arrangement in which Jews and Arabs would govern jointly. That was also the position taken by Judah Magnes; his post as president of the Hebrew University lent the idea international cachet, especially in the United States. It was a position that could not be ignored, but neither could it be accommodated. Ben-Gurion also had difficulty finding common ground with Tabenkin and his followers, who continued to oppose partition. Such was the state of affairs when Mapai convened its convention in Kfar Vitkin on October 25, 1942. It was the first step toward fracture in the party and a big step for Ben-Gurion on his road to leadership.

❖

He began his speech at the convention's first evening session, and continued it the next day. He spoke for a total of three hours. It was meant to be a "political overview," but he began by coupling, almost in the same breath, the danger Hitler presented to humankind and the Jewish people and the danger that loomed before the "collective soul" of the party as a result of the destructive and divisive passions that were raging within it. His thesis could be summed up in the words "there is no alternative," which he repeated again and again. There was no alternative to trusting that the British would agree to Jewish participation in the war against Hitler, in Jewish units, even if it were not a Jewish army assigned to defend Palestine. There was no alternative but to submit, for now, to the immigration quotas imposed by the White Paper. But all this held only during the war; Ben-Gurion's main interest was in what would happen thereafter.

The more he spoke, especially the next day, the more it sounded as if he was departing from his original plan for his speech and, in a fervor of free association, offering flashes of thoughts that appeared in his head. He evinced unbounded optimism and told one story after another; at times he peppered his Hebrew with Yiddish expressions, as he did when he was entirely at ease. He related what he had told an American official who had asked him why the Jews refused to give up their demand for a state: "When the United States revokes its own statehood, I will revoke the Jewish state."

He once again told the story of how he had heard from a Palestinian

Arab about the Nazi plan to exterminate the Jews of Poland, and reiterated that it was the duty of the able-bodied Jews of Palestine to volunteer for service in the British army. "All young men and women who are told to enlist and do not do so are deliberately or unintentionally Hitler's allies," he declared. Toward the end of his address he told, for the second time in recent weeks, a story proving that not all was lost. A young man had helped found a kibbutz in the Jezreel Valley; Ben-Gurion knew him because they were from the same town. That man had been the wild type; now he was almost sixty years old. He started taking driving lessons, and against the wishes of his comrades at the kibbutz, he enlisted in the British army. "When I heard that, I said, if we have men like that, there is still some hope." He was referring to Shlomo Lavi.[11]

Lavi hoped that his decision to enlist at such an advanced age would spur others to do the same. He also wanted to take part, within the scope of his capabilities, in the defeat of the Nazi enemy. He was placed in a transport unit in Italy. He spent most of the time being bored and hated it when the other men mocked him for his age; his commanders wanted him to manage the battalion library. He also had trouble adjusting to the vulgarity of his fellow soldiers. "The sweetest conversations are about prostitutes and things done with prostitutes," he related. He corresponded with his two sons at Ein Harod, Yeruba'al and Hillel. The exchange of letters brought them closer. Hillel wrote about life without his mother, who had died when he was a baby. When Yeruba'al also enlisted, Lavi wrote: "It is a direct result of my way in life. Had he not enlisted, I would have loved him less." The little political news that reached him at the front gave him cause for hope. "There is in any case a feeling that, since Ben-Gurion has started working energetically to repair the party, there are many changes for the better."[12]

"NOT MY DIRECT RESPONSIBILITY"

About six weeks later, the Jewish Agency Executive heard a summary of the information provided by the first people who had reached Palestine under the exchange of civilians with Germany. Eliyahu Dobkin, the member of the Executive who had overseen the debriefing, certified that the basic facts were undoubtedly true. "They put the weak into special structures and exterminate them with gas," he reported. "There are three furnaces at Oświęcim [Auschwitz]; they are now building two more, in which they burn the Jews." The testimony of the new arrivals confirmed secret information that the Jewish Agency already possessed. That report had come from a German source and had been conveyed through a representative of the World Jewish Congress in Switzerland, Gerhart Riegner.

As in the discussions of a Nazi invasion of Palestine, no one really knew what to do. The most practical proposal for saving Jews that was offered at the meeting was to remove Jewish children from the German zone of occupation and convey them to neutral states, with a commitment to take them back after the war. Moshe Shapira, a member of the Executive, spoke of saving half a million children in this manner. But no one had a clue how to actually carry out such a dramatic rescue operation. Ben-Gurion did not take part in this meeting because he was ill; Sharett also left after giving a political survey. Gruenbaum regretted their absence.[13]

The Jewish Agency issued a statement the next day, November 23, 1942, announcing that the Germans were systematically exterminating the entire Jewish population of Poland. It did not mention gas chambers. The leadership organized a series of public protests and mourning and prayer convocations; some people put black flags on their balconies. During the weeks that followed, the newspapers in Palestine wrote extensively about the murder of the Jews; headlines protested and lamented, with a great deal of "Zionist alertness." Ben-Gurion thought it was "huge." But after a few months had passed, the newspapers let up and sent the story to the inside pages. By the second half of 1943, the Holocaust was no longer considered a big story. Berl Katznelson, the editor of *Davar*, thought that the public was not interested in reading about the annihilation of the Jews. That was not true of every family. Whatever the case, what looked like indifference to the Holocaust and a lack of leadership was more than anything else helplessness, as Ben-Gurion wrote to Miriam Cohen in New York. In the meantime, he also turned to other matters.

❖

The Jewish Agency Executive established a Rescue Committee at the beginning of 1943. Ben-Gurion was not a member; Gruenbaum was the chairman.[14] When people approached Ben-Gurion with ideas for action or requests for help, he referred them to Gruenbaum or promised to speak to him himself. That was his explicit position up until the end of the war—the Holocaust was not under his purview. "There is a group of people who are specially designated to deal with it," he said to a delegation of Jews who had come to Palestine from Greece. A few months later, a delegation of rabbis came to see him and one of their questions was about the Rescue Committee. Ben-Gurion responded that he was not the right person to speak to, as he was a one-job man and was busy with other matters. "I doubt whether it is good to talk to me about that subject," he told them. He said the same to the members of his party: "The catastrophe of European Jewry is not directly my responsibility." When he saw those words in the minutes of the meeting, he corrected them by hand to "It is not my direct responsibility to publicize the catastrophe of European Jewry." Years later, when he was prime minister, he wrote: "I was not well-informed at the time in the matter of saving Jews under Nazi occupation. Although I was then chairman of the Jewish Agency Executive, the enlistment of the Jewish people in the demand for a Jewish state was at the center of my activity, and several members of the Jewish Agency Executive were much better informed than I was about what was being done then to save the Jews of Europe."[15]

One of the working documents of the Emergency Committee estimated the number of Jews slated for extermination to be seven million, and stated that no one should even dream of saving more than several tens of thousands. "What the Committee can do is only a drop in the ocean; anything more is self-delusion or salving the conscience, not any real action," it states. That was one good reason not to take responsibility for the Committee's work.[16]

Less than two months after the Jewish Agency issued its statement, Ben-Gurion could be grateful that his political instincts had impelled him to leave the rescue efforts for others. Yitzhak Gruenbaum became an enemy of the people. First he had to apologize for the fact that the Jewish Agency had not immediately made public the reports on the Holocaust that it had received from America. The charge was that they had been kept secret so as to cover up the failure to make plans to rescue European Jews. Gruenbaum hotly defended himself, and Ben-Gurion spoke up for him. All one had to do was read *Mein Kampf* to know that Hitler intended to exterminate the Jews, he said. At this point, the charges were not yet directed at Ben-Gurion, as he had just returned from the United States and had immediately reported to the Jewish Agency Executive what he had heard from Francis Kettaneh.[17]

There was one more reason to keep himself at arm's length from the Committee's work. On the assumption that it would be possible to save a handful of Jews, but not all of them, it would be necessary to determine whom to save. In other words, someone would have to decide who would live and who would die. The answer could be found in a five-page memorandum prepared by the Emergency Committee's coordinator. If it came to choosing between ten thousand Jews who would be beneficial to Palestine and the re-birth of the nation and a million Jews who would be a burden, the ten thousand should be saved, "despite the complaints and pleas of the million." The author of the memorandum stressed that it was most important to save young people, "because they constitute the best material for the community in Palestine," especially those who had undergone pioneer training. That had always been Ben-Gurion's position, but this Darwinist thinking inevitably caused him problems. He tried to keep things vague. He now stressed from time to time the importance of saving children. "We must save every Jewish child in Europe, and the place to save them is Palestine," he said in December 1942. But a few months later, he added: "I do not want to say what is more important, to build Palestine or to save a single Jew from Zagreb. It may well be that at times it is more important to save a single child from Zagreb."[18] A year later, he chose his words with maximum political caution: "We will not be able to save a million Jews. Of course we will also bring in Jews about whom we know explicitly that they will leave Palestine three months later, if the other alternative is that they will be killed there. But if the choice is bringing a Jew who immediately after the war will return to Romania and who will be here a foreigner and stranger, or to bring a Jew who will remain in Palestine, then we need to bring Jews who will remain here." He reiterated the need to bring children, as they could be educated not to leave the country.[19]

Once he stated who should be saved, he had to determine how to fund the rescue efforts. These included food packages, the smuggling of funds across enemy lines, and after that perhaps ransoming large numbers. An ideological debate quickly broke out over this question as well. Was it permissible to use for rescue the money that had been intended for national development? Gruenbaum asserted that the Zionist project took precedence. "I think that we need to state here—Zionism is above everything," he declared. Friends advised him to keep this opinion to himself, but he paid them no heed. The result was that he was accused of anti-Semitism. Ben-Gurion believed that the Jewish Agency should only devote itself to rescuing Jews by means of bringing them to Palestine.[20] The most difficult question of all came up again; Gruenbaum kept bringing it before the Rescue Committee as if for the first time: "What must we do?" Several plans aimed at saving tens of thousands of children were not implemented, in part because the British refused to grant immigration certificates.[21] Ben-Gurion thought principally about what needed to be done after the war, but as chairman of the Jewish Agency Executive he had no choice but to devote himself to the rescue issue. He, too, was soon sullied.

"A THOUSAND SHIPS"

On the day following the Jewish Agency's statement, Ben-Gurion appeared at Arthur Ruppin's Economic Research Institute in Rehovot. His speech proposed bringing a million Jews from Europe to Palestine. "They say that Hitler may annihilate two million, but whatever the case there will remain the problem of X million," he explained. He wanted them in Palestine, and as soon as possible. "The question that I place before the experts is what needs to be done so that we can bring them here at the same time, by marshaling a thousand ships all at once, a thousand Jews on each ship . . . what needs to be done for their conveyance, sustenance, and embedding them in the economy." He claimed that this could be done "immediately," but the plan could really only be implemented after the war.[22] It was his way of coping with his inability to save Jews from extermination—while it was still raging, he placed the Holocaust behind him and focused on the future.

The tendency to shunt the murder of the Jews from the present into the past was anchored in the Zionist and Jewish perception of time. Both built roads that led from the past directly to the future while circumventing the present. That explains Ben-Gurion's capacity, as the killing was at its height, for envisioning life after the Holocaust. In January 1942, he notified his colleagues that he intended from here on out to concentrate on planning. He would employ experts on land, water, production, security, and other fields. This work would take up all his time and he would be unable to perform any other task, with the exception of presiding over meetings of the Jewish Agency Executive itself. Alongside the plan for bringing over the first million Jews, which he commissioned from Ruppin's experts in Rehovot, he also ordered plans for shipping, housing, and other areas. Concerned about reports that the Arab birthrate was rising, he considered how Jews might be encouraged to have more children, and again examined the possibility of transferring the Arabs out of Palestine; this time, too, he hoped that the idea might be furthered with money.[23]

This gaze toward the future reflected not only powerlessness to save Jews but the need for hope. "We should not and must not lose hope in human conscience," he said in 1943. "In a world that is entirely malevolent we will have no restitution."[24] The extermination of the Jews was far from over when Ben-Gurion began pondering the reparations that the Jewish people would demand from Germany after the war.

❖

Some fifty thousand to sixty thousand refugees reached Palestine during the war. A bit more than sixteen thousand of them were smuggled in illegally. The Jewish Agency and other organizations in Palestine sent rescue agents to Istanbul and Geneva, and a few operated in other places as well. In the main, they provided assistance to refugees who passed through Turkey on their way to Palestine, by sea but also by land, via Syria and Lebanon. From time to time couriers made their way into the occupied lands; some of them took money and transit papers to Jews there and brought letters back. Thousands of Jews fled Poland, to Hungary and other places. About seven hundred children from Poland reached Palestine via Tehran.[25]

About half of these *ma'apilim* arrived under the aegis of the Revisionist movement and a variety of private agents; only about half were brought by the Haganah. Between March 1941 and March 1944, the climactic years of the war and of the Holocaust, the Haganah did not bring in a single boat of immigrants. Toward the end of the war the undercover immigration effort was renewed. At that time, there was already concern that Holocaust survivors would choose to settle elsewhere instead of in Palestine. "Had the gates to America opened wide after the war, it may well be that the masses of Jews would have flowed to America and only a minority would have come here," Ben-Gurion said to his party's convention. He believed, however, that America's gates would remain closed, because the Jews there were apprehensive about a massive influx of Holocaust survivors. It was essential, he thought, to portray the survivors as Zionists. "The fact that the Jews of Palestine were the leaders of the rescue efforts is an important Zionist asset," he said.

It was also the principal factor that impelled the Jewish Agency Executive to demand that the British permit them to send Jewish commandos from Palestine into Nazi-occupied Europe with the mission of establishing Jewish underground organizations. The Jewish Agency spoke of a thousand of these. Ben-Gurion thought it was a preposterous idea. "To found a commando force we first need a Jewish state," he maintained. But he did not hinder the operation. In the end, about thirty paratroopers, including three women, were put down by the RAF behind enemy lines in several Eastern European countries. Most of them set out on their missions between March and September 1944. Ben-Gurion briefed them prior to their departure. He told them to ensure that the Jews there knew that Palestine was their land and sanctuary, so that they would head there after the war. Some of the paratroopers made contact with Jewish communities; others carried out reconnaissance and sabotage missions. More than half of them were taken prisoner, and seven were executed. Their mission produced a national myth; as in previous cases, that was the principal good it did.[26]

About thirty thousand Palestinian Jewish men and women volunteered for service in the British military. They constituted only a third of those who said, at the beginning of the war, that they were prepared to enlist. In the final months of the war, the Jewish Brigade was finally founded; it numbered some five thousand recruits with their own banner and insignia bearing a yellow Star of David, a symbol of the war against the yellow star that the Nazis forced Jews in Germany and occupied lands to wear. Like the Jewish Legion of World War I, the Jewish Brigade's soldiers heard the last shots of the war. It was not the Jewish army that Ben-Gurion had wanted so badly. He had dreamed that the Jewish units would be the first to enter Berlin.[27]

His mood was grim. "He sat behind a bare wooden table, looking even smaller than he was," a visitor who came to see him in 1942 later recalled, "the white tufts of his hair springing belligerently and disconnectedly from his massive pate. His conversation was disjointed. It came in a series of barks and grunts . . . At one point he would appear to be deeply involved in what I was saying; at the next he would begin writing busily in a notebook as though I were not in the room at all."[28] His responses often indicated that he was at a loss. His inclination was to consider every idea brought before him, including one to dredge up German boats that had been sunk during the war and to refit them to bring Jews to Palestine. But in contrast with the fundamental Zionist policy of identifying rescue with immigration to Palestine, he also made an impassioned plea for Jewish refugee children to the Allies: "Bring them out of the Valley of Slaughter, bring them to neutral countries! Bring them into your own countries! Bring them here, to our homeland."[29]

One of the rescue agents in Istanbul, Ehud Avriel, later related how Ben-Gurion summoned him from time to time to report on his work. Ben-Gurion demanded information on what was being done behind enemy lines, took an interest in the smuggling of money and arms, and asked about especially secret and daring missions. He took particular interest in an operation to rescue several hundred Jews from Greece, carried out with the help of the Greek underground and British intelligence. Avriel's impression was that the time that Ben-Gurion himself had spent in Salonica enhanced his interest. He was well-informed and played an active role in contacts with British and American intelligence.[30] On three occasions during the war, he was involved in plans to save hundreds of thousands of Jews in exchange for money. All three failed. The Transnistria affair (Romania), the Europa Plan (Slovakia), and in particular the Trucks for Blood initiative (Hungary) dragged Ben-Gurion into a black hole of disaster.

"LIKE HELL"

Transnistria lies in southern Ukraine, to the west of Odessa. In October 1941, some two hundred thousand Romanian Jews were deported there. A few months later, only about seventy thousand were still alive. Approximately a year later, the pro-Nazi Romanian government, which controlled Transnistria, proposed to the Jewish Agency that it would free them at an estimated price, to begin with, of $400 per person, for a total of some $28 million. It was a fantastic sum, and there was nowhere to settle so many refugees, far exceeding the quotas set by the White Paper. Ben-Gurion presumed that the British would not permit bringing the Transnistrian refugees to Palestine, and that the plan was thus impossible to carry out. The Germans and Arabs were aware of the proposal and did all they could to stymie it. The United States opposed sending money to enemy states. In February 1943, the proposal was leaked to two Swiss newspapers and *The New York Times*, which seemed to put an end to it.

Ben-Gurion treated the matter in accordance with the principle that the Jewish Agency had adopted many years previously—it did not talk with foreign powers without the knowledge of the British. He greatly valued cooperation with the authorities and thus informed them of all such contacts; in any case, the British kept a careful eye on the Jewish Agency's activities and knew pretty much everything about it. The Romanian offer was unexpected, and Ben-Gurion was dubious from the start. He was then focused on an effort to bring five thousand Jewish children and accompanying adults from Romania to Palestine. "It does not solve the problem of the 5 million," he said, "but bringing 5,000 children is a huge thing. If we find a way to bring 5,000, we can demand that the British keep their promise—up to 24,000. Bringing 24,000 to Palestine now, that will be a huge thing. Again, it does not solve the problem of the millions. We will talk about the millions. But first we'll bring 5,000. That's urgent. Because we do not know how much time we have."[31]

A year later, about forty thousand of the Jews who'd been deported to Transnistria were gradually permitted to return to Romania, with the ransom paid by American Jewish organizations. The Jewish Agency budgeted several tens of thousands of dollars, perhaps more, to that end. Ben-Gurion asked the help of a group of industrialists and business leaders in Palestine. The Romanians' willingness to allow the Transnistria refugees to return in exchange for cash payment, despite the fact that the original plan had been leaked, posed a vexing question that no one agreed how to answer: could more have been done, perhaps earlier and with more money? There seemed to be no possibility of sending the refugees to other countries, such as the United States. In any case, as he continued to work on the rescue of children, an even more dramatic rescue proposal landed on his desk. It was also more fantastic and more tragic, because it seemed that all that was needed for it to succeed was money.

❖

A rabbi renowned for his learning and his hostility to Zionism lived in Bratislava, the capital of Slovakia. His name was Michael Dov Weissmandl. Slovakia was then a Nazi client state. Some sixty thousand of its Jews had already been deported and murdered; twenty-five thousand were still alive. In the summer of 1942, Weissmandl set up a Working Group, together with several other Jewish community leaders. One of them was Gisi Fleischmann, a woman who represented the Joint Distribution Committee. They were able to raise several tens of thousands of dollars and hatched a ransom deal with Dieter Wisliceny, Adolf Eichmann's deputy. As part of the process, Weissmandl presented himself as representing "World Jewry" and even forged a letter of authorization from himself, which he claimed to have received from Switzerland. Wisliceny took the money, apparently with the knowledge of his superiors. The deportations of Jews were halted and renewed, in alternation, over two years. Weissmandl and his colleagues believed that their ransom model could be expanded to all of Europe, and offered Wisliceny $2 to $3 million. That was later called the Europa Plan. Wisliceny demanded a down payment of $200,000. At this point, Weissmandl and Fleischmann began to shower the Joint and the Jewish Agency representatives in Istanbul with heartrending letters. Ben-Gurion was dragged into the affair.

A few of the Jewish Agency agents believed the calls for help from Weissmandl and his Working Group, and did all they could to persuade their superiors in Jerusalem to send the advance money that Wisliceny demanded. The plan to save the Jews of Slovakia and the Europa Plan to save all the Jews of occupied Europe did not require that the refugees be sent immediately to Palestine. That got around the major political obstacle, but placed it outside the purview of the Jewish Agency, as defined by Ben-Gurion—rescue through immigration to Palestine. Negotiating with the Nazis was forbidden but not impossible, as was transferring money to enemy countries.

A large part of the money that the Working Group asked for was sent to Bratislava, in cash, by means of smugglers. Some of the money came from the Jewish Agency budget, but most of it, so it seems, from the Joint. There is no information on how much was sent and when; there is no certainty that all the money reached its destination; in any case, it seems to have arrived too late.*

The historian Yehuda Bauer has linked the affair to Heinrich Himmler's plans to bring the war to an end as part of a separate peace between Germany and the Western powers. "No doubt, had Wisliceny obtained large amounts of money," Bauer writes, "the matter would have been raised again." Whatever the case, the Nazis suspended what had seemed like an offer to stop the murder of the Jews, and the deportations from Slovakia were resumed. Gisi Fleischmann and Rabbi Weissmandl were sent to Auschwitz. She was murdered there; he managed to jump out of the transport train and survived. After the war, he settled in the United States. He blamed the failure of the plan on the malice of the Zionists.[32] He meant Ben-Gurion as well.

The documentary evidence relating to the incident that has survived indicates that the initiative's legal and diplomatic aspect received attentive consideration from the Jewish Agency, with unhurried bureaucratic complacence that was sharply dissonant with the desperate cries for help in Weissmandl's and Fleischmann's letters and with the energy that Ben-Gurion put into party politics. The documents are not sufficient to determine with certainty if the Europa Plan ever had any real chance of succeeding. It may well not have, not so much because British and American intelligence knew about it,

---

* It is hard to compute how much money was taken from the institutions of the Zionist leadership in Palestine for the purpose of saving Jews. But it amounted to several million dollars, constituting about a quarter of the Jewish Agency's total budget. More money was spent buying land in Palestine. (Segev 1993, p. 102.)

but because no serious attempt was made to set it in motion. Ben-Gurion did not place himself at the head of the effort because he did not believe in it and did not believe that it offered a historical opportunity to save millions. Blinkered by his view that only handfuls of Jews, if any at all, could be saved before the war ended, he did not put sending money to Bratislava at the top of the Jewish Agency's priorities. He apparently never considered that the Europa Plan might somehow be connected to Himmler's strategy for ending the war. He did not seek out direct contact with the Germans. That being so, it is impossible to say with certainty that he tried every possible avenue to rescue Jews. Whatever the case, he soon found himself embroiled, for a third time, in another similar effort, even more horrific than its predecessors, and he managed it in a way that indicated that he had not learned much from the two previous affairs. In the meantime, he suddenly announced his resignation. His life was "like hell," he said. He meant not the Holocaust but his contention with Weizmann.[33]

"LIKE LOATHSOME CARRION, LIKE A TRAMPLED CORPSE"

The standard story was that they were fighting over the Biltmore Program. In the four months that had gone by since Ben-Gurion calmed down and consented to reassume his position as chairman of the Jewish Agency Executive, no subject roiled Zionist politics and the press more than Biltmore; the conflict was covered overseas as well and greatly interested the British intelligence services. In reality, the two Zionist leaders were not fighting over the Biltmore Program—they were fighting with each other. Once again, Ben-Gurion went on the offensive and Weizmann defended himself.

Ben-Gurion's major complaint remained unchanged: Weizmann was leading the Zionist movement without consulting him. "I am in despair," he said. During their face-to-face confrontation in New York, Ben-Gurion had concealed the offense he had taken from Weizmann. This time he did nothing of the sort. Weizmann had divested him of all influence, Ben-Gurion complained, recalling Weizmann's meeting with Roosevelt. "I would not have gone to the president without Weizmann," he claimed, adding: "I think he is the most harmful man in the Zionist movement." Katznelson lost patience: "There are now problems that are much more important than Weizmann," he rebuked Ben-Gurion. "The loss of European Jewry is a much more anti-Zionist factor than any other matter." In response, Ben-Gurion claimed that Weizmann had "handed over the defense of Palestine," meaning that he had sabotaged the negotiations with Churchill over the establishment of a Jewish fighting force by insisting on handling the talks himself. Soon the issue turned into one of the quasilegal inquiries that Ben-Gurion initiated from time to time. He sounded as if he had uncovered, for the first time, a horrible security scandal that mandated Weizmann's dismissal and disqualified him from all political involvement. Weizmann's conduct, he charged, displayed "the corruption of a guy lacking all sense of responsibility for anything." There was no alternative to recognizing him as president of the World Zionist Organization, but if it were just between the two of them, he would term Weizmann "loathsome carrion," he declared. He took the pejorative from the prophet Isaiah's prophecy of the downfall of the king of Babylon: "While you were left lying unburied, like loathsome carrion, like a trampled corpse" (Isaiah 14:19).

The use of this archaic curse, which can be found in the nineteenth-century Hebrew press, may indicate that Ben-Gurion carefully thought out his outburst at home. It was not always possible to know when he was in control of himself and when he was being carried away in the torrent of his emotions; he may well not have always known himself. In this case, he claimed that his decision to resign had taken form over years of emotional suffering; that may be further evidence that he carefully prepared this performance. "If I have transgressed, you can expel me from the party," he declared. "Expel me from the Histadrut, but I will not lend a hand to this regime . . . I will remain alone, I will do whatever work there is, I will plow or do any job."

One of the people who heard him intimated that Ben-Gurion's eruption had a "psychological cause"; a second reported what the streets were saying about the scandal—that Ben-Gurion wanted to usurp Weizmann. All refused to be forced into a choice between the two men, as Ben-Gurion was insisting. They demanded that he find a way to work with his rival. Ben-Gurion demanded that Weizmann come to Jerusalem for an inquiry. Weizmann demanded that Ben-Gurion come to London. Sharett, a great admirer of both, assumed the role of arbitrator. The result was that he lost the confidence of Ben-Gurion, who, Sharett related, subjected him to rigorous abuse: He started calling him by his last name rather than his first, Sharett related many years later. For a while, Sharett was clearly despondent, as if he were no longer worthy of Ben-Gurion's protection.

In February 1944, Sharett succeeded in negotiating a cease-fire between his two heroes, neither of whom came out the victor. Weizmann continued to conduct Zionist policy as he felt best, and Ben-Gurion continued to bolster his position in his party. As in the past, there was not a party member in even the most negligible branch office whose affairs were not worthy of the leader's attention. No detail was too marginal for him. He was now delving into Plato's *Laws*.[34]

❖

On May 24, 1944, a Jewish Agency rescue agent from Istanbul arrived in Jerusalem bearing information that Ben-Gurion referred to the next day as "fantastic." Adolf Eichmann was offering to rescind the transport to the death camps of a million Jews in exchange for ten thousand trucks and a considerable amount of goods such as coffee, tea, cocoa, and soap. The agent's name was Venya Pomerantz. He told Ben-Gurion that Eichmann had made the offer to two Jewish community leaders in Hungary, after telling them that he had already exterminated 3.5 million Jews. Eichmann's deputy, Dieter Wisliceny, who had played a role in the Europa Plan, was also present at the meeting. The Jews whom Eichmann was proposing to leave alive were to be sent to Spain and Portugal, not Palestine. Eichmann told the two Jewish leaders, Rudolf Kastner and Joel Brand, to convey the proposal to the Jewish Agency. Brand was dispatched to Istanbul to meet with the Agency's representatives there. Pomerantz believed the offer was a serious one; he was lucky in that he did not have to make a decision, only pass his impression on to Ben-Gurion and Sharett. The three of them pored over the proposal into the night. Ben-Gurion's spontaneous reaction was more wishful thinking than a plan of action: "If there is a chance of one in a million, we must grab it." He had never been in a position to make such a fateful decision. It was the third

proposal of its kind, and the first of them that had clearly come from Eichmann himself. Ben-Gurion may not have recognized the offer as another
Nazi attempt to orchestrate a separate peace. But he felt that the decision was
too big for him. He ruled that "the colleagues in London" should be informed,
by which he meant Weizmann and the high commissioner. "Without the
help of the government we will not be able to move," he maintained. Weizmann and Sharett had easy access to Foreign Secretary Anthony Eden, to
whom they spoke as fellow statesmen. Eden bamboozled them by offering
encouragement. Churchill and Roosevelt also knew about the offer; they
viewed it as an attempt to lure them into betraying the Soviet Union and
thus split the alliance against Germany. Nor did they know what to do with
the million Jews whom they would receive from Eichmann if no other country proved willing to take them in the end. Eventually, the same thing happened to Eichmann's proposal that had happened with the Transnistria
initiative—it leaked to the press.

Not all the members of the Executive agreed that the British should be
brought in, but Ben-Gurion overcame their reservations. That was a key decision, sufficient to stymie the deal. Together with Sharett and Eliezer Kaplan,
he handled the affair to the best of his judgment, with close attention to all
details. At no point did he backtrack on his position that everything connected to this matter had to be done with the knowledge and approval of the
British. He could have assumed that they would find out on their own, and
perhaps already had.

The Jewish Agency had no way to send the Nazis ten thousand trucks
and receive a million Jews in exchange without the Allies knowing and ap-
proving. But Ben-Gurion did not have to carry the deal out; all he needed
to do was play for time. That was how he saw it from the start. The Russians were not far from Hungary. It may have been the time for a grand
deception—to notify the British while still negotiating with the Germans
behind their back, through intermediaries in neutral states, or even directly. The leak to the press did not preclude that. The Germans sent more
and more signals; at one point, they invited a Jewish Agency agent in Istanbul to Berlin; after that they invited one of the leaders of the Jewish Agency,
as well as the Joint's European representative. The Jewish Agency believed
that the Germans would not insist on the trucks and goods they had speci-

fied, but would agree to take money instead. Perhaps an advance payment could be made. In the meantime, Eichmann permitted about two thousand Jews to leave Budapest on a special train, apparently to prove that his offer was a serious one. But Ben-Gurion opposed sending a Jewish Agency emissary to Berlin, and reported that to the British as well.

He and his colleagues had for years viewed themselves as a part of the legitimate regime in Palestine, and thus as partners in the war effort against Germany. That included the principle that no negotiations were to be conducted with the enemy. Their image of themselves as recognized leaders channeled them in the direction of routine diplomacy and limited their ability and inclination to resort to double-dealing and deception.

The Jewish Agency agents in Istanbul were more creative, and more daring. They twice sent Eichmann fictitious "interim agreements," so as to gain time. The Joint's representative in Switzerland, Sali Mayer, did the same. Eichmann later claimed that his offer had been a serious one. A memorandum drafted by Himmler on December 10, 1942, stated that Hitler himself did not rule out such a trade, on condition that it provide Germany with a large sum of foreign currency.[35] Ben-Gurion could not have known that, and the chances of exploiting the situation to gain time were not great; Ben-Gurion conceded it in advance.

❖

A few days after Eichmann's offer reached Jerusalem, Yitzhak Gruenbaum met with the American consul and asked that the U.S. Air Force bomb the railroad tracks leading from Hungary to Poland, as well as the Auschwitz death camp. The consul agreed to convey only the request to bomb the tracks; he had reservations about bombing Auschwitz and asked to receive that proposal in writing. Gruenbaum brought the subject before the Jewish Agency Executive. Most of its members, led by Ben-Gurion, opposed the idea. "We do not know the real situation in Poland—we cannot propose anything in this matter," he said. At the time, he was still hoping that the British would go forward with Eichmann's offer. Gruenbaum had proposed two months previously to seek direct contact with the Germans. But now he suspected that the offer was a "diabolical plot" aimed at making it easier for the Nazis to murder Jews. Best not to have any contact with them, he maintained.[36]

A week later, Ben-Gurion spoke at Mapai's Council. He began with a series of questions that also concerned him at that time. "Is our labor movement starting to come apart?" he asked. But he had not lost hope. "Has the nightmare that has oppressed us for many years come to an end? Are we waking up in the light, fresh and with new energy?" The Council ruled that the Faction, which supported Tabenkin, had, in practice, left the party, making the split official.[37]

❖

Several members of the Jewish Agency Executive feared that bombing Auschwitz would kill Jews; they made no distinction between bombing the railroad tracks and bombing the camp itself. Ben-Gurion summed up: "The opinion of the Executive is that we should not propose to the Allies the bombing of places where Jews are located."

Gruenbaum did not let up. To the best of his knowledge, the trains to Auschwitz were transporting twelve thousand Hungarian Jews each day. Bombing the tracks could at least slow the pace. In the meantime, further details about Auschwitz had become available—Gruenbaum's son was a prisoner there. Gruenbaum began seeking public support for his demand, and pelted pretty much everyone he knew, and many he did not, with telegrams, among them Churchill, Roosevelt, and Stalin.[38]

At some point, Gruenbaum managed to persuade Weizmann to demand the bombing of Auschwitz and the rail line leading to it. Foreign Secretary Eden promised to have it done. Eden wrote to Churchill, who favored the idea, but nothing came of it. Neither did the Americans take action, whether because it was not possible or because it did not fit in with their war plans. In the meantime, close to 450,000 Hungarian Jews were murdered.

Ben-Gurion did not conceal his chagrin that Gruenbaum had spoken to the American consul without asking him first, and had then gone on to lobby Weizmann, in breach of the decision made by the Jewish Agency Executive. He did not block the initiative, but treated it with indifference. About twenty years later, he wrote: "It was only natural that, for Churchill, saving England took precedence over everything else, and I am not certain that bombing Auschwitz would have saved Jews."*[39]

"WHAT HAVE YOU DONE TO US?"

In the meantime, two parallel election campaigns got under way, one to the Assembly of Representatives and one to the Histadrut. The question was how to bring Mapai's message to each and every worker. With the campaign he waged in Poland in 1933 in mind, Ben-Gurion set off for Haifa, to the home of the omnipotent local party boss, Abba Hushi. The goal was to bring 120,000 voters to the polls. He demanded that a special effort be made to reach new voters not affiliated with any party. Their votes were needed to replace those of the Tabenkin faction, which was running a separate slate called Ahdut Ha'avodah. "I want to make the message minimalist," Ben-Gurion declared. "A strong Histadrut. Without that, the state will not happen." Overflowing with confidence, he offered colleagues a challenge. If they ran the campaign as he told them, three weeks prior to the election he would deposit with the party secretariat a sealed envelope with his prediction of the election results.[40]

On July 10, 1944, Ben-Gurion spoke at a memorial ceremony for Theodor Herzl, marking the fortieth anniversary of his death. That same day, *Davar* reported on its front page that 1.5 million Jews had been murdered since the start of the war at the Birkenau death camp, part of the Auschwitz complex. Ben-Gurion remembered very well the trauma that the news of Herzl's death had caused him and his three friends, when he was eighteen years old. As might be expected, he shared with his audience thoughts about the history of Zionism, with an emphasis on the Jews of Hungary, where Herzl had been born. "This Jewish community is convulsing on the Nazi gallows, transported each day to slaughter in train cars of death," he said. His speech established the Holocaust as a central argument for Jewish independence in Zionist discourse. As part of this he also coined a unifying slogan whose spirit he had warned against in 1929: "The whole world is

---

* This assessment perhaps explains why the Jewish Agency made no serious appeal to the Soviet Union to bomb the rail line.

against us." The elections to the Assembly of Representatives were three weeks away.

"What have you done to us?" Ben-Gurion shouted. "You, the nations who love freedom and justice, the fighters for democracy, liberty, equality, socialism? What have you done to the Jewish people as you stand before the endless, unceasing flow of our blood, without lifting a finger, without offering help, without commanding the killer, in language he understands, Halt!" It had happened because the victims of the Holocaust were Jews, he argued. "Would you have acted in this way if they were burning, each day, thousands of women and elderly Americans, Englishmen, Russians? Would you be silent if each day they were smashing on the flagstones the children and babies of the Allies?"

The claim was a dubious one. The United States, Britain, and the Soviet Union, as well as dozens of other countries, hardly remained "silent" in the face of the slaughter of the Jews. They fought against Nazi Germany, and that was the only way to save Jews. In doing so, these countries lost tens of millions of civilians and soldiers.

Ben-Gurion's principal charge against "the whole world" centered on national honor and symbolism. "Why do you not allow us to avenge the blood of the millions and fight the Nazis as Jews in a Jewish army under a Jewish flag?" he asked. He reiterated the demand for vengeance and the affront to the Jewish nation: "Is our blood not as red as yours and our honor as dear to us as your honor is to you? Do we not have the right to fight and to die as Jews?" He had only disdain for the horror with which the world received the initial reports of the Holocaust. "Why," he accused, "are you desecrating our pain and wrath with insipid, worthless sympathy that is nothing but bitter mockery of the millions who are being burned and buried alive, day after day, in the centers of the Nazi inferno . . . ?" There was only one possible conclusion: "The hour has arrived for the historic demand of the Jewish people—the establishment of a Jewish state."[41] *Davar* covered the speech at length, on its front page. Its coverage was not directed at "the whole world" but at the Jewish voting public in Palestine.

❖

The elections were held at the beginning of August 1944. Mapai received more than 35 percent of the approximately two hundred thousand votes cast for the Assembly of Representatives. In the Histadrut elections, more than 52 percent of approximately one hundred thousand votes were cast for Mapai.[42] Ben-Gurion was pleased and checked into a small sanatorium on Mount Carmel for rest. Paula and Amos, who was on furlough from the army, stayed in a nearby hotel. On Saturday night, August 12, 1944, Ben-Gurion was wakened by one of his party's leaders, David Hacohen, who told him that Berl Katznelson had died two hours previously in the home of friends in Jerusalem. Ben-Gurion sat up on his bed, then fell backward, banging his head against the wall; Hacohen's impression was that he had ceased to think and see, nor did he know who was sitting before him. "He suddenly leaned his body and face on the sheet that was stretched over the bed, and the wails and groans of a wounded beast emerged from him. He dug his hands into the sheet, wrapped it around his head and shoulders, throttled his neck, banged his head against the mattress, and emitted disconnected words: "Berl, without Berl, how without Berl?" A few minutes later he recovered. "His face was very gray and grim," Hacohen related. Ben-Gurion dressed and asked Hacohen to drive him to Jerusalem; they picked up Paula and Amos on the way.

"A thick fog lay over Haifa," Amos later recalled. "There was an oppressive silence in the car. No one said a word." It was dawn by the time they reached Jerusalem. Katznelson was laid out in his bed. "Father was deathly pale," Amos said. "He gripped Berl's bed with all his might, until blood oozed from his fingers," he continued. "When a few minutes had passed, Father asked Mother and me to leave the room and allow him to be alone with Berl. We went out and moved a bit away from the door. We stood silently. We suddenly heard a heavy thud. We burst into the room in alarm. It was a horrible sight. Father was lying unconscious by the bed. Mother and I panicked. The awful thought went through my head that my father had also died." When he recovered, Ben-Gurion told Amos that Katznelson was the only friend he had ever had. "I think [my father] was more of a friend to Berl than to Paula," Amos said. It took months for Ben-Gurion to recover. "At least once a day he felt a need to ask Berl something," one of his party colleagues said.

During the four years that had gone by since Jabotinsky's death, Ussishkin, Rutenberg, and Ruppin, three of Zionism's founding fathers, had also passed on. Katznelson's death boosted Ben-Gurion's standing, just as Arlosoroff's murder had. Nearly forty years after entering politics, he was now, for the first time, his party's most senior leader. He brought with him a clear and solid view of what needed to be done, as well as a wealth of political experience, but he still had to work to be recognized as his party's undisputed leader. "Who will be our exemplar?" Shlomo Lavi eulogized Katznelson. "For whose pronouncements will we stand and wait? . . . To whose hands will we entrust the keys to our hearts? Who will stand up now to rebuke all the lies that have piled up in the field of our lives? . . . Who will tell us, from now on, if we are doing right or wrong?" Ben-Gurion was, at this stage, "the only one remaining to us."

So Ben-Gurion arrived at the end of the road to power. From this point onward his experience largely involved power's limits. Even before a hundred days of grace had gone by, he had to face the most terrible charge ever leveled at him: Joel Brand accused him and his party of the deaths of tens of thousands of Hungarian Jews.[43]

"WHERE WILL WE GET PEOPLE FOR PALESTINE?"

Soon after he arrived in Istanbul on a special plane provided by Eichmann, British intelligence officers abducted Brand and imprisoned him in Egypt for four months, to prevent his return to Hungary. When he was released and came to Palestine, he still believed that if he could return to Budapest with a positive response he could save the lives of tens of thousands of Jews, but if he were forced to remain in Palestine, they would all be sent to Auschwitz. In October 1944, he was invited to speak to the Mapai secretariat. He accused the party of mismanaging his mission. The party, he charged, would be held responsible for the lives of the Jews who would be murdered because of its mistakes, the principal one of which was loyalty to the British. He believed that the Jewish Agency had handed him over to the Mandate authorities, and he asserted that he should have been freed in a prison break. "You should have removed me from the jail by force, even with dynamite," he declared, "and sent me to Hitler. That was not done." But the most horrible mistake of all, he said, was that even now he was not being sent back to Hungary. It was still not too late, he maintained; Jews were still being murdered, and were being murdered that very day. He could save them.

Ben-Gurion's only response was a curt interpolation: "Why do you think they will stop murdering if you go back?" Brand reiterated that if he offered money or goods he could save Jews. "We've done that dozens of times and we have to continue to do so," he said. "I left my wife and children there. I am certain that, had I returned four months ago, I could have saved hundreds of thousands of Jews." The members of the secretariat tried to prove to him that he was mistaken. Ben-Gurion remained silent. They decided on a smaller meeting "to review things."[44]

❖

About nine million Jews lived in Europe on the eve of the war; approximately three million remained alive at its end. Most of them owed their lives to Germany's defeat, as Ben-Gurion had, in real time, believed would be the case. Some of them were saved thanks to assistance they received from countries and organizations, including the Joint, and thanks to several thousand good people, "righteous gentiles" as they are now called, in every country on the continent. There were also a handful of dramatic rescue operations, such as smuggling Jews from France into Spain, and from Denmark to Sweden. Only a relatively small number of survivors owed their lives to the Zionist movement's rescue efforts during the war. Ben-Gurion, whose outpourings of Zionist fantasy were almost boundless, conducted the rescue plans as a realist of narrow horizons and little faith. The result was a wound that remained open and painful for the rest of his life.[45] In the meantime, the war was approaching its end and Ben-Gurion delineated the principal problem that the Holocaust had created: "Each of us asks himself the question, Where will we get people for Palestine?"[46] Because, for him, the Holocaust was first and foremost a defeat for Zionism.

"The annihilation of European Jewry is the obliteration of Zionism," he had said in December 1942. In other words, it was a crime against the future State of Israel. "There will be no one with whom to build the country," he warned. Later he said: "The great enemy was Hitler. He ruined this country."[47]

That was not a gaffe, but rather a carefully reasoned historical narrative. "I see the terrible historical significance of the Nazi slaughter not as the frightening number of Jews who were massacred, but rather as the extermination of that select part of the nation that alone, among all the Jews, was capable and equipped with all the characteristics and abilities needed for the building of a state," he later wrote. "European Jewry was not only that which needed a Jewish state, but also possessed the material and spiritual tools needed for its establishment. The Holocaust, more than it was a mortal blow to the Jewish people, was a dangerous, if not fateful, subversion of Jewish national rebirth."[48] Over the years he repeated that thesis any number of times: "More than Hitler wounded the Jewish people he knew and hated, he devastated the Jewish state, whose arrival he did not anticipate."[49]

The defeat of Nazi Germany reminded him of the first Russian revolution, in 1905. Then, also, he heard the heartbeat of history and sensed that he could not rejoice with the crowds. On May 8, 1945, he wrote in his diary: "The day of victory—sad, very sad."[50]

PART II

THE LIMITS OF POWER

❖

BEN-GURION: What a disaster. That at such an important moment the country is led by fools who don't know what has been done here, what our future is.[1]

"Ben-Gurion Against Himself" (1964), as seen by Dosh

· **15** ·

MAPS

"IF WE HAD THE NECESSARY ARMS"

The winter of 1947 was one of the harshest in London's history; February was its cruelest month. The coal crisis was at its height, heavy snows blocked fuel trucks, unemployment continued to rise. On the thirteenth, Ben-Gurion arrived at the Dorchester Hotel for a meeting with Oliver Stanley, a senior figure in the Conservative Party. The fashionable hotel's heating was not working. "Stanley suggested, when I entered, that I keep my coat on," Ben-Gurion noted. "He himself sat in a heavy overcoat." Ben-Gurion's newsman's nose could appreciate the significance of such details. The British Empire was in the midst of a profound crisis and was about to come apart. The two men had met about two years previously, when Stanley held the post of colonial secretary. He had told Ben-Gurion on that occasion that the empire's days were numbered. Britain could not afford to lose the friendship of the

Arabs, but did not know how to decide between them and the Jews. That being the case, it would leave Palestine. The cost of keeping it did not seem worthwhile, especially given the economic crisis. Nearly a century of Britain's rule in India was also about to end. India was "the jewel in the crown" of the empire; Palestine was a trifle. In the meantime, it looked as if no one really knew what to do with it. A few months later, Ben-Gurion related that he had known as early as 1936 that "the Mandate was over," because the British reached the conclusion that they could not keep their hold on Palestine.[1]

He was now the most prominent leader not only of the Jews in Palestine but in the entire Zionist movement. That is how the British saw him—when, in March 1945, he was passing through Cairo, the police assigned a secret agent to shadow him. But he did not know how to move forward either, toward independence. His leadership displayed doubt, hesitation, uncertainty, inconsistency, contradiction, whims, and fantasies, swerving between politics, diplomacy, and terror. Despite the certainty that the British were seeking to end their rule, he placed himself at the head of a fight to "expel" them. What Stanley told him in May 1945 convinced him then that the war for control of Palestine was closer than ever.[2]

❖

Six weeks after the end of the war in Europe, Ben-Gurion rushed to the United States. A few days later, he convened a fateful meeting in the home of one of New York's affluent industrialists. It was the most important action he had taken up to this point. The idea apparently originated with Moshe Sneh, formerly Kleinbaum, who was then chief of the Haganah National Command. Sneh feared that, with the war over, the British would seek to destroy the Haganah. He demanded that Ben-Gurion raise $5 to $10 million for the organization. Ben-Gurion took a list of wealthy and trustworthy Jews, and asked Rudolf Goldschmidt Sonneborn to invite them.

Sonneborn, a first-generation American Jew born to immigrants from Germany, made his money in the petrochemical industry. He and Ben-Gurion were old friends—in 1919, when he was twenty-one years old, Sonneborn served as secretary of the Zionist Commission in Palestine. He reported from Palestine on the growing wave of Arab resistance that followed the Balfour Declaration, but minimized the danger. "Of course Arabs resent the fact that the country in which they live may be turned over to a newly born nation," he wrote. "But the average of that race is inferior even to our average Negro, and the race is entirely lacking in organizational ability, so that I believe there is very little to ever fear from them. Besides, they are a cowardly race." The richer he became over the twenty-five years that followed, the stronger became his support for the Zionist movement and the refugees from Nazi Germany. He invited the seventeen people Ben-Gurion had asked him to convene at his home on Sunday morning, July 1, 1945, on very short notice, from all across the United States and Canada. Worth in the aggregate many millions of dollars, they had only the vaguest notion why they had been bidden to come.

Ben-Gurion opened, as he often did, with the dawn of the Jewish nation. The men before him were the heirs of a historical continuum that began during the sojourn in the desert that had taken place five thousand years before, he told them. He confirmed that the Nazis had murdered between five and six million Jews; at that point, at least some members of his audience knew this only on the basis of newspaper reports. He had brought Eliezer Kaplan and Reuven Shiloah; he presented the latter as a member of the Jewish Agency's Department of Special Operations. They also surveyed the current situation for the guests. The meeting lasted all day, with a break for coffee and sandwiches. In the end, Ben-Gurion came to the main point. "I told those present that we would very soon be facing all the Arab armies, after the English left the country," he wrote many years later. "And while we were few, we could withstand them if we had the necessary arms." Up to this point, most of the Haganah's arms had been purchased in Europe; it sufficed only to fend off local gangs of Arab assailants. The United States was beginning to dismantle its military industries, he explained, and that meant that it was possible to obtain surplus equipment and machinery at a relatively low price. "But even 'inexpensive' can reach into the millions," he said. He presented the men with the question he had summoned them for: "Are you willing to provide the necessary money?"

He asked them for more than money. The purchase of the equipment needed to prepare the Haganah for war required covert activity that was liable to implicate those involved in serious violations of American law. His audience reacted with skeptical sympathy. Some of them wondered whether what Ben-Gurion was asking was consistent with their American patriotism. But not one of them refused; they all recognized his new standing as the leader of the Zionist struggle. Before they parted, he warned them that everything he said had to be kept entirely confidential. When he told the Mapai secretariat about the meeting, he said only that he had asked the Americans to support the struggle against the British.

This was the birth of what came to be called the Sonneborn Institute, a support group whose members raised money and sent to Palestine more or less everything that was needed for the war, including combat aircraft. It was all accomplished in coordination with Haganah personnel who came for that purpose from Palestine, often under cover, with forged papers, false identities, and secret codes. Instead of "dollars" they used the word "books." Some of the military equipment had to be smuggled into Palestine under the guise of spare parts for agricultural machinery. In time, the operation expanded into enlisting American volunteers who went to Palestine to fight in the Haganah's ranks.[3]

❖

Ben-Gurion had stopped in London on his way to America. Paula was meant to follow and join him. But just before she was to leave, she began to doubt whether he really wanted her to come. After several long, sleepless nights, she sent him a distraught letter that reflected their agonized relationship. "David, be *frank* with *me*," she pleaded. "Do you want me to come, will I not be in your *way*? I do not want to be in the same position as *1938*." She seems to have been referring to his affair with Miss May. "I do not want to be put in a *hotel* (like in a cage). I want to be partner of your concern. Am I asking too much? I ask for so little. Don't condemn me for my demands. I am only mortal. I have been deprived of happiness for more than 19 years. My demands are so small, can you give it to me. Consider all these and if you agree, let me know by wire. Forgive." He answered that she should come with him. A few days before the gathering at Sonneborn's home, the two of them paid a visit to Miriam Cohen, who had married in the meantime.[4] Anyone present could have used the opportunity to ponder the women in Ben-Gurion's life—they were young and displayed an interest in Zionism. The affairs did not endure for long; Cohen was not his last lover.

❖

The covert activity in the United States marked a dramatic shift in what had been Ben-Gurion's policy up to this time. No more did he advocate loyal cooperation with the British, as partners in government, operating openly and lawfully. Now he favored the prudent use of the arts of secrecy and subterfuge, and especially ambiguity of language. That seems to have been the main lesson he learned from Zionism's impotence during the Holocaust and the failure of its rescue efforts. Venya Pomerantz later recalled Ben-Gurion blowing up suddenly during a visit to Bulgaria in November 1944. "When and where, exactly, was it possible to save Jews?!" he exclaimed. Pomerantz listed several possibilities and Ben-Gurion fell silent. The next day, he placed his hand on Pomerantz's shoulders and said: "You know, Venya, I wasn't able to sleep last night. Our impotence during the Holocaust will not be repeated."[5]

On his way home from America on the *Queen Elizabeth*, which he insisted on calling by a Hebrew name, *Queen Elisheva*, he recorded in his diary a "Zionist postwar accounting." The pages are covered with numbers, arranged in columns, by country. According to his computation, about 1.1 million Jews remained in Europe, not including the USSR and Britain.

His immediate goal was to bring the survivors of the death camps to Palestine. In the autumn of 1945, some seventy thousand Jewish refugees were living in Germany, most of them in displaced persons (DP) camps in the American zone of occupation.[6] He set out to inspect the sites.

"A HUGE FACTOR IN OUR POLITICAL STRUGGLE"

The first DPs to recognize him on October 19, 1945, were so excited that they almost overturned the American military vehicle that brought him to one of the camps in Zeilsheim, an old town that by the late 1920s had become a western neighborhood in Frankfurt. When he entered the hall where he was to speak, they broke out in "Hatikvah." Many of them wept; "Ben-Gurion and I also cried," recalled one of his companions, Lt. Col. Rabbi Judah Nadich, General Dwight Eisenhower's adviser on Jewish affairs. "He spoke in Yiddish, in a choked and emotional voice. He tried to offer comfort and encouragement, but found the words to do so only with great difficulty. When he finished speaking, the crowd again gave him a standing ovation. It was an event that none of us ever forgot."[7]

❖

Early that evening he conferred with several members of a committee representing the camp's residents. He wanted to hear how many of the DPs were interested in and how many were capable of coming to Palestine. As Holocaust survivors, their plight was a humanitarian issue that could be used to further the Zionist cause. "I saw that it could be a huge factor in our political struggle," he said. To that end, the DPs themselves had to mobilize. The committee members were unanimous in telling him that only a handful would have any hesitations; the majority would come.[8]

A few days later, Ben-Gurion found similar support for Zionism in another camp, near Munich. The British offered fifteen hundred immigration certificates per month for the refugees; Ben-Gurion maintained that these should be rejected unless the White Paper quotas were rescinded. His position was roundly criticized by his colleagues. Moshe Sharett believed that such a move was liable to fan despair among the DPs; beyond that, it also contradicted the claim that the refugees were liable to die in the camps if they were not transferred to Palestine immediately. "How can we justify abandoning them?" he wrote. It was another debate over the human price that ought to be paid to advance the national struggle. According to Ben-Gurion, the representatives of the DPs told him: "We will wait. We will endure again what we have already endured, if it is vital for Zionism." He reached the conclusion that most of the DPs wanted to come to Palestine; the numbers he recorded changed from camp to camp, but ranged between 60 and 80 percent.[9]

He learned during his tour that a number of welfare organizations, Jewish and non-Jewish, were trying to get children out of the camps and into children's houses, often in other countries, where they could take refuge. Ben-Gurion opposed this vociferously. "It runs counter to Zionist interests," he asserted. "The children constitute political pressure . . . children specifically produce great pressure." He called the Zionist office in London. "For God's sake, stop sending the children away," he demanded. He said the same to Nadich. "First, do not permit taking out children—not a single Jew, not a single child, if it is not to Palestine." Many of the DPs also opposed removing the children.[10]

"I DID NOT HAVE THE COURAGE"

Before returning to Paris, he met with Eisenhower. "He did not impress me as a general, but rather as a consummately decent man," he later related. Ben-Gurion asked for a list of improvements in the food and living conditions supplied to the DPs. Eisenhower promised to make them. He also accepted Ben-Gurion's request to institute physical education programs in the camps, to open schoolrooms, and to fly in books from Palestine for the refugees. Most important, he asked that all the Jewish DPs in Bavaria be gathered together and settled in villages that would be evacuated of their German inhabitants for this purpose. There they would receive agricultural and paramilitary training and govern themselves until they were permitted to go to Palestine. In informing his colleagues about the conversation, he told them that he had, for all intents and purposes, proposed to Eisenhower the establishment of a Jewish state in Bavaria. The astonished general said it was a "new idea" and rejected the proposal, in part out of concern about the German reaction. He did, however, agree that the American zone of occupation would take in tens of thousands of Jewish refugees who had fled westward from Eastern Europe. Ben-Gurion saw this as an important achievement. "It is in the Zionist interest that there be a large Jewish presence in the American zone."[11]

Ben-Gurion's tour of the DP camps was thus much like that of a commander surveying his troops. He viewed the displaced Jews within the blinders of his Zionism; many of them felt alienated by his attitude. Those who managed to approach him tried to speak to him of the horrors they had endured; sometimes it seemed as if they needed nothing more than a friendly ear. But Ben-Gurion did not know how to offer paternal sympathy for their personal suffering; he could only see the Holocaust as a national catastrophe.

At Bergen-Belsen he encountered a cousin of his from Łódź, David Zoiraiv, who had been interned in Buchenwald and Auschwitz. "When he returned to Łódź," Ben-Gurion wrote in his diary, "he received word that his wife was alive. He went from camp to camp until someone told him that she was at Bergen-Belsen. He lives in building 67, apartment 11." Two years later, Ben-Gurion received a letter from the same cousin, who was then living in France. "When we last spoke at Bergen-Belsen," Zoiraiv wrote in Yiddish, "you promised that you would take me away from the land of blood. You took my second cousin from the Landsberg camp but you forgot me . . . I can believe that you forgot me because you are preoccupied with other things . . . I have already written you two letters, but I am sad to say there has been no reply . . . I asked that you do everything to get me out of there. I have nothing more to write than that. Be well and do not forget your cousin and his wife."*[12]

One of his aides, Ehud Avriel, later related that Ben-Gurion returned from the trip a broken man. "It seemed as if he had aged," Avriel wrote. "He went gray, as if he had lost his ability to live." Ben-Gurion himself said that he would have preferred to forget his experiences there.[13] He kept his distance from the suffering of the survivors he met. Yitzhak Ben-Aharon, a leader of Mapai's internal opposition, recalled: "I enlisted in the British army in 1940 and I was taken prisoner by the Germans . . . I returned sick and shattered after four years. I lost twenty-eight kilograms and I was sent to London for recovery. And I receive a telephone call. Ben-Gurion is in London and has to see me. He can't come to me. I should go to him." Ben-Aharon continued: "I'm still in uniform, limping on a cane, thin as a stick. He hasn't seen me for four years, and there were rumors that I had been killed after liberation. He leaps down the stairs, embraces me, and the first thing he says is, 'You know, Ben-Aharon, that we are in two different parties now?' That

---

* Another entry in Ben-Gurion's diary shows him helping another member of his family. "I learned that the daughter of Yeshayahu from Łódź has already left and is on her way to Bavaria. I gave orders to look after her." (Sheindele, the daughter of his eldest brother, Avraham, was married to a Bundist; the two of them chose to remain in Poland. Both apparently died in Auschwitz. (Ben-Gurion, Diary, Feb. 9, 1946, BGA; Hagani 2010, p. 172ff.)

was classic Ben-Gurion human relations." He publicly humiliated a celebrated underground fighter, Rozka Korczak, because she gave a speech in Yiddish, which he termed "a jarring, foreign language." His attitude toward Holocaust survivors may have been an attempt to conceal the fact that he found it difficult to look them in the eye; he may have been trying to repress the ineffectuality he had felt while the Holocaust raged, and to which they had been witness.[14]

And he did not go to Poland. He planned to do so at several junctures but each time canceled the trip, apparently because of technical difficulties. But about a year later, he said that a visit to the land of his birth would require more love than he was capable of mustering. He may have been plagued by his conscience. "I did not dare go there. I did not have the courage."[15] In contrast, he acted to boost the flow of Jews from Poland to Germany. This was called the Bricha operation, headquartered in Paris.

"THE MAXIMUM NUMBER OF JEWS"

The liberated City of Lights welcomed him. The French government was seeking to push Britain out of the Middle East, and many veterans of the French underground worked to aid the survivors of the Holocaust. One of the advantages the city offered was that Weizmann was in London. Paris thus became the capital of the Zionist underground in Europe. In practical terms, the movement operated as a tripartite operation, with the parts not always coordinated and sometimes in competition with one another—Bricha, the Organization for Illegal Immigration (in Hebrew, the Mossad Le'aliyah Bet), and the Haganah.

The term *bricha*, the Hebrew word for "flight" or "escape," designated the migration of Jews westward from Eastern Europe, but also the apparatus that organized and assisted their flight. "For me, there was a single nightmare," Ben-Gurion said a short time before the war ended, "that the Jews who were saved would not want to go to Palestine."[16] He viewed the refugees as a "Zionist fighting force," and thus, at his initiative, the Jewish Agency Executive decided to send emissaries to Europe to help them. In the autumn of 1946, the number of Jews in the DP camps rose to 175,000, and by the following summer they numbered 184,000. At the height of the operation, some 400 people were involved. As far as Ben-Gurion was concerned, Bricha had a single goal. "We see this matter as one of the political factors, if not the decisive one, in the difficult campaign that lies before us," he said.[17]

It was a national operation, with a political committee that reflected the political coalition that led the Jewish Agency. Its top commander was Shaul Avigur (whose name was still Meirov at the time), the chief of the Mossad for Illegal Immigration, founded in 1939. Ben-Gurion seems not to have intervened in its missions beyond the general instruction to get "the maximum number of Jews" out of Eastern Europe. It was, in a sense, a surrogate for the rescue that had not taken place during the Holocaust. "The common expression is after the Holocaust," said an article that appeared in *Davar* in 1947: "The fact of the matter is that European Jewry is still deep in the Holocaust." Ben-Gurion's role was largely to raise funds. Some of the outlays were paid for by American money, sent via the Joint; the Bricha also used Rescue Committee funds that had not been used during the Holocaust.[18]

❖

In addition to the Bricha operation, Avigur also directed the ongoing illegal immigration effort. That also required a clandestine network of operatives all over Europe, and tremendous daring as well, especially on the part of the refugees themselves. Some of the illegal immigration agents came from the ranks of the Haganah. Avigur was the type of man Ben-Gurion liked—down-to-earth, lackluster, addicted to secrecy. Ben-Gurion, who had opposed illegal immigration prior to the war, now lent his full support to the Mossad and intervened in the details of its activities. As part of this, he tracked the prices of the ships that the Mossad leased ("for 4,000 tons they asked for $150,000 here, as opposed to the American price of $145,000"). He knew that the best flag for the ships to fly was that of Honduras and that "each boat has a radio expert, two seamen for each lifeboat, to transmit a detailed description of the shore." This was just one of many technical jottings that show how deeply he was involved. As with the Bricha operation, the illegal immigration effort was run with a sense that the clock was running out. Jewish Agency emissaries confirmed Ben-Gurion's apprehensions that the survivors' morale was declining, along with their willingness to go to Palestine. This was liable to undermine the fundamental claims of Zionism; indeed, the British foreign secretary Ernest Bevin would soon ask why the Jewish survivors should not return to their former homes, just like the rest of Europe's refugees.[19]

❖

Ben-Gurion established his Paris headquarters at Le Royal Monceau hotel. Ho Chi Minh, the Vietnamese revolutionary, lodged a floor above him; their paths occasionally crossed. "He gave the impression of being a very nice man," Ben-Gurion later related. "During one of those conversations, he proposed that I immediately establish a 'Jewish government-in-exile' on Vietnamese territory. I thanked him and said that when the time came, I would consider his offer."[20]

"PLEASE STAY WHERE YOU ARE"

It was a midterm election year in the United States. President Truman needed every vote he could get to maintain the Democratic majority in Congress. In September 1945, it was reported that Truman had promised that he would get one hundred thousand DPs to Palestine. The British reacted in the usual way—they appointed a commission of inquiry. Its mandate was to propose solutions to the problem of the displaced persons, and to the Palestine issue as a whole. It was a joint Anglo-American body, with six representatives of each government. The composition showed that the British no longer assumed sole responsibility for the future of Palestine, and the United States was prepared to share the burden. The appointment of the committee was also seen as a test of whether the two countries could pursue a joint policy against the Soviet Union.[21]

In advance of the committee's tour of the DP camps, Ben-Gurion once again visited them, as part of the efforts to bolster the refugees' desire to settle in Palestine. "The Land of Israel calls you," proclaimed Yiddish-language posters that were put up at the camps. All the surveys of the question were conducted against the background of this campaign; they showed that most of the DPs did indeed want to go to Palestine.[22] Richard Crossman, a journalist and Labour member of Parliament who served as a member of the committee, asked himself whether the refugees would want to settle in Palestine if they were given a choice between it and the United States, but he knew that the question was irrelevant. The United States had agreed to take in only a small portion of the DPs.[23] For most of them, the choice was Palestine or a return to Communist Eastern Europe.

Extraordinary security measures were taken for the committee's visit to Palestine. When he went out to the balcony adjoining his room at the King David Hotel in Jerusalem, Crossman saw soldiers checking the garden with mine detectors. The public sessions were held at the YMCA building, on the other side of the street. "Here is a place whose atmosphere is peace," General Allenby proclaimed when he inaugurated the building in 1933, words that were inscribed on colorful ceramic tiles at the building's entrance, "where political and religious jealousies can be forgotten."[24] In the grim, very British lecture room where they held court, the members of the committee had no illusions that they could eradicate Palestine's religious and political antagonisms; they made do with the hope that they could prevent a rapid deterioration of the situation that would lead the country into disaster.

❖

On March 26, 1946, Ben-Gurion stood before a justice of Britain's Supreme Court and claimed that he had no idea what the Haganah was. The judge, Sir John Edward Singleton, was one of the committee's cochairmen. He did not believe Ben-Gurion. An impassive man who showed no trace of emotion and had no patience for those who wasted his time, "almost the caricature of a judge," as Crossman wrote, Sir John nevertheless went to considerable effort to get Ben-Gurion to acknowledge that the Jewish Agency ran the Haganah. He asked Ben-Gurion the same question nine times in a row, using almost identical language: Is or is not the Haganah under some sort of control by the Jewish Agency? Ben-Gurion said that the Jewish Agency dealt with defense—*haganah*, in Hebrew—but that he had no knowledge of an organization with that name.[25]

He was not enthusiastic about the formation of the committee, and for a moment even thought of boycotting it, but the chance that it might recommend sending the DPs to Palestine granted it importance. He prepared well for his testimony, as if he had to defend Zionism for the first time.[26] In fact, he said nothing new; at times he sounded as if he viewed the committee as a group of elementary school students paying a visit to a Zionist museum.

He was well aware of the intellectual difficulty the committee's members faced in trying to understand the special and unique connection between the Jewish people and Palestine. Therefore, he said, he would begin by telling them a parable about a large house with 150 rooms that had once been his family residence. They had been expelled from the house and the family's members dispersed. Someone else took over the house and after that it changed hands several more times. When the family finally returned, they discovered that five of the house's rooms were occupied by other people. All the other rooms were abandoned and derelict, not fit for habitation. "We do not want to remove you," the family's members told the tenants. "Please stay where you are, we are going back to these uninhabitable rooms, we will repair them." They renovated several of them and moved in. Then other family members joined them and they wanted to renovate more of the uninhabitable rooms. But the tenants said: "No, we are here and we do not want you; we do not live in them, these rooms are no good for any human beings but we do not want you to repair them, to make them better." Ben-Gurion concluded by saying: "In the neighborhood there are many big buildings half-empty, we do not say to them 'Please move over to that other big building.' No, we say 'Please stay here, we will be good neighbors.'"[27]

The members of the committee were meant to understand it as a love story. "You will find in no other country in the world people loving their country as the Jews love this country," Ben-Gurion told them. He evoked, as he was wont to do, his days at Sejera, making them sound like a spiritual, almost divine experience. "When I stood watch in the long nights in Sejera and looked at the skies I understood the magnificence of the full meaning of the book of Psalms, that the heavens are telling the glory of God, because I had never seen such glorious skies at night as when I was a watchman." At times he spoke, again, like a child who had lost his mother and received a stepmother in her place. "A man can change many things, even his religion, even his wife, even his name," Ben-Gurion told the committee. "There is one

thing which a man cannot change, his parents. There is no means of changing that. The parent of our people is this country. It is unique, but there it is."[28]
And just as a mother protects her child, so the Jewish community in Palestine would protect everything it had given birth to, he said elsewhere.[29]

The Holocaust took up only a paragraph or two of his presentation. He
repeated his assertion that a conspiracy of silence had surrounded the annihilation of the Jews. "I will tell you about only one of the feelings that I had
when I learned the full story of what happened to us," he added. "I felt happy,
along with my children, that we belong to a people who have been slaughtered, not to those who slaughtered us, and not to those who watched indif-
ferently."

He didn't leave out a single cliché. American children did not know when
the *Mayflower* set sail, but there was not a single Jewish child who did not
know when the Exodus from Egypt took place. And Palestine is not mentioned at all in Arab history. Not a single Jew settled in an Arab village, yet
the Arabs were attacking the Jews anyway. He explained to the committee
why that happened: the Arabs hated people who looked cowardly to them.
But there was no cause for concern, the Jews knew how to defend themselves,
he said, adding: "Even if sometimes they are attacking us we don't remember. We want to remember the good things, not the bad."[30]

While the committee was still hearing testimony in London, Crossman asked one witness what he would decide were he to have to choose between bringing one hundred thousand refugees to Palestine and establishing
a Jewish state. The witness did not have an answer. Ben-Gurion now took
the opportunity to answer the question for him. He said that the question
needed to be put to the refugees themselves. He knew what their answer
would be, he said, offering the committee another parable: "Suppose Hitler
had in his hand a hundred thousand Englishmen—prisoners—and he told
Mr. Churchill, either you give me the British Navy or we will slaughter all
these hundred thousand Englishmen. Would you ask Mr. Churchill this
question? I know what those hundred thousand Englishmen would answer.
Wouldn't they die gladly rather than renounce the British Navy?" He told
them about his time in London during the Blitz, and how much he admired
the resoluteness of the British. "There are hundreds of thousands of Jews . . .

who will give up their lives if necessary for Jewish independence, for Zion," he declared.[31]

One of the American members of the committee, James McDonald, saw "great strength and indomitable determination" in Ben-Gurion: "I can understand why he is so natural a leader." Crossman wrote, in contrast, that Ben-Gurion's testimony left a bad impression on the panel. It was a propaganda speech aimed at his own people, and the members of his audience had already had enough of such oratory. They especially disdained his attempt to evade responsibility for acts of terror. In his diary, he described Ben-Gurion as a local Lenin, referring to "the dictator who runs the Jews in Palestine, including the illegal army."[32] Weizmann, who spoke prior to Ben-Gurion, impressed the committee in particular with his sincerity, Crossman wrote. He was the first witness who explicitly acknowledged that the choice was not between justice and injustice, but between a larger and a smaller injustice. Weizmann "looks like a weary and more humane version of Lenin, very tired, very ill, too old and too pro-British to control his extremists," Crossman wrote.[33]

"A GENERAL HUMAN PHENOMENON"

The members of the committee tried to draw Ben-Gurion out of the routine Zionist manifesto he recited to them. Let's assume that Palestine is the only country that can take in these displaced persons, they asked. Why does that have to mean founding a Jewish state at the same time? What they were actually getting at was whether the Jewish people, now that they had lost six million of their number, still needed a state. Ben-Gurion responded just as he had before the Holocaust—only a Jewish state could constitute a Jewish national home for all those Jews throughout the world who for one reason or another wish to or must come to Palestine, he maintained. The Jews, he argued, could never really enjoy equal rights, because they were a minority in every country in which they resided. "It is a general human phenomenon," he explained. "Wherever you have two groups, one a strong group, powerful, and the other weak and helpless, there is bound to be mischief. The strong group will always take advantage of the weaker group, rightly or wrongly. You cannot expect human beings, human nature being what it is, people having power over other people, that they should not sometimes, not always, not necessarily always, abuse it."

The thesis of almost inevitable oppression that was the lot of every minority as a minority was not new in Ben-Gurion's thought. Three years before the Anglo-American Committee was formed, he warned the Assembly of Representatives that Britain's policy was leading to a binational Arab-Jewish state, in which the Jews would be consigned to a ghetto. "A Jewish ghetto is everywhere that there is a Jewish minority," he declared. "Every Jewish minority is, by its very nature, nothing but a hostage that is sometimes treated mercifully and sometimes given protection and sometimes abandoned, in accordance with the needs of the rulers and the majority, whether to plunder, persecution, or slaughter."[34]

The members of the committee then wondered how a Jewish-majority state in Palestine could ensure equal rights for the Arab minority that would live among it. Ben-Gurion responded that there was no reason for concern. The Arabs of Palestine, he proclaimed, would never be a minority, as they were part of the Arab world, with its hundreds of millions of inhabitants who would surround the Jewish state. The members of the committee were not convinced—not because they thought he was lying, or perhaps not only because they thought he was lying, but because it was one of the principal internal contradictions in his argument, one that he did not reconcile to their satisfaction.[35]

Crossman was appalled by the double game Ben-Gurion played after the Holocaust—obedient recognition of British rule, along with terror aimed at bringing it to an end. Neither the Irish nor the Boers had done such a thing, he wrote. They dared to take up arms against a large imperial power and received the fruits of their daring. "I formed the view that Ben-Gurion and his directives should have had the courage to break openly with Weizmann," he wrote, "to go underground and together with the Irgun [Etzel] to raise the standard of revolt."[36]

That is exactly what Ben-Gurion did, while continuing to play his double game.

❖

On the afternoon of Monday, July 22, 1946, more than ninety people were killed when a bomb went off in the southern wing of the King David Hotel. Most of the dead were Britons, Jews, and Arabs; the wing housed the offices of the British administration and army. At the time, it was the most lethal terror attack in history, and it remained so for many years thereafter. It was carried out by members of Etzel.[37] When it happened, Ben-Gurion was on his way from New York to Paris.

❖

When World War II broke out, Etzel accepted Ben-Gurion's "dual formula," and suspended, for the most part, terror against the British. The organization's commander, David Raziel, even fell in Iraq in the service of the British. Menachem Begin, who reached Palestine in 1942 and was chosen Etzel commander at the end of 1943, declared a revolt against British rule. "There is no longer a cease-fire between the Hebrew nation and youth and the British administration in Palestine, which is turning our brothers over to Hitler," he wrote. He was referring principally to the White Paper immigration quotas. "The British regime completed its shameful betrayal of the Hebrew nation and there is no moral basis for its existence in Palestine."[38] The revolt he led was aimed, for the time being, at British rule in Palestine, not at Britain itself, as its soldiers battled the Nazis. As in Jabotinsky's days, the difference between what Begin and Ben-Gurion said was mostly a matter of style and tactics; their national goal was shared.

Etzel soon launched a series of terror attacks against the British, which included placing bombs in government offices and police stations. The militia sabotaged bridges, railroad tracks, and telephone lines. Some of its members were captured and, in a few cases, executed. The terror campaign undermined the Zionist movement's contacts with the British; in London, it threatened to end the negotiations for the establishment of the Jewish Brigade.[39]

But Ben-Gurion's principal concern was Etzel's political influence—the organization's terror attacks were accompanied by an ongoing propaganda campaign. Its operations were not aimed only at the British. They also sought to gain Etzel and the Revisionist movement prestige in the Jewish public, at the expense of the labor movement. Begin was also looking over his shoulder at an even more militant terror faction that had split away from Etzel in the summer of 1940, Lehi. The name is the Hebrew acronym of Freedom Fighters for Israel; the British called it the Stern Gang. The organization specialized in bank robberies and assassinations of British officials. In August 1944, Lehi operatives threw a bomb at the high commissioner's car, and in November they assassinated Lord Moyne, then the most senior British official in the Middle East. The contest of Zionist patriotism that had characterized local politics in Jewish Palestine in the 1930s returned. In the 1940s, however, it was also a struggle over who would rule the Jewish state that would be born after the war. The labor movement referred to Etzel and Lehi as the "breakaway" movements, and Ben-Gurion sought to smash them.[40]

The decisive discussion came at an open meeting of the Histadrut membership, a few days following Moyne's murder. He proposed dismissing from their jobs "everyone connected to these gangs," even if he or she had not personally committed a terror attack but was only involved in advocating for the militias. The same was true of schoolchildren. Those engaged in propaganda for the militants—for example, by putting up posters—should be expelled from school. He called on children to turn in their parents who had helped the dissidents by giving them money, even if only under coercion. He demanded that people not provide refuge to members of the breakaway groups who were fleeing from the police. And he said that they should be turned in to the authorities. He termed them bandits and murderers, "some are maniacs and some charlatans."

Not all his associates agreed. Some feared a civil war, and others found it difficult to break free of the long-standing Jewish communal proscription on turning Jews over to non-Jewish authorities. But the "terror gangs" were also a threat to the labor movement, Ben-Gurion stressed. He told his people that it was time to make a decision: "either terror or an organized labor movement."

Shlomo Zemach objected that his rhetoric was liable to backfire. "When you besmirch the honor of these youngsters and call them all sorts of horrible names, the natural response of the masses is to defend them, and in doing so to be forgiving of their actions." In any case, going after the dissidents was considered dirty work, and as such it was carried out by "volunteers" who ostensibly operated at the Haganah's behest. They were called Mishmar Ha'uma, the National Guard. About two hundred people were put through a five-day course that trained them in security, counterterrorism, detective work, and surveillance, as well as in how to abduct and interrogate the dissidents, which often involved torture. The result was the Hunting Season, or the "Saison," as it came to be called. According to the *Haganah History Book*, about seven hundred names were handed over to the British secret police, and about three hundred people were arrested. Some thirty children were expelled from school.[41]

The operation against the dissidents prompted Etzel and Lehi to carry out joint operations. In July 1945, they together blew up a railroad bridge.[42] Both organizations also held talks with the Haganah, and at one point everyone reached a consensus that the internecine war was detrimental to the national cause. Eliyahu Golomb, who was understood to be the uncrowned commander of the Haganah, died in June 1945, leading to greater involvement by Ben-Gurion in the organization's activities.

Moshe Sneh, the chief of the Haganah National Command, was then thirty-six years old, a former Polish army officer and leader of the Zionist movement there. He was a physician by training. Ben-Gurion valued his astuteness, as well as the political advantage he offered. Affiliated with the parties and factions of the center-right, Sneh did not belong to the labor movement. As such, he was not involved in the movement's tangled intrigues, plots, and battles of competing interests. He was thus on good terms with his fellow Polish Zionist Menachem Begin. At the end of 1944, the two men talked about a possible alliance between Etzel and the Haganah.[43] After the war, Ben-Gurion authorized Sneh to sign a cooperation agreement with Etzel and Lehi. "The two rival factions should be invited for full cooperation, on condition of unitary authority and absolute discipline," Ben-Gurion wrote to Sneh. His reason: "We require a constant effort to ensure the unity of the Jewish community in Palestine, and above all among its fighters, for the sake of the war." The cooperation freed him of the need to defend the much-reviled policy of the Saison, and deprived the separatist organizations their monopoly on the revolt against the British. Up to that time, the Palmach's fighters had had to make do largely with helping along the Holocaust survivors who had reached Palestine's shores in illegal immigration ships. That was uplifting and humanitarian work, but it generally did not require much heroism. Now, in October 1945, the Jewish Resistance Movement was born.

❖

Not all terror attacks were carried out jointly, but for the most part they were coordinated and received sanction in principle from a civilian committee with a mysterious and somewhat puerile name—the X Committee. Ben-Gurion set it up himself; its composition reflected that of the Zionist coalition. He lent a hand to the Jewish Resistance Movement partly in preparation for his final and decisive round against Weizmann, who opposed terror.

He was in a fighting and autocratic mood. "His manner of speech is simply inhuman," Moshe Sharett wrote to Moshe Sneh. "If you agree with him eighty percent and differ twenty percent, or agree with his main point and argue a minor point, or agree in general but differ on a specific detail—he immediately focuses all his fervor on that twenty percent, that minor point, or that detail, and the altercation is so powerful that it is as if the dispute were over one hundred percent." Sharett was particularly aggravated by Ben-Gurion's attitude. "You never manage to get out a complete sentence with him," he griped. "He immediately interrupts, latches onto a word he doesn't like, confronts and rages."

On October 7, 1945, Ben-Gurion sent Sneh a letter he signed with the pseudonym "Amos's father." According to the letter, "The response is not to be limited in this country to immigration and settlement. It is necessary to use sabotage and reprisals. Not personal terror, but reprisals for every Jew who is murdered by the White Paper authorities. Every act of S [that is, sabotage] needs to carry great weight and make a great impression. Care should be taken to avoid human casualties to every extent possible." When he told his party colleagues about this letter a few months later, he stressed that he worded it with great care. He did not mean to issue an absolute prohibition against actions liable to lead to a loss of human life. Rather, his directive was to avoid this to every extent possible.[44] During the months that followed, he tried to conduct the terror campaign from Paris. In doing so, he sent out contradictory messages and lost control of the resistance.

"I HAVE A PLAN"

In mid-June 1946, members of the Palmach blew up eleven bridges. It was the Resistance Movement's most daring operation up to that point. The next day, Etzel operatives abducted five British officers. That was the underground faction's response to a death sentence the British had imposed on two of its men. The abduction of the officers was understood to be part of the rivalry between Etzel and the Palmach, despite the coordination between them. Ben-Gurion demanded that the Jewish Agency Executive condemn the kidnapping and promise to help the authorities apprehend the perpetrators. But two weeks later, he wrote to Sneh: "English newspapers are reporting that you are threatening to take action against Etzel if the officers are not released. They should be demanded to release them, but all internal conflict is definitely not desirable now."

A few days afterward, on June 29, 1946, the British authorities sent seventeen thousand troops on a search-and-seize operation aimed at crushing the Jewish Resistance Movement. This included arresting several Jewish Agency leaders, among them Moshe Sharett, Yitzhak Gruenbaum, and David Remez. The Jews called the operation the Black Sabbath. Ben-Gurion, then in Paris, was at the top of the British wanted list.[45]

It was already close to midnight when word reached Paris about what was happening in Palestine. The news was first broadcast by the BBC, and then also arrived via a secret wireless communications system Ben-Gurion used for contacts with Palestine. Ben-Gurion was in his hotel, surrounded by his aides. He looked dazed and asked Ehud Avriel to take him for a drive around Paris. During the ride, he did not emit a sound. A few hours later, as dawn broke, Avriel returned him to the hotel. Only at this point did he finally speak. "I'll tell you what needs to be done," he said, as if it were an original idea that had suddenly come into his head. "We need to establish a Jewish state."

Black Sabbath, or, as Ben-Gurion termed it, "the pogrom arranged for us by [Prime Minister] Mr. Atlee," was another seminal public trauma suffered by the Jews of Palestine while Ben-Gurion was outside Palestine, like the terror offensive of 1929 and the anxiety brought on by what seemed to be an impending Nazi invasion. For the first time since his Sejera days he felt

personally unsafe. His people warned him not to go to Palestine or to London, lest he, too, be arrested.[46]

❖

Two months after Black Sabbath, on July 1, 1946, Sneh ordered Begin "to
carry out that little hotel thing at the earliest opportunity." The hotel in question was the King David. The attack was planned collaboratively by Haganah and Etzel experts; Etzel assumed responsibility for the actual execution.
The X Committee had previously signed off on an attack on "a central institution of government." It may well be that the committee's members did not
know that this meant the King David Hotel. Perhaps they did not want to
know, or perhaps they were not officially told. Ben-Gurion knew about the
plan. On July 6, 1946, he wrote to Sneh: "Your proposal exceeds the framework of the five provisions and cannot be accepted. Operate only within the
five provisions." He was referring to the operational guidelines that he had
sent Sneh the previous October, which had included a warning to refrain, as
far as possible, from life-threatening actions. He would later be able to claim
that he tried to prevent the attack. But the letter was not particularly vehement. Whatever the case, he took off hastily the next day for the United
States, where the arms of the British law could not nab him.

Chaim Weizmann happened to be in Palestine that week. He put pressure on Sneh to reduce terror to the minimum; at one point, he threatened to
resign if his demand was not met. Sneh told Begin to postpone the King
David operation. On July 20, he wrote to him: "If you still take account of
my personal appeal, I hereby beseech you to suspend the activities that are
currently pending for a few more days." He asked Begin for a postponement,
not a cancellation, and he asked rather than ordered. He did not direct him
to hold his fire and did not warn that violating his request would bring on a
renewal of the Saison.[47]

❖

In America, Ben-Gurion met with Jewish leaders and several government
officials, but he does not seem to have been all that busy. He had time to buy

books, and also asked his secretary to send him other books from Palestine. He may have feared that his American exile would last a long time. He also dealt with his shopping list from home—bed linens, tablecloths, and towels.

He soon bucked up his spirits and made a full recovery, just as he had done in 1929. "I have a plan," he informed Paula. *The New York Times* reported from London that he was free to go there and would not be arrested. His response: "I am grateful to the government for this generosity. I hope that I will not require it much longer." Less than three weeks later, he was back in Paris. He heard about the bombing of the King David on the morning he arrived. He updated himself on the details, including Sneh's role, and then cabled the Jewish Agency Executive: "I do not want to be and cannot be responsible, and neither am I prepared or able to bear the moral burden alone." He may have intended the cable for British eyes. In any case, he shared responsibility. To be able to carry on his work, he had to place the full blame on Begin, and that is what he did. Sneh, who came to Paris, received his full backing, just as David Remez had following the Solel Boneh scandal; it was Ben-Gurion's way of extricating himself from such situations.[48]

❖

He sent the plan he had told Paula about to a number of prominent people, and submitted it to the Jewish Agency Executive, which convened in Paris. Palestine on both sides of the Jordan would become a neutral zone, free of foreign armies, and divided into two states, Abdulliya (after King Abdullah of Transjordan) and Judea. Abdulliya would be composed of those areas populated by Arabs, in the center of Palestine (including Jenin, Nablus, and Ramallah), with six hundred thousand to seven hundred thousand inhabitants all told. Judea would receive unsettled areas to the east of the Jordan River, the Jordan Valley, and the area around the Dead Sea. Neither country would maintain an army, only the forces necessary to maintain internal order. Each would set its immigration regulations for itself. Disputes between the two would be mediated by the United Nations. The Christian holy sites would be under control of the churches.

Different versions of the plan have been preserved. The main point was partition, one that would not require population transfer. Practically, the plan accomplished nothing, except perhaps to answer a need Ben-Gurion felt to regain control over events following Black Sabbath, just as he had sought to do following the 1929 disturbances. In keeping with that, he took care to keep playing a double game, or, as he put it, "Neither Masada," by which he meant a fight to the death, "nor Vichy," by which he meant capitulation. He himself saw "at least one merit" to the plan, as he wrote: "It will expose the lie in what Mr. Bevin and his supporters are saying, to the effect that they are in Palestine in order to bring about peace between Jews and Arabs."[49] Both Abdulliya and Judea would soon be forgotten, because one of the participants in the Jewish Agency Executive's deliberations in Paris would set in motion a decisive process.

❖

Nahum Goldmann, a rising star in Zionist diplomacy who generally worked from the United States, was sharp of mind and well connected, crafty and with a great zest for life. He had long advocated partition; the most prominent Zionist leader in America, Abba Hillel Silver, opposed it. In Paris, Goldmann explained to the Executive's members that President Truman was getting sick of Palestine and that the coming congressional elections might offer the last opportunity to achieve something for Zionism, the least of a few possible evils. As Goldmann did his best to persuade them, he was informed by telephone from Washington that the White House would, in a few days' time, announce its position on the issue. He offered to take the first plane to Washington to influence the deliberations at the last moment, but conditioned his offer on being authorized by the Jewish Agency Executive to inform the American government of its consent to the establishment of a Jewish state in a part of Palestine.

Most of the Executive's members, from both Palestine and the United States, agreed. Ben-Gurion resented it. It was a historic step that he had not initiated or led; the ambitious Goldmann was claiming that he could achieve, in just three days, what the Zionist movement in Palestine had not in three decades. Ben-Gurion haggled a bit over the precise wording of the authority invested in Goldmann; he was liable to soon find himself facing the opponents of partition in Palestine and would be expected to defend the mission. The presence of Sneh, who supported the initiative, gave it a patriotic stamp of approval. The result was that the Jewish Agency Executive voted by a large majority to authorize Goldmann to tell the White House that it was prepared to discuss "a viable Jewish state in an adequate area of Palestine." The Zionist leadership had taken the same position before the Anglo-American Committee, but the Paris decision had the character of a binding parliamentary resolution, the first of its type in the history of the Zionist movement.*

Goldmann set off immediately for Washington and returned less than a week later. His talks with Under Secretary of State Dean Acheson and the president's adviser on Jewish affairs, David Nyles, succeeded in getting the White House to endorse, for the first time, the establishment of a Jewish state in Palestine, as well as the settlement of one hundred thousand displaced persons there. Goldmann, much like Weizmann, had a dramatic flair. He related that Nyles, Ben-Gurion's old acquaintance, had dissolved into tears when he learned of President Truman's decision to support partition, crying out in Yiddish: "Had my mother only heard that we will have a Jewish state!" Weizmann liked to lend the story of the Balfour Declaration a similarly mythic cast.[50]

"LOVE AND LOYAL ESTEEM"

In October 1946, Ben-Gurion made his third visit to the DP camps in Germany. It was a few days before his sixtieth birthday. The visit was part of an election campaign—the camp inmates were about to vote in the elections for the next Zionist Congress, scheduled for December. More than eighteen thousand of the fifty-three thousand DPs voted for his party, making it the largest faction in the camps.[51]

The first Zionist Congress to convene after the Holocaust brought about

---

* Ben-Gurion abstained in most of the votes, so as to underline his displeasure with Weizmann's continuing involvement in Zionist statecraft. In its decision—which was not put into writing, for reasons of secrecy—the Jewish Agency Executive also resolved not to renew the terror campaign against the British. (Ben-Gurion 1993a, p. 99; Ben-Gurion 1993b, p. 329.)

twenty-five hundred delegates and guests to Basel, more than had attended any of the previous twenty-one Congresses. The delegates ostensibly had the discretion to vote for any of a number of alternatives for Jewish life in Palestine. Among these were an extension of the Mandate, international trusteeship, a joint binational regime, or the partition of Palestine into provinces or cantons or autonomous regions linked in a federative arrangement, perhaps as part of a larger regional federation. Echoes of the debate over partition reverberated in Basel, but in practical terms the idea that the Jewish state would include all of Palestine had become an anachronism by, at the latest, the eve of the previous Yom Kippur, on October 4, 1946. That day, four weeks before the midterm congressional elections in the United States, President Truman had issued a statement of support for the Jewish Agency's plan to establish a Jewish state in a part of Palestine.[52] By that he meant the partition proposal that Goldmann had brought from Paris that summer.

The delegates to the Zionist Congress were thus divided largely over the question of how to pursue the effort to establish a state—moderately and gradually, as Weizmann wished, or with a certain measure of belligerence and force, as Ben-Gurion proposed. In the three years since Ben-Gurion had referred to Weizmann as "loathsome carrion" and "a trampled corpse," relations between the two had not improved. But Weizmann may well not have been surprised when he received, just prior to the Congress, a letter reminiscent of the love letter Ben-Gurion had sent him ten years previously. "You remain for me (and, I am sure, not just for me) the chosen man of Jewish history, who symbolizes like no other Jewish suffering and greatness," he now wrote, "and wherever you are, you will have the love and loyal esteem of me and the members of the generation that followed you."

The political program that Ben-Gurion proposed to Weizmann was worded as one of those convoluted sentences seemingly meant to enable him to say "I told you so" no matter what happened, just as Ben-Gurion liked to do. "If England does not want to or cannot maintain the Mandate," he wrote, "and if neither is it prepared or willing to leave Palestine (and it is clear to me that it does not wish to do so, although I would not be concerned if it left, but I will not oppose it remaining), it may do so only under one condition (to the extent that it depends on us): it must agree to the establishment of a Jewish state, even if not in all of Palestine, immediately or following a brief transition period acceptable to us." In other words, either the Mandate would continue in all of Palestine, or there would be a Jewish state in part of it. His qualification ("to the extent that it depends on us") made no reference to the Arabs. "By this point, our opposition to the present regime has gained us honor in the eyes of the Arabs . . . ," he told Weizmann. "I have no hopes that the Arabs will help us obtain a state, but I am sure that, if a Jewish state is established, the Arabs will be our best friends."[53]

There was no political need for this letter. It principally evinced the confusion that pervaded the Zionist movement as the Congress approached. Ben-Gurion may also have meant to sweeten for Weizmann the bitter pill of his impending dismissal by the Congress. And it may also have been a sign of a real inner conflict about deposing the man who had been Zionism's public face for three decades. Whatever the case, the turmoil at the Congress lent the rivalry between the two the character of a parliamentary cockfight.

The split in Mapai divided its faction at the Congress into two as well. Most of Mapai's members accepted Ben-Gurion's position on the struggle for independence, but most also opposed his demand for Weizmann's removal. As in the past, they refused to choose between the two and wanted both. They decided to support Weizmann, on condition that he lend his support to Mapai's party line. It was a blow to Ben-Gurion. He responded as he always did. "I will not serve on the Executive so long as Weizmann serves or will serve as president," he informed his party, heading to his room to pack his bags.

The usual flurry ensued, producing a welter of legends. According to one version, Paula entered the plenum and collared a delegate. "He has gone mad," she said. Someone rushed Golda Meir to the venerable Drei Könige hotel, where Ben-Gurion was supposedly lodging in the same room that Herzl had stayed in during the First Zionist Congress. Other associates also arrived, and according to one of them, there was "shouting that reached the heavens." The loudest shouts came from Ben-Gurion and Eliezer Kaplan, who supported Weizmann. One person who was present later reported that their bellows verged on turning into a fistfight, and would have had Meir not physically separated them.*[54]

The uproar was gratuitous, because Weizmann's supporters were unable to garner enough votes to reelect him, bringing an end to his Zionist career. His greatest enemy was not Ben-Gurion but Abba Hillel Silver, who headed the largest faction in the Congress, the General Zionists. Like Ben-Gurion, Silver also advocated a tougher line toward the British. Weizmann was politely shown the door; he turned down a proposal to assume the post of "honorary president" of the Congress, with the Congress deciding that it would not elect a president at all at this time. Charming and ironic to the end, Weizmann bade farewell to the delegates from the dais with a maxim he said he had heard from his mother: "It is easier to swim in the sea than in a bathtub." Then, leaning on his aides, he made his way out of the hall, beaten and humiliated, but also regally, on his way into the history books. Ben-Gurion was reelected chairman of the Jewish Agency Executive. The power relations in the movement required Ben-Gurion to head a coalition that constricted his freedom of action, but he assumed the security portfolio.†[55]

❖

The shock, horror, and sense of guilt that afflicted the Christian world after the Holocaust produced profound sympathy for the Jewish people as a whole and the Zionist movement in particular. This helped further the movement's diplomatic and public relations campaigns, despite the fact that, after three decades of Zionism in Palestine, it was still not clear when exactly the Jewish state

---

* One of the sources for this account of the imbroglio is worth mentioning not because of the details of the story but rather because of who witnessed it—Shimon Peres, then twenty-three years old. Ben-Gurion had directed that young people should be included in the Mapai delegation. Moshe Dayan was also at the Congress. (Bar-Zohar 2006, p. 98; Ben-Gurion to Moshe Sharett, Nov. 7, 1946, in Ben-Gurion, Diary, BGA.)

† The Congress's first decision was to demand that Palestine be constituted as a Jewish state. Its second decision was that the state would be established *in* Palestine—in other words, not necessarily in all of it. This acceptance of the principle of partition was also implied in its rejection of Ahdut Ha'avodah's demand that the Congress explicitly state that its intention was Palestine "complete and undivided." (Aharon Zisling to the Zionist Congress, and "Decisions of the Zionist Congress, Political Program," Proceedings of the 22nd Zionist Congress, pp. 500, 575, CZA J28.)

would be born. But there was no longer any doubt that it would be—the so-cial, cultural, political, economic, and military infrastructure of the state-to-be was already solid, and the Jewish population's sense of national community was adamant. There is thus no basis for claiming that the state was founded as a result of the Holocaust; the British played a much larger role. The DPs com-prised only about 10 percent of the "first million" that Ben-Gurion fantasized about bringing to Palestine on boats "immediately after the war." They would not suffice to create a Jewish majority in the country. But no other country in the world wanted them and no one knew what to do with them. For Ben-Gurion, they were the vanguard of the Zionist struggle. It was his principal achievement at that time. The Zionist project and the struggle against the Brit-ish had become one and the same, as was put on display a few weeks prior to the Congress when, in a single night, eleven new Jewish settlements went up in the Negev region.[56] The British were still in Palestine despite themselves. In the ten years that had gone by since Arab terror had taught them that Palestine was not governable, they had postponed their exit primarily because of the world war; now that the war was over, they hadn't a clue as to how to leave.

Then, in an unexpected twist, on the eve of the Mandate's end and the inevitable war against the Arabs, Ben-Gurion tried to revive the historic alli-ance between Zionism and the British Empire, on the basis of the original Mandate. He wanted the Mandate to continue because the Haganah was still not prepared for war with the Arabs, and he was not yet prepared to lead it into war. The British did not want to acknowledge that they had failed. "We are the only group in the entire Middle East that wants to be and can be your friends," Ben-Gurion said to Colonial Secretary George Henry Hall in June 1946. "We have not only a common interest, but also common values." In a conversation with a senior Colonial Office official he proposed a "loyal alliance" and declared: "You can trust us." He noted that Britain could main-tain military bases in Palestine.[57]

When he spoke of common values, he meant labor values. While in op-position, the British Labour Party had supported free Jewish immigration to Palestine as well as population transfer there. But when the party formed its postwar government, it did not keep its promises. That was a good reason "to get rid of the British," as many of Palestine's Jews maintained. Hostility to the British focused in particular on the foreign minister Ernest Bevin.

Golda Meir wrote: "I do not know if Bevin was a bit mad or merely anti-Semitic, or both"; Ben-Gurion said that Bevin was "mad with hatred of the Jews and Zionism."[58] Nevertheless, he tried to entice him into staying. The Jews represented Europe in the Middle East, he assured Bevin, and they would always remain the only European nation in the region.

Impervious to Zionism, pessimistic, and often downright crude, Bevin put many hours into these conversations with Ben-Gurion, almost like an inveterate gambler unable to acknowledge that the game was over. At this point, both the Zionists and the British were committed to partition; the question was the borders. The British tried their best to get Ben-Gurion to commit himself to precise boundaries, but refused to show him their own map. This cat-and-mouse game lasted for a few days, until Bevin suddenly capitulated and announced, to the astonishment of his aides, that he was prepared to show Ben-Gurion his own partition lines. Ben-Gurion agreed to respond to what he saw. The map Bevin showed Ben-Gurion was that of a previous scheme. In keeping with his promise, Ben-Gurion marked out a line on the map with his finger, indicating what the Zionist movement could accept.

The next day, a British official produced another map and asked Ben-Gurion if the partition line it showed accorded with what he had drawn with his finger the previous day. Ben-Gurion, surprised and not amused, confirmed that it was his partition map.[59]

Sir Norman Brook, who had engineered the ploy, was then at the beginning of his tenure as Cabinet secretary. He seems to have been one of the officials who inspired the mythological figure of "Sir Humphrey" from the BBC series *Yes, Prime Minister*. Brook reported to the Cabinet about the map, and news of it reached the high commissioner in Jerusalem as well. The high commissioner asked for, and apparently received, a copy.[60] When he met with Foreign Secretary Bevin the next day, Ben-Gurion said: "I want you to know what I believe is the position of our people. If a Jewish State, including the area which I have outlined yesterday—that is, the whole of Galilee, the whole of the Negev, with the exclusion of the central part containing some 600,000 Arabs—will be set up, our people will accept this compromise, although they will not be very happy about the operation."[61] He made only one condition in exchange for putting off independence and extending the Mandate regime—control of immigration.

❖

It was the next day that Ben-Gurion had his frigid encounter with the Conservative Party's Oliver Stanley at the Dorchester. Despite the freezing temperatures, the tenor of the conversation was pleasant. "The current situation is impossible, insulting, and humiliating for England," Stanley said, adding reluctantly that it would be best for Britain to leave Palestine, but on condition that its withdrawal be part of a sensible partition plan and not look as if Britain were running away. He asked how he could help; Ben-Gurion asked him to coordinate a meeting with Churchill, who was now in opposition. Stanley said that he would be seeing Churchill that afternoon and would ask him. But this attempt to get to Churchill was no more successful than previous ones.

Ben-Gurion's day was far from over, however. Late that evening he went to the House of Lords for a talk with Lord Chancellor Sir William Jowitt. Simon Marks had set up the meeting, meant to be a last-minute attempt to avert war in Palestine. At close to midnight, the two of them reached agreement on the wording of a statement that Ben-Gurion permitted Jowitt to present to the Cabinet the next day. It proposed that the Mandate would be extended for another five or ten years; over the next year or two about one hundred thousand Jews would be allowed to enter Palestine, apparently at a rate of about four thousand a month. Thereafter immigration would continue in accordance with the country's ability to absorb it. The White Paper restrictions on the purchase of land and on settlement would be rescinded. Ben-Gurion undertook not to declare independence for five years and made it understood to Jowitt that he would act against terror and cease illegal immigration. "We met just in time," Jowitt said. Weizmann had never agreed to less than this, but in Ben-Gurion's case it is hard to believe that he thought it was really possible to avoid a war over Palestine. Whatever the case, the British Cabinet was indeed fed up with the Mandate, as Ben-Gurion had heard from Stanley, and resolved to hand the Palestine question over to the United Nations.

Ben-Gurion endured severe pain from the horrible cold. He had to spend several days in bed, and longed for Tiberias's hot springs.[62]

PARTITION

"CAN WE SURVIVE?"

Ben-Gurion spent the last weekend of November 1947 at the Kalia Hotel, on the north end of the Dead Sea. "I was with my wife, my son, and my little granddaughter," he later recounted. "Late at night people woke me up and told me about the UN decision. The laborers from the Dead Sea Works quickly arrived and danced all night." He was referring to Resolution 181 of the United Nations General Assembly, convened at one of the World's Fair pavilions in Queens. The great majority of the organization's member states supported the decision, which called for the partition of Palestine into two states. When Ben-Gurion reached his office the next day, he found the courtyard of the Jewish Agency building packed with dancers. "Every Jew in Jerusalem celebrated and danced," he related. "I never before saw such Jewish joy. And I was perhaps the only Jew who did not dance. Not because I did not appreciate the UN decision like the others, or that I wanted a Jewish state any less than they did. Rather, it was because I knew what awaited us before the state would arrive, and what awaited the state when it was established." He told his daughter Renana: "Who knows if some of the dancers here will not fall in battle."[1]

A few months later, he concerned himself with the question of what would happen in Palestine if the Jewish community were suddenly annihilated, as had happened with the Jews of Europe. It was, he said, a "brutal question," and he presented it to the members of his party. As they did their best to recover from the queasiness that must have overcome them, he explained that it might not necessarily happen the way it had in Europe. "If, God forbid, there was some catastrophe, say a geological catastrophe, or a political one, and the community was wiped off the face of the earth," he wondered, "would the Jewish people have the ability to reestablish one?" No other person involved in Jewish local politics in Palestine could have raised such a question; he answered it in the negative: the Zionist enterprise could not be re-created. His pessimism lent realistic credibility to the optimism he often displayed.[2] It was only natural that he take upon himself to prepare the Jewish public for war. He had no doubt that he was the right man for the job. "All my time in Palestine I was somewhat involved in defense," he wrote. Many years later, he explained: "I dealt with defense while still in the town of my birth, and when I worked at Sejera, I was placed face-to-face with death and came to understand the necessity of self-defense."[3] He knew nothing about leading an army into war.

❖

When he returned from London in February 1947, he estimated that it would be two years before war broke out in Palestine, and as such he embarked on a leisurely study of the security situation. "I am not making it my top priority right now," he told the members of his party. The party's immediate problems were more important, but he also promised to look closely at what was happening in the Haganah. It seemed to him that not everything there was as it should be, "and that, too, is a serious matter," he said.[4]

He termed the months he spent on this his "seminar." Each day he summoned Haganah leaders, one after the other, and presented them with questions that elicited smirks from some and alarm in others. He had no clue as to the state of the Haganah and how it needed to prepare for war. The structure and chain of command, personnel and the training of commanders, equipment and arms, strategy and tactics—it was all new to him.[5]

As he had often done before, he familiarized himself with the subject by setting down endless details in his diary. That was how he had prepared for the great election battle in Poland in 1933. Just as he had carefully recorded the votes each party could count on in each neighborhood, and how many Zionist memberships could be sold in each town, he now wanted to know everything: rifles and provisions, helmets and cigarettes, medications and socks, vehicles and cannon and military chaplains. There was barely a subject that did not appear as data in his diary—myriad figures, more numbers, and names as well. The numbers seemed to give him a grip on the subject he wished to internalize, and also provided self-confidence and perhaps a sense of control. Like the books that he purchased, the numbers also fed his passion for retention.[6] Sometimes he encouraged his interlocutors in his "seminar" to evaluate the personalities and capacities of their colleagues; he also asked about their party affiliation. From time to time he returned to the central question: "Can we survive?"[7]

One of the founders of the Haganah had summed up the situation for him in 1938: "Chaos. There is no military spirit. There is no plan nor any thought about bad times, especially the case of war." That had also been the situation in the world war, when Ben-Gurion feared that Germany and Italy would help the Arabs annihilate the Jews of Palestine.[8] The seminar of 1947 indicated that he did not prepare the Haganah for the coming war, just as he had not prepared it previously for the challenges of the 1920s and 1930s. Taken together, the details he recorded in his diary revealed an alarming picture.

The Haganah still largely comprised some twenty thousand volunteers, who were meant, in time of need, to defend their own settlements and neighborhoods; it now became, as well, something like a civil guard. About six thousand of them spent a day or two a week training and were termed the Field Corps. Some two thousand volunteers served in the Palmach and were, as Ben-Gurion put it, "semi-mobilized." The closest thing to a real military force, they spent half their time training, and they could be deployed outside their communities. Several of the Haganah chiefs whom he interviewed complained of a lack of antitank and antiaircraft weapons, but Ben-Gurion discovered that most members of the organization had not even been issued a rifle.[9]

In parallel with his personal inquiry, Ben-Gurion employed an American colonel named Mickey Marcus, who issued a lethal report. There was not a single full battalion that could be sent into battle, Marcus informed him.[10] Yitzhak Rabin, already then a Palmach commander, later wrote: "There is no way to escape the sad truth—in the face of huge political decisions and the danger of an Arab invasion, we were not properly prepared. Too much time was wasted."[11]

Ben-Gurion was dumbfounded. "I discovered that we were unready to an extent far beyond what I had imagined," he wrote.[12] The use of the first-person plural allowed him, as usual, to avoid pointing to the person principally responsible. He remarked that it had been that way "for many years"; in his absence, Moshe Sharett also addressed security issues. But, as chairman of the Jewish Agency and the holder of the security portfolio, Ben-Gurion had the overall responsibility. When he wrote a few weeks later that the Haganah "is not fit for its mission," he thought it best to add, cautiously: "That is not criticism of the past, but rather concern for the future."[13] He took it upon himself to reorganize almost everything from the ground up.

Less than a month after the partition resolution, Ben-Gurion was already offering excuses for neglecting the Haganah. "I ask myself how it happened that at this critical time we find ourselves unprepared, when the Haganah has been in existence for twenty-some years," said Moshe Shapira, a member of the Jewish Agency Executive. Ben-Gurion replied: "I ask Shapira to cease criticizing the past at this time. I have just as much to say about the past as anyone else—but what good will that do?"

He was not good at dealing with criticism. As in the past, he argued not only that "we are all guilty," but also "I told you so." He was not a general, he said, and did not want to be one. "I am not a military expert and war is not my profession," he declared.[14] Despite that, he had been the only one to discern the real danger, already two years previously, he stressed. For seventy years ("since Petah Tikvah's inception"), the Jewish community had needed to defend itself only against the Arabs of Palestine. But it would soon face the combined armies of the Arab states, mainly Egypt and the emirate of Transjordan, which would invade the Jewish state and seek to destroy it. That was an entirely new situation. He had begun warning about it in 1945, but he claimed no one had listened: "I sought to bring the Zionist movement to the realization that the security of the Jewish community is at this hour the central, vital, decisive issue, which determines everything else. Apparently the Zionist movement was not then prepared to hear such things."[15]

He also accused the Haganah's commanders themselves. The officers he interviewed were overly optimistic and did not understand how great the danger was, as he did. They thought only of the Arabs of Palestine, not the Arab armies from outside. "I was not persuaded by those optimistic answers," he said. He went so far as to send back the budget request they submitted to him, because in his estimate it did not provide for current needs. Sounding like a foreign correspondent, he asked Sneh, "Why did you not take action in your time to improve the command?" Sneh, who no longer headed the Haganah, responded that they had put their trust in the British army, and that seems to have been the principal reason for the Haganah's feeble state—the Jewish Agency leadership had made a point of not absolving the Mandate authorities of responsibility for security.

At one point, his seminar left him despondent. He urgently called in Golda Meir, who was at the time filling in for Sharett as head of the Jewish Agency's Political Department. She came to his home that evening and found him in the midst of an anxiety attack—he paced his room, which was almost completely dark. "What will happen? I know now what the Haganah is, more or less. We will face a war," he muttered. "I can't sleep at night. I'm going mad. What will become of us?" Meir was flattered that she was the one he chose to pour his heart out to: "He apparently knew that even if he told me all the truth, I would not despair," she wrote. Before she left, he said to her: "You know, it takes a lot of courage to be frightened."[16]

Beginning in 1945, he had indeed concluded that the Haganah would have to fight the Arab armies, and he had worked to strengthen it, particularly by enlisting support in America. He understood that the Haganah would have to be rendered fit to fight the impending war, but he did not have the military experience needed to do that, as he himself said.[17] It thus seems that he needed to do more than just prepare the Haganah for war, after neglecting it so far. He also had to prepare himself. Everything now happened at a spectacular pace. The war broke out just a few months later; the efforts to upgrade the Haganah into a combat force were still then far from successful. In the meantime, he fought his political rivals.

"CHOOSE BEVIN AND BEGIN"

On Wednesday morning, April 16, 1947, four Etzel men were taken to the gallows at the Acre prison and executed. One of them was Dov Gruner, who had been sentenced to death by a British military court for his part in an attack on the Ramat Gan police station. The terror operations carried out by Etzel and Lehi increased in number and severity week by week. Approximately three weeks after Gruner's hanging, an Etzel contingent broke into the Acre prison and freed a few dozen of their comrades, as well as a couple hundred Arab prisoners. Three of the perpetrators were captured and sentenced to death. To prevent their execution, Etzel kidnapped two British sergeants as hostages.[18]

UNSCOP, the United Nations Special Committee on Palestine, was in the country during the search operation for the abducted men. Its task was to draft a UN resolution in advance of the decisive General Assembly session on Palestine's future. Ben-Gurion feared that the terror campaign would hurt the chances of achieving a UN decision friendly to Zionism. He also feared that the terrorists would try to blow up the al-Aqsa mosque.[19]

The bold militancy of the underground organizations gained them much popularity; Dov Gruner metamorphosed into a national hero after his hanging. The dissidents were making the Haganah envious, Ben-Gurion noted.[20] He now loathed them even more than during the Saison. "The issue has taken on the form of a war for the rule of the state that has not yet been established," he declared.[21] He wanted to "uproot them," and thought of two ways of doing so: "either kill them all or imprison them all." For the moment, he recommended a more limited action, but "without blows, hands or fists, rifles or pistols, I don't see how we will be able to stand against them."[22] As in the past, there were members of the Mapai secretariat who warned against civil war, but Ben-Gurion was adamant: "If our doom is that we cannot withstand

Etzel without civil war—there will be civil war." To those who were appalled by the idea, Ben-Gurion proposed "sending the keys to Mr. Begin" and fleeing for their lives, because Etzel was "a gang of Jewish Nazis." Two days later, he added: "They must be wiped off the face of the earth, this gang."[23]

❖

The circumstances that produced these outbursts were indeed extraordinary. On July 18, 1947, an illegal refugee ship named the *Exodus* arrived in the port of Haifa with forty-five hundred Jews on board. It was meant to be the most conspicuous ship in the history of the illegal immigration operation, "one of the greatest manifestations of the Jewish struggle, Jewish pride, and the connection to the Land of Israel," as Ben-Gurion put it. It was also meant to be the labor movement's ultimate response to Etzel and Lehi's terror operations. A highly visible sign bearing the name of the Haganah was hung on the ship. The Mandate authorities decided to send the passengers back to France, their point of departure. This response, it was hoped, would sweep the public up into the national struggle and unite their ranks. But a few days later, the three participants in the break-in to the Acre prison were executed. The next day, Etzel announced that it had killed the two sergeants. Their bodies were found in a woods near Netanya, hanging from a tree. It was the most fearsome terror operation since the bombing of the King David Hotel. Ben-Gurion was incensed. The murder of the sergeants, he claimed, had caused the world to forget the great and tragic struggle of the *Exodus*.[24]

As a Zionist idealist, Ben-Gurion found it difficult not to be impressed by Gruner's idealistic dedication, which challenged his self-image and his responsibility as a national leader. "I am full of admiration for Gruner, but I will not spend even a moment exerting myself to prevent his hanging," he said, adding, "He is indeed a hero and is giving his life. But those who sent him are, in my opinion, the enemies of the Jewish people, and they are the ones responsible for it." After the hanging, Ben-Gurion meditated on the similarities and differences between Zionism and other nationalisms, between heroism and criminality. "Gruner was hanged a martyr," he said to the Mapai Council, "and with Hitler there were also young men who joined, perhaps were killed in that movement, in the name of their ideals—and we can appreciate Gruner's heroic act, how he ascended the gallows heroically, but not make him an example for youth, because the thing he ascended the gallows for is tainted, objectively."*[25]

❖

On the left, criticism came mostly from Ahdut Ha'avodah, which continued to oppose partition and preferred, in the meantime, a continuation of the Mandate, and from Hashomer Hatza'ir, which advocated a binational arrangement. Echoes of Weizmann's moderation could be heard here and there; its major spokesmen were the members of Aliyah Hadashah, a small party of peace seekers, most of them immigrants from Germany.[26] There were a few intellectuals who roused Ben-Gurion's ire, because he had no recourse against articles in *Ha'aretz*. Two days after Gruner's execution, he read a piece that enraged him, probably not just because of what it said, but also because of who wrote it: Shlomo Zemach.

At the time, Zemach's primary occupation was writing and editing. He opposed the terror of Etzel and Lehi, but did not recant his opposition to the various partition plans that Ben-Gurion had promoted. "I saw the horrible danger of exacerbating the conflict needlessly," he later wrote. From time to time he published articles to that effect in *Ha'aretz*. Without mentioning Ben-Gurion by name, he accused him of introducing "recklessness" into Zionist policy. Zemach reiterated his proposal to extend the Mandate, as long as it enabled "Zionism to grow."[27]

Zemach's articles annoyed Ben-Gurion, in part because he himself had tried unsuccessfully to further just such an arrangement, and he set out to humiliate Zemach—as he knew how to do so well. He first told his colleagues on the Mapai secretariat who the man was, as if Zemach were an unknown. He recounted his party affiliations beginning in 1906, and added: "I do not know where he is now." His tirade sparked a comic debate over what party Zemach might have joined by now. "I know him, he is actually

---

* Winston Churchill said something similar about Gruner in Parliament: "The fortitude of this man, criminal though he be, must not escape the notice of the House." (Gilbert 2007, p. 263.)

from my hometown," Ben-Gurion said, demanding to "fortify the public against sick responses like his." Zemach's proposal required the Jewish people to choose Bevin or Begin, he maintained. The middle road that he represented made it possible to reject both.[28]

The line that Ben-Gurion espoused at this point required patience and restraint—which made it hard to defend. Still, he continued to promote illegal immigration and settlement, and could point to some not insignificant achievements. During that same period, about seventy new settlements were founded, most of them kibbutzim. Between the summer of 1945 and the British evacuation of May 1948, some seventy thousand Jews set out for Palestine on sixty-five crossings; most of them were intercepted along the way and sent to transit camps in Cyprus.[29]

"A NEW HISTORY"

UNSCOP pursued its task of preparing a UN General Assembly resolution much in the way the Anglo-American Committee had in 1946. It held hearings, where Ben-Gurion once again declaimed his house parable. But the Special Committee worked in a very different context—Palestine would soon be without a sovereign, and the United Nations had to decide who would rule there. The Arabs, speaking in the name of the majority and invoking democratic principles, remained opposed to partition. They demanded independence in all of Palestine. Nearly a decade before, Ben-Gurion had threatened to prevent that by force.[30] The DP camps in Europe were still full. Some of the UNSCOP investigators went to Haifa to see the *Exodus*.[31]

In September 1947, a majority of the Special Committee's members voted to recommend the partition of Palestine into two states. Ben-Gurion was elated. "It is truly the beginning of the Redemption, and even more than the beginning," he wrote to Paula, making rare use of a rabbinic expression referring to the Messianic process. A few days before the vote, he said: "It may well be that the age of miracles has not yet passed, and it may well be that one of the greatest miracles in world history will happen soon, in our day." As he saw it, it was a moral victory. "Throughout our history the Jewish people have never once achieved what we have now," he declared. "A new history is now beginning." He attributed particular importance to the inclusion of the southern Negev Desert region in the Jewish state. "True, we will have to change one verse in the Bible," he commented after the vote, "not 'from Dan to Be'er-Sheva' but 'from Dan to Eilat.'" He still had to reconcile the opponents of partition. To that end, he tried to whip up enthusiasm in his party. "The wonder has come to be," he declared. Instead of saying that the United Nations had decided to partition Palestine, he said that it had decided "to reestablish the State of Israel." At another opportunity he referred to the new Jewish state as "New Judea."

Passage of UNSCOP's recommendations required the support of two-thirds of the delegates of the countries represented in the UN General Assembly. Moshe Sharett, the Zionist "foreign minister," oversaw a large staff of lobbyists in New York. He also conducted rocky contacts with the administration in Washington.

The trump card that Sharett and his staff were able to play remained Chaim Weizmann. "Despite [his] not serving in any post," Abba Eban wrote, "foreign statesmen stood before him with a strange mixture of awe and reverence." Weizmann spoke before the General Assembly and conferred with President Truman. Ben-Gurion called it "the greatest political campaign in our nation's history, at least in the last 2,000 years." He made a point of using Sharett's first name and indicated that he would be the foreign minister in his government.[32] He made no mention of Weizmann's role. American Jewish leaders joined the effort; they had the next year's elections in mind.

All this was happening against the backdrop of the Cold War. In May 1947, the Soviet Union's permanent representative to the United Nations, Andrei Gromyko, surprised the General Assembly by giving a speech sympathetic to Zionism's aims in Palestine. During a long meeting with Gromyko, Ben-Gurion spoke of the socialist values that guided his movement. To persuade the Russian diplomat that a binational state was not a possibility, he quoted, as he always did in this context, what he had heard from Musa al-Alami.[33]

❖

The partition lines that the UN approved were meant to be peaceful borders, and they would be very difficult to defend in wartime. They were also very bad in terms of Zionist demography—too many Arabs would remain within the Jewish state. According to UNSCOP's figures, there would be almost as many Arabs as Jews, about half a million, including some 90,000 Bedouin. In contrast, the proposed Arab state would have 735,000 inhabitants, of which only about 10,000 would be Jews. The numbers Ben-Gurion used were a bit more optimistic, with the Jews constituting some 60 percent of the population of the proposed Jewish state. But even this majority was too small, he asserted. The danger was that "a Jewish minority in our house of representatives could join with the Arab bloc to constitute a majority and assume control." He supposed that this would not happen, at least not immediately, "whether because the Arabs will boycott elections for a time, or what is more realistic, that no significant Jewish minority would lend their hand to such a betrayal." Yet, he maintained, "there can be no stable and legitimate Jewish state so long as there is a Jewish majority of only sixty percent." A million and a half Jews would have to be brought in over the coming ten years to boost the Jewish majority, he asserted.[34]

The demographic threat to the Jewish state would be even more grave were the Jewish state to expand its territory at the expense of the Arab state. Ben-Gurion offered contradictory messages in this regard. About four months prior to the partition resolution, he recalled the first convention of the old Ahdut Ha'avodah in 1919, which had demanded the establishment of a Jewish state in all of the Land of Israel, including territories east of the Jordan—the Hauran, Bashan, and Golan plateaus—and northward to the southern approaches to Damascus. "I believe that to this day," he said.[35] As the campaign in the United Nations reached its climax, he declared that the Jewish state would not try to capture territory designated for the Arab state, despite the fact that Jewish settlements would remain there. A few days after the resolution was approved, he said that the new state needed to hold back the opponents of partition who were still dreaming of "our undivided homeland."[36]

That same day, however, Ben-Gurion reflected on the philosophy of history with his party colleagues. "The borders of the land under Jewish rule—from the time of the judges to Bar Kokhba—changed all the time . . . ," he said. "In ancient times the boundaries of Jewish independence retreated and advanced in accordance with constant political change." He noted that the

Warsaw, 1904, farewell from
Shmuel Fuchs (left)
(BEN-GURION HOUSE)

Istanbul, 1913, with Yitzhak Ben-Zvi
(right) (BEN-GURION HOUSE)

Jerusalem, 1924 (ISRAEL GOVERNMENT PRESS OFFICE)

Cairo, 1918, in a British army uniform
(ISRAEL GOVERNMENT PRESS OFFICE)

Tel Aviv, 1924
(BEN-GURION HOUSE)

**Tel Aviv, 1933,
with Paula, Amos,
and Renana at
their home**
(ARYEH BEN-GURION /
BITMUNA)

Vienna, 1935, with Rega Klapholz (left) (COURTESY OF EDNA RAZ)

Petra, 1935, with Paula (BEN-GURION HOUSE)

Jerusalem, 1944, in the high commissioner's greeting line (SCHWARZ / BITMUNA)

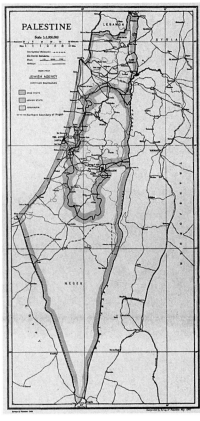

London, April 1947, Ben-Gurion's partition map
(THE NATIONAL ARCHIVES [UK] CO 537/2344)

Jerusalem, 1947,
following the UN
partition resolution
(BEN-GURION HOUSE)

Tel Aviv, May 14, 1948, after
signing the Declaration of
Independence
(FRANK SCHERSCHEL / ISRAEL
GOVERNMENT PRESS OFFICE)

On the way to Eilat, 1949
(DAVID ELDAN / ISRAEL GOVERNMENT PRESS OFFICE)

Somewhere in Israel, 1957 (IDF ARCHIVE)

Tel Aviv, 1954, with Nehemiah
Argov (BEN-GURION ARCHIVE)

With new immigrants from Yemen, 1950
(DAVID ELDAN / ISRAEL GOVERNMENT PRESS OFFICE)

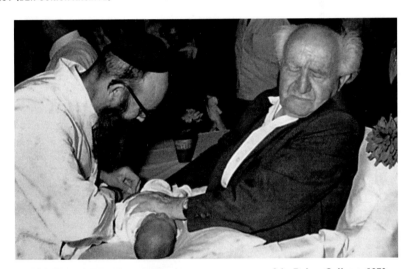

Sde Boker College, 1970
(ARYEH BAR-LEV / COURTESY
OF THE BAILY FAMILY)

Sde Boker, 1954, checking the
teeth of a sheep, with Paula
(FRITZ COHN / ISRAEL GOVERNMENT
PRESS OFFICE)

Jerusalem,
October 1951,
with Franklin
Roosevelt Jr. and
John F. Kennedy
(FRITZ COHN /
ISRAEL GOVERNMENT
PRESS OFFICE)

Tel Aviv, 1951, returning
with Paula from a visit to
the United States
(HANS PINN / ISRAEL
GOVERNMENT PRESS OFFICE)

Paris, 1960, with President de Gaulle
(FRITZ COHN / ISRAEL GOVERNMENT PRESS OFFICE)

CLOCKWISE: **Street in Berlin, plaque in London, promenade in Paris**

Somewhere at sea, 1949

Jerusalem, 1962,
in the Knesset, with
Golda Meir
(FRITZ COHN / ISRAEL
GOVERNMENT PRESS OFFICE)

Herut election poster, 1959; Ben-Gurion
says to Menachem Begin, "You are a
clown!"
(THE MENACHEM BEGIN HERITAGE CENTER)

Sde Boker, 1962
(FRITZ COHN / ISRAEL GOVERNMENT PRESS OFFICE)

Observation point in the
Negev desert, 1968
(FRITZ COHN / ISRAEL
GOVERNMENT PRESS OFFICE)

boundaries of the Jewish national home had been reduced "to a fourth" of their original size since the Balfour Declaration. The UN partition boundaries were, he thought, a possible stage in the process of expanding the state's territory, just like the partition boundaries that the British had proposed ten years previously; then, too, he had justified his support of partition by using the same Messianic term that he now used: "I believe that a Jewish state is the beginning of the Redemption." Geographically he was correct—the territory that the UN assigned to the Jewish state was more than twice as large as that which the British had offered in their partition plan.[37] From this point on he was guided by a strategic aspiration that accorded with what had been the Zionist dream from the start—maximum territory, minimum Arabs.

❖

During this same period, he received a number of plans for organizing the army, but only shortly before the UN vote, on October 6, 1947, did he call on a man named Efraim Ben-Artzi to urgently draw up a plan to deal with the worst-case scenario: "The Arab world . . . is liable to attack the Jews in Palestine, whether with the goal of repressing and subjugating it, or even to destroy it." By "the Arab world" he meant the Arabs of Palestine with the aid of one or more Arab states. The purpose of the plan was "to mobilize the full capacity of the Jewish community (economic, technical scientific, and military) to defend the population and conquer the country, all or in greater part, and to maintain the conquest until an authoritative political agreement is reached."

Many years later, Ben-Artzi recalled this improvised meeting. "We need to prepare for war," Ben-Gurion told him, as if he had suddenly come to that realization that same day. "How do we set up an army and what do we do with the underground militias, how do we mobilize the Jewish people?" Ben-Artzi asked: "A war against whom?" Ben-Gurion replied: "All the Arab countries." Ben-Artzi, a man of experience, asked to receive written instructions. Ben-Gurion tore a page out of the notebook he had in front of him and began to write. He wanted a plan within three days. Ben-Artzi claimed he had no idea why Ben-Gurion had waited until the last minute, and why he had suddenly called him in, of all people. He probably knew, in fact—he was one of the senior Haganah men who had volunteered for the British army, rising there to the rank of lieutenant colonel, the highest rank achieved by an officer from Palestine. It took him six days to draw up a plan of twenty-eight pages, in addition to several appendixes. It was comprehensive and detailed in a way that Ben-Gurion could appreciate.[38]

"OFFENSIVE DEFENSE"

It was a relatively quiet year; tensions between Arabs and Jews centered largely on criminal violations. The day after the UN decision, at about the same time that Ben-Gurion reached the Jewish Agency building's courtyard after his stay at Kalia and found himself among circles of dancers, two buses, one from Netanya and one from Hadera, were making their way to Jerusalem. Arabs opened fire on them near Petah Tikvah, attacking first one bus and then the other. Five passengers were killed on the spot and nine wounded. One of the dead, Nehama Cohen, came from a Zionist dynasty that included both Ahad Ha'am and Yitzhak Rabin. A report Ben-Gurion received a few days later said that the attack had been a robbery, "ostensibly in response to the UN decision." The report offered a long list of offenses, among them robbery and murder, committed by the same gang, all of them apparently with criminal intent.[39]

A few weeks after the partition decision, Ben-Gurion drove from Jerusalem to Tel Aviv. Because the road was no longer safe that winter, he joined one of the guarded convoys that were now the only way to travel between the two cities. The car he took was equipped with iron panels and reinforced glass; the Jewish Agency referred to the vehicle as "Weizmann's armored car." Not far from Bab al-Wad, later called Sha'ar Hagai, where the road emerges from the hills onto the coastal plain, the convoy came under fire. "We were attacked from the mountain and four were wounded," Ben-Gurion wrote. A bus was disabled. "It was a horrible onslaught, from both sides," a Jewish Agency official who traveled with him related. "Ben-Gurion suddenly opened the door and jumped out of the car. I thought he had gone mad." He wanted to see what had happened. British soldiers who suddenly appeared out of nowhere returned fire, and the convoy went on its way.

Before leaving Jerusalem with his convoy, Ben-Gurion had met with an official of Hadassah, the American women's Zionist organization, and described the situation to her with a single word: "War!" For the time being, the Arabs were limiting themselves to terror attacks, he reported. In the past two weeks, ninety-four Jews had been killed and a hundred wounded. There would soon be a real war.[40] He told the official that Hadassah had to fund all medical services in the country.

When the convoy stopped at a strategic point, called Latrun, to care for the wounded, the high commissioner's convoy passed by on the road. He now understood why British troops had been nearby: "It seems as if His Excellency had stationed forces by the Bab al-Wad forest." His Excellency was the last high commissioner; a few months later he went home, and Ben-Gurion reached the pinnacle of his life.[41] He later referred to the war he conducted during this period as an "improvisation."[42]

❖

December 1947 was a horrible month; Ben-Gurion had not experienced such catastrophes, and he was now commander in chief. The conflagration broke out in Jerusalem. The Arab Higher Committee, which represented the Arabs of Palestine, responded to the partition resolution by declaring a three-day protest strike. In the morning hours of Tuesday, December 2, 1947, an Arab mob emerged from the Jaffa Gate and headed toward Princess Mary Street, a commercial thoroughfare. By evening, some forty Jewish stores had been looted, and some of them burned. One of those who witnessed the attack was Eliyahu Elyashar, a merchant and public figure. He appeared before the Security Committee, a political body that replaced the X Committee. What upset him was not the attack as much as the Haganah's incompetence. The contingent that had been assigned to protect the storekeepers fired only two shots and left the site. "How can a commander leave a battle?" he asked, demanding an investigation.

The attack plunged the storekeepers into despair; some of them proposed asking Etzel to take responsibility for security in the city. Ben-Gurion did not say much when the Security Committee met to address the situation. He suggested that maybe not all the facts were clear and promised an investigation. "Every failure must be looked into. This matter demands a thorough and rapid examination and it will be checked." According to the *Haganah History Book*, "The Arab attack made a harsh impression on the entire country and abetted the spread of the riots to other cities in the country and to its roads."[43]

Rendering the roads that connected Jewish settlements impassable was one of the principal goals of the Arab terror campaign; even convoys like the one Ben-Gurion traveled in were no longer safe.[44]

❖

Ben-Gurion solicited proposals for a response, or, as he wrote, something like the choice of medications that a pharmacy offers to a doctor.[45] The staff of the Jewish Agency's Political Department recommended restraint, on the grounds that the leader of the country's Arabs, Mufti al-Hussayni, was interested in escalation. On the opposite side, some of Ben-Gurion's Arab affairs advisers proposed an aggressive reaction, in particular dealing a mortal blow to the Arab economy, and especially to Arab transport.[46]

The Haganah also proposed a punitive response, terror against terror. "If these things continue around Tel Aviv, we must make reprisals against the Arabs in such a way that will deal a heavy blow to a village such as Salamah and expel its inhabitants," declared Israel Galili, head of the organization's National Command. That same night, Haganah personnel set fire to fifteen automobiles in the Arab city of Ramla. A report given to Ben-Gurion a few days later stated that in the previous two weeks, the Haganah had carried out fourteen actions against Arabs. Etzel and Lehi had carried out only five, but killed more.[47]

The high commissioner, Sir Alan Cunningham, complained to Golda Meir that the Haganah was pursuing an "aggressive defense." According to a report of the conversation, he was furious. Meir confirmed that this indeed would be the tactic from now on. "We will defend ourselves and, quite explicitly, not only when they attack. And if dozens of Arabs get killed— that's exactly what we want." Cunningham cited an up-to-date count of 96 Jewish and 106 Arab casualties. Some were innocent. What would the world think? "We are prepared to stand before a world court tribunal for our actions," Meir replied. That was from this point forward Ben-Gurion's doctrine as well.[48]

❖

Two days after the conversation with Cunningham, Ben-Gurion said to two top Haganah officials: "It seems to me that we need to reexamine the security plan. We may have been too optimistic and did not properly evaluate the Arab plan." That same day he wrote in his diary that the kibbutz Kfar Yavetz was under heavy attack; two days earlier, he had written: "Bat Yam is cut off and surrounded by gunfire." He told the leaders of the Haganah: "I have doubts about the effectiveness of reaction after an act—it is liable to be interpreted as aggression, fanning the flames, widening the disturbances. We need to pursue a tactic of offensive defense. To deal a decisive blow with each onslaught, destroying the place or driving out the inhabitants and capturing the place."[49] Ben-Gurion had thought since the 1930s that Arab terror required "aggressive self-defense," but this was the first time that he numbered driving Arabs out among the goals of such actions. In the weeks that followed, Ben-Gurion reiterated this doctrine several times. In a talk with two top Haganah officials, Yigael Yadin and Galili, he named villages that needed "to be taught a lesson."[50]

On December 30, 1947, thirty-nine Jewish workers were killed at the Haifa oil refinery; some of their Arab fellow workers murdered them as a spontaneous retaliation for the slaying of six of their number in an Etzel operation. The Haganah staged a reprisal against Balad al-Sheikh, the village where many of the refinery workers lived. According to the *Haganah History Book*, six were killed, including women and children.[51] Members of the Security Committee criticized the operation; Ben-Gurion responded that although it was possible to refrain from attacking generally nonhostile villages, there was no way, during a military operation, to tell which individual Arabs were friendly and which hostile. "We are making war, and no war is conducted that way," he said. Yes, he agreed, there was injustice in this, but "otherwise we will not stand." He remarked that when a city is bombed from the air, what is hit is not a military target "but children who have not sinned." A few hours previously, he had heard something similar from one of his Arab affairs advisers, Gad Machnes: "A brutal and strong response is needed . . . If the family is known, attack it without mercy, women and children included. Otherwise the response is not effective. At the place of the action there is no need to distinguish between guilty and innocent." Ben-Gurion adopted the approach. In reference to the Balad al-Sheikh operation he said: "In Haifa there was a great slaughter. It is not good that the Arabs see us undefended. This is not Hebron. Haifa is a Jewish city and it is best to do this immedi-ately." A week later, he repeated this before a party forum.[52] He thus associated himself with the expulsion and flight of the Arab population.

"IN THE MOST COLLEGIAL WAY"

In January 1948, thirty-five Palmach and Field Corps troops were killed on their way to reinforce the besieged Jewish settlements of the Etzion Block, south of Jerusalem. A month later, a huge explosion shook Ben-Yehuda Street in downtown Jerusalem, killing dozens. "I never imagined such destruction," wrote Ben-Gurion, who rushed to the site. "I could not recognize the streets—horror and dread."[53] Less than three weeks later, a car bomb blew up in the Jewish Agency compound; a senior official was among the nine people killed. Ben-Gurion made a point of mentioning that the car belonged to the U.S. consulate—it was flying the American flag and driven by the consul's regular driver. But the fact that the vehicle had been allowed to enter the building's courtyard was seen as yet another blow to the Haganah's prestige in Jerusa-lem.[54] The road from the coastal plain into the city was practically impassable, as were the arteries connecting the country's center to the Negev and the Galilee. Convoys that tried to make their way to Jerusalem were forced to turn back; dozens of people were killed. Ben-Gurion was stressed and short-tempered: "I am not able to look at anything now except through the lens of security," he said.[55]

On March 19, 1948, Shlomo Lavi was working in the small experimen-tal garden at Ein Harod, where he was trying to grow subtropical plants. He heard an exchange of gunfire from the slopes of Mount Gilboa, to the south-east. It was a Field Corps operation against an Arab village, Zar'in. Just as he was watering the last tree he had planted, the body of his son Yeruba'al was brought to the kibbutz—he had been killed in the battle. Yeruba'al was twenty-four years old; in his youth he worked in the sheep pen and, like his father, had served briefly in the Jewish Brigade. Lavi sat by his eldest's body, knowing that his younger son, Hillel, was fighting there as well. A few hours later, the battle was still raging and he had not heard a thing from Hillel. Finally, he appeared; he already knew of his brother's death. "His helmet on his head and his rifle in hand," Lavi wrote, "in silence the young warrior stood before his father and before his brother, lips pursed, nobility and heroism frozen on his face. The son stood for a few moments, looking, thinking whatever he was thinking, planning whatever he was planning, and then finally he said, 'Father, I am going back.' He meant that he was returning to his unit. Lavi, committed to the end to pioneering Zionism, the labor movement, the kibbutz, and Ben-Gurion, responded: "Go back, son, go back." Yeruba'al was one of the nine hundred Jews killed since the UN approved the partition resolution.[56] The next day, it seemed as if the partition plan was about to fall apart.

In Washington, the Haganah did not look like a fighting force, certainly not one that could win a victory. The State Department feared that the United States would have to rescue the Jewish state from defeat, because if the Arabs were to win the war, they would open the Middle East up to the Soviet Union. The United States thus withdrew its support for partition and proposed to the UN Security Council that a temporary trusteeship be established in Palestine. Ben-Gurion heard of it on the radio. A trusteeship instead of independence after the loss of close to a thousand Jewish lives could mean the end of his leadership. He issued a press release rejecting the proposal and did his best to broadcast confidence and responsibility. "I was not party, on November 29, to the Jewish community's huge cheers, and I will not be party today to dejection, if the American announcement has dejected the community," he said. He had a good idea of what would happen—presidential elections were eight months away, so any such initiative would quickly be shelved.[57] But he could not disregard the widespread dejection.

❖

He tried to boost the public's morale. With the armies of the neighboring Arab states poised to invade, he promised that he would "not only engage in defense tactics" but would "crush the enemy wherever we find him," even outside the boundaries of Palestine.[58] He celebrated the last Pesach Seder before declaring Israel's independence with Haganah troops in Jerusalem. The decisive stage of the war had not yet begun, but he would soon be fantasizing about its end, still in the spirit of the Haggadah: "We will bomb Port Said, Alexandria, and Cairo, and that's how we will end the war, settling our forefathers' accounts with Egypt." That same month the Haganah captured, razed, and evicted the inhabitants of half a dozen Arab villages lying close to the Jerusalem–Tel Aviv road. Along with a number of other actions, Operation Nachshon, as it was called, was meant to open the road to traffic. Several supply convoys succeeded in getting through, but even after the operation the road into the city was passable only intermittently.[59] In the meantime, his colleagues in the leadership tried to limit his powers.

The membership of the Jewish Agency's Security Committee reflected the makeup of the Zionist coalition. It was meant to direct security policy and oversee its execution. Ben-Gurion provided the committee with a number of strategic overviews, but kept quite a bit from them as well. From time to time the committee's members protested: "I have a right to ask why we are even being convened. I am not prepared to be a travesty," one of them complained. Ben-Gurion reminded them that none of them was a Napoleon or a Montgomery. But he, unlike them, had recently learned how to manage the situation. He agreed to the establishment of a sort of war Cabinet, a coalition of thirteen members, which later came to be called the People's Administration, or sometimes simply "the Thirteen." Ben-Gurion recognized their authority, but also made it clear to them that they were not a command authority. A corporation required an administrative board, he said, but a war had to be commanded by a single man. That man was the chairman of the Jewish Agency.[60]

His need to bolster his position as commander in chief did not arise simply because of the grumbling he heard in the Security Committee. His principal concern was the Palmach's insubordination and what he saw as the political ambitions of its commanders. He appreciated the force's military abilities, but saw them as an undisciplined and rowdy band of men and women. They idolized Stalin's Red Army and owed allegiance to Yitzhak Tabenkin; he saw them as no less dangerous than Etzel.

The Palmach's first commander, Yitzhak Sadeh, began in 1945 to serve as the Haganah's acting chief of staff. The chief of staff himself, Ya'akov Dori, was in the United States at the time. Ben-Gurion had known Sadeh since the 1930s; his roots in the rebellious Labor Battalions led Ben-Gurion to mistrust him. When Ben-Gurion met with him during his "seminar," Sadeh was harshly critical. "We have lost this entire year—nothing has been done—the Jewish Agency Executive is largely to blame." In an article he published in the autumn of 1946, Sadeh had accused "the leadership" of defeatism and asserted that military discipline could not be a goal in and of itself. There were things that even the Zionist Congress could not force him to do, he wrote.[61] Ben-Gurion brought Dori back. Sadeh remained, for a time, without a post.

When he was preparing the Haganah for the war, Ben-Gurion preferred officers who had served in the British army and the Jewish Brigade, such as Efraim Ben-Artzi. He especially valued the military discipline they brought with them. His inclination was to fill senior command posts with officers loyal to Mapai. At the beginning of December 1947, when he refused to appoint Sadeh to a new position, he found himself up against Israel Galili.

With twenty years of experience in the Haganah, almost from its inception, Galili was seen as the final authority in the National Command. As such, he shared responsibility for the state of the organization. And he, too, was in Tabenkin's camp. Tabenkin and Hashomer Hatza'ir would soon found Mapam, the United Workers' Party, Mapai's major rival on the left. Relations between Ben-Gurion and Galili grew increasingly strained.

Ben-Gurion had named Galili chief of the National Command, the body that oversaw the entire Haganah organization, but almost immediately began trying to revoke the appointment. He promised "to consult in the most collegial way" with Galili and the National Command, but noted that wartime was not peacetime and that there was a need for "decisive rule." If he thought it necessary to make a decision contrary to Galili's position, he would do so. Several months went by; the war intensified and Ben-Gurion had difficulty overcoming the opposition of the high command.[62]

At ten in the morning on May 3, 1948, while conducting a meeting of the General Staff, Galili received notification from Ben-Gurion that, as of noon, his appointment as chief of the National Command was terminated.

It was an impulsive, personal, political move, not one that could enhance the Haganah's fighting ability. "My dismissal from my post immediately undermined the army's General Staff in a difficult and dangerous way," Galili later wrote. "The chiefs of the General Staff branches found themselves suddenly without coordination, without synchronization, without command, and without knowing why."

A generals' revolt broke out. The members of the General Staff sent Ben-Gurion a letter declaring that if Galili were not restored to his post, they could not be responsible for the consequences. Ben-Gurion found himself without a command echelon. Less than two weeks before the expected invasion of the Arab armies, he also threatened resignation. "I have spent forty-two years on defense in this country, but that can also be done without me, and now it depends on you," he told his colleagues in the People's Administration. But they did not want to choose between Ben-Gurion and Galili, just as his own party had not wanted to choose between him and Weizmann. Ben-Gurion was compelled to ask Galili to come back, without receiving a formal appointment, and Galili agreed.[63]

"DEAD CITY"

On May 1, 1948, as evening approached, Ben-Gurion, accompanied by a Haganah commander, set out to tour Haifa's Arab neighborhoods. "A terrifying and fantastic sight," he later wrote in his diary. "A dead city—a corpse of a city. In one place only we saw two old men sitting in a half-empty store, and in an alleyway we encountered an Arab woman, leading her son." Other than that, he saw only stray cats. According to his diary, he was stunned: "How could tens of thousands of people, without any sufficient reason, leave their city, homes, and wealth in such a panic?" He was especially surprised that Haifa's wealthy inhabitants had gone. "Was it really fear?" he wondered.[64]

What he saw in the abandoned city that evening may well have been "terrifying and fantastic," as he wrote, but it could not really have surprised him. Just a few weeks earlier, two members of the Haganah's intelligence service had briefed him on the Arab flight, including from Jaffa and Haifa. One of them predicted that the two cities would be left entirely empty if there was a food shortage.[65] "Masses of Arabs have fled," he wrote regarding Haifa's Wadi Rushmiya neighborhood; about two months after his evening visit to the deserted city, he was informed that a total of fifteen thousand Arabs had vacated it.[66]

Ezra Danin, one of his Arab affairs advisers, later related that Ben-Gurion saw the great Arab flight from Haifa with his own eyes. "We stood on the balcony of the Eden Hotel," Danin recounted, "and we saw the convoys of the city's Arabs heading for the port. Once or twice Ben-Gurion asked, 'How many have gone? How many remain?' Some of those present thought that we should hold them back. Ben-Gurion asked: 'If they want to go, why should you impede them?'"[67]

When he returned from his trip to Haifa, he laid the foundation for the perpetuation of the tragedy of Palestine's Arabs. "It is not our job to see to the return of the Arabs," he declared. At one of the first meetings of Israel's Cabinet, he reiterated this position: "When they flee—we don't need to run after them." The last of the Arab inhabitants of Haifa to leave had good reason to flee for their lives from their neighborhoods in the lower city—the Haganah was bombarding them from the upper slope of Mount Carmel with mortar fire.[68]

During the months that followed, he continually tracked the flight of the Arab population. "No Arabs are to be seen at Tzemach," on the southern shore of Lake Kinneret, he said, and of Jaffa's abandoned Salamah neighborhood he wrote: "Only one blind old woman remains."[69] From time to time he cited the Arab flight as one of the Haganah's achievements, to counterbalance reports of heavy blows the organization had suffered. In one speech he named eighteen Arab villages that had been emptied of their inhabitants, and said that these represented just a small proportion of the villages that had been evacuated out of fear. "Presumably many Arab villages will not be left deserted and Jewish boys will go in, and they have already gone into a number of villages," he related.[70] "In many of the western neighborhoods you don't see a single Arab, and I don't think that will change," he reported after a trip to Jerusalem, and added: "Now when I go to Jerusalem, I feel like I am in a Hebrew city. There are no foreigners. One hundred percent Jews. Since Jerusalem was destroyed in Roman times it has not been as Jewish as it is now." And that could be only the beginning, he promised. "What happened in Jerusalem and what happened in Haifa can happen in large parts of the country, if we endure. And we will succeed and endure, if we so desire," he declared. "And to so desire means to make a supreme effort, like that made by a nation fighting a life-or-death war."[71] The war would bring "a great change in the distribution of the Arab population," and victory depended on that, he estimated.[72]

Like the expansion of the partition borders, Ben-Gurion viewed the depletion of the Arab population as a historical process that would take place gradually. The poet Haim Gouri once noticed on Ben-Gurion's desk, between the green velvet blotter and the glass that covered it, alongside a photograph of Berl Katznelson, a piece of paper displaying a typescript verse from the book of Exodus. It was God's promise to drive foreign nations from the Land of Israel and give it to the Jewish people: "I will not drive them out before you in a single year, lest the land become desolate and the wild beasts multiply to your detriment. I will drive them out before you little by little, until you have increased and possess the land" (Exodus 23:29–30).[73] In many cases there was no need to issue an explicit order to expel Arabs—the spirit of the message conveyed by the commander in chief was sufficient.

❖

The ideological intent that had impelled him for many years had its roots in the struggle for Hebrew labor, which aimed to expel Arab workers from Jewish farming villages, and in his belief that there was no basis for peace with the Arabs. "I always thought, my entire life I have thought, that if we tell a Jew to come to Palestine, it means we are telling him to risk his life, because there will be a war here," he said in February 1948. "I thought that before these events," he continued. "When I had just come to Palestine I knew that." He intuited that the British evacuation offered an opportunity that might not return. "Whatever we don't do in the months to come will not get done for, perhaps, hundreds of years. I have no doubt that the next six months will determine the fate of the Jewish people, perhaps for hundreds of years, perhaps for thousands. We must know that it is an arduous effort, a financial effort, a human effort."[74]

Causing the Arabs to flee as a war aim also reflected the old dream of

population transfer. That issue came up again in advance of the UN partition resolution. Ben-Gurion told UNSCOP what he had said many times in
the past, that the establishment of a Jewish state in Palestine did not require
such a transfer. He assured his party, however, that he had said that for political reasons, even if he really believed it. "It would be convenient if there
were no Arabs here, but Arabs can be here," he said, "and we can settle another
four million Jews." When, however, he tried to prove that Jews and Arabs
could overcome their animosity, just like other nations that have gone from
war to peace, he once again chose to cite the 1923 peace agreement between
Greece and Turkey, which was followed by a massive population exchange.[75]

❖

A formal written order to expel Arabs from entire villages seems to have first
been given as part of Plan Dalet issued in March 1948; by then, tens of thousands of Arabs, perhaps more, were no longer in their places of residence. The
plan came together under the guidance of Yigael Yadin, who was then chief
of the Haganah's operations branch. Its principal goal was to defend the
partition boundaries against the invasion of Arab regular and semiregular
forces, but it also spoke of the possibility of fighting outside those lines, in
part in order to defend Jewish settlements that were meant to be included
within the Arab state. The strategy that the plan laid out was in line with the
offensive defense that Ben-Gurion demanded, and thus included operations
against "enemy settlements within or close to our defense system, with the
goal of preventing their use as bases for active armed forces." The targets and
operations for this purpose were primarily of two types: "The destruction of
villages (burning, bombing, and mining the ruins), especially with regard to
settlements that we are unable to maintain permanent control of." Nothing
was said about what would happen to the inhabitants of these villages. Other
villages were not slated, apparently, for "destruction" but rather for "eradicat-
ing and taking control," after being surrounded and searched. "In the case of
resistance, the armed force is to be destroyed and the population expelled
beyond the state's borders," the plan said of these villages.

Plan Dalet charged local commanders with responsibility for the villages
within their sectors. "The villages, in your sector, are to be captured, cleaned

out, or destroyed—decide for yourself, in consultation with your advisers on Arab affairs and the officers of the intelligence service," it stated. The commander of the Etzioni Brigade, operating in the Jerusalem region, also received sanction, in case of need, "to limit, as per your ability, the cleansing, seizing, and destroying of enemy villages."[76] Commanders were supposed to have the assistance of Arab affairs advisers connected to the Jewish Agency's Arab Department who were equipped with "village files" containing intelligence and general information about each village. Ben-Gurion demanded that these advisers also be given the authority to decide themselves to "get rid of" a village "that interferes with the plans of the Hebrew community or commits a provocation."[77] If commanders and advisers had doubts about how to treat any given village, they could be helped by the tenor of the messages conveyed by their supreme commander, Ben-Gurion. Yadin added an appendix to the plan in which he laid out the means to "break the spirit" of the population of "enemy cities," some of which he named. He noted the option of expelling Arabs from their homes and cutting them off from the essential services detailed in the order itself, including water and electricity. Other plans recommended a variety of ways of sowing terror among the Arabs, including using whisper propaganda, a well-known method of causing people to flee, as Ben-Gurion learned from his advisers.[78] News of Haganah actions against Arab villages spread rapidly even without a deliberate whisper campaign. The attack on the village of Deir Yassin by Etzel and Lehi combatants on April 9, 1948, became a symbol of brutality, especially against women and children. Ben-Gurion approved a Jewish Agency condemnation of the attack, and had the statement sent to King Abdullah of Transjordan; the Haganah also issued a condemnation. No such statement was issued in Ben-Gurion's own name.* During his visit to Haifa, he was told that the

---

* In his memoirs, Ben-Gurion wrote at great length about the involvement of the village of Deir Yassin in attacks on Jewish neighborhoods, but in general he stayed away from addressing what happened during the capture of the village. After the war, he opposed his justice minister's demand to bring the perpetrators of the deed to trial, and later refrained from replying to a letter he received from Martin Buber protesting a plan to build a Jewish neighborhood over the village's ruins. (Ben-Gurion 1971a, p. 346; Segev 1986, p. 88; Pinchas Rosen and Ben-Gurion to the Cabinet, Sept. 19, 1948, ISA.)

panic in the wake of the attack on Deir Yassin had caused the Arab flight from the city.[79] A few days later, Arabs attacked a convoy on its way to Hadassah Hospital on Mount Scopus. Most of the passengers were Jewish civilians, among them doctors and nurses. Seventy-eight were killed. It was another blow to the Haganah in Jerusalem. The conquest of Arab villages created a new and promising geopolitical situation, vital to the realization of the Zionist dream. Benny Morris, a historian of the War of Independence, has estimated that, during the six months that preceded the end of British rule, between three and four hundred thousand Arabs fled or were uprooted.[80]

"I RECEIVED TIDINGS"

The British Empire's Union Jack was to be lowered for the last time over Government House in Jerusalem, and the high commissioner was preparing to leave Palestine forever. It was scheduled to happen on Friday, May 14, 1948. In the meantime, the United States was pushing for a three-month cease-fire. That period would allow the Haganah to get stronger; according to Ben-Gurion, it was not yet prepared for war. "At this moment we do not have the necessary strength to withstand a possible invasion," he stated five days before the neighboring Arab armies began their invasion. But the proposed cease-fire would also have required putting off the Jewish state's declaration of independence. For Ben-Gurion, that was the proposal's major shortcoming. Hundreds of thousands of Arabs were still in their homes; the cease-fire was meant to keep them there and to allow the refugees to return.[81] Ben-Gurion thus opposed the cease-fire and insisted on declaring independence immediately, despite the expected cost in human life.

He believed he was acting in the name of the yearnings of generations of Jews; that was his lifelong belief. At this decisive moment, then, he did not act like a "computing machine," as he once said. It was not an engineer's cold calculation that impelled him, but rather a mysticism of national redemption, perhaps a faith that the declaration of independence would call up the nation's hidden powers of bravery and belief and fighting spirit. Some four months later, Ben-Gurion confirmed that "there were serious reasons not to declare independence," since at the time ten American bombers could have prevented it, and the United States was capable of sending fifty of them without batting an eyelash. It was a decision made in a state of uncertainty. In such cases, he said, one chooses on the basis of "deliberations, guesses, and feelings." The declaration of independence was, most likely, also meant to rehabilitate his own prestige, damaged by the Haganah's failure and the generals' revolt. There was another reason as well—Menachem Begin threatened that if Ben-Gurion did not declare independence immediately, he would do so himself.[82]

When Ben-Gurion said that the Haganah was not prepared for war, he chose his words very precisely. The key phrase was "at this moment," meaning that the Haganah could grow stronger as it fought. Because at this stage, Ben-Gurion knew something that most people did not—in a few days' time, large quantities of arms and ammunition would begin to arrive in the country. This included aircraft, which had already been purchased in Europe. The arms that made Operation Nachshon possible arrived four days before it began.[83] Among the factors in Israel's victory, arms procurement was no less important than the flight of the Arabs.

❖

Most of the money came from America. Golda Meir succeeded in raising an almost inconceivable sum, in the terms of that time, from America's Jews—about $50 million, of which about $30 million was designated for Palestine. "Without it I don't know how we could have come out of the War of Independence," she said.

Ben-Gurion kept track of every dollar, but, as was the case with the Bricha and illegal immigration operations and often with land purchases, arms procurement required more than just money. For this new operation he employed some of the same people who had worked in the illegal immigration organization. Like that operation after the world war, arms and equipment purchases involved extended covert operations that demanded resourcefulness, daring, subterfuge, imagination, and a lot of luck. Ben-Gurion kept his eye on every step along the way.

Ehud Avriel, who made initial contact with an armaments factory in Czechoslovakia, later told of the telegrams Ben-Gurion peppered him with "by the hour." A few weeks before Operation Nachshon, Ben-Gurion wrote to him: "I am worried and stunned that I have not received any news from you. Can you obtain heavy weaponry? And what everything depends on, combat aircraft." He instructed him to cable a reply with the words "I am healthy" if the answer was positive, or "I am being hospitalized" if it was negative. "Those missives really scared us," Avriel said. When Avriel visited Palestine, Ben-Gurion wanted to hear everything, just like during the Bricha operation. One story Avriel told him was about how he had gotten around a bureaucratic obstacle that had come up with the Czech manufacturer. The factory was permitted to sell its products only to governments; prior to independence, Avriel did not represent a government. During the Bricha operation, however, he had obtained stationery from the Ethiopian embassy in France, which he had used to type forged laissez-passers for refugees. The Czechoslovakian foreign minister, Jan Masaryk, an old acquaintance of Ben-Gurion's, helped Avriel compose an arms order in the name of the Ethiopian government, and Masaryk's secretary typed it up on the stationery that Avriel supplied her with. At the bottom of the order she typed the name of Emperor Haile Selassie. To Avriel's astonishment, Masaryk signed the document—but with his own name rather than the emperor's. It was enough for the factory.[84] Alongside overseas procurement, Ben-Gurion worked to expand the arms industry in Palestine, and followed its production on an almost daily basis.

The opportunity to bolster the Haganah could have served as a justification for putting off the war, so as to gain time, but the risk Ben-Gurion decided to take was not an unfounded one. "I received tidings of the arrival of the first cannon," his diary states; three weeks later, he wrote: "Ten Messerschmitts from Europe," meaning fighter aircraft. Two weeks later, he wrote: "Our air force should bomb and destroy Amman."[85]

That same day, Ben-Gurion offered his party's Central Committee a survey of the security situation. He had been warning about an invasion of Arab armies for seven years, yet four days before it was set to begin, by his estimate, he spoke of it only as a possibility, not a certainty. Four days before that he had suddenly asked Yadin: "Will the neighboring countries fight?"[86] He may have meant Transjordan specifically—a compact had been reached with King Abdullah, according to which he would refrain from attacking and would receive in return that part of Palestine that the UN had designated for the Palestinian Arab state. Golda Meir arrived late at the meeting—she had been conferring with the king. She passed a note to Ben-Gurion: Abdullah, she wrote, claimed that no agreement had been reached. That was not unexpected. With a growing tide of refugees inundating his country, many from Haifa, Jaffa, and other cities taken by the Haganah, Abdullah could not permit himself to take a course different from the other Arab states.*

Ben-Gurion immediately left the meeting, rushed to Haganah head-quarters, summoned its top people, and demanded of them, among other things, "to plan a campaign against a full-scale Arab invasion," as if no such plans had been made already. There was enough personal gear for soldiers, he recorded, except for socks and blankets.[87] In the meantime, the Central Committee continued its deliberations. The record of the meeting has not survived in its entirety, so it is not certain that the resolution to declare independence was put to a vote and approved; in any case, there were not many opponents.[88]

He was careful to include not just his party but also the People's Administration—the Thirteen—in decision making. Two of that body's members were not able to reach Tel Aviv from Jerusalem, and one was in New York. His political acumen prompted him to create the sense that everything was open for discussion and that his colleagues were free to reach decisions on the basis of their best judgment, with no pressure from him. The next day, he permitted Yadin and Galili to brief the members of the People's Administration. The two of them appraised the Haganah's chances against the Arab armies as "pretty much even."

The members debated; some of them thought there were good reasons to postpone independence.[89] Some of the decisions were made by vote. The decision to reject the cease-fire proposal and declare independence was reached by consensus, without a vote; some of the members seem to have capitulated to pressure from Ben-Gurion. Pinchas Rosen, a German-born

---

* An Egyptian pilot whose plane was shot down over Tel Aviv related in his interrogation that the refugees were spreading stories of atrocities; Ben-Gurion received similar intelligence from Lebanon. (Ben-Gurion, Diary, May 15, April 5, 1948.)

jurist who was still called Rosenblüth at the time and who generally took a moderate line in Weizmann's spirit, demanded that the official document, Israel's Declaration of Independence, explicitly lay out the country's borders. It was a legal issue that was impossible to avoid, he maintained. Ben-Gurion replied: "Everything is possible. If we decide here that we won't say what the borders are, then we won't say." Five of the nine participants in the meeting voted to support Ben-Gurion's position on the border issue, and the matter remained open, to be decided by the war. One day around that time, he flew from Tel Aviv to Jerusalem and back. Upon his return he wrote: "The flight took 35 minutes. How small our country is."[90]

❖

On May 14, 1948, *Davar*'s front page ran a small item quoting sources in Cairo: Egyptian army forces would cross the border into Palestine one minute after the end of the British Mandate, at midnight. The real war had begun. Just before striding into the Tel Aviv Museum to declaim the Declaration of Independence, Ben-Gurion learned that Haganah forces and members of the kibbutz Kfar Etzion, just south of Jerusalem, had surrendered after a two-day assault by forces of Abdullah's army and local Arab attackers. "The defenders have been butchered by the Arabs," he wrote in his diary, and also "cheering and profound joy in the land, and again I am a mourner among the joyous, as on November 29." He began a new journal, recording: "At 4 p.m. Jewish independence was declared and the state was founded. Its fate lies in the hands of the security forces."[91]

The declaration, redrafted by Ben-Gurion the previous night, contained a commitment to freedom and equality for all—including Arab citizens—and a call for peace.

❖

A few days later, Shlomo Lavi received word from the Negev: his younger son, Hillel, had also fallen. On the way to the front, Hillel had run by chance into his girlfriend; the two had been separated for a time but the unexpected encounter had reignited their love. He was not yet nineteen years old. "I will not eulogize Hillel, as one does not eulogize a soldier when he falls," Lavi said at the gravesite. "I will lament only myself. From now on, whose face will light my days as my boy could?" Addressing his two sons and the other soldiers who had fallen and would still fall, he declared: "The State of Israel is being founded . . . Your greatest dreams, our dreams, are becoming reality, and you have not seen it and will not see it . . . We will be your heirs. How bitter and frightening that thought is."[92] Hillel had been born in August 1929; in Hebron on that same day, dozens of Jews had been slaughtered by Arabs.

· 17 ·

WAR

"BLESSED IS THE NATION"

In the afternoon hours of September 8, 1948, the prime minister and his wife hosted leading public figures at a reception at Government House, a three-story building that had once belonged to a family of the Templer sect in Tel Aviv's Sarona neighborhood. The upper floor housed the prime minister's office.[1] Ben-Gurion was now interim prime minister and minister of defense. It was the first event of its kind since the declaration of independence; the guests included Cabinet ministers, the top commanders of the Israel Defense Forces (IDF), as the Haganah was now called, the leading Israeli and American Jewish Agency officials, newspaper editors, authors, artists, and actors. "The refreshments were light and sparse," Moshe Gurari, a veteran Jewish Agency official, later recalled, but spirits were high and the guests animated. Everyone crowded around Ben-Gurion, who stood in one corner, dressed in a gray suit, shaking the guests' hands "with unconcealed indifference." Earlier that day, Ben-Gurion had spoken at length with the U.S. special representative to Israel, later the ambassador, who warned him against violating the cease-fire that the sides had agreed to.

He suddenly vanished. The guests speculated about where he had gone; a few were offended and left. Gurari went to Ben-Gurion's office. He found him "immobile, gazing into space." Gurari tried to get him to return to his guests. Ben-Gurion referred to the event with distaste in Yiddish as a *hasenah*, which literally means "wedding" but connotes mindless revelry. He spoke of the families who had lost loved ones in the war and how they would react were they to see him at this party. "How many sacrifices we have made and how many more will we offer on the altar of this country?" they would ask, he thought. He sometimes attended the funerals of soldiers, or appeared at gatherings where bereaved parents were present, he said, "and I always wonder—no one has yet attacked me, no one has tried, in his sorrow and grief, to cast a stone at me, no one has raised his voice to me, and no one has shouted in his pain: 'You wanted a state and we are paying the price.'" He showed Gurari a book that a poet, Reuven Grossman, put out in memory of his son, Noam, who had been killed just north of Jerusalem, along with fifteen other soldiers. Some of them had been captured by Arabs, tortured and murdered, and their bodies mutilated. It was one of the war's most searing failures. Yitzhak Rabin, the IDF's operations chief in the Jerusalem sector, believed that Grossman's contingent had been assigned an impossible task; some would later term it a suicide mission. Ben-Gurion received a report on the incident. When he took hold of the book, Gurari recalled, his hands shook and his voice choked. He read Grossman's dedication out loud: "At your order he fought, at your order he fell, may your name be blessed!" Ben-Gurion hid his face in his hands and Gurari's impression was that he was crying. "It is immense, sublime, unbelievable," he wept. The book included a poem the father wrote, with the title "For This I Thank You, God." In a letter to the poet and his wife, Ben-Gurion wrote: "I am moved and shaken to the depths of my heart. Blessed is the nation that has sons like Noam, doubly blessed is the nation that has parents like you."[2]

Ben-Gurion's readiness to send people to their deaths in a war against the Arabs, and his ability to do so, singled him out from all other Jewish leaders. Together they were principal components of his leadership, and were anchored in his unshakable belief in Zionism. Yigael Yadin later remembered that Ben-Gurion did not generally ask how many soldiers were expected to die in a particular operation.[3] At times the responsibility was almost too heavy to bear; he found himself consoling friends and colleagues in the Israeli leadership. Among the fallen were brothers of both Yadin and Moshe Dayan, as well as one of Yitzhak Ben-Zvi and Rachel Yanait's two sons. Yitzhak "did not shed a tear and discussed the situation—but his pain was no less than Rachel's," Ben-Gurion wrote after returning from a consolation visit to the home of his old friends. They believed that their son had used his last bullet to shoot himself in the head, so as not to fall into the hands of the Arabs. He was to have been married just a few days later, Ben-Gurion noted.[4]

The fact that the political elite participated in the nation's grief must have deflected many of the accusations that Ben-Gurion had expected to hear. Quite naturally, he needed support of the type he received from bereaved parents like Shlomo Lavi and Reuven Grossman, who later changed his last name to Avinoam—meaning "Noam's father." He glorified the heroism of the fallen and declared: "Everything now for the war."[5]

❖

He made a point of meeting with IDF commanders each day. He generally radiated self-confidence and self-control, but on occasion he fell apart. Yadin recalled him as a strong man who was difficult to oppose because, while he sometimes raised his voice, most often he did not. He sometimes sat in a discomfiting and unexplained silence, or suddenly began to talk about the Bible. According to Yadin, he did so mostly when people tried to tell him something he did not want to hear. Furthermore, the fact that the prime minister and commander in chief recorded everything people told him in his diary unsettled and awed those who met with him. Many conversations with him had to be conducted at dictation speed, Yadin recalled; he frequently interrupted to ask questions. When he looked up from his diary to indicate disagreement, he would blink nervously. "It was a very strange characteristic," Yadin recalled. "People who knew him were not disturbed," he said, "but most people could not take it, and it was very difficult for them to question his decisions." Many decisions seemed to grow out of things he had just at that moment written down. Yadin believed that Ben-Gurion organized his thinking by writing.[6] He listened to his officers, but, as one of them said, in the end he consulted only with himself.[7]

He generally did not end a conversation with an order, related Moshe Carmel, commander of the northern front. He would simply say what he wanted done, assuming that his intention had been understood and would be carried out. At times he spoke cryptically, in hints. "You'd understand what he wanted and what his intention was," Carmel said, "but in a way that you could not afterward maintain that you had heard something or other explicitly."*[8]

At times he made decisions that ran counter to the tactical views of his officers, on issues including the deployment of forces, timing of action, and targets. He demanded taking the Arab position at Latrun no fewer than six times, so as to open up the road to Jerusalem. He feared that Jewish Jerusalem could not endure the siege if the position were not captured, and would fall to the Arabs. All six times the mission failed. It was his most blatant intervention in military operations. Yadin tried to explain to him that he was wrong, both about the capacity of Jewish Jerusalem to withstand the siege and about the IDF's capabilities. The effort to save Jerusalem would lose the rest of the country, he claimed. Some of their meetings deteriorated into shouting matches and ended with frayed nerves. Yadin, one of the most senior figures in the Haganah, maintained that the arguments were due to the fact that Prime Minister and Defense Minister Ben-Gurion had not a clue about logistics and their operational implications. Ben-Gurion also lost his temper when Yitzhak Rabin told him that it was impossible to capture Latrun. "Yigal Allon should be shot," Ben-Gurion fumed. Allon was the commander of the Palmach. "I was in shock," Rabin wrote. "I was speechless. With difficulty, I mumbled, 'Ben-Gurion, what are you saying?!' And he did not take it back: 'Yes, what you heard!' he repeated."

---

* That was how he spoke and argued at Cabinet meetings as well. He almost always worded himself in a way that left him an escape hatch, such as "I myself believe that there is a chance of winning, but if Mr. Gruenbaum were to put a question about it to me, I would not commit myself." He had done the same as secretary of the Histadrut. (Ben-Gurion to the Cabinet, Sept. 21, 1948, ISA; Mordechai Bentov, interview transcript, BGA.)

Yadin termed Ben-Gurion's insistence on conquering Latrun an "obsession," but gave in. The repeated defeats there took a toll of hundreds of men. Soon thereafter, with great effort, a different road to Jerusalem was paved, and given the name the Burma Road.*[9]

His incessant intervention in the conduct of battle identified him with such failures. In the meantime he had to defend his authority; he had never faced a tougher test.

"THE HOLY CANNON"

During the first half of June 1948, an agreed cease-fire gradually came into effect. The UN Security Council sent a Swedish mediator, Count Folke Bernadotte. One Saturday, Ben-Gurion appeared before the Mapai Council to survey the situation. He termed the cease-fire an initial victory; the fact was that it looked more like a defeat. His party comrades did not complain, but they must have been expecting Ben-Gurion to explain what had happened. He called on his audience to stand in memory of Shlomo Lavi's two sons, and then took a personal tone, asking for understanding, almost apologizing. During his fifteen years of membership in the Jewish Agency Executive, he had not held any portfolio, and the "war portfolio" had been placed in his hands only two years previously, he said. He had not agreed to accept it because he was a general, he said; on the contrary, there was no portfolio he was less suited for. He had no knowledge of military matters, he reiterated; he knew only what any person could read in books and in newspapers. He had agreed to take responsibility for security only because, like every profession and field of knowledge, military science was largely "a matter of common sense." He had begun his new career with study, recalling the seminar he had conducted for himself. "We have still not learned the craft of war," he

---

* Some of the men who fought at Latrun were sent there immediately upon their arrival in Israel, without any training. Ben-Gurion accepted responsibility: "We had no choice," he later said. "Jerusalem was in danger." Rabin told him that the immigrant soldiers were demoralizing his battalion. The debacle at Latrun was in part due to a failure of intelligence. (Moshe Shapira and Ben-Gurion to the Cabinet, June 2, 6, 8, 1948, ISA; Ben-Gurion, Diary, June 14, 1948, BGA; Ben-Gurion to the Mapai Council, June 19, 1948, in Ben-Gurion 1982a, p. 538; Ben-Gurion to the Knesset, Jan. 4, 1950, *Divrei Haknesset*, 3, p. 434ff.; Shamir 1994, p. 249ff., p. 7ff.)

claimed, using the plural. As in the past, he declared, "We are all to blame." He then moved on to a "delicate" question that many believed should not be brought up at all, he said, but he was not deterred by it, just as he was not afraid of bitterer and more dangerous matters. The issue was the Palmach.

He had thought out his speech very carefully. He began by praising the Palmach and its soldiers, and said that he had excellent relations with its commanders. Unfortunately, however, they were trying to turn the force into a "private preserve." He would not allow that to happen, he said. One person present warned of a "war of passions."[10] Ben-Gurion was prepared for a double war of passions.

That same Saturday during the cease-fire, a ship carrying several hundred immigrants and a large quantity of arms and ammunition approached the country's shores. Its name was the *Altalena*, Ze'ev Jabotinsky's pen name; it arrived under the auspices of Etzel. The story began on the day after the declaration of independence, when Begin proposed to sell the boat to the government.[11] The deal did not go through, but in the weeks that followed, negotiations were held with Begin over the allocation of the arms the ship would bring—80 percent for the IDF, 20 percent for Etzel in Jerusalem. The negotiations reached an impasse just a few hours before the ship arrived. Ben-Gurion brought the issue to the Cabinet for a decision. "I am prepared to act, and that means to shoot," he said, but he was willing to do so only with the Cabinet's approval. The ministers authorized the IDF to prevent the unloading of the arms from the ship, if possible without violence, "but if its order is not obeyed, force is to be used." The decision passed unanimously.[12] The problem of the Palmach fell on the government's table almost at the same time as the *Altalena* did.

❖

The ship first anchored across from Kfar Vitkin. A web of contacts attempting to resolve the problem failed and shots were exchanged. The passengers were removed, as were most of the arms. Begin boarded and the ship set sail for Tel Aviv. At 2:00 a.m., Ben-Gurion was woken and informed of the fact. The next day, the Cabinet again convened. Ben-Gurion had lost all interest in negotiation. "It is an attempt to destroy the army. It is an attempt to murder the state," he said. "These are the two questions and with both of them there cannot be, in my opinion, any compromise. And if, to our great tragedy, we need to fight for it, we must fight. The moment the army and the state surrender to another armed force, we are done for." He told his ministers that there had been dead and wounded on both sides in the exchange of fire on the beach at Kfar Vitkin.

Not all the members of the Cabinet agreed with him, but in the meantime, Yadin drafted an order for military action against "the enemy," as he called the ship. The aim was "unconditional surrender, by all means and by all methods." By a majority of seven to two, the Cabinet resolved that the ship be turned over to the authorities.[13] Ben-Gurion proceeded to General Staff Headquarters and ordered Yadin to act. Yitzhak Rabin commanded the operation itself. "Jews shooting Jews, for many hours," he later wrote. "Jews wounded and killed by the bullets of other Jews." But Ben-Gurion had no qualms. He wrote: "Day of Etzel . . . the ship is in flames."[14]

❖

The smoke that rose over the *Altalena* had not yet dispersed when Ben-Gurion went back to subduing the Palmach. The compromise that put an end to the generals' revolt in May did not end the political tension and personal hostility between Ben-Gurion and the Palmach; he aimed to disband it and to integrate its personnel into the IDF chain of command. Thus, for the second time in two months, with the war still far from over, Ben-Gurion again got caught up in a conflict with the army leadership. The clash revealed the limits on his power and forced him to ask for the government's support. The Cabinet decided to set up what came to be called the Committee of Five. He had only himself to blame for permitting the Palmach to build up so much political power. While none of the Cabinet ministers chosen to inquire into the issue had anywhere near Ben-Gurion's standing, they interrogated him and the army leadership as if they were of equal status.

The committee spent three days hearing testimony. Israel Galili explained the damage done to the army's fighting capabilities after he'd been removed as chief of the National Command; Yadin complained about Ben-Gurion's intervention in the conduct of operations and offered a detailed account of his incessant pressure to take Latrun. Everyone claimed, some explicitly and some implicitly, that Ben-Gurion appointed only Mapai loyalists to top command positions. Ben-Gurion claimed that the Palmach served Mapam's interests. He claimed that military defeats were due to the Palmach's refusal to obey his orders.[15] He did not look like a national military leader but rather like a politician who had miscalculated his rivals' strength. The investigation was humiliating, the committee's recommendation a heavy blow.

After accepting, in effect, every one of the claims of the rebels, the committee drafted a plan to reduce the powers of the defense minister. He would be forbidden to interfere with the army's operational considerations and to make appointments opposed by the chief of staff, and disputes about appointments were to be brought before the ministerial committee. Minister of the Interior Yitzhak Gruenbaum, who chaired the inquiry, presented a summary of the recommendations to Ben-Gurion and asked him if he had anything to say. "I have no comments," Ben-Gurion responded, and left the room. Gruenbaum soon received the expected letter from Ben-Gurion—the recommendations the committee was preparing, he claimed, were pushing him out of the Defense Ministry and government.[16]

The next step was not unexpected, but it was nevertheless dramatic—Gruenbaum sent Moshe Sharett to Ben-Gurion, to persuade him to relent. Sharett found him at his home, in serious mental distress; a doctor was in attendance. When he reported back to the committee, Sharett said he had found Ben-Gurion in a state of nervous breakdown. He used the same biblical word that Berl Katznelson had once used to describe Ben-Gurion's state, "tottering limbs and bitter grief," a combination of physical debilitation and mental enfeeblement. "I could not get into a conversation with him," Sharett related. "I tried to speak to him, but could not get him into a conversation about the subject that is of interest to us. When Sharett asked him if he was still prime minister, Ben-Gurion responded: "No."

Yadin also came to talk to him. Paula tried to keep him away. She screamed that Yadin was to blame for his distress and tried to kick him out. Yadin insisted that he had to see him and Paula told him to try, but that Ben-Gurion would not want to see him. She was right. Yadin went up to him and found him lying on a couch. When Ben-Gurion saw him, he turned his face to the wall. "Listen, history will not forgive you," the acting chief of staff said to the prime minister's back. Ben-Gurion did not want to talk to him.[17]

❖

At the time Ben-Gurion took action against the Palmach and Etzel, victory in the war was still distant. He needed successful battles. The ideological and political identity fostered by the Palmach threatened the standing of Mapai and its leaders in the larger labor movement. Begin was dragged into the *Altalena* episode by extremists in his own movement. They sought to force the arrival of the ship not just on Ben-Gurion's government but also on Begin. He had already agreed to integrate Etzel's combatants into the IDF and to place them under the army's authority—on condition that his men serve together in two battalions and receive the arms they needed to carry out their operations. There is not the slightest indication that any of them was plotting to "destroy the army" or "murder the state." They were no danger to its sovereignty; at most, they threatened to weaken Ben-Gurion's leadership and that of his party. Both Etzel and the Palmach were tied to movements that represented different social sectors and values with very different views and economic policies than those of Mapai, but they were all committed to the fundamental principles of Zionism, and in that sense they all operated under the same roof; hence there was no reason to use force against them while the war was still raging. Both organizations turned the actions against them into powerful myths for their supporters.

Ben-Gurion tended to become addicted to his hatreds, and to defend his decisions passionately. The morning after the attack on the *Altalena*, he said, "Blessed is the cannon that bombed that ship. The cannon is worthy of standing in the Temple, if it gets built." Supporters of the attack on the ship soon came to call it the "holy cannon."[18] Maybe he used such great force against Etzel so that he could threaten the Palmach with turning the holy cannon against it as well. Whatever the case, Etzel was a relatively easy target; the principal political enemies, as he saw it, were the leaders of the Palmach and Mapam.

"IT'S IN YOUR HANDS"

He was out of action on every front, including—exceptionally—writing in his diary, for a full three days. Some members of his Cabinet took advantage of his absence to put their frustrations into the minutes of Cabinet meetings. Minister of Health Shapira said, "Were I responsible for the atrocity of Latrun, my conscience would torture to my last day." Minister of Agriculture Aharon Zisling, of Mapam, proposed Ben-Gurion's ouster. He argued that the prime minister was on bad terms with the entire army, not only the Palmach, a veiled implication that his penchant for trusting his intuition may have inflated the number of dead. Ben-Gurion, he charged, was seeking one-man rule, free of criticism. He did not know how to work with people, another minister said, and wanted only yes-men around him. Sharett told the government that Ben-Gurion was hugely insulted and that the issue at hand was whether the government wanted to do without him. And then the Cabinet decided to call him back.[19]

When he returned, he seemed to have recovered from his tottering limbs and bitter grief. He calmly went about his regular business and led a discussion of the design of the country's flag and seal. For a moment it seemed as if this, too, was not his day—he wanted only a single blue Star of David in the upper corner of a white flag, and rejected the proposal to add seven golden stars, as Herzl had proposed. Gold is ugly, he declared. But he lost the vote—the government decided that there would be seven stars, and that they might be golden. For the state seal, Ben-Gurion now demanded two lions bearing the Ark of the Covenant, but agreed to a compromise: instead of the lions there would be the Menorah, the sacred lamp of the Temple, as it appears on the Arch of Titus in Rome, and there would be no golden stars. It was a promising start.

He opened the discussion of the Defense Ministry in a similarly conciliatory tone. He did not reject the government's right to dismiss him, he said, and for a moment it seemed as if he were encouraging his colleagues to do so. No man is irreplaceable, he said, and offered a favorite example. For many years, he told them, people thought that no one could take Chaim Weizmann's place. But when he was compelled to leave his post, the Zionist movement did not collapse. "It's in your hands," he concluded. But that was only his opening gambit.

The principal question was whether the defense minister was the commander in chief and what authority lay with the ministerial committee. It soon became clear that the Cabinet ministers were not seeking the most effective way of directing the war. They wanted a compromise formula that would keep Ben-Gurion at the helm. Gruenbaum suddenly remembered that, formally, the recommendations made by the Committee of Five regarding the Palmach had not yet been approved by the whole Cabinet and were thus null and void. Another minister quickly added that, if that were the case, they could simply be filed away. Ben-Gurion made an offer: "I'll be happy to bring every difficult matter here," he said, meaning to the full Cabinet, "so as to make things easier, because such matters require collective responsibility."

At this point, he offered them his vision of the war and the peace that would follow. The war should go on for another month or so and then "come to an end with a bombing of Damascus, Beirut, and Cairo until they no longer have any desire to provoke us to war, and will make peace with us." Because that was the goal of the war: peace. "We must gain the hearts of the Arabs," he said, "and there is only one way that we can teach them to respect us. If we don't blow up Cairo, they will think that they can blow up Tel Aviv." All that remained was to find the right words to define the powers of the defense minister; Ben-Gurion promised to consult with a committee of ministers "as needed."[20]

At the end of the year, in advance of the elections to the Constituent Assembly, which were held while the war was still in progress, ugly exchanges of insults over the Palmach question continued to be recorded in the Cabinet's minutes, but the force was disbanded anyway. Thousands of people never forgave Ben-Gurion for it to their dying days. In the elections, the Marxist Mapam won 19 seats in the 120-member Constituent Assembly, which soon transformed itself into the First Knesset, Israel's parliament. That made it the second-largest party, after Mapai's 46 seats.[21]

The political tone of the critique of his conduct of the war made it easier for Ben-Gurion to fend it off. He was determined to run the war himself, using the working methods he had adopted many years before. "In security affairs, nothing is general, everything is details," he told his colleagues. "The only thing I need to address is the details." From time to time he issued a threat, saying he would not consent to work any other way; if he couldn't do that, he'd find himself another job, he said.[22] And so the war, like the seminar that had preceded it, looked like a new edition of the great election campaign in Poland.

"THEY SHOULD BE TRANSFERRED TO TRANSJORDAN"

In the meantime, combat had resumed in full force, on all fronts. During the ten days between the breakdown of the first cease-fire and the beginning of a second one, the IDF conquered Nazareth, Ramla, and Lod, but failed in another attempt to take Jerusalem's Old City. Beirut and King Farouk's palace in Cairo were bombed by airplanes purchased only a short time before—three B-17G Flying Fortresses. "Our pilots are enthusiastic," Ben-Gurion wrote. The next day, Damascus was also bombed, "finally," Ben-Gurion wrote.[23]

Ramla and Lod were "thorns," as Ben-Gurion put it at one Cabinet meeting, and he ordered them demolished forthwith.[24] In May and June 1948, the two towns were bombarded from the air, but were not captured. "We have decided to help [Etzel] cleanse Ramla," Ben-Gurion told the Cabinet two days after the state was declared.[25] At the beginning of June, he was still griping that Yadin "did not appreciate" the importance of the Ramla-Lod front. In the end, he had to wait for about six weeks, until both were conquered in Operation Danny. Three of its best-known commanding officers were Moshe Dayan, Yigal Allon, and Yitzhak Rabin, all of them Palestine-born. Two days later, Ben-Gurion marveled at the "audacity of the *tzabarim*," the term, literally meaning "prickly pear cactus," that was used to refer to native-born Israelis. "It was an immense deed that stunned the town" of Lod, he told the Cabinet.[26]

He met Rabin and Allon just outside the conquered town at noontime on July 12, 1948. Rabin later related that he asked Ben-Gurion what to do with Lod's Arab inhabitants, and that Ben-Gurion waved his hand in a manner that Rabin interpreted as a directive to expel them; Rabin later claimed that Ben-Gurion had given an explicit order to do so. For his part, Allon told

Ben-Gurion that the inhabitants "were inclined to leave," and that all they wanted was for the IDF to release those it had arrested in the town. According to Allon, Ben-Gurion told him: "I advise you to free the prisoners," giving him a wink. "I was very much impressed," he said. "There was actually an understanding between me and Ben-Gurion that it was best if they left Lod . . . I tell him: I understand. So the pace will speed up. And he said: Yes. It was one of those exchanges of two sentences, and that was the end of the matter." Allon ordered the army "to encourage, with vehicles and even with buses and trucks, the exodus from Ramla to the front line facing Latrun." Later he would say that he commanded the army "to let them go." Allon claimed that he and Ben-Gurion also hoped that the flow of refugees would make it more difficult for the Jordanian army to advance.[27]

The need to ask Ben-Gurion what to do with the Arabs arose in part because of an order issued in the name of the chief of staff a few days earlier, on July 6, 1948. The order explicitly forbade the razing of villages and towns and the expulsion of Arabs other than during actual battle, "without special sanction or an explicit instruction from the minister of defense, in each and every case."[28] At 1:30 p.m. on July 12—that is, apparently, immediately after Ben-Gurion left—Allon signed an order that also bears Rabin's signature. It consists of two provisions: "1. The inhabitants of Lod are to be expelled quickly without any attention to sorting by age. They are to be directed to Beit Nabala. 2. For immediate execution."[29]

The great expulsion began on July 13, a day after Ben-Gurion's visit. The next day, he told the Cabinet that, according to a report he had received that morning, not a single Arab remained in Ramla and Lod. He claimed that, on the day of the deportation, only three to five thousand remained in Lod. "Many fled beforehand," he claimed—that is, before his visit to Allon and Rabin's command post.[30] The editors of his war diary, published by the Israeli Ministry of Defense's publishing arm, determined that most of the inhabitants of the two cities left, "whether willingly or by force," on July 14 and 15, 1948, *after* the cities were captured.[31] On July 15, Ben-Gurion quoted a Jordanian cable referring to thirty thousand refugees from Ramla and Lod moving in their direction. Regarding this, he wrote: "They should be transferred to Transjordan."[32] Finance Minister Eliezer Kaplan told his colleagues that he asked Ben-Gurion what the fate of the cities' inhabitants would be, and that Ben-Gurion's response was that the young men would be taken prisoner and that the rest should be "encouraged to leave the place," but Israel would have to see to the provisioning of those who chose to stay. Zisling said he read that wording as a warning that meant "save your lives while you can and flee." His party, Mapam, had received an independent report describing "the expulsion of the Arabs of occupied Lod and Ramla."[33]

One of the operation's field commanders, Shmaryahu Gutman, composed a detailed report of the incident immediately after it happened. His account largely confirms the version offered by Allon, Gutman's commanding officer. The battle for Lod was a difficult one; the IDF encountered opposition. At one stage the Israeli forces succeeded in confining thousands of the city's men in a mosque. They were permitted to leave and return to their homes, on condition that they and their families leave the city within a few hours. According to Gutman, "They greeted the edict about leaving with immense enthusiasm and rejoicing. They feared that the city would be destroyed in the battles that would continue there . . . It was as if they were fleeing from hell, from the vale of battle." He recalled them advancing in a long convoy toward the Jordanian lines, their wagons laden with their belongings and livestock. "There was not a man who was not overloaded, and even each child bore something, a basket of food, a jug of water, coffee implements, and the like." The city emptied out entirely. "A strange stillness pervaded the streets . . . as if after a pogrom," Gutman wrote. The inhabitants of Ramla were taken to the Jordanian border by bus.[34]

"GENERATIONS OF WEEPING"

On September 26, 1948, Ben-Gurion proposed to the government that Israel break the second cease-fire and conquer Latrun.[35] The Jordanians had already disregarded the truce by bombing Jerusalem's water main, killing several Israeli soldiers. The Cabinet refused his proposal. He later said the decision would cause "generations of weeping." The expression soon found a foothold in Israeli politics and myth to the point of becoming a persistent irritation, constantly resurfacing and refusing to disappear into the depths of history, just like the attack on the *Altalena* and the dismantling of the Palmach.

A few days previously, the UN mediator, Bernadotte, and his deputy were murdered in Jerusalem. The killers were members of Lehi. Bernadotte had put together a new peace plan that required Israel to agree to the return of the Arab refugees. The plan also proposed a new set of boundaries—the Negev would go to the Arabs and the Galilee to the Jews; Jerusalem would become an international city. Ben-Gurion ordered the Lehi disbanded and launched a manhunt against its partisans. He proposed to the Cabinet an antiterror law that some of its members felt contradicted their fundamental values—it included a death penalty and granted the defense minister great latitude. The debate over his proposal once again demonstrated that his colleagues feared that he was seeking unlimited powers.[36]

Under the circumstances, most of the Cabinet ministers were not inclined to accept his proposal to take Latrun. The operation Ben-Gurion proposed was a local one, "a small Arab pocket that needs to be done away with," as he put it.[37] "Latrun is Jerusalem," he said, but the six previous failures to capture it did not encourage the operation's opponents to sanction a seventh attempt. Bernadotte's murder also mandated refraining from any further provocation against the United Nations and the United States.

He hoped that the Arab reaction to the operation he proposed would restart the war throughout the country. For some months he had felt that a long truce was liable to strangle Israel economically; the number of enlisted troops was one hundred thousand, and he warned that their release could not be postponed for long. The war might last for five years, he feared. "If I were an Arab, I wouldn't let it end," he said, adding: "The object is not to capture Ramla or Lod, but to win and achieve peace."[38]

He tried to convince the members of the Cabinet that restarting the war had further important advantages for Israel, most importantly the chance to "cleanse" the Galilee of one hundred thousand refugees who were there at the time. An empty Galilee could not be achieved without war, he said. With a war, and without a great effort, "the Galilee is cleansed." He described the "cleansed Galilee" as a "dowry." Beyond that, he mentioned the chance to conquer the Negev and to move the state's border eastward, at least to the central mountain ridge. At this meeting he made no mention of the conquest of Jerusalem's Old City, Bethlehem, or Hebron. In his diary he wrote: "I proposed attacking and capturing Latrun." In response to those Cabinet ministers who were apprehensive about the UN, he said, "Let's assume that the operation will not be legal—but reality is reality."

The legal aspect was not Moshe Shapira's main concern; he and several of his colleagues did not trust Ben-Gurion. The plan is very nice, Shapira said, but if every war went according to plan, no country would ever lose one. Seven members of the Cabinet voted against the proposal, defeating it.[39]

At one Cabinet meeting, Ben-Gurion said: "I have no detailed comprehensive plan."[40] That was the case with the war as a whole. He had a minimum goal, which was an independent state able to defend itself, preferably devoid of Arabs. Most of the other ideas he brought up were more in the nature of improvisations and sudden flashes of inspiration, which at times contradicted one another. Part of this was a long string of definitions of victory, including "a huge bombardment" of Arab capitals, some of which were carried out, and the conquest of Nablus—which did not happen—with or without the entire area he referred to as the Triangle. "The conquest of the Jenin-Tulkarem-Ramallah-Jerusalem Triangle is compulsory, as soon as possible," he said a month after independence. He always used the term "the Triangle" to refer to an area in Judea and Samaria in the center of the country, but not always to the same area. The conquest of Nablus, or alternatively the entire Triangle, was meant to ensure victory in Jerusalem, and thus in the entire country. Sometimes he meant gaining control of the road into Jerusalem and sometimes the capture of the city itself, with or without the Old City.[41]

These inconsistent and unsubstantiated impulses all date from the five months between May and October 1948, and resulted not from difficulties and changing circumstances but his inclinations and intuitions, and the absence of any comprehensive strategy. Along the same lines, he offered incongruous national messages. "We can conquer all of Palestine," he once said. "We can also reach Nablus—Damascus, too, in my opinion. We can extend the borders to the Litani River." In his view, "we deserve all of the western Land of Israel," by which he meant the area between the Jordan River and the Mediterranean, but if he were given the choice between conquest of that territory and the partition borders of 1947 with peace, he would take a "clipped state."[42] At the Cabinet meeting of September 26, he only proposed capturing Latrun; he hoped that the operation would restart the war, but that was not its main goal.

A few days later, he tried to prove that there had actually been a majority for his Latrun initiative, because Sharett in fact supported it. According to the minutes of the meeting, that was not correct. It didn't really matter, as during the course of the week the matter became less important to him. We won't reopen the debate, he said, offering, as if it were an afterthought, "We don't need Latrun."[43] Instead, he proposed conquering the Negev. This time he did not tell the Cabinet that he wanted the war to start up again. Instead, he explained that the Egyptians were blocking access to Israeli settlements in the south, and they needed to be relieved or evacuated. He stressed that it was possible to defeat the Egyptians and take control of the entire area between Jerusalem and Aqaba. A few members of the Cabinet thought they were hearing something much like the proposal they had rejected just a few days earlier; Shapira again expressed a lack of confidence in Ben-Gurion and demanded more information. Ben-Gurion promised that, as long as Jordan, Iraq, and Syria did not come to the Egyptians' aid, "we will not do anything to them and the campaign will be limited to the south." A majority voted in favor. The decision was tantamount to finally giving up on the conquest of the Old City in Jerusalem.[44]

During the months that had passed since Israel declared independence, several attempts to break through the Old City walls had failed. The Jewish Quarter had surrendered at the end of May and most of its residents were taken prisoner by the Jordanians.[45] But Ben-Gurion did not make conquering the Old City a high priority. While still waiting for the UN to approve the partition resolution, under which Jerusalem and its environs would not be included in the Jewish state, he said explicitly that he had no intention of conquering the city, including its western Jewish neighborhoods. This could have been an attempt to improve the chances that the resolution would pass, but he offered a classically Zionist justification for his position. "If we expand Jerusalem in all directions, it will include many Arab villages, and the Jewish majority will become a minority," he explained.[46]

He fixated on opening the road to Jerusalem because he saw the connection between the Jewish state and the Jews living on the city's west side as a matter of national importance. He was well aware of the city's religious significance, but did not personally feel its holiness. It was a stronghold of Haredi Judaism, and Ben-Gurion feared that Jewish extremists were liable to stage attacks on the holy places of other religions. He was not eager to assume responsibility for Jesus's tomb, he said some time later at a Cabinet meeting; Begin needed to be watched to keep him from blowing it up.[47] In the time leading up to the declaration of independence, he said that tranquillity in Jerusalem was more important than access to the Western Wall. "It's not a tragedy if we don't go to the Western Wall for three months," he said.[48] After the state was established, he continued to display a degree of indifference with regard to Jerusalem, as he had since his arrival in Palestine.

"WE'LL ACCEPT THE CURRENT SITUATION"

A few months following independence, the government resolved to agree to the partition of Jerusalem between Israel and Jordan. The IDF did not accept the decision. "Moshe [Dayan] believes that we can try to conquer the city," Ben-Gurion recorded in his diary; Dayan wanted two battalions for the purpose.[49]

Three weeks later, Ben-Gurion rejected Dayan's request that he sanction a second attempt to take the Beit Jala ridge, not far from Bethlehem; the first attempt had failed the previous night. Ben-Gurion's reasoning was political. He explained that Israel's control of the city of Jesus's birth was likely to anger the Christian world, and that given the tension between King Abdullah of Jordan and Egypt, there was a chance that the king would not intervene to aid the Egyptians in the Negev; it was best not to anger him. One of the members of the IDF staff, Baruch Rabinov, later recalled that Ben-Gurion asked Dayan to explain his request to the General Staff. He preceded Dayan's presentation with his own explanation of why he was opposed, but said that, as a democrat, he would accept the will of the majority. Five of those present supported Dayan's proposal and five were opposed, with Chief of Staff Yadin among the latter. Only nine of the men present were members of the General Staff; one of the others was Shaul Avigur, who was invited out of respect for his personal standing. He favored the operation. Ben-Gurion wanted a clear majority against it, Rabinov recalled. He thus called in the chief of staff's attaché to express his opposition, as well as his own military attaché, Nehemiah Argov. The former favored the operation; Argov refused to offer his opinion. "Then Ben-Gurion blew up," Rabinov related. "He shouted: 'I am astounded by your lack of political judgment,' and ruled that the operation would not be carried out."

According to Rabinov, Dayan did not intend to conquer Beit Jala alone, but the Old City as well. On Sunday, Ben-Gurion went to Jerusalem and toured the Jordanian lines on the east side of the city. His impression was that they were very well ensconced and that, from a military point of view, it would be very difficult to eject them. He also expressed his concern that the Jordanians would bomb the Hebrew University on Mount Scopus. He reported to the Cabinet only that Dayan wanted to conquer Beit Jala, but most of what he said was aimed at justifying his opposition to conquering the Old City. A few days later, he made another argument: to take the Old City, he told the Cabinet, it would be necessary also to conquer Jenin and Nablus and other places, but at this point the army needed a rest.[50] There was another reason, also: "We don't want to get tangled up with the Jordanian army," he said. That same day, however, Yadin also told him that Jerusalem could be taken. "If we get to Nablus, Ramallah will fall of its own accord and Jerusalem will be liberated." A few days later, he was growing more skeptical— driving the Arab forces from Jerusalem would require unlimited time, but the United States was acting to block Israeli conquests. The question remained open. A few weeks later, Israel and Jordan held talks over a list of issues in Jerusalem, including control of the rail line into the city, access to the Hebrew University compound on Mount Scopus, and Latrun. Before agreements were reached, Ben-Gurion maintained that "if it works out, the Jerusalem problem is solved." He made no mention of the Old City; for all intents and purposes, he had conceded it.*[51]

❖

A few months after the war ended, he was still fantasizing to his colleagues about the Old City emptying of Arabs; only international teams would remain there, to guard the holy places. Israel would supply them with electricity.

---

* The agreement with Jordan moved the boundary with Israel to the east; as part of this, Israel agreed to take control of a cluster of Arab villages in Wadi Ara, and promised not to expel their inhabitants. (Segev 1986, p. 27.)

He told the Cabinet ministers not to repeat his idea in public. "There are certain things that it would be very bad to say," he explained, but if such a proposal were to come from "some gentile," Israel would agree. In a more realistic vein, he said: "We will not agree to fight for the Old City. That means we'll accept the current situation."[52]

Palmach veterans later claimed that Ben-Gurion missed a chance "to conquer the capital."[53]

"HUGE ZIONIST ASSET"

The final battles took place in the Galilee and the Negev. Years ago, during the great debate over the partition plan the British had proposed, Ben-Gurion had written in his diary that, were he to have to choose between the Galilee, which the plan made part of the Jewish state, and the Negev, which was not included, he would choose the Galilee without hesitation. In June 1948, he said that he would rather have the Negev. But he wanted both. When the war broke out, he declared: "If we do not stand firm in the desert, we will not stand firm in Tel Aviv."[54]

He said it was the most momentous decision he had made since he declared independence. He traveled to the Negev to instruct Allon on how to conquer it, just as he had instructed Yadin on how to conquer Jerusalem. The Negev sparked his imagination in part because he saw it as "an area empty of people," as he put it, an echo of the Zionist dream of a virgin and unpopulated Palestine.[55] The Negev was a "huge Zionist asset," he maintained; all it lacked was water. There might well be oil underground; five million Jews could be settled there; of these, two million would work in agriculture and three million in manufacturing. At one Cabinet meeting he spoke eloquently about Kurnub (Mampsis or Mamshit), the ruins of a Nabatean city southeast of Be'er-Sheva. A full three hundred thousand families could be settled there, and the government office complex could be located there as well.[56] The landscape was beautiful. But Allon sent his troops in the direction of El Arish, in Sinai. He hoped to capture Gaza. President Truman demanded that the IDF be returned to Israeli territory, and Ben-Gurion acquiesced; Allon rushed to Tel Aviv, but failed to change the decision. He never forgave Ben-Gurion for that.[57]

When Ben-Gurion heard that the IDF had reached Eilat, he was beside himself with joy. "This may be the greatest event of the last few months, if not of the entire war of independence and conquest," he wrote in his diary. He recalled his two trips to Eilat, in the company of Berl Katznelson, and set out on a third. Now it was an official victory tour—three airplanes containing an entourage of senior officers and officials, a press officer, and a cook; they flew over Masada. The prime minister dressed in khaki for this visit, but also sported a keffiyeh, as he had when he went with Katznelson. At one spot where the plane landed, he found himself facing a large lake and green wood, but it was a mirage.[58]

❖

During this period, he lodged at the Miriam, a small family hotel near General Staff headquarters in Ramat Gan. He generally slept very little; he was one of those leaders who instructed his people to wake him up at night. He knew how to control his weariness—he stopped smoking, did not drink much coffee, and took sleeping pills.[59] Gershon Zak, an educator and the founder of the Israeli navy, remembered seeing him lying crosswise on his bed, reading the works of Josephus, the author in whose works he had found his Hebrew name. "You can actually see all the military actions of that time and you can learn a lot from it," Ben-Gurion told him.[60] He may also have played chess, as he sometimes did to take his mind off his worries.[61] He frequently spent his weekends in Tiberias. By Lake Kinneret, which had given him poetic inspiration when he was twenty-two years old, he could devote himself to his thoughts. In December 1948, he wrote in his diary: "It is almost unbelievable: along the way from Tel Aviv to Tiberias, there are almost no Arabs." Four weeks later, he wrote: "A wonderful day. Will the war end today?"[62]

He spent much time thinking, writing, and talking about his relation to war and the military. "Every war is a horrible and terrible catastrophe, not just for the defeated but also for the victors," he said. "War is a cruel waste of blood, destruction of property, loss of spiritual and material resources." But since the day he was excluded from Bar Giora and Hashomer, he was irresistibly drawn to the practice of soldiering and command; he frequently spoke nostalgically about his brief and largely inactive service in the Jewish Legion, one of the seminal experiences of his life. He read a great deal of military literature.[63] "War is a nation's supreme test . . . ," he wrote. "Not a test of strength, but a test of will." It was nevertheless important for him to distance himself from ideological militarism. "There is a historical philosophy that sees war as man's highest destiny," he said. He was referring to the Nazis and Arabs. "This philosophy is an abomination to Judaism as we understand it and as it was understood, I believe, by the prophets and sages of the Bible." At a Cabinet meeting he remarked, "An army is the most dangerous thing there is in the world." He feared a military coup and opposed ending the death penalty in the army, which would leave it defenseless against "scoundrels," as he put it. He cited reports of abuse and looting committed by the IDF in Jerusalem. "That is why the army must be placed under civilian control," he said. The need to subordinate the army to civilian institutions was the principle; the immediate corollary was that he had to control the army himself. Victory had challenged his image of himself as the supreme commander in a just war. "The bitter question has arisen of acts of looting and rape in the conquered cities," he wrote in his diary two months after independence was declared.[64]

❖

The greatest spoils fell to the state itself. They included Arab houses and land, farm machines, vehicles, and money deposited in bank accounts—all this was private property. The war's expenses preoccupied Ben-Gurion and sometimes caused him hard nights. The shortage of money was a nightmare that did not let him sleep, he told his Cabinet ministers. At one point, however, he came to the conclusion that the war was profitable; the country spent less than it gained from it, he said. He meant, among other things, the development of military industries, as well as the trains and army camps left behind by the British, in some cases without compensation.[65] He was enthusiastic when the airport at Lod was captured. "Who knows if the government of Israel would be able to build such an airport in the next ten years," he wrote. It was worth millions, he told the government, adding: "I have learned that war is not just waste."[66] But he also learned something about the avarice of conquerors. About a decade later, he told of the massive looting that was, he said, an outbreak of the Jewish community's most primitive instincts. "No group was immune to it," he said. Some Hebrew University faculty members entered the abandoned homes of Arab intellectuals, took their books, and deposited them in the National Library.*[67]

The subject came up for discussion in the Cabinet several times; Ben-Gurion expressed revulsion and shock. "I was devastated when I heard about these acts," he said. "It undermined my confidence in victory." It was, he said, "a bitter surprise"; it was not how he had imagined Jewish morality to be. "I was confronted with moral flaws of a sort I had not suspected existed, and they are a serious military blemish," he wrote at another opportunity, warning that "a person who abuses a non-Jew will abuse a Jew as well."[68] Greed, he said, led to murder. Minister of Agriculture Zisling described several "almost Nazi" acts committed by soldiers. Commissions of inquiry were set up on at least two occasions.[69] Ben-Gurion also asked about it, at his own initiative: "Is it true that horrible acts were committed in the Galilee?"[70] In the summer of 1949, he wrote: "A shameful atrocity: Battalion 22 in Be'er-Sheva apprehended an Arab man and woman. They killed the man and they (twenty-two men) discussed what to do with the woman. They decided and carried out their decision—they washed her, sheared off her hair, raped her, and killed her." He noted that the battalion commander was sentenced to seven years in prison.[71]

Following instances of rape in the occupied cities, and with the possibility that Jerusalem and Nazareth might be taken, he ordered that every Jew, and especially every Jewish soldier, caught in an act of rape, looting, or desecration of a holy place, Christian or Muslim, should be shot "without mercy." He ordered a poem by Natan Alterman execrating the murder of Arab civilians to be distributed to soldiers. Prior to this he overruled an order by the military censor forbidding *Davar* to publish the poem.[72]

---

* His archives contain two sheets of paper inscribed with verses from the book of Joshua, from the story of Achan, a man who was sentenced to death after he stole a fine mantle as well as silver and gold from the conquered city of Jericho, instead of leaving them "to the treasury of the Lord," as Joshua ordered before the city's wall fell. The first of these documents bears the date of the expulsion of the inhabitants of Lod and Ramla. (Verses from Joshua 6, BGA, general chronological documentation.)

Alongside the moral debasement of war crimes and his constant concern that the world see Israel as just, there were political considerations. About two weeks after Eilat was taken, Yigal Allon tried, without success, to persuade him to conquer the central mountain region, including East Jerusalem, and to make the Jordan River Israel's eastern border. Allon proposed that the Arab refugees who had fled to this region from elsewhere in Palestine should be forced eastward into Jordan.[73] A few days previously, Ben-Gurion had told the Cabinet that Allon had suggested that a whisper campaign be used to cause the Arab inhabitants of the south to flee. Ben-Gurion now made it sound like an unacceptable tactic.[74] By this point, hundreds of thousands of Arabs had already been uprooted. Ben-Gurion distinguished between those who left their homes in fear of the Israeli army and those who stayed "and our army forced them out," as he put it, adding somewhat philosophically, "That can be prevented, there is no need to make them flee." In this context he offered the Cabinet his version of what had happened in Lod and Ramla. "The residents were given explicit orders not to flee, and it turned out that they were forced out," he said. He tried to distance himself from the expulsions and created the impression that he had gone to Lod only a few days later.[75] The Nakba, as the Palestinian Arabs called their tragedy, haunted him until the end of his life.

"YOU MADE WAR—YOU LOST!"

Since the beginning of the twentieth century, tens of millions of human beings had been murdered or turned into refugees after being expelled from their homes, mostly in Eastern Europe. But the tragedy that the world has never ceased talking about is that of the Palestinian Arabs. Perhaps that is because people on every continent have displayed a special sensitivity regarding everything that happens in the Holy Land. Ben-Gurion was thus called on, time and again, to explain and justify what had happened under his leadership. But, as a person who truly believed, as a Zionist, Jew, and human being, that he was an exemplar of morality, he had trouble reconciling the expulsion of the Arabs with the humanist values he claimed to live by.

Not long after he became prime minister, it was proposed that he establish his official residence in a grand house in Jerusalem's southern Talbiyeh neighborhood. It was a two-story stone structure with an outside staircase that granted it a majestic look; a stone arch shaped like a huge horseshoe faced the entrance. The house was shaded by pines and cypresses; a palm, an olive tree, and a lemon tree also grew in the yard. Like many houses in that area, it had been built in the 1930s, and like the others it was the very picture of Levantine affluence, with nods to English and French culture. Most of Talbiyeh's residents belonged to the Christian Arab elite, among them officials in the British administration, physicians, attorneys, and businessmen. There was no more prestigious neighborhood in Jerusalem. Its streets were nameless and its houses unnumbered; one simply had to ask, for example, for "Anis Jamal's house," which was the house that was proposed as Ben-Gurion's residence. Jamal had made his fortune in the insurance and tourism businesses. His wife hailed from the Russian aristocracy; the actor and author Peter Ustinov was her cousin. A few Jews also lived in the neighborhood. One of them, the publisher Reuven Mas, headed the Jewish residents' committee there. Both the Jews and the Arabs lived with an illusion of multicultural coexistence in the world's most cosmopolitan city—for as long as it lasted. At the end of 1947 the bubble burst.

In January 1948, Mas lost his son Danny, who had commanded a group of soldiers who, on their way to relieve the Etzion Block, were killed by Arabs. About four weeks later, *Davar* reported that "a Haganah vehicle drove through Talbiyeh yesterday afternoon and called on the residents to evacuate the neighborhood. Many of the Arabs left." Some of them returned later, for a short time, under the protection of the British authorities. When that happened, *Davar*'s correspondent wondered whether "perhaps we erred . . . when we proclaimed by loudspeaker that the Arabs had to evacuate Talbiyeh entirely." But the Arabs soon fled once more; most of them left behind nearly all their belongings, from grand pianos and wedding dresses to tennis rackets and kitchen utensils and books and family photograph albums. Many of the Arab houses came into the possession of Jews who also came from the elite, among them politicians, judges, and professors at the Hebrew University.

Ben-Gurion had already toured Jerusalem's abandoned neighborhoods; he refused to move into the Jamal mansion. Shlomo Arazi, the official in the prime minister's office who had offered him the house, later recalled the reason Ben-Gurion gave for turning it down—it was improper for the Israeli prime minister to live in a private residence confiscated from an Arab. At that time, the State of Israel had already taken possession of tens of thousands of houses confiscated from Arabs, but Ben-Gurion wanted to draw a line between himself and all that. He preferred to establish the prime minister's residence in Rehavia, in a house that the state rented from the widow of a senior official in the British administration who had been killed in the bombing of the King David Hotel.[76]

He was entirely at peace with the fact that the Arabs had been displaced—between 500,000 and 600,000 of them at his estimate, according to others about 750,000. That was the price of Jewish independence in the Land of Israel, "a captured land," as he put it. "War is war," he added.[77] His colleagues supported him. One termed the exit of the Arabs a divine miracle, a second remarked that the country's landscape was much finer without them, and Shlomo Lavi said: "The transfer of the Arabs out of the country is in my eyes one of the most just, moral, and correct things that needs to be done." That had long been his opinion, he remarked, meaning that he had held it even before his two sons were killed. Ben-Gurion agreed with his friend Yitzhak Ben-Zvi, who was concerned about the number of Arabs who remained in the State of Israel, about 100,000 of them. "There are too many Arabs in the country," Ben-Gurion declared.*[78]

Ben-Gurion always denied that the Arabs had been forced to flee. At times he claimed that "no refugee fled from the State of Israel. All the refugees who fled from the territory assigned by the UN decision to the Jewish state did so during the period of the British Mandate." In fact, close to half of them became refugees after the state was founded, but Ben-Gurion claimed that these people were not refugees—they were enemies.[79] Yet the refugees and their plight gave him no rest. Ghost cities and abandoned villages drew him in; again and again he wandered their streets, as if seeking to confirm with his own eyes that no Arabs remained there, and perhaps also in response to his need to persuade himself that he had not lent a hand to expel them.

---

* The IDF later conducted an inquiry into why such a large Arab population remained in the Galilee, despite the fact that "our forces tried to get rid of it and frequently did by other than legal and gentle means." The report quotes an order to commanders "to assist the inhabitants to leave the captured territories." (Yitzhak Moda'i, "Mivtza Hiram," IDFA 189.922/1975.)

"The city is almost empty" was how he summed up a visit to Jaffa, whose destruction he had fantasized about ten years previously. "Here and there an Arab in a tarbush," he wrote. In Ramla he searched for but did not find the house in which, in 1906, he and his friends had composed the Po'alei Zion manifesto. The building should have been preserved, he complained.[80]

Just as he did after his tour of the abandoned Jewish neighborhoods in Haifa, he claimed that he could not understand why the Arabs had fled. It was an "astonishing phenomenon," he said. It was important for him to state that, unlike the Jews, the Arabs had abandoned entire cities "with great ease," even though there had been no danger of destruction or slaughter; in Jaffa there had not even been any shortage of provisions. "There may well have been cases where they were helped a bit to flee, he said, "but, fundamentally, this really was an inexplicable phenomenon. They were not driven out of Jaffa. They fled even before Jaffa was conquered. They fled Haifa, fled Tiberias, fled Safed. It is a strange thing that is worth researching sociologically."[81]

He offered an explanation of his own: the flight of the Arabs, he claimed, showed that the Arab national movement was not based on positive ideas, whether cultural, economic, or social. All it had was religious hatred, xenophobia, and the ambitions of its rulers. A nation cannot fight for such notions, he said, because no fellah will want to die for them. "History has now proven," he declared, "who is really connected to this land and for whom it is nothing but a luxury that can easily be done without."[82]

It was a flattering thesis, but not an accurate one. The Arabs of Palestine wanted to prevent the establishment of Israel but were unprepared to do so, in terms of both organization and leadership. They had not yet recovered from the suppression of the Arab Revolt by the British, less than ten years previously. In their final months of ruling Palestine, the British did almost nothing to stop the flight. During their three decades of rule, they did not institute mandatory education, with the result that only three out of every ten Arab children had gone to school; the rest grew up unprepared for modern national life, especially in the villages but also in the outlying neighborhoods of Haifa, Jaffa, and other cities. In contrast, nearly every Jewish child went to school, and most adults had done so in their countries of origin.[83]

Yitzhak Ben-Zvi once quoted an Arab acquaintance who described the conflict over Palestine as a confrontation between a million fellahin and a million Einsteins.[84] Even so, tens of thousands of Jews were forced out of their homes.

Mayor Daniel Auster of Jerusalem reported to Ben-Gurion that a "mass psychosis to flee" had overcome the city's Jews; Ben-Gurion ordered that Jews should not be allowed to leave the city—they were meant to defend it with their bodies. He also rejected a proposal to evacuate the city's children. As with the evacuation of the Jews from Palestine during World War I, and in keeping with his position on rescuing children from the Nazis in 1938 and the children in the DP camps, he took the position that removing Jerusalem's children was tantamount to surrender to the enemy and thus should not be allowed. Furthermore, he said, there was no safe place anywhere in Palestine to accommodate children.[85]

Some of the Haredim living in Meah She'arim had raised white flags in surrender, Ben-Gurion reported, but Jews were driven out of their homes in Tel Aviv as well, and abandoned settlements that had become symbols of the Zionist enterprise, such as Masada and Sha'ar Golan, two kibbutzim located just south of Lake Kinneret. Their inhabitants had no desire to die, either. Ben-Gurion commented that he did not know how he would have reacted in their place.[86] The inhabitants of the kibbutz Nitzanim, in the south, were taken prisoner by the Egyptians. By the end of the war, about sixty thousand Jews were refugees, uprooted from neighborhoods, cities, kibbutzim, and other farming communities.[87] "Had the mufti captured the Old City in Jerusalem, he would have massacred all the Jews," said Ben-Gurion, and the mufti would have done the same had he reached Tel Aviv. Ben-Gurion later latched on to the claim that the Jews asked the Arabs to stay and that they fled only because they had been ordered to do so by their mufti. As usual, he remarked in this regard that the Zionists should be grateful to the mufti for all the mistakes he made.[88]

He wanted to believe that the Arab refugees would be absorbed by the neighboring countries so that the refugee problem would disappear of its own accord. "Everything will calm down and dissipate," he said. The Foreign Ministry fashioned this illusion into a political forecast. Ben-Gurion, who had devoted his life to achieving Jewish sovereignty, in fulfillment of the dispersed Jewish nation's long-held dream, failed to appreciate the unifying force of exile and the longing for the Palestinian homeland. At least one member of his Cabinet, Zisling, reminded him of that. "Hundreds of thousands of Arabs, they and their young children, will become our enemies. Just as we imbibed from our sufferings the feeling of a need for war, so they will bear within them the desire for revenge, reparation, and return."[89] But Ben-Gurion believed that time worked in Israel's favor. A million Jews, he maintained, would come in place of the Arabs.*

He sometimes brought up for discussion the possible return of the refugees, including those from Ramla and Lod, but these were largely diplomatic gestures aimed at enhancing Israel's image around the world; Israel at that point had not yet been accepted into the United Nations. "South Africa needs not compassion, help, and money, so it can allow itself to thumb its nose at the world," Ben-Gurion said. "We are not in the same position." That was also the reason that he averted, almost at the last minute, the deportation of the Arabs of Nazareth, in contradiction of the orders of the local military commander. At the time, he was also waiting for Israel's request for a loan of $100 million from the United States to be approved; it was just two weeks before the elections to the Constituent Assembly.[90] Thousands of refugees tried to infiltrate over the borders in order to return to their homes; preventing the return of refugees after the war, and the expulsion of "infiltrators," was an explicit Israeli policy that perpetuated their tragedy. Nevertheless, Ben-Gurion ordered that only "infiltrators" be deported, not refugees who had left their homes but remained within the borders of the State of Israel.[91] Once, in an especially emotional outburst, he spoke to them in the second-person plural, as if they had suddenly appeared in the Cabinet room: "You made war—you lost!"[92]

---

* The deportation of Ben-Gurion himself in 1915, "never to return," as the Ottoman document put it, became fixed in his mind as having occurred on the same date as Israel's establishment. "I was deported on May 15," he said at a Cabinet meeting in which the fate of the refugees was discussed. But the date he cited was incorrect. (Ben-Gurion to the Cabinet, June 25, 1961, ISA.)

"OUR SECRET WEAPON"

Levi Eshkol later related that, at his most difficult moments, Ben-Gurion used to hum to himself "It Is Burning," a 1938 song about the burning of a Jewish town. The residents call on their Jewish brethren to put out the flames with blood. From time to time he mentioned the Holocaust, generally as part of a political argument. "We will not go like sheep to the slaughter," he said during one of his last conversations with the high commissioner.[93] Hitler was not entirely original in his attempt to destroy an entire people, he also said: the Muslims had preceded him, he maintained, listing a long series of war crimes committed by Muslims from the time of Muhammad to the mufti's activity in Nazi Berlin. He also described the Arabs alternatively as Hitler's teachers, helpers, and pupils. They all knew only one way to solve the Jewish problem—total annihilation, he said. At such moments, he sounded as if this were his personal war against the Nazis.[94] He termed the aerial bombardment of Tel Aviv that took a toll of dozens of lives an "Egyptian Blitz."[95] As during the London Blitz, he sometimes refused to go down into a bomb shelter during the bombing, and as he had then, he took pride in it. "I see a psychosis of bombing" was how he responded to a proposal to move his office to a protected location. "I have more experience of this than all of you—I lived through it in London. The bombings are not so horrible."[96]

His admiration for Britain, its history, its culture, and its heroic spirit, remained undiminished, despite the fact that the British were supporting King Abdullah of Jordan's Arab Legion. He told the government almost nostalgically about England's finest hour, including the enlistment of British women in the war effort. "In London there was not a bus that was not run by women, from the driver to the ticket vendor. The same was true of the weapons factories." He maintained that women should be mobilized the same way in wartime Israel. In the dispute over his powers as commander in chief, Churchill's name often came up as an example of a civilian military leader whom Ben-Gurion sought to emulate.[97] He made "blood, sweat, and tears" speeches and often made use of the English term "D-Day."[98] When he stressed time and again that Israel needed to be prepared for a second Holocaust, he heightened the victory achieved under his leadership. In doing so, he fostered two myths that were seared into Israeli identity: the few versus the many, and the good versus the evil.

Before, during, and after the war, he often said that 700,000 people were facing off against 30 million, one Jew for every 40 Arabs. That heightened the danger and the victory as well.[99] That was both correct and incorrect. In Palestine, the demography changed rapidly. The Arab exile left a large Jewish majority, and over the course of 1948 more than 120,000 Jewish immigrants arrived.[100] Israel's fighting forces and those of the Arab states had an almost equal number of troops, as Ben-Gurion himself had explained at the end of 1948. "Up to this point the view was that the Arabs are the many and we the few, but that view is not correct. It is correct with regard to the total number of Arab inhabitants, but not with regard to the army fighting us." Both sides fielded about 100,000 soldiers; the IDF steadily grew stronger, thanks to equipment from overseas. But the Israeli version of the story, as a battle between an Israeli David and an Arab Goliath, was more potent than the numbers, and it was correct in some individual battles. Ben-Gurion continued to promote it for many years after the war.[101] From the vantage point of history, he told how it had all begun: "It was only thanks to the victory of Hebrew labor that a Jewish state was founded." In response to a letter he received about the subject, he repeated this no fewer than six times.[102]

He claimed again and again that the IDF's strength derived from Israel's moral superiority. "Our human material . . . has much greater moral and intellectual capacity than that of our neighbors," he maintained. He reiterated that countless times.[103] His belief in the IDF's moral preeminence was anchored in the moral and intellectual inferiority he had attributed to the Arabs for many years. "The Arabs are not sophisticated as we Europeans are," he said in this regard. After the war, he declared: "Other than Turkey, these nations are not able to fight."[104] He sometimes cited the difference between Israeli and Arab attitudes toward human life: "For our adversaries, the number of losses is not critical—they have many millions." At times he praised the way the Arabs fought, but even then as a way of magnifying the IDF's victory. Sometimes he boasted: "Up until now I thought that our secret weapon is our spirit, and that is indeed true," he said, "but our even more secret weapon is the Arabs: they are more bumbling than I can put into words."[105]

But he could also offer more mundane reasons for the Israeli victory, most specifically arms purchases, and the aid that Israel received from American Jewry, which included soldiers, military experts, and money. He once put it simply: "We won because the Arabs were exceptionally weak."[106]

❖

The war ended in March 1949, sixteen months after it began. The Arab states were unable to conquer Israel, and in the months that followed, armistice agreements were signed and temporary borders established—the so-called Green Line. It more or less coincided with the partition line that Ben-Gurion had marked off with his finger on the map Bevin had placed before him seven years previously. Jerusalem was divided between Israel and Jordan. The country's territory was about 40 percent larger than that awarded to the Jewish state in the UN partition resolution, with the additions providing Israel with the territorial continuity it would have lacked under that plan. The Arabs were left as a small minority in Israel, in keeping with the goals Ben-Gurion had spoken of since 1937. Those were the war's major achievements. "Outside of sorrow for the sons who fell, we have nothing to be sorry for in this war," he said.[107]

A few weeks before the war's end, Ben-Gurion wrote in his diary: "Peace is vital, but not at any cost." In the years that preceded independence, countless ideas about the disposition of Palestine had been suggested—partnerships, federations, partitions, autonomies, cantons, mandates, and trusteeships, almost every possibility imaginable. Some of them provided for settling the Jews in Europe's DP camps in Palestine. But none of the arrangements proposed as a way of averting war would have promised independence with a Jewish majority, which was Zionism's fundamental demand. War was probably inevitable, as Ben-Gurion himself had always maintained. "The war was a necessity foreseen," he said.[108] As he saw it, it was one of those historical moments in the life of a nation, a singular moment that would never occur again. It required a courageous decision, a violent and brutal one, that would serve as a new start and a transition into another and better age. At this stage, there was no reason to believe that the Arabs would willingly come to terms with a Jewish state in Palestine, so it was necessary to impose the state by force.

When Ben-Gurion led his generation into war, he took a calculated risk that was meant, in part, to improve the partition boundaries, while paying the price that this required. The price was heavy—close to six thousand Israeli dead, almost one out of every hundred, among them two thousand civilians. One out of every three of that toll was killed in Jerusalem or in the Negev. There were also twelve thousand wounded.*[109]

It may well be that the high number of casualties on the Israeli side was due to Ben-Gurion's failure to establish an army earlier, and on his insistence on conducting the war largely by himself. The glory of victory enhanced his political standing despite his faulty conduct of security affairs before the war and his flaws as a commander in chief during its progress, the exceptions being establishing a military industry and obtaining arms from overseas. He radiated khaki-tinged optimism. "One day a young amputee came to me, actually running," he told the Cabinet. "They made him a temporary prosthesis and he felt excellent. I was intoxicated by what I saw." He told of the cooperation between an English factory that made prostheses and his plans to found a similar one in Israel. "We will have an excellent plant," he promised; it opened a year and a half later.[110] It was a period of uncertainty—no one knew how to move forward to a permanent status agreement with Israel's neighbors. "The Arabs don't believe us, and I can understand that," Golda Meir said. Ben-Gurion responded: "Even more Jews don't believe us."[111] That was not accurate, but it reflected the sense of disappointment that had begun to gnaw at him. It was not the country he had hoped to found and lead.

---

* The losses incurred by the Arabs of Palestine remain unclear. They may have been greater than Israel's losses. The armies of the Arab states, taken together, seem to have lost fewer men than the Israelis. (Ben-Gurion, Diary, April 27, 1953; Sivan 1991.)

· 18 ·

NEW ISRAELIS

"LIKE WAR"

In the latter part of December 1949, the millionth Jew arrived in Israel. "It is good to be a million," cheered the poet Natan Alterman. A modest ceremony was held on the deck of the ship that was to set out to bring the first members of the second million. They were meant to be the fuel, the oxygen, the electricity, and the lifeblood that would propel the new country forward. But most of the Jews who arrived in the years that followed were broken people, emotionally in particular. They were penniless refugees, Holocaust survivors and Jews from the Islamic world. Like the archetypical kiosk proprietors who arrived in the 1920s, most of the newcomers had no interest in and no capacity for settling the land as pioneers or defending it as soldiers. They disappointed as "human material"; Ben-Gurion referred to them as "human debris." He longed for Zionism's primal era. "There was a different sort of human material in the country then," he said.[1] The Jews of the United States, the human material that he would have welcomed, continued to choose to remain in America; the Soviet Union's Jews were not allowed to leave. It was one of the major challenges Israel faced in its early years. It vexed Ben-Gurion and eroded his ability to lead the country.

The period was one of the most difficult of Ben-Gurion's life. Israel's economic frailty endangered its very existence; and even after the armistice, war with the Arabs had become routine. Only one out of every three Israelis voted for Mapai, but almost everything seemed to depend solely on him. The enormous responsibility sapped his strength. His fatigue mounted year by year. As prime minister, he reached the pinnacle of his career, but attaining that post also marked the beginning of his decline. As the Zionist dream achieved its goal, it lost its heady potency; what it now needed, principally, was a manager.

❖

They came in a huge tidal wave; the rate of their arrival recalls the million Jews whom Ben-Gurion once said he wanted to bring, all at once, on a thousand ships. By the end of 1950, Israel's Jewish population had doubled; Ben-Gurion noted that the number of Jews who had arrived in the state's first thirty months was equal to the number who had arrived in the thirty years of the British Mandate—about half a million. He calculated that were the United States to increase its population proportionally, it would have to take in thirty million people in a year. "Of all the miracles in our history, none has been like this one," he wrote in his diary. He told the Knesset that history had never seen such a small country, in a state of war, absorb so many immigrants.[2]

As in the past, they came for many reasons. The war in Palestine had caused Jews in Arab countries to be labeled enemy agents and to become targets for revenge. Jews in Eastern Europe, which had in the meantime fallen under Communist rule, also encountered animosity. All of them longed for a better life, free of prejudice and persecution. Some experienced a Zionist awakening of a religious or secular kind, in many cases as a response to the Holocaust. Not all came willingly. Israel urged them to leave, made the necessary arrangements, and paid for passage, in direct contact with national leaders who sought to rid their countries of their Jews. A few countries demanded that Israel pay for each exit permit, the price in dollars ranging from two to three figures per head. Ben-Gurion said it was blackmail, but declared: "Immigration is not an economic matter. It is more like war." That summed up his views on Israel's national security.[3] The thirty-year-old Zionist enterprise, including the expulsion and flight of the Arabs and the victory in the War of Independence, was not able to guarantee the country's existence. His aim was four million Jews. "It's a life-or-death question for us," he wrote.[4] And, for him, almost all the newcomers, Holocaust survivors and Jews from the Islamic world, were foreign and alien. They were Jews, he said, "only in the sense that they are not non-Jews."[5]

The Jews from the Islamic world were needed as a replacement for "the selected members of the nation," as Ben-Gurion referred to the Holocaust's victims, who were Eastern European Jews endowed with the capacities needed for building the Jewish state. They had stood "at the forefront of the Jewish people," he wrote, "both in quantity and quality," and were the "prime candidates for immigration." But they were murdered: "The country came into being and did not find the people who had awaited it."[6] The Zionist movement thus had to seek out the Jews of the Islamic lands, "something to fill up, at least a bit, the empty space left by the victims of the Holocaust."[7] Up to that point, the Zionist leadership had evinced only a marginal, folkloristic interest in these communities.

Prior to World War II, Ben-Gurion had not seen them as real partners in the Zionist enterprise. "We gave no attention to what was going on in Persia and Iraq," he later recounted. He seems to have become aware of them gradually, during the war. As he increasingly grasped the scale of the slaughter of Europe's Jews, he began to consider bringing the Jews of Yemen and Morocco to Israel.[8] But, as he saw it, the Jews of the Arab countries were a poor substitute for the murdered Jews of Europe. In recent centuries, he explained, the Jews of the Islamic world had played only a "passive role" in the history of the Jewish people. The lands in which they resided were replete with ignorance, poverty, and slavery, and had fallen far behind the European nations, who had experienced rapid progress. "The state of the Jews is like the state of the gentiles," he said. "The divine presence withdrew from the eastern Jewish communities and they had little or no influence on the Jewish people."[9] They thus had no place in his Zionist dream, nor that of other members of his generation. "We came here as Europeans," he maintained. "Our roots are in the east and we are returning to the east, but we bear European culture with us. We will not want to cut off either our ties or Palestine's ties to European culture."[10] That was the common wisdom in the Zionist movement, advocated by Ze'ev Jabotinsky as well. "We, the Jews," he said, "have nothing in common with what is called 'the east,' thank God."*[11]

Ben-Gurion also had an aversion to the Holocaust survivors who were settling in Israel. "Among the survivors of the German concentration camps," he said, "were people who, were they not what they were—hard and bad and egotistical people—would not have survived, and everything they endured purged their souls of all good." He was disappointed. For many generations the Jews had been a nation without a country, he pondered; now there was a danger that they would have a state without a people.[12] He wanted to upgrade the human material coming into Israel, and quite naturally thought of the United States. "North America," he wrote, "settled by waves of immigration from all the European lands and some Asiatic ones, along with the blacks who were brought as slaves from Africa, is a melting pot similar to Israel." The usual term for this was the "melding of the exiles." It was an attempt to assimilate the newcomers into Israeli society and make them forget where they came from "just as I have forgotten that I am Polish," as he told the Knesset. The idea itself had been with him for many years, appearing in a draft constitution he had published twenty-five years previously. He sometimes put it in biological terms—the children of the next generation were meant to be New Jews, those Israeli natives whose physical prowess as laborers, fighters, and heroes so enthralled him.[13]

---

* Ben-Gurion's first encounters with non-Ashkenazi Jews were in Izmir and on the deck of the ship that brought him to Palestine for the first time. "They dress like Arabs," he remarked at the time. In 1951 the Jews from Arab countries made up about half of the immigrants. That proportion rose in the years that followed—more than 70 percent in 1951–53, up to a height of 90 percent in 1955. (Ben-Gurion to his father, undated, in Erez 1971, p. 71; Ben-Gurion, "Netzah Yisra'el," in Ben-Gurion 1964a, p. 157; Ben-Gurion to the Cabinet, July 12, 1950, ISA; Cohen-Friedheim 2011, p. 318; Ben-Gurion, Diary, Nov. 13, 1951, BGA.)

"TWO NATIONS"

Cabinet ministers and Knesset members, the press and sociologists often spoke patronizingly about the Jews of the Islamic world, sometimes in racist terms.[14] For the most part, Ben-Gurion spoke of how foreign he felt them to be. "We are alien to them and they are alien to us," he said. From time to time he also used the expressions "two tribes," "two peoples," and "two nations." Thousands of years separated the two, on the one side the "cultured and educated," on the other "primitive Jews." The Yemenite father, he maintained, "does not look after his children and family as we do, and he is not accustomed to feed his children fully before he eats himself."[15] He once apologized for bringing up a subject that was not easy to speak of around the Cabinet table; he tried to persuade his colleagues that outhouses rather than bathrooms should be built for such immigrants. "These people do not know how to make hygienic use of a toilet in the home," he argued. "Maybe we can educate the next generation in that. But not this generation." Golda Meir differed, but Ben-Gurion stood his ground—an indoor toilet would be a catastrophe for them.[16]

But, most of all, he feared that the Jews of the Arab countries would not contribute to the country's defense and might actually be detrimental. That was one of the chilling predictions he shared with his Cabinet in a frank moment. He had no doubt that the Arabs were readying themselves for another round of war, and as such he did not dismiss the possibility that Israel could be destroyed. But instead of fortifying its military, the state was investing in the absorption of immigrants who did nothing to bolster the army. "A mob will not fight in the conditions that we will have to fight in for our survival, and the ingathering of the exiles is bringing us a mob," he said.[17]

❖

Briefings by the IDF's chief of staff Yadin and his deputy, Mordechai Maklef, painted a grim picture for the Cabinet. Eight out of every ten new recruits had arrived in Israel less than two years before their induction; 90 percent of them did not know Hebrew. "The intelligence level is very low," Yadin told the ministers, possibly referring to the amount of schooling they had received.

"It is so low," he said, "that it constitutes a security risk." He meant soldiers from North Africa in particular. Ben-Gurion spoke of a "substandard generation." He added that "almost all those who are going into the police force, like those going into the army, are refuse." He feared that the IDF's ethnic composition was detrimental to its qualitative superiority. "If our army as a whole gets to the level of the Syrian army, we're done for," he told his ministers. He repeated that sentiment a few months later: "Our entire advantage, our entire defense, is built solely on our quality, that our soldier is superior to the Arab soldier . . . that is our most precious asset."[18]

He meant not only the inferior combat capacities of the recruits; they were undisciplined as well. They committed crimes against Arabs. In a passage that the editors of his war diary omitted when they prepared it for publication, he described soldiers who had come from North Africa as "difficult human material." Specifically, "their cultural level is low, they use knives, there are cases of rape."[19] When a Cabinet minister questioned him about this information, Yadin confirmed it. These were Jews, he suggested by way of explanation, who had been oppressed by the Arabs and now suddenly found themselves with the upper hand.[20] Ben-Gurion hoped the education that the IDF provided to Jews from Arab countries would counteract their criminal inclinations. "To teach a young man from these countries to sit on a toilet like a human being, to wash himself, not to steal, not to grab an Arab girl, rape her, and murder her—that comes before everything else." For a brief moment he felt an unexpected longing: "We don't have the boys who grew up here," he said, mentioning specifically the Palmach soldiers who had completed their service and been discharged.[21] He suggested a special appeal to the Jews of the West to send Israel young people "of high quality." Foreign Minister Moshe Sharett told the Soviet Union's deputy foreign minister, Andrey Vyshinsky, that Israel needed Jews from Russia, because it could not depend on the resilience of Moroccan Jews.[22] Another security risk was the physical resemblance between Jews from the Arab countries and the Arabs living in Israel. People might think that an Arab attacker was a Jew and thus not be on guard. "Is it such a big deal to go into a movie theater, throw a bomb, and run away?" he asked.[23] Arab terror brought back the atmosphere of the years preceding the War of Independence— during the five years following the war, about 175 Israelis were killed in such attacks, on average almost three a month.[24]

He wrote that the problem was a "racial" one, putting that term in quotation marks. He reluctantly suggested that, in Israel, "an ostensibly 'superior' race, the Ashkenazi race, stands out and in practice leads the nation, as
opposed to an eastern race of "'inferior level.'"[25] More than fifteen years later,
he would say, "We did not take care of them," and ten years after that he
would admit, "We greatly sinned against some eastern Jews."[*26]

"I AM ASHAMED"

The first several tens of thousands to arrive, both Europeans and Asians, were
settled in homes that had emptied of their Arab residents. This completed a
population transfer. Some of the deserted Arab villages were in very poor
physical shape. Just as Shlomo Lavi had once complained about the state of
the Arab houses into which the Ein Harod settlers moved, Ben-Gurion lamented the filthy and fly-ridden state of the shacks and shambles that the
Arabs had left behind. "The more property, the more worry," he remarked.[27]
When the Arab homes were filled and the tidal wave of immigrants continued, they were settled in tent camps; many had at first to make do with living
conditions no better than those in the Arab refugee camps that had been set
up in neighboring countries, and harsher than those of the DP camps in
Europe and the detention camps in Cyprus.

Ben-Gurion took a great interest in the camps for new arrivals; the reports he received told him of great hardship. The tents were densely packed
together; the camps lacked running water and adequate sanitary facilities.
The provisions supplied to the immigrants were insufficient and the specific
food items provided were not what many of them were used to eating. Many
of the immigrants brought illnesses with them. Ben-Gurion received data on
the large number of tuberculosis cases. "An eight-year-old girl with active
tuberculosis sleeps in the same bed with her brothers and sisters, six of them
in a tiny room," he wrote in his diary. The disease was especially common

---

* Shlomo Zemach compared Ben-Gurion's attitude toward the Jews of Arab lands with his
attitude toward the Arabs. He had initially argued that peace with the Zionist movement
would raise the level of the Arabs. That was an "idiotic claim," Zemach said. "We've now
reached the level that we have 'Jewish Arabs,' and we Ashkenazim are treating them condescendingly." (Zemach 1996, May 3, 1963, p. 64.)

among newcomers from Yemen and Turkey. There were other epidemics as well, among them polio and eye ailments. There were not enough doctors, medical equipment, or medicines. There were schools for only some of the children, and many of the teachers lacked appropriate training. Many of the residents of the camps had no work, and none of them knew how long they would be there. They were subject to the whims of officials who could not communicate with them in their languages, and were at the mercy of swindlers, scalpers, and party hacks. Understandably, the immigrants were depressed, resentful, and frustrated. Ben-Gurion also received a report on a burgeoning amount of prostitution.[28]

At the end of 1949, nearly one hundred thousand immigrants, or one out of every ten Israelis, were living in the camps. Given that tens of millions of indigent refugees had roamed through Europe after the Holocaust and the world war, it was not a big story. But placed against Ben-Gurion's expectations and his definition of the Jewish state's purpose, the situation in the camps bordered on a humanitarian disaster. In summing up the first year of Israel's independence, he acknowledged that the country's absorption efforts had failed. As usual in such cases, he spoke in the plural. "It turns out that we are not yet prepared for this task," he said.[29] Speaking to the Knesset in January 1950, he accused the kibbutz movement of neglecting the absorption effort. "I am ashamed" of them, he said, as if he were not responsible for the government's immigration and absorption efforts. Unsurprisingly, he set off a storm of protest.[30]

In February 1950, Ben-Gurion decided to devote himself to a study of the absorption problem. As he did when he prepared his seminar on the Haganah, he drafted a list of questions.[31] He was cognizant not only of the plight of the Jews of the Arab lands but also of the need to improve their public image and to facilitate their integration into Israeli society. He compared racist acts against them to those committed by whites against blacks in Africa.[32] He did not want to be a racist, but in his view there was a real cultural problem that he had not anticipated prior to the Holocaust. Just as, not wanting to be a prophet of war, he repeatedly declared his belief in peace, he also proclaimed again and again that the Jews from the Islamic world were not inferior to European Jews, and that it was only a matter of time until the two merged into a single nation. "There is no basis for the assumption that the Jews of North Africa, or of Turkey, Egypt, Persia, or Aden are qualitatively and fundamentally different from the Jews of Lithuania, Galicia, and America," he said when he introduced the compulsory military service law to the Knesset, adding, "In them, too, are hidden rich springs of pioneering capacity, springs of heroism and creation. If we invest here, as well, the efforts we made with Jewish youth in the lands of Europe—we will receive the same welcome results."[33]

A visit to one of the camps led him to the conclusion that the IDF needed to be mobilized to deal with the situation. The army needed to provide not only water and medical services, but also counseling and instruction. The army would be the real melting pot that would forge everyone "through Jewish brotherhood and military discipline . . . into a nation renewing its youth."[34] He proposed conscripting the immigrants for labor "without individual profit" under a military or "paramilitary" regime that would give them a working knowledge of Hebrew and "national discipline." It was an echo of the "large commune" or "labor army" that he had suggested twenty-five years previously. A special committee was set up to study the idea, but it met with considerable opposition and was dropped.[35]

In May 1950, the people in the immigrant camps began to be transferred into new facilities that were called *ma'abarot*. Living conditions were meant to be better, and their residents were supposed to work in government employment programs, paving roads and planting trees. Within a few months, more than a hundred ma'abarot had been established, home to some eighteen thousand families and a total population of about fifty thousand. The reports Ben-Gurion read continued to be a source of great concern. He was informed that the infant mortality rate in the ma'abarot was twice that of the rest of the country. A few months later, he wrote: "The comrade in charge of the ma'abarot notes a frightening moral decline—they don't work, sell food to children, black market, gangsters." The transit camp population had risen by then to some one hundred thousand, but only a third of the adult men had jobs. The reports did not improve: "The ma'abarot are a cancer," he wrote in his diary in 1952. The following year he was told that tens of thousands of Israelis were starving; 90 percent of them were Jews from the Islamic world. One Mapai leader warned that the ma'abarot "are poisoning the air," by which he meant that they were endangering Mapai's standing; he demanded that they be dismantled. Some of the ma'abarot, established on the margins of cities, transformed in time into poverty-stricken neighborhoods.[36]

In the first half of April 1950, an organization representing Yemenite immigrants sent a complaint to the police minister regarding the disappearance of a five-month-old baby who had been hospitalized. "All trace of the baby has been lost and the father's searches have produced nothing," the complaint said. The police did not immediately investigate despite reminders that the organization sent. In the meantime, further cases came to light of Yemenite babies who had disappeared after being taken for medical care. A rumor soon started spreading that there was an organized operation to abduct Yemenite infants and sell them into adoption, in Israel and in other countries. This scandal would metamorphose into a myth that haunted the country for many years thereafter. Later investigations found that most of the children, several hundred of them, had in fact died and had been buried, but the parents were not notified.[37]

Bringing hundreds of thousands of Jews to Israel in such a short period of time, before homes and jobs and hospitals and schools had been prepared for them, was a direct outgrowth of the Zionist faith of Ben-Gurion and his contemporaries. They believed in the "liquidation of the Diaspora," meaning an end to Jewish life outside the Jewish state.[38] As he saw it, the country's needs justified the suffering that was involved in absorbing the masses who arrived. "Had we not brought them in in an insane way," he said, "had we not brought 700,000 Jews in then without thinking about it twice, 700,000 Arabs would inevitably have returned. There's nothing we could have done to stop it. By bringing in 700,000 Jews, we blocked the way for them."[39]

The winters of 1950 and 1951 were particularly harsh; heavy snow fell almost all over the country. Public censure of the immigrants' treatment grew more vehement, eventually leading some to demand that the immigration rate be slowed. "We are destroying and enfeebling these people," said one senior absorption official. The key concepts in the debate were regulation and selection, meaning that only those who had potential for successful absorption and who could meet the country's needs should be allowed to immigrate. Ben-Gurion was adamant: "People can live in tents for years. Anyone who doesn't want to live in one shouldn't come."[40] Those who wanted to limit immigration were racists, he charged. "They see no need for the blacks, these niggers, they see no need for this whole business," he said disgustedly.[41] In line with his policy since the days of the Bricha, he ordered that immigrants be brought in as rapidly as possible, on the grounds that they later might not be able or willing to come. Reports sent by Israel immigration emissaries in Morocco might well have reminded him of the early reports he had received during World War II. One of them asked: "Have we done and are we doing everything possible, even under current conditions in Israel and our difficult financial position, to save those children and families who can be saved?" It was a question pervaded by the memory of the Holocaust.[42] In the same context, Ben-Gurion also pushed for a higher birthrate.*

At the same time, large numbers of young men, veterans of the war, were discharged from the army; many could not find work. The country was living largely off loans and grants from overseas, and it funded part of its budget deficit by printing money and a mandatory bond issue. In April 1949, Ben-Gurion announced an austerity program that included strict price controls and the rationing of food, services, and raw materials, as well as foreign currency controls.[43]

"A MINIMUM FOR ALL"

At times he said that he did not understand the laws of economics, that they were a "sham" that he didn't get. His contribution during Cabinet meetings on economic matters largely took the form of questions and trivial interjections, some of them comic. "King Solomon did not wait for private capital, and neither can we," he asserted at one meeting.[44] Just as the inadequacy of his military knowledge on the eve of the war led him to grasp at the fine details of army operations, he now regaled the Cabinet with data on the inventory of soap and pickled fish, milk powder and iron, fodder and tea, nylon

---

* A year after independence, Ben-Gurion announced a prize of one hundred Israeli pounds for every mother who had given birth to at least ten living children. Arab women were also eligible, but the assumption was that Arab families of this size included more than one mother, so the chance that any one of them would win the prize was not high. (Ben-Gurion to the Cabinet, July 5, 1949, ISA; Ben-Gurion to Bluma Klein (Herzl), Sept. 22, 1949, BGA; Dorit Rosen, interview transcript, BGA; "Beshulei Devarim—Hapras Lemi?" *Davar*, Nov. 14, 1949.)

stockings and false teeth. He grasped the general picture only vaguely; he was aware of the cost of the Zionist enterprise, but did not really understand the economic systems needed to fund it and propel it forward. "You talk without understanding the issue," Finance Minister Kaplan rebuked him.[45]

The austerity policy grew out of an almost mystical belief in the power of bureaucracy to control market forces. Part of it involved a debate over fundamental ideological principles. Ben-Gurion declared that Israel was not a socialist country, but not a capitalist one, either. His government did not seek to impose equality on society, he promised—not yet. But neither was it prepared to permit "abundance for the few." The goal was "a minimum for all." He argued with the advocates of free enterprise, and sought to draw lessons from the American New Deal. He believed the public would cooperate, but he was wrong. The common wisdom was that the bureaucracy that enforced the austerity regulations was corrupt; everyone who was able to do so got around the rules. A black market bloomed and operated, almost completely in the open, in every economic sector. It was for all intents and purposes a mass act of middle-class civil disobedience.[46] He had a hard time accepting this. "Horrible," he said. "This is, after all, our economy and our honor . . . this phenomenon sullies the country's reputation." He declared that he would stand at the vanguard of the war against the black market, despite the political risk involved. "I will go all out against the black market," he said. "Find someone else to deal with the other stuff."*[47]

The black market gradually came to an end as the economic situation improved. In the meantime, tens of thousands of public housing units were built for the inhabitants of the immigrant camps. Hundreds of new settlements were also founded for them, many of them along the country's borders.[48] All this was meant to be part of a "profound human revolution," as Ben-Gurion termed it, and a fundamental transformation of human values.

He would soon have to address a traumatic identity crisis with particular

---

* The IDF Archives preserves copies of thank-you letters that Paula Ben-Gurion sent to several of her overseas acquaintances after receiving packages of food and clothing, items she could not have obtained legally in Israel. She also frequently requested gifts from her husband's aides and associates—warm winter pajamas from one, a refrigerator from another, a set of dinner plates from a third. (Paula to Teddy Kollek, Dec. 1, 1953, Rachel Gindi to Paula, Nov. 8, 1960, IDFA 492/2011; Robert Szold, interview transcript.)

impact on Israel's Yemenite Jews. "I have a weakness for Yemenites," he wrote. "They are different from all the other communities I am acquainted with."[49] But his acquaintance with them was superficial, replete with prejudice. His attempt to smelt them in his Israeli melting pot almost toppled his government.

"FOR US IT IS BARBARIC"

The Yemenites were seen as authentic, as a surviving remnant of the biblical Hebrews. Indeed, many of them knew Hebrew, even if they spoke it with a heavy accent that was difficult for others to understand. Yitzhak Gruenbaum, the first minister of the interior, believed that uprooting them from their homes in Yemen and bringing them to Israel would be harmful both to them and to Israel, and others agreed. But Ben-Gurion ordered that they all be brought in, every last one. Their "children are dying like flies," he maintained. "We must save them." Many of them were hospitalized as soon as they arrived. He went to visit them. "It is one of the most frightening things I have ever seen," he said immediately thereafter, in a powerful and emotional speech. The children he saw looked more like skeletons than human beings, he related. "The spark of life could be seen only in their eyes, the eyes of Jewish children, precious children, and Jewish doctors and nurses are caring for them with devotion, with love." It was like a revelation: "I was horror-stricken and stupefied by that great and terrible vision. Yes, these are the birth pangs of the Messiah."[50]

He had been acquainted with Yemenite Jewry since they were first brought to Palestine at the beginning of the twentieth century as a substitute for Arab laborers; he seems never to have forgotten the role they played in the campaign for Hebrew labor.

His expectation that the IDF would serve as a melting pot was realized at a very slow pace, at best. But he promised the maximum—one day the IDF would have a chief of staff "from among our Yemenite brothers," he wrote to Yisrael Yeshayahu, a Yemenite member of the Knesset for Mapai. It was a prediction he often repeated. He also sought a Yemenite candidate for the post of Israel's president.[51]

Women sent as soldiers to the camps counseled women and taught Hebrew, but Ben-Gurion wanted a more fundamental change. "The abyss between Yemenite men and women is terrible," he wrote. One of the things he was referring to was the marriage of young girls, an accepted practice in Yemen. "For us it is barbaric," he said at a Cabinet meeting.[52]

When he directed Yadin to deploy the army to extricate the Jews of Yemen from the ignorance he attributed to them, he warned him: "The soul of the Yemenite must be understood and his habits must be treated with respect, and they should be changed with good manners and by presenting an example."[53] But by the time the directive made its way down to the field, it had become a deliberate effort to impose secular education on the Yemenites. Their "primitiveness" was equated with their religious lifestyle. Boys and girls were put into coeducational classrooms and boys were required to cut off their sidelocks and to stop putting on tefillin, worn by Jewish men during morning prayers. The food they were given did not always meet their standards of religious dietary observance. One IDF officer working in the camps persuaded its residents to use contraception to lower the birthrate.

Ben-Gurion was shocked when he heard about the secular coercion in the camps. "These are horrible things," he said. "Not letting someone put on tefillin is an act fit for Sodom and Gomorrah." If it turned out to be true, he added, "not only will the government not survive, neither will the country."[54] He agreed to set up several inquiries and promised the minister of religion, Yehuda Leib Maimon, of the United Religious Front, "I will not take part in any government that is responsible for such actions." Without waiting for the outcome of the official inquiry, he sent several army officers to the camps. They reported back that the stories about secular coercion, including the cutting off of sidelocks, were baseless. Other inquiries confirmed the stories.[55]

The affair quickly ballooned into a power struggle over the souls of the inhabitants of the camps, and threatened to turn into a crisis of national identity. "We now face a situation in which an entire generation of religious children has been done away with," said Minister of Health Moshe Shapira, also of the United Religious Front. They had, he said, "been taken from their parents" and sent to secular schools. You could already see Yemenite Jews smoking on the Sabbath, he complained. It was, he said, "a death sentence against religious education." He was especially furious about the religious schools sponsored by the labor movement via the Histadrut, which competed with those run by the religious movements. Ben-Gurion refused to give in on this point. "You have no monopoly over religious Jews," he declared again and again. He claimed that the Yemenites were more tolerant than Shapira and the other members of his party.*[56]

Nevertheless, he tried to confine the dispute. When Shapira demanded that parents be allowed to choose freely what schools their children would attend, Ben-Gurion immediately agreed. "I am with you," he said, maintaining that the Yemenite community should be provided with religious education as they understood it, as long as it included basic core studies, including arithmetic. This brought the issue back into the realm of political give-and-take. "I presume that if there is goodwill, we will be able to reach a fair arrangement on this matter," he said, summing up an especially acrimonious Cabinet debate.[57] He was acutely apprehensive about a culture war, which would, he said, "be a greater danger than any external enemy."[58]

"WERE I RELIGIOUS"

On October 28, 1952, Ben-Gurion went to the home of Rabbi Avrohom Yeshaya Karelitz, who was commonly referred to as the Hazon Ish, that being the title of his magnum opus on Jewish religious law. He was one of the great halachic minds of his generation. The audience visit lasted only about fifty minutes, but was as much the subject of anticipation as a historical summit conference. Ben-Gurion's military secretary, Nehemiah Argov, had visited the rabbi for a preliminary meeting. When they arrived, a huge crowd stood in front of the house. Ben-Gurion brought his aide Yitzhak Navon. Both of them wore hats. The Hazon Ish, then seventy-five years old, lived in quite ascetic conditions. He received them in his one-room home; it was furnished with a bed and a bookcase; they sat at the dining table. Ben-Gurion said that he had come to ask how religious and nonreligious Jews could live together in Israel. The rabbi responded with a story from the Babylonian

---

* Ben-Gurion argued that the Yemenite Jews were tolerant because, unlike Polish Jews, they had not been influenced by the fanaticism of the Catholic Church. (Ben-Gurion to the Cabinet, Jan. 18, 1951, ISA.)

Talmud (Sanhedrin 32b) about two boats on a narrow river; if they both try to pass, they will both sink. Likewise, if two camels meet on a narrow and steep ascent and both try to pass, they will both fall. If one ship or camel bears a load and the other does not, the one without the load should allow the one with the load to precede it. According to Navon, the rabbi explained: "We religious Jews are like the camel bearing the load. We bear the yoke of many commandments. You must clear the way for us." On Navon's account, Ben-Gurion responded by tapping himself on the shoulder and saying: "And does this camel not bear a yoke of commandments? Is the precept to settle the land not a commandment? . . . And what about the boys whom you so oppose, who stand on the borders and protect you, is that not a commandment?" The Hazon Ish objected that many Israelis drove to the beach on the Sabbath instead of praying and studying. "It is outrageous and shocking to see such desecration of the Sabbath in the land of our forefathers," he said. "I don't drive to the beach on the Sabbath," Ben-Gurion responded, but he said that others should be allowed to do so. "It's their right," he said, adding: "Do you think that if they do not go to the beach, they will go to synagogue?" The rabbi said: "We believe that a day will come when everyone will observe the Sabbath and pray." Ben-Gurion responded that he had no objection, but that this could not be forced on people. "There should be no religious coercion and no antireligious coercion, each person should live as he sees fit." But the rabbi could not accept that. They parted without having reached an agreement, but they established the foundation for a working relationship. The encounter reinforced Ben-Gurion's belief that it was useless to get into debates over principle with Orthodox Jews. He recalled that the Hazon Ish had listened to him with a droll smile. "He has the face and eyes of a spiritual man," he reported. But he made no mention himself of the parable of the ships and the camels. He viewed the Hazon Ish's willingness to receive him at his home as an achievement in and of itself. Another Haredi leader, Yitzchok Zev (Velvel) Soloveitchik, known as the Brisker rabbi, refused.[59]

❖

His connections with the leaders of the religious public had always been based on four principles. First, the nature of the relationship between religion and state should not be defined by law. To every extent possible, theological debates should be avoided. Differences should be settled politically.

Second, there is no symmetry between religious and secular Jews. The religious population was divided into a number of different groups, but they all shared a willingness to defend the fundamentals of their faith zealously. Most nonreligious Jews were not so fervent. The Haredi welfare minister, Yitzhak-Meir Levin, told the Cabinet: "If we face the choice of transgressing the laws of Moses or the laws of the state, we will violate the laws of the state, not those of Moses." Nonreligious Jews did not generally face such a dilemma.[60] "I am familiar with your view of Judaism," Ben-Gurion wrote to a well-known rabbi, "and while I dispute some parts of that view, I would never reject it as worthless . . . in contrast, you are obliged to reject any view that is inconsistent with tradition as you understand it." The upshot was that nonreligious Jews could make more concessions, as they had done on the eve of the partition resolution of 1947, when they consented to leave a monopoly over marriage and divorce to the official rabbinate. So it was also when Ben-Gurion agreed to exempt yeshiva students from military service. His critics called that capitulating to religious extortion and preferring religious strictures to the conscience of the individual. Golda Meir warned that there were members of Mapai who were prepared to launch a religious war.[61]

The third principle was that the state should provide basic religious services to its observant citizens, without regard for their political position or the composition of the governing coalition. One of these was religious education.[62] The fourth principle grew out of Ben-Gurion's many years of political experience—it is easier to work with religious politicians in the government than with a religious opposition, because when they were Cabinet ministers they had more to lose and were thus less combative. It was this insight that once led him to offer Yeshayahu Leibowitz a place on Mapai's Knesset slate. Leibowitz, a respected scientist, was active in a small religious party. He claimed that he told Ben-Gurion that he would accept the offer on three conditions, one of them being separation of religion and state. Ben-Gurion responded: "I will never agree to separate religion from the state. I want the state to keep religion in a grip."[63]

❖

His partnership with the religious parties went from one crisis to another. In the initial years following independence, there was no subject that occupied the government more often. The debate over the observance of the Sabbath in public spaces seemed at the time to be one of the country's life-or-death issues. Minister of Religions Maimon wanted to forbid all transportation on the Sabbath, including private vehicles. Ben-Gurion warned the religious Cabinet ministers not to go too far with their demands: "If the aim is to give the rabbis additional legal authority—it won't go through." Whatever the case, he reiterated from time to time: "We see a need for us to sit together, if that is possible."[64] He generally came toward the religious parties, often using a conciliatory tone that could even be obsequious. "I am not a religious person," he said, "but were I religious, I would seek a way to adapt religion to the needs of the state, because, if there is a conflict, the state will win." He claimed to be trying to prevent such conflict. If that were possible, "we will be happy," he said.

So they argued again and again over the demand to forbid the importation of pork (Ben-Gurion was opposed); to establish a religious university (he opposed that as well); to open Knesset sessions with a prayer given by a rabbi (also); to close stores on the Sabbath, to prevent public transportation from running on the Sabbath, and to require special permits for work on the Sabbath (he agreed); to establish special units for religious soldiers and to end autopsies (he opposed); to exempt religious soldiers from the IDF's swearing-in ceremony (he opposed); and to end the death penalty (as he favored doing).[65]

On occasion he tried to demonstrate that he knew traditional Jewish texts better than they did. It was usually a mistake. Such moments sounded like the conversations he sometimes conducted with intellectuals—he spoke philosophy, they spoke politics. But for the Haredim, who rejected Zionism, Ben-Gurion was tantamount to a foreign ruler who was imposing horrible strictures on the Jews. Living in Israel, they felt like they were living in the Exile, Ben-Gurion wrote.[66]

It was a long series of power struggles. They sometimes sent thousands of demonstrators into the street. The compromises reached under Ben-Gurion's leadership exhibited his political acumen, his experience, and, more than anything else, his patience. He was at his best with religious politicians.

A great portion of the agreements were reached by allotting public money to religious programs and institutions.[67] That enabled him to further other national issues that were more vital, as he saw it. But the partnership was not an easy one to manage. On more than one occasion he pumped himself up with fighting spirit, as he knew how to do. Once he warned that, if he did not resist the demands of the religious parties, Israel would end up with two governments, just as the Catholic Church had had two popes in the fourteenth century. He said that anarchy was a worse danger than the enemies' weapons, and declared that his religious colleagues had caused a crisis more severe than that of the *Altalena*.[68] Once or twice he resigned. Then they compromised and everything was as it had been before, as if nothing had happened. Soon the government would collapse over economic policy; elections were held in July 1951.

❖

At that time, long speeches at mass rallies were still customary. But this time—a first—it was not an ideology that was being voted up or down, but rather a leader. Mapai placed Ben-Gurion front and center in its election campaign. As always, he put great effort and much time into the fight, meticulously tracking all the arrangements. His appearances drew huge crowds. Many of those who attended could not yet understand what he was saying, because their Hebrew was not yet fluent; they did not come to listen but to see him. For the first time he tried an American election campaign standard, "five minutes in a car," as he put it. He went from one ma'abarah to another, showed himself but did not speak, and rushed on to the next camp. The residents greeted him as if he were the Messiah, wrote one journalist, Amos Elon.[69] Ben-Gurion attended weddings and circumcision ceremonies, and, less than three months before the election, he set out on a victory tour of the United States, which included meetings with President Truman and Albert Einstein and an open-air car ride from the Waldorf Astoria hotel to City Hall. Three weeks before the election, he wrote in his diary: "I gave a directive to build an additional room for a Yemenite woman with three children in Kfar Uriah Bet, whose husband has another wife with four children."[70]

Mapai remained the largest party. It received more than a quarter of a million votes and 45 of the 120 seats in the Knesset, leaving its strength almost unchanged. As in the past, that was not enough to form a government without partners. Most of its voters were newcomers. The centrist General Zionists gained strength among established Israelis after speaking out against the government's economic policy and mass immigration. "We did not receive a majority, we are far from a majority," Ben-Gurion said, but he consoled himself with the fact that the party had gained strength in several cities. "A great victory for the party, a failure for the country" was how he put it.[71] Given that he was the emblem of the founding of the state and its victory in the War of Independence, it was to a great extent his personal failure.

The alliance with the religious factions, which joined the new coalition, proved itself once more. All parties understood one another, as Ben-Gurion had said even before the election.[72] His religious colleagues shared the burden of their joint government's failures. In 1953, Ben-Gurion's policies were dealt a heavy blow when, for the first time, the number of Jews who left Israel to live elsewhere—most of them of European origin—exceeded the number of immigrants who arrived.[73] On this point it was important for him to remind future readers of his diary how this had come to be: "What needs to be remembered is that the Jewish public that needed a state, and was capable of building one and likely to do so, was exterminated by Hitler."[74]

"TIME MUST BE FOUND!"

The transition from the era of the Jewish Agency and the National Council to the era of independence went fairly smoothly, almost without disturbance. The institutions of the state-in-the-making, some of them put in place under Ben-Gurion's leadership, proved themselves—in the areas of justice, education, health, and community organization, among others. Ben-Gurion was the leader and symbol of this continuity. His style of working and making decisions as prime minister was not fundamentally different from the way he operated as head of the Jewish Agency—he assumed an almost unbearable load.

About four months after the war's end, he had one of those days that impelled him to write down, as one of his first tasks as prime minister: "Time must be found! How to manage within the bounds of twenty-four hours in a day!" That morning he paid a visit to a police force training base. He drove back with Moshe Dayan, at the time the commander of Jerusalem and coordinator of the armistice agreements. Dayan briefed Ben-Gurion on the tensions on the border with Syria and in Jerusalem. Jordan was trying to wriggle out of an agreement that granted Israel access to the Hebrew University's buildings on Mount Scopus, which after the war remained an enclave under Israel's control, surrounded by Jordanian territory. Dayan proposed opening the road to the enclave by force. "He is not afraid that a war will break out," Ben-Gurion remarked. When he returned to his office, he found someone waiting to see him—a procurement agent who had just returned from overseas and reported that France was prepared to sell armaments to Israel. Ben-Gurion wrote down the list of what France was offering. It was also possible now to obtain Sherman tanks at $27,000 each, he noted. Someone who had returned from Argentina told him that the Jews there were living in fear—the regime there was "para-Nazi." Then a "tree expert" arrived and received a chunk of the prime minister's time. That afternoon he presided over the Cabinet meeting that made the decision to bring the Jews of Yemen to Israel. Among all this he also found time to address a request he had received from a girl named Roni Baron from Tel Aviv. "If I had my own car," he wrote to her, "I would be happy to take you to your preschool every day and take you home from there as well. But, as defense minister, I unfortunately cannot permit your uncle to take you in an army vehicle, because the car belongs to the people and the country." That evening he hosted an American couple in his home.[75] It was an exhausting but not unusual day.

His mornings generally began with Paula in the kitchen—they slept in separate rooms. She made him a mixture of soft cheese and fruit that she called "kooch-mooch." He listened to the morning news on the radio and looked at *Davar* and other daily newspapers. While he also served as minister of defense, his principal workplace was the prime minister's office, first in Tel Aviv and then in Jerusalem. As always, he dressed carefully. Only in the summer did he allow himself to work without a tie. If there were no trips or meetings on his schedule, he for the most part stayed in his office. He read and wrote a great deal. During the course of the day, he drank Turkish coffee or apple cider. If he needed one of his aides or a secretary, he went out to them—the office was not equipped with an internal telephone system and he did not like to talk on an external line. This put a lot of power in the hands of Nehemiah Argov, his military secretary. Argov operated as a chief of staff, summoning the people the prime minister wanted to see and scheduling those who wanted to see him. It was not that easy to control the flow—the Israeli establishment was still small, everyone knew everyone else; many belonged to the generation of leaders led by members of the Second Aliyah.*

With hundreds of thousands of new Israelis coming into the country, this group tended to close ranks. Ben-Gurion, who throughout his political life tried to be as accessible as possible, agreed even now to take up almost every issue. Many people asked for his help in getting around bureaucratic obstacles that were impeding projects or to offer him their solutions to national problems. Many citizens wrote to him about their personal problems— one complained about a leaky roof and another was distraught because his wife had left him.†

One of his secretaries would forward such requests to municipalities and government offices, but sometimes people appeared in person at the prime minister's office, and if Ben-Gurion encountered them by chance in the anteroom or corridor, he would sometimes stop to hear what had brought them. From time to time he would spot a letter on one of the tables, pick it up, and take an interest in it as if he had suddenly put his finger on one of the country's most pressing and fundamental problems. That may have been what prompted Roni Baron's letter, in which she asked that her uncle be permitted to take her to preschool in his army vehicle. On the average, he replied to two such letters each day; at his death they numbered some twelve thousand.[76]

He ran the weekly Cabinet meetings skillfully. He generally arrived prepared, with a mastery of the subject, firm positions, and for the most part knowing what the decision would be. He permitted the Cabinet members to speak only in turn; if they deviated from the subject or from the rules of

---

* Close to 100 of the 120 members of the Second Knesset were men who, like Ben-Gurion, had been born in Eastern Europe; one out of every three, Ben-Gurion among them, had been born in the previous century. (http://main.knesset.gov.il/Pages/default.aspx/.)

† He received many letters from overseas as well. Some advised him to order a retrial of Jesus. (Ben-Gurion, Diary, March 18, 1949, BGA.)

debate, Ben-Gurion would impatiently threaten to cut them off. But if they spoke to the issue at hand, he respected their right to disagree with him.[77] He loathed verbose presentations but was good at summing up the positions of speakers, generally in a dispassionate way devoid of side comments or personal jabs. He did not encourage humor. The minutes of Cabinet meetings exude historical awareness—everyone knew that they were setting precedents for how Israel's government would function for generations. Ben-Gurion generally spoke last; he often tried to frame what significance the issue at hand had for the country's future. On occasion he offered autobiographical anecdotes. At other times he was unable, or unwilling, to keep himself from interpolating a fierce objection. He was good at formulating motions to be voted on and followed the rules meticulously in conducting votes. The most extreme motion was always put to a vote first. Frequently, he did not vote himself, as if he were merely chairman of the meeting and a neutral director of the discussion. In many cases he imposed his position on his colleagues; in other cases he was compelled to compromise with them.*

He generally defended his decisions passionately, and only occasionally admitted mistakes, as he did six months after independence. It had been a mistake, he admitted, to include in the Declaration of Independence a deadline for the promulgation of a constitution. He said it had been a misunderstanding. "I edited the Declaration on May 13 in my room, and I know that that was not what was intended," he told the Cabinet.[78] He did not want a constitution.

And he was infuriated by legal constraints on "the sovereignty of the nation and the state." Jurists needed to be subordinate to history, not the other way around, he maintained, as part of his response to his justice minister's demand that he delineate the country's borders. "The law is whatever people determine it to be," he insisted.[79] Jurists were a nuisance, as far as he was concerned. "They don't know the meaning of statesmanship," he griped. "Policy is made by policy makers, not by legalists." He sometimes extended his critique to include judges. "I think that I am capable of understanding

---

* On at least four occasions he had to fight to enforce his prohibition on smoking at Cabinet meetings. As a former smoker, he knew it was possible to survive for several hours without a cigarette. (Ben-Gurion to the Cabinet, Aug. 31, 1950, Oct. 19, 1952, March 27, Nov. 6, 1955, ISA.)

things as well as the best judge in the world," he said at a Cabinet meeting. "The most knowledgeable person in the world knows not just the law but also has common sense."[80] He frequently disparaged the low quality of most lawyers, and once said baldly: "I absolutely hate that profession." Zerach War-haftig, a religious Zionist member of the Knesset and jurist, attributed Ben-Gurion's attitude to his failure to complete his legal studies in Turkey.[81]

As in the past, he continued to view the country's moral image as a matter of existential importance. "If our moral purity is marred, we will lose the love of the Jewish people and the friendship of the few nations on whom our standing in the international arena depends," he later wrote.[82] But he frequently averted his eyes from supposedly patriotic crimes committed, ostensibly, in the service of the state, including war crimes.

On December 9, 1949, the United Nations General Assembly decided that Jerusalem and its environs would become a *corpus separatum*, an entity under an international regime. In response, Ben-Gurion decided to move the Knesset and ministries, which had operated in Tel Aviv thus far, to Jerusalem. The only exception was the Ministry of Defense and, for the time being, the Foreign Ministry. His concern was that if the General Assembly's decision was not met with such a response, it would reconfirm the partition decision of November 1947 and require Israel to withdraw from all the territories designated for the Arab state that the IDF had since captured. But making Jerusalem Israel's seat of government was liable to be seen as a provocation aimed at nearly every other country, and thus seemed risky. "In the past three years I have from time to time faced unpleasant and difficult, not to mention fateful, decisions," he wrote in his diary. "I don't know if I have faced a more difficult decision: to flout the United Nations, to face [the ire of] the Catholic, Soviet, and Islamic worlds."[83] Moving the Knesset and ministries to Jerusalem, and formally designating the city as Israel's capital, did not accomplish anything more than negligible diplomatic damage. Ben-Gurion could tell himself that he had been right.

He generally went home to rest in the early afternoon. He ate quickly, apparently without deriving much pleasure from the meal; Paula served him and sat down to eat only after he finished. Then he would go up to his bedroom and read. Sometimes he fell asleep; he was able to refresh himself with catnaps of ten to twenty minutes.

Later in the afternoon he returned to his office, staying until sundown. He participated in many events and ceremonies; when he came home, he would again shut himself up with his books, sometimes well past midnight. He did not sleep well.[84] As prime minister, he continued to avidly peruse catalogues from Blackwell's, Oxford's legendary bookstore, and often placed them on the tops of piles of state documents that demanded his attention. He seems not to have given much thought to the question of who ought to be paying for the books he ordered and how it would be done. One of his secretaries recalled that the governor of the Bank of Israel tried to impress on Ben-Gurion that he was violating the law, as the foreign currency controls then in force forbade him to buy the books he so desired. Ben-Gurion either failed to comprehend what the problem was, or acted as if that were the case. At least some of the books were paid for, it seems, by Lord Marcus Sieff of Marks & Spencer, who made frequent trips and contributions to Israel. At one point, Ben-Gurion was given a legal budget for purchasing "professional literature." His aide Yitzhak Navon wrote in his diary about a loud argument between Ben-Gurion and Paula. "I asked where the money for all the books was coming from, and he said it was his own money," she told Navon. "Trust me," she added in Yiddish, "he can't fool me. I said to him: it's government money."*[85]

"I WANT TO GET TOGETHER WITH YOU"

Paula was an intelligent woman and politically engaged. She was opinionated, controlling, curious, short-tempered, and frank, and sometimes spoke bluntly. Navon recalled "unending provocations." He recalled that she "was never boring, and you could never know what to expect with her. She put on no airs, never dissembled, and said out loud what we only thought of, as we were well-mannered. She was not."[86] Once she told UN Secretary-General

---

* Navon had worked previously with Foreign Minister Sharett. He was sent to Ben-Gurion as a teacher because he knew Spanish and the prime minister had suddenly conceived a desire to read a book in Spanish about Spinoza and *Don Quixote* in the original. In the end, Navon stayed on as an aide. Ben-Gurion was an extremely diligent and analytic student, Navon related in his memoirs, but he had a horrible accent. (Navon 2015, p. 83ff.)

Dag Hammarskjöld that he should get married; she knew very well, of course, why he was single.

Guarding her husband's health and guaranteeing that he could rest were her life missions. As part of that, she jealously protected her position as his gatekeeper. She occasionally tried to prevent visitors from going up to his room, lest they disturb him, even if they were invited guests. She first asked what brought them, and when they descended from his room, she demanded to know what he had told them.[87] She seems to have been especially jealous of his closest aides. She frequently called his office during the day, sometimes, apparently, out of boredom. Unlike Ben-Gurion, she inquired into the private lives of his secretaries. She asked about Nehemiah Argov, who was not married, where he had spent the previous evening, and with whom.[88]

A Yemenite maid, standard in many Israeli middle-class homes, cleaned the house, cooked, did the laundry and ironing, and even polished Ben-Gurion's shoes. Paula had received Mazal Jibli from her friend Esther, the wife of the painter and diplomat Reuven Rubin. Jibli recalled that Ben-Gurion loved her traditional Yemenite *jahnun*, served with a tomato sauce. He didn't like gefilte fish. Ben-Gurion was generally polite to her; he often washed his own dishes. Paula could be stricter, but always apologized afterward. When Jibli occasionally slept over, she shared Paula's room. Her salary was paid by the Defense Ministry.[89]

Her impression was that Paula saw her daughters as rivals. That was especially true of Renana, Ben-Gurion's favorite. Jibli described a game of infiltration—Renana would open the door to the house, ask in a whisper or with sign language where her mother was. Jibli would indicate that Paula was in the back room and Renana would leap up the stairs, very quickly, before her mother could stop her. Sometimes Paula even kept Ben-Gurion's brothers and his sister Tzipora from seeing him. When he received women guests in his study, Paula would send in the maid to check to see if everything was in order. Jibli recalled a childish sort of game between him and Paula—he would lie down in his room, she would go up to see if he needed anything, and he would pretend to be sleeping like a baby. She did not have the same central role in his life as he had in hers. He seems never to have consulted her before an important decision. Their relations became a matter of routine. "Maybe he loved Paula when they were young," Jibli said.[90]

❖

Every so often Ben-Gurion would get together with a woman named Rivka Katznelson. In contrast with his relations with other women, that with Katznelson continued for almost forty years. It began in 1926, when she was nineteen and he about forty. She seems to have been his first extramarital romance, and it continued until the very end of his term as prime minister. Only his connection to Paula lasted longer. Rivka was a distant relative of Berl Katznelson, and spent most of her life working as a journalist for publications sponsored by Mapai. That included editing the monthly women's magazine *Dvar Hapo'elet*; she also served as a literary critic. Twice married, with two sons, she kept company with poets, actors, and other members of Tel Aviv's secular and unconventional bohemian community. Her relations with Ben-Gurion are documented in a large quantity of diaries, poems, and scraps of paper she placed inside notebooks and pads and among loose papers. Many of them were composed as letters to him, but she did not send them all, as she herself once told him.[91]

When it was opened after many years, her archive revealed a love story that did not bring her much satisfaction. She liked him when she first saw him at a political rally, she later related: "That large head with the huge forelocks—there was something cute about it." Her diaries, and the love poems she wrote him, evince a longing for a more total relationship, both intellectually and sexually. He did not respect her political admiration for him, nor did he satisfy her passions as a woman. Once he told her that she had eyes like Berl Katznelson, but an entry in her diary from 1928 complained that he could not tell the difference between her body and that of any other woman. That was a searing and mortifying insult, she wrote. She knew that he would set aside only a small, dark corner for her. She accepted that as a fact, but not submissively. When they met, he seems to have spoken a great deal, while she was relegated to listening. "You never saw me, you did not want to hear what I had to say, and my dreams held no interest for you," she wrote. He wanted a "little woman," she claimed, and she did her best to be one, but it "cast a shadow over her personality and inner soul." Their relationship apparently cooled for a time, but she spent her fortieth birthday with him in his house, and in the months that followed she wrote with wonder about the "revival of female desire that you aroused in me after years of cold-heartedness and communion with myself."[92]

Over the years her expectations and disappointments and love seem to have blended so completely that it is difficult to discern what her relations with him really were and what part of it was imagined.[93] The impression is that, in general, the two had brief trysts in his home when Paula was not around, or at hotels overseas. "His time was short, his passion impatient, and he didn't like love games," she wrote. Ben-Gurion, she later said, was "hungry." He "rushes, pounces, embraces, kisses, exposes himself, seeking release and nothing more."[94] His love was entirely "a love of animal urges," she related. "He did not know if I was married, did not know that I had children, did not ask and gave no thought to me. It didn't interest him. He wanted me, only wanted me."[95]

During and after the War of Independence, she had assignations with Ben-Gurion "in his military hideouts," and apparently also in his office; Argov was the principal go-between during the 1950s. "Nehemiah would call and say: Rivka—the Old Man needs you. I'll arrange it, come," she related.[96] She felt used: "Time and again I could not respond to his thirst for a quick bite when he saw me," she wrote, adding, "It may have disappointed him." Her papers include several letters that he wrote her, once a month, during 1963, on the prime minister's official stationery, in which he asked her to call one of his aides at his office to set up the next assignation. "I want to get together with you," he wrote to her, taking care to note that it was for "a talk."

According to Katznelson, his life with Paula was piteous. She saw his attitude toward Paula as "a man's desire for a woman," as well as for the mother's love he had lacked in his childhood, but without a trace of real interest in her. Paula served him, "as devoted as a faithful dog," Katznelson wrote, and he was grateful. In his old age he depended on her, and he seemed attached to her as well. They lived together for many years and had children together, but on the basis of his relationship with her, Katznelson maintained that Ben-Gurion had never reached "the depths of the satisfaction of masculine eros," and never knew a woman "to the depths of her sexuality." Not even Paula. In this sense, "he died a virgin," she wrote. Katznelson once asked Ben-Gurion to expedite the funds for a periodical she edited. Ben-Gurion reacted as if she had demanded money for their liaison. "You have humiliated me utterly," she wrote to him. "He may have loved me, or perhaps something sensuous flickered within him toward me, and he knew my devotion and sincerity," she wrote to the poet and literary scholar Simon Halkin. "I do not know if I loved Ben-Gurion. I did not fight to see him frequently, I did not struggle to claim him for myself. He was on some far horizon of my life, and so I was in his life." She did not want to be remembered as his mistress.[97]

19

ANXIETIES

"I NO LONGER HAVE THE STRENGTH TO WORK"

On one of the last autumn days of 1951, Ben-Gurion watched a parachuting exercise in the Upper Galilee. Something went wrong and two paratroopers plummeted to their deaths before his eyes. "We stood there and saw how the second plane cut them down and they fell," related Yigael Yadin, who was still chief of staff at the time. "And we were the first to get there. They were still warm." Ben-Gurion looked at them and remarked: "You know, they look as if they were alive." Yadin responded: "Yes, but they're dead." And Ben-Gurion said: "It's my first time seeing dead people." He wrote in his diary: "I was horribly depressed by the catastrophe. I am not sure that we are not responsible."

The two paratroopers, Michael Neuman and Haim Hayat, were not in fact the first dead people he had ever seen, but at that time he had a tendency to link routine events in the present to past experiences, often reliving those older events in the process. It was as if he was adapting them for reuse, to neutralize the disheartening power of more recent incidents. On the first anniversary of the paratroopers' deaths, he spoke to the Cabinet about the two Jewish laborers who had been killed before his eyes at Sejera, some forty years before.[1] He faced some tough challenges at the time, among them several tempestuous political battles, but only a few could have come as surprises; like the deaths of the paratroopers, most of these challenges brought back memories of the past.

The burden of history sapped his strength. After the struggle to establish the state, the war, the absorption of hundreds of thousands of refugees, and countless other matters, he took it upon himself to lead a policy of conciliation between Israel and West Germany, setting off one of the most critical and agonizing controversies in Israeli history. The emotional energy it demanded was matched only by the debate over partition. The exertion would soon exhaust him, mentally debilitating him, impeding his ability to think clearly and function properly. He complained frequently that he felt weak, while also voicing his disappointment and anxieties. Some of the latter grew out of realistic assessments of facts on the ground, but others were delusional. Here and there were indications that he was cut loose from reality. He had experienced flashes of disorientation in the past, but they had never come in so concentrated a way. He slid into a mood in which he began summing up his life and preparing for its end. Never had he been more pessimistic about Israel's chances for survival. He felt an urge to begin all over again. Aware of what was happening to him, he would soon collapse and go off to raise sheep in the desert. In his imagination, it was as if he had returned to Sejera.

❖

In August 1950, he was examined by a cardiologist from Boston. "My heart is fine," Ben-Gurion wrote in his diary.[2] On occasion he mentioned aches and ailments he had suffered from since childhood.[3] According to his diary, he was bedridden every few months, although he generally did not specify with what. He sometimes required hospitalization. He complained of lumbago that would render him unable to stand up. At one point, he reportedly came down with Ménière's disease, an inner ear disorder that can cause dizzy spells. His doctors sometimes ordered him to miss Cabinet meetings.[4] He also suffered from mental distress, and spoke about it frequently; the historical process he led caused him much anxiety.

"New catastrophes, no less horrible, can occur," he said a while after the end of the War of Independence, "and the tiny and dispersed Jewish people can be destroyed and eradicated to the last person." A few months later, he told the Cabinet: "I have a Zionist sensibility and I go through the country and I am terrified and horrified." He was referring to the fact that most of the country's Jews were concentrated in the Tel Aviv metropolitan area, while the rest of the country was almost empty.[5] "I always worried that the entire Zionist project would in the end come to one tiny building, and indeed it is producing a single large city with a hinterland," he said. He proposed closing Tel Aviv to immigrants. They would destroy it, he feared, and warned that the neglect of other parts of the country was liable to undermine the moral foundation of the Zionist enterprise.[6] "Something has happened," he explained. "The country is producing thorns and thistles and the mice are multiplying. It's horrible to see the land."[7] He asked the country's chief forester, Yosef Weitz, to plant a billion trees over the decade to come. Weitz suspected that the prime minister was playing a joke on him and asked himself whether Ben-Gurion had lost his senses.[8]

In January 1950, he offered the Cabinet a very pessimistic view of the state of the IDF. As he had many times in the past, he divested himself of responsibility. "I want to remind the Cabinet that I always stressed that I was not dealing with establishing an army, but rather with war," he declared. "That was the main consideration. To fight and to win. We had no time to prepare and train an army." A few weeks later, he repeated this, and later in the year he wrote: "I lay sick in bed . . . I will leave for a vacation soon, because I no longer have the strength to work." He was absent for a month, during which he wrote a brief introduction to one of his books, *When Israel Fights*.[9]

A few months later, he had again descended into what Katznelson and Sharett had in the past described with the biblical phrase "tottering limbs and bitter grief." At the end of November 1950, he wrote to Chief of Staff Yadin that he was "obliged to 'disappear' for two or three weeks," because he had not relaxed enough on his recent vacation in Tiberias and could not return to work without additional rest.[10] Two days later, he was at the National Archaeological Museum in Athens. He also visited the Acropolis and went to see a tomb said to be that of Agamemnon. He had two companions and security guards; Paula did not join him. The Prime Minister's Office did not provide advance notice of his trip or details about his movements.

❖

The next stop was Oxford. The British minister in Israel acknowledged that the visit might indeed seem odd at first glance, but he persuaded his superiors in London that the Israeli prime minister really did not want to see anyone, only browse at Blackwell's, "his spiritual home." The minister confirmed that Ben-Gurion was extremely fatigued. He indeed spent most of his time in the store's dusky basement, surrounded by piles of books, leafing through them and reading. Alongside the Greek classics, this time he also took an interest in contemporary works of philosophy, among them books by Martin Heidegger, Ludwig Wittgenstein, and, in particular, Karl Popper. He may have met with Isaiah Berlin. He also informed his old friend Doris May that he was in the country, and may have seen her. Perhaps, nostalgically, it took him back to the time of the Blitz, when he had also had a lot of time to read. *Ha'aretz* thought the trip was "bizarre"; for *Ma'ariv* it was "eccentric." The newspapers did not know just how right they were.

Despite the rumors that he would soon return, Ben-Gurion proceeded to the south of France. While vacationing at Antibes, between Cannes and Nice, he suddenly had the urge to learn to drive. It happened one day when Ehud Avriel was behind the wheel of one of the two cars the party was using; a detachment of French security guards was in the other one. Ben-Gurion asked: "Is it difficult to drive?" Avriel said it was very easy, to which Ben-Gurion responded: "Maybe you can teach me?" Avriel agreed; the Israeli secret service agent who was in the car with them did not object. Ben-Gurion began receiving daily driving lessons on the Riviera coastal road, generally early in the morning. The French security detail went along to clear the road for him.

The key word in this story may be the one that Ben-Gurion used in his letter to Yadin, in which he said he was "obliged" to take a trip because of his fatigue, making it sound as if he did not really want to go. So perhaps it was no coincidence that he asked to learn to drive at just this juncture. "He enjoyed so much his ability to operate that vehicle and cause it to move in the direction he determined," Avriel later related. "It gave him great satisfaction." Three weeks had gone by. The day after returning from France, he chaired a Cabinet meeting; in a discussion about the food shortage, Ben-Gurion asked why geese were not raised in Israel.[11]

"WHAT WILL HAPPEN TO OUR GRANDCHILDREN"

He was no more optimistic when he returned. "There is no greater concern in my life than the country's survival," he said a few weeks later, "and I cannot conceal from my colleagues that I am overcome with profound apprehension."[12] He began to speak about wanting to retire; several leaders of his party explained to him that it was simply not possible. But even his colleagues in the Cabinet began to notice that his strength was leaving him. In the meantime, Ben-Gurion estimated that the Cold War was liable to deteriorate into a military confrontation between the United States and the Soviet Union, in which Israel would be destroyed.

"I am full of trepidation about what will happen to our grandchildren," he said. A nuclear missile might misfire; "only a tiny deviation, we are not a large country, it would be enough to destroy Tel Aviv and its surroundings and that would almost finish us off." An atom bomb on New York could leave Israel without Jewish support. "What will be the fate of our small country?" he asked, but there was no answer. "I have said all this not to state a fact, but to express very difficult thoughts," he remarked.[13] Israel stood on the edge of an abyss, he told the government: "The country faces serious danger and can blow to pieces at any moment."[14]

❖

Like most of the world's small countries, Israel tried at first to remain nonaligned, but as the Cold War intensified it was compelled to declare its position between the Western and Eastern blocs.

Ben-Gurion liked to hark back to his seminal visit to Lenin's Soviet

Union in 1923. He noted that the Red Army had lost millions of soldiers in its effort to eradicate Nazi Germany; the Soviet Union had supported the establishment of the State of Israel, and had permitted Czechoslovakia to supply Israel the arms that had enabled it to win the War of Independence. The Soviets had also permitted several Communist countries to allow tens of thousands of their Jewish citizens to settle in Israel. But the difficulty of remaining truly nonaligned led him as early as 1949 to assert that "in the ideological debate, Israel is democratic and anti-Communist." He referred to Stalin's Soviet Union as a house of bondage built on murder and deception. He was especially resentful that the approximately two million Jews living there were not allowed to come to Israel. Most Israelis agreed with him.[15]

Then the Korean War broke out. The United States and its allies fought under the flag of the United Nations; Ben-Gurion proposed sending an IDF force to fight alongside them. "In my opinion, it is in our interest to take part in this war," if only symbolically, he asserted. He cited the need to raise the spirits of Soviet Jewry. "The Jews of Russia will be delighted if the Koreans are taught a lesson by the American army," he said; the Jews of Romania would be similarly cheered. America's Jews would be proud to see Israel's flag flying as part of the UN force. He was thinking of a contingent of 100 or 150 troops. It could be a replay of the Jewish battalions of World War II. It would be a great thing for the Jewish people, he said on a third occasion: "Jews need to feel that their country is 'cool.' That's very important." His Cabinet ministers seem to have had trouble believing their ears. All of them, led by Foreign Minister Sharett, rejected his proposal categorically; only with great difficulty did he get them to agree to propose to the UN that Israel dispatch a medical support team to Korea.

He was furious, as if the government had abandoned the Jews to a catastrophe. "On this matter I do not have a clean conscience with regard to the Jewish people," he said. He compared North Korea to Nazi Germany. In this fantasy, Israel's Jews were no longer unable to help their brethren, as they had been during the Holocaust. Yet Israel's government was now too cowardly to do so. "I feel miserable in this government," he said. But he acknowledged that the majority had a right to err. Four months later, he proposed that Israel declare war on Germany.

The rejection of the proposal to fight alongside the Americans in Korea did not change what was then called Israel's "orientation." Israel's place was alongside the United States. West Germany wanted to be there as well; its leaders believed that the road to Washington went through Jerusalem. That was the basis for cooperation between the two countries.[16]

In contrast with his proposal to send troops to fight in Korea, Ben-Gurion did not intend to attack Berlin. He was seeking his way around a legal problem. Israel had not been at war with Nazi Germany and thus could not demand reparations. It was a new incarnation of the proposal he had once made to declare war on the British Empire. The Foreign Ministry's director-general pleaded with him, apparently in something of a panic, to discard the idea. Ben-Gurion held to it with all his might at first, but after a lengthy discussion he agreed to postpone a Cabinet vote, to enable further consideration.[17]

Contact with Germans was viewed then as an insult to the victims of the Holocaust, as well as to the honor of the Jewish people and the State of Israel. It was the third of a trio of the most sensitive and unrelenting issues that Ben-Gurion had to keep returning to his entire life, the other two being partition and religion-state relations. He managed all three of them successfully, combining his persuasive powers with political maneuvering. He understood the emotional difficulty that motivated the opponents of his policy, disdained their political considerations, and refused to accept that contact with Germany was immoral. The clichés that his opponents used, including "Remember what Amalek did to you" (Deuteronomy 25:17) and the interdiction against Spain that the Jews had observed since their expulsion from that country in the fifteenth century, were voiced at one of the Cabinet's first meetings.[18] Ben-Gurion put it in a nutshell at another: "There is a well-known saying: 'Money has no odor.'"[19]

But the differences ran very deep. They recalled the debate over the Haavara Agreement with Nazi Germany. As they had then, they cut across party lines, including Mapai. "There is a mental gulf and we cannot bridge it," Foreign Minister Sharett declared. He also feared that the Germans would wiggle out of reaching an agreement with Israel, leaving it without both money and honor. He warned that Israel's demand to receive reparations from Germany was liable to lead to a demand that Israel pay reparations to Arab refugees. But in February 1950, Ben-Gurion succeeded in pushing through the Cabinet a decision to hold direct talks with West Germany and to notify the public of the fact.[20]

He compared his utilitarian attitude toward relations with Germany with his attitude toward what he called "Hitler's Holocaust." That came in a private conversation with Leivick Halpern, a Yiddish poet and playwright living in the United States. Ben-Gurion told him that Israelis did not live the Holocaust the way Halpern himself did. He explained: "More than that, we live the life that we make here. Not that we think any less of the tragedy and its danger. But we are on guard not against the things that happened to us in the past but toward the things that we need to do." Of himself he said: "The distant past, when we lived in our land, is closer to me than the recent past."[21]

In the wake of the official contacts, Ben-Gurion estimated that, as an opening offer, the Germans were proposing to provide Israel with merchandise worth $5 million, to be supplied over five years. Apparently, even at this point, there was an understanding that this would include the provision of military equipment.[22] Public opposition was reaching its peak. Sincere emotional revulsion in some cases was combined with political subterfuge; Ben-Gurion was not always able to distinguish between the two. As part of his campaign, he had to plumb the uttermost depths of Israeli identity.

❖

The first round was fought in the Mapai Central Committee, and Ben-Gurion won. It was a very long and painful debate, one that required the clarification of fundamental values—the state versus conscience, utility versus morality, emotion versus rationality, revenge versus hope, the past versus the future. A number of Holocaust survivors who opposed any talks with Germany shared their horrifying memories with their colleagues. Everybody there was aware of the anti-German atmosphere being fanned by the daily newspapers, most of which opposed the negotiations. Mapai was thus fighting not only for its soul, but also for its political future. Ben-Gurion stressed the financial aspect of the deal time and again. "If we don't know that we are talking about serious sums, we won't conduct any negotiations," he promised. The goal of the agreement was to prevent the Jews from returning to the situation they were in before the Holocaust: "We do not want the Arab Nazis to come and slaughter us," he said. The debate continued into the night. By a vote of forty-two against six, the Central Committee endorsed the negotiations.[23]

"GREAT MENTAL DISTRESS"

The seventh of January 1952 was a cold and rainy day in Jerusalem. The Knesset opened its session a few minutes after four in the afternoon. Menachem Begin declared his allegiance to the Knesset, staging a return after a self-imposed exile from the chamber following the results of the elections to the Second Knesset. His party, Herut, had fallen to a bit more than half its previous strength. It was a heavy blow, especially given Begin's charisma and his talent for firing up the masses, stoking their patriotic emotions and their chauvinistic passions. The struggle against German reparations offered him a chance to rehabilitate himself. He hoped to return to his time as the commander of Etzel. He called the plan to negotiate with Germany a "Holocaust."

After his swearing-in ceremony, Begin left the Knesset and walked down to Zion Square, at the other end of Ben-Yehuda Street in downtown Jerusalem. Thousands of his supporters had gathered there. He spoke to them from a hotel balcony adjacent to the Square. "Tonight the most shameful event in our people's history is slated to occur," he began. In his speech, he told of how German butchers had drowned his father in the river running through the city he lived in in Belarus, along with five hundred other Jews. He did not actually know for sure that the story was true, but he shouted: "There is no German who did not murder our fathers. Every German is a Nazi. Every German is a murderer. Adenauer is a murderer." And Ben-Gurion, "the little despot and big maniac," as he put it, was about to take money from them. "Because that's the way they think: money, money, money," Begin screamed, promising that the proposed agreement with Germany would not come to be. "All of us are willing to give our lives for that! Over our dead bodies! There is no sacrifice we will not make to thwart this intrigue."

Meanwhile, in the Knesset, Ben-Gurion was reiterating Israel's demands of Germany. He said that his government believed that it had a duty to reclaim the wealth lost by the victims of the Nazis at the earliest possible opportunity. He spoke for about twenty minutes, without being interrupted. His statement was factual, devoid of pathos. The debate that followed, as expected, exuded demagogy. The first speaker related that his young son had asked him how much the family would get for Grandma and Grandpa.

At Zion Square the rain intensified and Begin was approaching a frenzy. Someone came out to the balcony and handed him a folded note. Begin opened it very slowly, studied it with an expression of great concentration, and then announced that he had just been notified that the policemen on the crowd's perimeter were armed with German-made tear gas canisters, full of "the same gas that choked our fathers." But he would not be deterred, he promised: "We will go to concentration camps, to torture chambers . . . It will be a war of life and death . . . Even if I am sentenced to die, even if I am sentenced not to see my young son . . . there will be a boycott of Germany forever and ever . . . A government that enters into negotiations with it is criminal! Ben-Gurion—a criminal!"[24] He then called on the crowd to accompany him to the Knesset: "Walk with me and do not fear the gas grenades."

The police operated under its deputy chief, Amos Ben-Gurion. The force was not properly prepared. Thousands of demonstrators broke through barriers, advanced on the Knesset building, and began to throw stones. The chamber was on the ground floor, with windows facing the street. The stones shattered the windows and landed in the chamber; shards of glass began to cover the desks and the floor. One member was hit in the head by a stone. Policemen ascended to the roofs of nearby buildings and began to cast gas grenades into the crowd. The overpowering fumes seeped into the Knesset chamber. Members began pushing toward the exit. There were screams and curses. The police did not use live fire on the demonstrators, but hundreds were wounded. Some of them, both demonstrators and police, were brought into the building to receive first aid; Paula Ben-Gurion helped care for them.

Ben-Gurion himself went out to the street and returned to the building, went out and back in again. When he was told that his son's forces were not stopping the crowd, he wanted to alert the IDF, but he didn't know the telephone number. "I wanted to call the army," he told the Cabinet. "They couldn't make the connection right away, because my military secretary was not at work at the time. Only the military police showed up. That was not enough power, because they could send only fifty people. I asked to be connected immediately, once again, to the commander. They made the connection and the army arrived. The army didn't do a thing, but the very fact of its appearance had a psychological effect on the demonstrators." His memory processed the incident and turned it into a rescue operation that succeeded thanks to his presence of mind. Many years later, he wrote: "Had I not used an army force to prevent the mob from breaking into the Knesset, there would have been a massacre of the members."[25]

Sixty-one members of the Knesset voted to authorize the body's Foreign Affairs and Defense Committee to decide the issue; fifty voted against. It was a narrow victory for the coalition. Some representatives of the coalition parties voted no, but the religious parties, Mapai's partners, stood by him.*[26]

❖

The attack on the Knesset building was one of a series of more violent actions aimed at halting conciliation with the Germans. On April 16, 1953, Jascha Heifetz, one of the century's greatest violinists and a warm friend of Israel, played a concert at Jerusalem's Edison Cinema. One of the pieces on the program was a sonata by Richard Strauss. Strauss was a German composer who had supported the Nazi regime during its first two years in power. After the concert, Heifetz returned to his room at the King David Hotel. A stranger, armed with an iron bar, was waiting for him at the entrance. He struck Heifetz's hand and fled. The next day, Ben-Gurion told Heifetz that had the violinist asked him in advance, he would have advised against including the piece in the program. "Humans are not rational creatures but rather irrational, and emotions have an important place in life," he said. Following the attack, he advised Heifetz to continue his planned series of concerts, and to include the Strauss piece. He ordered that the violinist be provided with bodyguards, and promised that he himself would attend a concert.[27] A Holocaust survivor placed a bomb next to the Foreign Ministry's

---

* In advance of the vote, Ben-Gurion did a head count and believed that he had a seven-vote majority for commencing negotiations with the Germans, but five of those votes came from Arab members of the Knesset. He noted that there were also Arab members opposed to negotiations. (Ben-Gurion to the Cabinet, Jan. 6, 1952, ISA.)

offices in Tel Aviv. Israelis were also involved in an attempt to assassinate the West German chancellor Konrad Adenauer in Germany.[28]

But violence was not the main problem. The biggest difficulty was that there were no conventions about what was forbidden and what was permitted in relations with Germany. Nearly every day there was a decision to be made in this regard, and given the lack of parameters, each case had to be addressed separately, as if it were the only issue that required the government to make a historic decision between good and evil. The cases ranged from the export of oranges to Germany to the import of German books. It was not a rational and consistent policy-making process; instead, it involved a bundle of doubts and misgivings, fumblings, intuitions, internal contradictions, and a lot of politics; Ben-Gurion took part in all this.[29]

He believed that not every German was guilty of the Nazis' crimes, just as not every Jew was guilty of killing Jesus. But at one Cabinet meeting he said: "It could happen that tomorrow Nazi Germany will return."[30] The reparations agreement was signed in September 1952. According to the agreement, West Germany was to finance part of the resettlement in Israel of uprooted Jewish refugees, and to compensate individual Jews in Israel and other countries. Many Israelis continued to see it as a disgrace.[31] The reparations improved Israel's economic condition and expedited its recovery from austerity. The personal compensation that Israeli citizens received from Germany widened the inequality gap between those of European origin and those from the Islamic world.

The heavy load that Ben-Gurion bore as both prime minister and defense minister led to "great mental distress." In the summer of 1952, he raised the possibility that he would give up one of the portfolios. It was one of the rare cases in which the minutes of a Cabinet meeting show him to have uttered a few words in Yiddish. Two weeks later, he fell ill for ten days.[32] In addition to his struggling with fatigue, he felt that "the people" were not living up to his pioneering expectations of them. A British journalist, Jon Kimche, Jewish and sympathetic to the Zionist cause, told him of his impressions from a visit to Israel. The atmosphere was replete with resentment and disappointment, he said. People did not talk about the establishment of the state and the war's achievements; instead, they complained about the corrupt administration and considered leaving the country. Similar things could be heard in Ben-Gurion's closest circle of associates. "Stories about corruption," Navon wrote in his diary. "You could lose your mind. Will I ever succeed in explaining to BG what our country looks like? Can he do anything about it?"[33] Ben-Gurion realized that "the moral situation is bad," but what he meant by that was mostly that citizens' national identities were weak. He tried to go back to his role as a Zionist preacher, but, he said, "young people do not want to go to the Negev, many are leaving."[34]

During these months, he devoted himself to an exhausting political and ideological struggle to nationalize the school system. Schools had, up to this point, been run under the patronage of political parties; Ben-Gurion wanted to put the state in charge. He found the time and strength to draft, himself, the minimum core curriculum: Hebrew, Bible, Jewish literature, physical education, sciences (including Jewish and world history and Israeli and global geography), pioneering and labor education (agriculture and handcrafts), love of the homeland, Jewish values, and loyalty to the state. He stressed that the state would sponsor religious and Arab schools. While he did not specifically list mathematics, he thought of it as part of the sciences; he made no mention of English. Here Ben-Gurion emerged as the generation's educator and a national ideologue seeking to instill in his people a system of values and a new identity. It was not easy to overcome the objections of those members of his own party who warned that the State Education Law would rob Mapai of one of its most important means of influence—its party-affiliated school system—and strengthen the religious parties by providing them with state funding for schools that taught their ideology.[35]

Crime also depressed him, and the black market hurt his pride. The courts were overly lenient, he grumbled again and again.[36] It was a philosophical debate as well—Ben-Gurion preached law and order, and argued that law enforcement was too liberal. "It is acceptable for a criminal to sometimes receive a larger punishment than what he deserves," he said. "It's not only the murderer who is a human being, so is his victim. A raped woman is a human being as well, and a murdered child is a human being also . . . Better for there to be an error and for the guilty person to spend a little more time in jail, but in the meantime hundreds more people will not be murdered." Overly lenient judges should themselves be put on trial, he said.[37]

He linked the crime rate to a wave of political thuggery that was sweeping through the country. Religious extremists set fire to secular bookstores and even plotted to throw a smoke grenade into the Knesset chamber. Antireligious fanatics placed a bomb by the home of the religious transport minister because he ordered that public transportation should not run on the Sabbath. Anti-Communist zealots, some of them Lehi veterans, left a bomb in the yard of the Soviet legation in protest of that country's oppression of its Jews. All these, Ben-Gurion claimed, threatened to rip the fabric of national sovereignty. In practice, such ideological crimes were part of the struggle for power in the country. He made several unsuccessful attempts to eliminate his opponents on the right and left, one of them a move to outlaw the Communist Party. The debate over this proposal revealed, once again, a totalitarian element in his leadership. "If there is a need for detention camps, I will set them up, and if there is a need to shoot, I will not be afraid to do so," he told his party.[38] He had previously tried to shut down the Communist newspaper, *Kol Ha'am*, with a lawsuit, but he lost the case. The Supreme Court ruling against him became one of the cornerstones of freedom of the press in Israel.[39]

"THERE HAS NEVER BEEN SUCH A MIRACLE"

One day, apparently in September 1952, Ben-Gurion was on his way back to Jerusalem from a military exercise in the Negev. About thirty miles south of Be'er-Sheva, "in the middle of the desert," Yitzhak Navon wrote, he noticed a small shack and several tents. He ordered the driver of his jeep to halt, and when he got out, he found himself facing a group of about a dozen young men and a young woman. They told him that at the end of the War of Independence they had decided that it was not enough to conquer this area. "We came to settle it," they told him. Ben-Gurion asked which political party's settlement movement they belonged to; they responded that they had no political affiliation. He was beside himself in wonder. "There has never been such a miracle," he proclaimed. "Representatives of all parties unite for a pioneering cause." He asked where they were from. Most had been born in the country; six had been intelligence officers. One was from South Africa, another from Poland. They shared their dream with him—they wanted to set up a goat and horse farm and to be cowboys. Thus the name they chose for

their settlement, Sde Boker, the cowboy field; the name also sounded something like the place's Arab name. They were idealists and adventurers, romantic reformers and self-searchers, like Ben-Gurion himself and other
settlers had been for the last seventy years. A primal landscape encircled
them; a colorful cliff face rose in the distance. Not far to the south lay a huge
and breathtaking crater. If they could get enough water from the nearby
town of Yeruham, they would try to grow fruit trees, they said. Ben-Gurion
promised to visit them again. He spoke about them all the way to Jerusalem,
Navon recalled. "They are doing exactly what must be done now," he said, "to
settle the desert." He decided to join them.[40]

The story is captivating, but not accurate. There is also disagreement
about when exactly it took place; Ben-Gurion himself offered several different dates.[41] Whatever the case, he knew about Sde Boker before he met its
settlers for the first time—one of the founders of the group was the brother
of his aide Ehud Avriel. The settlement was founded with an official ceremony that was covered by the press; one of the speakers was the general of
the Northern Command, Moshe Dayan. The press followed the settlement's
progress. A young woman from the group who was out herding sheep was
murdered by Bedouin in September 1952, and in December a young man
was shot dead in an ambush.[42] Ben-Gurion knew all this when he first met
the Sde Boker settlers. Later that week, he learned that Ehud Avriel's mother
had died, causing him to once again lose himself in memories of his own
mother. "The mother is perhaps the only 'absolute' in human life. In the more
than fifty-five years since my mother died (I was a ten-year-old boy), the pain
and loss has not entirely left me, and I still remember my mother in all her
great and profound loving-kindness," he wrote. That same week he asked the
Histadrut and the Jewish Agency to compute his pension and accumulated
vacation days for his thirty years of work. He asked that the money, amount-
ing to about IL 7,000, the equivalent of about thirty monthly salaries as a
member of the Knesset, be paid to Paula.[43]

In October 1952, he again fell ill; he had a hard time keeping up his diary. "I didn't open a notebook," he wrote. "A few things (little and fragmentary) were written on scraps of paper and copied on a typewriter. Most of the
things were not written down at all because of all the pressure and for other
reasons."[44]

That same month he made a sort of farewell speech that began with "the first Hebrew warrior," Abraham, and continued with "five of the most important and decisive engagements" of the four thousand years since then. All were contrary to accepted logic, out of a Jewish imperative and hidden capacities that no outsider could comprehend, he said. All five occurred under his leadership. The establishment of Israel, he said, was the most fantastic event in history. He surveyed some of the central actions of his government, among them the reparations agreement with Germany and the establishment of an air force. He found the earliest depictions of combat planes in the Psalms (18:9ff.) and the second book of Samuel (22:9ff.)*[45]

❖

His historical lectures grew longer and became a central element of Cabinet debates. At times he seemed to be reliving his days as a laborer at Kfar Saba, and once he seemed to be arguing again for the principle of restraint he had championed in the 1930s. Sometimes he embarrassed his colleagues. He drew one of them into a long debate over Noah's ark, and once voiced his skepticism that the Jews in the European ghettoes had ever rebelled against the Nazis, as was commonly told. In that case he corrected himself, but once he sent out a letter that his staff apparently did not intercept in time, including this reflection: "Hitler was not an anti-Semite. Hajj Amin al-Hussayni, who was no less a Semite than any of us, was one of Hitler's friends and helpers."†[46]

It was a time when history, biography, and politics frequently mixed; Ben-Gurion had to explain again and again why Jerusalem's Old City had

---

* In his diary he erred, citing 2 Samuel 23 instead; that chapter contains King David's final words.
† There was at least one other contemporary statesman who had a tendency to equate political history with the events of his own life—Winston Churchill. In one of his speeches in Parliament, he went out of his way to praise Israel. He spoke in the first person, and the members of the house could have received the impression that he was relating an episode out of his own biography. He began with the Balfour Declaration, and mentioned his political and emotional support for Zionism time and again. On the fifth anniversary of independence, Ben-Gurion copied Churchill's speech into his diary, in English. (Ben-Gurion, Diary, May 15, 1953, BGA; Ben-Gurion to the Cabinet, May 24, 1953, ISA.)

not been conquered. He once tried to justify it with a detailed, emotional, and apologetic speech to the Knesset. It boiled down to the fact that the IDF did not have the needed forces, because it had to defend many settlements around the country. "It is impossible to hold Jerusalem if one does not hold the entire country," he said, citing the conquest of Jerusalem by the Roman army. "The Romans deprived us of liberty and destroyed our land, but they knew how to make war, and we should learn from an enemy who knows how to run a war," he said. "The Romans did not go to conquer Jerusalem first, the opposite is true. They left Jerusalem for last . . . and only after they had conquered the country did they besiege Jerusalem." It was an issue that would keep rearing its head for years to come.[47]

In November 1952, Chaim Weizmann died. He had served as Israel's first president. According to his diary, the news "devastated" Ben-Gurion. Yitzhak Navon wrote: "I am keen to know what he thought at that moment."[48]

Golda Meir had attributed to Weizmann the statement that, unlike Ben-Gurion, he would be incapable of sending people into war.[49] That may well have been true, but Weizmann had never faced such a dilemma, because he had been a statesman without a state. The top Zionist leadership had seen no other relationship that crumpled under such a heavy load of passions. Weizmann's role in history ended shortly after Israel declared its independence. Ben-Gurion reached the height of his achievement at that same time. His gradual decline lasted for twenty-five years. Weizmann was blessed with a brief decline, less than five years, but during that time he was compelled to live like an exile in his own country.

He had a hard time getting used to the fact that he no longer led the Zionist movement, and tried to intervene in Israel's foreign policy. Ben-Gurion reprimanded him. The country didn't really even need a president, he said.[50] He briefed Weizmann about government policy only rarely. President Weizmann was elderly and half-blind, and very weak, but Ben-Gurion humiliated him as if he still saw him as a political threat. It began when he didn't invite Weizmann to add his name to the Declaration of Independence. Weizmann did not participate in the ceremony, because he was in the United States at the time. Ben-Gurion mentioned him in the speech he gave after the declaration, but rejected all appeals to leave a space for Weizmann to sign. He had no obligation to do so. Meyer Weisgal, Weizmann's aide, proposed

adding his name to the declaration, as a symbolic gesture, on the tenth anniversary of independence—five years after the president's death. He reported
that Ben-Gurion told him: "Weizmann doesn't need it."[51]

A few days after Weizmann's death, Ben-Gurion again astonished the
country and the rest of the world with an original and fantastical initiative. He
offered Israel's presidency to Albert Einstein, who did not even speak Hebrew.
Abba Eban, Israel's ambassador to Washington, recalled that Ben-Gurion
told him of the idea by telephone and instructed him to call the professor.
As Eban pondered how to address the absurd directive he had been given, the
proposal was broadcast on the radio. A short while later, his phone rang
again. Einstein was on the line. Would the ambassador please get the idea
out of Ben-Gurion's head? he asked. It was absolutely out of the question.
Eban could tell from Einstein's voice that he was dumbfounded.[52]

Einstein's refusal did not lower Ben-Gurion's spirits. According to Navon,
he had not really expected him to agree. His next choice was Yitzhak Ben-Zvi.
The two men had a long history, dating back to when Ben-Zvi excluded Ben-
Gurion from Hashomer. Ben-Gurion now offered an honor that, as he saw
it, was devoid of any real content. For Ben-Gurion, it was historical justice.
"Ben-Zvi and Rachel arrived," he wrote the next day, "overjoyed."[53]

In May 1953, Ben-Gurion was back at Sde Boker, marveling as if it were his
first time there. He had not seen a pioneering project anything like Sde Boker
during his forty-seven years in the country, he wrote to its settlers after his
return home. "I have never envied another person . . . but during my visit
with you it was difficult to repress a feeling something like jealousy—why
did I not have the opportunity to take part in such an endeavor?" Sde Boker
"is the pinnacle of pioneering Zionism in our day," he told the Cabinet.[54] By
now, his strength was running out. It was a rapid process; tension along the
borders speeded it.

"I CAN'T GO ON"

Soon after the end of the War of Independence, Ben-Gurion set down in his
diary a strategic assessment he had heard from Ambassador Abba Eban. "He
sees no need to run after peace. The armistice is enough for us. If we run
after peace, the Arabs will demand a price—borders or refugees or both. We

will wait a few years."[55] They waited. On a few occasions, Ben-Gurion had to defend his position in the Cabinet. "On what basis do you propose that we conduct negotiations?" Ben-Gurion asked one of his ministers. "Should we bring back the refugees, the 1947 borders, should we give up Jerusalem, give up the Negev? Egypt will no doubt demand vehemently that we give up the Negev." A few months later, Ben-Gurion reiterated that he always favored peace, but that "there are limits to our desire for peace with the Arabs." He had used almost those same words more than thirty years previously. As in the past, he was piqued by claims that Israel was missing chances for peace.[56]

Other governments and individuals sometimes tried to further contacts between Israel and its neighbors, officially and openly in Lausanne, Switzerland, and secretly on other occasions. It was not hard to make such contact; the problem was the price. For a short time, Israel agreed to discuss the possibility that one hundred thousand refugees would be allowed to return.[57] There was also talk of a corridor through the Negev that would connect Egypt and Jordan, and that Jordan would receive free access to Haifa's port. The assassination of Jordan's King Abdullah I in July 1951 made it difficult to continue the talks with that country.[58]

Ben-Gurion did not rush to respond to a proposal from the president of Syria, Husni al-Za'im, that the two leaders meet. One thing Syria offered to talk about was the possibility that it would take in up to 350,000 Palestinian refugees. Ben-Gurion preferred to sign an armistice agreement first. Za'im was assassinated soon thereafter and his offer was forgotten.[59] Such events confirmed the basic assumption about the conflict that Ben-Gurion had long adhered to: "The people who make Arab policy today will agree to make peace with us if we go to Madagascar or some other place and leave their country." Madagascar, an island off Africa, occurred to him because of an early Nazi proposal to send Germany's Jews there. And, as many times in the past, he did not forget to cite the lesson he had learned from Musa al-Alami.[60]

It was not by chance that he again mentioned this Palestinian leader. While Israel signed armistice agreements with its Arab neighbors, it did not do so with the Palestinian people. Tens of thousands of them, uprooted during the war, were trying to return to their homes. Like after the partition decision of 1947, it was not always possible to distinguish between acts of theft, robbery, sabotage, and murder committed with criminal intent and the acts of national resistance. As the Haganah had done in the 1930s and 1940s, the IDF staged operations meant to punish, avenge, and deter.

On February 5, 1951, a thirty-nine-year-old immigrant from Hungary who lived in a house on the edge of the abandoned Arab village of Malha, next to Jerusalem, was murdered. The assailants raped his wife and ransacked their home. The IDF proposed a retaliation aimed at the Jordanian army; Ben-Gurion opposed that and ordered the army "to blow up the adjacent village responsible for the crime," as he wrote. The name of the village was Sharafat, where he had once sat under the oldest oak tree in Palestine with Musa al-Alami. An IDF force penetrated the village and attacked several houses. The Jordanians reported a dozen dead, including three women and five children, and several wounded. This became the standard Israeli method of operation, meant, according to Moshe Dayan, "to set a high price on our blood." Alongside its punitive and deterrent rationale, the price tag was in keeping with the biblical injunction of "an eye for an eye."[61]

The army, the police, and later the Border Guard, a force established specifically for this purpose, tried to halt the return of refugees and expelled many of those who managed to infiltrate Israel.[62] It was a major mission for the security forces. A related mission was the expulsion of large numbers of Bedouin from the Negev. These efforts were only partially successful; in the five years following the War of Independence, about twenty thousand Arabs managed to return to their homes.*[63]

At the end of 1952, Ben-Gurion asked to be excused from chairing a Cabinet meeting. "I have no strength left," he explained. His load was beyond anything a human being could bear, he said. "I do not know how many more days I can go on like this," he wrote in his diary. He received another two-month leave from his responsibilities as prime minister, and suggested that Minister of Finance Levi Eshkol fill in for him.[64] The next evening, he went to see a show at the Cameri Theatre, resuming his youthful hobby of drama criticism. The play was good, and the production nice and appropri-

---

* The expulsion of Palestinian infiltrators led to the death of hundreds of them and involved acts of abuse. A member of the Knesset's Foreign Affairs and Defense Committee asked for Ben-Gurion's response to a report that infiltrators were being tortured during interrogation, including by having their fingernails pulled out. Ben-Gurion promised to investigate the report. (Ben-Gurion to the Foreign Affairs and Defense Committee, June 20, 1950, BGA.)

ate for the material, he said of George Bernard Shaw's *St. Joan*. He went to the Tiberias hot springs; the members of the Cabinet came to have dinner with him.[65] But this time also the vacation did not last long. At the beginning of February 1953, he appeared at a Cabinet meeting and proposed an invasion of Jordan, with the purpose of conquering or destroying the town of Qalqilya.

The day before, a cargo train on its way from Haifa to Lod was attacked. A mine knocked three cars off the tracks, after which assailants fired on the train. No one was hurt, and the train was back on its way a few hours later.[66] Several of the ministers opposed the proposed action. One said that it was not worthwhile conquering Qalqilya, because Israel would have to withdraw afterward, which would be a humiliation. Ben-Gurion said that the town did not have to be captured, only destroyed. The inhabitants would flee and they would have nowhere to come back to. The minister without portfolio Pinhas Lavon (Mapai) expressed concern that women and children might be killed. As in the past, Ben-Gurion responded that there was no way to prevent women and children from being hurt when an Arab village was attacked. He spoke vehemently: "If I were to act according to Pinhas Lavon's logic," he charged, "I could reach the point of saying that people should not have children because children can turn into criminals, a boy can be an idiot, a child could come down with polio, there are any number of such cases . . . If we were to work according to that logic, we would not have a country."

As he often did, he stressed the weight of responsibility on his shoulders. "When I send a platoon of soldiers to guard the border, there is risk involved, and when, unfortunately and painfully, I receive a report that a person has been killed, I feel responsible for that loss of life." The Cabinet authorized him to plan a major military action, but to his chagrin it required him to bring it to the Cabinet for approval before carrying it out. As a result of the tension, he did not resume his vacation. He went back to work for, in his words, "as long as my strength lasts."[67] This time he had enough strength for five months. Then, at the end of a long monologue advocating a resumption of work in King Solomon's copper mines, he said: "I must have a vacation. I can't go on." He proposed that Moshe Sharett fill in for him as prime minister and Pinhas Lavon as defense minister. He promised to make himself available to the chief of staff and ministers, on condition that they allow him at least two weeks of rest. The Cabinet approved a vacation of "about" eight weeks.[68]

A few months later, he again took a trip to Sde Boker. This time it was to look into what sort of work he could do there. "They had already heard rumors that I wanted to come," he noted. He asked about the water problem and grazing, and gave them IL 1,200 for the purchase of two camels; the sum was equivalent to almost five months of a Knesset member's salary.[69] He asked if the crater could be filled with water.[70]

"EVERY WORD IS TRUE!"

During the vacations he took in 1953, Ben-Gurion again devoted his time to studying the state of the IDF. "The inquiries lasted for more than six weeks," he later said. "I not only looked into the Defense Ministry, but also went from place to place, to every army camp. I made a thorough investigation. Mordechai Maklef managed to make some improvements during his single year as chief of staff. He also upgraded the national security conception that had guided Ben-Gurion since the 1930s, "aggressive defense" or, as it was termed in the 1950s, "preventative war and preemptive strike."[71] But the reports received might have reminded him of his seminar of 1947, when he learned about the Haganah's sorry state. There was an ominous disparity between the IDF's strength and that of the Arab armies.

Moshe Dayan, then chief of the IDF's operations branch, told the Cabinet that tensions along the border with Jordan had not been as high since the War of Independence. He was concerned not only by the incidents of murder and robbery, but also by the failure of all efforts to prevent them. The army had deployed fourteen hundred ambushes to capture infiltrators, but most of them failed because, Dayan said, the soldiers were insufficiently trained. Most ambushes and hot pursuits had failed—only thirteen of the forty-two offensive missions assigned to the IDF that year had achieved their objectives. An IDF study in 1954 again found that "the high percentage of backward immigrants in the IDF has a negative effect on the quality of the army in comparison with the War of Independence."[72]

One report contended that if revolutionary changes were not made, the Arabs would surely win the next war. "The picture is appalling," it stated.

Before conveying his findings to the Cabinet, Ben-Gurion warned the ministers that they should prepare to be stunned. The report he would make included terrifying information that would shock them. They should "gird their loins," he told them, because they would need to make heroic efforts to see the situation as it was. Of himself, he said: "While I am no coward, my eyes went dark." Two days later, he offered a similar survey of the army to the Knesset's Foreign Affairs and Defense Committee. The educational level of a large proportion of the IDF's soldiers was, he said, "almost like that of the Arabs." Once again, and even more so than in the past, the ministerial responsibility for this state of affairs was entirely his, but instead of addressing it, the Cabinet debate detoured into an elucidation of the fundamentals of Zionism's attitudes toward the Arabs. Ben-Gurion again harked back to his early days in Palestine. The question had not bothered him until two Jews were killed right by him, he said, but "since then it has pursued me."[73]

One Cabinet minister demanded a clear answer to the question of whether Israel would win the next war. Ben-Gurion first responded that the country was "prepared" for war, but subsequently merely offered one of those convoluted statements that always left him an opening for claiming that everything that happened had been anticipated. "Only a giant fighting a dwarf, or an idiot, can say with one hundred percent certainty that he will win . . . but to the extent that probabilities need to be considered, in a matter of this sort about which there is nothing other than probabilistic computation, I am more or less certain that in a wartime confrontation between us and the Arab world, we will win."[74] A few weeks later, he coined names for two air force jets, calling them *Sa'ar* and *Sufah*, two Hebrew words meaning "storm" or "tempest." He took the names from Psalm 83:16: "Pursue them with your tempest, terrify them with your storm." The entire psalm "matches our situation today," he noted. It is indeed a psalm replete with fear, implying that the Jewish people can do nothing to save themselves; everything is in God's hands.[75]

Before the year was out, Ben-Gurion made more proposals to capture Jordanian territory, including the town of Tulkarem and East Jerusalem's Sheikh Jarrah neighborhood. When he was told that three Israeli soldiers had been killed, he proposed "an aggressive action by a large force on the other side" of the border. He told Sharett that what he meant by that was the conquest of Hebron. He termed it "a means of defense."[76] These ideas were not carried out.

His willingness to invade Jordan reflected his contempt for the armistice lines. "When I look at this strange and ridiculous map . . . I see it not as a Jew but also as an Arab. He, too, cannot accept it." By 1951 at the latest, the IDF completed a plan to conquer the West Bank, should Iraq invade Jordan. But during one of his historical lectures to the Cabinet, Ben-Gurion contested the thesis that the IDF had missed an opportunity to conquer the West Bank during the War of Independence, and argued that not doing so had given Israel a major advantage. Had all the Arab territories to the west of the Jordan River been captured, he argued, the number of refugees would have risen from 800,000 to 1.5 million. "That would not add to our strength and would not bolster our position in the world." As in the past, it was important for him to stress, over and over again, that the Arabs had fled and had not been expelled, but this time he suddenly added: "This small country, which has many enemies in the world, will suffer greatly from these refugees in the future. The world is not easily adjusting to the fact that hundreds of thousands of refugees have been expelled from their homes. It is a fact that hundreds of thousands of people were expelled from their homes. The world has still not come to terms with that."[77]

The world also took an interest in the fate of the Arabs who remained in Israel. Most of them were put under military control, including the Arabs of Iqrit, a Christian village in the Western Galilee, not far from the Lebanese border. The village was conquered by the IDF in November 1948, and its inhabitants were forced to move to another village. Ben-Gurion had approved the expulsion in advance, but said that the Arabs should be told that "we will be willing to discuss their return, as soon as the border is secured." When they were not, however, permitted to return, they petitioned Israel's Supreme Court, which ordered the authorities to allow them back. The IDF nevertheless refused; a part of the village's lands had in the meantime been allocated to Jews. Three months later, the IDF blew up most of the houses in the village, but left the church at its center standing. The operation took place on Christmas Day 1951. Ben-Gurion claimed that neither he nor the chief of staff had ordered the village's demolition; it was done, he said, "by the army," adding, "An inquiry is being conducted into the matter." Several Cabinet ministers criticized the operation, especially in light of the protest issued by the Vatican. Iqrit's inhabitants refused to accept offers to settle them in another location, and thus became symbols of the Palestinian national struggle.

Ben-Gurion cited their position as proof of what he had always thought. "You can't buy the Arabs," he declared; it was "simple human logic" that "the Arab must be on the side of his people and want to see Israel destroyed." It was one of those discussions that dragged its participants toward a debate over the foundation stones of the conflict over Palestine. Ben-Gurion, still sunk in his memories, did not spare the ministers a single one of the seminal experiences that had shaped his attitude toward the Arabs. He repeated the stories as if he were telling them for the first time, beginning with his classmate in Istanbul who had been happy to hear that Ben-Gurion had been expelled from Palestine.[78]

The refugees took an ever more central place in his conception of Israel's security, and, even more important, in his mind. "It is the harshest problem we have, the source of all evil," he said. They were at present the principal enemy. He described them as desperate people, without any hope, acting on their emotions, irrationally. He returned to the subject a few weeks later. The refugees would not disappear for many years to come, he feared, perhaps not for generations. A war might change the country's borders, but there would still be refugees, maybe even more. The key sentence was: "I know of no remedy for this."[79] For the time being, he restricted himself to punitive actions against villages from which terrorists set out on attacks, and demanded that he be authorized to act as he saw best. When Moshe Sharett asked if he would consult with the Foreign Ministry about it, Ben-Gurion replied: "I will no longer consult with the foreign minister, I will not consult with the members of the Cabinet. I will provide the Cabinet with a report every Sunday." Sharett protested; Ben-Gurion repeated: "I will do this at the behest of the Cabinet and will not consult with it any longer."[80]

Israel's reprisals coincided with the efforts to build the IDF up into a fighting force, but many continued to end in failure. In the meantime, they led to the establishment of special forces composed of soldiers whose mentality, methods, and self-image reflected an audacious patriotism in the spirit of the Palmach and American action movies. They specialized in raids over the border and on occasion killed civilians. But, unlike the Palmach, Unit 101, commanded by Ariel Sharon, did not foster political subversion against Ben-Gurion. On the contrary, Ben-Gurion admired these commandos and would protect them to a point that can only be explained by his weakness of mind at the end of 1953. He lied for them, to the public and to the Cabinet as well.[81]

❖

On the night prior to October 13, 1953, Palestinian guerrillas crossed the border from Jordan into the Israeli town of Yehud, north of Lod. The assailants cast a hand grenade into one of the houses. Susan Kinyas, a thirty-two-year-old immigrant from Turkey, and two of her children, born in Israel, were killed—Binyamin, a year and a half old, and four-year-old Shoshana. Other Israeli civilians had been killed in similar attacks in other places in the months preceding this incident. The statement issued by the IDF spokesman referred to it as Yehudiya, the name of the Arab village that stood there before the War of Independence.

At the time, Ben-Gurion was on leave from both his posts. He was in Tiberias, where the IDF was conducting training maneuvers, when the incident occurred. His stand-in as defense minister, Pinhas Lavon, Chief of Staff Maklef, and Operations Chief Dayan were also there. They consulted and decided, in response, to attack a Jordanian village, Qibya. The mission was assigned to a combined force that included a contingent from Unit 101, under Sharon's command. The operational order that Sharon gave to his men included an instruction to maximize casualties and property damage. The force first shelled the village with mortar fire and then went in. It planted explosives on about forty-five of the village's houses and blew them up. About seventy Arabs were killed, most of them women and children. It was the most deadly such incident since Deir Yassin.[82]

Four days later, Ben-Gurion chaired a Cabinet meeting, after returning from his vacation. He began by stating: "I was on vacation and no one needed to ask me whether to carry out a reprisal or not. Had I been asked, I would have said to stage one." In cases like these he knew how to choose his words with great precision. He did not say that he had not been asked, but neither did he reveal that he had taken part in making the decision. He expressed no reservations about the action, but claimed that it had not been carried out by the IDF, but rather by Israelis living along the border. "The army really did not do it," he said again. "The regular army is not capable of doing that. Just as we have set up a special border police force against infiltrators, there is also something special for reprisal actions. That is not a matter for the regular army . . . We do not do reprisal operations with the army. We cannot say that the army exists for that purpose." In the future as well, he said, "settlers" rather than the army would carry out such operations. He stressed that the Cabinet ministers should hold to this version of events unequivocally. "Whether or not anyone believes it is unimportant," he said. He was in a belligerent mood. He had something to say about George Washington's army ("entirely a mob") and a few blunt words in Yiddish on the positions taken by *Ha'aretz* and its editor, Gershom Schocken. Sharett spoke with Ben-Gurion before the meeting. "I found him glowing, as if everything were just fine," Sharett wrote. He said that Ben-Gurion had a trait that astounded him—he was impervious to reality.[83]

The ministers knew Ben-Gurion was lying. They agreed that it was best to issue a denial, but felt uncomfortable with the fact that the prime minister would not tell them the truth, either. At one point, he tried to give them the impression that he had heard about what had happened only the next day, on the Jordanian radio station that broadcast from Ramallah, in the West Bank. Some of them, led by the head of the religious Zionist Mizrahi movement, Moshe Shapira, forcefully condemned the operation. Ben-Gurion demanded that they approve a statement attributing the operation to inhabitants of the border region, "most of them Jews from the Arab countries or survivors of the Nazi concentration camps." Minister of Justice Pinchas Rosen commented, almost apologetically: "It is not good for the prime minister to issue a statement that is not true." Ben-Gurion replied: "Every word is true!"[84]

Israel had regularly denied its involvement in incursions into Arab villages even before the government issued its denial about the Qibya attack. Civilians living on the border indeed took part in some such operations at the time.[85]

"MY WHOLE BODY TREMBLES"

A few days following the attack on Qibya, Ben-Gurion called in Ariel Sharon. It was largely a get-acquainted meeting with a man he mistakenly referred to as "Aharon" in his diary. Sharon was the son of farmers who had immigrated to Palestine during the Third Aliyah, but he had not been born at a kibbutz and had not served in the Palmach. That was a big advantage in Ben-Gurion's eyes. He had been wounded twice during the War of Independence, reaching officer rank by the end of his service. After the war, he studied agriculture and Oriental studies at the Hebrew University. Ben-Gurion hoped to build the IDF with people like him. "At one of my meetings with him in his library," Sharon later related, "he invited me into his bedroom, sat on the standard-issue bed, went to the cupboard, opened it, and took out a Czech rifle, one of those we received in 1948. The rifle mechanism was still covered with grease, and Ben-Gurion caressed it, speaking wistfully about his service in the Jewish Legion and then going directly into the pride he felt at there being Jewish soldiers, Jewish pilots, Jewish paratroopers."

He wanted to know everything about Unit 101 and its men. Were they disciplined, were they angered by his denial of their operation in Qibya? Sharon replied that his men would be angry if the government were to decide to restrain its response to Arab attacks, but would remain disciplined and would not act of their own volition. No, they were not upset when Ben-Gurion's lie was broadcast.[86] Sharon probably told him what he later told one of his biographers: "We went into each room. We illuminated it with a flashlight and only afterward did we take the house down. No one answered our questions as to whether anyone was at home. Most of the inhabitants apparently really fled. Otherwise the catastrophe would have been much greater. We did nothing brutal. On the contrary: one officer heard a girl crying in a house that was about to be blown up. He went in and took the girl out. On the street we encountered a boy wandering there and we told him where to flee to."[87]

He described the operation as a military one in every respect, and boasted about the combat tactics they had used, focusing on the element of surprise— they penetrated the village before opening fire. "We were determined there to turn the village into a pile of rubble," he said. True, the Israeli forces were spotted about an hour before the attack began. "The Arabs shot like madmen," Sharon said. But the Israelis did not return fire. Silence causes panic, he explained. "Qibya's fall was not a result of being broken physically. I don't think a single Arab was killed in Qibya before it was captured. They were broken mentally." He described his men's motivation: "We reached the conclusion that the principal factor is their sense of self-respect, which is the major spur to fight. Love of the homeland and national spirit do not really affect fighting . . . There isn't any Zionism. In many cases people think—what will the guy lying to my left think of me. A soldier who knows that he constantly has to account for himself to the social environment in which he lives will do everything to excel, and not to dishonor himself."[88] Moshe Dayan was also pleased. "From a military point of view it was an operation of the first order," he wrote. "Our men took control of the village and acted as if it were their own." The village's houses were blown up "without anyone thinking that there were still people in a few of them."[89]

No one was held accountable for Qibya. Lavon became defense minister in his own right, and Dayan chief of staff, while Sharon embarked on a promising military career. Ben-Gurion protected them and in doing so extricated himself from a bind as well. He had done the same thing in the 1920s with David Remez, who shared responsibility with him for the Solel Boneh scandal. And he did it also with Eliyahu Golomb, his co-neglecter of the Haganah in the 1930s, and Moshe Sneh after the King David Hotel bombing. The message conveyed from the top echelons of the IDF down to its rank and file was that when an operation failed or disgrace threatened, the thing to do was to lie and evade responsibility.

Foreign Minister Sharett's role in the episode reflected his pathetically weak character. He claimed to have first heard of the murder at Yehud in the evening; he was very busy that day, he explained. He learned of the killings at the same time that he was informed of the plan to carry out a retaliation operation, at a chance encounter with Lavon during a meeting of Mapai's Political Committee. Sharett did not oppose the operation at that juncture, but, by his account, the next day he informed Lavon that he had changed his mind. When he learned that the IDF was about to act anyway, he sent a letter to Ben-Gurion informing him that he was no longer functioning as his stand-in. After the attack, he asked himself why he had not called an emergency Cabinet meeting. Had he known in advance what the results of the operation would be, he maintained, he would not have hesitated to get the ministers out of their beds. He helped Ben-Gurion draft his untruthful statement.[90]

Sometimes it seemed as if Sharett were following a path of his own, more cautious and considered than Ben-Gurion's. But, in large part, it was a difference of style more than substance; they followed the same path. Sharett also believed that the conflict with the Arabs could not be solved and that all that could be done was to manage it. A month after independence was declared, while the war still raged, he wrote that the evacuation of Arabs from their homes was "the most spectacular event in the contemporary history of Palestine—more spectacular in a sense than the creation of the Jewish state."[91] He did not reject reprisal operations in principle.

Relations between him and Ben-Gurion had their ups and downs, and highlighted their fundamental character traits. Sharett was awed by Ben-Gurion, to the point of self-negation; Ben-Gurion appreciated Sharett's abilities but was less taken by his personality. He recorded in his diary a telling comment on Sharett that he heard from an acquaintance: "He doesn't have the divine spirit, but he is a good minister, of the craftsman type." In a letter to Paula he wrote: "He is not a man of vision, his thinking is not deep . . . he is unable to make decisions on matters that require great mental and moral courage. But he knows his work. He is a man of many talents and he is dedicated and committed to his work, and it seems to me that he himself knows that he requires guidance."

Neither was Ben-Gurion's attitude toward Sharett free of biographical baggage. Like Ben-Gurion, Sharett had arrived in Palestine in 1906, though not as a lone young man of twenty but rather as a twelve-year-old boy who arrived with a supportive family. Unlike Ben-Gurion, he had never known financial straits in Palestine—his family was well-off. Sharett knew Arabic and felt well integrated into the country. His family had spent two years living in an Arab village. He had been a graduate of the prestigious Herzliya Hebrew Gymnasium high school's first class and served as an officer in the Turkish army. After his military service, he enrolled at the London School of Economics. He knew languages and attended concerts. All this made him a member of the Second Aliyah aristocracy. He married Shaul Avigur's sister; one of his sisters married Eliyahu Golomb and another Dov Hoz, all three men among the founders and leaders of the Haganah. In the history of the Zionist elite in Palestine they were known as the "four brothers-in-law." Sharett had been mentored by Berl Katznelson, Haim Arlosoroff, and Chaim Weizmann. Ben-Gurion began from nothing and built himself up. He seems to have felt a need to look down on Sharett.

When his retirement approached, Ben-Gurion suggested that Levi Eshkol replace him as prime minister rather than Sharett—a good choice. He did not offer Eshkol the Defense Ministry. Sharett was deeply wounded and Eshkol rejected the offer. Sharett was the fallback, and would become the next prime minister. Ben-Gurion offered the defense portfolio to Lavon.[92]

It was an unfortunate outcome. Sharett was too weak, Lavon and Dayan too strong. Lavon, the first Mapai Cabinet minister to be born in the twentieth century, was considered a rising star. He had behind him many years as a party and Histadrut functionary and no few admirers. As a member of the Knesset, he was known as a gifted orator. He tended toward moderate positions on political issues, in the spirit of Hapo'el Hatza'ir. In May 1948, he seems to have been among the few Mapai leaders who opposed declaring independence, in the hope that war could be averted. Prior to being appointed defense minister, he tended to support Sharett's more cautious line. When Ben-Gurion went on vacation and Lavon filled in for him as defense minister, he adopted Ben-Gurion's line. He accepted responsibility for the Qibya operation. Ben-Gurion nurtured him as an ally. Relations between Lavon and Sharett were bad, and Ben-Gurion knew it. He also knew that Lavon drank too much and Ben-Gurion heard warnings about his growing extremism.[93] Sharett was apprehensive about Dayan. He had known him for many years and thought him "crooked and perverse," a man whose integrity was "extremely flexible," he wrote, adding: "Who knows what complications and crises await us." Other Cabinet ministers also feared Dayan. It was a good reason not to appoint at least one of them, unless Ben-Gurion intended to ensure that the government could not function without him. Whatever the case, the hopeless weakness of the troika that Ben-Gurion left behind him would soon require his return.[94]

❖

Before he left, Ben-Gurion presented the Cabinet with an eighteen-point farewell program for rehabilitating the army, including a reduction in regular manpower. He estimated that it would be at least two years before the Arabs would launch a second round; in the meantime, the army had to depend to a large extent on its reservists. He stressed the importance of the armored corps, but believed that the army should depend mostly on its air force. He ended with a rare expression of self-criticism: defense affairs require a full-time minister, he said; he had also been preoccupied with other matters. "In that sense, I betrayed my trust," he said.[95]

The legacy he left his successors on security matters reflected a nightmarish fantasy about the country being overrun with Palestinian Arabs. It was good reason not to revoke the military control imposed on Israel's Arab citizens, as Lavon had proposed. "The minute we do away with the restrictions on the movement of Arabs, the number of Arabs will double every year, because Arabs in the Triangle will move to Haifa and Tel Aviv and work there, and others from over the border will move into their villages . . . The danger is that if there is freedom of movement, those 600,000 or more refugees living on our borders will cross the border and enter the villages that have emptied."*[96]

During one of his last appearances in the Cabinet's meeting room, Ben-Gurion suddenly went off on a reverie about the sea. "The sea is endless," he said. "It is a place where we can expand the country." He seems to have meant some sort of imperial expansion, on the British model. Up until three centuries ago, the British had been a nation in their land, but then it expanded. "It provides political power and security as well," he said. "And we need to take advantage of the German reparations for this purpose. If we can obtain ships in Germany, we need to buy the maximum amount."[97]

The news that he was leaving everything in order to settle "in the middle of the desert" spread fast through the political system. At first the story sounded baseless and mysterious. The press referred obliquely to what Ben-Gurion had told the Cabinet about his fatigue and mental distress, and more explicit

---

* To bring home how profoundly concerned he was that a majority of the Galilee's inhabitants were Arabs, he used a Nazi term, saying that "the Galilee is *Judenrein*"—that is, "purged of Jews." (Ben-Gurion to the Cabinet, Nov. 8, 1953, ISA.)

information spread by word of mouth. *Davar* tried to squelch the rumors in an article that censured other newspapers and demanded that they restrain themselves. "Let us suppose that the truth is that D. Ben-Gurion wishes to cease his activity in Israel's government for a year or two," the Histadrut daily speculated. "Let us suppose that this indeed has psychological and physical motives, after the great tension of the last six years." *Davar* had broken the taboo, and everyone in Israel began gossiping freely about the prime minister's mental state.

He did not hide the problem. "I can no longer take the mental pressure regarding what I do in the government," he wrote to President Ben-Zvi. The decisions he had to make, he explained, often sealed the fates of others. He had to choose between sometimes dangerous alternatives in given situations. This required inner concentration and maximum mental and psychological acuity. "There are apparently limits that have been placed, at least in my case, on the psychological effort that I am capable of." He later offered a more detailed account of the difficulty of discerning good from evil. "I am so tense that I am not sure that I am able to weigh things in a responsible way," he said, "and sometimes there are questions upon which the fate of the country depends."[98]

Yitzhak Navon recalled a Friday night at the home of Renana, Ben-Gurion's daughter, who was a microbiologist. The guests debated whether humans or machines are smarter. Ben-Gurion said that humans are, on the grounds that a human being can make a machine but a machine cannot make a human being. He walked out to the balcony and Navon followed him. Ben-Gurion sprawled on a couch there. It was a warm evening; they listened silently to the chirping of the crickets. Suddenly Ben-Gurion said: "When I need to decide something, I think of a particular solution. If I feel a kind of electricity run through my whole body, if my whole body trembles, I know that the solution is correct. It has never led me wrong." On at least two other occasions he described his decisions as the result of sudden illumination, and then he also maintained that "this way I have never made a mistake."[99]

At about that same time, his aides noted his attraction to mysticism. As his retirement approached, he seems to have developed a predilection for it. One of his close associates, Ya'akov Herzog, told Sharett that Ben-Gurion showed him a twenty-volume set of the *Zohar*, the classic work of Jewish mysticism, which he intended to take with him to Sde Boker. He declared, "ceremoniously and adamantly," that he intended to embark on a serious study of Kabbalah and understand it thoroughly. Herzog, whose father was the chief rabbi of Israel, knew other people whose absorption with the higher celestial spheres had led them to lose their minds. He worried that the same thing would happen with Ben-Gurion and suggested that they think about how they could ensure that Ben-Gurion would remain anchored to reality. Sharett reassured him, reminding him of Ben-Gurion's fascination with the philosophy of ancient Greece and India.*[100]

The members of Mapai competed with one another over who was best able to persuade Ben-Gurion that he could not abandon his country and his party. They were, quite naturally, looking after their own interests as well. One of them showed himself to be a true friend, though, by proposing that they should let him go. It was Shlomo Lavi. "It's done," he said. "We should accompany him, as good and devoted friends should accompany such a friend . . . These are the intuitions of a great man, not everyone can reach him and understand them."[101]

Three weeks later, Ben-Gurion asked for permission to hand the keys to his house over to the Cabinet secretary. This should be seen as a "natural request," one Cabinet minister suggested. "We know the background. I will not speak about it now."[102] Ten days later, he left Tel Aviv. On his first day of work at Sde Boker, he cleaned manure out of the stables. "It's interesting that my first job in Palestine was also carrying manure," he pondered.[103]

---

* In April 1953, Ben-Gurion met "an expert in palmistry," as he put it. He permitted the expert to photograph his hand. "He is certain that, from the signs on the hand, it is possible to tell not only a person's character, but also what will happen to him in the future, and the length of his life," he wrote. (Ben-Gurion, Diary, April 28, 1953, BGA.)

20

THE NASTY BUSINESS

"I HAVE BECOME A BROTHER TO JACKALS"

Reporters staked out around the Ben-Gurion home in the early morning of December 14, 1953, noticed that the lights went on at 6:00 a.m. Paula, in blue pajamas, stepped out onto the street and asked some police guards to help her with the final packing. Packages and bundles were loaded onto a pickup truck, as were a kerosene heater, blankets, and pillows. Then came crates upon crates of books. An industrious correspondent for *Ma'ariv* jotted down some of the authors and titles: Einstein, the Bible with Shmuel Leib Gordon's commentary, Oswald Spengler's *Decline of the West*, Indian philosophy, the poetry of Judah Halevi, histories of Greece and Rome, the *Zohar*. In the meantime, Renana arrived, as did a number of Mapai functionaries and Ben-Gurion's aides. Ehud Avriel showed up with his brother, Haggai. A gaggle of schoolchildren gathered on the sidewalk, satchels on their backs, and neighbors emerged. One of the reports said that there were tears in the eyes of some of the onlookers.

Ben-Gurion had received piles of letters from citizens pleading with him to stay on, many from children and teenagers. The two large afternoon newspapers were full of separation anxiety. "As he goes," the editor of *Ma'ariv* wrote, "we are overcome with the fear that from now on our lives will seem drab and routine." Cabinet Secretary Ze'ev Sherf, who regarded Ben-Gurion as the Messiah himself, hoped with all his heart that his savior had only gotten a bit weary and would quickly return. The opposition press attributed his exit to his failures in government and told him not to return—they thought the whole thing was a political gambit. Many suspected that he was not moving to Sde Booker permanently, although his diary entry for that day indicates that he indeed intended to do so.[1] On the other hand, he had said publicly on any number of occasions that his retirement would last for a year and a half, two years, or three; he made no commitment to stay at Sde Boker. In general, his relations with the kibbutzim were not good. He appreciated their role in Zionist settlement of the land, but seems to have been skeptical about their value as social institutions. "I give much credit to and very much respect the equality and moral values of the commune," he wrote a while after his arrival in Sde Boker, "but I think it is a serious mistake, both theoretical and practical, to make equality the central and fundamental value." Some kibbutzim had rebelled in the 1920s against the authority of the Histadrut and Mapai; politically, he saw them as a hostile force. When he told the Knesset that the kibbutzim had not taken in enough immigrants, he added that they had also not sent enough volunteers to fight in the War of Independence; not long thereafter he demanded to receive a list of kibbutzim that employed Arabs.[2]

As the Cold War intensified, many kibbutzim were beginning to come apart at the seams. Pioneering comrades who had lived together communally, sharing the same dream, suddenly discovered that ideas were stronger than friendship. They began to trade blows over who represented the absolute good and who utter evil—Stalin or Eisenhower. Suddenly the members of each camp could not stand the members of the other. They could no longer bring up children and raise cows together, nor could they eat together. A line was literally drawn down the middle of some communal dining rooms to separate the adherents of Soviet-aligned Mapam from the members of American-aligned Mapai; it was called the Thirty-Eighth Parallel, after the line that divided the Korean Peninsula into Soviet- and American-controlled zones after World War II.

In some cases husbands and wives separated and children had to choose not only between their mother and father but also between the Russians and the Americans. For Ben-Gurion, it was "the greatest disaster that has ever happened to our movement." In the big picture, it followed the lines of old battles for political control of labor Zionism. Shlomo Lavi, who had never recovered from the previous conflict that split Ein Harod, now got into fist-fights with some of the young people "trained in jujitsu" at his kibbutz, as he wrote in *Davar*; it was fathers against sons. They did not even comprehend how fond he was of them and how much he loved the kibbutz he had helped found.[3] Ben-Gurion tried to encourage him: "The kibbutz is the most won-derful thing that has happened to our nation, and has made a decisive contribution to the genesis of the pioneering movement," he wrote to his friend.[4] Lavi was then, at the age of seventy, a member of the Knesset for Mapai. He did not stand out in that body; most of his speeches dealt with economics and agriculture. Once he inserted himself into a rather macabre debate between the parents of a fallen soldier and a kibbutz over who should determine whether or not the soldier would be buried in the kibbutz ceme-tery. He suggested that the decision should be left to the soldier's family.[5] In May 1954, while driving, Lavi hit a road worker and killed him. Lavi sunk into deep depression and his friends feared he might do something to him-self. Ben-Gurion quickly sent him a book of his essays, with a personal dedi-cation: "With love and admiration." Lavi was convicted only of not honking in warning and was fined.[6] Ein Harod soon split into two kibbutzim and its land was divided between them.

This was the background to Ben-Gurion's decision to join Sde Boker. He chose this specific commune not just because it was isolated and full of pio-neering spirit, and not just because he dreamed of a new beginning. The important point was that, during its first years, Israel's "first cowboys," as *Davar* referred to them, did not yet call their settlement a kibbutz. Its mem-bers were sworn individualists, just like Ben-Gurion himself. As such, they termed themselves a group of workers in a communal agricultural settlement, or an "agricultural cooperative." They refused to join or align themselves with any of the settlement movements.[7] That was what won his heart and responded to his longing for a national, nonpartisan form of pioneering activity.

❖

He emerged from his house in a dark suit, wearing a blue tie with white polka dots. His official car waited for him on the street, as did a convoy of a dozen other vehicles, carrying security guards, a construction engineer, an electrician, and photographers. Mazal Jibli, the faithful housemaid, also came along to help them through their initial days at Sde Boker. When the caravan reached Be'er-Sheva, they stopped at a local café. The mayor came to greet Ben-Gurion, as did many of the city's inhabitants. Moshe Dayan also made an appearance. They reached Sde Boker in the early afternoon, during a rainstorm. More reporters and photographers were waiting for Ben-Gurion by the cabin that Solel Boneh had built for the new settler couple. It consisted of a small bedroom for Ben-Gurion, a study with room for about a thousand books, a corridor, a somewhat larger bedroom for Paula, an alcove, a small kitchen, a shower, and a bathroom. A solar water heater stood on the roof, "a new invention," Ben-Gurion noted. There was also a gas oven that took a lot of work to light. Paula immediately set to organizing the cupboards; the rest of the party helped Ben-Gurion arrange his books. They ate lunch in the communal dining room; the main course was lamb cutlets.

The dozen or so members of the cooperative had had to approve the membership of the new couple. Some were opposed, because the constant hubbub they would bring with them would ruin the community's pastoral atmosphere. The community would always be full of security personnel, VIPs, and the press. In the end, they gave their consent, and accepted Ben-Gurion's offer to put in four hours of work a day for the collective.[8] On his first day, when he was taken to spread manure in one of the fields, the work exhausted him. The next day he plowed. "The work was even harder," he wrote to Amos, "because we plowed with a single mule, and one of us drove the mule and the other held the plow. But holding on is not enough. It takes no little strength to ensure that the plow doesn't slip over the earth but stays deep and turns over the clods along the desired furrow." Ben-Gurion and his partner shared the two tasks. It was cold, and the wind was full of dust. "After work I felt as if my bones were breaking," he told his son, but in his diary he wrote: "We will win out over nature!" Two weeks later, he fell ill; a doctor was called in from Be'er-Sheva.[9] After he recovered, he worked at an easier job, in the sheep pen.

He tried to convince himself that he was living a good life, and that is what he told the many Israelis who wanted to know how he was. On one of his first nights there, he slept for six straight hours, for the first time in fifteen years. True, he had taken a sleeping pill, he wrote, but he had done that in the past as well, and it hadn't helped. He wrote to Moshe Sharett that he felt more or less as he had on his first day in Palestine. In another letter he wrote, "I feel here like in the old days at Sejera."*[10]

But Sejera had been a joyful place in the ascent of a boy of twenty; he arrived at Sde Boker as a broken and declining man of sixty-seven. He had not willingly left the government; he did so with great and profound sorrow, as he wrote to President Ben-Zvi, because he had reached the conclusion that he was no longer capable and, most important, that it would not be right for him to carry on. It was a "sad admission, but I have no choice," he wrote to the Mapai Central Committee; to several of his Cabinet ministers he wrote that his retirement was an "unpleasant necessity." He said the same on the radio and in a farewell letter to the IDF. When Shaul Avigur tried to persuade him to remain, his eyes filled with tears. "You do not know to what extent my strength is gone," he said, in Avigur's account. "I would betray my trust if I were to stay on."[11]

About ten days after he began to work, he recalled a horrible verse from the book of Job. It came to him when he and Haggai Avriel were sowing orache, also called saltbush, a flowering plant that sheep graze on. "Wasted from want and starvation, they flee to a parched land, to the gloom of desolate wasteland, they pluck saltbush and wormwood," he quoted Job 30:3–4. In the Bible with Gordon's commentary that he took with him to Sde Boker he could read that the verses describe the dramatic reversal of Job's fortunes,

---

* Among the young people working at Sde Boker, Ben-Gurion discovered Eliezer Regev, who had been born at Sejera. He was the grandson of the farmer Avraham Rogachevsky, who had employed him there. (Ben-Gurion to Ya'akov Regev, Nov. 11, 1967, BGA; Sheleg 1998, p. 132.)

from a time when he was honored by great and important people, to now being scorned and disgraced. Just before this verse appear the lines "But now those younger than I deride me," and soon thereafter: "They have thrown off restraint in my presence . . . I looked forward to good fortune, but evil came . . . I have become a brother to jackals."[12]

A trip he took in the surrounding area depressed him. The desert's spaces were huge, and "you don't know why they were created," he wrote. "At times the question has come to me, during these trips, if I did not make a mistake when I insisted on the conquest of the Negev." His answer was in the negative, that he had not erred, but the question kept coming up. Here and there he found settlements that aroused his enthusiasm, but they were isolated oases.[13]

"THE DEVOTION OF YOUR YOUTH"

At first they had no telephone. He was entitled to one as a former member of the Knesset, and he applied to that body to receive a line. In the meantime, he had to communicate by Morse code. Shlomo Gazit, the chief of staff's bureau chief, told him that he could not receive a radio phone because there were only five of them in the entire IDF.[14] An airstrip was built nearby, where a Piper could land and take off; the army regularly patrolled the area, to ensure his security.*

His aides continued to manage his affairs as if he had not retired. Teddy Kollek, director of the Prime Minister's Office, and Military Secretary Argov frequently visited him to update him on government affairs and to find out what he needed. From time to time he summoned Cabinet ministers to urge them to carry out all sorts of plans he concocted in his head.[15] Newspapers and mail came from Be'er-Sheva. He received thousands of letters, from Israel and overseas. He did not at first have a secretary to vet the letters for him, so he took it upon himself to answer them all, dozens every day. People wanted to know what he was doing, what he felt, and what he thought about

* The Be'er-Sheva police sent him a trained watchdog named Eldad. Ben-Gurion carefully recorded all the words the dog knew. He was a good dog, he wrote the next day, but asked that Eldad be taken back, as he had barked all night. (Ben-Gurion, Diary, Jan. 18–19, 1953, BGA.)

myriad subjects. Some asked his help in solving personal problems.[16] His handwriting was difficult to read; he wrote his replies in a notebook with numbered pages. He placed carbon paper between the pages, so that a copy of each reply would be preserved in his archives. Later he stopped answering them all and a personal secretary helped him.*

He wrote articles for *Davar* and put a lot of effort into a lengthy piece for *The New York Times*. Upon his arrival, he handed over to the commune's treasury close to half of his salary as a member of the Knesset, of which he formally remained a member throughout his sojourn at Sde Boker, and from time to time he was asked to intervene in the community's internal matters. But all in all he had little contact with the others in the community, eating only occasionally in the dining hall. He showed up for the first wedding to be conducted there wearing a tie and a military windbreaker; Paula came in a coat with a fur collar; they looked very out of place.[17] His closest friends there were Yehoshua Cohen, who was responsible for his security, and his wife, Nehama. Once a day, Ben-Gurion went out for a walk. When he wanted to leave the confines of Sde Boker, special security arrangements had to be made and Cohen accompanied him. Over time the two became close friends; he knew that Cohen had been a member of Lehi, but saw him as an idealist. Ben-Gurion had, in the past, displayed admiration for other members of Lehi and Etzel. Only later did he learn that Cohen had been involved in the murder of Count Bernadotte, the Swedish UN peace envoy.†

❖

Paula was miserable and lonely. When they left Tel Aviv, Ben-Gurion gave her one of his collections of articles and wrote a dedication: "To Paula with love. I accounted to your favor the devotion of your youth, your love as a bride, how you followed me in the wilderness in a land not sown." It was a

---

* For a short time he tried, unsuccessfully, to learn how to type. His secretary rejected his repeated requests to learn how to drive a jeep. (Elhanan Yishai, interview transcript, BGA.)
† Cohen did not himself tell Ben-Gurion about his involvement. Ben-Gurion learned of it through one of his biographers, Michael Bar-Zohar, who found Cohen's name on a list of suspects that Ben-Gurion had written in his diary immediately after the assassination. (Bar-Zohar 1977, p. 836.)

quote, Jeremiah 2:2, a speech by God to the Israelite nation. It did not make her feel better. "What does he think, that he's Tolstoy?" she protested. He did not compel her to come with him, but he refused to change his plan. It was just like the beginning of their life together in New York, when she was pregnant and he left her so he could serve in the Jewish Legion. Perhaps her exile in the wilderness was like her exile in snowy Płońsk, some thirty years previously.

She hated every day of it. She especially suffered during the time they lacked a telephone. The food served in the communal dining room was horrible; Paula barely touched it.[18] Drivers from the Defense Ministry would bring her food packages containing items she had ordered, including fruit and wine. Bread was sometimes parachuted to her from an airplane.[19]

He seems to have softened toward her in those months, and when she went away, he felt intense longing, as during their early time together. Once, when she made a trip to Tel Aviv, he wrote to her: "After you left I became very sad. I feel as if the house is empty; a thick cloud covers the sky." He ate in the kitchen, the food was not bad, he told her, "but when I returned to my room I felt horrible loneliness and I lost all desire to read. The house is very quiet, but it is an oppressive quiet, not a relaxing one." He hoped that she would enjoy Tel Aviv, see the children, and that "this time" she would not find a reason to argue with Renana. A week later, he wrote to her again. "It is very sad without you," he told her, and added that "today I planted two trees next to the cabin." Yitzhak Navon related that sometimes, on trips outside Sde Boker, "he would put his head in her lap and nap, while she placed her hand on his head and stroked him fondly." Sometimes she talked to friends about how much he hurt her and she broke out in tears.*[20]

❖

He spent most of his time after work in the company of a rising tide of innumerable visitors. He complained about the inconvenience; he did not want

---

* In August 1954, Miss May visited Ben-Gurion at Sde Boker. The only thing he wrote about it in his diary was "she argued about Qibya." It is not clear whether Paula was home that day. (Ben-Gurion to Paula, Jan. 13, 18, 1954; Navon 2015, p. 111.)

to see them all, did not know them all, did not want to know them all, among the latter all sorts of zany inventors and nuisances. A man by the name of Moshe Dweik harangued him about a number of topics and demanded "to look into the state of the army." Ben-Gurion said that he looked strange but also seemed to be sincere and honest. But he told his visitor that, were he minister of defense, he would not permit Dweik to conduct an investigation of the army. Dweik was offended, it seems. "I will not come again unless I am called," he said proudly, and went. Three years later, he appeared again in Ben-Gurion's life, unannounced, with a bomb.[21]

Photographers from around the world trekked out to the desert to immortalize the famous shepherd among his lambs. "My hope is that they will forget about me in a week or two," he wrote. On the other hand, he did not instruct the Prime Minister's Office to put an end to the visits.[22] For the most part, the pilgrims seem to have been to his liking. Not a month had gone by before Minister of Finance Eshkol arrived to consult with him about the defense budget; Ben-Gurion opposed cutting it. A party leader came to ask his advice about the coalition negotiations, and shortly thereafter President and Mrs. Ben-Zvi came for a visit, followed by Prime Minister Sharett and his wife. "It occurred to me that he might get disgusted with the whole thing very quickly," Sharett said to his colleagues.[23]

A few days later, Ben-Gurion flew to Tel Aviv to visit Paula, who had been hospitalized.*

He went to his home in Tel Aviv, where he met with Pinhas Lavon and Shimon Peres, director-general of the Defense Ministry. Two weeks later, Chief of Staff Moshe Dayan came to Sde Boker; from that point onward the two of them met once every few weeks, sometimes alone and sometimes along with others.[24] The country was awash with rumors that Ben-Gurion intended to return to government.

A prematurely mature fifteen-year-old, a member of the Masada Scout troop, sent him a pointed letter from Jerusalem. "I fear that in going to Sde Boker, you have left behind in Tel Aviv not only the prime minister, but also the leader within you," the boy wrote, adding, "And I regret that." He called

---

* Paula sometimes had herself hospitalized for no reason at all, as a way of getting her husband's attention. (Jibli, interview transcript, BGA; Navon 2015, p. 110.)

on Ben-Gurion to lead Israel's youth in a war against corruption, vapidity, and careerism. He presumed that Ben-Gurion could still do this, despite the "mistakes" he had made. He thus insisted on an answer: "Was 'Sde Boker' the retreat and surrender of a weary, broken, and disheartened man, or was it a stage and link in a leader's struggle?" If the former, "I can do nothing but eulogize the leader who broke," but if the latter, "it is my opinion that you are obligated to answer this letter." He apologized for his letter's disrespectful tone, but added, "Neither of us needs decorum." He made a point of noting that he did not number himself among Ben-Gurion's admirers, and signed "In appreciation, but not without reservations."

Ben-Gurion replied less than five days later. "I enjoyed your style of writing," he complimented the boy, Amos Oz. But he corrected him: it was not the job of young people to fight corruption; their job was to engage in pioneering settlement. He left his correspondent's main question unanswered, "for my own reasons," as he put it.[25] In fact, he had a great desire to impart his vision to his country's youth; he may have hoped that his move to Sde Boker would set off a massive wave of pioneer settlement. If so, he was disappointed.[26] Whatever the case, thirteen years after he traveled the country as a Zionist preacher, he prepared for another round.

"WHO WILL BE THE DICTATOR?"

In the mid-1950s, Israeli high school students began adopting elements of style imported from the United States. It was an American dream that Ben-Gurion himself had adopted in his youth and fostered his entire life. Now, cut off entirely from this ambience—clothing, hairstyles, films, songs, and expectations from life—Ben-Gurion believed that he could galvanize young people to enlist in a new pioneering movement. The best way to do so, he thought, was to bring several thousand of them on trains and buses to an open area in central Israel where he could make a speech.[27] It was meant to be a momentous event; he dreamed of a national, nonpartisan "youth front." He was thinking of a mass youth movement, under state control, with links to the Ministry of Defense and the army. The scheme worried his rivals in the labor movement and in the Knesset; some saw it as the first step toward a dictatorship.[28]

A few weeks before the convocation, while he was working in the sheep pen, he picked up a ewe to hand her over to be sheared and felt a pain in his back. He went on with his work, picking up a second ewe. "When I wanted to take a third ewe, I felt horrible pain and I was barely able to walk home," he wrote. It was his first attack of lumbago since his trip to the United States three years previously. He was hospitalized at Tel Hashomer, just outside Tel Aviv. Preparations for the youth convocation continued in the meantime. He was still hospitalized when the appointed day arrived, but insisted on going anyway. He arrived leaning on a cane.[29] It was a humiliating event. Very few of the young people who came saw him, and it is doubtful that many heard him—the loudspeakers did not work properly. He told his audience that they had a choice between "career and calling." The speech lasted for about an hour and a half. At the end a huge fire inscription was lit, spelling out the slogan "To the farm, to the frontier."

The young people interrupted him, and worse yet jeered. Not because they were Communists, as one of his aides maintained, but because they were teenagers and he did not speak their language. The only thing he said that received thunderous applause was his plea to increase the birthrate.*[30]

Dayan did all he could during that period to give Ben-Gurion the feeling that his leadership was vital and that the public wanted it. Sharett feared that the chief of staff was seeking to replace the country's leadership.[31] For his part, Ben-Gurion not only aimed for a new leadership, but also fantasized about a new sort of regime. His Youth Front was meant to be part of a larger Popular Front.

❖

Three elections were to take place in the coming year—for the Histadrut, municipalities, and the Knesset. Ben-Gurion still had no equal as a political campaigner, and the Mapai leadership did not find it difficult to enlist him

---

* A young newspaper reporter who wrote a rhymed account of the event reported that, on their way there, the young people sang Frankie Laine's "Kiss of Fire." Prime Minister Sharett planned to listen to a recording of the speech on the radio, but he couldn't make it through to the end. It was too full of "eternal truths," he said. (Kabalo 2003, p. 123ff.; Moshe Sharett, Diary, June 10, 1954, in Sharett 1978, p. 544.)

in the effort. Partisan politics was an elixir of youth for him. He was able to set aside his mental fatigue for at least a period of time. Again, he was replaying an event in his past, and took up the challenge with vigor and nostalgia. "I do not know what can be done among the shopkeepers," he wrote, just as he had during the great battle to "conquer Zionism" in 1933. He made a condition for his participation: Mapai would have to adopt his demand to change the Knesset's electoral system, with the aim of turning a multiparty system into a two-party system. Mapai agreed.[32]

It was a subject that had long preoccupied him, but it came to a head largely because of the coming elections. "This existing system of government," he argued, "undermines democracy, divides the people, weakens government, creates endless crises, increases extortion, and educates to irresponsibility." He predicted "a catastrophe for the state and for the nation" if the existing system remained unchanged, warning that "it could lead to destruction." The principal danger, he said, was that Israeli society was still then, to a large extent, "a welter of tribes and rabble." He wanted a "British regime," in particular a two-party system. The person who took responsibility for this project was Ehud Avriel. His impression was that Ben-Gurion saw this as a "magic key to paradise." A number of Mapai leaders suspected that its main purpose was to circumvent the party, or at the very least to replace them with the younger cohort that Ben-Gurion had begun to gather around him. They resolved to call Ben-Gurion in for "clarifications."[33]

The term "front" had a pronounced antidemocratic flavor. Some members of the young guard, who tried to enhance their power by virtue of their close relationship with Ben-Gurion, indeed tended to disregard the rule of law. Ben-Gurion's opposition to a constitution, and his tendency to place "national interest" as he defined it above the law, encouraged some of them to advocate one-man rule.

In a conversation with several leaders of one of the settlement movements, Ben-Gurion was asked if it would not be best for Israel to be run by a dictator, at least for a time. Ben-Gurion asked: "Who will be the dictator?" They replied: "You. Take over the government, for a while not necessarily in accordance with democratic procedure, until everything is okay." It apparently was something he had thought of before, because he was ready with a response about why it was not a good idea. "I'll tell you what the problem with a dictatorship is," he said. "If we always knew that the dictator would be elected in a democratic process, that wouldn't be so bad. But we don't know who will be dictator. It could be me, it could be you, and it could be the most undesirable person in our nation or another nation. Therefore, even if it could be an excellent solution, it would be a national catastrophe that should never be abetted."[34]

Similar to the Youth Front, the National Front that Ben-Gurion had in mind remained a fantasy, indicating the weakness of his position vis-à-vis the party apparatus. The democratic system remained unchanged, and prone to weakness. Ben-Gurion could not have imagined that the backdrop to the coming election would be a historic trial that revealed to the public a horrifying affair from the Holocaust. He was well acquainted with it, and wanted to believe that it would never emerge from oblivion to haunt him. But its hero, Israel Rezsö Rudolf Kastner, was a prominent Mapai functionary.

"I KNOW NOTHING ABOUT THE KASTNER AFFAIR"

Kastner was a newspaper reporter by profession; a short time after he settled in Palestine, his name appeared on a list of journalists recommended to Ben-Gurion to lead the public relations aspect of the War of Independence. Ben-Gurion recorded his name with no comment—his negotiations with Adolf Eichmann to save a million Jews were passed over as if they had never happened. Ben-Gurion also included Kastner on Mapai's slate of candidates for the Knesset, another partner in a failed enterprise who received his backing. Kastner did not make it into the Knesset, but he was appointed press secretary for the ministries headed by Dov Yosef of Mapai.[35] Prior to that, when he started working among Mapai's Hungarian-born members, Kastner was asked to explain his actions, including testimony he gave at the Nuremberg trials in favor of several top figures in the Nazi extermination apparatus. He naturally stressed his role in saving Jews. There were many people who owed their lives to him, but also many others who believed him to be a traitor and Nazi collaborator who had hidden from the Jews of Hungary what he knew about what awaited them, and thus ostensibly prevented them from defending themselves.

One day these accusations and others appeared in a pamphlet written by a Hungarian Jew in Jerusalem, Malchiel Gruenwald, who had it typed up and mimeographed at his own expense. He distributed the pamphlet to several hundred residents of the city. Among his claims was that Kastner had accepted bribes to save Mapai functionaries from the Nazis. "Dr. Rudolf Kastner should be liquidated," he wrote. The sorry-looking pamphlet required no response, and many people indeed advised Kastner to ignore it. But Attorney General Haim Cohn insisted on suing Gruenwald for libel.

Politically, it was a big mistake. Gruenwald's attorney, Shmuel Tamir, was a fierce antagonist of Ben-Gurion. A former member of Etzel in his early thirties, he was ambitious, uninhibited, and a brilliant demagogue, with a penchant for political trials. He knew how to turn his defense of Gruenwald into a lawsuit against Mapai as a whole. He depicted the negotiations with Eichmann as a direct continuation of the Haavara Agreement of the 1930s and the failure to rescue Jews from the Holocaust. It was, he charged, part and parcel of the policy of collaboration with the British Mandate authorities and the reparations agreement with West Germany. At that time, Israelis still did not know how to grapple with the Holocaust; the tendency was to envelop it in a great silence. Tamir forced Israelis to face up to a subject that was very hard for them to accept—that Jews had cooperated with the Nazis. It was a troubling, impassioned, almost pornographic story, and Tamir told it over the space of several months. He spoke of the *Judenräte*, the Jewish councils the Nazis set up in every ghetto and community they conquered; the *kapos*, the Jewish prisoners placed in command positions in concentration camps; Mapai and a mysterious train of gold. The District Court in Jerusalem in effect accepted each of Gruenwald's claims and ruled that Kastner "sold his soul to the Devil." Prime Minister Sharett thought the verdict was a "nightmare" and an "atrocity." His name starred in the courtroom, nearly every day. He came out sounding not only like a partner of Kastner's but of Hitler himself. Ben-Gurion claimed to have had no part in the incident. "I know nothing about the Kastner affair," he wrote.[36]

❖

Sharett tried, during this time, to persuade himself that there was life after Ben-Gurion, but he had a hard time making his way through the thicket of intrigues and plots laid by Minister of Defense Lavon and Chief of Staff Dayan. Partners in contempt for the law and for truth, they hated and undermined each other, but shared a contempt for Sharett.[37] They lied to him time and again, to each other, and to IDF officers, in particular, so it seems, when it came to intelligence. The result was a sinkhole of a scandal, even more damaging than the Kastner affair. It was given a number of different names, but needed none. When Israelis said "the Affair," everyone knew exactly what they meant.

Ben-Gurion seems to have heard of it first from Dayan: "An inexplicable order from Pinhas Lavon during Dayan's absence regarding an operation in Egypt that failed, and which people should have known would fail. Criminal recklessness."[38] Dayan may very well have lied to Ben-Gurion as well. Whatever the case, it was a fairly dubious description of what had happened, but not the first or last to be offered. It haunted Ben-Gurion for the rest of his life, first bringing him back into power, then sending him packing. Like the Kastner affair, it had its roots in another fiasco, which Ben-Gurion was also indirectly responsible for.

"INCOMPARABLE IDIOCY"

In the summer of 1954, a huge dread came over Israel's government. Two years after the Free Officers coup in Egypt, which brought Gamal Abdel Nasser to power, Britain was preparing to withdraw from that country, including the Suez Canal. Lavon reminded his colleagues what that meant: "Egypt is now up against Tel Aviv." He proposed that Israel "go crazy," by which he meant that it would unilaterally withdraw from the armistice agreement with Egypt and seize the Gaza Strip. The Cabinet rejected the proposal.[39]

In the early afternoon hours of Friday, July 2, 1954, a booby-trapped package blew up in a post office in Alexandria. Twelve days later, bombs were placed in two American libraries, one in Alexandria and one in Cairo. The perpetrators were apparently working for IDF intelligence. They were Egyptian Jews, some of whom had been trained in Israel. The mission, so the IDF intelligence chief Binyamin Gibli was said to have claimed, was to "undermine the West's confidence in the existing regime by creating public

538 ■ A STATE AT ANY COST

insecurity . . . and thus preventing the provision of aid to Egypt." An order
preserved in the IDF Archives states that the attacks were meant to sabotage
the agreement under which Britain would evacuate its troops from Egypt. In
the days that followed, bombs went off in two Egyptian cinemas. Two more
bombs failed to go off, one in a Cairo train station and the second at the port
of Alexandria. A few days later, an attempt to place a fire bomb in an Alexandria cinema was foiled when the charge went off before it was supposed to.
The person carrying it was badly burned, taken to the hospital, and placed
under arrest.[40] Two members of the cell were sentenced to death and executed; one killed himself. Some ten spent many years in prison.

❖

It was all meant to remain a state secret. The press was only allowed to hint
at what had happened. Military censorship was imposed at first in the hope
that the accused men in Cairo could be saved, and afterward to protect those
involved. But Israel was small, with an elite that was like a family, so the *Esek
Bish*, the "Nasty Business," quickly became the talk of the town. One Cabinet minister said that he felt "a bit like an idiot," because when he came
home his family spoke to him about the snafu in Egypt; a second minister
said: "Every kid is talking about it in the street." Minister of Justice Rosen
said that if someone in the army could have proposed "such an idiotic plan,"
as he put it, "it means that there is a military junta in the IDF that is conducting its own policy of its own volition."[41] At the time, he was still under
the impression that the operation had been carried out "behind the backs of
the prime minister and minister of defense."

Nehemiah Argov quoted Ben-Gurion as saying that the operation of the
group in Egypt was unjustified "militarily, morally, and politically." He speculated how Lavon, "who everyone says is smart," could arrive at "such a foolish" decision. But his focus was largely on the operational aspect. "It's
incomparable idiocy," Ben-Gurion said, according to Argov. "Such an operation can never remain a secret. Because of the Americans and the British, not
the Egyptians, and in all these cases we end up battered and lose everything."[42] As with the Kastner affair, Ben-Gurion tried to distance himself
from what had happened.

But the fiasco in Egypt was not the first of its type. About two years previously, Israel had recruited several Jews in Baghdad as saboteurs. The purpose of these acts remains a matter of controversy, but one aim was apparently to aggravate relations between Iraq and the United States. That ring was also uncovered, and some of its members were apprehended and executed. Ben-Gurion was prime minister and defense minister at the time, while Binyamin Gibli headed the General Staff's Intelligence Department. Despite the botched operation in Baghdad, Gibli was allowed to remain in the army and was promoted to head of military intelligence, where he coordinated the "shameful business" in Egypt. The operation in Egypt seems to have been planned before Ben-Gurion retired to Sde Boker.[43] The use of agents there did not require his approval, but here, too, the spirit of the message conveyed by the commander in chief was in the air. The operation in Egypt was almost a precise copy of the botched one in Iraq.[44]

Here and there attempts were made to connect the failure in Egypt with the previous one in Baghdad, and to pin them both on Ben-Gurion. Ben-Gurion vehemently denied all responsibility. In a book he wrote about the affair, Ben-Gurion maintained that nothing regarding the incident in Iraq was at all like the one in Egypt. The Iraqi affair, he claimed, was in fact "a frame-up against a number of young Jews, and no one from Israel had any connection to it."[45]

But the major scandal was the operational failure, not the ideas that produced it. The central question was: "Who gave the order?" Gibli claimed that he operated the Egyptian ring in accordance with explicit instructions he received from Lavon. Lavon denied it.[46] Prime Minister Sharett asked Israel's chief justice, Yitzhak Olshan, and the former chief of staff Ya'akov Dori to determine who gave the order. The two were unable to provide an answer. They summed up their investigation in tortuous statements: they could not be certain that Gibli had not received a directive from Lavon, but neither could they say for sure that Lavon had not issued one. This left open the possibility that Gibli had received a directive from Dayan. Sharett wrote down the three conclusions that the Olshan-Dori report led to: Lavon, Dayan, and Gibli all needed to go.[47] Not only because it was the right thing to do, but because if they were not dismissed, the responsibility would devolve on Sharett himself. Sharett claimed that Lavon had not told him about the sabotage ring in Egypt.

But Sharett was not strong enough to dismiss any one of the three, especially with a general election looming. Lavon's case was especially fraught, because Sharett received warnings that Lavon would kill himself if he were forced to resign.[48] Sharett filled page after page in his diary with agonized doubts. Much of what he wrote was pathetic, some quite dramatic. Lavon had proved that there were "Satanic elements" in both his character and his mind, Sharett said to a leader of his party. According to Sharett, Lavon had "plotted atrocities" that had been averted only thanks to the opposition of the chiefs of staff, who themselves were primed for "anything hotheaded." Dayan was prepared to steal planes and abduct officers from trains, but he was shocked by an idea to fire asphyxiating gas into the Gaza Strip. Maklef was horrified when Lavon ordered him to disseminate toxic bacteria along the frontier of the Syrian demilitarized zone. Lavon was responsible for the outrage in Cairo even if he did not give the order, Sharett maintained, as he had created an environment that enabled "insane actions" of his own devising.[49]

Lavon protested the findings of the investigation that Sharett instigated, and demanded Gibli's ouster. "I witnessed an eruption of blind fury," Sharett related. "During our conversation he went time after time to the whiskey cupboard, poured glass after glass, drinking cognac without stopping. It is a horrible thing to see a person in such disgraceful dissipation."[50] Gibli also reacted as if the world had collapsed around him when Sharett told him that he had to be transferred to a different position. "I saw the abyss," Sharett wrote.[51]

❖

While they all were waiting for the verdict in the trial of the agents in Cairo, Gibli was implicated in another botched operation, when five soldiers sent covertly into Syria to service an Israeli surveillance apparatus were apprehended. One of them, Uri Ilan, killed himself in prison. An investigation of this operation revealed, according to Sharett, that it had been organized "with appalling irresponsibility," verging on criminal negligence. The abyss before him grew deeper. Several Mapai leaders were afraid to get rid of Lavon, fearing that he would make everything about the fiasco in Egypt—as well as other such failures—public. "I am like a sleepwalker these days," Sharett told his diary, "terrified and lost in a maze, utterly destitute." He felt he was "suffocating, with no way out."[52]

Under the circumstances, there was only one man who could save the party and the IDF.

"IT IS UNFORTUNATE THAT YOUR DESTINY LED YOU TO AMERICA"

Ben-Gurion had thought that Sde Boker would be his haven from mental distress, but from the first day there he realized he had been mistaken. Sharett's impression was that Ben-Gurion suffered from a "psychological complex" and was seeking "an outlet for anxiety." Avriel told him that Ben-Gurion was "irritable and depressed" because he believed that Israel was in danger of being obliterated. His health also troubled him. In August 1954, he referred in his diary to a series of radiation treatments he received in the hospital, but offered no details. "It is difficult to see the lion in a cage, when he ostensibly put himself there," Nehemiah Argov wrote.[53] He often said that his beloved hero was not meant to be a shepherd, "not even for two or three years." Ben-Gurion spent most of his time among his books, wandering the paths of history and reliving his past.

On one of his last days at Sde Boker, he was suddenly cast many years into his past, reliving one of his seminal friendships. It was entirely unexpected. Yehuda Erez, who edited his writings, was in New York, and ran into Shmuel Fox. He told Erez that he had a bundle of letters he had received from Ben-Gurion, and consented to return them to his old friend. Ben-Gurion was thrilled. "It is as if I returned to my youth and reencountered you then in Płońsk," he wrote to Fox. He was astonished that Fox had kept the letters for so many years, and was even more astonished that his friend had not told him about the letters when they had met, if only infrequently, in New York. Now he picked up the friendship where it had left off, as if they had never parted. He told Fox about their mutual friend, Shlomo Zemach, who had made a name for himself as a novelist, and about the political rivalry between them. Perhaps Zemach had changed his views since the founding of the state, but Ben-Gurion was not sure of that because they had not met since, even though they lived in the same country. "I'd very much like to get together with him," he remarked.

Fox responded with a six-page letter; only the beginning was in Hebrew, the rest in Yiddish. He began by explaining why he had not returned the letters to Ben-Gurion earlier. Without that chance meeting with Erez, he wrote, he would not have dreamed of parting with them. They were dear to him, because they reminded him of the spiritual revolution he had experienced when he escaped the suffocating atmosphere of his parents' home and discovered Zionism and socialism. "And you were my guide along that road," he wrote. Bialik's "Scroll of Fire," which Ben-Gurion had so carefully copied out for him, was especially precious. That was something you never forget all your life. He had never thanked Ben-Gurion for the poem, because he had not known how to do so. It was such an intimate gift that he, Fox, had never dared to mention it when they met afterward. He quoted a line from one of his own poems: "Do not ask the secret of my love; lay your head on my chest and listen to the murmurs of my heart."

He had closed his dental clinic, he related; he now lived off the rent from an apartment building he had purchased. He was not wealthy, but not poor, either. He belonged to half a dozen socialist organizations that also promoted Yiddish culture. He sometimes still wrote and published poems. He had belonged to the Spinoza Club until it closed. So the years had gone by; old age had pounced on him, bringing loneliness in its wake. His son Emanuel and his family lived in a different city. For forty years Fox had been friends with Mani Leib, a Yiddish poet. A great poet, Fox wrote. They were neighbors; they got together every day and read together. But he had now passed on.

Ben-Gurion did not answer immediately. "For reasons that a person far away will not understand," he had been compelled to return to the Ministry of Defense, and his letter was thus delayed, he apologized. He also offered some good news—he had seen Shlomo Zemach a few days ago. "I was in Jerusalem and on the drive from my hotel to my office I saw him standing in the street," he related. He told his driver to stop. Getting out of the car, he approached his friend, whom he had not seen for many years. "I was sorry to see he had aged considerably, and to hear that he had been ill," Ben-Gurion wrote. "His face, as I saw it now, worries me."

Fox had spent his life as a Diaspora Jew rather than a Zionist, and

Ben-Gurion felt that his boyhood friend owed him an explanation. "As best I remember, we decided, the three of us, you and Shlomo and I, to go to Palestine," he wrote. "I recall that, like Shlomo and I, you were an anti-Ugandist, and in protest against Uganda we reached the conclusion that the best way to fight the opponents of Zion was to move to Palestine. Do you remember that? What led you to go to England first?" Almost half a century had gone by, but it still grated on him. "Fate apparently separated us, things happened that none of us could have anticipated," he wrote. He offered news of Płońsk: to the best of his knowledge, only two or three Jews remained there. But, unlike his friend, he refused to be pessimistic. War is not an eternal fact of life, only a present necessity, until peace arrives, he wrote. The thread that connected the Jewish people in Israel with the Jews of the Diaspora was Hebrew education, he maintained. "The Jewish people will rise, and it is unfortunate that your destiny led you to America, but what is done is done," he acknowledged. He hoped that Fox would at least come for a visit.*[54]

❖

At the beginning of January 1955, Ben-Gurion asked Sharett if Dayan had had a hand in what happened in Egypt. There was no reason to assume that Dayan had not known about the agents and the mission they were assigned. Like Ben-Gurion, who had claimed that he had not known about the Qibya operation because he had been on vacation, Dayan claimed that, at the time of the operation, he had been in the United States. That was not exactly true—the attack on the post office in Alexandria had occurred some ten days before he departed.[55] He could have aborted the rest of the operation after the first incident, but he did not do so. Perhaps he presumed that the operation would delay the British withdrawal from Egypt, and he might have assumed that it would lead to Lavon's ouster. It is inconceivable that Gibli would have set such an operation in motion at his own initiative. If he had not received the order from Lavon, he received it from Dayan.[56] Sharett told Ben-Gurion that the army was reckless; Ben-Gurion rejected the characterization.

---

* Fox died a year later. He never visited Israel. (Ben-Gurion, Diary, July 23, 1956, BGA; Mordechai Striegler, interview transcript, BGA.)

Sharett said that in the IDF there was "no such thing as truth." Ben-Gurion agreed with that: "It's horrible in the extreme," he said.[57]

Events then proceeded rapidly. Lavon resigned as defense minister and the Mapai leadership could not find a replacement acceptable to Dayan. Elections were five months away. In the meantime, the Kastner trial, as it was called, even though Kastner was not the defendant, was moving to center stage. As it proceeded, the public began to identify Mapai with the failure to save Jews from the Holocaust. On the evening of February 17, 1955, Golda Meir and the Histadrut chief Mordechai Namir paid a visit to Ben-Gurion. They demanded that he return to government as minister of defense. "I was deeply moved," Ben-Gurion wrote in his diary. "I decided that I must accept the call and return to the Defense Ministry. Defense and the army are above all." The next day, he was surprised to hear from Paula that the radio had already announced his return the previous day. "I began receiving congratulatory telegrams," he remarked.[58]

Sharett was also moved, as he wrote in his diary. "Ben-Gurion has returned to government, returned as a member of the Cabinet and not as prime minister, returned ostensibly as my subordinate. Who could have thought it possible? Could I have ever conceived of such a thing? Could he have ever conceived of such a thing? Could anyone?" He praised Ben-Gurion in the Knesset for having answered the call of conscience, seeking to intimate that Ben-Gurion accepted responsibility for Lavon's appointment; he praised Ben-Gurion's "gallantry." He sought, so he said, to stress that Ben-Gurion had accepted "the imperative of subordination." But he also knew that he had embarked on "a new Via Dolorosa." He expected "excruciating vicissitudes" on a daily basis and presumed that Ben-Gurion would always get what he wanted. Whenever he needed to, he would simply threaten to return to Sde Boker.[59]

"HEIGHT OF HEROISM"

Some twenty-four hours after Ben-Gurion returned to the Cabinet as minister of defense, the IDF staged an incursion into the Gaza Strip. It was called Operation Black Arrow. The UN partition decision had designated Gaza and a strip of territory around it as part of the Palestinian Arab state; during the War of Independence, Egypt captured most of it. The armistice agreement

Israel signed with Egypt in February 1949 left the area in Egyptian hands. At the time, about three hundred thousand Arabs lived there, some two-thirds of them refugees. Ben-Gurion's decision to refrain from conquering Gaza was castigated by his opponents, on a par with his failure to capture the Old City of Jerusalem. His political rivals, from Menachem Begin to Yigal Allon, often accused him of defeatism. The record of his war diary and his pronouncements at Cabinet meetings were full of contradictions regarding the desire, need, and possibility of taking Gaza, or as one source puts it, to "do away" with it.*

The debate brought home a dilemma that the Zionist movement had faced from the start—more territory came with more Arabs. In time it became clear that the number of refugees in the Gaza Strip was far larger than the government had thought when it discussed the issue, which was a very good reason not to annex the territory.[60]

Infiltrators and terrorists soon began crossing the border from the Gaza Strip into Israel, harrowing the new settlements Israel had established nearby. It was a direct continuation of the war for Palestine; most of the attackers were refugees. Some of them operated in the service of the Egyptian army. Lavon and Dayan, separately and together, repeatedly proposed an invasion of the Gaza Strip. Sharett was opposed, and Ben-Gurion arrived from Sde Boker to support him.[61] But within hours came a new and particularly provocative attack: this time the terrorists from Gaza broke into the army's top secret microbiological research institute only twelve miles from Tel Aviv and stole some documents. Now not even Sharett could object to action in the Gaza Strip.

Operation Black Arrow was the largest reprisal action since independence. Commanded by Ariel Sharon, now a battalion commander in the paratroopers, it ended with eight Israelis and thirty-seven Egyptians dead,

---

* At one Cabinet meeting, Ben-Gurion recounted what he had thought about the Gaza issue during the war. "It would be good if we could eject the Egyptians from Gaza as well," he said, "but we would not take Gaza, for it is doubtful whether Gaza should be within the bounds of our country, and it is very doubtful whether anyone would allow us to make Gaza part of our country." He added, parenthetically, "According to the Bible, we also deserve Sinai, but war does not go according to the Bible." (Ben-Gurion to the Cabinet, Jan. 2, 5, 1949, ISA; Ben-Gurion, Diary, Oct. 18, 1948, BGA.)

almost four times the estimate that Ben-Gurion and Dayan gave Sharett before the action.[62] "The battalion remembers no operation this severe," Sharon told Ben-Gurion.

He wanted to know everything. Sharon provided him with a full account, kilometer by kilometer, fallen soldier after fallen soldier, with much drama and color. Ben-Gurion was dumbfounded. "It's almost a miracle that you got back," he said. Sharon promised him that his men could conquer the Gaza Strip.[63] "From a human military point of view, it was the height of heroism," Ben-Gurion told the Cabinet. "I cannot imagine any higher human heroism." Had the IDF had such a unit in the War of Independence, he added, all of Jerusalem would be in Israeli hands, and Latrun as well.

It was an important moment in Sharon's career. Only a handful of officers had direct contact with Ben-Gurion. In Ben-Gurion's eyes, Sharon was the archetype of the Hebrew warrior, a modern incarnation of Bar Kokhba. In a letter to Dayan, he lauded the "Jewish heroism" displayed by Sharon's battalion. He seems still to have believed Sharon at this stage. In the years to come he would discover that Sharon was a liar.

The Gaza operation was criticized in the Cabinet, especially because of its magnitude and the large number of dead soldiers. A few Cabinet ministers suspected that it was meant to drag Israel into a war. Ben-Gurion promised his colleagues that that was not the case. The Israeli people needed to be aware of "the limits of their abilities," Ben-Gurion said. But after the operation, he sent a letter to the chief of staff extolling the soldiers—among them, many immigrants—for their "unbounded" courage and devotion.[64] He admitted that he had not expected so many casualties. But he seems to have seen the cost as worthwhile, because the way the paratroopers had fought helped shape, he thought, a common Israeli identity. "You have no idea what a huge distance—Jewish and human—there is between us and the immigrants," he said emotionally, speaking again about "two nations." Service in the paratroopers gave "these Jews" a feeling that they, too, are "like us," he said.[65] His failure to enlist Israel's young people into his Youth Front made it all the more important for him to stress the army's capacity for forging the younger generation into a single nation and to instill it with a profound Zionist identity.

Sharon viewed Operation Black Arrow as a professional landmark. "The victory was principally an educational one," he said. He meant that it instilled in his men the aspiration to make direct contact with the enemy in a large-scale operation. In the meantime, his soldiers were gaining proficiency in what he described as a new vocation: "creating a wartime atmosphere."[66] Sharett argued that they had turned the urge for vengeance into a moral principle and a justification for their existence. "In every case in which an operation is rejected by the government, depression and anger pervade the battalion, and the whole unit turns into an engine of incitement and vilification of civilian rule," he said.[67] The man who symbolized the paratrooper unit and its values was not Sharon himself but one of its warriors, Meir Har-Zion.

❖

A scion of an old Jerusalem family, Har-Zion grew up in Ein Harod to become an almost mythical hero, in part because of the role he played in Sharon's Unit 101. Prior to his military service he hiked extensively around the country, largely disregarding the armistice borders. Once, he and his sister Shoshana found themselves in prison in Damascus, and another time he and a girlfriend crossed the border into Jordan to visit Petra. The city carved into red rock southeast of the Dead Sea was an object of desire for young Israelis, just as it had once attracted the young Ben-Gurion. In the 1950s, it became an element of Israeli youth rebellion, as many sought to break through the boundaries that closed Israel in on all sides. Making a trip there was a test of courage. Romantics, nationalists, and adventurers like Har-Zion dreamed of braving the dangers and seeing the mysterious Nabatean city in enemy territory. It was also their way of displaying their contempt for the cease-fire lines that divided Palestine. Few succeeded in reaching their destination; some were killed along the way.

In December 1954, Shoshana and a girlfriend went on a hike in the Judean wilderness. They crossed the border into Jordan and disappeared. A few weeks later, their bodies were found in the desert. Har-Zion, who had completed his military service by this time, set out with three other veterans of Unit 101 to avenge her. Sharon and Dayan knew about their plan. They tried to persuade the young men to desist but did not stand in their way. An

IDF unit equipped them with hand grenades; Dayan denied that they had been given the use of IDF vehicles. They crossed the border and captured five Bedouin, stabbing four of them to death and shooting one. A sixth Bedouin was sent to tell his tribe about the act. When they returned to Israel, they were arrested; the question was what to do with them. Prime Minister Sharett and Justice Minister Rosen demanded that they be brought to trial. Dayan refused to condemn the murder, saying only, "We do not propose to support acts of retaliation of this sort." He ruled that the four men had "exceeded their authority," but stressed that "most of them are officers and are the best and most idealistic of young men."[68]

It was, as it often was in the young State of Israel, a conflict between fundamental values. "I wondered about the nature and fate of this nation," Sharett wrote in his diary, "which is capable of fine delicacy of spirit, profound love of humanity, such sincere affinity for the beautiful and noble, and yet produces from among the ranks of its best youth young men who are capable of murder, in clear mind and cold blood." He asked himself which of these two souls, both to be found in the Bible, would win. He reminded Ben-Gurion of the debate over the policy of restraint in the 1930s and how they had held back the urge for revenge.[69]

Ben-Gurion, choosing his words carefully, asserted that no citizen should be allowed to take the law into his own hands. He proposed that the four murderers should be brought to trial; as in the past, he represented the authority of the state. But, also as in the past, he had trouble concealing his lenient attitude toward crime committed out of patriotic motives, in this case a crime committed by one of the IDF's most idolized warriors. "You can't see this as a simple case of murder, even though it is a murder," he said. At his suggestion, the Cabinet decided that he, Sharett, and Justice Minister Rosen would decide what to do. At an IDF General Staff meeting, Ben-Gurion said that the solution that was taking form was that the four men would be tried, but that after they were sentenced, they would be pardoned.[70] As he saw it, Har-Zion had fought for his country, and as such deserved his country's support. The four murderers wanted to appoint Shmuel Tamir, the star of the Kastner trial, as their defense attorney; the suggestion seems to have been Sharon's. Either way, the person who actually asked Tamir to take the case was the Knesset member Shlomo Lavi from Ein Harod. "They are our sons and we owe them the defense that they seek," the good kibbutznik mumbled uncomfortably. With a general election in the offing, the trial was about to turn into another political show. Tamir suggested a possible line of defense: "Just as Mapai officials sacrificed the paratroopers whom they sent into Budapest, so they are forsaking the IDF's finest warriors." According to Tamir, Sharon told him many years later that Ben-Gurion had presented him with an ultimatum. If the four men did not forgo Tamir's representation, Sharon's service in the IDF would come to an end. "I wanted to remain in the paratroopers so badly that I disgracefully agreed," he related. The four dismissed Tamir and were not brought to trial.[71]

A few months later, the issue returned to the Cabinet. "My conscience is uneasy," the justice minister said. Ben-Gurion was concerned that if the murderers were brought to trial, they would reveal information detrimental to the IDF. He reported that Sharon had been severely disciplined for not preventing the incident. Ben-Gurion's patience with patriotic criminals was again on display; Sharett remarked that he was highly emotional. The case seems also to have called up his long-standing sensitivity to the subject of motherhood. Shoshana's murder had plunged her mother into deep depression, he told the Cabinet. It was a double tragedy—she and her husband were divorced, and Shoshana was the only solace the family had. After he learned this, he had come to see the murderer as less responsible for his actions. "He did it mostly for his mother," Ben-Gurion said.[72]

❖

Soon after his return from Sde Boker, Ben-Gurion had to confirm the dismissal of the IDF's intelligence chief Gibli. It was not easy—he put it off, taking a lenient view of him as well. But in the end, he called Gibli in and informed him that "there is no alternative." Gibli said that he was being done an injustice. Ben-Gurion responded: "I don't want to go back to this matter. For me, it no longer exists. The minister of defense has left his post, that is something that doesn't happen every day, and I cannot do other than to preserve some sort of balance." He noted that Gibli was still young, and that it was not the end of his army career: "He would be found a different post and a new career as well." At this stage, that was the sum total of what he wanted to achieve—not to investigate what had led to the horrible fiasco in Egypt, not to find out who had given the order, who had lied and who had told the truth. He just wanted to get the entire incident behind him as quickly as possible, just as he tried to do with the Kastner affair. "I have no intention of inquiring into the past," he wrote to Dayan, "but rather to focus on the needs of the future."[73] At the Defense Ministry, Ben-Gurion was closer to the army than he had been in Sde Boker, and now came under Dayan's direct influence. Four weeks after his return to government, he proposed conquering the Gaza Strip.

· 21 ·

THE SECOND ROUND

"THE THIRD ISRAELI KINGDOM"

On one of the last days of March 1955, Minister of Defense Ben-Gurion received an urgent telephone call from one of the volunteer counselors at Patish, a farming village in the northern Negev, about twelve miles from the Gaza Strip. If he did not get there immediately, the counselor warned, the inhabitants would abandon their homes and head for Jerusalem to stage a protest in front of the Knesset. Ben-Gurion canceled all his appointments and set out for the tiny settlement. It was the first station along the road to a second round of war with the Arabs. Another Negev settlement was the second station; the third was Paris.

Most of the inhabitants of Patish had come to Israel from Kurdistan. One evening they were celebrating a wedding in one of the homes. Some sixty guests were still there just before midnight. Suddenly hand grenades flew through the window, along with automatic rifle fire. A volunteer counselor, Varda Friedman, was killed; some twenty guests were wounded. The assailants had come from the Gaza Strip. Friedman was from Kfar Vitkin, an established agricultural community in central Israel founded in the 1930s; she and her boyfriend had responded to Ben-Gurion's call to serve as unpaid counselors in communities of new immigrants. Ben-Gurion attended her funeral.

The atmosphere at Patish had been grim even before this attack, as one of the volunteers, Meir Rabinowitz, told Ben-Gurion. Most of the inhabitants had been sent there immediately after arriving in Israel. The homes that awaited them there were substandard; there was not a single flush toilet in the whole village, and only one shower. Neither was there electricity. The inhabitants worked as farmhands, but there was only enough work to employ them for two weeks out of every month; the rest of the time they were idle. Many came from cities and towns and did not want to be farm laborers. Terrorists had attacked the village several times. Many of the residents felt abandoned by the state and showed signs of despair; one once took his baby son to the center of the village and threatened to burn him. Many abandoned the place and tried to manage on the margins of Tel Aviv. Varda Friedman and her friends taught them to cultivate onions and potatoes.

The day following the attack on the wedding party, they all decided to leave. Rabinowitz was able to convince some of them that that was exactly what Nasser wanted. Ben-Gurion's visit reassured them a bit. Playing on the village's name, which means "hammer," Ben-Gurion declared: "There are many Patishes in the country, but there is also a heavy hammer that will shatter the boulders of our enemies." He promised to settle another thousand families along the Gaza Strip. As always, he took a personal interest in several of them and asked what they needed. Some of the inhabitants spoke only Aramaic, the language of Kurdish Jews. When he returned to Jerusalem, Ben-Gurion told the Cabinet that he had been wrong when he claimed that there were two nations in Israel. "There are many nations, distinct and different from one another, and there is almost no contact between them." He did not delude himself that his visit would persuade the inhabitants of Patish to remain. "They will flee and it will be a catastrophe," he told the General

Staff, with the same alarm he had displayed when the Jews of the Islamic world began arriving in Israel.[1]

About a year after the attack on Patish, a large wedding was being readied at the kibbutz Nahal Oz, founded in 1951 just a few hundred yards from the Gaza Strip border. Most of the initial members were of a background quite different from that of the residents of Patish—they were native-born Israelis, members of a youth movement affiliated with Mapai. Four couples were to be married on April 29, 1956. Moshe Dayan had been invited as guest of honor. When he arrived, he learned that the regional commander, Ro'i Rotberg, had just been shot dead. Rotberg had set out on horseback to chase away several Palestinian farmers from the Gaza Strip who had crossed the border to harvest wheat from Nahal Oz's fields. When he reached the invaders, he was shot and killed. His murderers took the body, mutilated it, and then handed it over to UN observers. Rotberg had been twenty-one years old, and left a wife and a young son. The eulogy Dayan gave at his grave turned the fallen man into an Israeli symbol. Dayan knew how to write—he wrote poetry as well. He described the war with the Palestinians as Israel's unavoidable doom: "We are a generation of settlers, and without helmets of metal and the muzzle of the cannon we will not be able to plant a tree or build a house," he intoned. It was not a new idea. Nor was he saying anything new when he declared that the millions of Jews exterminated in Europe "are looking at us from the ashes of Jewish history and commanding us to inhabit and raise up a land for our nation." Echoing Ben-Gurion many years earlier, he offered a pessimistic insight regarding the hatred of the Palestinians: "For eight years they have been living in refugee camps in Gaza, and before their eyes we are turning the land and villages where they and their forefathers dwelt into our possession." Quite naturally, hostility and a thirst for revenge were surging among them.

Rotberg himself had not realized this, Dayan intimated, implying that Rotberg was culpable for his own death. "The light in his heart blinded his eyes, and he did not see the glint of the blade," Dayan said. "The longing for peace deafened his ears and he did not hear the voice of the murderer lying in wait." Dayan depicted Rotberg as "a slender blond boy," apparently not physically sturdy enough, he said, evoking Samson's devastation of the Philistine city of Gaza (Judges 16:1–3): "The gates of Gaza were too heavy for his shoulders and overwhelmed him." Dayan did not say how it was that a "boy" so naïve, skinny, and weak had been made responsible for the region's defense, and did not explain who was guilty of not enabling his blinded eyes to properly make out the deadly hostility of the Arabs. Before speaking of Rotberg's blindness, deafness, and weakness, Dayan spoke of these same defects in the first-person plural. He meant Ben-Gurion.

UN Secretary-General Dag Hammarskjöld happened to be in Israel that week. He demanded that Israel agree to a set of arrangements that were meant to reduce tensions along its borders. Dayan opposed the provisions and feared that Ben-Gurion might accept them. Relations between the two men were strained as a result. "Ben-Gurion is deluding himself and we will pay a heavy price for such concessions," Dayan wrote in his diary before setting off for Nahal Oz. Ben-Gurion understood the eulogy for Rotberg perfectly, and before its publication demanded the omission of the words "The ambassadors of hypocrisy are plotting and calling on us to set aside our weapons." Hammarskjöld was not to be insulted, Ben-Gurion told the chief of staff. He no doubt meant also that his own authority was not to be undermined. Politically, Dayan was on the ascendant.[2]

Half a year later, Ben-Gurion and Dayan were sitting in a plane together, on a secret night flight to France. The chief of staff had brought with him two books about a tiny island, Tiran, located at the southern end of the Gulf of Aqaba. Along with another island, Sanafir, it was located in the middle of the narrow strait that connected the Gulf with the Red Sea. Whoever controlled the island could prevent ships from reaching Eilat. Ben-Gurion dismissed the books because they were based on a translation. He was acquainted with the original, written by Procopius of Caesarea, a sixth-century Byzantine historian, and had copied a passage into his diary in ancient Greek. It said that Tiran had once been an autonomous Hebrew province called Yotvat.*[3]

Soon thereafter, when the IDF took the island, Ben-Gurion wrote: "Eilat will again be the principal Hebrew port in the south, and Yotavat,

---

* Seven years previously, Ben-Gurion had told the Cabinet that there had been a "Jewish state" on the island until the Byzantine emperor Justinian conquered it. (Ben-Gurion to the Cabinet, Dec. 13, 1949, ISA; Ben-Gurion 1979.)

called Tiran, will return to be part of the third Israeli kingdom." That was the fantasy that put Ben-Gurion, Dayan, and Shimon Peres on that night flight to France.

"ALL LIT UP"

The day after the attack on Patish, Ben-Gurion summoned Dayan and put three questions to him: Could Israel quickly take control of the Gaza Strip? Was the IDF prepared for war with Egypt? Was the IDF prepared for war against all the Arab armies?[4] A few days later, he told the Cabinet that Dayan had answered all three questions in the affirmative and proposed "expelling the Egyptians" from the Gaza Strip. He presumed that such military action would also empty the area of the refugees who lived there. Most of the ministers were dismayed.

Some Cabinet members from his party supported his proposal. Golda Meir said: "I have been living a long time in fear, not of war but of peace," by which she meant the conditions of peace that the United States was liable to impose on Israel. But most of the ministers feared a full-scale war with Egypt, which could deteriorate into hostilities with Jordan and Syria as well. The principal problem was, as they saw it, the fate of the refugees. Some of the ministers feared that the refugees would not flee to Hebron, as Ben-Gurion predicted they would, but into Israel, inundating Be'er-Sheva and the entire Negev. That would double the number of Arabs in Israel. "We won't know what to do with them," one minister said.

Ben-Gurion intimated that they would not be allowed to do so. Nevertheless, another minister expressed his concern that, if Israel were flooded with Gaza refugees, "there will be a great extermination of those refugees and afterward we will be worse off." Moshe Shapira suggested that the refugees would not flee. "The only way to make them leave would be by murder," he said. He would vote to take Gaza only if it were decided that all the refugees who would not flee of their own volition, by his estimate two-thirds of them, would be allowed to remain under Israeli rule. The result was that a majority opposed the idea. The vote was nine against five. "We were thus saved from a disaster the end result of which no one could predict," Sharett wrote.[5]

Ben-Gurion devoted the major part of his strength and time in the summer of 1955 to the election campaign. In that capacity, he termed himself "Golda's deputy," as Meir headed the effort. "He has a hand in everything," *Ma'ariv* wrote. "Everyone attends to his advice concerning organization, propaganda, and public relations." The party sought to produce the maximum from his return to the leadership, making him its superstar. He traveled from city to city, speaking to rallies attended, so the press reported, by myriad Israelis. He flew to Haifa, appeared at five events, and then spoke for more than an hour before a crowd that he estimated at fifty-five thousand. "I have never seen such a huge crowd at a rally listen in that way," he wrote. One exhausting day he campaigned in the Upper Galilee. He had not worked so hard for a long time, he wrote. When, in the evening, he emerged from Kfar Giladi's dining hall, he saw a flying saucer in the sky. "I found him quite impressed by the experience," Sharett wrote. "It looked like a cigar, all lit up," Ben-Gurion said. He was not alone—a local teacher who was with him also saw the "flying object," as Ben-Gurion referred to it in his diary. The upper and lower ends looked like fish tails. It flew rapidly from north to south, along a straight line, and disappeared behind the trees that blocked the horizon.[6] About half a million people took part in the Histadrut elections and more than 57 percent voted for Mapai.[7]

Ben-Gurion and the party leadership made a great effort to win just as great a victory in the elections to the Knesset and municipalities. They saw the party and the state as a single entity. At the end of May, Israel was visited for the first time by a foreign prime minister, U Nu of Burma. His visit was produced as a mass celebration of national pride. Children were taken out of school and stationed along sidewalks to welcome the eminent visitor, waving little flags of his country. The Ministry of Finance announced that Israel would receive $70 million from Germany, a down payment on the reparations. Sharett and Ben-Gurion declared that, if Egypt did not desist from harassing ships sailing to and from Eilat, Israel would use force to keep the Gulf of Aqaba open. A week later, *Ma'ariv* offered a prominent headline quoting what Ben-Gurion had told an American journalist: "If they want to try at strength, they must know we will give them a good beating." Another large headline that day proclaimed that the Israeli navy would receive two destroyers from Britain by the end of the year. Moshe Dayan raised the Israeli flag at a ceremony marking their imminent arrival and lauded Britain's assistance in establishing the IDF. The next day, Ben-Gurion told an election rally in Jerusalem that Israel was close to producing atomic energy. "The United States has decided to deliver us a nuclear reactor, but even without it we could build such a reactor, because we have heavy water and uranium." He related that there was uranium "in every rock in the Negev," although in small quantities, making its production expensive. He was overseeing this project as part of his position as defense minister, he stressed, adding, "Without revealing secrets, I am convinced that the time is not distant when we will produce and exploit atomic energy." Two days later, he said on the radio that he would agree to return to the post of prime minister.[8]

There were thus good reasons for Israeli citizens to support Mapai. But two days before the elections, the newspapers reported that terrorists from Gaza had again attacked Patish, again tossing hand grenades into houses. Three Israelis were wounded, two of them critically. A *Ma'ariv* correspondent who visited the village the next day discovered by chance a bomb that had not gone off. Prior to this, *Ma'ariv* had reminded its readers that the platforms of the opposition Herut and Ahdut Ha'avodah parties demanded the annexation of the Gaza Strip.[9]

Mapai emerged from the election with forty Knesset seats, five fewer than before. Menachem Begin's Herut almost doubled its strength, receiving fifteen seats to become the second-largest faction in the new Knesset. Ben-Gurion, who intended to form the next government, did not take responsibility and displayed complacence. "I do not see in these elections a significant failure of the party," he declared. He attributed the weakening of his party to a confluence of "fortuitous factors," first and foremost the Kastner trial.[10] Three more months passed before he returned to the prime minister's chair. The coalition negotiations frayed his nerves, as well as those of Sharett, who continued in the meantime to serve as prime and foreign minister.

"AS IF I HAVE NO BRAIN"

On the morning of October 13, 1955, Ben-Gurion was scheduled to set out for Tel Aviv. At eight, his military secretary, Nehemiah Argov, arrived at the room at the Jerusalem President Hotel where Ben-Gurion was lodging, only to find that the prime minister's shoes, which he had left out to be polished, were still outside the door, along with the morning newspapers. Ben-Gurion, it seemed, had not even woken up yet. Argov went in, and Ben-Gurion emerged from the bathroom. He tottered for a few minutes and then col-lapsed. By the time a doctor arrived he had lost consciousness. The doctor managed to bring him to so that he could, with great effort, answer a few questions, but he then again plunged into insensibility. The medical team was alarmed in the extreme, Argov reported to Sharett. After treating and reviving Ben-Gurion, they ordered absolute bed rest for several days; he was not hospitalized. Sharett asked if it had been a heart attack; Argov replied that his heart was fine, "but it's something connected to the blood." Sharett sum-moned Ben-Gurion's personal physician, Dr. Moshe Rachmilevitz, who told him that Ben-Gurion had apparently suffered a stroke. He related that Ben-Gurion had complained of a sense of heaviness in his head, "as if I have no brain," in his own words. Ben-Gurion himself attributed the feeling to the sleeping pill he had taken the night before. Dr. Rachmilevitz was skeptical but did not entirely dismiss the possibility. In the meantime, it was quite possible that it could happen again. As such, Ben-Gurion had to be forbid-den to engage in "all work with responsibility"—in other words, he was not to engage in any physical, mental, or emotional effort.[11] He had several difficult months behind him.

❖

Since his return to the Defense Ministry, the conflict over Palestine had looked much like it had during the second half of the War of Indepen-dence—a confrontation between Israel and the Arab states, led by Egypt. But in large measure it was a continuation of the fifty-year struggle for the land. Most of the infiltrators and attackers who penetrated Israel from the Gaza Strip were refugees, as were the *fedayun* ("those who sacrifice them-selves") guerrillas, some of whom operated under the direction of the Egyptian army.[12]

The attacks increased, and, in tandem, so did the army's demand to be al-lowed to respond. Sharett did not oppose every reprisal operation on principle, but his inclination was to hold the army back. That was a source of tension between him and Ben-Gurion. A short time after the elections, Ben-Gurion declared at a meeting of his party's Central Committee that the Foreign Ministry existed to serve the Defense Ministry, not the opposite, and that the Defense Ministry was responsible for the well-being of Israel's population, not for what foreign diplomats might say or what *The New York Times* might write. He remarked that the foreign affairs portfolio, which Sharett had retained when he became prime minister, should be placed in the hands of "a worthy person," adding that he still did not know who that would be. "In this speech, the Old Man spoke out in the sharpest way against the Foreign Ministry, and hurt Father very much," Tzipora Sharett wrote to her children. "The entire scene was so appalling that even the newspaper reporters were ashamed to make it public." She offered her children a scoop that the journalists themselves might not have been aware of. "Ben-Gurion's speech was preceded by a personal message to Father, a note he sent him during that very same meeting, informing of his decision to return to Sde Boker. Father took Ben-Gurion's speech as that of a man pouring out his anger prior to his retirement." The next day, it turned out that Ben-Gurion was staying.[13] It would have been the right moment, and was likely the last possible one, for Sharett to break with Ben-Gurion and resign to preserve his honor and self-respect. But he stayed on.

At the end of that same month, the Cabinet approved a reprisal operation. An IDF contingent set out. After they had already crossed the Gazan border, an order arrived from Sharett to abort the operation. It turned out that as the operation was in its final stages of preparation, Sharett received a call from an American named Elmore Jackson, United Nations observer for the American Friends Service Committee, a Quaker peace and charitable organization. Seeking to promote a Middle East peace compact, Jackson had met with both Nasser and Ben-Gurion.[14] According to Sharett, Jackson had assured him that he was doing all he could to restore calm. As a result, Sharett, with Ben-Gurion's apparently reluctant concurrence, ordered that the operation scheduled for that night was not to be carried out. Dayan submitted his resignation the next day. Ben-Gurion summoned the Mapai members of the Cabinet, placed Dayan's letter on the table, and said that there had to be a clear line, either his or Sharett's. Then he walked out of the room. Sharett then obtained the Cabinet's approval for an operation to blow up the police station in Khan Yunis, a city in the southern Gaza Strip. It would be the IDF's largest operation since the War of Independence, and it ended with seventy Egyptians and one Israeli dead. Ben-Gurion observed the operation from close to the border, along with Dayan and Ariel Sharon.*[15]

The next Cabinet meeting was on a war footing; the IDF had called up reserves. "I did not sleep for two straight nights," Ben-Gurion related. He conjectured that the British were behind the rising tensions and listed three Israeli settlements that the Egyptians intended to attack—one of them was Sde Boker. One Cabinet minister asked about the country's food stocks, the water supply in Jerusalem, and the condition of Tel Aviv's bomb shelters. "We have what remains from the War of Independence," Ben-Gurion responded.[16]

In September 1955, Egypt announced that it had signed an arms deal with Czechoslovakia, which would include a supply of tanks and MiG aircraft. The country had already ratcheted up its restrictions on shipping to Eilat and signed a defense pact with Syria. Like the supply of arms to Israel during the War of Independence, the deal required the Soviet Union's sanction. The Russian penetration of the Middle East created a new and dangerous situation. Sharett called a special Cabinet meeting. The record shows that the ministers were in shock, especially because of the difficulty of obtaining armaments from the United States. In that regard, Ben-Gurion commented: "I am not so sure that we will not ever have to ask for arms from the Russians, if an opportunity rises." He did not say much more than this. At a certain point he blurted out: "If they really receive MiGs, I will favor bombing them. We can do it." Then he excoriated Nasser: "I have heard that he is a hypocritical liar," he said.[17] He collapsed in his hotel some ten days later.

❖

He was very sick. The political system began to prepare for the day after. "I was going mad with speculation," Sharett wrote. "Are we on the verge of a new catastrophe? And even if this is not a catastrophe, what if it turns out

---

* In a conversation with the men who took part in the operation, Ben-Gurion characteristically took a great interest in the role played by soldiers of Yemenite and North African origin. (Moshe Dayan 1976, p. 159.)

that Ben-Gurion is not capable of heading the government? Good God, what chaos."

The country was awash in rumors. An American news agency reported that he had had a stroke. The government had no choice but to issue a statement. The Government Press Office suggested saying that he had had a dizzy spell caused, according to his doctors, by an inner ear disturbance—in other words, an attack of vertigo, or perhaps Ménière's disease. Sharett consulted with Golda Meir, who said that the statement offered too much detail. "Everyone will say, dizziness, loss of balance—it means that the Old Man is not what he once was and that he needs to leave the ranks." Sharett called in the physicians. Dr. Rachmilevitz had not yet ruled out the possibility of a stroke, but agreed to sign the statement drafted by the Government Press Office. Paula also objected to all the detail. In the meantime, Ben-Gurion's condition improved. Sharett went to see him at the hotel. Suddenly there was an electrical outage, as occasionally happened in Jerusalem. "I saw his face by candlelight, wonderfully relaxed but sad," Sharett wrote. He was lucid and asked about the protracted and aggravating coalition negotiations. Tzipora Sharett said that even if Ben-Gurion recovered, he would never regain his previous stature. "The legend has lost its allure," she maintained. It had been "the greatest mistake of his life" not to remain at Sde Boker but to try to return to the helm.[18]

The growing friction on the Gaza Strip border faced Ben-Gurion with two sets of heavy pressures. Dayan and several political leaders were demanding war against Egypt, as soon as possible. They based their position in part on the "Czech deal," which meant, so Dayan said, that Egypt was preparing to destroy Israel. Most members of the Cabinet, led by Sharett and other Mapai leaders, opposed war. Ben-Gurion had difficulty deciding between them. Rather than leading, he was drawn in one direction and then in the other. His physical and mental frailty made it all the more difficult. He was unsure what to do, to go to war or not. His memory was also bad. He proposed capturing Gaza and fought for his proposal, but did not resign when it was rejected, just as he was actually not sure that it was the right thing to do.

He would soon order Dayan to plan a large operation to seize control of the Tiran Straits, but he did not allow it to be carried out.[19] It was not easy to hold Dayan back; the army was behind him.

"WITHOUT END"

When he returned from Sde Boker, Ben-Gurion found that Dayan was carrying out the eighteen-point program that he had left behind him when he retired. He could reassure himself that, in contrast with Sharett and Lavon, Dayan lived up to expectations. The chief of staff was acting in accordance with a strategic conception that Ben-Gurion himself had dictated to the Haganah during the period of terrorist attacks that preceded the War of Independence, what he had variously termed a policy of "first strike," or "offensive defense," or "initiated war."[20] In fact, Dayan pushed Ben-Gurion toward war.*

The Lavi Plan that the IDF developed under Dayan's leadership, in accordance with this conception, integrated a study from July 1954 produced by the General Staff's Planning Department under the title "Nevo." Its principal conclusion was a rather bleak one—time was working against Israel. To survive, it had to enlarge its borders. The forty-three-page document reflected an innovative approach to the concept of national security. The evaluation of strength and definition of goals was expanded beyond military capability to take into account political, demographic, and economic data and processes, from the health of the population to national morale, including education, culture, and values. The authors of the document also listed a number of advantages held by Israel's 1.5 million Jews, as civilians and soldiers, but they argued that Israel would have difficulty achieving its aims, most important of all "the Jewish settlement effort," within the armistice borders.

The document's economic chapter stated that if 2.5 million Jews lived within the state as defined by the armistice borders, per capita national product would decline "decisively" to the level of the Arab world. Furthermore, if

---

* As tensions increased, Ben-Gurion received a small request from Shlomo Lavi. Once a year he went on a hike in the south, along with some friends from Ein Harod with whom he had served in the army. They took automatic rifles and he used an ancient Mauser pistol dating from his time in Hashomer. Could David, whom he admired so much, help him out? The defense minister ordered that an Uzi submachine gun be given as a gift to Lavi, along with two magazines and three hundred bullets. (Lavi to Ben-Gurion, Jan. 7, 1956; Argov to the director of Israel Military Industries, Jan. 1, 1956, BGA.)

Israel were blocked from using the waters of the Banias and Hatzbani Rivers, which had their sources in Syria and Lebanon, half a million Israelis would not have enough food. Among the major dangers facing the country, other than the hatred of the Arabs, the report cited the composition of its Jewish population. During the coming several decades, about a third of Israelis would belong to "backward ethnic groups whose natural increase will be greater than the rest of the inhabitants." As a result, Israel was in danger of "Levantization," which could weaken social solidarity and strength. To achieve what the study called "qualitative enhancement," Israel would need the immigration of high-quality Jews from overseas, meaning mostly the United States and the Soviet Union. The economic forecast did not promise that they would want or be able to come. In any case, it asserted, "It is absolutely clear that, within the existing borders, there is no economic capacity for absorbing the desired population."

The question, according to the Nevo report, was thus not whether to enlarge the country's Green Line borders but when and where to do so. Strategic logic suggested that the country's borders should coincide with natural barriers, such as deserts, mountain ridges, and sources of water. Also, the borders should be as distant as possible from the areas where the Jewish population was concentrated and restrict the number of Arabs in Israel to no more than 20 to 30 percent of the population.

On this basis, the authors presented several alternatives. The best of them was that the border with Egypt should be set at the far end of the Sinai Desert, preferably on the bank of the Suez Canal. In the south, the border should lie beyond the desert reaches of Saudi Arabia, with the possibility of an "extension" that would enable Israel to control the Arabian oil fields. The recommended boundary with Syria would run somewhere beyond the Bashan highlands, while the border between Israel and Jordan should be set deep in the desert, far east of the Jordan River. The study offered less attractive alternatives as well, including one that would leave Israel with control only of the eastern shore of the Sinai Peninsula and the Straits of Tiran, including the island itself, along with the Hebron highlands and East Jerusalem.

Like the Cabinet ministers, the IDF's Planning Department also addressed the fate of the population that would, in all these cases, come under

Israeli rule. Control of all of Sinai, to the Suez Canal, was so desirable that it would be worth it for Israel to assume also the burden of ruling the Gaza Strip, with its entire population, "although a transfer would, of course, be desirable." A less comfortable option would be to evacuate the two hundred thousand refugees in the Strip "westward," which seems to have meant into the desert, or to create for them a "neutral political enclave." The added value of placing the eastern border beyond the Jordan River had to be balanced against the need "to control and eradicate a hostile population of more than 1.3 million." That did not seem like a practical option, or would not be until after Israel took in at least 2.5 million more Jews and transferred at least 50 percent of the Arab population to Iraq, in the framework of a "political settlement," a phrase the document placed within quotation marks. Moving the eastern border of Israel to that of Jordan would require Israel to "swallow" eight hundred thousand people, including the Palestinian population in the West Bank. Even after "maximum thinning," at least four hundred thousand would remain, leaving a total population in which there were only twice as many Jews as Arabs. The Hebron highland option would bring only two hundred thousand Arabs under Israeli rule, "if it is not possible to evacuate them." The ideal northern border would involve bringing only a relatively small number of Arabs under Jewish rule.

"A policy of thinning out [the Arab population] by means of evacuation or transfer," as the Nevo report put it, was meant to go hand in hand with a "large settlement effort," but the authors also proposed consideration of the political aspects of another possibility: the "creation of a neutralized Arab enclave in Transjordan and the Triangle, in the framework of a 'Palestinian state,' linked to Israel, that will also include the Gaza Strip refugees."[21]

The head of the Planning Department, who gave the name "Nevo" to the document, may have been thinking of Moses, who ascended Mount Nevo, east of the Jordan River, to gaze out over the Promised Land that he would not enter. There is no clear evidence of the extent to which the authors were influenced by the spirit of Dayan's order; perhaps they were seeking to please him. What is certain is that the IDF's top command advocated a larger Israel and sought to instill that view in the troops.[22] Ben-Gurion may or may not have been directly influenced by the Nevo report. Whatever the case, he viewed the Green Line as a temporary border, which is indeed how it had been designated in the armistice agreements. From time to time he pondered ways of correcting it.

❖

Chief of Staff Dayan, then about forty years old, a member of the second generation of the Zionist aristocracy, was already an object of adulation. Ben-Gurion considered him the ideal combination of farmer and warrior, the two essential sides of the New Jew. He was also impressed by Dayan's fascination with archaeology and the Bible, and recommended to him that he read Sophocles. Dayan had been born at the very first kibbutz, Degania, and grew up at Nahalal, another legendary pioneering settlement. His father was a leading figure in Mapai and represented the party in the Knesset. Dayan's trademark black eyepatch became a national symbol. An admired and charismatic commander, he was daring and adventurous, and seems to have been fascinated by danger and death. He often placed himself at the front line of battle, where he could smell the gunfire and absorb the smoke. One of his command assignments during the War of Independence was the conquest of Lod; on several occasions he was involved in the expulsion of Arabs.

He thought a lot about how Jews and Arabs might live together, but he remained largely ensconced in the Orientalist fantasy of the kindly landowner who treats his tenant farmers well or punishes them, as he sees fit. His biographer, Mordechai Bar-On, wrote that he had an "extreme aversion" to being under the sway of any form of ideology and aimed to constantly re-examine changing circumstances. But he was born into the Zionist creed and held fast to it to the end of his life. And, like Ben-Gurion, he was willing to pay any price that it demanded.

An arrogant romantic, who sought power, women, money, and glory, he was a slave to his desires and passions. Over his lifetime he betrayed his wives and children, the law, the truth, and himself as well. Averse to accepting supreme responsibility, he always needed to be under the authority of a prime minister. As Ben-Gurion aged, he became ever more dependent on this younger man, treating him with a great measure of indulgence. This included allowing his general to do what he had categorically forbidden officers affiliated with Mapam to do—engage in political activity.

Dayan's efforts to force Ben-Gurion into a full-scale war with Egypt produced a dialogue that sometimes looked like a cat-and-mouse game. Both men were cunning, but Dayan more so, and with impunity. "Once and for all, I have to try to give you some military education," he told Ben-Gurion imperiously on one occasion. Ben-Gurion responded that he was always prepared to learn, and for his part tried to give Dayan a lesson in national leadership. Dayan betrayed him, too, in the end.

Ben-Gurion started from the insight that, while Egypt could destroy Israel, Israel could not destroy the Arab state, even if it had the upper hand in a second round of war. "If war comes tomorrow and we win, we will face the prospect of a third, fourth, and fifth round, without end," he said, adhering to the fundamental approach that had guided him for many years. He reminded Dayan that every war causes a huge amount of destruction. It made no difference if Israel initiated the war or waited for the Arabs to attack, whether Israel lost or won—the damage the country would suffer would set it back by five to seven years. A preventative war was liable to prompt the intervention of a third party—he especially feared that Britain would come to the aid of Egypt and would in exchange receive control of the Negev. A war Israel initiated was thus liable to end in defeat; at the very least it would leave Israel in a worse position than it had been in before. The entire world would condemn it, even if, "in the best case," sanctions were not imposed on it. The immediate task was thus to obtain arms, not start a war.

If that were the case, Dayan asked, then what level of alert did the army need to be on? Ben-Gurion said that the question was a hard one, but he offered an answer. The army had to take into account the possibility of a sudden war, and needed to be able to mobilize the necessary reserve forces "in the shortest possible time." The army, including the reserves, needed to be well trained, its "armaments in good order," and have the needed fuel available. Furthermore, it needed to ensure that Israel's "moral climate" would enable the nation to face such a test.[23] Dayan was not convinced, but inferred from his talks with Ben-Gurion that there was nothing preventing him from pursuing what he called the "deterioration method." Israel did not need to stage any provocations, he explained to his men. It was sufficient to respond forcefully to every act of Egyptian aggression. "In the end, such a policy will, on its own, bring the tensions to the detonation point," he said.[24] But neither did he set aside the option of preventative war.

"WE WILL NEVER START A WAR"

Ben-Gurion returned to work three weeks after his collapse. "It is the first time since he fell ill that I have seen him standing on his feet, and I did not get the impression that he is standing firmly," Sharett wrote. The new government that Ben-Gurion had finally formed was supported by a coalition comprising two-thirds of the members of the Knesset, including Mapam and Ahdut Ha'avodah.[25] Sharett had lost the prime minister's post, but remained foreign minister. Prime Minister Ben-Gurion retained the Ministry of Defense. When he presented his government to the Knesset, he dressed in khaki; his face was pale and his voice muffled. A few minutes after he began to speak, he stopped, apologized, and then after a brief silence went on. The entire house held its breath, Sharett wrote. Everyone was preoccupied with the question that no one asked out loud: had he really returned? Meir related that, a few days previously, Ben-Gurion had shared with her his fear that he would not last long as the country's leader. He gave the rest of his speech sitting down, an unprecedented sight in the Knesset. But he seemed to recover toward the end of his address. "We have never and we will never start a war against anyone," he declared. He then walked firmly from the speaker's podium back to his seat at the Cabinet table. That night the IDF carried out an operation in the area of Nitzana, which was disputed between Israel and Egypt. Operation Har Ga'ash (Volcano) left some eighty Egyptians and six Israelis dead.[26] A few days later, Dayan again proposed to Ben-Gurion that Israel bring about a "large-scale confrontation" with Egypt, "at the earliest possible time." The goals of the war he was proposing had not changed—the conquest of the Gaza Strip and the Straits of Tiran.

Dayan pressed very hard, and employed the rest of the IDF leadership to help him. At one General Staff meeting, Ben-Gurion informally polled the generals. Every one of them favored a preventative war.[27] Yehoshafat Harkabi, who had replaced Binyamin Gibli as army intelligence chief, sent Ben-Gurion a memorandum in this spirit, as did the chief of the Shin Bet secret security service and Mossad, Isser Harel. Abba Eban, Israel's ambassador to Washington and the United Nations, agreed.[28]

During this period, the chief of staff of the United Nations Truce Supervision Organization in the region tried to put together an agreement that would reduce to a bare minimum the tensions in the Gaza Strip area. To that end, he met with both Ben-Gurion and Nasser. Among his proposals were joint Israeli and Egyptian patrols and the construction of a border fence. But Israel did not want joint patrols, which would constrain its freedom of action, and the Egyptians did not want a fence, which would grant the armistice line the nature of a recognized border between states.[29] UN Secretary-General Dag Hammarskjöld also traveled to the Middle East, as did a series of self-appointed mediators. One of the latter was Richard Crossman, who still felt he had a mission to save Zionism from Ben-Gurion and get it back on Chaim Weizmann's track. He also visited Nasser, but had no success and went home. Britain and the United States concocted a peace plan, which they gave the code name "Alpha." An American envoy named Robert Anderson, a former secretary of the navy, arrived in total secrecy, at the behest of President Eisenhower. He tried to arrange a meeting between Ben-Gurion and Nasser, perhaps even in Cairo. But all these efforts failed, because Israel wanted Egypt to recognize Israel's right to live in peace, while Nasser agreed to consider only proposals that Israel had refused to accept, among them Israel ceding the southern Negev and accepting the right of the refugees to return to their homes or accept compensation, as each one saw fit.*[30]

Ben-Gurion did not believe in these initiatives. "Nasser's face is not turned toward peace," he wrote in his diary. That was the fundamental assumption that guided him. Nasser knew how to make a good impression on his guests. They returned to Jerusalem with the feeling that he was not refusing to make peace. But, Ben-Gurion wrote, "his behavior over the years shows that he seeks war with Israel, and is only waiting for the day when he can be sure of his military superiority."[31] As time went by, he increasingly came to see Nasser as the principal factor in Israel's conflict with Egypt, and

---

* At one of those creative moments he sometimes had, Ben-Gurion fantasized about the possibility of digging a tunnel under the Red Sea that would provide Egypt with a direct link to Jordan; his models were the tunnels under the Hudson River in New York. (Ben-Gurion to the Cabinet, Aug. 28, Dec. 25, 1955, ISA.)

to a large extent with the entire Arab world. He read Nasser's book, *Philosophy of the Revolution*, just as he had read *Mein Kampf* in an earlier decade. "Nasser is now the greatest danger for us," he said.[32]

Against this background, the tension on Israel's borders continued. In December 1955, the situation on the Syrian border deteriorated, leading to a large Israeli reprisal at Lake Kinneret, where the two countries were at odds over fishing rights in the lake, among other issues. Some fifty Syrians and six Israelis were killed. Ben-Gurion seems not to have properly appreciated the dimensions of the operation or to have considered the possible implications with all due caution. Neither did he take account of an urgent appeal that reached him a day earlier from Sharett. The foreign minister was in the United States, closing an arms deal with the Americans. He asked Ben-Gurion to refrain from all military action until the deal was finalized. But Ben-Gurion listened to Dayan instead; he apparently wanted to humor Dayan after vetoing several other operations the chief of staff had proposed. The operations were aimed, in part, at furthering Dayan's "deterioration policy."

The Kinneret operation was condemned throughout the world. It roused protests in the Cabinet as well, among other reasons because Ben-Gurion had not brought the operation before the ministers for their approval. *Ha'aretz* ran an editorial with the headline "Dictatorship of the Prime Minister?" Ben-Gurion explained that, when the operation was approved, he was not only prime minister and defense minister, but in Sharett's absence was also acting foreign minister. He had thus consulted with himself. But his face was bleak, sad, and distressed during the debate; he seems to have regretted the operation. Ambassador Eban also sent him a sharply worded protest, but then defended the operation before the Security Council. Ben-Gurion's retort became an Israeli classic: "I fully understand your concern about the Kinneret operation. I must confess that I, too, began to have my doubts about the wisdom of it. But when I read the full text of your brilliant defense of our action in the Security Council, all my doubts were set at rest. You have convinced me that we were right, after all."

Here, too, hawkeyed and razor-tongued Tzipora Sharett offered a merciless but clearheaded account of the background to the operation. "It is difficult to understand what happened here logically," she wrote to her children. "I can say that what was at work here was the Old Man's age, the fallout from his recent illness, his weakening memory and capacity for considering the act from all sides, political and military, his old complex regarding your father, and above all else, the fact that he has been dominated by Moshe Dayan, who explicitly wants war." Ben-Gurion liked to play with soldiers and lived in an imaginary world, she wrote: "Not everyone is mad, but it is not hard to be dragged along by history." Sharett himself told the members of Mapai's Political Committee that even "the Devil himself" could not have recommended a more damaging operation than the one at the Kinneret. In response to a note from Navon, Ben-Gurion's aide, Sharett agreed to take back that metaphor.[33]

"IT'S A BEAUTIFUL OBJECT"

Operation Alei Zait (Olive Leaves), as the Kinneret operation was officially called, did not draw Nasser into war, but Syrian attacks on Israeli settlements increased. Like the conflict over fishing in the lake, disputes over grazing and harvesting rights in the Gaza Strip area led to a large operation that ended up killing dozens, most of them civilians, in that territory. In the months that preceded the operation, fedayun carried out a series of attacks on civilian settlements in Israel. They also planted mines and carried out ambushes. From behind the border, Egyptian soldiers sniped at Israeli patrols; an Israeli soldier was killed on March 1, 1956, and three days later three more were killed. The soldiers were driving away a flock of sheep that had crossed into Israeli territory, apparently as bait. The Egyptians then shelled a number of kibbutzim, including Nahal Oz. There were no casualties. In response, the IDF fired artillery at Gaza City. According to a report Sharett made to the Cabinet, thirty men were killed in the shelling, twenty-six of them civilians, as well as fifteen women and twelve children. More than a hundred people were injured. Ben-Gurion told the Cabinet that when the chief of staff informed him about the shelling, he ordered Dayan to desist. His reason, he explained, was that the target, an Egyptian army outpost, was located within a civilian area. Any light deviation in the direction of fire would mean that civilians would be hurt, Ben-Gurion said, and for that reason he ordered an end to the shelling.

Several members of the Cabinet agreed that the action had been necessary. "I want to say that I am not sorry about the Gaza matter," Golda Meir said. "I know that it might sound cruel. Children were killed. But the children of Kibbutz Ein Hashlosha are also children. I freely admit that I don't have any bad feelings about it . . . I am not saying that because in Gaza Arab children were killed and here we are talking about Jewish children, but because we did not start it. They need to know that they need to pay, and pay a high price." By this point, Ben-Gurion had reached the conclusion that there was no way of preventing fedayun incursions from the Gaza Strip; the only way to stop them was to undermine Nasser's regime.[34]

Nasser did not allow himself to be drawn into war this time, either, but he sent several fedayun squads into Israel. One of them managed to reach Shafrir (later renamed Kfar Chabad), just nine miles from Tel Aviv. The terrorists made their way into the synagogue of the village's vocational school while evening prayers were in progress, opened fire, and killed four students and a counselor.[35]

About two hours previously, the first six Mystère IVA fighter-bombers purchased from France arrived in Israel under a veil of the highest secrecy. Ben-Gurion drove to the Hatzor airbase, in the Negev, to watch them land. He was beside himself with excitement. When, standing in the air control tower, he heard the voices of Israeli pilots, a huge smile spread across his face. "It's a beautiful object," he told the Cabinet. "It was a pleasure to see them descend, one after the other." For a moment he sounded like a kid with a new toy. "You press a button and it throws rockets at an enemy plane," he marveled. Several selected guests watched the landing with him, including Israel's ambassador to France and France's to Israel. Foreign Minister Sharett was not invited.[36]

Following the attack on Shafrir, Ben-Gurion demanded a large-scale operation on a fedayun base in the Strip. He explained that Israel could not act against Egypt with the same kind of small detachments the Palestinian commandos used. Several ministers asked if he meant war and the conquest of the Gaza Strip. Ben-Gurion responded with an ambiguous statement of the type he had used in the past. "I do not favor us starting a war, although I am not opposed to carrying out an operation that might cause a war." In any case, he said, "the war is approaching us rapidly."

The Cabinet authorized him to make a decision about a reprisal operation as he saw fit, "in consultation with the foreign minister." Two ministers voted against the resolution; Sharett was one of them.[37] Two months later, he was dismissed. He heard about it from a columnist for *Ha'aretz*, Shlomo Gross, who called him to ask whether it was true that he was being appointed to the position of secretary of Mapai and that Golda Meir was replacing him as foreign minister. Tzipora Sharett had already heard about it from her friends.[38]

There was no easy way of getting rid of Sharett. As he had at other junctures, Ben-Gurion offered his colleagues a choice: him or me. Unlike in the past, his colleagues offered no opposition. Sharett felt that he had been done a terrible injustice. "Every day is a nightmare," he wrote. Before he was compelled to leave the Cabinet, he put in writing things he had never dared say so ferociously before. "I have thought about a long chain of fabrications and lies that we are to blame for and which cost us lives, and on excesses by our people that have caused the most horrible catastrophes, some of which have had repercussions on the entire course of events and contributed to the security crisis we find ourselves in," he wrote. "I warned against the criminal narrowness of our approach to state security, which leads us to impetuous and wild actions that destroy our political standing on the security front and which severely undermine our position."[39] With regard to the shelling of Gaza, he first wrote that it had been "wild and foolish"; a while later he wrote: "In my opinion, it was a criminal act." He argued that the "deterioration policy" had caused Israel to miss an opportunity to restrain Nasser, perhaps even to topple him. Nor could he resist putting down an embarrassing incident that revealed Ben-Gurion's poor memory. During a Cabinet debate, Sharett claimed, Ben-Gurion had demanded the establishment of an Israeli settlement in the demilitarized zone along the Egyptian border. When he was told that the Cabinet had long ago approved the proposal, he was surprised and said that, if that were the case, there was no reason not to found the settlement. But the settlement was already there. "I do not know if all members of the Cabinet have given proper consideration to these vicissitudes of memory, misleading reports, and wiles of concealment and disguise that were here demonstrated in such a measure of deterioration in the space of just a few minutes," Sharett wrote. He left the Cabinet feeling that his ouster was a catastrophe of history. "I am sad, sad, sad," he wrote.[40]

All this principally indicated that Sharett knew very well that he could not serve as foreign minister in Ben-Gurion's government. Just weeks later, Nasser provoked another dramatic crisis, of a sort that Golda Meir was much better suited to manage together with Ben-Gurion. It happened on July 26, 1956, in Alexandria. Nasser told an audience of three hundred thousand of the city's inhabitants that he was nationalizing the Suez Canal. *Ma'ariv* called it a bombshell; Israel, which up to that point had faced war with Egypt alone, suddenly found itself with two potential allies, Britain and France.[41]

"IS THAT GOOD OR BAD?"

About ten days after marveling at the sight of the first French warplanes to arrive in Israel, Ben-Gurion visited the Kishon port, just north of Haifa, to see the unloading of several dozen AMX-13 tanks that had arrived by boat from France. This was the first installment of a larger shipment that would arrive on several boats over the next several days. He was extremely excited, Dayan wrote, and boarded the ship to shake the hand of the French admiral and his officers. Dayan was excited as well, but tried to hide it.

It was meant to be a secret, but many people already knew about it, in part because Ben-Gurion invited selected guests to witness the arrival of the ships carrying the tanks. Natan Alterman was invited to memorialize the event in a poem. Ben-Gurion did not allow him to publish the work, but read it at a Cabinet meeting ("iron, much iron, new iron . . . and while it is all imagination—it is all already real . . ."). It was Alterman's best poem ever, he thought; at a later date, he also recited it before the Knesset. He proposed to the ministers that they cast lots to determine in what order they would come to watch the tanks unloaded, but they preferred that he decide.[42] Ben-Gurion made a point of welcoming each one of the ships; when one was late in arriving, he was upset and personally called the commander of Israel's navy to ask what had happened.*

---

* It was not easy for him to get hold of the commander. The girl who answered the phone asked for his name. He said, "Ben-Gurion." She asked which Ben-Gurion. He said, "The defense minister." She thought that was very funny. It took a while before he convinced her. "It was only after several further exchanges that she believed that it was really me talking, and then I received what I had asked for," he wrote. He also told the story to the Cabinet. (Ben-Gurion, Diary, Aug. 2, 1956, BGA; Ben-Gurion to the Cabinet, Aug. 5, 1956, ISA.)

The arms purchase agreements between France and Israel were signed before Nasser nationalized the Suez Canal. The negotiations between the two countries apparently received a push after the Czechoslovakian arms deal with Egypt. Dayan had informed the Cabinet as early as August 1954 that France was interested in selling arms to Israel. In April 1956, he explained France's motives: certain circles in the French army wanted Israel armed so that it would start a war with Egypt. That would ensure that Egypt would not intervene in the Algerian revolution against French rule. It was a French gamble that reminded Dayan of something he claimed to have once heard from Ben-Gurion: "Whoever bases his policy on Israel rather than the Arabs is either an idiot or a genius. The difference between a genius and an idiot is that a genius sees things before they happen."[43]

France had lent aid to the Zionist struggle before the establishment of the state, and during the War of Independence as well.[44] But in the 1950s, the road to obtaining French arms was a bumpy one. It required putting out cautious feelers to competing individuals in France, who had differing interests and approaches, among them politicians, officials, generals, and the heads of secret security agencies, many of whom were caught up in a web of conflicts, plots, and intrigues. Very few foreigners were able to divine how it all worked. One who did was Shimon Peres; he felt completely at home in the jungle of the Fourth Republic. He had a talent for precisely identifying who was a friend and who a foe, who a potential ally and who a likely turncoat, how much power each had, and what the weaknesses of each individual were. "In France there are three defense ministers," Ben-Gurion told the Cabinet in astonishment—of land forces, the navy, and the air force.[45] Peres's secret activity was an extension of the escapades of the Bricha and arms procurement operations that had preceded the state, among them covert operations and deceptions of all sorts, many of great imagination, ingenuity, and daring. Peres often spoke in the name of the survivors of the Holocaust, or on occasion in terms of socialist values—he always knew how to target the interests of his interlocutor. "The central figures in the aviation industry are Jews," he reported. Ben-Gurion asked: "Is that good or bad?" Peres said it was good.[46]

Ben-Gurion had discovered him at a young age. Peres had been only thirty years old when Ben-Gurion appointed him director-general of the

Ministry of Defense. Ben-Gurion's relationship with Peres, unlike that with Dayan, did not grow out of the younger man's biography. Rather, it principally derived from Peres's ability to get things done and his intellectual talents. Peres read widely and was willing to consider all options, as fantastical as they might seem. Peres was almost everything Dayan was not. He had been born in a town in Poland; he had arrived in Palestine at the age of thirteen and had lived on a kibbutz for a while, but did not fight in the War of Independence and never made it into the native-born elite. He remained something of an outsider his entire life, a Jew among Israelis; the accent he had in every one of the several languages he knew, Hebrew included, gave away that Yiddish was his mother tongue. Many treated him with contempt and hostility; almost to the end of his life he was identified more as a political intriguer than as a person who had made a huge contribution to Israel's security. He thus spent his life seeking love, or at least recognition and belonging. One of his most senior counterparts in France, Abel Thomas, attributed his success there to his inclination and ability to blend into whatever surroundings he found himself in.[47] His outsider position in Israel was an obstacle, but his foreign Israeli mien charmed France. There was probably no one in Israel who admired him as a politician and a friend the way Maurice Bourgès-Maunoury did; Bourgès-Maunoury was France's defense minister and later prime minister. Ben-Gurion's patronage was the source of his power, but Peres also felt a profound personal loyalty to his patron. Dayan's relations with Ben-Gurion were much more utilitarian. Together, Peres and Dayan led him into a war that he did not at first want.

❖

The summer found Ben-Gurion, as sometimes in the past, in a meditative, nostalgic mood. A day before Nasser's announcement about Suez, he was poring over Plato's position that rulers are permitted to lie in the service of their people. He wrote several lines of Greek in his diary. The news from Cairo did not distract him from critically engaging with a theory of the origins of the Jewish faith. Two days later, he avidly listened to the radio broadcast of the Israel national soccer team's game against the Soviets—Israel lost

2–1, but at halftime the two teams were tied at 0, and during the second half Israel played without its star, the goalie Ya'akov Hodorov, who had been injured. "It could be that the heat worked against the Russians, but our boys proved that they know how to try hard and succeed," he wrote in his diary.*[48]

Nasser's move to nationalize the Suez Canal did not spur him into immediate action. He presumed that the Soviet Union had sanctioned the move. As he put it, "Hitler has helped the Egyptian Mussolini." It soon transpired that the United States recognized, in effect, Egypt's right to nationalize the waterway. Ben-Gurion wrote: "It's worse than Munich. It's a knife in the backs of England and France and perhaps NATO as a whole." But he presumed that France and Britain would not dare take the canal by force, and that there was nothing Israel could do, either.[49]

"AN ENGLISH PLOT TO GET US IN TROUBLE WITH NASSER"

Dayan continued to press for an Israeli first strike. Plans had been ready since January of the previous year. A bombing campaign in Egypt might well kill tens of thousands, one of the plans stated; dozens of Israelis would die. Ben-Gurion continued to say no. Dayan's patience began to run out. "The question is what result you want to achieve," he said to Ben-Gurion at the end of July 1956. Ben-Gurion wanted "many small strikes that can be kept up and thus make life intolerable for them." Dayan was opposed. "If we kill five Egyptian peasants they won't mind," he said. "They'll shout 'the Jews are murderers,' but not one of them will really get upset." In fact, the "small strikes" that Ben-Gurion wanted would be interpreted as Israeli failures, Dayan added. The assumption would be that it had wanted to carry out a large operation but had been unable to do so, he maintained.[50] The question remained open for the time being.

---

* It was a return game—Israel had lost the first 5–0. The Cabinet devoted an extended discussion to the results, during which Ben-Gurion announced that he was considering establishing a national soccer team within the IDF. He said that he had not listened to the game because he knew Israel would lose. He had never been to a soccer game, he said, but he liked it when Jews beat gentiles and not the reverse. The discussion provided him with another opportunity to hark back to his trip to Moscow in 1923, and he did not let it pass by. (Ben-Gurion to the Cabinet, July 15, 1956, ISA.)

❖

Later that summer, Ben-Gurion found time to inquire about the condition of his friend Shlomo Lavi's eyes, as well as to copy out selections from Aristotle's letters in ancient Greek and to listen to a detailed report on a caterpillar that was ravaging the cotton crop. On August 24, 1956, he celebrated the fiftieth anniversary of his immigration to Palestine. Memories of his first hours in Jaffa overwhelmed him; his decision not to spend the Sabbath there but to leave the city immediately had, over the years, taken on an ideological cast. "Naveh Shalom Street, where Jews lived mixed in with Arabs, gave me a very harsh feeling of Exile," he wrote.[51] The exile imposed on the refugees of 1948 returned to disturb him, making him again feel a need to insert his own account of what had happened into the Cabinet record. As part of this, he asked Moshe Carmel, who had commanded the forces that took Haifa and was by that time transport minister, for an alibi. "Carmel must know what happened in Haifa," he said. "When the Haganah began to conquer the Arab parts of Haifa, they said to them, hand over your weapons and you can stay."

Doris May wrote to him from London. When he returned to the Ministry of Defense, he tried to persuade her to come work for him, and now she finally agreed to come for six months.[52]

❖

The French ambassador to Israel, Pierre Gilbert, an unabashed supporter of Israel, hosted Dayan and Peres for dinner and told them that only a joint French-Israeli operation could guarantee the canal's international status. The possibility that France would take action against Nasser, perhaps in cooperation with Israel, had already come up before. On September 1, 1956, word arrived from Paris that the scenario was feasible. Ben-Gurion was primarily interested in what Britain would do. He continued to presume that the British would not want to attack Egypt, and certainly not in cooperation with Israel.[53] Dayan said that the political risk of refraining from war was greater than the military risk that war would involve. Ben-Gurion rejected that presumption. For a moment it seemed as if he had adopted a strategy that he had first heard from the military historian Israel Beer: "Bleed the attacker from a defense posture and only then sortie and attack." But "generally," he added, he agreed with Dayan that the proper thing to do was "to go on the offensive, disrupt, deceive, surprise, and destroy the enemy, and that is possible, even if the enemy has an advantage in personnel and weapons."[54] He found it very difficult to formulate a consistent line of action. During the weeks that followed, it was thus Dayan who led the country to war. Ben-Gurion was not dragged along by the chief of staff against his will, but unlike in earlier times, when he was stronger, he now went along with Dayan more easily.[55]

In September 1956, he went to spend the Jewish holiday season at Sde Boker, his first visit there in five months. He found a forgotten volume of his diary from 1951 and recalled that he had seen *The King and I* in New York that year. He spent a long time meditating on the rule of the prophetess Deborah. He was stirred by a passage he found in Plutarch. He hosted George Orwell's widow and spent many hours in the company of the American journalist Drew Pearson and his television crew. The American presidential campaign interested him. "Ike's popularity is high and people think that there will not be war during his presidency," Ben-Gurion wrote. He began to think through the terms and substance of socialist Zionism ("what they said in the past and what they don't say today"), and he covered many pages of his diary with statistical and economic data, including the annual balance sheet of Solel Boneh. "A bathtub made in Israel is more expensive than one made outside the country," he wrote.[56]

In the meantime, deadly terrorist attacks continued, sometimes also originating on Jordanian territory.*

Dayan demanded authorization for reprisal actions. Ben-Gurion consented to only a few of them, and only some of those he brought before the Cabinet received its sanction. Some of these ended with heavy losses for the IDF—in September 1956, sixteen soldiers died in two reprisals. During one of them, Jordanians abducted several soldiers, then returned their bodies that

---

* Fedayun tried hard to attack Sde Boker. A car was blown up by a land mine planted about three miles from the kibbutz gate. Another mine was discovered before it went off. A terrorist was discovered and shot dead as he attempted to enter the commune. (Ben-Gurion, Diary, Aug. 15, 16, Oct. 15, 1956, BGA.)

evening. "The bodies were naked and horribly mutilated," Ben-Gurion wrote. "They cut off the penises." Dayan came to Sde Boker to explain why the operation had failed. "Ben-Gurion looked despondent," Dayan wrote, "sitting glumly between piles of books scattered around his workroom in the little hut; the air was heavy." In a diary entry dated September 22, 1956, Ben-Gurion noted: "According to the Hebrew calendar, I am seventy years old today."

Three days later, everything changed. Ben-Gurion was flown urgently from Sde Boker to meet with Peres. "What he told me may well be momentous," the prime minister wrote. His trusted aide had just returned from Paris. Peres said that France had concluded that it had to take action against Nasser, "with the knowledge and consent of the English. They want Israel to be involved, that too with the knowledge of the English."[57] The plan began to move quickly; Ben-Gurion followed all the details. He continued to believe the French and to be suspicious of the British. Dayan tried to reassure him, proposing that Israel, with British cooperation, bring about a new Middle East order. Nasser would be gotten rid of and Jordan partitioned between Israel and Iraq. Ben-Gurion could not conceive of why Britain would agree to such an arrangement. "I think it is an English plot to get us in trouble with Nasser and bring about an Iraqi conquest of Jordan," he wrote.*

But the desire for a new Middle East, and perhaps also the last several weeks of not seeing any clear way out of the corner Israel found itself in, finally led Ben-Gurion to adopt Dayan's plan and make improvements to it. The latter included a solution to the refugee problem. Two days later, he presented the plan to Ambassador Gilbert. Nasser would be ousted. Jordan would be partitioned, with its eastern side going to Iraq, which would make peace with Israel. The United States would fund the resettlement of the Palestinian refugees in the expanded Iraq. He also proposed a partition of Syria, with Israel annexing part of its territory.[58] That same day a French plane

---

* Israel's relations with Britain took a very bad turn at that time, following a major reprisal raid in which Israeli forces blew up the Qalqilya police station. Some one hundred Jordanians and eighteen Israelis died. A few weeks earlier, Ben-Gurion had told the Cabinet: "With all my confidence in the Israel Defense Forces and the Jewish people, I do not think we have the strength to fight the English." (Moshe Dayan 1976, p. 246ff.; Ben-Gurion to the Cabinet, Aug. 12, 1956, ISA.)

arrived to take him to the French capital, accompanied by Dayan and Peres. It was during this flight that he read Procopius of Caesarea's *History of the Wars*.

"WHAT IF NASSER DOESN'T FALL?"

It was not easy to cobble together this triple alliance. Ben-Gurion was housed in a private villa in Sèvres, a southwestern suburb famous for both its porcelain and the treaty signed after World War I between the Allies and Turkey. The illusion that the three countries could rid themselves of Nasser by means of an almost childishly simple stratagem lent the talks a "mythical" cast, as Ben-Gurion later told the Cabinet. The idea was that Israel would attack Egypt and that Britain and France would demand that the two sides agree to a cease-fire. Israel would consent on condition that Egypt also agreed, but Egypt would reject the ultimatum, providing a pretext for the two powers to join the Israeli offensive. All three countries wanted to depose Nasser. The French wanted Israel's help and agreed to provide assistance, but the Israelis wanted a joint action from the outset. Britain was inclined to agree to a joint Israeli-French action, but without its own direct involvement. The Israelis insisted that the British also needed to play a role, the logic being that, if Britain were involved, Jordan would be much less likely to enter the war on Egypt's side. Ben-Gurion hesitated long and hard before closing the deal. "What if Nasser doesn't fall?" he kept asking himself.[59]

Each of the three partners compromised on its opening position. Ben-Gurion agreed to make the first strike against Egypt, for all intents and purposes accepting Dayan's demand for a preventative war. Dayan promised that no more than 250 IDF soldiers would die. One of his subordinates, Shlomo Gazit, asked Dayan what the basis for this promise was. Dayan responded: "You yourself have seen and heard how apprehensive Ben-Gurion is about losses, and how unsure he is about the IDF's ability to win this war. I had no choice but to reassure him." He added that if Israel won, no one would take him to task about the number of soldiers killed, and if Israel lost, it would have much more serious problems to deal with. No one really knew what would happen afterward, but everyone believed that the principal goal would be achieved—Nasser would be done for. Dayan and Peres persuaded

Ben-Gurion that it was now or never. That was the major claim he made to the Cabinet a few days later.[60]

❖

Several members of the Cabinet were angry that they had not been informed of the contacts leading up to the pact. "Now you know," Ben-Gurion told one of them. He had brought most of them up to date before the meeting. He offered a fairly precise but not complete account of the plan. Getting rid of Nasser would guarantee freedom of navigation to and from Eilat; as part of the campaign, Israel would seize control of the islands in the Tiran Straits. He could not say who would receive the Sinai Peninsula after the war. As usual, he stressed that he could not promise anything for certain, and nearly every sentence he uttered was couched in a caveat. He presumed that the United States would be too caught up in the presidential election to intervene, and that the Russians were preoccupied with repressing the uprising in Hungary, but he could not really know how they would react. The "collusion," as he would later refer to the pact, was thus liable to ensnare Israel in conflict with the two superpowers, but the opportunity to put an end to Nasser's regime was worth the risk. He said again and again that Israel had been presented with an opportunity that it would never have again, although he refused to commit himself even to that statement. He did not tell his colleagues about the plans for a new Middle East order, but as always got carried away by his own arguments. Israel could destroy Egypt's army even without French and British assistance, he maintained. Israel didn't need them. "We'll do it like nothing," he asserted. The ministers could still vote down the plan, he said. That was not entirely true—all the preparations for war were in place and the reserves were already being called up.

Most of the ministers supported him. Golda Meir related how she had encountered battle-ready and well-prepared soldiers and her heart had broken; she said those final words in Yiddish. But Minister of Health Israel Barzilai, of Mapam, cited what Ben-Gurion himself had said just a few months earlier—the proposed war would only mark the start of an interim period, between the second round and the third. Ben-Gurion responded: "I'm not saying forever. There will be five to eight years of calm." He promised that there would not be heavy losses, but did not specify a number. He compared the war he was proposing to the creation of the state.

Someone asked what would happen in the Gaza Strip. Ben-Gurion said that the subject was an "embarrassing" one; he used the English word. "We must take it," he explained. "If I believed in miracles, I'd wish for it to be swallowed up by the sea." His constant doubts about conquering Gaza sounded much like his uncertainty about the conquest of the Old City of Jerusalem during the War of Independence. "I am so tense right now," he said. He promised to keep the leaders of the parties represented in the Knesset posted about developments, and he indeed did so. Even Menachem Begin was invited to his home for a visit, where he offered his best wishes for the IDF's success. During the days that followed, Begin called Ben-Gurion from time to time to provide him with information he had gleaned from the BBC.[61]

❖

The war began on the afternoon of October 29, 1956; Ben-Gurion was in bed with the flu. He had a high fever and was weak, but kept up with events. Unlike in the War of Independence, he did not interfere with the army's operations. Dayan was with the forces; Navon was the liaison with the General Staff and for the most part Ben-Gurion had to make do with what he learned through this channel. He waited impatiently for the British and French to intervene, and when they did not begin operations at the assigned hour, he ordered Dayan to bring the Israeli forces home and cancel the war. Dayan persuaded him to continue. "I was very anxious," Ben-Gurion wrote. He worried that the Egyptians would bomb Tel Aviv and the country's airfields. It took less than one hundred hours for Israel to capture the entire Sinai Peninsula and the islands of the Tiran Straits. Ben-Gurion sent a message to an IDF victory ceremony at Sharm el-Sheikh, on the peninsula's southern tip, that it was "the greatest and most glorious operation in our nation's history, and one of the most amazing operations in the history of all nations." He quoted several bellicose verses from the book of Exodus and added, "You have extended a hand to King Solomon." The manifesto ended with the promise that Tiran Island would remain part of the "Third Jewish Kingdom." He summed up the events of the previous two weeks in his diary with these words: "First the whole thing looked like a hallucination, afterward like an ancient tale, and at the end as the purest marvel."[62]

That same morning an official statement was issued regarding "unfortunate events in which several Arab civilians were killed and wounded." It was referring to the killing of close to fifty inhabitants, among them women and children, of the village of Kafr Qasim in central Israel, close to the border with Jordan. A contingent of the Border Guard, a force then under the command of the IDF, had lined them up and shot them to death because they had returned from work about half an hour after the start of the daily curfew. That day the curfew time had been moved up by half an hour all along the Jordanian border, but villagers working in the field had no way of knowing it. Ben-Gurion claimed that he heard about the incident only three days later. Navon described his reaction: "What? They killed Arabs? Where? Why?" He was shocked. "How can such a thing happen? They just killed Arabs for no reason? Soldiers shot them—why? What happened there? It's horrible! It's horrible!" He immediately ordered the appointment of a commission of inquiry.[63] But on the day of Operation Kadesh, as the Sinai Campaign was known in Israel, he had more serious things to worry about.

Even as Dayan was reading his victory speech at Sharm el-Sheikh, Ben-Gurion had in hand a threatening letter in Russian from the Soviet prime minister, Nikolai Bulganin. He demanded the immediate withdrawal of IDF forces from Egyptian territory "before it is too late." President Eisenhower also demanded withdrawal. But Bulganin's letter was of unparalleled ferocity, an almost explicit threat to destroy Israel. Ben-Gurion put off responding to the Soviet threat long enough to make a dazzling victory speech to the Knesset. He declared that the conquest of Sinai brought Israel to the place where the Jewish people had received the Torah. He also quoted, from the source, the account of the Jewish state on Tiran Island; the original Greek appears in the Knesset record. He gave the impression that the occupied territories would remain under Israeli control, at least until the signing of a peace agreement with Egypt. He would never agree for a foreign military force to be stationed there. The armistice agreement with Egypt was a dead letter, he said. "Our losses are few," he said, "about 150 dead."*

But the Soviet threat terrified him. "It was a nightmarish day," he wrote. "Bulganin's letter to me—a letter that could have been written by Hitler— and the ferocity of the Russian tanks in Hungary, show just what these Communist Nazis are capable of doing." He was very pale, Dayan wrote after leaving his room, "enraged like a wounded lion."[64] The withdrawal commenced a week later. The last Israeli soldier in Egypt left three months later, just before the Pesach holiday.

---

* In fact, the IDF dead numbered more than 170. Many years later, Ben-Gurion said that it was the one speech he regretted making. "I talked a little too much," he said. He was, he said, "drunk at the time." Ben-Gurion very seldom regretted anything he said or wrote. As such, his remorse over his victory speech is reminiscent of his comment that he would not repeat the eulogy of Herzl that he sent to Shmuel Fuchs when he was seventeen years old. (Ben-Gurion interview with Malcolm Stuart, April 1968, transcript, BGA, p. 83; Ben-Gurion interview with Levi Yitzhak Hayerushalmi, Feb. 28, 1972, BGA, p. 15.)

22

YES TO THE OLD MAN

"THE GREATEST POLITICAL MARVEL"

On April 24, 1958, Israel celebrated its tenth Independence Day—marked, as was customary, according to the Hebrew calendar. In the morning the sidewalks in downtown Jerusalem began to fill up with crowds jostling for a good place to watch the military parade scheduled for that afternoon. Entire families were there with folding chairs, food, and drink. There were tourists as well. The press estimated that a quarter of a million people watched the parade. What they saw were several dozen tanks, field artillery, vehicles of various types, and thousands of soldiers—armed men as well as women in below-knee-length uniform skirts. The opening ceremony was held at the new Hebrew University stadium at the campus in West Jerusalem. Ben-Gurion arrived in an official black American sedan. He and Paula were welcomed with a trumpet fanfare and applause from the throng filling the bleachers. It was a very hot and dry day; he wore a blue suit and white shirt, no tie. Even though his speech was not long, several of the soldiers standing at attention fainted and had to be removed from the ranks on stretchers.

Ben-Gurion had a great time. "The army's parade was excellent," he wrote in his diary. "I recall how, in earlier years, our boys did not know how to march. This time the parade was exemplary and impressive."[1]

Ten years and two wars after he declared the establishment of Israel, he had good reasons to feel satisfied. At the end of that same month, the country's population passed the 2 million mark, a threefold increase since independence; of these, 1.8 million were Jews. "In America, it was more than forty years after the War of Independence before the country had grown to such proportions," Ben-Gurion wrote in an introduction for a lavish coffee-table book of photographs of the country, exuding pride and optimism. The number of immigrants approached a million; more than one hundred thousand, mostly from Morocco and Romania, had arrived in 1957 alone. The great majority were already living in permanent homes, most of them in urban settlements. Almost five hundred new settlements had been established since independence, an average of almost one a week. Most of them were farming communities, including about a hundred kibbutzim. Close to 1.5 million citizens enjoyed medical care and health insurance. Israelis now lived longer than in the past, and infant mortality was on the decline. The number of children in elementary school had more than tripled, and the number of secondary school students increased by almost as much. Ben-Gurion kept the statistics regarding Jews and Arabs separate, but the Arab sector was also enjoying progress. Over the course of its first decade, the country had recovered from a severe economic crisis and a period of austerity and rationing. It was an achievement that Ben-Gurion could credit to one of the most important decisions he had gotten through the Knesset, with great effort—conciliation with Germany.

The Israeli nation was still a mixed multitude of identities, hailing from more than one hundred lands and speaking a babel of languages. Most of them were not fluent in Hebrew. But just a hundred years previously, Hebrew had not been the mother tongue of a single Jewish child, Ben-Gurion noted. The Zionist enterprise and the establishment of a Jewish state was "the greatest political marvel of the twentieth century," he maintained.[2]

A year earlier, he had offered the Cabinet a set of goals for the country's second decade. At the top of the list was increasing the number of Jews from two to three million.³ His high spirits were testimony to how ably he had managed the country in dangerous situations, including the withdrawal from Sinai and the Gaza Strip, and also to his survival of a terrible personal calamity.

❖

Soon after the occupation of Gaza, a military administration began to operate there, on an ostensibly temporary basis, without annexing the territory. "A temporary regime can last thirty or even fifty years," Ben-Gurion noted. Development Minister Mordechai Bentov of Mapam said: "If I could take the Gaza Strip together with all the Arabs living there and put them on an airplane and send them to Cairo, or to the UN secretary-general in New York, that would be a solution of sorts." His colleagues seem to have felt much the same.⁴

Ben-Gurion continued to be torn between the dream of holding on to the Sinai Peninsula, including its oil wells, and his aversion to annexing the Gaza Strip. At times he felt that Israel should retain control of the Gaza region, even if its population doubled the number of Arabs in Israel. The Palestinian refugees, however, should not be resettled in Gaza but rather in Iraq and Syria, he believed. Many shared his qualms, as if it would be their call, rather than an inevitable decision that might need to be taken under pressure from Moscow and Washington and other capitals of the world, including Paris. Shlomo Lavi pleaded with him not to remain in the Gaza Strip. "Better for us to be a smaller country and on our own than a larger country with a great enemy within," he wrote. "The most important part of what I am saying, or pleading: do not enlarge the minority that lives among us."

He really had no choice other than full withdrawal from the Sinai and Gaza. It was not easy; his surrender to superpower pressure set off a storm of opposition. One member of the Knesset shouted at him: "You defeated the IDF, not Nasser."⁵

He also had to give up on his dream of constituting a new Middle East.

❖

On the afternoon of October 29, 1957, Ben-Gurion sat in the Knesset, listening to a routine debate. Tempers were not particularly high—Golda Meir had offered a foreign policy survey, and representatives of the various factions were responding. Yitzhak Rafael of the National Religious Party suddenly noticed that someone in the visitors' gallery had thrown an object into the chamber. It was a hand grenade. "Gentlemen, a bomb!" he shouted, hitting the floor. A huge explosion shook the hall and smoke began filling the air. The grenade had been aimed at the Cabinet table. Moshe Shapira, minister of religions and of welfare, was badly wounded. Ben-Gurion was injured in an arm and a leg. Golda Meir and Transport Minister Moshe Carmel were also injured. All were rushed to the hospital.

The assailant was captured on the spot; several people in the gallery shouted, "Arab, Arab!" He was a Jew. His name was Moshe Dweik, the same man who had once shown up at Sde Boker and tried to press a welter of proposals on Ben-Gurion. At the time, Ben-Gurion thought he was strange, but sincere and honest.[6] Some guessed that he had thrown the bomb in protest against the withdrawal from Sinai and Gaza, in the spirit of the violence that remained a part of Israeli political life even after independence.*

It was the first anniversary of the beginning of the Sinai Campaign. Until it became clear that Dweik was a mentally ill Jew, it seemed reasonable to assume that he was an Arab avenger—it was also the first anniversary of the Kafr Qasim massacre.

"SIDE BY SIDE, IN ETERNAL REPOSE"

A few days after the attack in the Knesset, Nehemiah Argov took his pistol, placed it against his temple, and pulled the trigger. Two letters were discovered in the military attaché's apartment in Tel Aviv. In one he explained that he had killed himself because he had hit a bicyclist with his car earlier that day and feared that the victim would not survive or, even if he did, would remain incapacitated and unable to support his family. The second letter was addressed to Ben-Gurion. "The substance of my life was to serve you," he opened, and later repeated the sentiment, saying that he had sought to "de-

---

* Israel Kastner had been murdered in Tel Aviv just a few months previously.

vote" himself to him. It had been, he wrote, the greatest joy of his life. "It seems to me that three men in Jewish history have done the greatest deeds— the prophet Moses, King David, and David Ben-Gurion." He signed the letter "with love, Nehemiah." A few years earlier, Argov had written in his diary: "If anything remains to me in life, it is the fact that I have had the privilege of being a bit in the company of this great man. He fills my life. I thank him for that."[7]

His diary evinces utter faithfulness, to the point of self-abnegation. He kept a meticulous record of people who had tried, so he said, to lie to Ben-Gurion and treat him disrespectfully. He once had to hold himself back from beating Israel's ambassador in Washington, when the latter had criticized the prime minister. "My blood began to boil," he wrote. He reserved particular fury for Lavon, "that scum." He also referred to Lavon as a "political adventurist" and a "trampler of dead bodies," and called him "the most corrupt politician I have ever met." He had no doubts that the order for the bungled operation in Egypt had come from Lavon and, even worse, Lavon had begun to persuade himself that he had not given the order. "Astounding recklessness," Argov wrote.

Argov saw Lavon's appointment as defense minister as a disaster, one for which Ben-Gurion himself was partly to blame. In his diary he tried to make excuses for his boss, however: "He did not know Lavon and didn't know who he was." He sometimes wrote as if he were addressing Ben-Gurion directly. "It will be considered almost criminal that you did not recognize who this comrade really was at an earlier date," he wrote. In retrospect, he stated with no reservations, "It was a crime to hand over the most precious thing in the country to Pinhas Lavon." The only way Ben-Gurion could atone for his "crime" was to return to the leadership immediately, he wrote. "The works of your hands, Ben-Gurion, are drowning in the sea, and you are at Sde Boker." When Ben-Gurion's retirement showed no sign of ending, Argov wrote in his diary: "Have you resolved to abandon this country that you founded?" When Ben-Gurion realized that Lavon had to go, Argov wrote: "I had a feeling of joy. The Old Man is still so great."[8]

The connection between Argov and Ben-Gurion aroused the curiosity of many of their acquaintances. Yitzhak Navon described admiration to the point of renunciation of the self. According to Teddy Kollek, director of the

Office of the Prime Minister, Argov was "a man who lived and breathed only for Ben-Gurion." According to Yehuda Erez, the editor of Ben-Gurion's writings, Argov was "lovesick." Some of Ben-Gurion's acquaintances, Yigael Yadin among them, compared Argov's role in Ben-Gurion's life to Paula's—he saw to all his needs and blocked access to him. "Nehemiah was more possessive than a wife," recalled Ben-Gurion's grandson, Yariv Ben-Eliezer. "I think he developed a sort of jealousy and possessiveness toward Grandpa. Like women do, to a certain extent."[9]

Rivka Katznelson, who claimed to have introduced Argov to Ben-Gurion, also placed the relationship within what she saw as an "erotic dimension" of Ben-Gurion's addiction to his work. "Ben-Gurion loved Nehemiah," she wrote. "Nehemiah was gentle by nature, nice-looking, and short, and Ben-Gurion liked small women. He met him when he was already at the beginning of old age and Nehemiah was still young, and Ben-Gurion spread fatherly wings over him, a feeling that he missed with regard to his son, Amos, and trusted him not as a son but rather as a disciple, in the Platonic sense, as he understood it."*[10]

It was not easy to tell Ben-Gurion what had happened. While he lay wounded in the hospital, following the atrocity in the Knesset, his staff tried to keep it from him. The newspapers printed a special edition without word of the suicide especially for the prime minister. In the end, Dayan was assigned to break the news. Ben-Gurion responded much as he had when he learned of Berl Katznelson's death. "He sank onto the bed, turned his face to the wall, covered himself in his blanket, and did not turn to face us for many long minutes," Navon related. "We did not hear a thing, but we saw his body trembling ceaselessly, from uncontrollable weeping." In a eulogy he delivered to the Knesset, Ben-Gurion said: "Nehemiah was blessed with a precious and rare gift from God, the gift of great love. That was the flame that burned within Nehemiah always, and it was that fire that felled him, in love

---

* Ben-Gurion once gave Katznelson a copy of Plato's *Symposium*. After reading it, she told him to be careful. An old man's love for boys is stronger than his love for women, she warned him, because he served as a model for emulation for boys. That was a kind of eros that could drive one mad, she claimed. Ben-Gurion dismissed her concern. (Rivka Katznelson, interview with Shabtai Teveth, Oct. 2, 1977, BGA, Shabtai Teveth collection: subjects: Ben-Gurion and women.)

and agony." As he spoke, Ben-Gurion looked "ragged and broken, his voice crushed, and very, very old," Navon related. Navon presumed that Argov's death would shorten the prime minister's life. "I fear that the Old Man will never return to us and will never be what he once was," he wrote. "The cords of his heart were ripped out, his soul was torn, and he is now exposed to every wind."

In the days that followed, Ben-Gurion asked over and over again why Nehemiah had killed himself. He felt betrayed. According to Navon, "Ben-Gurion's pain did not let him rest, also because of the fact that he was open with Nehemiah, who knew everything about him. How, then, could Nehemiah have concealed such a fateful decision from him? Where was his friendship?" Navon quoted Ben-Gurion in his diary: "Had Nehemiah had a wife and children, he would not have committed suicide."[11] On another occasion, Ben-Gurion said: "Argov became part of me. Who conceived that Nehemiah had feelings and thoughts of his own. I didn't know—I hadn't a notion."[12] That was Ben-Gurion, not understanding those closest to him, and trying to slough off all guilt. The story of Argov's life, and the riddle of his death, produced many rumors over the years. One was that he had been the victim of Soviet blackmail because of his lifestyle.* Ben-Gurion asked to keep Argov's hat in his office, and told his staff that he wanted Argov's replacement to be young and married.[13] He was infuriated when Natan Alterman published a poem in Argov's memory, because the poet depicted his subject as a man who had sacrificed himself for a man he loved. The subtext of Alterman's poem was the Bible's story of the love between David and Jonathan. Ben-Gurion once told Navon that Jonathan was the most beautiful figure in the Bible, a man of true nobility, he said. Whatever the case, other than the companion of his youth, Shmuel Fuchs, Ben-Gurion loved Nehemiah Argov

---

* Argov's close friends claimed that he killed himself because of a "difficult romantic disappointment." Haim Israeli, who ran the defense minister's office, wrote to Elie Wiesel that "Nehemiah had an affair with a woman who was an IDF officer. The affair went on the rocks and years later the young woman worked in Jacqueline Kennedy's press office. According to Navon, Argov told him a few months before his suicide that he wanted to die. "I have nothing more to aspire to," he explained. "I have reached the acme of my life. What more can there be?" (Navon 2015, p. 194; Lam 1990; Bar-Zohar 2006, p. 274; Yisraeli 2005, p. 48.)

more than any other friend. "I am sorry to the point of death that I was unable to tell Nehemiah what I felt for him," he wrote.[14]

A short time later, Ben-Gurion said that when he died and was buried, Argov's bones should be reinterred next to his. "And lower our bones together, side by side, in eternal repose," he instructed. Paula was to be buried on his other side. He withdrew his request regarding Argov at the advice of the chief rabbi.[15] When he returned to work, he spent considerable time producing Israel's decennial celebration, which included a military parade.

"THIS JOURNALIST SHOULD BE IN A MENTAL HOSPITAL"

The country-in-the-making that Ben-Gurion led to independence stood on the foundation of liberal tradition that had guided the Zionist movement from its inception. He had no difficulty adopting the fundamental political values of the British administration, including recognition of the sovereignty of the parliamentary majority. Elections were free and generally conducted in accordance with the law. The State of Israel recognized the independence of the judiciary. That was not to be taken for granted—political and ideological disputes had more than once threatened the country's unity, and the hundreds of thousands of Jews from Communist Europe and the Arab states who populated the new country did not bring a democratic culture with them. Most of the world's inhabitants did not live in democratic countries, and in many countries democracy was still a new experience. It was thus of signal importance that the leadership generation led by Ben-Gurion identified with liberal values.

But just as he placed national interests above socialism, he also often gave them priority over democracy. His opposition to a constitution, he said, grew out of a fear that it would endanger his fragile cooperation with religious and Haredi leaders. But he also opposed a constitution because such a document would have made it harder for him to constrict human and civil rights and to bolster Mapai's hold on power. And he often identified his country's interest with that of his party. The secret security services chief Isser Harel used to provide him with political intelligence, including on Mapai. "There is already a serious crisis in internal relations at the top of the party," Ben-Gurion once recorded him as saying.[16]

His difficulty in fully internalizing the fundamental rules of democracy was often evident in his attitude toward the press and his attempts to constrain it. He was addicted to newspapers from the day he learned to read. Almost to the day of his death he published articles in the press and on occasion listed his profession as journalist. He had background talks with newspaper reporters, frequently gave interviews, and would send angry letters to newspapers. "This journalist should be in a mental hospital," he once wrote to the editor of *Davar*.[17]

The influence and power of the press increased as the years went by, and Ben-Gurion was not powerful enough to become an autocrat. There is thus no way of knowing for sure when the political system reflected his worldview as a democrat and when it was merely a result of his limited power. Whatever the case, the greatest proviso he placed on democracy was with regard to Israel's Arab citizens, who numbered some two hundred thousand in his time. They lived under military rule and were, in practice, second-class citizens. It was this situation that made the atrocity at Kafr Qasim possible.

"AN ARAB IS FIRST AND FOREMOST AN ARAB"

The military administration imposed restrictions on the freedom of movement and civil rights of a large proportion of the Arabs who had remained in Israel, or who had managed to make their way back in after the War of Independence. These restrictions contradicted both the spirit of and the specific promises contained in the Declaration of Independence but were justified on the grounds that they were required for defense. So long as the Arab world threatened to destroy the Jewish state, the Arabs living in Israel were seen as dangerous enemies, even if they were in fact a small and vanquished minority. "If anything happens," Ben-Gurion told the Cabinet at the end of 1953, "the enemy lives at home. If someone has an illusion that the Arabs will be loyal to Israel—that runs counter to human nature."[18] Military rule made it easier to expropriate land from Arabs. Some of that land was used to "Judaize the Galilee," as they said at the time. Ben-Gurion closely followed the construction of Jewish Nazareth Illit as a counterweight to historic Nazareth, inhabited by Arabs. The military government also made it easier for Mapai to win Arab votes. Its administration was arbitrary and at times corrupt, routinely harassing the population and, over the years, also carrying out some expulsion operations.

Israel's Arab citizens were allowed to vote and to be elected to the Knesset, and in that sense Ben-Gurion could claim that an Arab could in principle be elected prime minister or president, as he had often maintained. He exempted them from military service. Once, at a Cabinet meeting, he declared that, in the United States, a Jew or a black person could not be elected president. He did not believe in American civil rights, he said, perhaps thinking of the discrimination against blacks that he had seen with his own eyes during World War I. He also cited anti-Jewish bias in America.[19] One Cabinet minister said that Israel's Arabs were basically living in ghettoes; Ben-Gurion claimed that keeping them isolated protected their livelihoods, just like the first reservations set up for Native Americans in the United States did.[20]

Most critically, he saw them as a danger to the country's Jewish character. As the years went by, the debate over the military administration took a central place in public discourse, and not only on the left. The opposition leader Menachem Begin and his Herut party also opposed it. There were a number of reasons for this position, among them Begin's European liberal-national worldview. This led him on occasion to denounce antidemocratic measures taken by Ben-Gurion. A series of government committees studied the military regime. Some figures in both the IDF and government agencies that dealt with the Arab population, including the secret police (Shin Bet), recommended that it be ended. The assumption was that the integration of the Arab citizens into Israeli society would reduce the risk to security that they presented.[21] Ben-Gurion fought against every attempt to eliminate the military government, agreeing only to mitigate it. In 1962 he went so far as to threaten to resign over the issue. At the same meeting he said with foreboding that the Arabs would become a majority. "Their death rate is like that of the Jews, and their birthrate is without contraception," he warned. He argued heatedly that the military government was an expression of moral ideals. "The security of the State of Israel is the greatest moral foundation in the world," he maintained. One of the last speeches he made to the Knesset as prime minister centered on the continued need for military administration.[22]

Constantly labeling the Arabs as a fifth column also provided a retroactive justification for driving the Arab population away during the War of Independence. The Kafr Qasim massacre also had roots in the tenor of his rhetoric. "An Arab is first and foremost an Arab," he told the Cabinet a few days before the bloodbath.[23]

❖

The details of the atrocity came to light in stages.[24] When he informed the Cabinet of the murder of dozens of villagers, he termed it an "outrage," adding that it was "unprecedentedly reprehensible and deplorable." He gave the ministers the essence of the story. When the decision was made to move up the time of the curfew, the battalion commander had asked the regimental commander what to do with people who violated it. The former claimed that the regimental commander's response was: "I don't want any sentimentality. I don't want arrests." The battalion commander did not leave it at that. "Nevertheless?" he asked. The regimental commander silenced him with an Arabic expression: *Allah yerhamo*, meaning "May God have mercy on him." The battalion commander took this to mean "Do what you need to do." The regimental commander denied it, Ben-Gurion reported.*

The members of the Cabinet, some of whom had not had previous word of the incident, agreed that the soldiers involved should be brought to trial. They also agreed that the families of the dead should be given immediate advances on the compensation that they would eventually be allotted. A debate ensued on whether the incident should be made public. Ben-Gurion was in favor, arguing that it could hardly be concealed in any case. The Cabinet members spoke largely to the point, but every few minutes, Ben-Gurion interrupted the discussion to share his thoughts and feelings. "How could children be killed?" he asked. He answered his own question: "We have a wonderful army, but apparently there are cases and circumstances in which

---

* It seems that at least some of the soldiers who took part in the Kafr Qasim massacre were aware of a plan code-named Operation Hafarperet (Mole). According to this plan, apparently, in the case of war between Israel and Jordan, Arabs living in villages along the border between the two countries were to be driven out of their homes. (Reuven Rubik Rosenthal 2000, p. 14ff.; Ben-Gurion, Diary, July 14, 28, Aug. 16, 1958, BGA; Yitzhak Navon, Diary, July 13, 24, 1958, YNA.)

people lose their minds." It was an explanation that could absolve the IDF and himself of responsibility. He posed another question: "How could anyone give an order to shoot children?" A committee he appointed to investigate the incident found that the order had been illegal. Israeli society once again found itself agonizing over the "purity of arms" and human responsibility, culpability, and conscience in wartime. The debate recalled many of the same moral questions that arose in discussions of Nazi Germany.[25]

Ben-Gurion's position was unambiguous. "The soldiers are not guilty. They receive orders. The country is at war. Does every soldier have the right not to carry out an order because he sees it as illegal?"[26]

Ben-Gurion devoted much time to the trial and its aftermath, apparently without ever really grasping its significance. A ministerial committee found that what had happened at Kafr Qasim was not due to orders and directives from the general of the Central Region Command or his superiors, meaning Dayan and Ben-Gurion. Before consenting to this inquiry, Ben-Gurion conducted an investigation of his own. He reached the conclusion that the whole thing had been the result of an "unfortunate chain of events": the lack of caution with which the battalion commander, Colonel Yissachar Shadmi, had spoken; the stupidity of the commander in the field, Major Shmuel Malinki; and the sadism of one of the platoon commanders, Lieutenant Gabriel Dahan, and one of his soldiers, Shalom Ofer, the two most prominent perpetrators of the massacre. Had Malinki himself been at the site, the killings would not have happened. Had Shadmi spoken with greater care, Malinki would not have given the orders he gave. Had normal men been there instead of Dahan and Ofer, they would not have done what those two men did, even had Malinki ordered it.[27]

The Kafr Qasim case was heard by Judge Benjamin Halevi, who had been born in Germany. He ruled that a soldier is required to refuse a manifestly illegal order. He defined such an order graphically: "The hallmark of manifest illegality is that it must wave like a black flag over the given order, a warning that says: 'forbidden!'" It was also one of the principal messages that Israel was supposed to learn from the Holocaust. The major perpetrators of the massacre were sentenced to prison terms of up to seventeen years. But within three years, they were all free men; some resumed careers in the IDF or other security agencies. Malinki was appointed the security officer for the atomic reactor in Dimona. Ben-Gurion was still prime minister and defense minister at the time. "Only one person was hurt at Kafr Qasim, and that was me," he declared. "I was suspected of perpetrating murder." It was very peculiar, he said.[28]

Israel's tenth year was coming to an end. The country had never been stronger.

"I NEVER THOUGHT HE WOULD BE SUCH AN IDIOT"

The Sinai Campaign lowered tensions, especially on the Egyptian border, but did not bring absolute calm. The "second round" also proved that the IDF's fighting ability had improved a great deal since the War of Independence and early 1950s. This progress had taken place under Moshe Dayan's command. Israel received planes, tanks, and other sophisticated equipment from France, largely thanks to the exertions of Shimon Peres, director-general of the Defense Ministry and another Ben-Gurion appointee. The IDF was thus largely his personal achievement. Along with this, Ben-Gurion became increasingly taken with Ariel Sharon—the man, the warrior, the style, and the image.

Ben-Gurion's relation to Sharon grew closer as Dayan inserted himself into politics and demanded special, personal, indulgent, and, especially, careful treatment. Sharon, for his part, became for Ben-Gurion the central authority on IDF security thinking. "This guy is original," Ben-Gurion wrote. "If he were to get over his penchant for not speaking the truth and talking behind people's backs, he would become an exemplary military figure."[29]

In addition to demonstrating the IDF's strength, the war guaranteed Israel free navigation of the Gulf of Eilat. The Sinai Peninsula became a demilitarized zone and a UN peacekeeping force was stationed in the Gaza Strip. The window of opportunity that opened because of France's abortive attempt to capture Port Said made it possible to rescue several dozen of the city's Jewish residents and bring them to Israel.[30] Shimon Peres reported from Paris that the French were now prepared to demand that the British carry out their part of the plan, including the partition of Jordan between Israel and Iraq. Ben-Gurion responded there was no longer any reason to do so. It had all been based on the assumption that Nasser would be taken out of the equation, but that opportunity had been missed. The slow pace and hesitancy of the British prime minister Anthony Eden was to blame. "I never thought he would be such an idiot," Ben-Gurion told the Cabinet.[31] He had never managed to overcome his fundamental suspicion of Great Britain, which coexisted with his admiration of its regime, nation, and spirit. The attempt to get rid of Nasser, Israel's principal goal in the war, was quickly revealed as a foolish, embarrassing, and ultimately abortive collusion. Nasser emerged as the great victor. Britain and France had botched it and been humiliated. What remained was the question of how Ben-Gurion could have believed that two declining colonial empires could fashion a Middle East without Nasser, without Jordan, with a divided Syria and Lebanon, with a solution to the refugee problem, and with peace.

His worldview was forged in the colonialist nineteenth century. A strategy based on an elaborate intrigue fit in well with the long Zionist tradition of underground activity, especially in the area of arms purchases, in the spirit of Proverbs 24:6: "By stratagems wage war." But almost from the time he could think for himself, he was also fascinated by the wonders and innovations of the twentieth century. That may be the way to understand his willingness to involve Israel in such a dubious escapade. Because, just a few weeks previously, the Atomic Energy Commissions of France and Israel had reached an accord under which France would provide Israel with a small research reactor. The official agreement was signed just a few weeks after Israel's withdrawal from Sinai.*

The agreement laid the foundation for nuclear cooperation between the two countries. Ben-Gurion had known before the Sinai war that it was in the works.

---

* The nuclear agreement recalled Ehud Avriel's use of the Ethiopian emperor's name to obtain planes from Czechoslovakia on the eve of the War of Independence. "The radio announced this morning that the Bourgès-Maunoury ministry fell last night over the vote on Algeria," Ben-Gurion wrote in his diary. "I am afraid that Shimon Peres's trip to Paris the day before yesterday was useless." But Peres got the ousted French prime minister to sign the document and backdate it to the previous day, when he was still in office. (Ben-Gurion, Diary, Oct. 1, 1957, BGA; Bar-Zohar 2006, p. 297ff.)

"HOW TO DRAW SHOES"

One day, in the Sde Boker dining room, Yitzhak Navon told Ben-Gurion about a popular book he had read, replete with photographs and drawings. The title was *The Atom in the Service of Mankind*. The author was an Israeli engineer and educator named Shlomo Zeira. He wrote that he found it difficult to understand why countries fully aware of the horrors of the atom nevertheless spent hundreds of millions of dollars to manufacture the bomb. To explain why, he evoked J. Robert Oppenheimer's metaphor likening the nuclear powers to two scorpions in a sealed bottle. As each one fears the sting of the other, they circle each other, each one ready and willing to sink his sting into the other. Thus the fear of the use of a bomb by one hostile nation leads to its manufacture by another. Ben-Gurion asked Navon to obtain the book for him, and in a thank-you letter to the author said that he hoped to learn from it.[32] At the time, in 1961, he already knew a lot about nuclear power, and believed it to be essential to Israel's survival. He first invited an atomic scientist to speak to him a few days after the end of the War of Independence. Scientific and technological innovations fired his imagination from the day he saw his first automobile and his first telephone, apparently when he was sixteen. He never stopped marveling at human progress thereafter. In 1933 he arrived in London for the first time by air. During the flight, he had an idea that he quickly shared with Paula—he was certain that, someday, scientists would invent a "communication mechanism" that would make travel superfluous. "You'll sit in your room, press a button, and see the person you want to see who is at the other end of the world, and you'll speak with him the same way people talk to each other in the same room." Perhaps that eye contact would not even be limited to the planet Earth, he fantasized, but would reach Mars as well. It was very likely that it would happen even earlier than expected. But in the meantime, a new world war could break out and "destroy all of civilized humanity," as he put it, "and all that will remain will be Negroes in the heart of Africa and the whole thing will begin from the start."[33] His attraction to science and technology was part of his belief in progress, which he saw as humankind taking control of nature. This was also the spirit of his Zionist devotion to "conquering nature" and reshaping it. From Herzl's time, Zionism had identified itself with progress and the creation of a new world, which included living in a nation-state. It was a faith in a measurable, quantifiable world that could be described with facts and numbers, like the figures with which he covered so many pages of his diary. That was the goal of the study of Palestine he coauthored in 1918 with Yitzhak Ben-Zvi.

Science, technology, and military industry found new ways to collaborate in World War II, especially in the United States. Given the American dream that beat within him, it was only natural that Ben-Gurion would strive to establish a similar sort of collaboration in Israel, promoting technological and scientific research in the service of the army. The Haganah established a special department for this purpose, and a few weeks before the declaration of independence, a Science Corps was founded. At around the same time, he directed Ehud Avriel, who was still in Prague, to enlist Jewish scientists in the war effort. "This means scientists in the fields of physics, chemistry, and technology who can expand the capacity for killing large numbers of people, or the opposite, for curing people," he wrote. He added, "Both things are important."[34] In his war diary he sometimes made mention of combat "by scientific means," such as the use of bromine ("a substance that causes tears and kills"). In September 1949, Ben-Gurion noted in his diary that Ernst David Bergmann had brought from Argentina "a bit of thorium," a radioactive material that could serve as nuclear fuel. "America refuses to allow the manufacture of these things in other countries," he added.[35]

The pinnacle of cooperation between science and the U.S. military was the atom bombs that were dropped on Hiroshima and Nagasaki. Ben-Gurion made merely a concise note in his diary: "The war with Japan is over." He seems not to have immediately grasped the significance of the use of nuclear weapons. In 1950 he could still ask his Cabinet: "What difference does it make how you kill a person, with an atom bomb or some other weapon?"*[36]

---

* He sometimes cited Hiroshima to argue that it is not always possible to obey the biblical injunction that "a person may be put to death only for his own crime." In war, innocent civilians, women and children among them, inevitably become casualties. So it was during the Blitz on London, and so it also was in many of the IDF's reprisal actions. "Had Japan, with the consent of a large part of its populace, not attacked America," he later wrote, "the first atom bombs would not have fallen on Hiroshima and Nagasaki." (Ben-Gurion to the Cabinet, Oct. 25, 1953, ISA; Ben-Gurion to Enrico Pratt, Sept. 13, 1961, BGA.)

Toward the end of the War of Independence, Ben-Gurion mentioned the "incredible composition" of the atom "and its enormous hidden capacities when it is split and fused." A few weeks later, he was told that a number of scientists—chemists, physicists, and biologists—had organized to help Israel. One of them was Maurice Surdin, a key figure in the French atomic energy agency. Ben-Gurion wrote in his diary that Surdin was "the builder of France's atomic furnace," as he termed the reactor. One of Surdin's proposals was to build radar-guided rockets for Israel.

Surdin had grown up in Palestine as the son of the owner of a salt factory. He attended the Herzliya Hebrew Gymnasium high school in Tel Aviv before moving to France. Ben-Gurion heard that he was prepared to return. By the time Surdin arrived, Ben-Gurion had learned of another group of scientists who were prepared to work in the atomic field. Ben-Gurion was enthusiastic. "We stand before the greatest revolution in human life—the discovery of atomic energy and its use in the world economy," he wrote. Surdin told him about the nuclear physics laboratory he had worked in, and the costs of running such a facility with a staff of 3 or 4 senior scientists, 150 engineers, and another 300 to 400 employees. Ben-Gurion was impressed— Israel needed chemical, electrical, and technological industry, and principally people with the knowledge needed to work in these fields.[37] In the years that followed, he kept tabs on Israeli students pursuing scientific studies in Europe and the United States. One of them was his daughter Renana, who went to Paris for advanced training in microbiology "on assignment from the Science Corps," as he put it.[38] In November 1958, Ariel Sharon returned from his studies in England and Ben-Gurion wrote: "The new thing he learned was tactical warfare with short- and long-range atomic warheads."[39]

❖

He saw science as the pursuit of the truth. "One might almost say that he had a mystical faith in the power of and mission of science to solve what seem to be insoluble problems," wrote General Yohanan Ratner of the Technion—Israel Institute of Technology. When a religious educator told Ben-Gurion that he was disappointed with science, as compared to faith, Ben-Gurion responded: "I agree that science is not enough, but it is possible to be totally devoted to science as the highest expression of the human spirit, rising up and up."[40] Above all, he saw science as a means of advancing the Zionist project, a central source of the country's strength. He thus demanded that Israel's universities and research institutions work in the service of the country, in accordance with government policy.

He did not always have an easy time with what he was told by scientists and experts in general. He treated them much like he did lawyers. They did not always tell him what he wanted to hear and sometimes tried to force policies on him. When that happened, it undermined their status as experts. Every intelligent person was capable of deliberating on every subject, he insisted. When experts advised him not to do something he wanted to do, he sometimes claimed that they were outside their field of specialization. "If a cobbler tells Michelangelo how to draw shoes, that falls under his area of expertise," Ben-Gurion said, "but if he tells him how to draw a human expression, it's not his expertise." He sometimes insulted experts as if they were political rivals. "They are experts on their own subject and love it and see it as the sum total of everything," he maintained, even though in practice all that was needed was common sense.[41]

"INCREDIBLE AND ENORMOUS POWER"

Three months after his conversation with Surdin, Ben-Gurion made note of the fact that uranium had been discovered in the Negev. He mentioned it again two and a half years later, and four months after that wrote that "we need to obtain a million Israeli pounds for a reactor (heavy water and more) from the development budget."[42] In the autumn of 1954, large headlines proclaimed that Israel was extracting uranium and had developed a method for producing heavy water.[43] The IDF magazine *Bamahaneh* published a long article under the title "On the Verge of the Atomic Era," which opened with the sentence "The subject fell on the press like an atom bomb." Written by young soldiers, the piece was largely a paean to Ben-Gurion, who had not yet returned from Sde Boker at the time; it was perhaps another attempt to encourage him to do so.

"In the beginning was daring," the official weekly declared. "The man who dared was the man for whom daring was part of his character. We cannot today know or evaluate everything this man, David Ben-Gurion, did to establish the state and in the fateful years after World War II." The soldier-correspondents drove to Sde Boker to ask him, "How did we encroach on an area that is the preserve of the great powers?" Ben-Gurion replied: "You soldiers do not need to ask how we dared. You dared to face the Arabs in 1948."

The article quoted remarks made on the radio by Bergmann, chairman of Israel's Atomic Energy Commission: "With a quiver of respect, I name the man who, also in this field, created something out of nothing, David Ben-Gurion. He endorsed a plan that was brought before him by a group of young people who were not among the hesitant and doubtful, but rather instigated the establishment of the Atomic Energy Commission, and he encouraged our work with vision and love." The writers explained: "The experiments for the development of atomic energy were Ben-Gurion's 'obsession' . . . Among us, also, there was no lack of 'practical' people who were skeptical whether the huge outlays would in the end justify the effort." Bergmann remarked that atomic research in Israel was conducted in cooperation with France. French scientists worked in Israel, and Israelis went there. During the War of Independence, it had been French arms that made the breakthrough on the road to Jerusalem, ensuring that Israel had its capital, the writers quoted Ben-Gurion as saying. Many had forgotten that, they noted, but he remembered it very well.

He saw atomic energy as a stimulus for making the entire Negev bloom, he told them. They carried on in the same vein—it would also serve industry and medicine. A large part of the article was devoted to explaining what atomic energy was, with a diagram to elucidate the concept. The article was illustrated with a large photograph of Ben-Gurion in khaki, and stressed that the project, including the production of heavy water, had begun "largely" in the Ministry of Defense's research and planning branch. When he told the same story in the election campaign, Ben-Gurion added something new—the United States had decided to supply Israel with a nuclear reactor in the framework of its Atoms for Peace program.[44]

❖

In the same period, during the Cold War, Ben-Gurion spoke to the terror the world felt at the prospect of a nuclear confrontation between the United States and the Soviet Union. The last letter he received from Shmuel Fuchs was very pessimistic. Ben-Gurion tried to raise his spirits. "I am not a party to the pessimism that pervades your letter," he wrote. "The splitting of the atom brings with it not only the danger of destruction, but also a great blessing. War is not inevitable, and we are on the threshold of one of the greatest revolutions in human existence. When we know how to harness that atom to the needs of humankind, horizons we never dreamed of ten years ago will open before us."[45]

Ben-Gurion sincerely believed that atomic power could benefit humanity. At poetic moments he may also have believed that the atom would bolster the Zionist myth that the Jews were settling and cultivating a wasteland, empty of human habitation. He believed that there were as yet unexploited water resources in the Negev; he believed in piping water from Lake Kinneret to the Negev; he believed in desalination of seawater; and he believed in solar energy. But he believed even more in atomic energy, the "incredible and enormous power," as he put it. There can be no doubt that he also believed that, within a few short years, humankind would harness it for industry, agriculture, and transport, "just as it is already being exploited for the requirements of war," he promised. "What Einstein, Oppenheimer, and Teller, three Jews in the United States, have done, will be done also by Israeli scientists for their nation." In addition to being Jews, Oppenheimer and Edward Teller were among the fathers of nuclear weaponry, and Einstein had taken part in the initiative to develop it.*[46]

There is no reason to think that when Ben-Gurion offered Israel's presidency to Albert Einstein, his motivation was the advancement of atomic research in Israel. That was not the case, however, when Israel tried, in 1954, to persuade Robert Oppenheimer to join the Weizmann Institute of Science. Oppenheimer was being hounded at the time by Senator Joseph McCarthy. Teddy Kollek, the director of the Office of the Prime Minister, thought it was the right time to offer him a position in Israel. Prime Minister Sharett wrote that the first step would be to invite Oppenheimer to give the annual Weizmann Memorial Lecture. "Here we can take stock of him and see if we should talk

---

* Shimon Peres and Reuven Shiloah, one of the founders of Israel's secret security services, visited other American Jewish scientists as well, including Edward Teller. "My picture is the only one in Teller's room," Ben-Gurion wrote in his diary, noting that Teller was "an enthusiast for the Negev." (Ben-Gurion, Diary, Nov. 26, 1957, BGA.)

about a permanent relationship. In the meantime, the invitation itself would serve to honor him on behalf of the Jewish people and the State of Israel."[47]

Some two months after the war in the Sinai, Ben-Gurion learned that the proposed defense budget did not include a line for atomic research. "The subject is of general importance for medicine, agriculture, manufacturing, and energy," he said. "There is no need to say more. You all know what the atomic energy problem is." Israel might well need it even more than European countries did. "It has a military aspect as well," he added. Without mentioning France by name, he referred to "a large country that is prepared to assist us in all aspects of this matter, both with materials and technology." He referred to it as a "historic miracle." The project would take eight or nine years, he said, "although during that time science will progress and that might shorten the time before we achieve what we require." He cited a cost estimate, $50 million. "We need to build an entire city in the Negev," he said.[48]

"A CONSTANT NIGHTMARE"

Oppenheimer arrived after Israel and France signed their nuclear agreement, to participate in an international conference at the Weizmann Institute. His conversation with Ben-Gurion in the early summer of 1958 might have been decisive. "His outward appearance makes a tremendous impression; he has a noble face," Ben-Gurion wrote in his diary. "I had the impression that some sort of Jewish spark lit up in the man," he told the Cabinet. He had intended not to touch "on one question that should not be touched on with him," he continued, "the question of the atom bomb." As a general rule he did not talk about "such things" with Americans, he explained. That was all the more the case with Oppenheimer, who was in a very sensitive position in America. To his astonishment, Oppenheimer broached the subject himself. He warned Ben-Gurion that Egypt was liable to obtain nuclear arms.

"He said that he was horribly apprehensive about Israel's fate as a result of Egyptian-Russian relations, and especially the matter of the atomic reactor. He sees it as a great menace," Ben-Gurion related. Oppenheimer proposed that Israel bring the matter before the UN Security Council. "He is very naïve on political matters," Ben-Gurion remarked. But Oppenheimer also had a more practical proposal: "In his opinion, we must do everything to ensure that we have an atomic power station, as soon as possible," Ben-Gurion said. Weizmann had spoken to him about the subject in 1947, Oppenheimer related, but he himself had taken a negative view then. The only atomic power plants were in America at the time, and a small country like Israel could not afford one. But many things had changed since, and the technology had advanced. "It is a very consequential matter," Ben-Gurion repeated. "He is horribly apprehensive about Egyptian-Russian relations." The ministers could deduce from this that building an atomic power plant could help defend the country against nuclear weapons.

Because Oppenheimer brought the subject up, Ben-Gurion went on, "I spoke to him about it." He tried to persuade Oppenheimer that the Soviet Union was not seeking nuclear war. "I explained to him that Russia had no reason to put itself in danger in a world war, because they are certain that they will win in any case." He meant that they were certain that Communist ideology would be victorious in the world. Oppenheimer responded that that was correct only on condition that the Russians had no means of defense against atomic weapons. "But he believes that they may well have defensive means against an atom bomb, and not just the atom bomb but also the hydrogen bomb," he related. "He cannot say for sure that the Russians have such means. But he said that there may well be such a device, that can sense when an atom bomb or hydrogen bomb is sent from some location, and then they can send this device and the device will find the plane or the missile and blow it up on its path." If the Russians had such a thing, Oppenheimer said, there could be no guarantee that they would not go to war.

"What he said made me very worried," Ben-Gurion continued. "While I was worried before, after I heard this man say these things, it made me all the more worried." He had recently taken part in a study of Israel's chances of repelling an Egyptian and Syrian attack, he told the Cabinet, perhaps within the next two years. That was the time those countries needed to bring the equipment they were getting from Russia into use. The equipment included, he said, "missiles with nuclear warheads."

He told the story about Oppenheimer in reference to a Cabinet debate of four months previously, when Minister of Health Israel Barzilai of Mapam proposed that Israel support a Soviet initiative to create a nuclear weapons–free zone in the Middle East. Only the pro-Soviet Mapam and Ahdut Ha'avodah ministers supported the idea; the rest of the Cabinet, led by Ben-Gurion, rejected it. But Justice Minister Rosen took advantage of the debate to stress that he opposed Israel acquiring nuclear capability. "I must say that this matter gives me no rest," he told his colleagues. "If we were to decide here, or almost decide, to take certain steps toward the creation of atomic power for war needs, I do not know what might happen." Ben-Gurion quickly corrected him. "Atomic power for peaceful purposes," he stressed. He added: "I request that you not repeat your comment." Rosen went on. He knew that, in terms of its scientific level, Israel was capable of achieving a nuclear option, and while he accepted the prime minister's assurances that it was not doing so, it was nevertheless important for him to state that it would be extremely undesirable to move in that direction. "I am very concerned that we could turn into a country that Russia might seek to destroy," he said. Nevertheless, he ruled out the possibility that the Soviet Union would ever place so much trust in Egypt that it would turn that country into a "serious atomic power." Ben-Gurion responded in the spirit of Oppenheimer. "Are you certain that Nasser will not get an atom bomb?" he asked. "Are you certain that in some specific circumstances, when it wants to attack us, it will not receive an atom bomb? Can you swear to that? Are you sure? I ask you not to assume responsibility for that." Even if Egypt received only a nuclear reactor it would be dangerous, he said, adding: "Any sort of atomic power can be used to make an atom bomb."

The goal of "developing atomic power" was included in the ten-year plan that Ben-Gurion placed before the Cabinet in 1957. In response to a question from one of the ministers, he said: "I am excluding all the security matters; I am speaking at this point about atomic power for industrial needs." His conversation with the American atomic scientist a year later heightened his concern. "Even before the conversation with Oppenheimer, this thing was a constant nightmare for me," he said. "But in particular after that conversation, it gives me no respite." He shared his concern with his colleagues. "I thought," he said, quoting Proverbs 12:25, "that if there is anxiety in a man's heart, he should talk about it."

Minister of Education Zalman Aran asked if Oppenheimer knew what he was talking about, or was only offering a conjecture. "If it is a conjecture, I could have thought of it even without Oppenheimer," Aran said, apparently sarcastically. Ben-Gurion responded that the scientist needed to be taken with more weight than Aran. "He is informed about such matters. He knows what words mean. I only have the understanding of a common man. He knows the material well. If they bring a reactor and they bring experts, he knows what that means." In support of Oppenheimer's thesis and what he himself had said in the previous discussion, he repeated what he had heard from another American physicist and Nobel laureate, Isidor Isaac Rabi, to the effect that "every atomic reactor station has the possibility of manufacturing bombs."

Philip Sporn, president and chief executive officer of the American Gas and Electric Company, was also urging Israel to build a nuclear power plant, according to Ben-Gurion. He said that the British were offering to sell such a plant, but he dismissed the offer. "We will not be able to benefit from the English offer on security matters, as it is conditioned on oversight," he explained. Ben-Gurion's conclusion was that it was vital for Israel to build "a plant for the production of heavy water." He said that "an atomic plant can be made without heavy water, but it would be especially difficult for us." Heavy water could be obtained "inexpensively" from the United States, but its use would be subject to oversight, too. Until recently it had been possible to obtain heavy water from Norway, at a higher price, but without inspection. Now Norway, as a NATO ally, was itself requiring inspection. "We must proceed immediately to the construction of a heavy water plant, so that we not be dependent on others," he asserted. Several Cabinet members reminded him that Israel had already announced that it was capable of producing heavy water, but Ben-Gurion said that the quantities were small, for experimental purposes only.

It was a new subject; the record of the Cabinet's discussion shows that the ministers were confused about the terminology. Most of them had trouble fathoming what Ben-Gurion's actual intentions were, including with regard to his pronouncements about manufacturing and using heavy water. Some of the ministers suspected that Ben-Gurion was misinforming them, either intentionally or because he himself did not understand the concepts involved. The Mapam and Ahdut Ha'avodah ministers emerged as the bridgehead of opposition to the nuclear program. They took literally Ben-Gurion's statement that any atomic plant for peaceful uses could also serve as the foundation for a nuclear weapons program. In response to their questions, Ben-Gurion said that a heavy water plant would cost $10 million. "I think we can obtain that money from individuals," he added, meaning from donations. Interior Minister Israel Bar-Yehuda, of Ahdut Ha'avodah, countered: "I don't really know what that can be used for other than a bomb." Ben-Gurion responded, "It can be used for lots of things."[49]

❖

Work commenced on a nuclear reactor that year at a site in the northern Negev, not far from Dimona, a town built to house new immigrants. The project was carried out in accord with agreements Israel had signed with France both before and after the Sinai Campaign. After ten years of unremitting hostilities, Ben-Gurion believed even more strongly in the doctrine that he had held to for at least forty-five of his fifty years in the country—Israel's future depended on the Arabs concluding that the Jewish state could not be obliterated. He generally presented this as a condition for peace. "Peace with the Arabs will come—when we fortify ourselves and the Arabs realize that we cannot be destroyed, and when they have more liberal and democratic regimes that will provide for the needs of their people and understand the importance of peace."[50] Rosen continued from time to time to remind Ben-Gurion of his opposition to the nuclear project. During one of these conversations, Ben-Gurion told him: "We need deterrence, not victory in war. The Sinai Campaign will not happen again. We lost 175 men there, and 50 of them were hit by our own fire. That campaign will not recur. In every other campaign we will suffer much more serious losses, and we cannot afford to lose our best young men. So the most important thing is deterrence."[51] Rosen understood from this that the Dimona project was aimed at averting war. It was a manifestation of the security doctrine that Jabotinsky and Ben-Gurion had, in the 1920s, termed the "iron wall." But the key words that had motivated him since the 1940s were the ones he used when he told the Cabinet about his conversation with Oppenheimer: "a constant nightmare."

Because, despite his faith in progress and the future of the Zionist project, Ben-Gurion continued to live in constant dread that the country would be destroyed. It was a very real anxiety, with roots in the Holocaust. Like many Israelis, he invoked the Holocaust to back up his political claims. But while the Holocaust was used manipulatively, it also became a growing and central element in Israeli identity. It produced a fatalistic pessimism; a second Holocaust was always a clear and present possibility. "None of us can guarantee the country's survival," he said at the end of 1957. "I can only make every possible effort to ensure its existence. Whether we succeed or not does not depend on me." The lessons learned from the Holocaust thus played a central role in molding his security conception, which included the nuclear program. Berlin-born Ernst David Bergmann did not direct the project only on its scientific and practical side. He also formulated its ideological foundations. In the summer of 1966, he corresponded on the subject with the Mapam leader Meir Yaari. Like Ben-Gurion before him, Bergmann presumed that the Arab countries could achieve nuclear capability. He framed this conclusion as a lesson of the Holocaust. "The proliferation of atomic weaponry is unpreventable," he wrote, listing a number of countries that denied that they had developed nuclear arms but which should not be believed. One of them was India. "Every development in the area of atomic energy for peaceful purposes automatically leads any country toward atomic weapons," Bergmann maintained. He warned against hopes and illusions. "I cannot forget that the Holocaust arrived as a surprise to the Jews," he wrote. "The Jewish people cannot afford another such illusion."[52] Ben-Gurion could not have put it better. The Dimona project required great bravery on his part; deciding not to pursue it would have required even more courage.

"MAN OR WOMAN"

Two weeks after the tenth-anniversary parade, Teddy Kollek told Ben-Gurion that he was concerned about the mental state of Moshe Dayan, who had completed his term as chief of staff in January 1958. Dayan did not know what to do with himself. He had enrolled at the Hebrew University in the meantime. Kollek was a great expert at divining the moods of his acquaintances. "He is going through a very serious crisis," he maintained. "He feels neglected and not needed for anything." Moshe is depressed, his wife, Ruth, told Ben-Gurion. His studies were not enough for him. Nor was it pleasant for him to sit in class alongside young people in their twenties. He was suffering from head-aches as well, apparently the product of the wound that had cost him one of his eyes. Ben-Gurion heard from Shimon Peres that Dayan saw himself as a future national leader.

Dayan was forty-three years old, making him one of the younger figures in Israeli politics. While still in the army, he had begun to voice views that were seen as tantamount to an insurgency against Mapai's veteran leadership, Ben-Gurion included. The impression was that he was forming a young guard.[53] Despite the heroic aura that the Sinai Campaign had brought him, and perhaps precisely because of his fame, he had many foes. Levi Eshkol told Ben-Gurion that some people in the party were afraid that Dayan would stage a military coup. "I could not believe my ears," Ben-Gurion wrote. "I explained that the idea was absurd. Even if there was someone who would try to do it, the IDF would not put itself at his service." He might well have suspected that there was some truth to the rumor; in the past he had thought about it from time to time. Whatever the case, Eshkol's warning brought home what he had probably known even before—the members of the party leadership saw Dayan as a threat. When Ben-Gurion told Golda Meir that he intended to give Dayan a seat in the next Cabinet, she said that if that were the case she would not be there.*[54]

Dayan thus began his political career as a problem. Ben-Gurion held him in esteem but did not like him very much. "Moshe lacks love of people," he wrote in his diary; he had previously remarked to Navon, "The chief of staff loves the IDF but not its soldiers. But he is the best chief of staff we have had."[55] When Dayan was caught up in a particularly embarrassing scandal, he defended him.

Lieutenant Colonel Dov Yermia, a childhood friend of Dayan's, was married to a woman named Hadassah. She was his second wife, having served as his secretary during her army service. Dayan stationed Yermia on the Syrian border and his wife went to Jerusalem, where she enrolled at the Hebrew University. She lived in IDF officers' housing and soon grew intimate with

---

* Peres was an easier case. He simply told Ben-Gurion that it was time for him to be elected to the Knesset, and that after the elections he wanted to be appointed deputy defense minister. (Yitzhak Navon, Diary, May 3, 1958, YNA.)

Dayan; Yermia fomented a scandal. He sent abusive letters to Dayan, complained to Dayan's wife, Ruth, and also wrote to Ben-Gurion, demanding that he, the minister of defense, censure the former chief of staff.

Ben-Gurion, vacationing on Mount Canaan, near Safed, replied with a long and revealing letter, written by hand. He opened by assuring Yermia that he understood his pain, but even at this point intimated that Dayan was not solely to blame. "I know how deep and sensitive the personal side is in things of this type, and I am not claiming that you need to rage not only against the man but also against the woman (if in cases of this sort there is a logical basis for rage), and that you must understand that a woman is not private property but rather a free individual. That is none of my business." But Yermia was demanding that he withdraw his support from a man he termed an "arrogant hypocrite," Ben-Gurion went on, requiring him to make a distinction between the intimate and subjective side of the affair and its public ramifications.

"A man can be an ascetic and a saint his entire life but not be a successful public leader," he maintained, and the opposite was also true. He offered two examples—King David and the British admiral Horatio Nelson. "The authors and editors of the Bible were devotees of the Davidic dynasty," he began this section of his letter, "and their moral greatness is exemplified in the fact that they did not hide David's horrible and terrifying crime from the people." Not only against Bathsheba, the woman he lusted for, he wrote, but also against her husband, Uriah the Hittite, whom he sent to his death in battle so as to be able to steal his wife. What David did to Uriah, his servant and loyal soldier, was a thousand times worse than what he did to Bathsheba, he argued. Then Nathan the prophet bravely castigated him—but did not disqualify him from the kingship. To this day there is no king more venerated in Jewish lore, even though every Jew knows what David did to Bathsheba's husband. There was no reason to doubt that the story was true, unlike a number of other things in the Bible, he went on. And when David said that a person who does such a deed deserves death, the prophet responded, "You are the man." But he went on to say: "Even for your sin you will not die." As a result, David's line lasted until the destruction of the First Temple.

The second case involved the most admired man in British history, Ben-Gurion continued—Nelson, the hero of Trafalgar. "The entire English people knew what he did with the wife of the British ambassador (to the Kingdom of Naples, I believe), but this did not detract from the British people's gratitude to and admiration for their hero, despite, as you no doubt know, the puritanical views, or at least the expectations of public comportment, that prevailed in England during the age of Queen Victoria."

He knew that nothing he said would assuage Yermia's pain or anger, but the lesson of both these cases was clear. "It is unfeasible and, I think, wrong to examine the confidential intimate life of any person, man or woman, so as to determine their public standing and reputation," Ben-Gurion wrote. For that reason, he could not agree that the man who was the object of Yermia's fury, "and not without reason and justice," was a hypocrite. After all, Dayan did not play the role of a moral tribune and preacher on intimate matters, those between man and woman. "And the things he did, at the behest of the nation, he accomplished not only with great ability but also by putting his life on the line, and what he demanded of others he first demanded of himself, and in battle he went first, before his subordinates."

Here he repeated, almost word for word, his admonition about the need to keep the intimate and public aspects of a person's life separate. "It seems to me that you are mixing up two things that cannot be mixed," he wrote, reiterating, "with friendly sincerity," that he could not be a party to Yermia's "public vendetta" as much as he respected his feelings and understood what he felt. "I have replied to you after much inner hesitation," he concluded, "and if I have in some way hurt you, or if my words have pained you, I ask your forgiveness." He wished Yermia well and wrote, underneath his signature, "If you would like to see me in person, I will do so willingly."

A short time before his death, at an age of more than one hundred, Yermia said that the backing Ben-Gurion gave Dayan helped create an atmosphere of male chauvinism in the IDF and security forces. Here, again, the spirit of the leader engendered a value system in which certain things were permissible and others taboo. The two men continued to correspond. Yermia, who became a leading peace activist, wrote to Ben-Gurion about the injustices of the military regime imposed on Israel's Arabs. Ben-Gurion began his reply by saying: "If I was not aware of the emotional background of the resentment in your last letter, I would have thrown it into the wastebasket."[56]

❖

In the summer of 1958, Paula needed surgery; Ben-Gurion visited her often in the hospital. One of his drivers told Navon: "We visited her today. She walked down the stairs, chattering and talking. As soon as she heard him coming, she lowered her head, as if she were about to faint, sighed, moaned, and groaned. Ben-Gurion approached her tenderly, wanting to help her descend. She shouted at him: 'Go away, go home, immediately. Leave me alone, David.'" The driver thought she behaved despicably. The nurse also said that Paula felt just fine and that she was putting on a show, but she was afraid to tell Ben-Gurion himself. "Paula feels good objectively," Navon told Ben-Gurion, "but when she sees you she behaves the way she did today. She wants to be pampered, cared for, given attention. The nurse asked that you not take what happened today personally." Ben-Gurion was dumbfounded. "He sat there, pale, with a long face, and with great sorrow in his eyes," Navon recorded in his diary. "All he did was shake his head, without saying a word."[57]

Ben-Gurion was now primarily occupied with the construction of the nuclear reactor near Dimona. In 1959 he again got caught up in the enthusiasm of an election campaign. At the age of seventy-three, he led his party under the slogan "Say yes to the Old Man!" Mapai won 47 of the 120 seats in the Knesset, more than ever before. Having reached the height of his power, he commenced a campaign of self-destruction.

23

THE LAVON AFFAIR

"I DON'T TRUST MYSELF"

In the afternoon hours of June 16, 1959, the prime minister and defense minister cleared his schedule to have a long meeting with a well-known Romanian-born fortune-teller from Tel Aviv, Sally Linker. About sixty years old at the time, she was a "diviner of secrets," he wrote, in quotation marks, using a phrase that is used in the book of Jeremiah (11:20) to describe an attribute of God. They seem to have spoken in a mixture of French and Yiddish; Linker did not know Hebrew. "She did not look at me when she spoke, but rather at her fingers resting on her lap," he noted. She began by describing his character—he had will and energy, and was sometimes stubborn. He was often irate, as a result of weakness. He liked to be with people, but sometimes didn't want to see anyone. He had once had a strong emotion, a profound experience, and was unusually sensitive. He needed to develop good habits; badly fitting shoes were liable to tire him. Success was on the horizon. Four days hence he would have a good feeling.

Ben-Gurion carefully recorded everything she said, even unfinished sentences and single words. The impression is that she spoke in a trance of some sort. He asked her to read his thoughts about a number of people whose identity he did not reveal to her. She did not even get close to what Ben-Gurion felt about Lavon. "I have been disappointed with her," he wrote. But when a baby girl was born to Amos, he noted: "Ruth was born precisely four days after my conversation with the Romanian woman, who told me that something important and joyful would happen to me in four days." He continued to consult with her.

She was unmarried and childless, and had lived most of her life in a rented room full of rags, cats, and houseplants; she also painted. One of her neighbors was a Mapai member of the Knesset, Hannah Lamdan, who became Linker's patron and brought her along when she met her acquaintances.

Ben-Gurion was again reminded of her a few days after the election in which Mapai rose to forty-seven seats in the Knesset. "When she came to me a few months ago, she prophesied that things would be good, very good, after the election," he wrote. "But I did not pay attention, and even now I have my doubts as to whether there is really a human faculty for predicting the future."

He met with her twice more in 1960, recording political and diplomatic forecasts she offered. When she told him that he needed to deal severely with two or three people, he asked if they were foreign agents. She said they were not. He asked if they held political positions in Israel. She said they did, and again warned him that they were ambitious. She saw "a family problem," but also told him that "it will work out."

In three weeks there would be a change for the better, she promised him.

Less than a month later, Navon recorded in his diary an outburst from Paula, in the usual mixture of Hebrew, English, and Yiddish. "I can't take any more. I am fed up . . . You don't understand anything I say. He is so selfish, doesn't care about anything. It's only him . . . he doesn't care about the children. He doesn't love anyone, only himself. We've been married for forty years. That's enough. I can't stand it. But I'm the prime minister's wife. If I wasn't, I'd leave him."[1]

A few days later, he was received in the White House for a conversation with President Dwight Eisenhower. He also met with the West German chancellor Konrad Adenauer. When Ben-Gurion reported to the Cabinet on these meetings, he said, "I am now deathly weary, I don't trust myself . . . I am not sure of myself."[2] When he next met with Linker the Romanian, as she was known in Tel Aviv, she offered him several pieces of advice on how to surmount his fatigue.[3]

His final years as prime minister were one scandal after another; he became a prisoner of his whims and humiliated himself. This same period saw dramatic struggles over relations with Germany, control of Mapai, and the construction of the Dimona reactor, as well as a crisis in relations with the United States, now led by John F. Kennedy. All these were pieces of a puzzle that had the Lavon Affair at its center. His power eroded, his influence diminished, he turned spiteful and cantankerous, resentful and insufferable. In June 1963, he resigned from the prime ministership for the last time. In the ten years of life that remained to him, he became an Israeli King Lear.

❖

As prime minister, he attached great importance to relations with Germany, not just because of the economic benefits the ties produced, but also because they included, almost from the start, military cooperation. "I think Germany can be a great help to us, first of all in the military sense," he had told the Cabinet at the beginning of 1955. "It can provide us with raw materials and perhaps arms as well." The Mapai faction in the Knesset sent two emissaries to ask him to at least "lower the volume." Ben-Gurion responded vehemently, one of the members of the delegation later recalled. "Who are you to tell me who the Nazis were," he muttered, standing up and pacing. "My Sheindele, they killed her, and you're telling me, you don't understand a thing." But even as the uncle of his brother's beloved murdered daughter, as a Jew and an Israeli, he felt no inhibitions at all about the issue, neither emotional, moral, certainly not political; he had no pangs of conscience at all, he maintained.[4]

In December 1957, he told the Cabinet that Germany was prepared to sell Israel a submarine and to purchase Uzi submachine guns.[5] Two weeks later, Ben-Gurion informed the ministers that Chief of Staff Dayan was making a trip to Germany to further the submarine deal. The story leaked to the press. Ben-Gurion resigned, but formed a new government a few days later, identical to its predecessor. The ministers representing the left-wing parties committed themselves to supporting legislation imposing criminal penalties on Cabinet ministers who leaked information about Cabinet meetings.[6]

The big blast came in the summer of 1959, when *Der Spiegel* reported on the Uzi deal.

According to Ben-Gurion, the agreement was to supply Israeli-made hand grenades and Uzis, many of which had already been shipped, worth $40 million. He claimed that the Cabinet had sanctioned the deal, citing the minutes of the relevant meeting. The ministers representing Ahdut Ha'avodah and Mapam claimed that they had no memory of such a Cabinet debate; they would soon intimate that the record of the meeting had been doctored. Once again, the exchange was extremely emotional. "I don't see that in a real war five years from now we are assured victory over the Arab armies," Ben-Gurion asserted. "I do not believe that if, God forbid, our army was to fail, many Jews would remain alive, including old people, women, and children." That was why Israel required means of deterrence, he argued, adding that there was "only one place to obtain those means of deterrence: I do not see that it can be anywhere outside Germany."

One of the Mapam ministers claimed that Israeli-made Uzis would be used to arm the SS; Ben-Gurion responded that Germany of the Nazi era and Germany of the 1960s were two different countries. This affair, like others before it, fired up the public for only a short time; the opposition demanded that the deal be canceled, but the Knesset voted down the proposal.[7] The need to continually defend his German policy weighed on him, but it also helped him defend that very policy. The more he was attacked, the more motivation Germany had to come toward Israel.

"IN A PRIMITIVE COMMUNITY IT CAN HAPPEN"

Germany and its elderly chancellor continued to fascinate him. Israel's representative in Cologne, Felix Shinnar, frequently updated him on the chancellor and German politics—trends and interests, forces and factions, plots and intrigues, gossip—and offered his personal assessment of events in the country. Direct military contacts were conducted largely in regular meetings between Shimon Peres and the German defense minister, Franz Josef Strauss. They occasionally met at Strauss's home in a small Bavarian town, far out of sight. Strauss's German rivals considered him a dangerous militaristic nationalist, and many Israelis agreed. Peres admired him and, especially, his power. Over time, they became friends. Peres managed to bring Germany into the pact he was concluding with France. Strauss was interested, as he wanted nuclear arms to defend Germany against the Soviet Union. Both he and Peres believed in deterrence. Ben-Gurion recorded Peres as saying that Strauss supported Israel for two reasons—fear of Russia, which he hated, and admiration for the IDF. It was all done in coordination with Adenauer. "He saw the secrecy of the ties as particularly important," Ben-Gurion noted, because the arms deal also had opponents in Germany. A few days earlier, he had written to Adenauer that Israel was interested in conducting its atomic research in cooperation with "Europe." Several months later, Adenauer asked two Israeli diplomats how soon Israel would be able to produce nuclear arms, adding, "It would be good for your security if you had an atomic bomb."[8]

The contacts to bring the two old men together took a long time. They finally agreed that the meeting would be public and would take place on March 14, 1960, in New York. "We were staying in the same hotel," Ben-Gurion told his Cabinet. "I was two floors above him. I went to see him." The hotel was the Waldorf Astoria. Adenauer opened with a few sentences of admiration for Israel, and Ben-Gurion told him that the extermination of the Jews of Europe had dealt a mortal blow to the Jewish people, because it was the European Jewry, as opposed to the Jews of the Arab lands, who had the capacity to establish a state. He proposed that Germany give Israel a loan of half a billion dollars over ten years, $50 million a year, for the development of agriculture, industry, and shipping, and to ease immigrant absorption. "He agreed immediately," Ben-Gurion reported. He then asked for a small submarine, because British-made submarines were too large. Finally, he asked for air-to-air and surface-to-surface missiles, perhaps to be supplied by Germany in cooperation with France. Adenauer confirmed that he had already heard about the requests from Strauss and "it will be okay." It was only an oral promise. "I can't say whether he will keep it," Ben-Gurion said, concluding his report.[9]

It was a historic summit conference, but the two elderly men who had not met previously were at ease, as if they were old friends. They also traded opinions of world leaders, among them John Kennedy, who had not yet been elected. For the most part, Adenauer asked and Ben-Gurion answered. "What do you think, how many microphones are there in this room?" the chancellor suddenly asked. Ben-Gurion replied that he did not know how many, but he was certain that there were some. "He bent down and began to whisper in French, so that no one would hear," Ben-Gurion later told the Cabinet. Toward the end of the conversation, Ben-Gurion made a point of saying that he had already been attacked for meeting with Adenauer. But it was not in keeping with Jewish values to impose collective guilt on an entire nation; the chancellor thanked him. About three months earlier, Ben-Gurion had decided that Israel's secret security agencies would abduct Adolf Eichmann from his home in Argentina and bring him to Israel.[10]

❖

Some two months after the meeting at the Waldorf Astoria, Ben-Gurion wrote in his diary: "Isser's messenger came to me this morning to inform me that Eichmann was identified and captured and next week will be sent here, if they are able to put him on the plane . . . If there is no mistaken identification, it is a successful and important operation." About half a year before, Isser Harel had reported to him that the source for the information on Eichmann's whereabouts was the public prosecutor of the state of Hesse in Germany, Fritz Bauer. Ben-Gurion noted that Bauer was Jewish. "I suggested asking him not to tell anyone and not to demand [Eichmann's] extradition, but rather to give us the address and, if we find him there, we will capture him and bring him here," Ben-Gurion wrote. It is not clear whether this was the first time he had heard of the matter—Harel had received the initial information from Bauer two years previously. He sent one of his men to Argentina, but he was unable to locate Eichmann. "I can't say that the efforts were particularly thorough," Harel later admitted. That may have been no coincidence— Israel had not made much of an effort to locate Nazi war criminals.[11]

When Ben-Gurion was told that Eichmann could be apprehended, he saw a number of advantages in a trial in Israel. As he saw it, the trial was the most important thing, not the punishment that would be meted out; that is why he ordered that Eichmann not be liquidated in Argentina. He directed the minister of justice to conduct a trial that would lay out the entire story of the Holocaust, beyond Eichmann's own role.

A few months before Ben-Gurion ordered Eichmann's abduction, a wave of violence spread through Israel. It began in Wadi Salib, a formerly Arab neighborhood in Haifa.[12] Many of the rioters were Moroccan-born; they were protesting discrimination. In a letter to the chairman of the commission of inquiry set up to investigate the events, Ben-Gurion wrote, "An Ashkenazi thug, thief, pimp, or murderer would not be able to gain the sympathy of the Ashkenazi community (if there is indeed such a community), nor would such an idea even come into his head. But in a primitive community it can happen."[13]

He again became concerned about the increasing influence of the Jews from the Islamic world in Israeli society. He mentioned this once again a few days after he was informed that Eichmann had been apprehended.[14]

The wave of riots that began at Wadi Salib reinforced his conviction that it was imperative to bond Israelis together by means of an emotionally formative, sweeping, and unifying experience around a common catastrophe that taught the nation a moral. Alongside its effect on Israeli society, the Holocaust trial was meant to stress the justification for Zionism, to strengthen Israel's position in the world and put an end to the repeated claims that the government's German policy reflected an indifference to the Holocaust.

The impending trial did, in fact, reawaken interest in the Holocaust. When Ben-Gurion paid a visit to France, President Charles de Gaulle asked Ben-Gurion if more could not have been done to save the Jews. Ben-Gurion responded that the British were to blame. He concealed Israel's involvement in Eichmann's abduction and claimed that it had been carried out by "Jewish boys who were Holocaust survivors" who had been pursuing him for fifteen years. "They found him, brought him to us," he claimed. The French, as was their custom, showered him with honors of a sort that Ben-Gurion had never before received. "Drawn swords, blade at the nose," he related in wonder. De Gaulle promised to defend Israel; if Nasser destroyed Tel Aviv, it would cause a world war, he said. Ben-Gurion said that Israel was seeking nuclear capability. He mentioned nuclear research. De Gaulle was inclined to suspend cooperation in this area, but an arrangement was finally achieved, again thanks to Shimon Peres.[15] But, at this very moment, the ghost of the great fiasco of 1954 was rising from the dead.

"I SEE THAT THE AFFAIR IS ONLY BEGINNING"

In the first years after his return from Sde Boker, Ben-Gurion managed to take his distance from the collapse of the Israeli spy ring in Egypt. To the extent that it depended on him, the Nasty Business was dead and buried. In keeping with this, he was notably magnanimous to the two central perpetrators, Pinhas Lavon and Binyamin Gibli.[16] He appointed Dayan, who shared responsibility, to the Cabinet. Rumors and gossip spread through the army, and over the years it also reached politicians and journalists.

In May 1960, Lavon learned that an officer from IDF intelligence had lied to the Olshan-Dori committee that had been set up to investigate the affair. He claimed that Lavon had given the order, and backed up his testimony with forged documents. Lavon immediately went to see the prime minister and defense minister. Ben-Gurion ordered a thorough inquiry, and on the basis of its findings forced Gibli out of the army. Lavon was not satisfied. He demanded that Ben-Gurion clear his name by issuing a statement saying that he had been accused falsely. This was the opportunity to stop the snowball that was rolling toward him, but Ben-Gurion seems not to have yet properly appreciated just how much momentum the snowball had. Clearly, his political faculties were failing. He rejected Lavon's demand. The version of events that he adopted was reasonable: "Lavon did not give an explicit order to Gibli to carry out the 'nasty business,' but spoke to him in a way that led Gibli to presume that that was the defense minister's will. Only after the deed was done and the horrible results became clear did Lavon wash his hands of the matter."[17]

He needed to be cautious because Lavon was a more dangerous enemy than Gibli could ever be. Before demanding to be cleared, Lavon leaked the matter to *Ma'ariv*, at the time the daily newspaper with the largest circulation. The newspaper quickly became one of his principal allies. He also invited himself to a meeting of the Knesset's Foreign Affairs and Defense Committee.[18] He had a lot to tell them about Ben-Gurion's term of service. That was a good reason to strike a compromise with him and formulate a statement that they could both live with; it would have reburied the affair. But Ben-Gurion didn't do that. Instead, he told Lavon, "I never accused you, and if others did so, I am not a judge who can acquit you." Politically, it was an error.

Two of the heads of Mapai proposed a way out. Sharett would announce that had he known then what he knew now, his investigation might well have reached a different conclusion—that is, Lavon would have been exonerated. Lavon would accept this statement and the affair would be laid to rest. In fact, that is what happened. Sharett published an article to that effect and Lavon issued an appropriate statement. But Ben-Gurion missed the opportunity. He told them that they could do as they wished, but that it would not be in his name, with his sanction, or with his consent. From this point on he started behaving like a suspect; one day he suddenly ordered the Mossad archives to provide records meant to prove that he had not been involved in the explosions in Iraq years before the blunder in Egypt. "From the press I see that the affair is only beginning," he wrote in November 1960 to several leaders of his party.[19]

❖

The events that would soon upend the power relations in Israel's political system and lay the foundation for new ones did not reach the roots of the system's malfunction, or the ideological conflicts that produced them. As in the scandal's previous incarnation, the Nasty Business, the Lavon Affair centered on who had said what to whom and when, who had fabricated, forged, incited, and lied, and who had not—ostensibly. The stress was put on the politics—who would benefit from it, who would be harmed, who was on the rise and who in decline.[20] As in the past, the major question appeared to have been who gave the order. But the principal riddle in that amateurish scheme was barely discussed and in the end remained without any certain answer—how could anyone believe that planting a few bombs in a post office and library could prevent the British Empire from leaving Egypt?

The fact that the operation put the Jews of Egypt in jeopardy was no deterrent to Ben-Gurion; he viewed every Jew as a potential soldier in the service of the Zionist project. A tradition dating almost fifty years back, of defense based on irregular organizations, impelled the young IDF to try to make history with the tricks and stratagems of underground forces and covert operations. Other countries did the same. The Nasty Business in Egypt exemplified the youthful adventurism fostered by the Haganah and, in particular, the Palmach, and the conceit that Jews were mentally superior to Arabs. The defects in the IDF's combat readiness during the period that preceded the Sinai Campaign reinforced a penchant for concealing the truth and evading responsibility for failures. A comprehensive and full inquiry into the operation in Egypt, including its roots in Iraq, was thus liable to damage Ben-Gurion.[21]

As part of the arrangement for putting an end to the matter, the Cabinet appointed a committee of seven ministers to examine the issue. The intention was to clear Lavon. Ben-Gurion was opposed. He continued to demand a legal inquiry. His position led him to the verge of resigning. "I will not take part in anything now," he threatened, "neither debates nor votes."[22] The committee was appointed despite him, largely thanks to Eshkol's efforts. He managed to do what Ben-Gurion had tried to do since returning from Sde Boker—send the affair into oblivion.

"THE CRIMINAL ACT OF A MADMAN"

At the end of 1960, the Lavon Affair had become Ben-Gurion's primary obsession. People described him as agitated, unfocused, and belligerent.

He began to communicate almost entirely in writing with political comrades who had been by his side for decades. Apparently he spent a large amount of time drafting letters, just as the world discovered the secret nuclear reactor near Dimona. That was inevitable in a country in which everyone knew everybody else. French technicians and engineers had been a presence on the streets of Be'er-Sheva and Dimona for some time, and everyone thought they knew what had brought them there. In December, reports on the construction of the reactor began to appear overseas. *The New York*

Times said that the CIA chief had briefed President-elect John Kennedy about it.*

But the French were also worried about the news reports. Lacking any other option and with evident reluctance, Ben-Gurion informed the Knesset that Israel was building a second "research reactor" that would be completed no earlier than three or four years hence. It was intended solely for peaceful purposes, he declared, denying that Israel was building a nuclear bomb. Moshe Sharett wrote to his son that Ben-Gurion's statement was "untrue, as is his wont." A new question thus became part of the public discourse, to which *Ma'ariv* devoted a full-page spread: "Should Israel make an atom bomb?" The question was part of a symposium the newspaper sponsored, alongside the question of whether Eichmann should be executed. Ben-Gurion's statement averted an open confrontation with the United States for the time being, but behind the scenes the relations between the two countries took on a new and threatening dimension.[23]

❖

The Committee of Seven was slated to present the results of its investigation just two days after Ben-Gurion's statement. "The Old Man is very tense," Navon wrote. The reason was that, when Lavon appeared before the Knesset Foreign Affairs and Defense Committee, he had described a series of IDF fiascoes and failures—and criticized the nuclear policy led by Ben-Gurion and Peres. That, apparently, was his major sin, as Ben-Gurion saw it. The Dimona project had been controversial from the start; it was opposed in part on principled and policy grounds, but much of the antagonism was personal. Politicians, scientists, military figures, businessmen, and all sorts of visionaries

---

* Some of the information seems to have been obtained by the American embassy in Tel Aviv. Ambassador Ogden Reid was invited for a helicopter tour of the Negev; when he asked his escort what he saw there, not far from Dimona, he was told that it was a new textile factory. Ben-Gurion recorded in his diary that, at one meeting between them, the young ambassador had raised his voice; Ben-Gurion told him to leave the room at once. He had to remember that he was but an ambassador, and that when he spoke with the leader of a country, even a small one, he had to speak with all due civility. (Ben-Gurion, Diary, Jan. 5, 1961; Gris 2009, p. 90ff.)

and adventurers knew that they were witnessing the creation of a new entity of huge power and influence. They often acted as if they assumed that whoever controlled Dimona would control the country. Some opponents of the reactor thought it was too expensive; others warned that it would prompt the Arab states to get nuclear arms; others opposed nuclear weapons on moral and philosophical grounds; and still others were resentful of the rising strength of Peres, Dayan, and the rest of the "young guard." The position on the reactor taken by the leaders of Ahdut Ha'avodah, Israel Galili and Yigal Allon, recalled the clash between Ben-Gurion and the Palmach. Like many military leaders, Yitzhak Rabin among them, the Ahdut Ha'avodah leadership believed that the available funds should be put into strengthening the army, with the goal of conquering the West Bank, not spent on a nuclear option. The IDF chief of staff, Tzvi Tzur, promised Ben-Gurion that such an operation would take only two days. But the Ahdut Ha'avodah leaders did not reject out of hand the idea of developing a nuclear option.[24] Mapam opposed nuclear proliferation, in the spirit of the international left and the Soviet Union. Sharett wrote that the project was "the product of adventurism and arrogance" on the part of Ben-Gurion and Peres.[25]

His brief tenure as defense minister left Lavon as a secondary character in this drama, but from the start he had looked like a political rival to Peres and Dayan, and thus to Ben-Gurion and the nuclear project as well. "What Lavon told the Committee is the criminal act of a madman whose passions have driven him insane," Ben-Gurion maintained. "He should be brought to trial. There is a limit! My limit is when security is damaged."[26]

The Committee of Seven found that Lavon had not given the order and that the operation in Egypt had been carried out without his knowledge. Clearly stressed by the need to reveal the construction of the reactor, Ben-Gurion offered an emotional and fairly jumbled monologue that takes up fifteen pages of the minutes of the meeting. From time to time he lost his temper. In contrast with his past manipulative threats to resign, this time his speech sounded like a painful, almost desperate, cry for help. Again and again he faulted not only Lavon but also the Cabinet ministers. His principal claim was that Lavon had lied to the Foreign Affairs and Defense Committee, and that the members of the Committee of Seven had let "that heap of lies" pass. "It cannot be that you do not know that these are lies," he reprimanded them. "If you don't know, you are indeed too naïve." He described Lavon as a man without a conscience and "a new Stalin" who had disregarded the law of the land and deceived the prime minister. He responded to the incidents that Lavon had mentioned, including the covert operation committed by Israeli agents in Iraq in 1952. Lavon had claimed that these operations were "just like the one in Egypt." Ben-Gurion responded that "Lavon hasn't a clue what happened there."

The Iraq operation was only one of the things that rankled him. Several newspapers supporting Lavon accused Ben-Gurion himself of having given the order for the operation in Egypt. "Since I am the principal criminal, I am prepared to be put on trial," he said, "but not with Mr. Lavon. I am not willing to be associated with that man, not physically and not socially."

He ended as expected. "I am no longer a member of your government," he declared. It would be best for him to resign immediately, he said, but resignation was liable to be interpreted as part of the "atom issue"; neither did he want to cause an embarrassment for the Zionist Congress that was scheduled to convene in Jerusalem. So he would take a leave of absence. Justice Minister Rosen tried to say something, but Ben-Gurion interrupted. "My vacation begins at this moment," he declared, and without saying another word, he got up and left.[27]

❖

The resignation was seen as part of the generational struggle in Mapai. The Young Guard, or, as they were sometimes called, "Ben-Gurion's Boys," led by Dayan and Peres, were threats to the "middle generation," led by Finance Minister Levi Eshkol, Commerce and Industry Minister Pinhas Sapir, Foreign Minister Golda Meir, and Lavon himself. They all shared doubts about the Dimona project.

A few days later, Ben-Gurion raised the ante—he threatened to bolt Mapai.[28]

"INTERESTING AND SAD THINGS"

Some four months before the Eichmann trial opened, Adenauer celebrated his eighty-fifth birthday and Ben-Gurion sent him a laudatory letter, praising his efforts to restore German moral standards.

He told the chancellor about a plan to develop the Negev that included "a center of settlement between the new town we built five years ago, Dimona, and the Dead Sea Works." He may have meant Arad. Whatever the case, Adenauer already knew what was being built near Dimona. Ben-Gurion made no mention of the town when he told the Knesset about the construction of the reactor, but if he had not told Adenauer about it when they met at the Waldorf Astoria, the chancellor could have read about it in *The New York Times*.[29] The aid that the chancellor had promised for the development of the Negev could also fund the "textile factory" near Dimona. The code name in Germany for the oral agreement between the two old men was the *Geschäfts-freund*, the "Business Partners." But the money did not arrive.

❖

Ben-Gurion postponed his resignation to the end of January 1961, and continued to head an interim government. At the beginning of February, the Mapai Central Committee caved in to him and ousted Lavon from his position as secretary-general of the Histadrut.

Lavon's ouster gave Ben-Gurion a victory devoid of glory that undermined both his prestige and his mental state. Over the next three months he experienced "interesting and sad things," as he put it. His handwriting again became almost illegible, and the lines again started to slant down to the bottom of the page.[30]

❖

Six weeks after the beginning of the Eichmann trial, Ben-Gurion wrote to Felix Shinnar in Cologne: "The foot-dragging shakes my faith in the old man's promises. We spoke about a long-term loan . . . fourteen months have gone by already. You need to talk with the old man about whether the promise still stands." He demanded to know immediately if Israel would receive $50 million "in the next few days." Shinnar rushed to Adenauer and, three days later, informed Ben-Gurion that the chancellor had suggested waiting until the Eichmann trial was over. Shinnar told him, "It's out of the question," because Israel had already started spending the money that it had not received yet; Adenauer consented to order an initial payment "as soon as possible."[31] A short time later, Ben-Gurion met with Defense Minister Strauss in Paris; Peres was the only other person at the meeting. The official German report states that "Ben-Gurion spoke of the production of nuclear arms." Beyond this, he sought to gain Israel's admission into NATO.[32]

At the end of May 1961, he returned to the Waldorf Astoria in New York, this time for a meeting with President Kennedy.

❖

The meeting had been scheduled hastily; in fact, Ben-Gurion inflicted it on Kennedy. The purpose was to persuade the president, as quickly as possible, that Israel needed the reactor in Dimona. The young and inexperienced president was over his head in other issues, among them the crises in Cuba and Berlin. But Ben-Gurion put on the pressure. "I received instructions," Israel's ambassador to the United States, Avraham Harman, later recalled, "and when you received instructions from Ben-Gurion, you did what he said. You couldn't do anything about it." He employed all his talents and connections, but was able to arrange only a meeting in New York, not in the White House. Kennedy was on his way to Vienna, where he was to meet the Soviet premier, Nikita Khrushchev. Ben-Gurion did not get much from the president, who left no doubt that he would not permit Israel to develop nuclear weapons. When Ben-Gurion claimed that the project was meant for peaceful purposes, the president responded: "A woman should not only be virtuous but also have the appearance of virtue." He proposed placing the reactor under a regime of international inspections. Ben-Gurion agreed only to the involvement of a third country, perhaps Norway. He linked the reactor to a plan to desalinate seawater, but chose his words carefully: "That is Israel's principal and, for the time, only goal," he maintained, adding, "We do not know what will happen in the future. Maybe in three or four years we will need a plant for the production of plutonium." Ben-Gurion may have thought that he had gained time. He also asked for Hawk air-to-air missiles; Kennedy turned him down for the time being. Ambassador Harman had trouble pointing to any significant achievement: "Not much, not much," he said.[33]

"ONLY FELDENKRAIS CAN HELP ME"

Knesset elections were set for mid-August 1961; it would be the last time Ben-Gurion headed the Mapai slate. He had lost much of his capacity for sweeping it to victory. The news of Eichmann's capture and the establishment of the nuclear reactor did not help. Neither did the meeting with Kennedy or the launch of an Israeli-made rocket, the Shavit 2. Officially, the rocket was meant to be used for meteorological research, but Ben-Gurion and Peres had their pictures taken in front of it before it was fired; Ben-Gurion wore khaki. No other photographs were permitted for publication. The newspapers celebrated Israel's entry into the space age. Ben-Gurion told the Cabinet: "This thing has great military value, meteorology has nothing to do with it." He claimed that the timing of the launch was not deliberately set prior to the election, but was rather determined by Egypt's plans to put its rockets on display in a military parade. From a military point of view, Israel's launch was "far from perfect," as the director of the government company that built it, Meir Mardor, said. The Mapam and Ahdut Ha'avodah ministers protested that Ben-Gurion had not obtained the Cabinet's approval before the launch. One of them demanded that Ben-Gurion be put on trial for this omission. He was refraining from publicizing his demand only because of the elections, said Transport Minister Yitzhak Ben-Aharon.[34] Ben-Gurion told the Knesset's Foreign Affairs and Defense Committee that the rocket was not a military one.[35]

On the same day, Ben-Gurion gave the impression that he was particularly distressed. One government minister asked if he intended to revoke the Cabinet's decision to adopt the conclusions of the Committee of Seven. Ben-Gurion said that the decision was null and void. "Whether an order was given or not given interests me as much as the snows of yesteryear," he said, but he would not stop demanding a judicial investigation, unless a law were passed forbidding him to speak. The more he spoke, the more persecuted he felt. He seemed to be losing control of himself. "Everyone is coming out against the most criminal man . . . I know, I'm not just the greatest criminal in Israel, I am anti-Zionist, I'm anti-Israel."[36]

The election results were bleak for him. They reflected the affair and Lavon's dismissal, and especially disappointment at the Old Man who had, just two years previously, received more votes than ever before. Mapai lost five seats, its second-worst showing ever. For Ben-Gurion, it was a disaster. He predicted corruption and depravity and even more political blackmail; stability was done for, and the intrigues would be even uglier. "The State of Israel deserves pity," he wrote in his diary.[37] A few months later, he flew to Burma, seeking serenity in Buddhism.

❖

He was welcomed warmly and colorfully there. Since Prime Minister U Nu's visit to Israel in 1955, the two countries had forged relations that included military cooperation.[38] Following the official part of the visit, Ben-Gurion spent another week there as a personal guest of U Nu, in his home, for the purpose of delving into Buddhist teachings. U Nu provided three scholars for the purpose. One knew English; Ben-Gurion spoke to the other two through interpreters. They arrived each day and read passages from the wisdom of the great teacher. Two or three days later, he convinced himself that he had discovered a self-contradiction in the Buddha's doctrine that no one else had ever noticed. His teachers, and U Nu as well, politely suggested that he was wrong, but he defended his "discovery"; a Burmese newspaper got wind of their dispute. He might soon have caused a diplomatic incident; it transpired that the problem was a translation error.

"I learned a great deal from them," he said upon his return, giving the Cabinet a long lecture summing up the main points of Buddhist teaching. In the weeks that followed, he devoted himself to writing an article on Buddhism that was published in *The New York Times*.[39]

❖

At this time, he was utterly under the sway of a charismatic healer named Moshé Feldenkrais, who had managed to alleviate the lumbago that plagued

Ben-Gurion incessantly. A colorful and controversial figure, Feldenkrais first gained fame as a judo master in Paris. Born in Poland, he came to Palestine as a teenager after World War I. At the age of twenty-seven he went to France in the hopes of pursuing medicine, but instead ended up studying electrical engineering and physics. He lived in Scotland during World War II. Word reached Palestine that he was a rocket expert, so in 1950 he was invited to return and recruited for the Science Corps. *Dvar Hashavua* greeted his arrival with an article that touted him as a scientist in the ranks of the great figures of the time. It turned out that he did not know much about rockets, but one of his commanders, Aharon Katzir, told Ben-Gurion that Feldenkrais had crafted a method of pain reduction and suggested calling him in. At the time, Ben-Gurion was sick in bed and the Sinai Campaign was in progress. Feldenkrais's method was based on "coordinating body and mind," and Ben-Gurion agreed to try it. A year later, he wrote, "My back pains are gone and I am sure that they will never return." He recommended using the Feldenkrais Method in the IDF. "I believe, as he does, that one cannot separate body and mind."[40]

For a time, Feldenkrais visited Ben-Gurion on a daily basis, in the morning, for a session of forty-five minutes. Ben-Gurion would remain in his undergarments or pajamas until after the treatment. Feldenkrais "worked on his body" with his hands, as he said: "simple movements, pulling, pressing, touching." As part of the process, the therapist sought to imbue his patient with a sense and understanding of his body. He encouraged him to keep up his daily walk, and tried to teach him to control his memory. Sometimes Ben-Gurion opened up and shared intimate thoughts. According to Feldenkrais, they did not talk about politics, but he tried to get Ben-Gurion to rein in his outbursts. "Just the day before yesterday we spoke about the fact that you do things compulsively," he once reprimanded the prime minister after a furious exchange with Begin. "You talk before you think."[41]

Ben-Gurion continued the sessions for about fifteen years, almost until his death. He trusted Feldenkrais completely, submitting to his treatments as if the therapist were a physician. As part of this, he consulted with Feldenkrais about medications prescribed for him by the best doctors in Israel. The doctors were skeptical about the Feldenkrais Method and Ben-Gurion tried to persuade them that it worked. "You don't know anything about how the human brain operates," he once castigated two of them.[42] The pains returned, but he did not lose faith in Feldenkrais; in 1960 he wrote after a treatment that he felt like a new man. His dependence on the therapist deepened over the years. "I went to Be'er-Sheva today, to the hospital, to be examined for the source of the pains that overcome me from time to time in my left knee," he wrote in 1966. "They x-rayed me and gave me medication—I have doubts about its efficacy, but I am using it. I imagine that only Feldenkrais can help me."[43] He sent the healer to his Cabinet ministers, Moshe Dayan included, and to other high-placed figures. He also tried, with limited success, to obtain funding for the establishment of an Institute for the Coordination of Body and Mind. Feldenkrais claimed that he never requested and never received payment; in retrospect, it rankled him that Ben-Gurion never even asked about payment.

Nevertheless, Feldenkrais gained worldwide publicity. His method attracted followers, and he was seen as a man to whom the prime minister listened, in part because in July 1957 he began to teach Ben-Gurion to stand on his head.[44] Feldenkrais believed that he was helping Ben-Gurion live a childhood dream that had never been realized. He managed to impart the technique to the prime minister, but his dominant presence for some reason interfered with Ben-Gurion's ability to execute the movement. He kept falling down. "I couldn't do it properly in his presence," he wrote. But once, when Feldenkrais was away, he relaxed. "I discovered the right posture, tried it once more, and got it right," he related. "Now I stand on my head in my room with no fear that I will topple or roll over." At the time, he often lodged at the Sharon hotel in Herzliya. "Of course, it reached the newspapers," he wrote to his daughter. It was not a onetime sight. His headstands on the Herzliya beach, dressed only in a black bathing suit, attracted journalists, photographers, and curious onlookers; Paula encouraged them.[45] The photographs seem to have made him happy and proud; old age was beginning to concern him.

"IT SHOULDN'T HAPPEN TO A MAN LIKE THAT"

In June 1961, Ben-Gurion went to London in the hope of finally realizing one of his old dreams—a conversation with Winston Churchill. Israel's standing and his personal prestige now granted him access to world leaders as if he were one of them—he met Presidents Eisenhower, Kennedy, and de Gaulle, as well as Chancellor Adenauer, in the space of less than a year and a half. But of all the twentieth century's great leaders, with the possible exception of Lenin, who had so impressed Ben-Gurion in his youth, he admired none more than Churchill. At times Churchill angered him, but Ben-Gurion never doubted that the British leader was a great supporter of Zionism. Churchill embodied the heroic resilience that Ben-Gurion had experienced, along with the British, during the Blitz, as well as their political culture, which he so admired. Churchill's daughter, Sarah, and his son, Randolph, visited Ben-Gurion at Sde Boker and told him about their father's daily routine and state of mind; Ben-Gurion's impression was that Churchill was healthy and alert.[46] But the two men had never met—primarily because Chaim Weizmann had jealously guarded that connection for himself.

The British prime minister Harold Macmillan hosted him for lunch, Israel's ambassador to the Court of St. James, Arthur Lourie, later recalled. When Ben-Gurion and Lourie told Macmillan that they were on their way to visit Churchill, the prime minister cautioned them that he was eighty-seven years old and not in good condition. "We came to Churchill's apartment at Hyde Park Gate," Lourie recalled. "I have a very great admiration for your people and for you personally," Churchill said. It was a very nice beginning. But "it was almost impossible to get through to him. Not only did he suffer from deafness, but also from sclerosis." Ben-Gurion, with his high-pitched voice, spoke in English "that was probably hard for Churchill to understand—there was practically no real contact made between them." When they left, Ben-Gurion said: "It shouldn't happen to a man like that. It is horrible." According to Lourie, it was a shock, despite Macmillan's warning: "Ben-Gurion was still quite unprepared for what he found."[47]

Lourie may have been exaggerating. During their encounter, Churchill at least recalled that he had once written an article about Moses, a witty and political piece, in the early 1930s. Half seriously, half ironically, Churchill wrote that almost everything related about Moses's life, including the Ten Plagues and the parting of the Red Sea, had actually happened. He praised the Jews for having understood that there was only one God in the universe, but condemned them for trying to take that God only for themselves. But later another great prophet appeared who brought tidings of love and peace to the whole world.

Ben-Gurion was not acquainted with the piece; Churchill sent him a copy, along with a letter saying that he would not write it the same way now. "I think he thought that ending the article with Jesus constituted an offense against the Jewish people," Ben-Gurion said to the Cabinet. Or it might have been that, in a lucid moment, Churchill had thought that what he had written about the Jews' attempt to gain exclusivity over God was liable to be taken as criticism of their attempt to gain exclusivity over the Holy Land. "His mind is fine," Ben-Gurion told his colleagues, but added, "It's very sad to see this great man incapacitated. You need to shout when you speak with him. He smokes cigars and drinks whiskey. When I asked him how he was, he responded 'I am waiting,' meaning that he is waiting for death."[48]

❖

Some three months later, Ben-Gurion tried to settle an account between him and Shlomo Zemach that had remained open for too many years. He sent his boyhood friend a long, conciliatory letter. He had heard that a commemoration of Zemach's seventh-fifth birthday was to be held at the president's residence, he wrote. He was sorry that he would not be able to leave Sde Boker to attend, but when he returned to Jerusalem after the Sukkot holiday, he would invite himself for a visit, and hoped that his friend would accept an invitation to visit his own home. He wanted a friendly talk in which they would recall how they had founded the Ezra movement sixty-one years ago, and how "we both taught" Hebrew and "propagated" the language, first among the young people of Płońsk and then among the town's older inhabitants. His pointed use of the first-person plural was meant to correct the impression that Ben-Gurion had given at times in the past, when he told this story in the singular. He did not explain why he had to put their conversation off until "after Sukkot," when he himself would be celebrating his seventy-fifth birthday. It was the second well-wishing letter he had sent to Zemach in the space of two months—its brief predecessor had been written without warmth and had apparently wounded him.

In the second letter, Ben-Gurion mentioned the letters that Zemach had sent to Płońsk from Palestine. They had been very precious for him; he had saved them all and taken them when he went to study in Salonica and Istanbul. He named the guesthouse where he had stayed. The letters had been left in the room with all his other belongings when he set out for a visit to Palestine in August 1914. World War I had broken out when he was on his way and he had been unable to return and the letters had been lost. "I was very sad about the loss of your letters, which were written in a very clear hand, in vibrant, fluent, picturesque style, offering vivid accounts of your early days in Palestine," he wrote. He said that he had not thought then that Zemach would become "one of the pillars of contemporary Hebrew literature, of the generation of Bialik." When he moved to Jerusalem to work on the staff of *Ha'ahdut*, Zemach was already a "famous author," he wrote, and he had met other writers at his home. "I listened to the conversations without saying a word. I was very shy back then," Ben-Gurion wrote. He wanted to hope that Zemach's success as an author had its roots in their work together in Ezra. Then he repeated how much he regretted the loss of the letters, which were "living documents of the personal dawn of our lives and the lives of our generation, and also a turning point in Jewish history." He recounted the political debates they had conducted in their twenties, one siding with Po'alei Zion and the other with Hapo'el Hatza'ir. "For many years—not just a few—it seemed to me that an ideological and political barrier had risen between us. I was an activist and you inclined more to Magnes's way of thinking, and you did not look kindly on my political struggle." It was important for him to say that he had tied his politics to those of Berl Katznelson and that he had remained at Sejera longer than Zemach had. "I stayed there for two years," he claimed, almost doubling his time there, as he tended to do. His memory also misled him when he recorded the Hebrew date of his arrival in Palestine. He wrote that he had never dreamed in those days that he would see the State of Israel. It was a courteous letter, more personal than its predecessor, but its first three pages could leave no doubt that it had been written at the desk of the prime minister.

Then, on the fourth page of the five-page letter, Ben-Gurion was suddenly carried away by his youthful friendship. Zemach was once more the senior of the two. "In my memory, you live as the handsome youth of fifty-seven years ago, friend of my youth, beloved of my soul, a friend sharing the dreams and fantasies of adolescence," he told him. "I do not know why I am writing you these things," he continued, "but when I began to think about it, I was overwhelmed by memories of Płońsk and Warsaw." He also mentioned Shmuel Fuchs and Shlomo Lavi, as well as Rachel Nelkin, later Beit Halahmi, the girl he had loved in Płońsk, and other childhood memories.

One memory was stronger than all the others. It was when Ben-Gurion had saved Zemach from his father, after Zemach had stolen several hundred rubles from his father's money box to pay for his flight to Palestine. "You came to me in Warsaw, and I hid you with an acquaintance, because we feared that your father would quickly arrive and search for you," Ben-Gurion wrote. "And the next day your father indeed appeared in the Pronbuk home at Novolowsky 12 and pleaded with me to bring the two of you together, but I was afraid to do that and he embraced my knees and wept and it seemed to me that I would burst with sorrow and shame. Father Zemach pleading with a boy like me. In the end I consented, when he promised me that he would not take you back, only see you before you trip to bid you farewell."

Zemach was deeply hurt by this story, which had also appeared in the Płońsk memorial book that Zemach had himself edited, as well as in Ben-Gurion's memoirs. "I must say that Ben-Gurion is certainly not correct in his account of this event, when he relates that my father kneeled before him and kissed him and pleaded with him to tell where I was," Zemach dictated to his daughter. "It is simply impossible to conceive that my father fell on his knees. A Jew does not fall on his knees, all the more so a Jew like my father." He also denied that Ben-Gurion had arranged a proper farewell. "Such a thing never happened," he asserted.*[49]

At the end of his letter, Ben-Gurion stated for the third time that he had lost Zemach's letters; this time he sounded apologetic. He had carefully guarded them, he wrote, in that pension, the name of which, Tatar, he mentioned again,

---

* Ben-Gurion's biographer Michael Bar-Zohar has noted the affront that Zemach felt and pointed to a letter from Ben-Gurion to Fuchs that offers a different account of Zemach's father's visit to his room. "He spoke with me calmly and with no sign of excitement," Ben-Gurion wrote to Fuchs. This sentence does not prove that Ben-Gurion made up the other story; it might testify to an attempt to conceal the incident. According to Bar-Zohar, however, Ben-Gurion later apologized to Zemach. (Ben-Gurion to Shmuel Fuchs, Feb. 14, 1905, in Erez 1971, p. 49; Bar-Zohar 1977, p. 37.)

as if he were at a court hearing. He had left them in Istanbul when he departed for his summer vacation, not knowing that a world war would break
out. He fondly recalled "the beauty and goodness" of their youth in Płońsk,
and then mentioned Zemach's letters for a fourth time, and for the second
time wrote, "I remember you as a handsome and charming youth." He signed
off "Engulfed in love, longing, admiration, and the warmth of boyhood."
Zemach replied that true friendships are acquired only in youth, and that
views and ideas cannot harm them. On the contrary, "the older a man gets,
forces from deep within him take him back more and more into the world of
his boyhood and youth."[50] Thus the two began to share their old age, just as
they had shared their boyhoods and youth. And it reawakened the old jealousy
that had tormented them almost their entire lives.

· **24** ·

TWILIGHT

"WE LIVE IN THE AGE OF THE ATOM"

As 1960 approached, Ben-Gurion increasingly evinced signs of cognitive decline, and he gradually lost touch with reality. At the end of the summer of 1961, he responded to a request from *Look* magazine to forecast the state of humankind fifty years hence. He predicted that the Soviet Union would evolve into a democracy and that Europe would unite. He maintained that the world would be organized as a federation of autonomous polities united under a social-democratic regime, with a global police force that would resolve conflicts. Armies would be disbanded. The United Nations would establish a World Court with its seat in Jerusalem. Most of his other predictions had to do with scientific developments, in particular the enhancement of the human brain. New and powerful sources of energy would enable the desalinization of seawater and the "air-conditioning of the globe will grant all parts of the world a moderate climate." Humanity would settle the moon and Mars. He also prophesied the development of an injection that could change the color of human skin from black to white or the other way around, which would end the practice of racial segregation in the United States. The United States would be revamped as a welfare state. Average life expectancy would reach one hundred. It took him six drafts to put his prediction of the future in final form.[1]

Despite this vast optimism, he continued to be troubled by visions of a dark future. At the end of 1962, he grew distressed, once again, about the concentration of Israel's population in Tel Aviv, reiterating the fear he had felt since the 1930s that Tel Aviv would end up being a second Carthage. The danger had only grown since then, he said: "We live in the age of the atom— are we to mass everyone in one place so that the atom will annihilate them?"[2]

The compulsive behavior noted by Moshé Feldenkrais had always been part of his personality, central to his leadership style, along with his proclivity for provocative pronouncements, some of which were staged while others were uncontrolled.[3] The boundaries between statesmanship and politics, realism and fantasy, courage and adventurism, originality and obstinacy, were often blurred in his character. Many of the initiatives and ideas he proposed over the years made his acquaintances' jaws drop. But because he was such a venerated and powerful leader, a humorless one who often elicited awe, his pronouncements produced an impact that they did not always deserve. He once, out of the blue, proposed that Tel Aviv should be renamed Jaffa, or Jaffa–Tel Aviv.[4] In January 1952, he told the Cabinet that the only way to resolve the conflict with the Arabs was to convert them to Judaism. He solicited an expert opinion on that idea.

It was difficult to assess these and other proposals, because he presented them with great conviction and often vehemence, as if they were vital to the future of the country and society. That was the case when he tried to prove that Jewish religious law did not in fact prohibit the consumption of pork, or when he announced, on the basis of his own research, that the number of Israelites who participated in the Exodus from Egypt was not six hundred thousand, as the Bible says, but only six hundred or a bit more.[5] On any number of occasions he was carried away by his passion for disputation and victory and veered off into eccentricity. He thus invested an enormous amount of energy and time in skirmishes over what he thought was proper Hebrew usage.

❖

Soon after his failed attempt, in 1956, to establish a new Middle East, he embarked on further political initiatives that seemed fantastical even at the time. One of these had been brought back from Paris by Shimon Peres, according to which France would grant Israel control over French Guiana, turning that French territory on the southern shore of the Caribbean Sea, north of Brazil, into an Israeli colony. A team of Israeli experts were sent to Guiana to look into the matter. A few months later, he presented President Charles de Gaulle with a plan to solve the Algerian problem without ending French rule. It involved partitioning the area between the French and the Arabs and settling another million French nationals there.[6]

At around that time, the Mossad director, Isser Harel, claimed that Egypt's president, Gamal Abdel Nasser, had recruited German scientists for a project to build missiles that would be able to strike targets anywhere south of Beirut. Harel saw the project as a major threat to Israel. The press soon began publishing reports that presented the work of the German scientists as a continuation of the extermination of the Jews under Hitler. Ben-Gurion suspected that Harel was exaggerating, and replaced him with the chief of military intelligence, Meir Amit. Harel's dismissal set off a storm in Mapai, with some demanding Ben-Gurion's ouster. "Isser is going from one person to another and Golda is putting together a conspiracy," Navon wrote. He noted that Golda Meir opposed both military ties with Germany and the Dimona project; furthermore, she hated Shimon Peres, whom she saw as a threat.[7] Navon tried unsuccessfully to make sense of what he termed the "hidden psychological recesses" in the relations between Ben-Gurion and Meir. "When he seeks her favor, she thinks he is insincere; when he doesn't, he's ignoring her, and there's no end to it. Love, admiration, hatred, and jealousy merge one into the other, and the wretched romance of this couple has no remedy."[8]

His treatment of the hysteria regarding the German scientists showed that he was still capable of reasonable and pragmatic decisions. But Ben-Gurion also feared that the Adenauer era was coming to an end. He repeatedly inquired into the chancellor's health, fearing that his death would take with it the agreements with Israel. In 1961 he allowed Shimon Peres to propose a secret pact to Germany, according to which, in time of need, Israel would entertain a German request to establish military bases in Israel.[9] Just as the affair of the German scientists in Egypt was reaching its climax, a political crisis in Germany led to the resignation of Minister of Defense Franz Josef Strauss. Ben-Gurion feared the future of the Dimona project was in jeopardy. Simultaneously, President John Kennedy was demonstrating ever more determination to prevent nuclear proliferation, and demanded that the Dimona reactor be placed under outside oversight.[10]

On April 17, 1963, Egypt, Syria, and Iraq declared the establishment of a United Arab Republic. Its goals included "the liberation of Palestine." Two days later, Chief of Staff Tzur offered the Cabinet a survey of the development's significance, focusing on the danger it presented to the stability of the regime in Jordan, whose King Hussein was, Tzur maintained, in danger of assassination. He told the ministers that the IDF could, with a lead time of twelve hours, capture all of East Jerusalem with the exception of the Old City. With forty-eight-hour advance notice it could take the entire West Bank, in an operation that would last twenty-four hours. Ben-Gurion had pondered such plans any number of times over the years; he opposed the idea this time for the same reason he had in the past: "This time the Arabs won't run away," he feared.[11]

Golda Meir was in the hospital at the time, meaning that Ben-Gurion was also acting as foreign minister. In that capacity, he ordered that letters be drafted to several dozen prime ministers and presidents. The text was more or less identical, condemning the Arab intention of destroying Israel and demanding that the United Nations require the Arabs to make peace. The Foreign Ministry's staff wondered why Ben-Gurion had suddenly decided that this was necessary, but did not see it as a major deviation from diplomatic routine. In fact, Ben-Gurion was in a frenzy, firing off two letters—a total of sixteen pages—to President Kennedy. A Foreign Ministry official referred to the second of these as "sick."[12] The meaning of the letters was that Ben-Gurion might be prepared to compromise with the United States regarding the Dimona project.

"IT MAY NOT HAPPEN IN MY LIFETIME"

His first letter to Kennedy evinced anxiety and a state of emergency. He took the words "liberation of Palestine" that had been included in the declaration of the new Arab state as if they were an actual plan for an immediate attack on Israel aimed at destroying it.

"The 'liberation of Palestine' is impossible without the total destruction of the people in Israel," he declared. He quoted at length from one of Hitler's pronouncements about the extermination of the Jewish people. The nations of the world had treated Hitler's declaration "with indifference and equanimity, enabling the Holocaust," he wrote. "Six million Jews in all the countries under Nazi occupation (except Bulgaria), men and women, old and young, infants and babies, were burnt, strangled, buried alive."

To avert the catastrophe that the liberation of Palestine would bring on, Ben-Gurion demanded that Kennedy and Khrushchev issue a joint statement guaranteeing the integrity of all the countries of the Middle East, withdrawing aid from any country that threatened to attack any other, that maintained a state of war against another country, or that refused to recognize another country. He stressed that the declaration needed also to threaten sanctions for noncompliance. He noted that the Soviet Union was providing arms to Egypt and that the United States was giving economic aid. He knew the chances for such a declaration were not great, but he felt it was incumbent on him to tell the president that the situation in the Middle East had grown inestimably grim. He thus asked Kennedy to free up an hour or two of his time for a conversation about a possible way out of the situation. He would come to Washington on whatever day the president liked, "without publicity."[13] He drafted the Hebrew version of the letter himself and corrected it by hand. The Foreign Ministry staff was stunned, but prepared an English version for him and dispatched it to Washington.

At the next Cabinet meeting, Ben-Gurion focused on how the Arabs could be deterred from attacking Israel. Such a discussion would seem to have been mandated by the declaration of a new united Arab state, but Ben-Gurion intended a discussion of fundamentals that would produce a long-term road map, for a time when he would no longer lead the country. In other words, he wanted to establish his legacy in the area of Israel's security. He offered four alternatives for ensuring Israel's survival: public guarantees in the form of a joint Kennedy–Khrushchev statement; a military alliance between Israel and the United States, or alternatively a military alliance with France; full Israeli membership in NATO; or the development of a deterrent weapon of which Ben-Gurion was willing to say only that it required missiles. He stressed that his second alternative referred to an alliance, ratified by Congress, providing that an attack on Israel would be considered an attack on the United States. He had sought American guarantees since the 1950s, and had dreamed then of a military alliance with America as well. It was the only thing of any value, Ben-Gurion said in 1955. The military alliance he was speaking of at this point needed, by the nature of things, to include a provision about Dimona. It made Dimona out to be a sort of atonement for the sin that the Jewish people had committed over two millennia, the "sin of weakness," as Ben-Gurion had put it many years previously.[14]

In the meantime, Peres returned from Washington and reported to the Cabinet on his talk with Kennedy. The president asked him what he could tell him about Israel's nuclear plans, and Peres responded that Israel was not going to manufacture atomic weapons and would certainly not be the first country to introduce nuclear arms into the region. Kennedy also took an interest in why Harel was replaced, and in the work of the German scientists in Egypt. It was an official meeting, with Israel's ambassador to Washington, Avraham Harman, in attendance. "Kennedy looked less handsome than in his photographs," Peres told the ministers.[15]

During the next Cabinet meeting, Ben-Gurion was told that the American ambassador to Israel would be bringing him Kennedy's reply to his letter that afternoon. In the meantime, Ben-Gurion continued to impart his thoughts on the nature of the needed deterrent. "Either a political deterrent force or a military deterrent force. Because I don't want there to be a war," he said. Had Khrushchev accepted his proposal, he maintained, he would have agreed to a military alliance with the Soviet Union as well. But, just like Israeli membership in NATO, that possibility did not seem like a real option. For that reason, it was necessary to find out if it would be possible to receive "real help with deterrent arms." It was not a focused discussion; Ben-Gurion flitted from one subject to another.[16]

Kennedy's reply, which arrived that afternoon, was chilly, almost sarcastic. The president understood, of course, that Israel was concerned about the declaration of intent to "liberate Palestine," but, in his opinion, the practical implications of those words were no different from those of the innumerable similar statements the Arabs had made in the past. The United States remained as concerned about Israel's security and peace in the region as it had ever been. He did not think that a joint declaration by the United States and the USSR was a possibility, and even if it were, it would only enhance the USSR's importance in the eyes of the Arabs, thereby increasing Soviet influence in the Arab world. He did not understand what Ben-Gurion meant when he warned of an unparalleled increase in the gravity of the situation. He thanked the prime minister for his willingness to lay aside the urgent affairs for which he was responsible in order to rush to Washington, and perhaps if it were possible to have such a meeting without it being publicized it would even be helpful, but he knew from experience that that was not possible. Promising that American efforts to strengthen its ties to the Arab states would be to Israel's benefit, he concluded with the hope that they would remain in touch.[17] The letter could hardly have been more patronizing, given that Ben-Gurion had warned that Israel was in imminent danger of being destroyed. Affronted, Ben-Gurion forthwith began drafting his second letter, nine pages long.

"I felt somewhat disappointed when I read your message," he wrote, attributing this to his high expectations of Kennedy, based on his support for and assistance to Israel up to that point. It was a personal letter. He had spent decades living with the Arabs, he related, and had worked in the fields with Arab laborers. He had also studied with Arabs in Istanbul before World War I, and had spoken with Arab leaders before World War II. During the war, he heard many Arab leaders praise Hitler as a liberator of humanity, and pray for his success. He was not surprised. "Knowing them, I am convinced that they are capable of following the Nazi example," he wrote, claiming that Nasser was in fact adopting the National Socialist ideology of the Nazis. "I have no doubt that a similar thing might happen to Jews in Israel if Nasser succeeded in defeating our army," he declared. There was no certainty that such a thing would happen today or tomorrow, he added. "I am not so young anymore, and it may not happen in my lifetime," he continued. "But I cannot dismiss the possibility that this may occur, if the situation in the Middle East remains as it is—and the Arab leaders continue to insist on and pursue their policy of belligerency against Israel." It didn't really matter whether or not it happened during his lifetime, he explained. What was important was that there was a way to prevent it. He meant the joint U.S.–Soviet declaration he had described in his previous letter. He went on to lay it out in detail one more time. In his opinion, that was the safest way to ensure Israel's survival. Given Kennedy's opinion that such a declaration was not on the table, what remained was a "Bilateral Security Agreement" between Israel and the United States. Likewise, the United States would need to supply Israel with all the types of arms that the Soviet Union was supplying to Egypt.[18]

The Foreign Ministry's top officials convened to work together on the English version of the letter. One of them, Gideon Rafael, proposed that the letter not be sent. "We must not reach a point where the prime minister writes fantastic and sick things," he said. He showed the draft of Ben-Gurion's letter to Golda Meir, and she, still bedridden, was particularly shocked by the words "I do not know if the country will continue to exist after my death." She instructed Rafael to persuade Ben-Gurion to omit them, but Ben-Gurion agreed only to tone down the language. Ambassador Harman tried to make the letter even gentler. Ben-Gurion was furious when he heard of it, Navon wrote in his diary: "To hell with them—he shouted—and his face turned red. Idiots. They don't understand what they are saying." The Foreign Ministry cabled Harman a firm directive to convey the letter even if he did not agree with it.[19]

Fear of a second Holocaust might have been the principal justification for the establishment of the Dimona reactor. But Ben-Gurion's letter to Kennedy could also be read as a proposal to compromise on Israel's nuclear program in exchange for security guarantees. There can be no other interpretation of the security agreement he asked Kennedy for, because he had nothing to offer the Americans other than to give up the Dimona project. That was also how it was understood in Jerusalem.

❖

Foreign Ministry officials quickly jumped on the idea and began to craft a policy around it. Some of them had been opposed to the nuclear project from the start—the debate around it had penetrated their ranks as well. One proposed seeing the Dimona initiative as "an impetus for solving the fundamental security problem" that Israel faced; another proposed using it as a "bargaining chip." Gideon Rafael swiftly sent the ministry's director-general a draft security agreement to propose to Kennedy. The director-general, Haim Yahil, sent a few of his thoughts to Golda Meir. Israel needed to demand "concrete guarantees" for the country's security, with two foundations, he wrote. The first was sufficient Israeli power to hold back an attack during its early stages, until outside assistance could arrive. The second was an explicit and detailed agreement about assistance and joint planning of how it would be provided. Only such an arrangement could serve as a deterrent factor, Yahil maintained. He proposed to be frank with the Americans about what would happen if such an agreement was not offered. In its absence, he said, Israel would have no choice but to look after its own interests, and could not forgo the option of developing nuclear capability. If the United States proved willing to sign a deterrent agreement, or to bring Israel into NATO, the country could relinquish the option of a nuclear potential.[20]

Meir was inclined to agree. There was no reason to stop the work in Dimona, she said, but she also saw the reactor as a bargaining chip. That being the case, she proposed telling the Americans the truth. "If we deny that Dimona is there, then we can't bargain with it, because you can't bargain with something that doesn't exist," she explained. Ambassador Harman and the Israeli minister in Washington wrote to her to say that they had "taken note" of her position on the Dimona facility, and that they presumed that instructions for proceeding would soon be formulated in that spirit.[21]

Ben-Gurion's willingness, in principle and under certain conditions, to trade the Dimona project for a military alliance recalls his agreement to extend the British Mandate and put off declaring Israel's independence. He left the decision on the future of the Dimona project to his heirs, Dayan among them, but it is reasonable to presume that the two of them argued about the subject while he was still in office. Dayan's position was firm: "The most important thing that can change our security balance is the final product of Dimona," he maintained. "Nothing else can replace it and there is nothing else that can do the trick. As long as we face any sort of chance of reaching that, we need, in my opinion, to do everything to reach it and not to do anything that is liable to stand between us and that." He thought a military pact with the United States would be dangerous, and maintained that it should not even be discussed. Never before had such a fundamental and sharp disagreement divided Ben-Gurion and Dayan. Dayan was at the height of his power; Ben-Gurion could no longer withstand him. Peres thought that there was no chance of achieving a military alliance, but agreed to consider a compromise on developing the reactor in exchange for $1 billion that Germany was to give to Israel. "We have six million voters in Germany," he cynically remarked.[22]

The continuing controversy over Israel's relations with Germany frayed Ben-Gurion's nerves. He went to the Knesset and set off a scandal unmatched since the great reparations debate; some said that there had been nothing like it since the Knesset was first established.

"A MAN IS NOT ALWAYS RATIONAL"

The speech was prepared as a response to participants in a foreign policy debate, and was meant to be half an hour long. The text was handed out in advance. But Ben-Gurion managed to speak for only four minutes before screams of protest drowned him out. Ben-Gurion had declared, basing himself on an article published in a Revisionist newspaper in 1933, that Jabotinsky's supporters had lauded Hitler. During the uproar, several members of the Herut faction rose to their feet; Ben-Gurion's bodyguards went on alert.

Most of the Mapai members did not come to Ben-Gurion's defense. Instead, they sat in embarrassed silence. Meir even sharply dissented. The press reaction was harsh. One article caused Ben-Gurion to erupt like a volcano, this time in writing.[23]

Its author was Haim Gouri, the poet of War of Independence heroism, loss, and the brotherhood of warriors. He gained many admirers in the early 1960s when he wrote sensitive coverage of the Eichmann trial. "Unforgivable" was what he had to say about Ben-Gurion's Knesset speech. Ben-Gurion immediately sent off a letter to Gouri. "Begin is a classically Hitlerist type," he wrote. "Racist, ready to exterminate all the Arabs for the whole Land of Israel, ready to employ any means for his sacred end—absolute rule; I see him as a serious danger to Israel's situation, both internally and externally."

The letter went on for three pages. He had not been surprised by the bizarre charges Gouri had made, he remarked. It may well be that the Eichmann affair had left him with a trauma that "consciously or unconsciously affects things unconnected to the trial." He had no regrets about a single word he had said in the Knesset, he asserted, offering a long list of crimes he attributed to Begin, including the bombing of the King David Hotel, Deir Yassin, and the *Altalena*. He predicted that if Begin were to seize control of the country, "he will replace the army and police command with his own thugs, and rule as Hitler ruled Germany, suppressing the labor movement with force and brutality; his political adventurism will destroy the country."

The letter was delivered to Gouri early in the morning by a special messenger from the Office of the Prime Minister; apparently no one in the office had the presence of mind to keep it from going out. Gouri was alarmed in the extreme. The few people who knew about the letter feared that Ben-Gurion had lost his mental capacity for running the country.[24]

❖

A few days later, a press report outraged Israelis in a way unseen since the controversy over German reparations: Israeli soldiers, the public learned, were receiving military training in Germany.[25] United Press International was the first to report it. A few hours later, Meir rushed over to Ben-Gurion's home and demanded that he impose military censorship to prevent the report from being printed in Israel. Ben-Gurion refused. They argued about it until after midnight. Ben-Gurion stuck to his position, but agreed to hold a comprehensive discussion of Israel's relations with Germany. The report was published. Meir did not quit.[26]

Prior to the weekly Cabinet meeting scheduled for the next day, June 16, 1963, Ben-Gurion called in all the Mapai ministers and informed them that he had decided to resign that day. Unlike in the past, he did not say he was taking a leave of absence for a year or two, nor was he threatening resignation in order to get a demand met. He said, once more, that he no longer had the mental fortitude to bear responsibility. Some of the ministers insisted that he make do with a vacation; he gave in only to their plea that he remain a member of the Knesset. The ritual was a very brief one this time. In fact, everyone felt relieved. Ten days later, Levi Eshkol formed a new government. Navon asked Ben-Gurion why he had done it. "He raised his head and gave me a weary look. 'A man is not always rational,' he murmured." Isser Harel described him as a sad man, passive and withdrawn, and he was upset by his failing memory. Feldenkrais said that at about this time he heard Ben-Gurion ask Paula where in Tel Aviv they were living.[27] It was not a single thing that broke him in the end, but rather an entire range of tensions, anxieties, and people, from Lavon to Kennedy, from Dayan to Nasser. Taken together, it was now more than he could handle.

"I CANNOT DO OTHERWISE"

He resigned unwillingly. "To my great chagrin, I cannot do otherwise," he explained to the Cabinet ministers who tried to talk him out of it. He was profoundly sad to leave. "I was barely able to hold in my emotions and my tears," he wrote. One of the last acts he took as prime minister was aimed at guaranteeing Ariel Sharon's political future.[28] The first person he visited after resigning was Shlomo Zemach.

The two men had reestablished contact in January 1963. Ben-Gurion called to invite Zemach to attend the Bible study group that met at Ben-Gurion's home every Saturday night. "David invited me to come to his home and I accepted," Zemach wrote. "Perhaps there is a true feeling of youthful friendship in his desire to become closer to me," he wondered. "He is alone and all the splendor that surrounds him does not satisfy his needs." His sudden visit, immediately after his resignation, did nothing to change Zemach's feelings about him. "He spoke for an entire hour," Zemach wrote in his diary, "yet we did not touch on the main thing—what had brought about his resignation?" But he knew Ben-Gurion well, every "wrinkle in his soul," and that enabled him to sense that he was upset and "bitterly disappointed." And he feared that future events would be much worse than anything that had already happened. He seemed healthy. "I believe that he has put on weight and that his paunch is larger," Zemach noted. "But there is a hidden hesitation in his expression, some sort of inner anxiety, but I do not know where it comes from or what its nature is." During their conversation, Ben-Gurion "went off into higher spheres," Zemach related. He meant Ben-Gurion's interest in biology and related fields. Zemach did not believe that Ben-Gurion was really interested in science. "He was too quick to accept things he read and to lecture on them as if they were his own," the friend wrote. According to him, the limits of Ben-Gurion's intellect were now so starkly revealed that one couldn't help feeling sorry for him. Both of them had been well aware of those limits when they were young, Zemach wrote. "He knows it and he knows that I know." That was the reason for his great thirst for the spiritual, "the attraction to things he was not given," as his friend put it. When he launched into a discourse on cells and tissues and the cosmos and other such things, Zemach suspected that Ben-Gurion had lost his mind. "I sat there and pitied him," he related.

Ben-Gurion came to him "with zero strength," Zemach wrote. "He was lonely all his life. Perhaps I might have been a close friend, but things did not work out that way. No soul is close to him . . . Those who were close to him were, first of all, close to themselves, and used him for their own interests. In the great hubbub around him he stood alone and abandoned. That is his great tragedy." Zemach continued to follow Ben-Gurion and received the impression that he was having trouble adjusting to being a citizen, without the "trappings of office." Ben-Gurion began to write for *Davar*, a series of fairly long-winded articles about Israel's history. Regretfully, Zemach thought they were not very good. "They have no stature and no depth, no feeling and no thinking." He thought that the articles might be detrimental to Ben-Gurion's reputation. He regretted that and considered sending him "a few writing tricks" that would help him improve his style. "But I am afraid that he will take my advice not as it is intended."[29]

Less than a month later, their friend Shlomo Lavi died. "I am not concerned about myself," Zemach wrote. "But this generation—my generation—is gradually leaving us, one after the other." They had seen each other just a few days before; Zemach had congratulated Lavi on looking so well, but Lavi retorted that his look was deceptive—he was very ill. Zemach was not all that healthy himself; his doctors forbade him to travel to Ein Harod for the funeral. Ben-Gurion and Paula went; Ben-Gurion offered only a brief eulogy and looked distraught. Almost all the surviving founding fathers were there.[30]

❖

He was unable to disengage from politics; taking on the role of a gadfly who set off uproars, his actual influence was negligible. Four months after his retirement, Ben-Gurion called several dozen of his followers to his home and announced that he intended to run at the head of a new party in the next election. He was not inclined to return to the post of prime minister, but did not rule it out. "If I am called on to purify the turbid atmosphere, I believe I could not refuse to try," he wrote.[31] The result was that, thirty-five years after he and Berl Katznelson founded Mapai, the party, which was now run by Eshkol, expelled him.

Ostensibly it was all about the Lavon affair. Ben-Gurion insisted, incessantly, on investigating "who gave the order." Eshkol wanted the question out of the way and if possible forgotten. Ben-Gurion's endless demands, accusations, and protests seemed to be nothing more than an old man's self-destructive obsession. He claimed to want the truth—but most Israelis, including his admirers, were annoyed or pitied him; some tried to analyze what they regarded as the founding father's jealousy of his heir. Most people simply no longer wanted to hear about Lavon.

❖

Ben-Gurion ran for the Knesset at the head of a new party called Rafi, the Israel Workers List. Heading a slate that included Moshe Dayan, the former IDF chief of staff Tzvi Tzur, the author Yizhar Smilansky, and Shimon Peres, Ben-Gurion tried, at the age of seventy-nine, to project a young and technocratic image. In November 1965, the party won ten seats in the Knesset. It was a humiliating defeat; in June he had fantasized that his new party would win twenty or even twenty-five seats.[32] The Alignment, a joint Mapai and Ahdut Ha'avodah slate headed by Levi Eshkol, won forty-five seats. For the first time in his life in Israel, Ben-Gurion found himself in the opposition.[33]

"NASSER WON'T DO ANYTHING"

He did not go often to the Knesset, spending most of his time at Sde Boker. He wrote articles, worked on his memoirs, and received visitors, including the foreign press. He continued to receive dozens of letters each week from people who thought he could help them with all sorts of questions and personal problems. It was a medium that he continued to enjoy; he devoted several hours a day to answering his correspondence. His prestige far exceeded the ten seats his party had received. His successor was his greatest enemy now; in fact, his hostility toward Eshkol swelled to the point where he viewed the new prime minister as the people's enemy. When he was holding himself back, he limited himself to saying that Eshkol lacked "the moral and national qualities required of a prime minister." At more unbridled moments, he called him a liar, fraud, and coward. Zemach asked himself where his friend's "criminal vulgarity" toward Eshkol could possibly come from. As one might expect, he came up with a psychological explanation dating back to Płońsk. "The root and the source from which it derives," Zemach wrote, "is the empty heart that, seeking recompense for the insults of youth, finds them in the troubles of others and self-promotion."[34]

On the holiday of Sukkot, in the fall of 1966, some ten thousand people came to Sde Boker to celebrate Ben-Gurion's birthday. He told everyone that he was sixty years old—the number of years he had lived in the country. Israel marked the event as if it were a national holiday. The IDF organized a huge ceremony at Sde Boker's amphitheater, with speeches and an audiovisual display. Aharon Meskin, Habima theater's leading actor, pronounced just two sentences: "The nation loves you, Ben-Gurion. Thank you for all you have done and remain in good health in the future." He received thousands of congratulatory telegrams from all over the world. The Cabinet also offered its felicitations, after a debate over the wording. Eshkol forbade commending Ben-Gurion for the "development of the country," because he maintained that his own contribution to the country's development was greater.[35]

❖

In June 1967, tensions between Israel and Jordan worsened, largely because of terror attacks committed by young Palestinian Arabs, many of them the children of refugees displaced in 1948. At that same time, the questions of why Israel had not conquered the West Bank in the War of Independence and why the Old City of Jerusalem had been allowed to remain in Arab hands were again being debated in Israel. The *Ma'ariv* correspondent Geula Cohen, interviewing Ben-Gurion for Independence Day, posed a question that his grandson might ask him: "Grandpa, what are the borders of my homeland?" Ben-Gurion replied that the borders of the homeland corresponded to the Green Line, but did not rule out that those might change, just as borders had often moved during history. "We are interested in peace based on the status quo," he said, "but if the Arabs are not interested in peace, but rather in war, then we will fight, and then perhaps the status quo will be otherwise." It was the same answer he gave to Israeli citizens who posed the question to him, time and again. Cohen asked him if he would encourage an Israeli child to write a song of yearning for a united Jerusalem. "If he wants to write one, he can write one," Ben-Gurion replied, adding: "I will not write one." *Ma'ariv* also interviewed the former chief of staff Yigael Yadin on the same occasion. Yadin intimated that Ben-Gurion had not wanted to conquer the Old City. A military correspondent for *Ha'aretz* recalled that the attempt to take Jenin had failed.[36] The renewed preoccupation with the borders established by the victory of 1948 may have grown out of the gloomy atmosphere of the time.

When, in May 1967, Egypt announced that it was blocking the Straits of Tiran to Israeli traffic, Ben-Gurion was not alarmed. "In my opinion, Nasser won't do anything, because he's satisfied with having closed the Straits. That will enhance his stature," he wrote. He proposed a limited operation to open shipping to Eilat. Neither did he think that such an operation was urgent. "The army is wonderful, but in this age one shouldn't fight like David fought Goliath," he wrote.[37] He was presumably acquainted with the current strategy planned by the IDF—a surprise aerial attack to destroy the Egyptian air force. That, as he recalled, was how Egypt had been defeated in the War of Independence: "At the first moment, we defeated their air force," he once told the Cabinet; a few years later, he repeated that this was the way to defeat Egypt.[38] But, contrary to the opinion of the IDF's generals, and most politicians and pundits, and in particular unlike the frightened public, Ben-Gurion opposed an Israeli first strike. He feared that war against Egypt and Syria would lead to the conquest of the West Bank from Jordan—and with it the acquisition of more Arabs.

Neither did he see any immediate need to conquer Sinai or the Gaza Strip, nor did he think it would be worthwhile to capture East Jerusalem. He apparently knew that, six months hence, Israel's deterrent capability would improve dramatically, averting war.[39] In the meantime, Israel commenced a massive reserve call-up. Ben-Gurion thought it was a mistake. When he said as much to the chief of staff, Rabin panicked. He suffered a breakdown and required medical treatment.

Most Israelis had no clue that this was Ben-Gurion's opinion, as he did not state it publicly. They believed that the war was being delayed because Eshkol was waffling and weak. Ben-Gurion offered the prime minister no backing, and did nothing to cool down the bellicose atmosphere. When he heard that the world's socialist parties had issued a statement of support for Mapai, his comment was: "Mapai does not support the State of Israel."[40]

Neither did he use his influence to restrain the army, with the exception of that grim conversation with Rabin. When calls for Eshkol's replacement increased, Ben-Gurion agreed to receive in his home the most dangerous and repulsive man he had known before he decided that Eshkol was even more dangerous and repulsive—namely, Menachem Begin. Begin had first tried to pressure Eshkol to bring Ben-Gurion back into the Cabinet, but when Eshkol refused, he proposed that Ben-Gurion return as prime minister and lead the country into war. Only when they met did Begin learn, to his astonishment, that Ben-Gurion opposed going to war, in part because he feared it would lead to Israeli conquest of territories populated by Arabs.[41] Four days before the war began, Ben-Gurion copied into his diary numbers he found in a news clipping from nineteen years previously, according to which everyone was exaggerating the number of Palestinian refugees. Even the best binoculars would not be able to discern more than three hundred thousand of them, the clipping said. He himself generally spoke of six hundred thousand refugees.[42]

He supported replacing Eshkol, suggesting that Dayan serve as prime minister and defense minister; he also hinted that he would agree to reassume the post of prime minister if Dayan were to serve as defense minister. "As long as Eshkol is prime minister, we will descend into perdition," he wrote. Perhaps he thought that Dayan would operate under his guidance, or at least in coordination with him. But Dayan favored war and Ben-Gurion knew it. The attraction of getting rid of Eshkol seems, however, to have been irresistible. When Eshkol agreed, reluctantly, that Dayan could join the government as defense minister, Ben-Gurion gave his consent to this arrangement on condition that Peres tell Eshkol that Rafi did not consider him to be the right man to head the government.[43] Eshkol was now backed by a broad coalition, including Begin, who was appointed minister without portfolio.

The Six-Day War broke out as a result of repeated Palestinian attacks on Israel, and Israel's reprisals against Syria and Jordan. Nasser ostensibly acted in their support by mobilizing the Egyptian army. Israel's attack on Egypt on June 5, 1967, reflected the army's pressure on the Eshkol government to act, as well as widespread panic created by Nasser's threats to eliminate Israel.

"DEMOLISH THE WALL"

Ben-Gurion spent the first day of the war at his home in Tel Aviv. Dayan promised to visit and brief him. While waiting for him, Ben-Gurion started reading the new issue of a literary magazine, *Molad*, which had published a selection of the letters he had sent to Shmuel Fuchs in his youth. He read them avidly, as if encountering them for the first time. So his day passed, with his memories, cut off from everything that was happening, and Dayan did not show up. "He is bad-hearted," he once told Navon about Dayan.[44] The next day, Dayan sent a General Staff officer to inform him that the operation in the south had begun, in the air and on land. "I believe that it is a grave mistake," Ben-Gurion wrote. "The great thing that took place in the past week is Levi Eshkol's removal," he wrote.[45] He also opposed capturing the Golan Heights. But soon he, too, was swept up by that ecstasy produced by the victory and conquests.[46]

Journalists from around the world peppered him with questions about what should happen next. Ben-Gurion issued a public statement: he advocated withdrawal from the Sinai Peninsula as part of a peace treaty with Egypt that would guarantee free passage of ships coming to Eilat through the Tiran Straits and the Suez Canal. The Gaza Strip should remain under Israeli control. Israel should withdraw from the Golan Heights as part of a peace treaty with Syria. The government should negotiate with representatives of the inhabitants of the West Bank to establish an autonomous entity tied to Israel economically, with an outlet to the sea through Haifa, Ashdod, or Gaza. Palestinian refugees should be moved from the Gaza Strip to the West

Bank, with the refugees' consent and Israeli assistance. All the Jews who had once lived in Hebron should be permitted to return. Israel would protect the holy sites in Jerusalem and elsewhere that were now under its control; the IDF would deploy on the western bank of the Jordan River to guarantee the West Bank's independence from Jordan. There would be no negotiations over the future of the Old City of Jerusalem and its environs. From the time of King David it had been the capital of Israel, and so it would remain forever.[47]

The majority of Israelis thus moved, quite suddenly, from fear of another Holocaust to the verge of the messianic era. Ben-Gurion had gone through no few such sudden shifts in his personal life; he recalled one from the end of the War of Independence. "The entire Jewish population is drunk with victory," he wrote then. "A year ago, every Jew would have said that we have no chance, and today everyone is saying that no one can stand in our way."[48] He placed himself at the head of those who were demanding to move Jews into the Old City, as if he were seeking atonement for what he had decided not to do during the War of Independence. Less than two weeks after the war, he proposed demolishing the Old City wall. "It will unify Jerusalem and make it easier for it to expand to the east, south, north, and west," he argued. It was the most notable testimony yet to the weakness of mind that had, for several years, produced any number of fantastical proposals of this sort. As always, he held fast to his idea, reiterating it over and over again: "Demolish the wall." He claimed that the wall had no historical value, as it had been built only in the sixteenth century at the order of the Ottoman sultan.[49] It was not easy for him to live with the fact that the Old City had been taken under a government led by Eshkol, in which Begin served, in a war that he himself had opposed.

The conquest of the Old City corrected what many Israelis saw as the major shortcoming of the political order that Ben-Gurion had bestowed on the Jewish state nineteen years earlier; up until a few days before, Ben-Gurion had viewed the borders set in 1949 an acceptable basis for a final status arrangement with the Arabs. In this sense, the Six-Day War was the second round in the battle for Palestine; the Sinai Campaign now seemed like but an interim episode. The new situation sent him back to the dawn of Zionism. He was overwhelmed by a "profound and joyous experience," he wrote. "I experienced something so profound only on my first night after arriving in Petah Tikvah, when I heard the howling of the jackals and the neighing of the donkeys and I felt that I was in our nation's renewed homeland, not in exile in a foreign land."[50]

The sense that history was beginning again from the start led him to renew his acquaintance with Musa al-Alami, the man he had so often quoted over the intervening thirty years as proof of his contention that the Arabs did not want peace. Ten years before, he had told Navon that he missed Alami. He asked that he be found. Alami was in London; Ben-Gurion's attempt to speak to him by telephone seemed to be a metaphorical confirmation of his opinion on the chances for dialogue with the Palestinian Arabs, because the connection was bad. "He didn't hear me, although I heard him. It got a little better afterward, he heard me but I didn't hear him," Ben-Gurion wrote in his diary.[51]

❖

The conquest of the West Bank and Gaza Strip suddenly confronted Israelis with the truth about the conflict over Palestine, including the suffering of the refugees and their yearning to undo their national catastrophe and take back the parts of the homeland, the homes, and the property they had lost, beginning in 1947. Many Israelis felt that they had reached a historical crossroads that required them to make a choice. While the war was still in progress, an impassioned debate over the fundamental values of Zionist identity reignited. Few of the people involved offered real alternatives. One who did was Shlomo Zemach. The war made his views more extreme, as it did for many Israelis, both those on the left and, even more so, those of the center and right. Many longed for a new start, as Zemach did. "To go to the Arabs and say to them—we have been going the wrong way all these years . . . and now we have come to you, tribes of Arabia, to live under your protection."[52]

Ensuring a Jewish majority in a democratic Israel required the immediate immigration of two million Jews from other countries, or expelling the inhabitants of the West Bank and Gaza Strip, or giving up the captured territories, including East Jerusalem, even without a peace treaty. The idea of resettling in the West Bank the 1947–49 refugees living in Gaza was not carried out and in retrospect was the single greatest mistake of those years.[53] One Cabinet meeting also raised the possibility of asking Canada and Brazil to take in the Gaza refugees. Israeli Jews soon started settling in Judea and

Samaria, as they called the northern and southern parts of the West Bank, just as they had settled in the central and northern parts of Palestine during the sixty years since Ben-Gurion's arrival, "village by village." In that sense, the Six-Day War propelled the Zionist project forward, in the Ben-Gurion spirit. After visiting the Golan Heights in August 1967, he changed his mind and declared that Israel should never leave it, even in exchange for a peace treaty. In the months that followed, he began to voice a vague version of a formulation he had used in the past: "If I had to choose between a small Israel with peace and a large Israel without peace, I would prefer a small Israel." Those who were impressed by this statement did not know that he had never believed that peace was really possible. He had always dreamed of possessing the entire Land of Israel, and that continued to be his ultimate wish. "If only the government had the strength and will to hold fast to the occupied territories when our neighbors refuse to discuss peace with us," he wrote in July 1967. He maintained, as he always had, that Israel's survival depended on bringing in millions of Jewish immigrants. "If the Zionist movement had not made do with words, and instead every Zionist had come here, we would long since have become the majority on both banks of the Jordan, and Israel would have come into being prior to World War I and certainly before World War II," he wrote. "We must now principally see to a large wave of immigration from the prosperous world—the danger of war has still not passed."[54] He spent some three months in Tel Aviv, caught up in politics, the war, and the connection between them. Then he returned to Sde Boker, to write.

"MY PAULA ADMIRED YOU"

Paula died in January 1968 of a stroke. Israel's president and many Cabinet ministers and members of the Knesset attended the funeral. Prime Minister Eshkol was notably absent, but issued a statement of mourning; Menachem Begin was notably in attendance. The German ambassador also came. Ben-Gurion decided that she should be buried on the site that he had chosen for himself, on the top of a cliff overlooking a breathtaking desert view of the Zin riverbed. "I was always sure that I would die first," he said again.

He immediately returned to his work routine. "I did not notice that he was badly shaken after Paula's death," one of his bodyguards said. Yehoshua

Cohen of Sde Boker also received the impression that her death was not, for Ben-Gurion, a "geological fault line" in his life.*[55]

For the first time in his life, he was irrelevant, cut off from public life. Rafi turned out to be a passing episode. Most of its members voted to merge with Mapai and Ahdut Ha'avodah to form the Labor Party. Ben-Gurion led the rump that remained, under a new name, into the next election, winning only four seats, one of which went to Isser Harel. In 1970 Ben-Gurion finally resigned from the Knesset. On occasion he still received distinguished guests, among them the former German chancellor Konrad Adenauer. He continued to lash out at Prime Minister Eshkol, including in a thirty-three-page letter he sent to Golda Meir.[56] In addition to accusing him of lies and corruption, he now added "idiocy." At the Six-Day War victory parade, he sat in the audience instead of on the dais, apparently so as to avoid shaking Eshkol's hand. That seems to also have been the reason that he refused to accept the Israel Prize he had been awarded, at a ceremony that evening. Eshkol died a few months later, while Ben-Gurion was vacationing at the Tiberias hot springs. He refused to leave the resort to attend the funeral.[57]

When he said that he expected to die before Paula, he was presumably giving voice to a conviction that wives should not die before their husbands, any more than mothers should die before their small children. After Paula's death he stopped eating meat, just as he had when his mother died when he was a boy. In January 1973, at Sde Boker, he told Yehuda Erez, who was helping him write his memoirs, that he had wanted another child, but that Paula had not. Yitzhak Navon wrote in his diary that Paula told him: "I never told Ben-Gurion how many abortions I had. Three children are enough for me." On the second anniversary of Paula's death, two great-grandchildren were born to Ben-Gurion, a boy and a girl. He wished to tell Paula the news, his daughter-in-law recalled, but did not know how to reach her. "I think he began to die the minute she did," his grandson said.[58]

---

* About a year after her death, he evoked her name while seeking to persuade Begin to join his fight against Eshkol. "My Paula admired you, for some reason," he wrote to Begin. He did not deny that he disagreed with Begin about many things. Still, "on the individual level, I never had a personal grudge against you," he maintained, "and the better I have come to know you in recent years, the more I have come to admire you, and my Paula was very happy about that." (Ben-Gurion to Menachem Begin, Feb. 6, 1969, BGA.)

ANOTHER KIND OF JEW

"A HORRIBLE THING HAS HAPPENED"

On a summer Saturday in 1958, Ben-Gurion received a visitor from America. The guest professed that he was an atheist, and added that his wife was not Jewish. Their daughter adopted her mother's non-Jewish identity, but he had had his son circumcised. Ben-Gurion asked him why circumcision, if he was an atheist. "I don't know. I want him to be a Jew. There's something irrational about it," replied the guest, Cyrus Leo Sulzberger II of *The New York Times*. "What is Judaism?" Ben-Gurion asked him. Sulzberger said that he didn't know. The next day, Ben-Gurion told the Cabinet about the conversation. That same day the Cabinet addressed the question: Who is a Jew?[1]

He was one of those world leaders who believed that they could change the course of their people's history. His ideological resolve was unbending, his imagination unbounded. Both told him that everything was possible, and nearly every price seemed reasonable. It was the foundation of his strength as a leader—people believed in him because he believed in himself. His colleagues in the leadership thus allowed him to make some decisions on his own. His values and worldview were more like those of a British and American liberal than of the socialist he claimed to be, or the totalitarian that his enemies accused him of being.

During the thirty years that preceded the founding of Israel, he played a decisive role in moving the Zionist project forward and in establishing the political, military, social, economic, and cultural infrastructures that made it possible to establish a Jewish state as soon as the British left Palestine. His success was not complete, nor his power absolute, but during its first fifteen years, Israel grew stronger and, under his leadership, laid the foundations for its further progress after he left the scene.

He was much less influential over the Jewish people as a whole. The Zionist movement had always failed to persuade most of the world's Jews that it was right—that was its greatest failure. It proved helpless against Hitler and Stalin; that was its greatest tragedy. The Zionists were able to save only a small fraction of the Jews persecuted by the Nazis, and until many years after Ben-Gurion's time failed to persuade the Soviet Union to allow its Jews to settle in Israel. The war for Palestine put an end to the communal life of most of the Islamic world's Jews; most of them ended up in Israel. That was the longest-lasting imprint Ben-Gurion left on world Jewish history.

Both his admirers and his rivals agreed that he was his generation's most singular man. But, paradoxically, his uniqueness was almost a norm for many members of his generation. As Jews, they were anomalous in their non-Jewish surroundings; as Zionists, they were anomalous among Jews; as Israelis, they were anomalous in their Arab surroundings; as supporters of the labor movement, they were anomalous in Israel.

Ben-Gurion could conduct a philosophical debate with an atomic physicist on whether the cosmos is a mind, but he left some of the fundamental questions of Israeli existence unanswered.[2] The man who posed these questions with the utmost clarity was Shmuel Fox. Could the Jewish nation be reborn in its ancestral land without incurring the curse of having to live by the sword? What was the connection between Israel and the Jews of the rest of the world? And what was secular Judaism? Fox intimated that he might have settled in Israel had he had answers to these questions. Ben-Gurion chose to live there even though he thought that the country might well live from war to war for generations to come; he wanted to believe that he was a "secular Jew" even though he was unable to define what exactly it was that made a person a Jew. He also had a hard time defining who was a Zionist.[3]

❖

The British high commissioner Arthur Wauchope once asked him what the Jews were: A religion? A race? The British used the term "race" in the sense of both ethnic group and nation, which made the question even more complicated. "I said, number one, recognizing themselves as such," Ben-Gurion wrote, summing up his reply. "Number two, recognition by others, that is the refusal of the gentiles to recognize the Jews as English, French, German, etc."[4] He tried to tiptoe around the question as if it were a minefield. "A Jew is a Jew," he once pronounced at another opportunity. "I am a Jew and nothing else. It's enough to be a Jew." It was a problem that threatened political coexistence between secular and religious Jews.

Since Israel was defined as a Jewish state, it required a law laying out who was and who was not a Jew, among other reasons to determine who had a right to become an Israeli citizen. During the mid-1950s, there was a rise in the number of Eastern European immigrants who arrived in Israel with non-Jewish spouses, women in most cases. Ben-Gurion demanded that they be accepted as Israelis, "even if the woman is a German," he said. "Not every German is necessarily a Nazi."[5] They generally received Israeli citizenship under the terms of the Law of Return, which provided that every Jew, with minor exceptions, could become a citizen. According to Ben-Gurion, the law granted Jews a right that had always been "intrinsic to them" because they were originally from Palestine. That right had preceded the establishment of Israel and was constitutive of the state, he said. It was in this spirit that he fought for the law's poetic name.[6] The question was how to register the children of such mixed couples. The Interior Ministry classified the children according to their mother's religion, in accordance with Jewish religious law. In the winter of 1957, the issue came to a head in the case of Aharon Steinberg, a five-year-old boy whose parents lived in an immigrant camp not far from Pardes Hannah.

The father was a Holocaust survivor; his first wife and the three children he had had with her were murdered in Poland. He married again, this time a non-Jewish woman. They had two children. Aharon died a short time after his family arrived in Israel. Because he was the son of a Christian woman, and had not been circumcised, the parents' request to bury him in a Jewish cemetery was rejected by the Jewish religious authorities. But the Christian authorities refused to bury him in a Christian cemetery because his father was Jewish. The bereft parents bore their son's body to the local municipality building. A local rabbi ordered that the boy be buried outside the fence of the town cemetery, in an open field. The father was not permitted to say the traditional kaddish prayer. The story set off a public uproar. "A horrible thing has happened," Ben-Gurion told the Cabinet. "It is no wonder that it became a sensation. It is a stain not just on Israel but on Judaism as well. We have always spoken against anti-Semitism, against discrimination, and against racism." The debate over registration thus took on the dimensions of a national identity crisis.[7]

In March 1958, Minister of the Interior Israel Bar-Yehuda, of Ahdut Ha'avodah, ruled that any person who in good faith declared himself to be a Jew would be registered as a Jew, unless he could be proved not to be. The directive did not accord with Jewish religious law. The two religious Cabinet members resigned. The government did not fall as a result, but Ben-Gurion wanted them back in. At first he tried to pretend that the dispute was merely an administrative matter, and as such he focused on finding a formulation to permit registration in a way that would skirt the issue of the essence of Jewish identity. When that failed, he suggested that parents who declared in good faith that they were Jews would also be required to affirm that they did not adhere to a different religion, and to state that their sons were circumcised. The question remained open, not just because it did not require any external evidence of Judaism for girls, but also because the religious establishment's ritual circumcisers would most likely refuse to perform the operation simply on the basis of a parental declaration. Ben-Gurion proposed that the Cabinet solve this problem by instituting "national circumcision," which would be performed by doctors. The ministers held a lengthy debate over the significance of this surgical intervention; all of them were men, as Golda Meir was not present at the meeting. Ben-Gurion insisted circumcision be included in the definition of a child's Judaism with almost religious fervor. "This has been a sort of clear mark of Judaism for many generations," he declared. "I don't know if it began in the time of Abraham or not. I wasn't alive at that time. I don't know if the story told in Genesis is a legend, myth, or historical truth. I tend to think that it is historical, but for thousands of years it has been a clear mark among the Jews." He warned that if the State of Israel set it aside, the split within the Jewish people would grow deeper.

Ben-Gurion did not demand mandatory circumcision for boys of veteran Israelis. Uncircumcised boys of secular Jewish parents would still be counted as Jews. Cases of this sort were extremely rare in Israel, but Ben-Gurion fought for the principle.

"A Jew can be an unbeliever but still be a Jew," he maintained. He noted that other religions also practiced circumcision.[8]

The principal question remained unanswered, and the major goal continued to be political—to restrict the power of the official rabbinate. As part of this, Ben-Gurion sought not only to institute "national circumcision" but also to rule on the status of communities whose membership in the Jewish people was controversial—he insisted that the Karaites and Samaritans, two groups that split away from the main body of Judaism in ancient times, be accepted as Jews. While he always claimed not to believe in race theory, he said that "a Cushite woman can't be said to be Jewish"—referring to the woman whom Moses married according to the book of Numbers. Traditionally, the term "Cushite" was understood to mean "dark-skinned," and in the modern Hebrew of the time it was the equivalent of "Negro." But ten years later, he accepted the Jewish status of the Falashas, as the Jews of Ethiopia were called then. He claimed that he had not worked to enable them to immigrate to Israel because he did not know if they wished to do so.[9] Here, too, he seems to have operated as a politician facing off against a religious establishment that still refused to accept this group as Jewish. It was also as a politician that he had the Cabinet resolve to ask several dozen "wise Jews" to weigh in on the riddle of Jewish identity.

The question was put to fifty-one rabbis, philosophers, writers, and scholars, all of them men. Most lived in the United States or Europe. They were ostensibly asked only for their advice on the registration issue, but in fact they were asked to define who is a Jew. It may have been the only time in history that a government asked citizens of other countries to help it demarcate its own identity. The replies offered nothing new and did not provide a solution; ultimately, the initiative was no more than a curiosity.[10] This poll of "wise Jews" also grew out of Ben-Gurion's difficulty in coping with the question of marriages between Jews and non-Jews. He believed that life in Israel ensured that the children of such intermarriages would live as Jews, whereas the children of intermarriages living elsewhere would grow distant from Jewish tradition. He took a great interest in the fate of the thousands of Jewish children who had been saved from death during the Holocaust when Christian families and convents provided them with shelter. He saw them as a national asset. He warned against allowing them to be educated as Christians, and demanded that they be returned to their parents or placed in public institutions in Palestine.[11] But he opposed intermarriage in principle. "I think that it is not a good phenomenon," he said. "Not good, first, for the marriage itself. It causes a lot of complications. But there are exceptions."[12] On this point, he had trouble separating his role as a national leader from his own son's story.

"ENHANCE THE STOCK"

During the last week of January 1946, Amos Ben-Gurion telephoned his father to tell him that he had fallen in love and had decided to get married. He had already written to his mother. He was serving as an officer in the British army at the time. Two months previously, he had fallen ill and was hospitalized at a military hospital in Liverpool. His parents opposed the marriage. Ben-Gurion rushed to England to explain to him "the extent to which this is not desirable," principally for him and his future. The father was not optimistic. "I am not certain that I will manage to get him out of the mess he has gotten himself into," he wrote to Paula. The problem was that Mary Callow was not Jewish. She came from an Anglican family living on the Isle of Man in the Irish Sea. She was close to completing her nursing studies and had met Amos in the hospital. Their decision to marry certainly could make living in Palestine problematic for them, but it was even more of a problem for Amos's father, then chairman of the Jewish Agency Executive.[13]

Ben-Gurion's attitude toward marriages between Jews and non-Jews was fairly conservative. It was a phenomenon he had first encountered in child-hood. An uncle of Rachel Nelkin, the first girl he had loved, had married a non-Jewish woman and converted to Christianity. Shlomo Zemach later re-called that when the uncle, who lived in the Polish quarter of Płońsk, passed through the Jewish quarter, children would jeer him by shouting "Nel-kin the a-pos-tate." Sometimes he would need to call in the police to escape them. Ezra the scribe, the biblical figure whose name Ben-Gurion and his friends had chosen for their first organization, had commanded: "Now then, do not give your daughters in marriage to their sons or let their daughters marry your sons" (Ezra 9:12, 10:3). Ben-Gurion had been about eighteen years old when he read in a newspaper that Max Nordau, one of the leaders of the Zionist movement, was married to a non-Jewish woman. He was so upset by the news that he immediately wrote to his friend Shmuel Fuchs. Nordau had been mentioned as a possible successor to Herzl as president of the Zionist Organization. In a newspaper interview he said that his family life was liable to expose him to libels and slanders.

Ben-Gurion later told of the first time he had encountered an intermarried couple at Sejera. There was a Jewish teacher there who had married a non-Jewish woman. In 1936, Ben-Gurion had been told by Rabbi Yehuda Maimon, a prominent religious Zionist leader, that among the refugees arriving from Ger-many were at least a thousand gentile women. "I said that we will not do as the Nazis did," Ben-Gurion wrote. He asked Rabbi Maimon if he would not allot an immigration certificate to a German Zionist with a Christian wife. Maimon said he would do so, but that if he had only a single certificate to give, he would give preference to a Zionist without a Christian wife. Ben-Gurion recorded his answer without comment. Three years later, he rejected marriages between Jewish women and Arab men. "I am very much in favor not only of reaching an agreement, but also closer relations, contacts, and cooperation. But I am not now prepared for my daughter to marry an Arab, and not for religious reasons. I am not religious. And not for racial reasons, but because as I see it an Arab is still not on the human level that I would want for a man who marries a Jewish woman." In 1966 he asked his close associate Avraham Wolfensohn what he would say if his daughter were to tell him that she wanted to marry a non-Jew. Wolfensohn replied that he would not oppose it. Ben-Gurion asked: "Even if she were to fall in love with a Negro?" Wolfensohn said he would not oppose a marriage "to any man she falls in love with—I am opposed to racism." Ben-Gurion's reply was: "It's not that simple."[14]

That was why, partly because of his concept of Jewish identity, and partly because of the "libels and slanders" Nordau had cited, Ben-Gurion tried to persuade his son to leave his beloved. He referred to his meeting with Amos as a "hearing," as if it were a party caucus rather than a heart-to-heart conversation between father and son. "It would be useless, nor is there any reason, to get angry or reprimand him," he wrote to Paula. "Force and shouting won't change anything." He hoped that all was not yet lost, but didn't really believe that. "I think that the matter is not all that serious yet, although I am not certain that it is not serious," he wrote, composing one of those convoluted sentences that often served him in times of crisis. He tried to solve the problem with "friendly treatment, without any compulsion or duress," he wrote. He had not yet met Mary herself. He failed utterly.

He was late for the wedding—Amos and Mary were waiting for him on the track at the Liverpool railway station. They had already wed. "Mary made a good impression on me," Ben-Gurion reported to Paula cautiously. According to Amos, his father fell in love with Mary at first glance, and even whispered in his ear: "It's good, it's good, it'll enhance the stock." Ben-Gurion's report to Paula offered no physical description of their daughter-in-law. "She is an intelligent and strong-willed girl," he wrote. "She knows and understands what awaits here. She loves Amos profoundly and is ready for everything. She is concerned that her parents will not under any circumstance grant their consent to what she has done. And perhaps they will not want to speak with her. But her desire is to follow Amos like Ruth did in her time, to leave everything and become a Jewish woman in every respect." To stress her good influence on their son, he added: "Amos has stopped smoking. He promised Mary and me that he would not smoke anymore. He has also become more frugal."[15]

While he was still hospitalized, Amos was visited by Liverpool's chief rabbi, Isser Yehuda Unterman. Ben-Gurion sent him an emotional thank-you letter. "I will never forget this act of kindness," he wrote.[16] Following the marriage, Ben-Gurion asked Unterman to convert Mary, apparently hoping for a rapid process. The rabbi replied "with sorrow and offense," as he wrote in a letter that rebuked Ben-Gurion in a way not many others ever had. He was well acquainted with the intermarriage problem, Rabbi Unterman wrote, and he also knew Amos's story quite well. He had twice invited Amos to his home, once orally and once in writing. If he had come, he would almost certainly have spoken to Amos about his love for Mary when "it was still not too late." He speculated: "It is possible that something of what I said might have gotten to his heart, and at least he would not have taken such a hasty and impetuous step." He noted that he had, with God's help, succeeded in preventing a few other young men from "falling in the trap of a foreign woman," but Amos had not come. Unterman hinted that, as the leader of the Jewish people in Palestine, Ben-Gurion might bear some of the responsibility not only for his son's behavior but for that of Amos's entire generation: "How wonderful it is that we 'extremists' seek the company of young people and our hearts are full of fondness for them, to the point that we disregard some transgressions and sins; and they, the 'tolerant ones,' who preach open-mindedness, keep their distance from us. It is unfortunate." To the point, he instructed Ben-Gurion that a proper conversion could take years; he proposed finding Mary an appropriate teacher.

Ben-Gurion wrote to Mary that he was receiving a steady stream of congratulations on their marriage, and assured her that she would be warmly welcomed in Palestine. He promised to help her and indicated that he had three reasons to do so: "You, Amos, and baby." She was in the early weeks of pregnancy; Ben-Gurion hoped to arrange for her conversion prior to her arrival in Palestine and the birth of his grandchild. As luck would have it, a Reform rabbi from New York, Joachim Prinz, happened to be in London; he and Ben-Gurion were longtime acquaintances. Ben-Gurion invited him to his office and, according to Prinz, showed him telegrams from Paula in which she demanded a conversion. Amos should not dare return home with a non-Jewish wife who had not yet converted, she wrote, according to Prinz.

He promised to make it easy for Mary, but, he related, she did not make it easy for him. She said that it was her intention to live in Amos's country and to be part of his nation. She declared that she did not believe in the central tenets of Christianity, but refused to deny that, while living with her parents, she attended church. She also categorically rejected Rabbi Prinz's suggestion that she change her name to Miriam. Prinz convinced himself that she would not remain in Palestine, and gave her a conversion certificate. But, as he was a

Reform rabbi, the rabbinate in Palestine refused to recognize her as a Jew. Rabbi Prinz occasionally met Paula in later years, and wrote that she told him that she also did not consider her daughter-in-law a real Jew. Mary remained in Israel, and many years later underwent an Orthodox conversion.[17]

"I BELIEVE IN GOD"

Ben-Gurion worked on Yom Kippur and ate pork, but reference to the latter was removed from the collection of his letters to Paula that was published after her death.[18] That sort of partial and rather indeterminate "secularism" was practiced by many Jews, with individual differences. Berl Katznelson did not eat pork, but once, while in London, went to visit Karl Marx's grave on Yom Kippur. Yitzhak Navon attended synagogue on Yom Kippur, but spent the rest of the day listening to Radio Damascus, he wrote in his diary.[19] Ben-Gurion's attitude toward Judaism remained indefinite throughout his life, just as it had been from the day he arrived in Palestine. He was only rarely seen in a synagogue, and when he went, it was generally when he was overseas. He claimed that the first time he went to a synagogue service in Israel was on the day of the Knesset's inaugural session. He made a point of saying that he did not pray there. "I hope that your God will forgive me that transgression," he replied to a citizen who had written to ask him about the incident.[20] He sought the roots of his identity in the Hebrew Bible, to which his Zionism was also closely tied. "The endurance of the Jewish people," he once wrote, "is rooted in these two things: the State of Israel and the Book of Books."[21] He sometimes compared Zionism to religion, speaking of the "Zionist faith," and once even referred to the "Zionist commandments." He saw Zionism as "the light secreted in the soul" of the Jewish people.[22] But he did not leave it at that. During one of those innumerable debates over religion's place in Israeli public life, he offered a monologue that opened with what was almost a supplication: "I cannot say that the Torah came from heaven. The Torah was written by human beings. But its value is no less for having been written by humans. On the contrary, if it came from heaven, what portion does the Jewish people have in it? The greatness of the Jewish people is that it wrote this Torah . . . Some believe that the Torah came from heaven, but I do not believe that. I am another kind of Jew."[23]

That was a precise definition of how he felt, and even more so of what he hoped for. He wanted to be "another kind of Jew." But the fact that he did not believe that a scion of the Jewish nation had a right to affiliate with a different religion showed that he did not believe in an entirely secular form of Judaism. The same could be said of his opposition to intermarriage and his insistence on male circumcision. In a forlorn attempt to grapple with this contradiction, he once said, referring to the classic code of Jewish law, "The *Shulchan Aruch* is a Jewish value for me, but we are not obligated to live our daily lives according to its strictures."[24] And there was also God.

Ben-Gurion was no atheist—he never denied God's existence. But, influenced by Baruch Spinoza, he did not see God as a super-entity outside nature. His inclination was to identify God with Nature, including human existence. He believed that the Jewish people chose God before God chose the Jews. From the time when he first tried to put this idea into words, when he was eighteen, he had found proof of it in the text of the book of Joshua, "You chose God for yourselves" (Joshua 24:22), as well as in Deuteronomy 26:17–18. This thesis was important to him, because a nation that chooses its God is one that shapes its own historical destiny, just as Zionism advocated.

Spinoza was, as he saw it, "the greatest Jewish philosopher since the canonization of the Bible" until Albert Einstein. He also regarded Spinoza as the "first Zionist" of the last three hundred years. In one of the early articles he wrote after his retreat to Sde Boker, he demanded that Spinoza's works be translated into modern Hebrew, so as to rectify the injustice that the Jewish establishment had done him when it banned him and his works in perpetuity.[25] His article cited a theory that Spinoza's ideas derived from Buddhism; he was inclined to agree. But Buddhism seems to have fascinated him chiefly because he saw it as an ethical teaching devoid of God, maintaining that humankind could craft its own moral values and shape its own fate. "In my opinion, Judaism is a historical experience," he wrote in his diary, but he had trouble elucidating for himself what he meant by that. "God is a cosmic, universal, eternal being. It is true that the Bible is full of faith in the Creator, and there can be no doubt that Moses, Jeremiah, and the other prophets heard God's voice, but God did not speak to them. The whole story of the burning bush and Mount Sinai are episodes in Moses's history, not the history of God."[26]

His struggles with the nature of faith grew more profound as he aged, when he increasingly came to believe in the existence of a God of some sort, even if not the God of Jewish faith. "The Jewish faith is part of Judaism, but Judaism is not part of the Jewish faith," he wrote, "because Jewish faith has changed through different generations."[27] At the end of 1967, he wrote: "I believe in God, but on the matter of the 613 commandments there are different opinions . . . so the matter is not at all simple."[28] A year later, a visitor asked him if he believed in God. "The question is what you think when you say that word," he responded. "Most Jews see it as an old man with a big beard sitting on his throne. And he speaks . . . I do not believe that God spoke . . . but I also don't believe that there are only physical forces in the world. I cannot presume—and I asked one of the great men of science—that the brain is just a physical process." He was referring to Niels Bohr, a Danish physicist and Nobel Prize laureate of Jewish descent. When Ben-Gurion tried to persuade him that "the cosmos thinks," Bohr responded that there were only physical processes in the universe. "How, by a physical process, could Newton's brain arrive at such great innovations?" Ben-Gurion wondered. "Or Einstein's theory, or any other scientific discovery? There is a thing called mind, no matter what it's called, there is something higher than physical processes, in the entire universe."

He told of a visit to Uppsala, Sweden: "They showed me a machine that measures millionths of a second," he recalled. "I know that, theoretically, it is possible to divide a second not only into millionths but also into billionths and so on without end, but how do they do it?" The answer sounded simple: "They told me that the machine rotates very fast and that when I want to know, I stop it and then I know. And really, by this logic, that is a millionth of a second." He knew that he walked eighty paces a minute, he added, "but a second is a short time, and it can be divided by a million?!" He could not imagine that there was not some higher power, or "ruler" of all this, he asserted, "a thing we call mind, but the name is not what determines it and it is not just a physical process. That's that!"[29] In 1970 he enumerated a number of principles that he saw as "the eternal essence of Judaism." Among them were "Love your neighbor as yourself," and "Nation shall not lift up sword against nation." At the top of the list he wrote: "The belief in one God who creates everything."[30] He did not concede his desire to be "another kind of Jew," but he admitted that he could not be a wholly secular Jew, either.

His difficulty in defining his Judaism also made it hard for him to determine what relations ought to prevail between Israel and Jews who remained outside the country. His grandson Alon, whom Ben-Gurion had once referred to as half-Jewish and half-British, added a modicum of Zionist irony to this—he went to live in New York and for many years managed the Waldorf Astoria hotel.[31]

"SINGING 'HATIKVAH' IN CLEVELAND"

During his meeting with John Kennedy in 1961, the president pulled Ben-Gurion into a corner and, far from earshot of the other people in the room, told him: "You know, I was elected by the Jews of New York. I will do something for you." He meant something in the area of aid for Israel. Ben-Gurion was shocked. "I'm a foreigner; I represent a small state. I didn't come to him as a Jew, as a voter." He was doubly insulted, first as prime minister of Israel and second in the name of American Jewry.[32] Of course, he had known since World War I that that was how things worked. That was why he had then asked Ben-Zvi, who was in Washington during the war, if he had met "Woodrow," meaning President Wilson. He took for granted that the road to realizing the Zionist program ran through the White House, and that American Jews should provide help along that part of the road.

But over the years he at times wrestled with trying to delineate the division of Zionist responsibility between the Jews of the Diaspora and those living in Israel. It was a complicated and sensitive subject, replete with internal contradictions, highly charged with ideological emotions that metamorphosed over the years. Ben-Gurion and his colleagues in the Zionist leadership never tired of holding forth on the issue in books, articles, and speeches. It was not just a philosophical question; it preoccupied Israelis constantly.

❖

In the summer of 1962, Israel was roiled by the cases of two Jews. One was a ten-year-old boy, born in the Soviet Union, named Yossele Schumacher. The second was Robert Soblen, a sixty-year-old psychiatrist who had been convicted in the United States of spying for the Soviet Union. He had been sentenced to life in prison but had been released on bail while his appeal was being heard. Yossele was smuggled out of Israel to New York; Soblen fled to Israel.

The boy fell victim to a family dispute over his schooling. His grandfather wanted him to receive a Haredi religious education. At one point, members of the Haredi extremist Neturei Karta sect intervened and spirited him out of Israel, dressed as a girl. "In my opinion there has not been such a scandal in Israel since it rose again," Ben-Gurion said. He put the Mossad on the case. The Mossad chief, Isser Harel, showed the Cabinet broadsides and letters that Neturei Karta had written, in Yiddish, opposing Zionism. He charged them, among other things, with sabotaging the immigration of Jewish children from Morocco. The scandal set off an emotional debate over values that played on the bare nerves of Israeli "secular" identity. Yossele was seen as "the child of us all." Getting him back was portrayed as a national challenge of unparalleled importance. Everyone was asking "Where's Yossele?"

Ben-Gurion informed the Cabinet on July 1, 1962, that Yossele had been found in New York. He added that removing the boy from the United States and bringing him back to Israel required the consent of American immigration authorities. Later in his statement he said, as if it were a different subject, "At the request of the interior minister, I hereby announce that at 7:30 this morning, Dr. Soblen was flown to England . . . a physician was secretly sent with him, but he does not know that." Another secret that Soblen presumably did not know was one that Ben-Gurion kept from his Cabinet as well— one of the passengers on the flight from Tel Aviv to London was an American secret agent who had arrived specially from the United States to accompany Soblen on his flight back to the USA.

The fact that Soblen had been expelled from Israel on the same morning that Ben-Gurion told the Cabinet about finding Yossele Schumacher resulted from a diplomatic deal. Harel had phoned the Israeli ambassador in Washington to demand that he call Attorney General Robert Kennedy to make the appropriate arrangements for Yossele's return. Soblen, it seems, was deported precipitously, without even being given an opportunity to appeal, in response to an American demand, and in order to expedite the arrangements for Yossele's return. Ben-Gurion told the Knesset that he assumed personal responsibility for Soblen's deportation, despite the fact that he was Jewish.

He displayed considerable anger at a Cabinet meeting. "I think it is a disgrace to our country," he said. "There is a new Jewish hero, Dr. Soblen. A con man and swindler."[33] Soblen remained in London for a time. When the British authorities decided to extradite him to the United States, he took poison and died.

He was not the first Jewish criminal to seek refuge in Israel. The law said that they could be expelled, but in each case their stories revealed internal contradictions that challenged Israel's ideological commitment to serve as a sanctuary for persecuted Jews.[34] Ben-Gurion continued to see all the world's Jews as a single nation, and was convinced that the return to Zion manifested the interests of all Jews. This led him to divide the Jewish people into four categories: Zionists, sympathizers, the indifferent, and enemies. Most Jews were sympathizers or indifferent. There are few Zionists in the world, he remarked. He saw this principally as a Jewish, not a Zionist, failure. "All the millions of Jews of past generations who have prayed and longed and hoped and wished and ached and yearned to the death for a return to Zion did not bring a single Jew to the land," he said. "Has the Jewish nation returned to its land? Only a handful, individuals, a small number."[35]

His fundamental assumption was that the right place for every Jew to be was in Israel, and that their duty as Zionists was to settle there. In 1950 he declared that "the Arabs don't need to live here, just as an American Jew shouldn't live in America."[36] But the Zionist enterprise was very much dependent on the philanthropy and support of Jews who did not want to live in Israel. Ben-Gurion himself had experienced that dependency, during his long period of relying on his father. Many Jews feared that Zionism would jeopardize their standing as the citizens of their own countries, as Ben-Gurion very well knew. "The aspiration for Israel to be the world center of the Jewish people puts the rights of the Jews in the Diaspora at risk," he said. Many other Polish Jews regarded themselves as Polish patriots and never thought of leaving their country. So did Jews in Germany and other countries.[37]

The more secure his position as a local leader in Palestine became, the more Ben-Gurion was inclined to stress the duty of Jews overseas to assist in the realization of the Zionist project, even while remaining in their own countries. Less than a year after the Balfour Declaration, he proposed establishing a world Jewish congress with "governing power" recognized in international law; it would have the authority to levy taxes from the Jews of the world, with the money going to Palestine. In 1947 he returned to an old idea of his, describing the world's Jews as "hostages." They faced the danger of revenge attacks if Israel did not treat its Arab minority with "absolute justice."[38]

He knew that without the influence of American Jewry, including their money and their votes, Zionism would never achieve its goals. And he realized that many American Jews were more useful to Zionism there than in their historic homeland. He thus learned to flatter donors who helped his party; he used a lot of exaggeration, as he had learned to do in America. "I think that the participation of the American labor movement is actually more important than the diplomatic victory of the Balfour Declaration," he once wrote to an acquaintance in New York.[39]

The Zionist enterprise in Palestine thus had an interest in having Jews remain in other countries, and of wielding power and influence there. Ben-Gurion the ideologue did not want to admit this. "A Jewish Cabinet minister in England, or a Jewish viceroy in India, does nothing at all to solve the Jewish question," he wrote.[40] But, speaking as a "Zionist preacher" who sought to enlist maximal support, he once declared that Zionism was also bound to fight to ensure equal rights for the Jews of Poland, Russia, and "every other country." Political and economic rights were no less important than national rights, he said.[41] He sometimes maintained that the establishment of a Jewish state was not an end in and of itself, but rather only a stage in the Jewish people's redemption. "The state is not for the Jews of Palestine alone, nor can the Jews of Palestine alone establish and maintain it," he said. "The state is for the Jewish people and only if we mobilize the full capabilities of the nation will it come into being." That was at the beginning of 1948. "We would not prevail without the help of the Jewish people," he said; Golda Meir would later say the same. Just as Jewish supporters of Israel funded a large part of the War of Independence, in many cases in violation of American law, the nuclear reactor in Dimona would also be funded in part from contributions made by a select group of individual Jews around the world.[42]

This dependence was vital but frustrating, and sometimes humiliating. Ben-Gurion appreciated the solidarity he discovered among America's Jews, but sometimes he could not restrain himself, as when one philanthropist regaled him with a description of his vacation home not far from Chicago, which he had named Palestine. "And why don't you have a summer house in Tel Aviv and call it Chicago?" Ben-Gurion suggested.*[43]

Jacob Blaustein, the oil magnate and president of the American Jewish Committee, managed to obtain a written commitment from Ben-Gurion stating that Israel would not interfere with the lives of America's Jews and would not try to ensnare them with dual loyalties. Here, too, Ben-Gurion acknowledged the legitimacy of Jewish life outside Israel, in contradiction of the principles of Zionism.[44] But he also refused to recognize Diaspora Jews as Zionists and took pride in the fact that he had, many years before, put the word "Zionists" inside quotation marks when referring to Zionist activists around the world. Zionism in Palestine was, in his view, much more than Zionism elsewhere. "Singing 'Hatikvah' in Cleveland is a Zionist act," he said. "To fight and build the Negev—that's also a Zionist act, but is there not a difference between them?" Only a small number of American Jews agreed with him. Rose Halprin, the president of Hadassah, called his position childish.[45]

He kept abreast of the situation of the world's Jews, noting that the influence they wielded in their home countries could also be problematic. As part of this, he analyzed, with trepidation, the standing of America's Jews. There was no contradiction between being a Jew and being a citizen of the United States, he noted, and that was why Zionism could not succeed.[46] Every manifestation of anti-Semitism could, in contrast, be a "boost," as he liked to say. That was a fundamental idea of Herzl's: "The anti-Semites will be our most steadfast friends," he wrote. "The anti-Semitic countries will be our allies."[47] The Haavara Agreement between the Zionist movement and the Nazis, as well as the agreements to evacuate Jews from Eastern Europe and the Islamic countries after the Holocaust, were indicators of this thesis.

When the reparations negotiations with Germany ensued, it was of great ideological and political importance to Israel that it be recognized as the

---

* As prime minister, Ben-Gurion once returned a check in the sum of $10 that an American Jew sent him. "We cannot allow ourselves to be the objects of charity," he told the Cabinet. At the beginning of 1967, he traveled to the United States to raise money for Midreshet Sde Boker, an educational and research institution at the kibbutz. (Ben-Gurion to the Cabinet, June 1, 1952, ISA; Ben-Gurion to *Ha'aretz*, Jan. 23, 1967, BGA.)

representative of all the Holocaust's victims. This same principle once engendered a proposal to grant Israeli citizenship to each of the six million Jews who perished at the hands of the Nazis. Ben-Gurion expressed reservations but did not reject the idea out of hand. He feared that the Germans would see it as blackmail. It turned out that coordination with Jewish organizations outside Israel was a better way to get good results in the negotiations with the Germans.[48]

"COMING HOME"

Many of those who made their lives in Israel, whether they came by choice or ended up there as refugees, felt that they had had a better life in "Exile." Their difficult integration into Israeli society impelled Ben-Gurion to promote Israeli identity, especially among young people. It was one of the tasks he assigned to the army. The Jews of Israel, he maintained, are not "just a collection of Jews from the Diaspora," as he put it. "It is impossible not to see that what we have here is a Jewish nation, bearing the characteristics of an independent people." This approach also threatened a crisis with American Jewry.*

The need to persuade themselves that life in Israel was "fuller" than life elsewhere produced, among many Israelis, a tendency to look down on Diaspora Jews who had chosen to remain in their countries. Ben-Gurion shared this inclination. He on occasion voiced scorn for the Jews of the rest of the world, and sometimes he was ashamed of them. "What value do tailors and shoemakers have there?" he once asked Jewish labor associations in America. The Histadrut in Palestine, on the other hand, was working to create a more healthy social structure for the Jewish people, he maintained.[49]

"The most precious thing that the Zionist movement produced is not new ideas but a new human type," he said at Mapai's founding congress.[50]

---

* When Richard Crossman served as a member of the Anglo-American Committee that laid the groundwork for the UN partition decision, he came to the conclusion that the Jews of Palestine were crystallizing into a nation distinct from the Jews of the Diaspora, in part because of their willingness to fight for their independence, just as the Americans became a nation thanks to the blood they shed in their War of Independence. (Crossman 1946, p. 203.)

He himself was not a good example of the "new Jew" that Zionism took pride in creating in Palestine. He remained essentially a Polish Jew, as he said, with his feet planted firmly in a social, political, and mental establishment created in Eastern Europe. He never entirely shed what the poet Shaul Tchernikovsky had called "the imprint of his native landscape." Thick cords of memory and sentiment connected him to the days of his youth, and he was sometimes overcome by longing, as when he went to see *The Dybbuk* in Moscow. In 1950, after attending a production of *Tevye the Dairyman* in Tel Aviv, he wrote to the lead actor, Yehoshua Bertonov, that it had been one of the most profound and stunning events of his life.[51]

After settling in Palestine, he did all he could to maintain contact with the town of his birth, and his need to do so grew over the years. When his travels took him to Poland, he usually made a visit to Płońsk, even after his father left the town. When he told his father that he intended to visit, he said that he was "coming home."[52] Płońsk was his Jerusalem. He spoke Yiddish there. He wrote many of his letters to Paula in Yiddish as well. In Palestine he tried to deny his mother tongue, but as he grew older he became reconciled to it. In 1951 he supported doing away with a prohibition on producing plays in Yiddish, and at Cabinet meetings he sometimes peppered his speech with Yiddish expressions. It was the language whose accent could be heard when he spoke Hebrew or English.[53]

The limitations of Israel's ability to absorb all the Jews who needed it, and his inclination to give preference to those who could be useful, provided an even greater challenge to the explicit internal logic of the Zionist vision.

❖

At the beginning of the 1930s, Ben-Gurion was already well aware of the imperfections and internal contradictions of the ideology he had adopted in his youth. "All my life, for as long as I remember, I have been a Zionist," he said in 1940. "But I always struggle, I always see that in everything I do, in everything I think, I am still not a Zionist one hundred percent."[54] From time to time he felt the need to enhance his Zionist consciousness. "Every Zionist finds himself assailing the Zionist within him," he once said.[55] Late in life he began to say that he was no longer a Zionist. "I do not know the meaning and definition of the term 'Zionism,'" he wrote after the Six-Day War. "Once, in my youth, I thought I knew. Now I have my doubts about whether the word has any meaning at all."[56]

It was his principal weakness: he led a movement that never agreed on its fundamental principles.

"DEATH INTERESTS ME"

His schedule of meetings grew shorter, as did his diary entries.[57] In one of the last interviews he granted, he again told the story of the Arab student who had been happy about Ben-Gurion's expulsion from Palestine during World War I. He did not know what happened to that young man, he said once again. Maybe he had died in the meantime. Whatever the case, "he presented me with today's picture," he said.[58]

His bodyguards at Sde Boker and in Tel Aviv documented his routine. They saw to his meals and laundry and even ironed his shirts. Yehuda Erez noted with astonishment that Ben-Gurion was well dressed and perfectly shaven. He continued to work on his memoirs and to go out for his daily walk. Every few months he went to Jerusalem to visit Shlomo Zemach, who now complained of inactivity, boredom, and a weak heart. Ben-Gurion did not do much to improve his mood. "David was here for close to two hours yesterday," Zemach wrote in October 1968. "He has gained weight, his face has gotten lumpy, and he sat there and talked the whole time and said the same things he said so many times before and the same hyperboles and the same fabrications and his same 'me' with him in the center of all the events and the moving force behind them."

Zemach received the impression that Ben-Gurion enjoyed spending time with him, and when his bodyguard came into the room to remind him that he had to bring the visit to an end, Ben-Gurion "almost scolded him" and stayed put until the bodyguard returned and insisted that they go. Again he hurt his boyhood friend: "Of course, he reminded me of the hard times that my late father endured through a few low years," Zemach related. "Once again he talked about the time he spent at Sejera and his heroic deeds there; again he said that the thing he had wanted most was to be a farmer. He spoke about Yigal Allon and Moshe Dayan and Abba Eban and rounded it all off with Levi Eshkol. He said to me, 'I will go to the Knesset, because I must explain to the nation why I am demanding that Eshkol and the entire government be dismissed. Of course they'll say that I'm crazy, but I need to say what I think. It is my duty to say my word.'" But usually he was affable and pleasant, Zemach wrote, and was also happy to see his wife, Hanke.

Zemach and his wife were then living in a retirement home run by the Association of Israelis of Central European Origin. Ben-Gurion's appearances, with his bodyguards, attracted attention; Zemach always received and parted from him with great respect. When he left, Ben-Gurion said, "I now have another corner in Jerusalem." Zemach sensed that Ben-Gurion was very lonely and was in need of warm friendship. "And since boyhood friendship is forever, let us warm ourselves in its light," Zemach declared. Rachel Beit Halahmi also visited Zemach, and showed him a letter she had received from Ben-Gurion. "I have only two people in the world who are close to me," he wrote to her. "You, Rachel, and Shlomo Zemach." So it was for two and a half years. "This afternoon Ben-Gurion came by and spent an hour," Zemach wrote in December 1971. "His face is pale, his body stiff." He discerned "low spirits" and remarked that "everything goes very slowly."[59]

At about this stage, Yehuda Erez had to set aside his optimism and admit that Ben-Gurion was in decline. Several visitors who came to see him were troubled to find Ben-Gurion forgetful and confused; in some cases he did not recognize them. In February 1973, he was still planning to participate in a ceremony opening a new road in the Negev; everyone waited, but at the last moment his doctor forbade him to leave home.[60] He was under constant medical supervision, but generally not ill, and he felt fine, although pains in his hand made it difficult to write.[61] The newspapers were delivered every day, but his burning desire to keep abreast of events had dwindled; Erez noted that he was reading the issues of three days previously.[62] He spoke about the *Altalena* and Arlosoroff's murder, and finally revealed why he did not trust Yigal Allon: "He grew up with Arabs," Ben-Gurion said.[63]

In August 1973, he was still in Sde Boker; the heat and the stuffiness of his cabin were unbearable. The fan wasn't working. He lay on his bed, holding a jar for the sputum he coughed up. His bodyguards continued to see that he was properly dressed and clean. In coordination with the Defense Ministry, they encouraged his acquaintances to pay visits, to keep him from being lonely. One of his bodyguards, Aharon Tamir, offered Ben-Gurion a warm family atmosphere, inviting him for Friday night dinner at his home, where Ben-Gurion sat on the rug and played with Tamir's baby daughter. It was a great kindness on Tamir's part—during the final years of his life, nothing frightened Ben-Gurion more than the grim debilities of old age that awaited him. He tracked with awe Adenauer's aging process, and once wrote in his diary: "Adenauer is eighty-one years old, and intends to remain in office for another ten years. There is an injection in Germany that was first invented in Russia that invigorates the life of an old man." He told his personal physician, Dr. Chaim Sheba, to look into rumors he had heard of pills that could improve the memory, and sent another doctor to Switzerland for this purpose. "Death interests me," he once told Haim Israeli, the director of the Office of the Minister of Defense. "At my age, I know that I am approaching it." Were he to have the opportunity to live his life again, he said, he would study biology and investigate the human brain. As summer turned to autumn, Erez noticed that Ben-Gurion had stopped working on his memoirs; it was a sign that his end was near. "For eight months before he went, he no longer wanted to live. He had no desire, I remember that," his daughter-in-law Mary recalled. "It was hellish to see and hear Ben-Gurion in that state," Golda Meir said, "but it was for a short time." Two years earlier, he had written to her: "I am sometimes incredulous that I am still alive. Almost all my closest and dearest friends are no longer among the living."[64] One of the last letters he sent was to Miriam Cohen. "I'd like to see you," he wrote. The author Yizhar Smilansky (S. Yizhar) compared him to King Lear. Smilansky did not say which act of the Shakespeare play he was thinking of. Perhaps it was act 3, scene 2, in which Lear refers to himself as "a poor, infirm, weak, and despised old man," or perhaps act 4, scene 6, where Gloucester declares "The King is mad," and then considers: "Better I were distract; so should my thoughts be severed from my griefs, and woes by wrong imaginations lose the knowledge of themselves."*[65]

❖

---

* An old-timer from Płońsk once related that as a boy, Ben-Gurion acted in amateur theater productions at the firehouse, including *King Lear*. (Teveth 1977, pp. 39, 492.)

On October 6, 1973, the armies of Egypt and Syria launched a two-pronged attack on Israel; it was another round in the war that Ben-Gurion had taken into account when he began to act to achieve Jewish independence. More than twenty-two hundred Israeli soldiers were killed; only in the War of Independence did more die. Ben-Gurion spent the war at his home in Tel Aviv; Shimon Peres came by once or twice a day to tell him what was going on. A few days later, Ben-Gurion had a stroke, for which he was treated at Tel Hashomer hospital and then sent home. The hospital sent a doctor to examine him. "Ben-Gurion sat on the edge of the bed," the doctor wrote in his diary. "He stared without moving and the bedsheet was wet." Only men were with him, the doctor noted, apparently meaning his bodyguards. "Devoted, practical men of few words," as he described them. "I looked around, and the house seemed cold to me, lacking any sign of a woman or of gentleness, I didn't even see a tablecloth on the table or flowers, not even artificial ones." He sat facing Ben-Gurion but had trouble establishing contact. "Facing me was an old and weary lion," the doctor wrote. After performing a physical examination, he endeavored to check his patient's cognitive abilities. "What do you think of the war, Ben-Gurion?" he asked. "What war?" Ben-Gurion responded. The doctor was aghast. "I thought at that moment about those people whose flesh perishes, but their place in history remains."[66]

His eighty-seventh birthday was celebrated forlornly; he knew about the war. He signed a letter of condolence to an aide whose son had fallen, writing that this was the most serious and cruelest war so far.[67] One of the wounded was his grandson, Alon. At the end of November, Ben-Gurion suffered another stroke and was hospitalized. Most of the few visitors who were allowed to see him were unable to communicate with him.[68] Moshe Dayan was one of the last to come. "During his final days his mind was foggy," he wrote. "He was unable to speak, his eyes were closed, and his mouth pursed. He looked as if he were deep in thought, but not troubled. On the contrary, his face looked gentle and serene. He left the world calmly, his life slowly ebbing away."[69]

He died on Saturday, December 1, 1973, at close to 10:30 a.m. The Yom Kippur War, which ended five weeks earlier with survival, not victory, left the country deeply traumatized, and with the nebulous feeling that nothing would ever be the same again. Ben-Gurion's death at this moment thus took on symbolic significance; Israel parted not only from a man but from an entire sense of national being. Everyone connected his decision to be buried in the desert with his vision of making the Negev bloom. It is doubtful whether he thought that a national tomb would draw more settlers to the region than the few whom he had managed to inspire to come to the Negev when he was still alive. It seems more likely that what he had in mind was Chaim Weizmann's gravesite in Rehovot. Like Weizmann, he did not want to be buried in the shadow of Herzl, on the mountain bearing his name. Jabotinsky had already been reinterred and Eshkol buried there. Ben-Gurion also instructed that there should be no eulogies at his funeral, just as none were offered for his two friends at Sejera. The result was that the funeral consisted mostly of prayers. In a will he wrote just a few months before his death, he no longer fought to be identified as "another kind of Jew." He did not order any changes in the traditional religious service. At his death he was fairly well-off financially; a short while before, his future heirs began fighting over the inheritance, the house in Tel Aviv in particular. In the end, he left it to the state, to be opened to the public; he also left his papers to the state. In addition, he asked that the cabin at Sde Boker be preserved as it was in his lifetime.[70] He had lived a few years too long, but could have been grateful that he did not live to see Menachem Begin elected prime minister four years later. He probably never imagined that such a thing could happen, just as he never imagined that Begin, or anyone else, would ever sign a peace treaty with Egypt.

Shlomo Zemach died a year later. His quality of life had declined to substandard. He suffered from severe heart disease; by August 1973, he weighed only 117 pounds. "The thirst to write is of inestimable power," he wrote in his diary; they were the last words he wrote. He had last seen Ben-Gurion in December 1971. They each griped to the other about "the spiritual decline in the country." Ben-Gurion said: "If we do not remain decent, we will not remain here." Zemach agreed with him, perhaps for the first time since that day on the Płonka, seventy years before.[71]

NOTES

INTRODUCTION: IN THE FOOTSTEPS OF HISTORY

1. Ben-Gurion, Diary, Jan. 30, 1940, BGA.
2. Ben-Gurion, Diary, Feb. 5, 1940, and Nov. 29, 1940, BGA.
3. Ben-Gurion to Hazaz, July 10, 1968, BGA.
4. Ben-Gurion, Diary, May 2, June 10, July 16, 20, 1953, BGA; Ben-Gurion to Allon, May 11, 1953, BGA; Yehuda Erez, interview transcript, BGA.
5. Ben-Gurion, Diary, Feb. 5, 1940, BGA.
6. *Ma'ariv*, Jan. 6, 1967; Ben-Gurion to Rachel Mishal, Jan. 19, 1967; Ben-Gurion to Alexander Peli, Jan. 26, 1967; Ben-Gurion, Diary, Aug. 1, 1960, BGA.
7. *Davar*, Sept. 28, 1967.
8. Mordechai Ben-Tov, interview transcript, BGA.
9. Ben-Gurion to Shmuel Fuchs, Dec. 18, 1904, in Erez 1971, p. 39.
10. Yitzhak Lamdan 1955. The number of dead is computed according to http://www.izkor.gov.il/.
11. Ben-Gurion, Diary, May 8, 1948, BGA.
12. Whartman 1961.
13. Shachar 2002, p. 523ff.; Feldstein 1998, p. 354ff.
14. Ben-Gurion at the Mapai Council, Jan. 12, 1949, in Rafi Mann 2012, p. 247.
15. Ben-Gurion to the Cabinet, July 15, 1958, ISA.
16. Ben-Gurion at the Zionist Congress, Dec. 10, 1946, in Ben-Gurion 1993a, p. 249.
17. Ben-Gurion, Diary, May 14, 1948, BGA; Ben-Gurion 1969b, 1, p. 106; Cabinet meeting, Oct. 20, 1953, ISA.
18. Moshe Carmel, interview transcript, p. 54, BGA.
19. Ben-Gurion, Diary, March 1, 29, 1948, BGA.
20. Ben-Gurion to the Mapai Central Committee, Sept. 29, 1936, BGA; Ben-Gurion at the Zionist Executive, Feb. 11, 1945, BGA.
21. Ben-Gurion to the Mapai Central Committee, Sept. 29, 1936, BGA.
22. Ratner 1978, pp. 347ff., 382; Yanait, interview transcript, July 17, 1975, p. 13, BGA; Carmel, interview transcript, BGA.
23. Carmel, interview transcript, BGA.
24. Yanait, interview transcript, Jan. 11, 1978, p. 11, BGA.
25. Ben-Gurion with writers, March 27, 1949, BGA.
26. Ben-Gurion, Diary, Dec. 25, 1948, BGA; Ben-Gurion to Halperin, Sept. 21 and Oct. 10, 1948, BGA; Ben-Gurion 1954b; Ever Hadani 1955, p. 162.
27. Ben-Gurion, Diary, Dec. 26, 1953; Ben-Gurion 1954b; E. A. Simon to *Ha'aretz*, Dec. 24, 1953; *Panim el Panim*, Dec. 22, 1954.
28. Ben-Gurion 1958, pp. 92ff., 155ff.
29. Ben-Gurion, Cabinet meeting, July 7, 1957, ISA; Ben-Gurion at an IDF ceremony, April 27, 1955, BGA; Ben-Gurion, Diary, Sept. 18, 1967, BGA.
30. Ben-Gurion, Cabinet meeting, March 29, 1955; Babylonian Talmud, *Megilah* 16a.
31. Ben-Gurion to Moshe Sharett, June 25, 1937, in Ben-Gurion, Diary, June 25, 1937, BGA.
32. Peres and Landau 2011; Shilon 2013; Anita Shapira 2014; Goldstein (in process).

PART I: THE ROAD TO POWER

1. Ben-Gurion interviewed by Yosef Avner, Avraham Kushnir, and Tom Segev, *Nitzotz*, April 28, 1968.

1. THE VOW

1. Ben-Gurion interview with Ya'akov Ashman, Nov. 25, 1963, BGA.
2. Friedman 1994, p. 175ff.; Ben-Gurion 1963a, p. 31; Lavi 1957, p. 59.
3. Bartal and Gutman 2001.
4. Ben-Gurion 1974b, p. 18ff.; N. M. Gelber 1963, p. 24ff.
5. Ben-Gurion 1963a, p. 34; Lavi 1957, p. 15ff.; Ben-Gurion, eulogy for Lavi, July 12, 1964, BGA; Zemach 1983, p. 21; Michelson 1963, p. 125.
6. Zemach 1983, pp. 10, 18; Krieger testimony, Bracha Habas Archive, NL.
7. Habas 1952, p. 16; Memoirs of Avigdor Gruen, p. 9, BGA, subject file 470-1-18; Ben-Gurion, 1974b, pp. 9, 16, 19; Zemach 1983, p. 19; Ben-Gurion 1963a, p. 32.
8. N. M. Gelber 1963, esp. p. 169; Teveth 1977, p. 26.
9. Zemach 1983, pp. 20, 11, 23; Ben-Gurion 1974b, p. 14; Lavi 1957, p. 28.
10. Ben-Gurion, Cabinet meeting, Oct. 20, 1953, ISA.
11. Ben-Gurion 1961; Ben-Gurion at the Anglo-American Commission, March 11, 1946, in Ben-Gurion 2014, p. 939.
12. Ben-Gurion to Haim (last name not identified), Oct. 27, 1953, BGA, p. 31ff.; Philip Cruso, Yehudit Simhoni, Rachel Yanait Ben-Zvi, Geulah Ben-Eliezer, Emmanuel Ben-Eliezer, Yariv Ben-Eliezer, interview transcripts, BGA; Ben-Gurion to Golda Meir, Aug. 28, 1952; Ben-Gurion to Ehud Avriel, Sept. 11, 1952, BGA; Ben-Gurion to Shimon Shetreet, Aug. 2, 1961, BGA; Ben-Gurion to the Knesset, July 2, 1951, in Ben-Gurion 1957, p. 166; see also BGA, Shabtai Teveth collection, concepts, motherhood; Ben-Gurion to the Mapai Central Committee, March 7, 1948, BGA.
13. Ben-Gurion to the Jewish Agency Executive, Nov. 21, 1945, BGA; Teveth 2004, 4, p. 181.
14. Kavshana, interview transcript, BGA; Ben-Gurion to the Knesset, July 2, 1951, in Ben-Gurion 1957, p. 166; Ben-Gurion 1974b, pp. 8–32; Ben-Gurion 1963a, p. 31; on fights with non-Jewish children, see also Gruenbaum 1963, p. 94.
15. Ben-Gurion 1974b, p. 30; Zemach 1983, pp. 11, 16, 20.
16. Ben-Gurion 1974b, p. 31.
17. Ben-Gurion to Shmuel Fuchs, Dec. 14, 1904, in Erez 1971, p. 36; Ben-Gurion to Yitzhak Hildesheimer, Jan. 15, 1960, BGA; Teveth 1999, p. 29.
18. Ben-Gurion interview with Malcolm Stuart, April 1, 1968, BGA; *Nitzotz*, April 28, 1968; Ben-Gurion at the Sejera celebration, Sept. 25, 1962; Ben-Gurion interview with Ya'akov Ashman, Nov. 25, 1963, BGA; Bar-Zohar 1977, p. 26; Ben-Gurion to his wife and children, May 14, 1942, BGA.
19. Goldstein 2016; Laqueur 1972, p. 75ff.; Laskov 1999, 1, p. 393ff.
20. Ben-Gurion 1974b, p. 7.
21. *Hamelitz*, June 18, 1886.
22. Ben-Gurion 1974b, p. 16.
23. *Hamelitz*, May 12, 1898.
24. Zemach 1983, p. 24; Lavi 1957, p. 51.
25. Zemach 1983, p. 25; Ben-Gurion 1974b, p. 31ff.; Ben-Gurion to Hildesheimer, Jan. 15, 1960, BGA.

26. N. M. Gelber 1963, p. 24; Zemach 1963b, p. 168; Klinitz-Vigdor 1963, p. 228; Zalkin 2001, 2, p. 402.
27. Ben-Gurion to Shmuel Fuchs, June 28, 1904, in Erez 1971, p. 18.
28. Zemach 1983, p. 25; Lavi 1957, pp. 29, 63ff.; Shlomo Zemach to Shmuel Fuchs, Oct. 23, 1904, courtesy of Yoram Verete.
29. Zemach 1983, pp. 22, 19, 27; Shlomo Zemach to Shmuel Fuchs, two undated letters, courtesy of Yoram Verete.
30. Zemach 1983, p. 18; Zemach 1996, p. 225.
31. Shlomo Zemach to Shmuel Fuchs, June 1, 1904, and June 2, 1904, courtesy of Yoram Verete.
32. Ben-Gurion to Shmuel Fuchs, June 14, 1904, BGA, correspondence.
33. Zemach 1983, p. 21.
34. Lavi 1957, p. 30.
35. Lavi 1957, p. 49.
36. Lavi 1957, p. 30ff.; Zemach 1983, p. 20.
37. Shlomo Zemach to Shmuel Fuchs, June 13, 1904, and June 2, 1904, courtesy of Yoram Verete; Ben-Gurion 1974, p. 30; Lavi, "LeZikhro shel Simcha Isaac," *Davar*, April 20, 1936; see also Habas, "Ehad veDoro," *Dvar Hashavua*, Jan. 19, 1950.
38. Lavi 1957, pp. 63, 33ff.
39. Shlomo Zemach to Shmuel Fuchs, June 13, 1904, and Oct. 23, 1904, courtesy of Yoram Verete; Zemach 1983, p. 24.
40. Shlomo Zemach to Shmuel Fuchs, June 26, 1904, and Oct. 23, 1904, courtesy of Yoram Verete.
41. Zemach 1983, p. 30; Shlomo Zemach to Shmuel Fuchs, June 26, 1904, courtesy of Yoram Verete.
42. Habas 1952, facing p. 33; Ben-Gurion 1974b, p. 33.
43. Zemach 1983, pp. 24, 26; Ben-Gurion 1974b, p. 7; Habas, "Ehad veDoro," *Dvar Hashavua*, Feb. 6, 1950.
44. *Hamelitz*, June 18, 1896.
45. Zemach 1963a, p. 60; Zemach 1983, p. 25.
46. *Zikhronot shel Avigdor Gruen*, p. 4, BGA, subject files 470-1-18; Yatziv 1963, p. 235.
47. Avigdor Gruen to Theodor Herzl, 1901, in Ben-Gurion 1971a, p. 6; *Zikhronot shel Avigdor Gruen*, p. 4, BGA, subject files 470-1-18; Zemach 1963a, p. 41; Ben-Gurion 1974b, p. 27.
48. Ben-Gurion 1963a, pp. 35, 22; Ben-Gurion to Shmuel Fuchs, Feb. 6, 1905, in Erez 1971, p. 47.
49. Taub memoirs, LI, IV-104-543-1; *Hatzefirah*, Sept. 27, 1900.
50. Ben-Gurion 1971a, p. 10ff.; Ben-Gurion 1974b, p. 32ff.; Ben-Gurion to Emanuel Ben-Gurion, Aug. 11, 1968, BGA; Lavi 1957, p. 62; Holtzman 1993, p. 191ff.; Berdichevsky 1897.
51. Zemach 1983, pp. 24, 29.
52. Alroey 2008, p. 65.
53. Herzl 1989, p. 45.
54. *Hamelitz*, April 4, 1899; Stefan Zweig 2012, p. 158.
55. Stefan Zweig 2012, p. 158.

2. SCROLL OF FIRE

1. Ben-Gurion 1974b, p. 51.
2. Ben-Gurion to Shmuel Fuchs, June 2, 1904, in Erez 1971, p. 3.
3. Ben-Gurion 1974b, p. 37; Ben-Gurion 1971a, p. 11.
4. Ben-Gurion to Shmuel Fuchs, June 14, 1904, in Erez 1971, p. 13.
5. Ben-Gurion to Shmuel Fuchs, July 2, 1904, in Erez 1971, p. 3.
6. Avigdor Gruen to Theodor Herzl, 1901, in Ben-Gurion 1971a, p. 6.
7. Ben-Gurion to Shmuel Fuchs, Nov. 6, 1904, in Erez 1971, p. 31.
8. Ben-Gurion to Shmuel Fuchs, June 14, 15, 18, Nov. 6, 1904, in Erez 1971, p. 11ff.; Shlomo Zemach to Shmuel Fuchs, June 2, 1904, and July 13, 1904, courtesy of Yoram Verete; Zemach 1983, p. 30; Ben-Gurion 1971a, p. 11.
9. Zemach 1983, p. 30; Lavi 1957, p. 70.
10. Habas 1952, p. 40.
11. Ben-Gurion to Shmuel Fuchs, July 16, 22, 1904, in Erez 1971, pp. 21ff., 25.
12. Ben-Gurion to Shmuel Fuchs, Sept. 27, 1904, in Erez 1971, p. 29; Teveth 1977, p. 494.
13. Ben-Gurion to Shmuel Fuchs, Sept. 24, 27, Nov. 6, Dec. 14, 1904, in Erez 1971, pp. 28, 29, 31, 37.
14. Ben-Gurion to Shmuel Fuchs, Dec. 18, 1904, in Erez 1971, p. 39.
15. Ben-Gurion to Shmuel Fuchs, Jan. 22, 1905, in Erez 1971, p. 40.
16. Ben-Gurion to Shmuel Fuchs, Feb. 6, 14, 1905, in Erez 1971, pp. 47, 49.
17. Zemach 1983, pp. 28, 31; Shlomo Zemach to Shmuel Fuchs, Oct. 23, 1904, and Sept. 12, 1904, courtesy of Yoram Verete.
18. Lavi 1957, p. 66ff.
19. Lavi 1957, p. 73.
20. Zemach 1983, p. 23; Ben-Gurion to Shmuel Fuchs, Feb. 14, 1905, in Erez 1971, p. 49; Ben-Gurion to Shmuel Fuchs, July 22, 1904, in Erez 1971, p. 25.
21. Ben-Gurion to Shmuel Fuchs, July 22, 1904, in Erez 1971, p. 25.
22. Zemach 1996, p. 225.
23. Ben-Gurion to Shmuel Fuchs, Sept. 27, Nov. 6, 1904, in Erez 1971, pp. 29, 32.
24. Ben-Gurion to Shmuel Fuchs, Nov. 6, 1904, in Erez 1971, p. 31.
25. Ben-Gurion to Shmuel Fuchs, Nov. 20, 1904, Jan. 22, 1905, in Erez 1971, pp. 35, 41.
26. Ben-Gurion to Shmuel Fuchs, Nov. 6, 1904, Jan. 22, April 2, 1905, in Erez 1971, pp. 31, 41, 55.
27. Ben-Gurion to Yitzhak Fuchs and Lipa Taub, Feb. 21, 1905, in Erez 1971, p. 43; Ben-Gurion 1949, 3, p. 140; "Mah Helkenu," *Hatzefirah*, May 4, 1905; Ascher 1994, p. 157ff.; Ury 2012; Alroey 2008, p. 47; Ben-Gurion to Shmuel Fuchs, May 9, 1905, in Erez 1971, p. 57.
28. Ben-Gurion to Ussishkin, March 30, 1905; Ben-Gurion to Shmuel Fuchs, April 2, Jan. 2, 1905, in Erez 1971, pp. 52, 55, 40; Alroey 2011, p. 170ff.
29. Shlomo Zemach to Shmuel Fuchs, undated; Shlomo Zemach to Shmuel Fuchs, Aug. 17, 1906; Shlomo Zemach to Shmuel Fuchs, Oct. 23, 1904, all courtesy of Yoram Verete.
30. Shlomo Zemach to Shmuel Fuchs, Oct. 21, 1906, courtesy of Yoram Verete.
31. Ben-Avram and Nir 1995, pp. 96, 80; Segev 2000, p. 249ff.; Ben-Gurion 1971a, p. 372ff.; Ben-Gurion interview with Oryan, Nov. 12, 1969, HICJ.
32. Shlomo Zemach to Shmuel Fuchs, June 2, 1904, courtesy of Yoram Verete; Ben-Gurion to Shmuel Fuchs, June 2, July 22, 24, 1904, in Erez 1971, pp. 8, 25, 27.

33. Ben-Gurion to Shmuel Fuchs, Nov. 6, 14, Dec. 14, 1904, and Ben-Gurion to Shmuel Fuchs, Feb. 14, 1905, in Erez 1971, pp. 31, 36, 50; Zemach 1963, p. 38; Shlomo Zemach to Shmuel Fuchs, June 2, 1904, courtesy of Yoram Verete; Shlomo Zemach to Shmuel Fuchs, Jan. 9, 1906, courtesy of Yoram Verete.
34. Blatman 2001, 2, p. 493ff.; Frankel 1990, p. 147ff.
35. Mintz 1986a, p. 33ff.; Ben-Gurion 1971a, p. 16; Teveth 1977, p. 75.
36. Ben-Gurion 1971a, p. 16; Ben-Gurion to Shmuel Fuchs, Feb. 6, 14, April 2, 1905, in Erez 1971, pp. 47, 49, 55; Zoref 1965, p. 266ff.
37. Ben-Gurion 1971a, p. 13; Ben-Gurion 1974b, p. 41.
38. Ben-Gurion to his wife and children, May 14, 1942, BGA; Ben-Gurion 1971a, p. 8.
39. Ben-Gurion to Shmuel Fuchs, May 9, 1905, in Erez 1971, p. 58.
40. Lavi 1957, pp. 68, 75ff.
41. Shlomo Zemach to Shmuel Fuchs, two undated letters, courtesy of Yoram Verete; Ben-Gurion 1971a, p. 16.
42. Yosifon 1963, p. 197ff.; Ben-Gurion interview with Ya'akov Ashman, Nov. 25, 1963, p. 7, BGA; Ben-Gurion to Moshe Nahmanowitz, Oct. 15, 1961, BGA; Teveth 1977, p. 75; Ben-Gurion 1974b, p. 41; Ben-Gurion to his wife and family, May 14, 1942, BGA.
43. Hirsch Nelkin to Rachel Nelkin, March 23, 1906, and Elazar Nelkin to Rachel Nelkin, March 27, 1906, in Rachel Beit Halahmi 2006, p. 40ff.; Rachel Beit Halahmi 1963, p. 363.
44. Hirsch Nelkin to Rachel Nelkin, March 23, 1906, and Elazar Nelkin to Rachel Nelkin, March 27, 1906, in Rachel Beit Halahmi 2006, p. 40ff.; Rachel Beit Halahmi 1963, p. 363.
45. Ben-Gurion to his wife and children, May 14, 1942, BGA.
46. Habas 1952, facing p. 32.
47. Elazar Nelkin to Rachel Nelkin, March 27, 1906, in Rachel Beit Halahmi 2006, p. 45ff.
48. Ben-Gurion to Emmanuel Ben-Gurion, Aug. 11, 1968, BGA.
49. Ben-Gurion to Rachel Beit Halahmi, Dec. 26, 1953, BGA.
50. Lavi 1957, p. 75.
51. Ben-Gurion 1949, 3, p. 140.
52. Rachel Beit Halahmi 2006, p. 79; Yehezkel Beit Halahmi 1963, p. 369; Zoref 1965, p. 103ff.
53. Translator's note: The passages from Bialik's poem are quoted, with minor revisions, from Atar Hadari's translation of the poem in *Songs from Bialik*, Syracuse, N.Y.: Syracuse University Press, 2000.
54. Bialik 1942, p. 88; Ratosh 1974; Fichman 1974, pp. 309ff., 314ff.; Moked 2014, p. 23.

3. BIRDS

1. Zemach 1983, p. 61; Ben-Gurion 1971a, p. 18.
2. Ben-Gurion 1974b, p. 57ff; Teveth 1977, p. 502, note 34; Alroey 2004, p. 79ff.
3. Ben-Gurion to his father, Aug. 21, 28, 1906, in Erez 1971, p. 65ff.
4. Ben-Gurion to his father, undated, in Erez 1971, p. 70.
5. Ben-Gurion to his father, undated and Oct. 1, 1906, in Erez 1971, pp. 71, 75.
6. Ben-Gurion to his father, undated, in Erez 1971, p. 70.

7. Memoirs of members of the Second Aliyah, BGA, subject file 377, M.T. 62; Memoirs of Tuvia Solomon, in Yaari 1974, p. 245ff.; Mordechai Eliav 1978, p. 3ff.

8. Ben-Arieh 1999, p. 120.

9. Carmel 1999, p. 143ff.; Laskov 1999, 1, p. 351ff.

10. Ben-Arieh 1999, pp. 78ff., 113; Ben-Arieh 1977, p. 317ff.

11. Laskov 1999, 1, p. 354.

12. Carmel 1973, p. 198ff.

13. Berlowitz 2010, p. 100ff.; Dinur 1954–61, 1, p. 194ff.

14. Tzachor 1994, p. 15.

15. Laskov 1999, 1, p. 387; Ben-Artzi 1999, 2, p. 356.

16. Kressel 1953, p. 12.

17. Ben-Gurion to his father, undated and Oct. 11, 1906, in Erez 1971, pp. 71, 75; Lavi 1957, pp. 15ff., 168; Zemach 1965, p. 62ff.; Kavashna, interview transcripts, BGA.

18. Rachel Beit Halahmi 2006, p. 79; Ben-Gurion to his father, Sept. 7, 1906, in Erez 1971, p. 69.

19. Ben-Gurion interview with Malcolm Stuart, 1968, interview transcripts, p. 48, BGA; Ben-Gurion interview with Avraham Avi-hai, HIJC-OHA, p. 49.

20. Ben-Gurion to his father, undated, in Erez 1971, p. 70; Ben-Gurion 1971a, pp. 23, 69, 76; Ben-Gurion to Hazaz, July 10, 1968, BGA.

21. Alroey 2002, p. 33ff.

22. Alroey 2004, pp. 169, 128, 208ff.; Yanait Ben-Zvi 1962, p. 86; Ben-Gurion interview with Levi Yitzhak Hayerushalmi, Feb. 28, 1972, BGA; Zemach 1983, p. 33.

23. Yanait Ben-Zvi 1962, p. 86; Yanait interview, July 17, 1975, p. 2, BGA; Erez 1971, p. 76.

24. Teveth 1977, p. 503, note 17; Alroey 2004, p. 27; Ben-Artzi 1999, 2, p. 358; Lavi 1957, p. 176; Anita Shapira 1980, 1, pp. 100, 272.

25. Zemach 1965, p. 196.

26. Ben-Gurion interview with Malcolm Stuart, 1968, p. 48, BGA.

27. Ben-Artzi 2002, 2, p. 356.

28. Yanait Ben-Zvi 1962, p. 94.

29. Ben-Gurion to his father, Oct. 11, Dec. 16, 18, in Erez 1971, pp. 75, 89, 91.

30. Ben-Gurion 1916a.

31. Ben-Gurion to Shmuel Fuchs, Jan. 2, 1907, in Erez 1971, p. 93.

32. Ben-Gurion to his father, Sept. 13, Nov. 8, 1906, in Erez 1971, pp. 74, 82; Yanait Ben-Zvi 1962, p. 94; Ben-Gurion 1916a; Ben-Gurion 1971a, p. 18; Ben-Gurion 1974b, p. 30.

33. Ben-Gurion 1916a.

34. Ben-Gurion to his father, Dec. 16, 1906, in Erez 1971, p. 89; Ben-Gurion 1916a.

35. Ben-Ami, interview transcript, BGA.

36. Philip Cruso, Shaul Avigur, and Ya'akov Katzman, interview transcripts, BGA; Zemach 1996, p. 226.

37. Katzman, interview transcripts, BGA.

38. Ben-Gurion to his father, July 24, May 5, 1907, in Erez 1971, pp. 108, 120.

39. Ben-Gurion to his father, Oct. 16, 1906, Aug. 25, 1909, in Erez, 1971, pp. 80, 140; Ben-Gurion to Ralph Goldman, Sept. 3, 1951, BGA.

40. Ben-Gurion to his father, Feb. 8, May 23, 1907, in Erez 1971, pp. 103, 107.

41. Ben-Gurion to Shmuel Fuchs, Jan. 2, 1907, in Erez 1971, p. 94.

42. Ben-Gurion to his father, Oct. 15, 1909, in Erez 1971, p. 145.
43. Ben-Gurion to his father, Aug. 4, 1907, in Erez 1971, p. 109.
44. Zemach 1965, p. 107ff.
45. Lavi 1957, pp. 253, 257ff. 329.
46. Rachel Beit Halahmi 2006, p. 76.
47. Ben-Gurion to his father, Oct. 16, 1906, in Erez 1971, p. 80.

4. FOREIGN LABOR

1. Ben-Gurion to his father, Oct. 19, Nov. 8, 1906, in Erez 1971, pp. 76, 83.
2. Ben-Gurion to Shmuel Fuchs, Jan. 2, 1907, in Erez 1971, p. 93.
3. Ben-Gurion to his father, Dec. 18, 1906, May 13, Nov. 7, 1907, in Erez 1971, pp. 91, 105, 112; Ben-Gurion 1916a.
4. Ben-Gurion to Shmuel Fuchs, Jan. 2, 1907, and Ben-Gurion to his father, May 13, 1907, in Erez 1971, pp. 93, 106.
5. Ben-Gurion to Shmuel Fuchs, Jan. 2, 1907, in Erez 1971, p. 93.
6. Ben-Gurion to his father, June 30, 1909, in Erez 1971, p. 133.
7. Ben-Gurion interview with Malcolm Stuart, 1968, p. 44, BGA.
8. Ben-Gurion to his father, Oct. 19, 1906, in Erez 1971, p. 77.
9. Ben-Gurion interview with Levi Yitzhak Hayerushalmi, 1972, BGA; Ben-Gurion to Israel Shohat, Jan. 15, 1956, BGA; Habas 1952, p. 108.
10. Ben-Zvi 1945.
11. Ben-Gurion 1971a, p. 23ff.
12. Gorny 2002, p. 440; Karlinsky 2000, p. 149ff.
13. Ben-Gurion 1916a; Ben-Gurion at the Sejera celebrations, Feb. 25, 1962, BGA.
14. Yitzhak Kavashna, interview transcript, BGA.
15. Ben-Gurion during Education Month, 1941; Ben-Gurion 2008, p. 379.
16. Ben-Gurion, Diary, Nov. 20, 1927, BGA.
17. Lavi 1957, pp. 219, 254ff.
18. Lavi 1957, p. 334ff.
19. Horwitz 1981, p. 124ff.
20. Ben-Gurion 1925; Ben-Gurion 1931, p. 92; Ben-Gurion, "Hapo'el Ha'ivri Veha'aravi," in Ben-Gurion 1931, p. 105; Sheffer 2015, p. 34.
21. Ludvipol 1901.
22. *Hatzefirah*, April 25, 1890, June 9, 1890, April 7, 1891, April 11, 1891, Dec. 9, 1891, Jan. 31, 1892, and more; Israel memorial website for fallen soldiers, www.izkor.gov.il, and the National Insurance Institute of Israel's memorial website for victims of terror and hate crimes, http://www.laad.btl.gov.il.
23. Anita Shapira 1992, p. 84ff.
24. Ahad Ha'am, "Emet Mi'eretz Yisra'el" and "Hayishuv Ve'apotrosav," 1949, pp. 29, 236; Gorny 1975, p. 82; Rokach to Levontin, May 20, 1886, quoted in Anita Shapira 1992, p. 507, note 14.
25. Giladi 1999, 1, p. 503ff.; Ahad Ha'am, "Hayishuv Ve'apotrosav," 1949, p. 225.
26. Gorny 1975, p. 72ff.; Yosef Lamdan 1999, p. 215ff.; Frankel 1990, p. 149; Segev 2000, pp. 150–51.
27. Epstein 1907, p. 193ff.

28. Anita Shapira 1992, p. 95ff; Moshe Smilansky to Ahad Ha'am, Sept. 6, 1913, National Library of Israel, Ahad Ha'am Archive, 7912119.
29. Moshe Smilanksy 1936a, p. 42; Anita Shapira 1992, p. 509, note 48.
30. Herzl 1989, p. 52.
31. Anita Shapira 1992, pp. 89, 91.
32. Ben-Gurion 1971a, pp. 49, 470, 516.
33. Yosef Haim Brenner, quoted in Anita Shapira 1992, p. 85; Moshe Smilansky 1936b, p. 214; Zemach 1965, p. 105; Horwitz 1981, p. 122; Eliezer Ben-Yehuda and Yehiel Mihal Pines to James Finn, Aug. 17, 1883; Druyanov 1909, 1, p. 96.
34. Ben-Gurion 1932, p. 7; Kressel 1953, p. 13.
35. Ben-Gurion 1932, p. 4; Ussishkin, "Haprogramah Shelanu," 1934, p. 118; Ben-Gurion to Shmuel Fuchs, Jan. 22, 1905, in Erez 1971, p. 41.
36. Moshe Smilansky 1936b, p. 214.
37. Moshe Smilansky 1936a, p. 214.
38. Ben-Gurion 1911c.
39. Ben-Gurion 1910a.
40. *Hapo'el Hatza'ir*, Aug. 31, 1908; Zemach 1965, p. 154.
41. Ben-Gurion 1932, p. 3; Ben-Gurion 1916a, p. 102ff.; Penslar 1991.
42. Ussishkin, "Haprogramah Shelanu," 1934, p. 117ff.
43. Vladimir Dubnow to Simon Dubnow, Oct. 20, 1882; Laskov 1982, pp. 507, 522.
44. Ben-Gurion 1972, 2, p. 48ff.; Teveth 1977, p. 583ff.
45. Teveth 1977, p. 101.
46. Ben-Gurion to his father, Oct. 19, 1906, in Erez 1971, p. 78; Ben-Gurion 1971a, p. 25.
47. Yanait Ben-Zvi 1962, p. 86.
48. Teveth 1977, p. 581ff.
49. Ben-Gurion to his father, Dec. 18, 1906, in Erez 1971, p. 91.
50. Ben-Gurion to his father, Jan. 15, May 13, 1907, in Erez 1971, pp. 97, 107; Ben-Gurion 1971a, p. 32.
51. *Yiddisher Kempfer*, Jan. 18, 1907, in Teveth 1997, p. 104.
52. Dinur 1954–64, 1, p. 203ff.; Tsoref 1998, p. 15; Lev 1983, p. 135ff.
53. Habas 1952, p. 108.
54. Lazar 2012, p. 49ff.
55. Ben-Gurion interview with Levi Yitzhak Hayerushalmi, 1972, BGA; Erez 1971, p. 77.
56. Ben-Gurion 1971a, p. 35.
57. Ben-Gurion to his father, Dec. 16, 1906, Feb. 8, May 13, 1907, in Erez 1971, pp. 96, 101.
58. Ben-Gurion to Yitzhak Ziv-Av, July 13, 1964, BGA.

5. SEJERA

1. Hareuveni 1999, p. 33; Burkhardt 1822, p. 333; Yankelevitch 2001, p. 97ff.
2. Ben-Gurion to his father, Feb. 1, 1909, Feb. 1, 1908, in Erez 1971, pp. 166, 124.
3. Ben-Gurion to Shimon Kesselman, Feb. 28, 1962, BGA; Ben-Gurion 1916a, p. 106.
4. Anita Shapira 1992, p. 89; Kayla Giladi testimony, Bracha Habas Archive, NL; Yankelevitch 2001, p. 111ff.
5. Ben-Avram and Nir 1995, pp. 96, 80; Segev 2000, p. 249ff.

6. Ben-Gurion 1916a, p. 102, BGA; Ben-Gurion to his father, Nov. 7, 1907, in Erez 1971, p. 112; Ben-Gurion at the Sejera celebrations, Sept. 25, 1962, BGA.

7. Ben-Gurion at the Sejera celebrations, Sept. 25, 1962, BGA; Ben-Gurion to Yitzhak Ziv-Av, Sept. 2, 1973, BGA; Ever Hadani 1955, p. 222.

8. Ben-Gurion 1971a, p. 34; Ben-Gurion at the Sejera celebrations, Sept. 25, 1962, BGA; Zemach 1983, p. 33.

9. Ben-Gurion 1971a, p. 32, Teveth 1977, p. 137.

10. Zemach 1983, p. 68ff.; Ben-Gurion at the Sejera celebrations, Sept. 25, 1962, BGA; Kayla Giladi testimony, Bracha Habas Archive, NL.

11. Yankelevitch 2001, p. 108ff.; Ben-Gurion to his father, May 5, 1908, in Erez 1971, p. 120.

12. Ben-Zvi et al. 1962, p. 17; Ben-Gurion 1911, "Reshit haShmirah ha'Ivrit," BGA, Sejera subject file; Ben-Gurion 1971a, p. 36; Alroey 2009, p. 77ff.

13. Ben-Gurion at a party in honor of Eliyahu Krause, Nov. 15, 1951, BGA.

14. Ben-Gurion 1955b, p. 311ff.; Ever Hadani 1955, p. 223ff.; Ben-Gurion 1971a, pp. 17, 37, 44ff.; Ben-Gurion at the Sejera celebrations, Sept. 25, 1962, BGA.

15. Ben-Gurion at the Sejera celebrations, Sept. 25, 1962, BGA; Ben-Gurion to his father, Feb. 1, 1908, in Erez 1971, p. 116; *Hador*, Jan. 24, 1950; Ben-Gurion, Diary, Jan. 21, 1955, BGA; Ben-Gurion to Larna Yashar, Dec. 6, 1970; Ben-Gurion to David Goldman, March 2, 1969, BGA.

16. Michaeli 1991, p. 136.

17. Ben-Gurion to his father, Nov. 7, 1907, May 5, 1908, in Erez 1971, pp. 112, 120; Rachel Beit Halahmi 2006, p. 90.

18. Rachel Beit Halahmi 2006, pp. 76, 80ff.; Ben-Gurion to his father, May 13, 1907, in Erez 1971, p. 106; Teveth 1977, pp. 502, 148, 520, note 28.

19. Teveth 1977, p. 147ff.; Zemach 1983, p. 68.

20. Ben-Gurion to his father, June 30, 1909, Jan. 21, 1910, in Erez 1971, pp. 136, 149.

21. Teveth 1977, p. 143.

22. Ben-Gurion 1971a, p. 44ff.; Yanait Ben-Zvi 1962, p. 96ff; Ben-Zvi et al. 1962, p. 20; Michaeli 1991, p. 42ff.

23. Ben-Gurion 1971a, p. 46ff.; Ya'akov Webman testimony, BGA, subject file 34/242405; Korngold, Ministry of Defense Memorial site, http://www.izkor.gov.il/HalalView.aspx?id=506380; Shweiger, Ministry of Defense Memorial website, http://www.izkor.gov.il/HalalKorot.aspx?id=506518; Melamed, Ministry of Defense Memorial website, http://www.izkor.gov.il/HalalView.aspx?id=506083.

24. Ben-Zvi et al. 1962, p. 20; Lev 1983, p. 135ff.

25. Yanait Ben-Zvi interviewed by Nahum Barnea, *Davar*, Nov. 23, 1979.

26. Yanait Ben-Zvi and Avigur, interview transcripts, BGA.

27. Ben-Gurion, Cabinet meeting, Sept. 23, 1952, NA; Ben-Gurion to the Jewish Agency Executive, April 6, 1941, in Ben-Gurion 2008, p. 342.

28. Search for the Hashomer Archive, Ben-Gurion subject file; Ben-Gurion to Israel Shohat, Jan. 15, 1956; Israel Shohat to Ben-Gurion, April 12, 1957, BGA; Ben-Gurion, Diary, April 26, 1957, BGA.

29. "Israel Shohat Mesaper al Manya," *Davar*, Nov. 27, 1959.

30. Ben-Gurion to his father, July 29, Sept. 26, Oct. 15, 1909, in Erez 1971, pp. 138ff., 112, 142, 143; Ben-Gurion to his father, Jan. 21, 1910, in Erez 1971, p. 149.

31. Ben-Gurion to his father, Aug. 21, 1909, in Erez 1971, p. 140; Ben-Gurion 1971a, p. 48.
32. Ben-Gurion to his father, Nov. 14, Dec. 25, 1909, Jan. 21, 1910, in Erez 1971, p. 146ff.
33. Ben-Gurion to his father, May 9, 1909, in Erez 1971, p. 128; Ben-Gurion 1916a, p. 103ff. Ben-Gurion to donors, Sept. 24, 1970, interview transcript, BGA, file 39, "Ben-Gurion with journalists"; Ben-Gurion 1971a, p. 34.

6. DEPORTATION

1. Ben-Gurion to his father, March 31, 1909, in Erez 1971, p. 127.
2. Naor and Giladi 1993, p. 60ff.; Bloom 2008, p. 212ff.
3. Naor and Giladi 1993, p. 72ff.
4. Ben-Gurion, "Reshit Avodati Hasifrutit," April 1920, BGA, general chronological documentation 206; Ben-Gurion at the jubilee celebration for *Ha'ahdut*, July 10, 1960, and March 25, 1962, BGA; Ben-Gurion 1971a, p. 50ff.; Yanait Ben-Zvi, 1962, p. 85; Zerubavel 1953.
5. Yanait, interview transcript, July 17, 1975, p. 10, BGA; Witztum and Kalian 2013, p. 46.
6. Yanait Ben-Zvi 1962, p. 134.
7. Ben-Gurion 1910c.
8. "Telegram," *Ha'ahdut*, March 31, 1911.
9. Ben-Zvi 1967, p. 174ff.
10. "Megamatenu," *Ha'ahdut*, July–Aug. 1910; Yanait Ben-Zvi 1962, p. 133; Ben-Zvi at the Po'alei Zion Convention, April 23, 1910; Tsoref 1998, p. 34.
11. *Hatzvi*, Jan. 27, 1909.
12. Bloom 2008, p. 112ff.; Rosenman 1992, p. 27.
13. Bloom 2008, p. 318ff.
14. Ben-Gurion at the Council of the Po'alei Zion organization, *Ha'ahdut*, Nov. 11, 1910; Nini 1996, p. 18ff.; Ben-Gurion 1912; Ben-Gurion 1971a, pp. 34, 324.
15. Gorny 1988, p. 75.
16. Yehoshua 1971, 4, p. 32; Kroyanker 2005, p. 264; Genichovsky 1993; *Josephus*, 1956, 2, p. 539, 3, p. 105; Yanait Ben-Zvi 1962, p. 103; Holtzman 1993, p. 193.
17. Reuveni 1932, pp. 41, 151, 165, 211, 214.
18. Ben-Gurion 1911a; Ben-Gurion 1911b; Ben-Gurion 1911c.
19. Zemach 1983, p. 75.
20. Ben-Gurion and Shlomo and Hemda Zemach to Rachel Beit Halahmi, undated, GSA, Rachel and Yehezkel Beit Halahmi file; Yehoshua 1971, 4, p. 32.
21. Ben-Gurion 1910a; Yosef Lamdan 1999, 1, p. 225.
22. Haver 1910.
23. Ben-Gurion 1911b.
24. Yanait Ben-Zvi 1962, p. 156.
25. Ben-Gurion 1910b.
26. Ben-Gurion to Po'alei Zion in the United States, Dec. 25, 1906, BGA.
27. Ben-Gurion to Rachel Beit Halahmi, undated, GSA, Rachel and Yehezkel Beit Halahmi file.
28. Ben-Gurion to his father, Aug. 6, 1911, in Erez 1971, p. 156.
29. Ben-Gurion to his father, Oct. 11, 1911, in Erez 1971, p. 156.
30. Ben-Gurion 1971a, p. 50ff.; Ben-Gurion to Hazaz, July 10, 1968, BGA.
31. Ben-Gurion 1971a, p. 52; Ben-Gurion to Eliyahu Elyashar, May 19, 1964, BGA.

32. Ben-Gurion to his father, March 3, 1912, in Erez 1971, p. 203.

33. Stroumsa, interview transcript, p. 40, BGA; Ben-Gurion ("Dan") 1911e.

34. Ben-Gurion to his father, April 21, 1912; Ben-Gurion to Ben-Zvi, March 31, June 28, 1912, in Erez 1971, pp. 212, 216, 220; Ben-Gurion, "Reshit Avodati Hasifrutit," April 1920, p. 3, BGA, general chronological documentation, 1919–20; copy of forged diploma, "Ishur Limudim Vetziyunim shel Ben-Gurion Miturkiyah Beshanim 1912–1914," BGA.

35. Memoirs of Avigdor Gruen, p. 9, BGA, subject file 470-1-18; Ben-Gurion to his father, Jan. 28, 1912, in Erez 1971, p. 188.

36. Ben-Gurion to his father, Sept. 28, Nov. 25, Dec. 7, 1911, Jan. 18, Jan. 28, Aug. 12, Sept. 2, 1912, in Erez 1971, pp. 163, 179, 183, 176, 186, 221, 231, 234.

37. Ben-Gurion to his father, Nov. 25, 1911, July 26, 1912, in Erez 1971, pp. 176, 228.

38. Stroumsa, interview transcript, p. 9, BGA; Yanait Ben-Zvi, interview transcript, Nov. 16, 1976, p. 6, BGA; Ben-Gurion to his father, Feb. 5, 1914, in Erez 1971, p. 295.

39. Ben-Gurion to his father, July 15, 1912, in Erez 1971, p. 226.

40. Ben-Gurion to Zerubavel, Jan. 26, 1912, in Erez 1971, p. 184.

41. Stroumsa, interview transcript, p. 3, BGA; Ben-Gurion to Ben-Zvi, Feb. 11, March 8, March 31, 1912, BGA; Ben-Gurion to David Bloch-Blumenfeld, June 6, 1913, in Erez 1971, pp. 194, 210, 273, and editor's note, p. 170.

42. Ben-Gurion to his father, April 1, May 3, 1912, in Erez 1971, pp. 194, 214, 217.

43. Ben-Gurion to his father, July 15, June 28, Aug. 12, 1912, in Erez 1971, pp. 219, 226, 235.

44. Ben-Gurion to his father, July 13, 15, Oct. 15, 1912, in Erez 1971, pp. 225ff., 241.

45. Ben-Gurion to his father, Oct. 15, Nov. 5, Nov. 12, 1912, in Erez 1971, pp. 241ff., 245, 246.

46. Stefan Zweig 2012, p. 115.

47. Ben-Gurion 1971a, p. 56.

48. Ben-Gurion to Bloch-Blumenfeld, Dec. 21, 1912, in Erez 1971, p. 250.

49. Ben-Gurion to his father, June 28, 1912, in Erez 1971, p. 220.

50. Ben-Gurion to his father, Dec. 29, 1913, in Erez 1971, p. 293.

51. Ben-Gurion to his father, Dec. 11, 1913, Feb. 5, 1914, in Erez 1971, pp. 291, 294.

52. Yanait Ben-Zvi, interview transcript, Nov. 16, 1976, p. 6, BGA; Ben-Zvi 1967, p. 201ff.; Ben-Gurion 2008, editor's note, p. 300.

53. Ben-Gurion to his father, Sep. 23, 1912, March 2, April 3, April 20, 1913, in Erez 1971, pp. 239, 263, 264, 268.

54. Ben-Gurion to his father, April 23, May 21, 1913, in Erez 1971, pp. 269, 272.

55. Ben-Gurion to his father, July 26, 1912, July 12, 1914, in Erez 1971, pp. 228, 317; transcript of grades, May 15, 1952, BGA, personal documents; Baron 2008, p. 80ff.; Ben-Gurion to Rachel Beit Halahmi, Oct. 5, 1913, GSA, Rachel and Yehezkel Beit Halahmi file.

56. Baron 2008, p. 92ff.

57. Stroumsa, interview transcript, p. 8, BGA.

58. Israel Shohat, "Shelichut Vaderech," in Ben-Zvi et al. 1962, p. 35ff.; Ben-Gurion to Bloch-Blumenfeld, June 6, 1913, in Erez 1971, p. 237; Ben-Gurion to his father, July 31, 1913, in Erez 1971, p. 276; Ben-Zvi 1967, p. 201ff.

59. Ben-Gurion, "Likrat He'atid," in Ben-Gurion 1931, p. 1ff.

60. Y.Z., "Michtav Miyafo," *Ha'ahdut*, Dec. 30, 1914; *Hapo'el Hatza'ir*, Jan. 1, 1915, p. 16; Giladi and Naor 2002, p. 457ff; Teveth 1977, p. 265.
61. Ben-Gurion 1914; Mintz 1988, p. 69ff.
62. Reuveni 1932, pp. 105, 151ff.
63. Ben-Bassat 2014, p. 52ff.
64. Y.Z., "Michtav Miyafo," *Ha'ahdut*, Dec. 30, 1914; Ben-Zvi 1967, p. 201ff.
65. Memorandum to Djemal Pasha, Feb. 21, 1915, BGA; Ben-Gurion 1972, p. 50; Ben-Gurion 1971a, pp. 50, 76ff.; Ben-Zvi 1967, p. 217ff.; Yanait Ben-Zvi, interview transcript, Dec. 6, 1976, p. 7, BGA.
66. Morgenthau to Louis Marshall, Sept. 16, 1914, and other documents, LPA P3/710; Ben-Gurion and Ben-Zvi to Glazebrook, end of 1917 (?), BGA, correspondence 1915–1917; Ben-Gurion, Diary, March 29, 1915, BGA; Ben-Gurion 1971a, p. 73; Ben-Zvi 1967, p. 217ff.; Teveth 1977, p. 293; Friedman 1991, p. 168ff.
67. Elam 1984, p. 22ff. Shmuel Katz 1993, p. 37.
68. Ben-Gurion and Ben-Zvi to Djemal Pasha, Feb. 21, 1915, BGA; Ben-Gurion and Ben-Zvi to Brandeis, 1916, BGA, general chronological documentation; Ben-Zvi 1967, p. 223; Ben-Gurion 1971a, p. 222.
69. New York Passenger Lists 1820–1957, Patris, David Bengorion [*sic*], May 16, 1915, ancestry.com; David Green-Ben-Gurion Registration Card, June 5, 1917, United States World War I Draft, FamilySearch.org.
70. Ben-Gurion 1971a, p. 75; Ben-Gurion to Eliezer Canaani, May 13, 1964, BGA.
71. Ben-Gurion, Diary, May 3, 1915, BGA.
72. Ben-Gurion, Diary, April 3, 13, 14, 28, May 15, 1915; Ben-Gurion to Shmuel Fuchs, Jan. 2, 1907, in Erez 1971, p. 93; Ben-Gurion, "LeYahadut America," Sept. 3, 1950, in Ben-Gurion 1962a, 2, p. 366.

7. NEW WORLD

1. Ben-Gurion 1971a, pp. 79ff.; Ben-Gurion, Diary, May 17, June 2, 1915, BGA.
2. Ben-Gurion interview with Avraham Avi-hai, Aug. 23, 1972, HIJC.
3. Ben-Gurion 1971a, p. 76.
4. Ben-Gurion, Diary, May 27, 1915, BGA.
5. Ben-Gurion, Diary, May 15, 17, June 1, 5, 7, 9, BGA; Mintz 1983, p. 181ff.
6. Ben-Gurion, Diary, May 27, 1915, BGA.
7. Ben-Gurion, Diary, May 26, 1915, BGA.
8. Ben-Gurion, Diary, May 29, July 4, 5, 1915, BGA; handwritten correction to the diary, BGA, Shabtai Teveth collection, people; Ben-Gurion to Shmuel Fuchs, Jan. 29, 1955, BGA; Ben-Gurion 1971a, p. 16; Berl Cohen 1986.
9. Shmuel Fuchs to Ben-Gurion, May 14, 1955, BGA.
10. Jonathan Shapiro 1971, p. 90ff.; Tuchman 1981, p. 208ff.
11. Po'alei Zion communication 18, June 28, 1915, BGA, general chronological documentation; Ben-Gurion and Ben-Zvi, "Hehalutz: Printsipn un Aufgaben," in Basok 1940, p. 14; "Di Yesodos fun 'Hekhalutz,'" 1917, BGA, general chronological documentation; Ben-Gurion, Diary, Aug. 9, 1915, BGA; Ben-Gurion to Ben-Zvi, Aug. 9, 1915, BGA; Ben-Zvi 1967, p. 230.
12. Guttman, interview transcript, p. 17, BGA; Cruso interview transcript, BGA; Ben-Gurion to Ben-Zvi, Dec. 13, 1915, March 8, July 19, 1916, BGA, general chronological

documentation; Ben-Gurion to Hirsch Ehrenreich, Jan. 6, 1916, in Erez 1971, p. 333.

13. Ben-Gurion and Ben-Zvi to Brandeis, 1916, BGA, general chronological documentation.

14. Ben-Gurion 1971a, p. 81; Ben-Zvi 1967, p. 226.

15. Ben-Gurion, Diary, Nov. 9, 1940, BGA; Ben-Gurion to Ben-Zvi, Feb. 3, 1918, BGA, general chronological documentation.

16. Ben-Gurion, Diary, July 8, 1915, BGA.

17. Ben-Gurion to Hirsch Ehrenreich, Jan. 6, 7, 1916, BGA; Erez 1971, pp. 333, 334; Teveth 1977, p. 552.

18. Y. Z. Rabinowitz, "Hakdamah," p. D, and Yehoshua Tohn, "Mesirut Nefesh," p. 17ff.; Frankel 1958, p. 88ff.

19. Zerubavel et al. 1916.

20. Ben-Gurion, Diary, May 15, 1916, BGA.

21. Ben-Gurion to Ben-Zvi, June 22, May 9, 1916, BGA.

22. Ben-Gurion, "Likrat He'atid," in Ben-Gurion 1931, p. 1ff.

23. Ben-Gurion to Ben-Zvi, May 9, 1916, BGA; Chashin and Ben-Gurion 1916, p. 8ff.; Ben-Gurion to his father, July 1919, BGA.

24. Mordechai Eliav 1980, p. 13.

25. "Peace Army for Palestine," New York Times, April 27, 1917; Ben-Zvi 1967, p. 232.

26. Ben-Gurion to his father, Dec. 5, 1919, in Erez 1971, p. 442; Ben-Gurion 1971a, p. 85.

27. Reinharz 1993, pp. 31, 114; Segev 2000, p. 33ff.; Teveth 1977, p. 374.

28. "Britain Favors Zionism," New York Times, Nov. 9, 1917; "Zionists Get Text of Britain's Pledge," New York Times, Nov. 14, 1977; Segev 2000, p. 50.

29. Ben-Gurion at the Po'alei Zion Convention, Yiddisher Kempfer, Oct. 27, 1916.

30. Ben-Gurion 1971a, pp. 92, 98ff.

31. Ben-Gurion 1971a, pp. 86, 97ff.; Samuel Schulman, "Jewish Nation Not Wanted in Palestine," New York Times, Nov. 25, 1917.

32. "Jewish Socialists Acclaim Zionism," New York Times, Nov. 30, 1917; Ben-Gurion to his father, Dec. 5, 1919, in Erez 1971, p. 445.

33. Ben-Gurion 1971a, p. 86; Avrech 1965, p. 13; Erez 1953.

34. Avrech 1965, pp. 13, 21; Yiddisher Kempfer, Dec. 14, 1917.

35. Mordechai Eliav 1980, p. 19.

36. Ben-Gurion and Ben-Zvi 1918; Ben-Gurion to his father, July 1, 1919, BGA.

37. Ben-Gurion and Ben-Zvi 1918, p. 318ff.; Ben-Gurion, "Livirur Motza Hafalahin," "Letoldot Hafalahin," Ben-Gurion 1931, pp. 13ff., 26ff.

38. Ben-Gurion and Ben-Zvi 1980, pp. 44ff., 122, 228; Ben-Gurion, "Gevulei-Artzeinu Ve'admatah," Ben-Gurion 1931, p. 34ff.

39. Ben-Gurion to his father, July 1, 1919, BGA; Ben-Gurion to his father, Dec. 5, 1919, in Erez 1971, p. 445.

40. Ben-Gurion to the Cabinet, Aug. 9, 1949, NA; Reinharz 1993, pp. 81ff., 167ff.; Shmuel Katz 1993, p. 103ff.; Elam 1984.

41. Ben-Zvi 1967, p. 237; Elam 1984, p. 183ff.

42. Ben-Gurion to Kaplansky, Oct. 21, 1918, BGA; Ben-Gurion 1971a, p. 155; Ben-Gurion to the Po'alei Zion Central Committee, Jan. 18, 1918, in Erez 1971, p. 335.

43. Ben-Zvi 1967, p. 237; Ben-Gurion 1971a, p. 98.
44. Ben-Gurion to Paula, June 25, 1918, in Erez 1971, p. 369.
45. Elam 1984, p. 190; Ben-Gurion to the Mapai Central Committee, March 7, 1941, in Ben-Gurion 2008, p. 252ff.
46. Ben-Zvi to Yanait, June 14, 1918, in Tsoref 1998, p. 81; Ben-Gurion to Paula, June 1, 3, 13, 20, 24, 1918, April 15, 1919, in Erez 1971, pp. 348, 350, 353, 367, 416; Paula to Ben-Gurion, June 5, 28, 1918, April 15, 1919, BGA; quoted also according to Ben-Gurion to Paula, June 1, 1919, letters by Ben-Gurion to Paula from his period of service in the British Army and the Jewish Legion, May 30, 1918–July 20, 1919, BGA, personal archive of Yehuda Erez.
47. Ben-Gurion to Paula, Aug. 6, 1918, April 15, 1919, in Erez 1971, pp. 348, 416, quoted also according to Ben-Gurion to Paula, April 15, 1919, letters from Ben-Gurion to Paula from his period of service in the British Army and the Jewish Legion, May 30, 1918–July 20, 1919, BGA, personal archive of Yehuda Erez.
48. Paula Ben-Gurion, July 9, Aug. 17, 8, 29, June 29, Aug. 17, July 21, 1918, BGA; Ben-Gurion to Paula, June 13, 1918, in Erez 1971, p. 353.
49. Ben-Gurion to Paula, June 14, 21, 15, Sept. 7, 1918, in Erez 1971, pp. 355, 364, 357, 389, quoted also according to Ben-Gurion to Paula, June 15, 1918, letters by Ben-Gurion to Paula from his period of service in the British Army and the Jewish Legion, May 30, 1918–July 20, 1919, BGA, personal archive of Yehuda Erez.
50. Ben-Gurion at a gathering of recruits, April 20, 1943, in Ben-Gurion 1949, 3, p. 132.
51. Tsoref 1998, p. 78; Ben-Gurion, Diary, July 16, 23, 1918, BGA; Segev 2000, p. 74.
52. Ben-Gurion to the Cabinet, Sept. 7, 1950, ISA.
53. Ben-Gurion 1971a, p. 96.
54. Ben-Gurion to Kaplansky, Oct. 21, 1918, BGA.
55. Ben-Gurion, Diary, Aug. 12–28, 1918, BGA; Ben-Gurion to Tzipora and Moshe Koritani, Dec. 29, 1918, in Erez 1971, p. 408.
56. Ben-Gurion to Yanait, Oct. 21, 1918, in Erez 1971, p. 399.
57. Ben-Gurion to Paula, Sept. 17, 1918. Note that a photocopy of the original, preserved in BGA, bears the date Sept. 5, 1918, and is corrected in Ben-Gurion's handwriting to October 5. Several words cannot be deciphered. Ben-Gurion to Paula, Sept. 23, Oct. 2, 3, 1918, in Erez 1971, pp. 389, 390, 392, 394; Paula to Ben-Gurion, Sept. 13, 1918, BGA; Ben-Gurion, Diary, Oct. 2, 1918, BGA.

8. AUTHORITY

1. Ben-Gurion, Diary, Nov. 7, 1923, BGA; "Red Moscow a Whirl on Revolution Day," *New York Times*, Nov. 8, 1923.
2. Ben-Gurion 1971a, p. 181; Histadrut Council, Nov. 8, 1921, BGA; David Zakai, interview transcript, BGA; Ben-Gurion to the Histadrut founding convention, Nov. 28, 1920, in Erez 1972, p. 41.
3. Ben-Gurion, Diary, Oct. 18, 19, 1918, BGA; Anita Shapira 1988, p. 48; Ben-Gurion to the Mapai Convention, Aug. 23, 1946; Ben-Gurion 1993a, p. 154.
4. Ben-Gurion 1971a, p. 110; Tzachor 1981, p. 17ff.; Anita Shapira 1980, p. 121ff.
5. Shiloni 1985; Segev 2000, p. 65ff.; Ben-Gurion to Paula, July 16, 1919, in Erez 1971, p. 426.

6. Ben-Gurion to Paula, Nov. 18, 1918, in Erez 1971, p. 400.
7. Ben-Gurion to the Thirteenth Congress of Po'alei Zion, version 2, p. 25, BGA; Ben-Gurion to Paula, March 3, 1919, in Erez 1971, p. 414.
8. Ben-Gurion to the Thirteenth Congress of Po'alei Zion, Feb. 22, 1919, BGA.
9. Tzachor 1981, p. 38.
10. Ben-Gurion 1971a, p. 118.
11. Ben-Gurion 1971a, p. 116ff.; Yitzhak Ben-Zvi to Rachel Yanait, Nov. 24, 1918; Ben-Zvi 1967, p. 263.
12. Tzachor 1981, pp. 25, 140.
13. Ben-Gurion to Paula, March 3, 1919, in Erez 1971, p. 413.
14. Paula to Ben-Gurion, Sept. 14, 1918, March 1, Nov. 15, Sept. 24, July 30, 1919, Sept. 30, Oct. 30, 1918, BGA.
15. Paula to Ben-Gurion, April 7, 1919, Nov. 15, 1918, June 23, 1919, Nov. 22, 26, 1918, June 26, 1919, BGA; Ben-Gurion to Paula, May 17, July 16, 1919, in Erez 1971, pp. 420, 426.
16. Paula to Ben-Gurion, April 11, 1919, BGA; Ben-Gurion to Paula, April 15, May 17, 1919, in Erez 1971, pp. 415, 420; Ben-Gurion to his sister Tzipora, Dec. 29, 1918, in Erez 1971, p. 409; Ben-Gurion to Paula, May 8, 1919, Nov. 18, 1918, in Erez 1971, pp. 400, 409, 418; Ben-Gurion to his father, July 1, 1919, BGA.
17. Teveth 1977, p. 19; Ben-Gurion, Diary, Dec. 7, 8, 12, 13, 1918.
18. Teveth 1977, p. 476; Ben-Gurion to his father, Nov. 24, 1919, in Ben-Gurion 1971a, p. 153.
19. Ben-Gurion to the Provisional Committee, July 9, 1919, CZA J1/8777.
20. Intelligence reports from meetings, copies in English, BGA, general chronological documentation, 1919–1920.
21. Ben-Gurion 1971a, pp. 130, 143; Segev 2000, p. 122ff.
22. Teveth 1980, p. 65; Barnea 1981, p. 156.
23. Minutes of the Ahdut Ha'avodah Executive, Jan. 20, 1921, BGA, minutes, Ahdut Ha'avodah; Ben-Gurion to Po'alei Zion in New York, Oct. 10, 1920, in Erez 1972, p. 8.
24. Ben-Gurion to David Eder, Sept. 12, 1919; Ben-Gurion to David Blumenfeld, Sept. 16, 1919; Eder to Ben-Gurion, Sept. 17, 1919; Ben-Gurion to the Provisional Committee, Sept. 30, 1919, BGA.
25. David Yizraeli to Ya'akov Ettinger, Nov. 28, 1919, BGA; Glass 2002, p. 199ff.
26. Ben-Gurion, Diary, April 12, 1919, Oct. 19, 24, 1924, BGA.
27. Segev 2000, p. 133ff.
28. Ben-Zvi, Diary, ed. Rachel Yanait Ben-Zvi, manuscript in YBZ, p. 4ff.; Moshe Smilansky 1921; Ben-Gurion, Diary, July 13, 1922, BGA; *Kontres* 19, Jan. 1923.
29. Ben-Gurion to the Executive of the Provisional Committee, June 23, 1919, *Hadashot Miha'aretz*, July 4, 1919; Ben-Gurion 1919.
30. *Doar Hayom*, April 28, 1920.
31. Y.K., "Aleinu Levater Hapa'am," *Doar Hayom*, April 20, 1920.
32. Yemima Rosenthal 1979, p. 43; Teveth 1980, p. 59.
33. Dinur 1954–1964, 1, 2, p. 665; Ben-Gurion to Po'alei Zion, New York, Oct. 19, 1919, in Erez 1972, p. 8.
34. Minutes of the Eighth Session of the Provisional Committee, Oct. 22–23, 1919, CZA J1/8782.

35. Yemima Rosenthal 1994, p. 165ff.
36. *Kontres* 47, July 1920; Ben-Gurion to Po'alei Zion in America, Jan. 6, Feb. 10, 1921, in Erez 1972, pp. 2, 5; Segev 2000, p. 144.
37. Ben-Gurion to his father, Sept. 7, 1920, in Erez 1972, p. 17; Ben-Gurion at a press conference, July 27, 1946, in Ben-Gurion 1993a, p. 91; Ben-Gurion to his father, Oct. 5, 1920, in Erez 1972, p. 24; Ben-Gurion to Rachel Yanait Ben-Zvi, Oct. 9, 1910, in Erez 1972, p. 26; Ben-Gurion to Shlomo Kaplansky, April 24, 1923, in Erez 1972, p. 125; Reader's card, BGA, general chronological documentation, 1921–22.
38. Ben-Gurion to Rachel Yanait and Ytizhak Ben-Zvi, Jan. 21, 1921, BGA; Ben-Gurion to Rachel Yanait, Oct. 9, 1920, in Erez 1972, p. 26; Berl Katznelson to Ben-Gurion, Oct. 2, Nov. 22, 1920, BGA; Moshe Shertok to Ben-Gurion, June 1, 1921, in Moshe Sharett 2003, p. 190; Teveth 1980, p. 119.
39. Dinur 1954–64, 2, 1, pp. 128ff., 148; Moshe Shertok to Ben-Gurion, June 1, July 24, 1921, in Moshe Sharett 2003, pp. 190, 274; Rivka Hoz to Eliyahu Golomb, July 25, 1921, in Moshe Sharett 2003, p. 276.
40. Tomaszewski 2001, p. 421.
41. Final report, Jan. 1, 1922, JDC Archive, AR 1921/1932, file 130.
42. Ben-Gurion to Zalman Rubashov, Dec. 14, 1921, in Erez 1972, p. 92.
43. Ben-Gurion to his father, June 6, 1921, March 23, 1922, in Erez 1972, pp. 66, 97.
44. *Hatzefirah*, May 3, 4, 1921; Zemach 1983, p. 116.
45. Moshe Shertok to Geula and Yehuda Shertok, May 7, 1921, in Moshe Sharett 2003, p. 166; Segev 2000, p. 173ff.
46. "Lefanim Ulahutz," *Ha'aretz*, May 9, 1921; "Lechol Beit Yisra'el," May 1921, *Knesset Yisra'el*, 1949, p. 45.
47. Ben-Gurion to the Zionist Executive, July 12, 1921, in Yogev and Freundlich 1984, p. 283; Ben-Gurion to his father, Aug. 5, 1921, in Erez 1972, p. 76; Moshe Shertok to Eliyahu Golomb, May 19, 1971, in Moshe Sharett 2003, p. 229.
48. Berl Repetur, Zvi Lieberman, Walter Preuss, interview transcripts, BGA; Ben-Gurion, Diary, April 3, 1922, BGA; Ben-Gurion to his father, March 28, 1922, in Erez 1972, p. 97; Teveth 1980, p. 619, note 34.
49. Ben-Gurion, Diary, Feb. 11, 13, 15, 16, March 20, April 5, 1922, BGA.
50. Ben-Gurion to the Council of the World Union of Po'alei Zion in Vienna, Sept. 1, 1921, in Erez 1972, p. 80ff.; Tzachor 1981, p. 206ff.
51. Ben-Gurion to a Po'alei Zion delegation, March 16, 1920, in Haim Golan 1989, p. 189ff.; Gorny 1973, p. 175.
52. Ben-Gurion to his father, Aug. 5, 1921, March 28, 1922, in Erez 1972, pp. 76, 98; Moshe Sharett to Eliyahu Golomb, Nov. 20, 1921, in Sharett 2003, p. 92.
53. Paula to Ben-Gurion, Sept. 10, 1921, BGA.
54. Ben-Gurion to his father, June 6, Aug. 5, 1921, March 28, 1922, in Erez 1972, pp. 66, 76, 97; Binyamin Ben-Gurion interview with Shabtai Teveth, BGA, Teveth collection, file 1100.
55. Ben-Gurion, Diary, April 8, 7, 24, 5, 29, June 26, 1922, BGA.
56. Ben-Avram and Nir 1995, p. 10.
57. Adams, Frank, et al. 1928, pp. 14, 707.
58. Nordheimer 2014.
59. Avraham Tarshish interview transcript, BGA; Anita Shapira 1989, p. 157ff.

60. Lavi 1968, p. 8.
61. Lavi 1947, pp. 58, 63.
62. Lavi 1947, pp. 67, 115, 120; Stein 1984, p. 56ff.
63. Ben-Gurion eulogy for Shlomo Lavi, 1963, http://www.en-harod.org.
64. Lavi 1947, pp. 129, 287, 156, 162.
65. Lavi 1947, p. 193; Avraham Tarshish, interview transcript, BGA.
66. Lavi 1947, pp. 135, 136, 193; Ben-Gurion to the Histadrut Executive, May 15, 1923, BGA.
67. Lavi 1947, p. 189; Ben-Gurion, Diary, Jan. 14, 1922, BGA; Avraham Tarshish interview transcript, BGA; Dov Hoz to Rivka Golomb, Pesach 1921, BGA, Dov Hoz personal archive.
68. Tzachor 1990, p. 128ff.
69. Ben-Gurion, Diary, Oct. 9, 1922, BGA.
70. Ben-Gurion to the Histadrut Executive, Dec. 13, 1922, April 11, 1923, BGA; Lavi 1947, pp. 185, 195; Ein Harod, Tel Yosef, and [Jezreel] Valley Settlement file 1921–23, BGA, Yehuda Erez personal archive.
71. *Miheienu—Iton Gdud Ha'avodah* 40, June 21, 1923, Labor Archive edition, 1971.
72. Ben-Zvi and others at the secretariat of the Histadrut Executive, June 15, 1923, BGA; Sternhell 1986, p. 262ff.
73. "10,000 Men Working on Moscow's Big Fair," *New York Times*, July 22, 1923.
74. Ben-Gurion 1971a, p. 220ff.; Frederick Kisch to the first secretary, July 6, 1923; Ben-Gurion to Paula, Aug. 14, 1923; Ben-Gurion to the members of the Histadrut Executive, Aug. 14, 1923, Ben-Gurion to the Histadrut Executive, Aug. 24, 1923, BGA.
75. Gorny 1971, p. 120; Ben-Gurion to a Po'alei Zion delegation, Nov. 11, April 11, 1920, in Haim Golan 1989, p. 46.
76. Ben-Gurion interview with Dov Goldstein, *Ma'ariv*, Sept. 28, 1966; Ben-Gurion 1971a, p. 380.
77. Ben-Gurion 1971a, p. 453; Ben-Gurion at a gathering of enlistees, April 20, 1943, in Ben-Gurion 1949, 3, pp. 142, 155.
78. Ben-Gurion to the Provisional Committee, Feb. 24, 1920, CZA J1 8785/6; Ben-Gurion to the Fourth Congress of Ahdut Ha'avodah, Sept. 7, 1924, in Ben-Gurion 1955a, p. 221; Ben-Gurion to a Po'alei Zion delegation, March 17, 1920, in Haim Golan 1989, p. 201; Ben-Gurion 1925; Kolatt 1988, p. 118ff.; Sternhell 1986, p. 269.
79. Ben-Gurion to a rally in Tel Aviv, *Davar*, April 18, 1928; Ben-Gurion to the Mapai Council, March 7, 1941, in Ben-Gurion 2008, pp. 248, 376; Berl Repetur, interview transcript, BGA.
80. Berl Repetur, Akiva Govrin, interview transcripts, BGA.
81. Ben-Gurion 1971a, p. 228ff.; Ben-Gurion, Diary, Sept. 1, 1923, BGA.
82. Ben-Gurion, Diary, Aug. 30, 31, Nov. 7, 1923, BGA; "Red Moscow a Whirl on Revolution Day," *New York Times*, Nov. 8, 1923.
83. Ben-Gurion 1971a, pp. 232, 237, 241; Rotberg report on the Moscow Fair, secretariat of the Histadrut Executive, Feb. 8, 1924, BGA.
84. Elazar Galili 1988, pp. 27, 31; Elazar Galili interview, Jan. 4, 1976, conversation 14, HIJC-OHA; Ben-Gurion, Diary, Jan. 26, 1924, BGA.
85. Ben-Gurion 1971a, p. 262ff.

86. Ben-Gurion 1971a, p. 245.
87. Ben-Gurion 1971a, p. 268.

9. SCANDALS

1. Ben-Gurion, Diary, March 20, 1926, Oct. 17, 1924, BGA.
2. Ben-Gurion to the offices of the World Union of Po'alei Zion, March 8, 1926, in Erez 1972, p. 309; Ben-Gurion to Meir Sheli-Bogdan, March 15, 1926, in Erez 1972, p. 311; Ben-Gurion, Diary, Jan. 21, Feb. 2, BGA.
3. Teveth 1980, p. 180ff.; Tzachor 1981.
4. Ben-Gurion, Diary, Oct. 7, 1922, BGA.
5. Ben-Gurion, "Haroshet," in Ben-Gurion 1955a, p. 216ff.
6. Ben-Gurion to the Zionist Executive, May 27, 1924, BGA, general chronological documentation; Ben-Gurion to the secretariat of the Histadrut Executive, June 30, 1924; Ben-Gurion 1925.
7. Yitzhak Lufban, "Hasbarah," *Hapo'el Hatza'ir*, Dec. 26, 1924.
8. Ben-Gurion to the secretariat of the Histadrut Executive, April 26, 1924, BGA; Ben-Gurion to Ben-Zvi, July 18, 1924, BGA, general chronological documentation; Ben-Gurion 1971a, p. 313.
9. Ben-Gurion, Diary, April 3, July 6, 1924, BGA.
10. Ben-Gurion, Diary, June 5, 1924, BGA.
11. Ben-Gurion, Diary, Feb. 17, 1922, BGA; Ben-Gurion 1971a, p. 205.
12. Berl Repetur, interview transcript, BGA.
13. Berl Repetur, interview transcript, BGA.
14. Ben-Gurion, Diary, March 22, 24, 25, 27, 1924, BGA.
15. Erez 1953.
16. Mordechai Ish Shalom and Yehiel Duvdevani, interview transcripts, BGA.
17. Ben-Gurion to David Zakai, Oct. 26, 1924, in Erez 1972, p. 242; Ben-Gurion to Meir Sheli-Bogdan, Dec. 17, 1924, in Erez 1972, p. 282.
18. Ben-Gurion to MacDonald, July 25, 1923, in Erez 1972, p. 140; Ben-Gurion to the National Council, Aug. 21, 1923, in Erez 1972, p. 149; Ben-Gurion 1971a, p. 220; Shchori 1990, p. 272ff.
19. Ben-Gurion, Diary, Oct. 9, 10, 1926, BGA.
20. Ben-Gurion to David Zakai, Oct. 26, 1924, in Erez 1972, p. 240; Ben-Gurion to Ze'evi, Nov. 19, 1924, in Erez 1972, p. 262; Ben-Gurion to Meir Sheli-Bogdan, Dec. 31, 17, 1924, in Erez 1972, pp. 288, 282; Ben-Gurion, Diary, Jan. 7, May 26, 1925, BGA; Teveth 1980, pp. 186, 252.
21. Isser Harel, interview, GMA, LMA, oral documentation, fourth interview, p. 18; Anita Shapira 1988, p. 63.
22. Nakdimon and Mayzlish 1985, p. 241ff.; Dinur 1954–1964, 2, 1, pp. 227, 252; Segev 2000, p. 208ff.; Ben-Gurion to the Assembly of Representatives, *Ha'aretz*, March 8, 1922; Barzilay 1985; Ben-Gurion, Diary, July 1, 1924, BGA.
23. Nakdimon and Mayzlish 1985, pp. 197ff., 224ff.; Katzman 1985.
24. Ben-Gurion, Diary, April 28, 1924, BGA.
25. Decisions of the Histadrut Council, April 27–29, 1924, minutes, June 14, 1924, p. 2, BGA, Teveth collection, concepts, faction; Ben-Gurion, Diary, April 28, 1924, BGA.

26. Sprinzak to the Histadrut Convention, Feb. 20, 1923, BGA, Teveth collection, concepts, faction; Ben-Gurion and Sprinzak to the secretariat of the Histadrut Executive, June 25, 1924, BGA.

27. Ben-Gurion to the Histadrut Executive, May 26, 1922, BGA; Ben-Gurion, Diary, Oct. 10, 1929, BGA; Ben-Gurion to David Zakai, April 24, 1924, BGA.

28. Manya Shohat to Ben-Gurion, July 23, 1926, and Ben-Gurion to Manya Shohat, July 26, 1926, in Reinharz et al. 2005, p. 184.

29. Shohat 1962, p. 69ff; Shaul Avigur, interview transcript, p. 7ff.; BGA; Dinur 1954–64, 2, 1, p. 234ff.

30. Ben-Gurion to the Third Histadrut Convention, July 10, 1927, BGA.

31. Ben-Gurion 1971a, p. 317.

32. http://history.state.gov/milestones/1921-1936/immigration-act.

33. Tomaszewski 2001, p. 422; Ben-Avram and Nir 1995, pp. 107, 193; Lissak 1994, 2, p. 173ff.

34. Ben-Gurion to the Agricultural Center, March 7, 1924, BGA; Ben-Gurion to the Hehalutz Central Committee, April 9, 1924, in Erez 1972, p. 205.

35. Ben-Gurion, Diary, April 7, 1924, BGA; Ben-Gurion to the Hehalutz Central Committee, Berlin, April 9, 1924, BGA; Ben-Gurion to the Hehalutz Central Committee in Russia, June 26, 1924, in Erez 1972, p. 221; Ben-Gurion, Diary, May 5, 1924, BGA.

36. Ben-Gurion to the Zionist Executive, Nov. 18, 1924, in Erez 1972, p. 260.

37. Giladi 1973, p. 47.

38. David Izmozhik, "Lo Yoshieinu Zeh," *Hayishuv*, Aug. 6, 1926; Giladi 1973, p. 47.

39. Ben-Gurion 1949, 5, pp. 58–59.

40. Ben-Gurion to his sister Tzipora, Nov. 19, 1924, in Erez 1972, p. 263.

41. Ben-Gurion to his father, Aug. 5, 1921, in Erez 1972, p. 76.

42. Ben-Gurion interview with Noah Orian, Nov. 12, 1969, HIJC; Teveth 1980, photographs; Giladi 1971, p. 131; Geula's report card, 1927, BGA, general chronological documentation.

43. Yigael Yadin, interview transcript, BGA.

44. Barel 2014, p. 68ff.

45. Ohana 2003, p. 57ff.; Keren 1988, p. 112ff.

46. Ben-Gurion to a gathering of fishermen, Dec. 23, 1943, in Ben-Gurion 1949, 3, p. 193.

47. Ben-Gurion, Diary, Sept. 13, Nov. 6, 1924, BGA.

48. Ben-Gurion, Diary, Dec. 3, 1925, BGA.

49. Moshe Smilansky to the Assembly of Representatives, according to *Davar*, Jan. 18, 1926; Ben-Gurion, Diary, Jan. 8, 1926, BGA.

50. Zemach 1983, pp. 76, 92, 102ff., 108, 115, 130; Zemach to Ben-Gurion, April 12, 1920, BGA; Ben-Gurion to his father, Aug. 5, 1921, in Erez 1972, p. 76.

51. Zemach to Ben-Gurion, Feb. 22, 1926, LMA 104IV, file 6; Ben-Gurion, Diary, March 3, 1926; BGA subject file, Smilansky, Moshe, suit against Ben-Gurion.

52. Avodah Ivrit Bamoshavot 1911–34, BGA, subject files; *Davar*, Dec. 28, 1927; *Ha'aretz*, Dec. 29, 1928.

53. Ben-Gurion, "Hapoe'l Ha'ivri Veha'aravi," "Avodah Ivrit o Me'urevet Bamoshavot," in Ben-Gurion 1931, p. 105ff.; "Al Bit'hon Hayishuv Vetafkid Hasochnut Basha'ah Zo," Oct. 20, 1929, BGA.

54. Ben-Gurion, "Avodah Ivrit o Me'urevet Bamoshavot," in Ben-Gurion 1931, p. 170; Ben-Gurion 1932.

55. Ben-Gurion, Diary, July 13, 1922, BGA; Ben-Gurion at the Ahdut Ha'avodah Convention, *Kontres* 119, Jan. 21, 1923; Teveth 1985, p. 100ff.

56. Ben-Gurion, "Al Hafelah Ve'admato," in Ben-Gurion 1931, p. 61.

57. Ben-Gurion, "Gevulei Artzenu Va'admatah," Ben-Gurion 1931, p. 34; Ben-Gurion, Diary, July 1, 1924, BGA; Tsoref 1998, p. 56.

58. Ben-Gurion, "Al Hafelah Ve'admato," "Al Gevulei Ha'aretz," "El Hapo'alim Ha'aravim," "Shnei Gormim," in Ben-Gurion 1931, pp. 61, 62, 67ff., 72ff., 98; Ben-Gurion to the secretariat of the Histadrut Executive, March 30, June 16, 1924, BGA; Ben-Gurion to Yitzhak Ben-Zvi, July 18, 1934, BGA; Ben-Gurion 1971a, pp. 269ff., 312.

59. Ben-Gurion, Diary, April 3, 1924, BGA.

60. Ben-Gurion, Diary, March 20, 21, Dec. 1, 1924, Jan. 10, 1925, BGA.

61. Berl Repetur, interview transcript, p. 130, BGA.

62. Memoirs of Avigdor Gruen, p. 16, BGA, subject file 470-1-18.

63. Ben-Gurion to his father, Nov. 24, 1919, in Ben-Gurion 1971a, p. 154ff.

64. Ben-Gurion to his father, Oct. 5, 1920, in Ben-Gurion 1971a, p. 159ff.

65. Ben-Gurion to his father, Sept. 17, 1920, in Ben-Gurion 1971a, p. 159ff.

66. Ben-Gurion to his father, Sept. 30, 1931, in Erez 1972, p. 90; Ben-Gurion to Tzipora, Aug. 23, 1922, in Erez 1972, p. 112; Ben-Gurion to Tzipora, Aug. 8, 1922, BGA; Hagani 2010, p. 16ff.

67. Ben-Gurion to his father, March 28, 1922, in Erez 1972, p. 99.

68. Ben-Gurion to his father, Aug. 4, 1923, BGA; Ben-Gurion to his father, July 2, 1924, in Erez 1972, p. 225ff.

69. Ben-Gurion, Diary, July 12, 14, 18, 1925, BGA.

70. Ben-Gurion, Diary, April 5, 1926, BGA.

71. Ben-Gurion, Diary, June 6–7, 1926, BGA.

72. Ben-Gurion, Diary, June 12, 1924; Dov Hoz to his wife, Pesach 1921, BGA.

73. Giladi 1971, p. 128ff.

74. Lissak 1994, 2, p. 214ff.

75. Ben-Gurion to an Ahdut Ha'avodah assembly, Oct. 26, 1926, in Greenberg 1989, p. 24ff.; Ben-Gurion, Diary, July 22, 1924, BGA.

76. *Ha'aretz*, Jan. 17, 1926; Ben-Gurion, Diary, Dec. 30, 1925, BGA; Cahan, "The Palestine Labor Movement," *Forverts*, Dec. 10, 1925.

77. Giladi 1971, p. 138ff.

78. Ben-Gurion, Diary, Jan. 16, May 22–25, 1924.

79. *Kontres* 290, Jan. 21, 1927; Histadrut Council, Feb. 2, 1972, BGA, general chronological documentation; Ben-Gurion to Sprinzak at the Histadrut Council, Feb. 1927, BGA; Ben-Gurion, Diary, Feb. 2, 1927, BGA.

80. Ben-Gurion, Diary, March 10, 1927, BGA; Ben-Gurion, Yosef Sprinzak, et al. at the Histadrut Executive, March 24, 1927, BGA; *Davar*, March 11–14, 1927.

81. Ben-Gurion, Diary, June 20, 1922, BGA; Teveth 1980, p. 242ff.

82. Ben-Gurion, Diary, Jan. 7, 1926, BGA; Accounting Department to Ben-Gurion, July 1, 1924, BGA, general chronological documentation.

83. "Al Dargat Hamaskoret Vetashlumeha Bamosdot Hahistadrut," *Davar*, June 13, 1927; Teveth 1980, pp. 356, 381ff.

84. Ben-Gurion 1971a, pp. 569, 334, 546, 311, 333ff.; Ben-Gurion, "Likrat Have'idah," in Greenberg 1989, pp. 44–49; Ben-Gurion to the Zionist Executive, Nov. 18, 1924, in Erez 1972, p. 260; Ben-Gurion, Diary, July 22, 1924, BGA.
85. Erez 1972, p. 368; Segev 2000, p. 2.
86. Yemima Rosenthal 1979, p. 136.
87. Ben-Gurion, Diary, June 14, 1927, BGA.
88. The Third Histadrut Convention, July 1927, Ben-Gurion, minutes, pp. 14, 27, 36, 42, 43.
89. Arlosoroff and Katznelson at the Third Histadrut Convention, July 7, 1927, BGA minutes, pp. 30ff., 45.
90. Proceedings of the Third Histadrut Convention, July 22, 1927, BGA, minutes, p. 265; Avizohar 1990, p. 71.

10. UNIFICATION

 1. Ben-Gurion, Diary, Nov. 12, July 9, Sept. 8, 1935, BGA.
 2. Haim Israeli, interview transcript, BGA.
 3. Ben-Gurion, Diary, May 25, 1928, BGA; Ze'ev Sherf, interview transcript, BGA; Anita Shapira 1980, p. 295.
 4. Data from the National Insurance Institute Memorial Site, http://www.laad.btl.gov.il.
 5. Ben-Gurion and Jabotinsky at the National Council, Oct. 16, 1928, CZA J1/7232; *Davar*, Oct. 18, 1928; Ben-Gurion, "Al Hakotel Veha'ikar," in Ben-Gurion 1931, p. 256; *Doar Hayom*, Oct. 17, 1928; Jabotinsky 1953, pp. 251–60.
 6. *Doar Hayom*, July 4, 1929; Jabotinsky 1932.
 7. Lavi 1947, p. 277.
 8. Hillel Cohen, 2013; Segev 2000, p. 295ff.
 9. Ben-Gurion, Diary, Sept. 4, 8, 9, Oct. 11, 1929, BGA; Ben-Gurion, "Al Me'ora'ot Av," "Birurim," "Darkeinu Hamedinit la'ahar Hame'ora'ot," "Hamediniyut Hahistzonit shel Ha'am Ha'ivri," "Avtonomiah Le'umit Vayahasei Shekhenim," in Ben-Gurion 1931, pp. 173, 181, 165, 224, 129, 264, 214, 130; Ben-Gurion to the Histadrut Executive, Sept. 5, 1929, BGA.
10. Ben-Gurion 1971a, pp. 388, 472; Ben-Gurion, "Al Me'ora'ot Av," "Darkeinu Hamedinit la'ahar Hame'ora'ot," "Nokhah Ha'emet," in Ben-Gurion 1931, pp. 175, 125, 142.
11. Ben-Gurion, Diary, April 11, 19, May 12, June 28, July 2, 28, 1933, BGA; *Davar*, March 21, 1933; *Hazit Ha'am*, Nov. 4, 1932; Teveth 1980, p. 541ff.; Shmuel Katz 1993, p. 825ff.; Bechor et al. 1985, p. 39ff.
12. Ben-Gurion, "Hasihah," Ben-Gurion 1931, p. 151; Ben-Gurion 1971a, pp. 337ff., 298ff.
13. Ben-Gurion, Diary, Nov. 5–7, 1929, May 5, 1930, March 11, 1936, BGA; Ben-Gurion to the National Council, Oct. 15, 1928, CZA J1/7232; "Darkeinu Hamedinit la'ahar Hame'ora'ot," in Ben-Gurion 1931, pp. 226, 168; Teveth 1985, p. 152ff.
14. Ben-Gurion, "Autonomiyah Le'umit Vayahasei Shechenim," in Ben-Gurion 1955a, p. 79ff.; Teveth 1985, p. 118ff.
15. "Al Bit'hon Hayishuv Vatafkid Hatziyonut Basha'ah Zo," Oct. 20, 1929, BGA.
16. Ben-Gurion, Diary, Nov. 3, 8, 1929, BGA; Ben-Gurion, "Hanahot Lekevi'at Mishtar Mamlachti Behetem Latvi'ot Hamandat Leshe'ifot Ha'am Ha'aravi Veletzarchei Ha'aravim in Ba'aretz," Nov. 23, 1929, BGA; Ben-Gurion, "Hamediniyut Hahitzonit shel Ha'am Ha'ivri," in Ben-Gurion 1931, p. 182ff.; "Al Bit'hon Hayishuv Vatafkid Hatziyonut Basha'ah Zo," Oct. 20, 1929, BGA.

17. Ben-Gurion to the Ein Harod Convention, 1924, in Ben-Gurion 1931, p. 7.

18. Ben-Gurion, "Tazkir Lava'adat Hahakirah," Dec. 24, 1929, in Ben-Gurion 1931, p. 208.

19. Dinur 1954–64, 2, 1, pp. 298, 359, 417ff.; Dinur 1954–64, 2, 1, p. 1296; Segev 2000, p. 194.

20. Ben-Gurion, Diary, July 14, 1924, Nov. 3, 5, 1925, May 10, 1929, BGA; Dinur 1954–64, 2, 1, p. 258ff.; Dinur 1954–64, 2, 3, p. 1294.

21. Ben-Gurion, Diary, Sept. 21, 1929, BGA.

22. Dinur 1954–64, 2, 1, p. 424ff.

23. Ben-Gurion, "Hakamat Ko'ah Tzva'i Yehudi" (Sept. 6, 1963), in Ben-Gurion 1963b.

24. Ben-Gurion, Diary, Sept. 9, 1929, BGA; Ve'idat Ha'ihud, 1/1930/-5-7, BGA; *Davar*, Jan. 8, 9, 1930; Teveth 1980, p. 482; Gorny 1973, p. 315ff.; Avizohar 1990, p. 62ff.; Erez 1971, p. 95, editor's note.

25. Segev 2000, p. 335ff.

26. Ben-Gurion, "Shtei He'arot Lavikuah Hapolitit," "Nochah Ha'emet," "Mizrah Uma'arav," in Ben-Gurion 1931, pp. 234, 241, 247; Ben-Gurion to the Mapai Council, Oct. 25, 1930, BGA.

27. Ben-Gurion et al. at the Mapai Council, Oct. 25, 1930, BGA.

28. Ben-Gurion, Diary, July 10, 17, 1930, BGA; Ben-Gurion to his father, June 5, 1929, in Erez 1974, p. 50; Ben-Gurion to Paula, July 17, 1939, in Erez 1974, p. 97; Ben-Gurion to Golomb, July 17, 1930, in Erez 1974, p. 112; Ben-Gurion to his father, July 29, 1930, in Erez 1974, p. 113.

29. Ben-Gurion to Paula, Aug. 27, 1930, in Erez 1974, p. 53; Elam 1990, pp. 211ff., 292ff.; Segev 2000, p. 332.

30. Teveth 1980, 2, pp. 492, 639.

31. Ben-Gurion, Diary, June 29, 1929, BGA.

32. Paula to Ben-Gurion, Aug. 10, 1930, BGA.

33. Elam 1990, p. 125.

34. Ben-Gurion to Paula, Aug. 12, 1929, in Erez 1974, p. 66; Ben-Gurion, "Al Bit'hon Hayishuv Ubitzrono," in Ben-Gurion 1931, p. 187.

35. Ben-Gurion, Diary, Dec. 26, 1930, BGA; "Me'eretz-Yisrael," *Ha'olam*, July 26, 1929; Elam 1990, pp. 139, 353.

36. Fisher 1994, p. 286; Weizmann to Felix M. Warburg, Jan. 16, 1930, in Litvinoff 1978, p. 201.

37. Elam 1990, pp. 266, 361; Ben-Gurion to colleagues, Sept. 2, 1930; Erez 1974, p. 134.

38. Ben-Gurion interview with Noah Orian, Nov. 12, 1969, HIJC-OHA 10 (56), p. 7; Ben-Gurion, Diary, July 29, 1930, July 11, Aug. 15, 1931, BGA; Ben-Gurion 1971a, p. 480ff.; Ben-Gurion 1973, p. 140.

39. Elam 1990, p. 360ff.

40. Ben-Gurion 1971a, p. 578; Ben-Gurion 1932, p. 16ff.

41. Ben-Gurion to Paula, May 11, 1933, in Erez 1974, p. 252; Teveth 1980, p. 578.

42. Ben-Gurion, Diary, Sept. 10, April 29, 1931, BGA; Teveth 1980, p. 574ff.

43. Ben-Gurion, Diary, April 19, 23, 29, 1931, BGA.

44. Ben-Gurion to Klapholz, Sept. 27, 1932, BGA; Ben-Gurion, Diary, Sept. 10, 1932, BGA.

45. Ben-Gurion to Heschel Frumkin, Sept. 16, 1930, in Erez 1974, p. 145; *Davar*, Feb. 13, 1933; Daniel Heller 2017, pp. 16ff.

46. *Davar*, March 21, 1933.

47. Ben-Gurion to Klapholz, June 26, 1933, BGA.

48. Ben-Gurion, Diary, May 10, 1933, BGA.

49. Haim Ya'ari, interview transcript, BGA; Ben-Gurion, Diary, Aug. 26, 1932, April 22, 1933, BGA.

50. Ben-Gurion, Diary, March 1, April 8, May 9, 18, June 6, 1933, BGA; Ben-Gurion to Israel Marminsky, June 5, 1933, in Erez 1974, p. 296.

51. Ben-Gurion, Diary, June 7, 1933, BGA.

52. Ben-Gurion, Diary, May 26, 27, 1933, BGA; Baruch Azanya, Haim Ya'ari, interview transcripts, BGA.

53. Yemima Rosenthal 1979, pp. 222, 295.

54. Oznia, interview transcript, BGA.

55. Ben-Gurion to Paula, April 25, June 2, 1933, in Erez 1974, pp. 240, 192; Hillel Dan, interview transcript, BGA; Ben-Gurion, Diary, June 6, 1934.

56. Ben-Gurion, Diary, April 7, 24, May 24, 30, 1933, BGA; Ben-Gurion to Klapholz, April 29, 1933, BGA.

57. Ben-Gurion 1933; Ben-Gurion, Diary, April 22, 23, May 1, 7, 9, 24, 27, 29, June 15, 3, 1933, BGA; Dan, interview transcript, BGA.

58. Ben-Gurion, Diary, July 27, 1933, BGA.

59. Ben-Gurion, Diary, June 17, 23, 27, 1933, BGA; Ben-Gurion to Paula, March 26, 1933, in Erez 1974, p. 317; Bechor et al. 1985, pp. 17, 39ff.; Eliyahu Dobkin, Anshel Reiss, interview transcripts, BGA.

60. Ben-Gurion, Diary, June 17, 23, 27, 28, July 3, 1933, BGA.

61. Ben-Gurion to Klapholz, July 7, 1933, BGA.

62. Ben-Gurion, Diary, July 3, 1936.

63. Ben-Gurion, Diary, July 26, 1933, BGA; Dan, interview transcript, BGA.

64. Teveth 1987b, p. 25ff.

65. Ben-Gurion to Klapholz, August 19, 1932, BGA.

66. Ben-Gurion to Klapholz, Dec. 18, 1933, BGA.

67. Ben-Gurion to Klapholz, Feb. 19, July 8, 1934, BGA.

68. Teveth 1987b, p. 98; Rega Klapholz, subject file, Shabtai Teveth archive, BGA.

69. Klapholz to Baratz, Feb. 15, 1936, courtesy of the Degania Alef Archive; Baratz's letters to Klapholz, 1932–34, courtesy of Oren Baratz.

70. Ben-Gurion, pocket diary, Aug. 28, 1933, BGA; Teveth 1987, p. 68; Ben-Gurion to Klapholz, July 1, 1933, BGA.

11. CONVERSATIONS

1. Ben-Gurion, Diary, April 16–20, 1935, BGA; Katznelson, Diary, April 16–20, 1935, CAHJP, 4-006-1924-263; Padeh 1993, p. 203; "Be'ayat Hakarka'ot: Hanegev Ve'akabah," submitted to Louis Brandeis, June 4, 1935, in Ben-Gurion 1972, p. 321ff.

2. Ben-Gurion to Paula, Sept. 6, 1933, in Erez 1974, p. 354.

3. Ben-Gurion 1972, p. 435ff.; Ben-Gurion, Diary, Sept. 14, 1935, BGA; Ben-Gurion 1971c.

4. Ben-Gurion, Diary, Aug. 30, Sept. 7, 1935, BGA.

5. Ben-Gurion to the Histadrut Convention, Jan. 10, 1934, in Ben-Gurion 1972, pp. 11,

13; *Davar*, Jan. 14, 1934; Ben-Gurion to Edmond de Rothschild, Jan. 5, 1934, in Ben-Gurion 1972, p. 4ff.; Ben-Gurion to Louis Brandeis, Jan. 5, 1934, BGA.

6. Ben-Gurion to the National Council, Dec. 12, 1938, BGA.

7. Ben-Gurion to Edmond de Rothschild, Jan. 5, 1934, in Ben-Gurion 1972, p. 4ff.; Ben-Gurion to Louis Brandeis, Jan. 5, 1934, BGA.

8. Ben-Gurion to Shmuel Fuchs, Dec. 14, 1904, in Erez 1971, p. 391; Ben-Gurion 1971a, p. 312.

9. Ben-Gurion to the Mapai Council, Oct. 26, 1933, BGA; Ben-Gurion to members of Hano'ar Ha'oved, Dec. 4, 1937, in Ben-Gurion 1974a, p. 460; Ben-Gurion to Zionist emissaries in Warsaw, April 19, 1933, and Ben-Gurion to Mapai members, July 9, 1933, in Ben-Gurion 1971, pp. 611, 644; Ben-Gurion, Diary, April 22, 1933, BGA.

10. Ben-Gurion to Chaim Weizmann, Oct. 26, 1933, in Erez 1974, p. 360; Anglo-American Committee of Inquiry 1946, 1, p. 185.

11. Segev 1993, p. 18ff.

12. "Mistorei Hatransfer," "Ervat Haha'avarah," *Hayarden*, Nov. 10, 13, 1935.

13. Ben-Gurion to the National Council, *Davar*, Dec. 17, 1935; Ben-Gurion to the Jewish Agency Executive, Nov. 23, 1935, BGA; Ben-Gurion to the Political Committee, May 4, 1936, in Ben-Gurion 1973, p. 143.

14. Ben-Gurion to the Political Committee, April 7, 1936; Ben-Gurion to the Jewish Agency Executive, May 19, 1936; Ben-Gurion to Zalman Shazar, May 31, 1936, in Ben-Gurion 1973, pp. 113, 203, 225; Segev 1993 pp. 42–43, 31ff.

15. Ben-Gurion to the National Council, May 5, 1936, p. 164; Ben-Gurion and Moshe Shertok to the high commissioner, July 9, 1936, in Ben-Gurion 1973, pp. 162, 322.

16. Ben-Gurion to the Zionist Executive, Dec. 29, 1935, in Ben-Gurion 1972, p. 566; Ben-Gurion to the National Council, Dec. 12, 1938, BGA; Ben-Gurion to the Zionist Executive, Oct. 3, 1938, in Ben-Gurion 1982b, p. 290; *Davar*, Nov. 16, 1938.

17. Ben-Gurion to the Zionist Congress, Aug. 24, 1933, in Ben-Gurion 1971a, p. 661.

18. Ben-Gurion at the Mapai Council, Jan. 19, 1933, BGA.

19. Ben-Gurion, Diary, Dec. 12, 1933, June 1, 1935, June 11, 1937, BGA.

20. Halamish 1993, p. 98ff.

21. Segev 2000, p. 394ff.; Katznelson to the Mapai Central Committee, July 18, 1934, in Ben-Gurion 1972, p. 127.

22. Ben-Gurion to Simon Marks, Dec. 31, 1935, in Ben-Gurion 1972, p. 570.

23. Ben-Gurion, Diary, Dec. 19, 1938, BGA; Ben-Gurion to Paula, March 23, 1938, Ben-Gurion 1982b, p. 168.

24. *Davar*, March 1, 1935.

25. Jabotinsky, "Der Krieg," *Der Moment*, April 14, 1933, JIA, articles, 119/1933.

26. Ben-Gurion, Diary, June 27, 1933, BGA; Teveth 1982; Bechor et al. 1985; Shmuel Katz 1993, p. 885ff.; Yemima Rosenthal 1979, pp. 276, 277, 279; Segev 1994, p. 16ff.

27. Ben-Gurion, Diary, Sept. 13, Oct. 3, 4, 9, 1934, BGA; Shmuel Katz 1993, p. 885ff.

28. Ben-Gurion to the Mapai Central Committee, Oct. 28, 1934, BGA.

29. Weizmann to the Zionist Congress, Aug. 10, 1937, in Ben-Gurion 1974a, p. 416.

30. Ben-Gurion, Diary, Sept. 4, 1934, July 20, 1936, BGA; Ben-Gurion 1971a, p. 477; Yegar 2011, p. 163ff.

31. Jabotinsky 1949, p. 207.

32. Jabotinsky 1953, p. 251ff.; Ben-Gurion, "Al Me'ora'ot Av," in Ben-Gurion 1931, p. 177ff.

33. Ben-Gurion to Jabotinsky, Oct. 28, 1934, and Jabotinsky to Ben-Gurion, Oct. 29, 1934, in Ben-Gurion 1972, pp. 199, 214; Ben-Gurion, Diary, Oct. 31, 1934, BGA; Ben-Gurion, Diary, Oct. 28, 31, 1934, BGA; Jabotinsky to Edna Ya'akobi, Nov. 4, 1934, JIA, letter 2393; Shmuel Katz 1993, p. 927ff.

34. Ben-Gurion, Diary, Nov. 1, 1934, BGA; Shaltiel 1990, p. 437.

35. Ben-Gurion to Berl Katznelson at the Mapai Central Committee, Feb. 21, 1934, BGA; Ben-Gurion 1972, p. 182ff.; Ben-Gurion, Diary, Oct. 24, 29, Nov. 8, 1934, BGA; Berl Katznelson, Diary, Nov. 8, 1934, LPA, 4-006-1924-263.

36. Ben-Gurion to Amos, Nov. 8, 1934, in Ben-Gurion 1972, p. 229; Ben-Gurion to Amos, May 7, 1935, BGA.

37. Ben-Gurion to the Cabinet, Jan. 23, 1951, ISA.

38. Ben-Gurion to Paula, June 18, 1936, in Ben-Gurion 1968, p. 154.

39. Mary Ben-Gurion, interviewed by Shabtai Teveth, May 6, 1974, BGA, Teveth collection, file 361.

40. Amos Ben-Gurion interviewed by Dov Goldstein, *Ma'ariv*, Oct. 17, 1986; Ahuvia Malchin, Haim Cohn, Geula Ben-Eliezer, interview transcripts, BGA; Ben-Gurion to Paula, June 4, to Amos, July 27–28, to Renana, March 1, 1938, and Jan. 8, 1939, in Ben-Gurion 1968, pp. 171, 220, 274; Ben-Gurion to the Cabinet, Jan. 23, 1951, ISA.

41. Renana Leshem–Ben-Gurion interviewed by Ze'ev Segal, *Bamahaneh*, Nov. 24, 1976.

42. Ben-Gurion, Diary, Nov. 7, 1934, BGA; Shmuel Katz 1993, p. 923.

43. Yemima Rosenthal 1979, p. 296; *Davar*, March 26, 1935; Ben-Gurion, Diary, Sept 7, 1935, Aug. 16, 1939, BGA.

44. Ben-Gurion to the Mapai Central Committee, July 6, 1938, BGA.

45. Ben-Gurion, Diary, April 20, 1936, BGA.

46. Teveth 1985, p. 285ff.

47. Ben-Gurion, Diary, April 20, May 31, 1936, Dec. 16, 1938, BGA; "Od Kever Ahim," *Davar*, April 20, 1936; Heschel Yeivin 1937, p. 1ff.

48. Yemima Rosenthal 1979, pp. 259, 265.

49. Ben-Gurion to the Mapai Central Committee, Sept. 29, 1936, in Ben-Gurion 1973, p. 443.

50. Ben-Gurion to the Mapai Central Committee, July 6, 1938, BGA; Ben-Gurion to Moshe Sharett, in Ben-Gurion, Diary, June 26, 1937, BGA; Teveth 1987b, p. 155ff.; Segev 2000, pp. 370–71.

51. Stern 1974, p. 15; Ben-Gurion to the Jewish Agency Executive, May 19, 1936, in Ben-Gurion 1973, p. 200; *A Survey of Palestine*, 1946, 1, pp. 141, 185.

52. Ben-Gurion to the Mapai Central Committee, Sept. 29, 1935, BGA; Segev 2000, p. 350ff.; Ben-Gurion to the members of the Zionist Executive in London, Nov. 2, 1933, CZA S25/4224; Ben-Gurion, Diary, June 25, 1937, BGA.

53. Ben-Gurion to the Jewish Agency, May 19, 1936, and to Moshe Sharett, Aug. 2, 1936, in Ben-Gurion 1973, pp. 198, 356.

54. Ben-Gurion, Diary, Sept. 4, 1934, BGA; Ben-Gurion 1972, p. 163ff.; Ben-Gurion to Arthur Wauchope, July 29–30, 1934; Ben-Gurion to Judah Magnes, Sept. 7, 1934, in Ben-Gurion, Diary, BGA; Moshe Glickson to Moshe Shertok, Feb. 28, 1946 (Conversations with Arabs, 1934–45), CZA S25/8085; Meetings with Arabs, April 23, 1936, CZA S25/10188; Ben-Gurion to the Jewish Agency Executive, May 19, 1936, in Ben-Gurion

1973, p. 198ff.; Ben-Gurion 1967, p. 19; Lazar 2012, p. 11ff.; Ben-Gurion to the German and Austrian Immigrants Association, March 20, 1941, in Ben-Gurion 2008, p. 299; Ben-Gurion to the Cabinet, Jan. 20, 1952, and April 26, 1953, NA; Ben-Gurion to Martin Buber, Feb. 24, 1958, in Ben-Gurion, Diary, Feb. 24, 1958, BGA; Ben-Gurion interview with Walter Laqueur, 1960, BGA; Ben-Gurion, interview with *Nitzotz*, April 28, 1968.

55. Ben-Gurion with the high commissioner, July 29–30, 1934, CZA S25 17/1; Ben-Gurion, Diary, Aug. 11, 1936, Nov. 26, 1938, BGA; Segev 2000, pp. 365, 382.

56. Ben-Gurion, Diary, June 18, Aug. 16, 1936, BGA; Ben-Gurion to the Mapai Central Committee, July 6, 1938, BGA.

57. Elam 1979, p. 58ff.

58. Ben-Gurion, Diary, June 1, May 20, 1935, April 22, 1936, BGA.

59. Ben-Gurion, Diary, May 17, 1935, July 23, 1936, June 6, 1935, BGA; Ben-Gurion 1973, p. 380; Ben-Gurion, Diary, May 19, 1935, BGA.

60. Ben-Gurion, Diary, March 6, Aug. 22, 1936, BGA; Ben-Gurion to the Mapai Central Committee, Sept. 11, 1936, in Ben-Gurion 1973, p. 430.

61. Ben-Gurion, Diary, May 23, July 1, June 11, 1935, BGA.

62. Ben-Gurion, Diary, May 21, July 1, Oct. 12, 1935, BGA; Ben-Gurion to Amos, July 27, 1937, in Ben-Gurion 1968, p. 176; Segev 2000, p. 397ff.

63. Ben-Gurion, Diary, June 30, 1937, BGA.

64. Ben-Gurion, Diary, June 8, 1936, June 9, 1937, BGA.

65. Ben-Gurion, Diary, Oct. 16, 1935, BGA.

66. Ben-Gurion, Diary, Nov. 15, 1935, BGA.

67. Ben-Gurion, Diary, June 14, 1936, BGA; Ben-Gurion to Paula, June 14, 1936, in Ben-Gurion 1968, p. 151.

68. Ben-Gurion, Diary, June 10, 11, 1936.

69. Weizmann and Ben-Gurion conversation with William Ormsby-Gore, June 30, 1936, in Ben-Gurion 1973, p. 308ff.; Rose 1990, p. 200.

70. Ben-Gurion to the Mapai Central Committee, July 9, 1936, in Ben-Gurion 1973, p. 326ff.; Ben-Gurion to the Histadrut Convention, *Davar*, Jan. 14, 1934.

71. Ben-Gurion to the Mapai Central Committee, Sept. 29, 1936, in Ben-Gurion 1973, p. 445.

72. Segev 2000, pp. 387–88.

73. Ben-Gurion, Diary, July 10, 11, 14, 17, 1936, BGA; Ben-Gurion to the Mapai Central Committee, Sept. 29, 1936, in Ben-Gurion 1973, p. 445.

74. Ben-Gurion, Diary, Dec. 23, 24, 1936, BGA.

75. Ben-Gurion, Diary, Jan. 25, June 2, 23, 1937, BGA; Ben-Gurion to Paula, June 22, 29, 1937, in Ben-Gurion 1968, p. 174; Ben-Gurion to Chaim Weizmann, Aug. 22, 1937, in Ben-Gurion 1974a, p. 422ff.

76. Royal Commission 1937, pp. 306, 394.

77. Ben-Gurion to Amos, Oct. 5, 1937, BGA; Ben-Gurion to the Jewish Agency Executive, June 12, 1938, BGA; Ben-Gurion to the Mapai Central Committee, Feb. 5–6, 1937, in Ben-Gurion 1974a, pp. 26, 60ff., 370.

78. Ben-Gurion, Diary, July 3, 1937, BGA.

79. Ben-Gurion, Diary, July 6, 23, 1937, BGA.

80. Ben-Gurion, Diary, July 11, 12, 3, 1937, BGA.

81. Ben-Gurion, Diary, July 12, 1937, BGA.

82. Royal Commission 1937, p. 390ff.
83. Ben-Gurion, Diary, July 4, 6, 1937, BGA; Ben-Gurion to Amos, July 27, 1937, BGA.
84. Dotan 1979; Avizohar and Friedman 1984.
85. *Davar*, July 13, 1937.
86. Ben-Gurion, Diary, July 3, 1937, BGA.
87. Ben-Gurion to Moshe Sharett, June 26, 1937, BGA.
88. Rachel Yanait, interview transcript, July 17, 1975, BGA.
89. Ben-Gurion, Diary, June 11, 1937, BGA; Ben-Gurion to the Mapai Central Committee, July 1, 1937; Ben-Gurion to the World Union of Po'alei Zion, July 29, in the Congress plenum, Aug. 7, Dec. 12, 1937, in Ben-Gurion 1974a, pp. 165, 334ff., 392; Ben-Gurion to the Zionist Executive, March 10, 1938, in Ben-Gurion 1982b, p. 132.
90. Herzl 1960, 2, p. 74.
91. Ben-Gurion to the World Union of Po'alei Zion, July 29, 1937, in Ben-Gurion 1974a, p. 366.
92. Ben-Gurion, Diary, July 17, 1937, BGA; lists by Ben-Gurion of Arab villages in the north, BGA, subject files 19, 27; Ben-Gurion to the Jewish Agency Executive, June 12, 1938, BGA; Yossi Katz 2000, p. 68ff.
93. Ben-Gurion to members of Brit Shalom, in "Hapo'el Ha'ivri Veha'aravi," in Ben-Gurion 1931, pp. 105, 182ff.
94. Ben-Gurion to Berl Katznelson, Nov. 19, 1930, in Erez 1974, p. 166.
95. Ben-Gurion, Diary, Nov. 12, 1935, BGA; Ben-Gurion and Moshe Sharett to the high commissioner, July 9, 1936, in Ben-Gurion 1973, p. 324.
96. David Hacohen, interview transcript, BGA; Anita Shapira 1980, pp. 559, 608; Ben-Gurion, Diary, July 12, 1937, BGA.
97. Lavi 1947, p. 283; Lavi to his sister, Aug. 13, 1937, in Lavi 1968, p. 311.
98. Zemach 1983, p. 153ff., 164; Anita Shapira 2004, p. 78ff.
99. Zemach 1983, pp. 153ff., 164, 174; Anita Shapira 2004, p. 78ff.; Govrin 2008, 3, p. 365ff.
100. Ben-Gurion, Diary, Aug. 12, 1937, BGA.
101. Ben-Gurion to Paula, Nov. 7, 1937, in Ben-Gurion 1968, p. 214.
102. Ben-Gurion to Geula, Feb. 18, Sept. 26, 1938, BGA.
103. Segev 2000, p. 413; Wolfensohn 2014, p. 189.
104. Ben-Gurion, Diary, Oct. 7, 1937, Jan. 2, 1939, BGA; Ben-Gurion to the Jewish Agency Executive, June 12, Dec. 11, 1938, BGA; Segev 2000, p. 403ff.; Teveth, "Gilgulei Hatransfer Bamahshavah Hatziyonit," in Teveth 1999, p. 245ff.; Morris 2000, p. 23ff.; Messer 1996, p. 19.
105. Ben-Gurion to Paula, March 1, Oct. 1, 1938, in Ben-Gurion 1968, pp. 219, 235; Ben-Gurion to Renana, Sept. 30, 1938, BGA.
106. Paula to Ben-Gurion, Oct. 25, 1938, in Teveth 1987b, 3, p. 266.
107. Doris May to Ben-Gurion, June 9, 1938, BGA.

12. WINDS OF WAR

1. Yitzhak Avneri 1987, p. 126ff., 1929; David H. Shapiro 1994, p. 165ff.; Zertal 1990, p. 87ff.; Ofer 1988, p. 474.
2. Ben-Gurion at a party with colleagues, Sept. 8, 1939, BGA.

3. Elam 1979, pp. 74ff., 101ff.; Ben-Gurion, Diary, Oct. 19, 1935, April 11, 1937, BGA; Ben-Gurion to the International Union of Zionist Labor Parties Council, Aug. 18, 1936, in Ben-Gurion 1973, p. 381, BGA.
4. Ben-Gurion, Diary, April 19, 1939, BGA.
5. Ben-Gurion, Diary, July 1, 7, 1935, Feb. 24, Dec. 5, 1936, May 5, 1939, BGA; Ben-Gurion to the Zionist Executive, March 22, 1937, in Ben-Gurion 1974a, p. 103.
6. Ben-Gurion, Diary, April 7, 1939, BGA; Ben-Gurion to the National Council, Dec. 12, 1938, BGA; Golani 2008, p. 340ff.
7. Ben-Gurion, Diary, Jan. 16, 1939, BGA.
8. Ben-Gurion to Paula, Sept. 14, 1937, in Ben-Gurion 1968, p. 196; Ben-Gurion, Diary, Jan. 15, 1939, BGA.
9. Ben-Gurion to Zalman Shazar, in Ben-Gurion, Diary, May 31, Dec. 9, 1936, BGA; Ben-Gurion to Paula, Oct. 7, 1938, in Ben-Gurion 1968, p. 238.
10. Ben-Gurion, Diary, Dec. 16, 1938, April 30, June 13, 1939, BGA.
11. Shoshana Vardinon interviewed by the author, Feb. 23, 2013.
12. Ben-Gurion, Diary, March 20, April 27, 1937, BGA; Binyamin Eliav 1990, p. 101ff.
13. Ben-Gurion, Diary, July 4, 1939, BGA; *Davar*, July 5, 6, 1939.
14. Ben-Gurion to the Mapai Central Committee, Jan. 31, Feb. 5, 1934, in Ben-Gurion 1972, p. 17ff.; Ben-Gurion to the Mapai Central Committee, June 29, 1938, in Ben-Gurion 1982b, p. 220ff.
15. Ben-Gurion at a party with colleagues, Sept. 8, 1939, BGA.
16. Ben-Gurion, Diary, Dec. 16, 1938, BGA.
17. Ben-Gurion, Diary, July 22, 1937, Sept. 27, 29, 30, Oct. 17, 1938; Binyamin Eliav 1990, p. 134ff.; Dinur 1954–64, 2, p. 1063ff.
18. Dinur 1954–64, 2, p. 833ff.; Ben-Gurion, Diary, Dec. 16, 1938; June 6, 13, 1939, BGA; Ben-Gurion to the International Union of Zionist Labor Parties Council, Aug. 18, 1936, in Ben-Gurion 1973, p. 380; Ben-Gurion to the Zionist Congress, Aug. 18, 1939, in Ben-Gurion 1987, p. 505.
19. Ben-Gurion to Arthur Wauchope, April 2, 1936, BGA.
20. Ben-Gurion, Diary, Dec. 12, 1938, BGA; Ben-Gurion to the Mapai Central Committee, Dec. 15, 1938, in Ben-Gurion 1982b, p. 416.
21. Ben-Gurion, Diary, Dec. 10, 1938, BGA; Ben-Gurion to the Jewish Agency Executive, Dec. 11, 1938, in Ben-Gurion 1982b, p. 408.
22. Ben-Gurion to the Jewish Agency Executive, June 26, 1938, in Ben-Gurion 1982b, p. 219ff.; *Davar*, July 12, 1938.
23. Ben-Gurion to the Mapai Central Committee, Dec. 10, 1938, BGA, Mapai minutes; Ben-Gurion at the Zionist Congress, Aug. 18, 1939, and at the World International Union of Zionist Labor Parties Council, April 26, 1939, in Ben-Gurion 1987, pp. 506, 271.
24. *Davar*, Aug. 7, 1938; Ben-Gurion, Diary, Sept. 20, Oct. 14, 1939, BGA; Ben-Gurion to Paula, Sept. 20, 1938, in Ben-Gurion 1968, p. 231.
25. Ben-Gurion, Diary, Sept. 20, 1938, BGA; Ben-Gurion to Paula, Sept. 20, 1938, in Ben-Gurion 1968, p. 225.
26. Ben-Gurion, Diary, Sept. 23, 27, 1938.
27. Ben-Gurion, Diary, Nov. 30, Oct. 1, 1938, including Ben-Gurion to Amos and Geula, BGA.

28. Ben-Gurion to the Mapai Central Committee, Dec. 7, 1938, in Ben-Gurion 1982b, p. 397; Avizohar 1987, "Hatziyonut Halohemet," in Ben-Gurion 1987, p. 22.

29. Yitzhak Avneri 1987, p. 129; Ben-Gurion, Diary, Dec. 10, 1938, Jan. 3, 1939; David H. Shapiro 1994, p. 165ff.

30. Ben-Gurion, Diary, Feb. 16, 1939, BGA; Segev 2000, p. 415ff.; "Policy in Palestine on the Outbreak of War," Sept. 26, 1938, NA (UK) FO 371/21864 E5603/G; Chamberlain to the Ministerial Committee on Palestine, April 20, 1939, NA (UK) CAB 24/285 C.P. 8939.

31. Ben-Gurion, Diary, June 18, 1936, BGA; Ben-Gurion to the Jewish Agency Executive, Nov. 6, 1939, in Ben-Gurion 1997, p. 237.

32. Ben-Gurion, Diary, March 7, 1939, BGA.

33. Ben-Gurion, Diary, March 13, Nov. 8, 1939, and Ben-Gurion to the Zionist Congress, Aug. 28, 1939, in Ben-Gurion 1987, pp. 200ff., 507.

34. Ben-Gurion to youth organizations, May 24, 1939, in Ben-Gurion 1987, p. 327ff.; Ben-Gurion to the Jewish Agency Executive, Oct. 20, 1938, in Ben-Gurion 1982b, p. 346; Ben-Gurion to the Zionist Congress, Aug. 21, 1939, in Ben-Gurion 1987, p. 523.

35. Ben-Gurion, Diary, May 4, 1939, BGA; Yitzhak Maor, interview transcript, BGA.

36. Ben-Gurion to the Zionist Congress, Aug. 19, 1939, in Ben-Gurion 1987, p. 512.

37. *Davar*, Jan. 31, 1939.

38. Ben-Gurion to the Jewish Agency Executive, Sept. 17, 1939, BGA.

39. Ben-Gurion at a Zionist assembly for the unity of the Jewish community, April 13, 1941, in Ben-Gurion 2008, p. 350.

40. Ben-Gurion to Paula, Jan. 1, 1939, BGA; Ben-Gurion to security personnel, Sept. 8, 1939, in Ben-Gurion 1949, 3, p. 14; Ben-Gurion, Diary, Sept. 11, 1939, BGA; Ben-Gurion to the Histadrut Executive, Sept. 11, 1939, in Ben-Gurion 1997, p. 71.

41. "Some Notes on the Jewish Military Effort," July 31, 1940, BGA, general chronological documentation; Ben-Gurion 2008, p. 63ff.

42. Ben-Gurion, Diary, April 1, 1939, BGA; Ben-Gurion to youth organizations, May 24, 1939, in Ben-Gurion 1987, p. 328; Ben-Gurion to the Mapai Central Committee, Sept. 12, 1939, in Ben-Gurion 1997, p. 76.

43. Undated data, CZA J1/6283/1; Volunteer Declaration, May 18, 1939, CZA J/1 33.549; Ben-Gurion, Diary, Nov. 15, 1939, BGA.

44. Ben-Gurion, Diary, April 30, 1939, BGA; Ben-Gurion et al. to the Jewish Agency Executive, Sept. 17, 1939, BGA.

45. Ben-Gurion, Diary, Sept. 28, Oct. 9, 1939, BGA.

46. Ben-Gurion, Diary, Oct. 7, 1939, Jan. 21, 1940, BGA.

47. Ben-Gurion, Diary, Oct. 18, 1939, BGA; Avizohar 1997, p. 6ff.

48. Ben-Gurion, Diary, Nov. 14, 15, 1939, BGA; Ben-Gurion to Eliyahu Golomb, in Ben-Gurion, Diary, Nov. 23, 1939, BGA.

49. Stern 1974, p. 100ff.

50. Menachem Ussishkin to the Zionist Executive, March 14, 1940, BGA.

51. Avizohar 1997, p. 27ff.

52. Slutsky 1973, 3, p. 141.

53. Avizohar 1997; Werner Senator to the Jewish Agency Executive, April 8, 1940, in Ben-Gurion 1997, pp. 17, 488.

54. Avizohar 1997, p. 27; Slutsky 1973, 3, p. 137.

55. Avizohar 1997, p. 29; Ben-Gurion to the Mapai Central Committee, Dec. 7, 1938, in Ben-Gurion 1982b, p. 397; Ben-Gurion, Diary, June 20, 1939, BGA.

56. Ben-Gurion, Diary, Oct. 12, 1939, BGA.

57. Rachel Yanait, March 8, 1978, p. 10ff., interview transcript, BGA.

58. Ben-Gurion, Diary, Jan. 31, 1940, BGA.

59. Ben-Gurion, Diary, Nov. 30, 1939, BGA; Organization Department to the Jewish Agency Executive, Jan. 24, 1940, Richard Lichtheim reports, Jan. 1, 1940, BGA, subject file: Holocaust of European Jewry.

60. Ben-Gurion to the Smaller Zionist General Council, March 14, 1940, in Ben-Gurion 1997, pp. 469, 475.

61. Ben-Gurion to a meeting of the Smaller Zionist General Council, Feb. 29, 1940, in Ben-Gurion 1997, p. 457ff.

62. Avizohar 1997, p. 26; Teveth 1987b, 3, p. 341.

63. Mortimer 2010, p. 28.

64. Ben-Gurion to Paula, Sept. 8, 1941, in Ben-Gurion 2008, p. 81.

65. Ben-Gurion, Diary, Sept. 11, 12, 14, 15, 1940, BGA; Ben-Gurion to the Mapai Central Committee, Feb. 19, 1941, in Ben-Gurion 2008, p. 199.

66. Ben-Gurion to Paula, May 31, Sept. 16, 1940, in Ben-Gurion 2008, pp. 38, 91.

67. Ben-Gurion 2008, p. 81.

68. Ben-Gurion to the Mapai Central Committee, Feb. 19, 1941, and Ben-Gurion to Paula, July 1, 1940, in Ben-Gurion 2008, pp. 5, 51, 81, 230; Arthur Lourie, June 7, 1976, interview transcript, BGA.

69. Ben-Gurion to Paula, Sept. 8, 1940, and Ben-Gurion to the Smaller Zionist Executive, Feb. 24, 1941, in Ben-Gurion 2008, pp. 5, 81, 230; Ben-Gurion, Diary, June 7, 1940, BGA.

70. Ben-Gurion to Blanche Dugdale, Sept. 21, 1940, BGA, Teveth collection, subject file: Churchill; Ben-Gurion interview with Noah Orian, Nov. 12, 1969, p. 11, HIJC-OHA; Ben-Gurion to the Mapai Central Committee, Feb. 19, 1941, in Ben-Gurion 2008, p. 205.

71. Ben-Gurion to the Jewish Agency Executive, Feb. 16, 1941, in Ben-Gurion 2008, p. 185.

72. Ben-Gurion, Diary, Sept. 22, 1940, BGA; Wolfensohn 2014, p. 189.

73. Ben-Gurion to Paula, Sept. 16, 1940, in Ben-Gurion 2008, p. 91.

74. Arthur Lourie interview with Teveth, July 18, 1977, and Lourie to Teveth, Aug. 18, 1977, BGA, Teveth collection, people; Teveth 1987, p. 351; Doris May to Lourie, March 31, 1942, July 2, 1944, Shabtai Teveth collection, files 1198, 1205, 1206, BGA.

75. Ben-Gurion, Diary, Nov. 12, 13, 19, 1940, BGA; Ofer 1988, p. 50ff.; Slutsky 1973, 3, p. 152ff.

76. Ben-Gurion to members of Hashomer Hatza'ir, March 13, 1941, in Ben-Gurion 2008, p. 279.

77. Ben-Gurion to Paula, Sept. 8, 1940, in Ben-Gurion 2008, p. 81, and the note on p. 200; Ben-Gurion, Diary, Sept. 22, 1940, BGA.

78. Ben-Gurion with members of Hakibbutz Ha'artzi and with the German and Austrian Immigrants Association, March 11, 13, 1941, in Ben-Gurion 2008, pp. 279, 273ff., 289.

79. Ben-Gurion, Diary, Sept. 11, 18, 1940, BGA; Meeting at the Jewish Agency office, Sept. 18, 1940, in Ben-Gurion 2008, p. 92ff.; Ben-Gurion 2012, pp. 520, 526, editor's note no. 6.

80. Ben-Gurion, Diary, Oct. 15, 1940; Ben-Gurion to Paula, Nov. 9, 1940, and Ben-Gurion to the Jewish Agency Executive, Feb. 16, 1941, in Ben-Gurion 2008, pp. 138, 197; Ben-Gurion, Diary, Oct. 6, 1940, BGA.

81. Ben-Gurion to Paula, July 1, 1940, and Ben-Gurion to the Jewish Agency Executive, Feb. 16, 23, 1941, in Ben-Gurion 2007, pp. 51, 182, 222; Ben-Gurion, Diary, Oct. 4, 7, 1940, BGA; "*Excambion* Brings Mrs. Ratherborne, M.P.," *New York Times*, Nov. 25, 1941.

13. ZIONIST ALERTNESS

1. *Davar*, Feb. 21, 23, 1941; Ben-Gurion to the Mapai Central Committee, March 5–8, 1941, BGA; Ben-Gurion to the General Zionists, April 10, 1941, Ben-Gurion 2008, p. 348.

2. Ben-Gurion to the Jewish Agency Executive, March 14, 1941, in Ben-Gurion 2008, p. 292; Ben-Gurion 2012, p. 305.

3. Ben-Gurion to the Mapai Central Committee, Feb. 19, 1941, BGA; Ben-Gurion 2008, p. 274.

4. Segev 1991, p. 60; Ben-Gurion, Diary, Sept. 19, 1939, Nov. 22, 1940, BGA; Ben-Gurion to the Mapai Central Committee, Feb. 19, 1941, in Ben-Gurion 2008, p. 207; Ben-Gurion to Paula, May 31, 1940, BGA; Weizmann to Moyne, June 21, 1941, Letters and Papers of Chaim Weizmann 1979, p. 156ff.; Litvinoff 1988, p. 377ff.

5. Ben-Gurion, Diary, Nov. 22, 1940, BGA; Moshe Sharett to the Jewish Agency Executive, April 27, 1941, BGA; Ben-Gurion to the Zionist Executive, May 7, 1941, and Ben-Gurion to members of the Haganah, March 26, 1941, in Ben-Gurion 2008, pp. 397, 324.

6. Segev 1993, p. 68; Moshe Sharett and Ben-Gurion to the Jewish Agency Executive, April 27, 1941, BGA.

7. Ben-Gurion to the Mapai Central Committee, March 5, 1941, and at a meeting of the Mapai Central Committee, Feb. 19, 1941, in Ben-Gurion 2008, pp. 244, 208.

8. Ben-Gurion to the Mapai Central Committee, Feb. 19, 1941, in Ben-Gurion 2008, p. 244.

9. Ben-Gurion to the Mapai Council, March 5, 1941, in Ben-Gurion 2008, p. 244ff.; Ben-Gurion 1949, 3, p. 58.

10. Ben-Gurion to the Mapai Council, March 7–8, 1941, to the General Zionists, April 10, 1941, at a monthly seminar, April 1941, in Ben-Gurion 2008, pp. 254, 252, 249, 349, 378, 299.

11. Ben-Gurion to the Mapai Council, March 8, 1941, to the Jewish Agency Executive, April 6, 1941, to the Mapai Council, March 7–8, 1941, to the German Immigrants Association, March 11, 1941, to Hitahdut Bnei Hamoshavot, April 14, 1941, in Ben-Gurion 2008, pp. 253, 342, 252ff., 254, 273, 347, 360, 255.

12. Ben-Gurion to the Mapai Convention, June 22, 1941, and to the Jewish Agency Executive, March 16, 1941, in Ben-Gurion 2008, pp. 426, 291.

13. Ben-Gurion to the Mapai Council, March 5, 1941, to members of the Haganah, March 26, 1941, to the Jewish Agency Executive, May 16, 1941, in Ben-Gurion 2008, pp. 243, 324, 408.

14. Ben-Gurion to the German Immigrants Association, March 20, 1941, to Rabbi Berlin, April 2, 1941, to the Jewish Agency Executive, April 6, 1941, in Ben-Gurion 2008, pp. 306, 337, 343.

15. Ben-Gurion to the General Zionists, April 10, 1941, and to the Mapai Central Committee, Feb. 19, 1941, in Ben-Gurion 2008, pp. 348, 218.

16. Ben-Gurion to the Jewish Agency Executive, March 23, 1941, in Ben-Gurion 2008, p. 309ff.

17. Ben-Gurion to the German Immigrants Association, March 11, 1941, and to Hashomer Hatza'ir, March 13, 1941, in Ben-Gurion 2008, pp. 264ff., 281.

18. Ben-Gurion 2008, p. 148, editor's note; Ussishkin and Ben-Gurion to the Jewish Agency Executive, March 16, May 16, 1941, in Ben-Gurion 2008, pp. 292, 409.

19. Ben-Gurion to the Jewish Agency Executive, March 23, 1941, to Hitahdut Bnei Hamoshavot, April 14, 1941, to the Jewish Agency Executive, June 15, 1941, Yitzhak Gruenbaum to the Jewish Agency Executive, April 6, 1941, in Ben-Gurion 2008, pp. 313, 361, 427, 340ff.; Elam 1979, p. 150ff.

20. Shlomo Zemach to Ben-Gurion, undated, BGA, Shabtai Teveth collection, persons; Zemach 1983, p. 171; Zemach 1996, p. 289.

21. Ben-Gurion and Eliezer Liebenstein to the Mapai Central Committee, June 25, 1941, BGA; Ben-Gurion to Paula, Aug. 19, 1941, BGA; Ben-Gurion 2012, p. 258, editor's note; Ben-Gurion to the Jewish Agency Executive, Oct. 4, 1941, BGA; Rose 1990, p. 234; *Davar*, Feb. 14, 1964.

22. Ben-Gurion, Diary, July 9, 29, 1942; Ben-Gurion to the Jewish Agency Executive, Oct. 6, 1942, BGA.

23. Ben-Gurion to Moshe Sharett, Feb. 8, 1942, in Ben-Gurion 2012, p. 337.

24. Ben-Gurion, Diary, Dec. 30, 1941, BGA.

25. Ben-Gurion, Diary, Dec. 21, 31, 1941, and Shabtai Teveth collection, people, Nyles, BGA.

26. "A Zionist Army?" *New York Times*, Jan. 22, 1942.

27. Ben-Gurion to Berl Locker, Dec. 27, 1941, BGA; Ben-Gurion, Diary, Dec. 27, 1941, BGA.

28. Conversation with Henry Morgenthau, Jan. 6, 1942, Ben-Gurion to Langer, Jan. 19, 1942, interview with members of the staff of the coordinator of information, Jan. 13, 1942, in Ben-Gurion 2012, pp. 276, 315, 304.

29. Ben-Gurion, Diary, December 2, 1941, Jan. 6, 1942, BGA; conversation with Ambassador Bullitt, Feb. 10, 1942, in Ben-Gurion 2012, p. 348.

30. Ben-Gurion, Diary, Dec. 28, 1941, Jan. 2, 10, 1942, BGA; Ben-Gurion to Arthur Lourie, Jan. 27, 1942, BGA.

31. Ben-Gurion, Diary, Dec. 6, 27, 1941, BGA.

32. Ben-Gurion, Diary, May 5, 1942, BGA; Ben-Gurion to Berl Locker, Jan. 26, 1942, and Ben-Gurion to Doris May, Feb. 13, 1942, in Ben-Gurion 2012, pp. 324, 372.

33. Ben-Gurion to Arthur Lourie, Jan. 1, 1942, in Ben-Gurion 2012, p. 257.

34. Ben-Gurion, Diary, Sept. 8–11, 1935, July 14, 1936, BGA; Ben-Gurion to Miriam Cohen, April 24–27, 1942, BGA, Shabtai Teveth collection, 1206, 1205; Teveth 1987b, p. 402ff.

35. Ben-Gurion to Fritz Simon, Jan. 11, 1942, Ben-Gurion to Paula, Jan. 25, April 22, 1942, in Ben-Gurion 2012, pp. 288, 323, 428; Paula Ben-Gurion's will, May 19, 1942, BGA, general chronological documentation, April–May 1942.

36. Ben-Gurion to Renana, Feb. 18, 1942, Ben-Gurion to Paula, March 24, 1942, in Ben-Gurion 2012, pp. 370, 396.

37. Weizmann 1949, p. 426ff.; passage from *Trial and Error* that was not included in the book, Weizmann Archive, 1-2948; Ben-Gurion, Diary, Dec. 1, 2, 1941, BGA; Ben-Gurion, memorandum, Dec. 5, 1941, in Ben-Gurion 2012, p. 169ff.

38. Ben-Gurion to John Winant, Jan. 19, April 15, 1942; Ben-Gurion to Felix Frankfurter, April 16, 1942; Ben-Gurion to Moshe Sharett, Feb. 8, 1942; Ben-Gurion to Samuel Rosenman, Feb. 10, 1942; Ben-Gurion to Berl Locker, Jan. 4, 1942, in Ben-Gurion 2012, pp. 414, 418, 337, 342.

39. Chaim Weizmann to Vera Weizmann, April 29, 1920, in Reinharz 1978, p. 347.

40. Letters and Papers of Chaim Weizmann 1977, pp. 342–43.

41. Meeting in Wise's office, June 27, 1942, in Ben-Gurion 2012, p. 518ff.; *Biltmore Program*, May 10, 1942, BGA, general chronological documentation, April–May 1942; Ben-Gurion to the Biltmore Conference, May 10, 1942, in Ben-Gurion 2012, p. 435ff.; *Test of Fulfillment*, BGA; Ofer 1988, p. 235ff.; Ben-Gurion to the Jewish Agency Executive, Oct. 4, 1942, BGA.

42. *Davar*, May 14, 1942; Ben-Gurion to Paula, May 14, 1942, and to Geula, May 19, 1942, BGA; Ben-Gurion, 2012, p. 449ff.; Hagani 2010, p. 169ff.

43. Ben-Gurion to the Jewish Agency Executive, May 12, 1942, BGA; Ben-Gurion to Chaim Weizmann, June 11, 1942, BGA.

44. Chaim Weizmann to Ben-Gurion, June 15, 17, 1942, Ben-Gurion to Chaim Weizmann, June 16, 1942, in Ben-Gurion 2012, pp. 495ff., 500ff., 507.

45. Ben-Gurion to Stephen Wise, June 19, 1942, in Ben-Gurion 2012, p. 501; Chaim Weizmann to Stephen Wise, June 20, 1942, in Michael Cohen 1979, p. 311ff.; Nahum Goldmann, interview transcript, BGA.

46. Meeting in Wise's office, June 27, 1942, in Ben-Gurion 2012, p. 518; English original, "Special Meeting, June 27, 1942," BGA.

47. Weisgal 1971, p. 175.

48. Louise Levinthal, interview transcript, BGA, p. 6.

49. Weizmann to Lewis Namier, June 27, 1942, in Michael Cohen 1979, p. 317.

50. Ben-Gurion to American members of the Zionist Executive, Aug. 3, 1942, in Ben-Gurion 2012, p. 585; Chaim Weizmann to Stephen Wise, June 20, 1942, and to the Jewish Agency Executive, Oct. 22, 1942, in Michael Cohen 1979, pp. 312ff., 359ff.

51. Ben-Gurion to Felix Frankfurter, June 22, 1942, in Ben-Gurion 2012, p. 511; unidentified signature to Sir George Gater, July 14, 1942, NA (UK) CO 733/462/7; Weizmann to Lewis Namier, June 27, 1942, in Michael Cohen 1979, p. 317; Lord Halifax to the Foreign Office, June 1, 1942, NA (UK) FO 371/31379.

52. Ben-Gurion to Arthur Lourie, July 1, 1942, BGA; Ben-Gurion, Diary, July 1, 1942, BGA.

53. Memorandum on the Defense of Palestine and the Jews, July 2, 1942, BGA, general chronological documentation, June–Aug. 1942.

54. Ben-Gurion to Felix Frankfurter, July 6, 1942, in Ben-Gurion 2012, p. 550.

55. Ben-Gurion to Moshe Sharett, July 8, 1942, in Ben-Gurion 2012, p. 555.

56. "May We Present," *The Rotarian*, Jan. 1942, p. 5; *New York Times*, April 1, 1976; Watts 1942.

57. Kettaneh 1942.

58. Minutes of conversation with Francis Katany [*sic*], July 29, 1942, BGA, general chronological documentation, June–Aug. 1942.

59. Ben-Gurion to the Jewish Agency Executive, Oct. 6, 1942, BGA.

60. Anshel Reiss, Shraga Netzer, Baruch Azanya, Rose Halprin, interview transcripts, BGA.

61. Apolinary Hartglas to the Jewish Agency Executive, Sept. 11, 1940, BGA; Porat 1986, p. 30.

62. "Extinction Feared by Jews in Poland," *New York Times*, March 1, 1942.

63. Ben-Gurion to convention of Pioneer Women, June 14, 1942, BGA, record of meetings.

64. "Allies Are Urged to Execute Nazis," *New York Times*, July 2, 1942; Bauer 1987, p. 61ff.

65. Press conference, July 20, 1942, and Ben-Gurion to Eliezer Kaplan, July 8, 1942, in Ben-Gurion 2012, pp. 572, 556; "Nazi Punishment Seen by Roosevelt," *New York Times*, July 22, 1942.

66. Elam 1979, pp. 166, 139; Weizmann to Moshe Sharett, Aug. 12, 1942, Michael Cohen 1979, p. 344; Ben-Gurion to the Jewish Agency Executive (USA), Aug. 3, 1942, and to the Emergency Committee, Sept. 17, 1942, in Ben-Gurion 2012, pp. 586, 619.

67. Ben-Gurion to the Mapai Council, March 5–8, 1941, in Ben-Gurion 1949, 3, p. 58.

68. Ben-Gurion to the Jewish Agency Executive, Oct. 6, 1942, BGA; Ben-Gurion to the Emergency Committee, Sept. 17, 1942, in Ben-Gurion 2012, p. 620.

69. Ben-Gurion, Diary, Sept. 20, 1942, BGA.

14. HOLOCAUST AND SCHISM

1. Goldblum report, undated, BGA, general chronological documentation; Ben-Gurion to Miriam Cohen, Feb. 1, 1943, BGA; Avihu Ronen 1986, p. 76ff.

2. Yitzhak Gruenbaum and Moshe Shapira to the Jewish Agency Executive, June 30, 1942; Y. Eshed to the Council of Hakibbutz Hameuchad, July 5, 1942, in Brenner 1984, pp. 106, 129, 180; "Hatza'ah Letochnit Hibul Ba'aretz Lemikreh Shetikabesh al yedei Ha'oyev," Jan. 19, 1942, BGA, general chronological documentation; Yoav Gelber 1990a; Kanaan 1974, pp. 137, 139, 168, 209; *Davar*, Nov. 5, 1942.

3. Ben-Gurion with representatives of party branches, Oct. 13, 1942, BGA; Ben-Gurion at the Moshavim Convention, Oct. 10, 1942, *Davar*, Oct. 11, 1942; Ben-Gurion to Katznelson, Oct. 5, 1942, BGA, general chronological documentation.

4. Anita Shapira 1980, p. 674ff.; Ben-Gurion, Diary, Oct. 23, 1942, BGA.

5. Ben-Gurion to the Mapai Council, Jan. 1944, in Ben-Gurion 1949, 4, p. 102ff.; Ben-Gurion to the Jewish Agency Executive, Oct. 11, 1942, BGA.

6. Zemach 1983, p. 172; Ben-Gurion to the Mapai Council, March 6, 1944, BGA.

7. Ben-Gurion on Herzl Day, July 10, 1944, BGA; Ben-Gurion at the Am Ve'admato exhibition, March 2, 1945, in Ben-Gurion 1949, 3, p. 225; Ben-Gurion to Ben-Zion Katz, Sept. 1, 1957, BGA.

8. Ben-Gurion to the Mapai Convention, June 12, 1941, and to the General Zionists, April 10, 1941, in Ben-Gurion 2008, pp. 426, 348; Ben-Gurion to the Mapai Convention, Oct. 25, 1942, in Ben-Gurion 1949, 4, p. 89; Ben-Gurion to a gathering of Mapai activists, Sept. 8, 1942, BGA.

9. Zemach 1983, p. 174.

10. Ben-Gurion with party branch representatives, Oct. 13, 1942, BGA.

11. Ben-Gurion to the Mapai Convention, Oct. 25, 1942, and with party branch representatives, Oct. 13, 1942, BGA.

12. Lavi 1968, pp. 322ff., 355.
13. Ben-Gurion to the Jewish Agency Executive, Nov. 22, 1942, BGA; Ben-Gurion to Miriam Cohen, Nov. 23, 1942, BGA; "Yediot al Ma'asei Hazeva'ot Lehashmadat Yehudim Ba'artzot Hakibutsh mipi Anshei Hakevutzah Sheba'ah Misham," Nov. 23, 1942, BGA, general chronological documentation.
14. Porat 2009, p. 449ff.
15. Ben-Gurion, Diary, Nov. 11, Dec. 21, 1942, July 6, 1943, Sept. 14, 1944, BGA; Ben-Gurion to Agudat Israel, Oct. 29, 1944, BGA; Ben-Gurion to Mapai activists, Dec. 8, 1942, BGA; Ben-Gurion to Yehoshua Kastner, Feb. 2, 1958, BGA; Morgenstern 1971, p. 60ff.
16. Ben-Gurion to the Jewish Agency Executive, Dec. 6, 1942, BGA; Segev 1993, p. 99.
17. Ben-Gurion with Mapai activists, Dec. 8, 1942, BGA.
18. Ben-Gurion with Mapai activists, Dec. 8, 1942, BGA; Ben-Gurion to the Mapai Central Committee, Aug. 24, 1943, BGA.
19. Ben-Gurion to the Jewish Agency Executive, July 23, 1944, BGA.
20. Ben-Gurion to the Mapai Central Committee, Aug. 24, 1943, BGA.
21. Gruenbaum to the Zionist Executive, Jan. 18, 1943; Dobkin to the Histadrut Executive, Dec. 12, 1942, BGA; Ben-Gurion to the Jewish Agency Executive, July 23, 1944, BGA; Porat and Weitz 2002, p. 119; Segev 1993, p. 97ff.; Porat 1986, p. 173ff.; Friling 1998, p. 350ff.
22. Ben-Gurion to the Economic Research Institute, Nov. 24, 1942, BGA; Ben-Gurion to the Mapai Convention, Oct. 25, 1942, in Ben-Gurion 1949, 3, p. 98ff.; Dvora Hacohen 1994b; Ben-Gurion to Mapai activists, Dec. 8, 1942, BGA; Ben-Gurion to the Mapai Convention, Oct. 25, 1942, BGA.
23. Ben-Gurion, Diary, Nov. 23, Aug. 2, 1943, BGA.
24. Ben-Gurion to the Jewish Agency Executive, Jan. 16, 1942, BGA; Ben-Gurion, Diary, Oct. 25, April 7, May 2, 1943, BGA; Segev 1993, p. 102ff.; Ben-Gurion, "Teshuvah Ledivrei Hashalit," Assembly of Representatives, March 24, 1943, p. 3, BGA.
25. Porat 1986, p. 201ff.; Segev 1993, p. 84.
26. Ofer 1988, p. 470ff.; Ben-Gurion to the Mapai Convention, Oct. 25, 1942; Segev 1993, p. 86ff.
27. Ben-Gurion to the Mapai Convention, Oct. 25, 1942, in Ben-Gurion 1949, 4, p. 66.
28. Eban 1977, p. 43.
29. Friling 1998, p. 421ff.; A. Gasner to Ben-Gurion and Ben-Gurion to Gasner, Sept. 1, 14, 1943, BGA; Ben-Gurion to the Assembly of Representatives, Nov. 30, 1942, BGA.
30. Ehud Avriel, interview transcript, p. 32, BGA; Friling 1998, p. 381ff.
31. Porat 2011, p. 119ff.; Ben-Gurion to industrialists and business leaders, Sept. 23, 1943, BGA; Ben-Gurion to the Jewish Agency Executive, Nov. 10, 1935, in Ben-Gurion 1972, p. 504; Ben-Gurion to the Mapai secretariat, Feb. 10, 1942, BGA.
32. Friling 1998, p. 335; Bauer 1994, p. 100.
33. Ben-Gurion to the Jewish Agency Executive, Oct. 26, 1943, BGA.
34. Ben-Gurion to the Political Committee, June 16, Nov. 3, 1943, BGA; "Zionist Disagreements: Mr. Ben-Gurion Resigns," Times (London), Oct. 29, 1943, NA (UK) CO 733/462/7; Reuven Rubik Rosenthal, personal communication with the author; Ben-Gurion, Diary, Feb. 18, 1943, BGA; Moshe Sharett 1978, 1, p. 184.

35. Bauer 1994, p. 191ff.; Friling 1994, p. 229ff.; *Attorney General v. Adolf Eichmann*, 1962, p. 133; Himmler, memorandum, Dec. 10, 1942, BB Sammlung Schumacher R 187/240.
36. Yitzhak Gruenbaum to the Jewish Agency Executive, April 2, May 1, 25, 1944, BGA.
37. Ben-Gurion to the Mapai Council, May 31, 1944, BGA.
38. Porat 1986, p. 401.
39. Yitzhak Gruenbaum, Ben-Gurion, et al. to the Jewish Agency Executive, June 11, 1944, BGA; Bauer 2015; Friling 1998, p. 771; Frister 1987, p. 289; Ben-Gurion to Binyamin Nahari, Feb. 10, 1965, BGA.
40. Ben-Gurion, Diary, May 13, 1944.
41. Ben-Gurion on Herzl Day, July 10, 1944, BGA; Ben-Gurion at the "Am Va'admato" exhibition, March 2, 1945, in Ben-Gurion 1949, 3, p. 225.
42. Stern 1974, p. 191ff.
43. David Hacohen 1974, p. 85; Amos Ben-Gurion interview with Dov Goldstein, *Ma'ariv*, Oct. 17, 1986; Shlomo Lavi to Leah Meron-Katznelson et al., Aug. 1944, *Ma'arachot* 1968, p. 350ff.; Ze'ev Sherf, interview transcript, cassette 97, p. 5, BGA.
44. Joel Brand and Ben-Gurion to the Mapai secretariat, Oct. 17, 1944, BGA.
45. Segev 1993, p. 76ff.; Ben-Gurion to Mapai activists, Dec. 8, 1942, BGA; Anita Shapira, "Berl, Ha'antishemiyut Vehasho'ah," in Porat 2009, p. 237ff.
46. Ben-Gurion to the Jewish Agency Executive, Sept. 8, 1944, afternoon, BGA.
47. Ben-Gurion to the Cabinet, March 29, 1955, ISA; Segev 1993, p. 97.
48. Ben-Gurion to Israel Galili, Jan. 29, 1960, BGA.
49. Ben-Gurion 1964a, pp. 167, 177.
50. Ben-Gurion, Diary, May 8, 1945, BGA; Ben-Gurion to Paula, May 11, 1945, BGA.

PART II: THE LIMITS OF POWER
1. Ben-Gurion interviewed by Yosef Avner, Avraham Kushnir, and Tom Segev, *Nitzotz*, April 28, 1968.

15. MAPS
1. Ben-Gurion to the Mapai Council, Aug. 8, 1947, and to the Assembly of Representatives, Oct. 2, 1947, in Ben-Gurion 1993b, pp. 278, 379.
2. Ben-Gurion, Diary, Feb. 13, 14, 1947, BGA; Ben-Gurion 1993a, p. 364ff.; Ben-Gurion 1969b, p. 65; Watching report, March 17–20, 1945, NA (UK) FO 141/1056.
3. Ben-Gurion, Diary, May 21, 1945, BGA; Ben-Gurion 1963b, April 24, 1964; Slater 1970, pp. 21–28ff.; Rudolf Sonneborn to Amalie Katz, April 4, 1919, http://rudolfsonneborn .blogspot.co.il/2008/03/letter-18-march-20-1919.html; Ben-Gurion to the Mapai secretariat, Nov. 22, 1945, BGA; Ben-Gurion 2014, p. 574; Haim Slavin, Adolf Robison, Ira Eisenstein, interview transcripts, BGA.
4. Paula to Ben-Gurion, date unclear, 1945, IDFA, Ben-Gurion deposit, selected documents from file 3469-800/1973.
5. Ben-Gurion 2014, p. 130.
6. Ben-Gurion 2014, p. 227ff.
7. Judah Nadich, interview transcript, BGA.
8. Weitz 1980, p. 53ff.; Ben-Gurion to the Mapai secretariat, Nov. 22, 1945, BGA; Judah Nadich, interview transcript, BGA; Ben-Gurion to the Jewish Agency Executive, Feb. 24, 1946, BGA; Segev 1993, pp. 115ff., 120; Zerach Warhaftig, interview transcript, BGA.

9. Ben-Gurion to the Mapai Central Committee, Nov. 22, 1945, BGA; Moshe Sharett to Moshe Sneh and Shaul Avigur, Sept. 27, 1945, courtesy of the Moshe Sharett Heritage Association; Ben-Gurion, Diary, Oct. 20, 26, 1945, BGA; Kenan 1991, p. 343ff.

10. Ben-Gurion to the Jewish Agency Executive, Nov. 21, 1945, BGA; Ben-Gurion 2014, p. 544ff.; Ben-Gurion to Paula, Feb. 9, 1946, in Ben-Gurion, Diary, BGA.

11. Ben-Gurion to the Jewish Agency Executive, Nov. 21, 1945, BGA; Ben-Gurion 2014, p. 544ff.; Ben-Gurion to Paula, Feb. 9, 1946, in Ben-Gurion, Diary, BGA.

12. Ben-Gurion, Diary, Oct. 27, 1945, BGA; Zoirav to Ben-Gurion, Nov. 2, 1947, BGA.

13. Avriel, interview transcript, BGA; Ben-Gurion to the Mapai secretariat, Nov. 22, 1945, and to the Jewish Agency Executive, Nov. 21, 1945, BGA.

14. Ben-Gurion 2014, p. 398; Ben-Aharon, interview transcript, BGA; Ben-Gurion to the Histadrut Convention, Feb. 1, 1945, BGA.

15. Ben-Gurion to the Jewish Agency Executive, Nov. 22, 1945, BGA; Ben-Gurion, Diary, Feb. 3, 1946, and Ben-Gurion to Paula, Feb. 9, 1946, BGA; Ben-Gurion at the final session of the International Union of Zionist Labor Parties Convention, Dec. 24, 1946, BGA, Shabtai Teveth collection, file 162, item 256192.

16. Ben-Gurion to the Jewish Agency Executive, Feb. 11, 1945, BGA.

17. Ben-Gurion to the Zionist General Council, Dec. 11, 1945, BGA; Kenan 1991, p. 351ff.; Slutsky 1973, 3, p. 1036; Dobkin to the Jewish Agency Executive, April 30, 1946, BGA; Segev 1993, p. 123ff.

18. Ben-Gurion to the Mapai secretariat, Nov. 22, 1945, BGA; Bauer 1974, pp. 120, 126, 304; "Hagolah Hayehudit be-1946," *Davar*, Feb. 4, 1947.

19. Bauer 1974, pp. 269, 262; Ben-Gurion, Diary, Oct. 3, 1945, Jan. 20, 22, 25, June 24, Sept. 24, 1946, BGA.

20. Ben-Gurion 1993a, p. 192.

21. Ben-Gurion, Diary, Sept. 13, 26, 1945, BGA; Nachmani 1987, p. 65ff.

22. Ben-Gurion 2014, p. 692; Segev 2010, p. 79; Crossman 1946, p. 102; Kenan 1991, p. 343ff.

23. Crossman 1946, p. 71.

24. Segev 2000, p. 348.

25. Ben-Gurion to the Anglo-American Commission, March 26, 1946, *Public Hearings Before the Anglo-American Committee of Inquiry*, in the possession of the author, p. 11ff.

26. Ben-Gurion, Diary, Feb. 13, 1946, BGA.

27. Ben-Gurion to the Anglo-American Commission, March 11, 1946, *Public Hearings Before the Anglo-American Committee of Inquiry*, in the possession of the author, p. 3.

28. *The Jewish Case*, 1947, pp. 69, 64.

29. Ben-Gurion to the Anglo-American Commission, March 26, 1946, *Public Hearings Before the Anglo-American Committee of Inquiry*, in the possession of the author, pp. 13, 19, 15; Ben-Gurion to a public assembly, Oct. 10, 1946, in Ben-Gurion 2014, p. 1030.

30. Ben-Gurion to the Anglo-American Commission, March 11, 1946, *Public Hearings Before the Anglo-American Committee of Inquiry*, in the possession of the author, pp. 9, 15, 16, 20; *The Jewish Case*, p. 74.

31. Ben-Gurion to the Anglo-American Commission, March 11, 1946, *Public Hearings Before the Anglo-American Committee of Inquiry*, in the possession of the author, p. 25ff.

32. Crossman 1946, p. 138.

33. Crossman 1946, p. 115ff.

34. Ben-Gurion, "Teshuvah Lidvar Hashalit," Assembly of Representatives, March 24, 1943, p. 6, BGA; *Public Hearings Before the Anglo-American Committee of Inquiry*, in possession of the author, p. 5ff.

35. Ben-Gurion to the Anglo-American Commission, March 11, 1946, *Public Hearings Before the Anglo-American Committee of Inquiry*, in the possession of the author, pp. 24ff, 30, 36.

36. Kaplan to the Jewish Agency Executive, May 29, 1946, BGA; Crossman 1946, p. 156ff.

37. Hoffman 2015, p. 298ff.

38. Alfasi 1994, 3, p. 172ff.

39. Ben-Gurion to Harold MacMichael, April 21, 1944, CZA S25/197.

40. Slutsky 1973, 3, p. 531.

41. Slutsky 1973, 3, p. 530ff.; Ben-Gurion, Diary, Sept. 24, 1946, BGA; Ben-Gurion to the Histadrut Convention, Nov. 26, 1944, in Ben-Gurion 1949, 2, p. 289ff.; Lapidot 1994.

42. Stern 1974, p. 210.

43. Moshe Sneh and Menachem Begin, Oct. 9, 1944, CZA S25/206.

44. Responses to questions from the public, April 18, 1947, p. 10, BGA.

45. Shaltiel 2000, pp. 213, 255, 257, 277.

46. Avriel testimony, in Ben-Gurion 1993a, p. 60; Ben-Gurion, Diary, July 8, 1946, BGA.

47. Shaltiel 2000, pp. 276, 268.

48. Ben-Gurion to Moshe Sharett, July 24, 1946, CZA S25/10016; Ben-Gurion, Diary, Sept. 12, 1946, and Ben-Gurion to Paula, July 8, 11, 1946, BGA.

49. Ben-Gurion to Felix Frankfurter, July 17, 1946, BGA; Ben-Gurion to the Mapai Convention, Aug. 23, 1946, BGA 1993a, p. 158.

50. Ganin 1978, p. 227ff.; Ben-Gurion 1993a, p. 98ff.; Segev 2000, p. 49.

51. Mordechai Surkis, interview transcript, p. 2, BGA; Ben-Gurion at Zeilsheim DP camp, Oct. 14, 1946, in Ben-Gurion 2014, p. 1043; *Proceedings of the 22nd Zionist Congress*, p. 21, CZA J28.

52. Harry S Truman to Clement Attlee, Oct. 3, 1946, FRUS, Vol. VII, document 544, p. 703.

53. Ben-Gurion to Chaim Weizmann, Oct. 28, 1946, in Ben-Gurion 1993a, p. 221ff.

54. Ben-Gurion to Zalman Rubishov, Dec. 20, 1946, in Ben-Gurion 1993a, p. 288; Ben-Gurion, Diary, Sept. 14, Oct. 1, 1946, BGA; Mordechai Surkis, interview transcript, BGA; Moshe Gurari, interview transcript, p. 2, BGA.

55. Ben-Gurion to the Jewish Agency Executive, Dec. 29, 1946, Ben-Gurion 1993a, pp. 297, 232; Chaim Weizmann to the Zionist Congress, Dec. 11, 1946, in *Proceedings of the 22nd Zionist Congress*, p. 341, CZA J28.

56. Ben-Gurion 2014, p. 1030ff.

57. Ben-Gurion with George Henry Hall, June 20, 1946, BGA, Shabtai Teveth collection, people, Crossman; Ben-Gurion to Arthur Creech Jones, Jan. 2, 1947, in Ben-Gurion 1993a, p. 309; Ben-Gurion at the Royal Institute of International Affairs, Oct. 12, 1945, BGA.

58. Meir 1975, p. 154; Ben-Gurion, Diary, Aug. 28, 1947, BGA.

59. "Palestine: A Study of Partition," April 1947, NA (UK) CO 537/2344.

60. Brook at Cabinet, Feb. 14, 1947, NA (UK) CAB/195/5; colonial secretary to high commissioner, Feb. 17, 1947, NA (UK) FO 371 618736; John Gutch to Trefford

Smith, Feb. 25, 1947, NA (UK) CO 537 2326; Horowitz 1951, p. 172ff; Segev 2000, p. 482ff.

61. Ben-Gurion to Ernest Bevin, Feb. 12, 1947, in Ben-Gurion 1993a, p. 354.

62. Ben-Gurion to Paula, in Ben-Gurion, Diary, Feb. 14, 15, 1947, BGA; Cabinet, Feb. 14, 1947, NA (UK) CAB/195/5; Ben-Gurion to William Jowitt, Feb. 13, 1947, BGA; Lord Chancellor memorandum, Feb. 14, 1947, NA (UK) PREM 8/627; Ben-Gurion to the Mapai Council, Aug. 9, 1947, 1993b, p. 284.

16. PARTITION

1. *Ha'aretz, Davar,* Nov. 30, 1947; Ben-Gurion to Eliezer Whartman, memoirs of the signers of the Declaration of Independence, BGA; Ben-Gurion to Haganah personnel, Jan. 15, 1948, in Ben-Gurion 1951, p. 37; Ben-Gurion 1993b, p. 503, editor's note.

2. Ben-Gurion to the Mapai Council, Aug. 8, 1947, BGA.

3. Ben-Gurion to the Security Committee, June 7, 1947, BGA; letter to members of the Palmach, Oct. 17, 1948, BGA; Ben-Gurion to the UN Committee, July 7, 1947, in Ben-Gurion 1993b, p. 263; Ben-Gurion 1963b, Aug. 2, 1964.

4. Ben-Gurion to the Mapai secretariat, March 15, 1947, BGA; Ben-Gurion, Diary, June 4, 1947, BGA; Directives to the Haganah Command, June 18, 1947; Avizohar 1993, p. 48; Ben-Gurion 1993b, p. 305ff.

5. Ben-Gurion to the Mapai secretariat, Oct. 30, 1947, in Ben-Gurion 1993b, p. 440; Zvi Ayalon, interview transcript.

6. Barel 2014, p. 91ff.

7. Ben-Gurion, Diary, March 26, April 9, 25, May 6, Dec. 29, 1947, March 28, 1948, BGA; Ben-Gurion 1993b, p. 143, editor's note 3; Ben-Gurion 1969b, p. 69ff.

8. Ben-Gurion to Paula, Oct. 7, 1938, in Ben-Gurion 1968, p. 238; Ben-Gurion, Diary, Dec. 16, 1938, BGA.

9. Ben-Gurion, Diary, March 26, 1947, BGA; Ben-Gurion 1993b, p. 142ff.; Ben-Gurion 1969b, p. 78.

10. Ben-Gurion, Diary, May 27, 1947, March 2, 1948, BGA.

11. Moshe Shapira and Ben-Gurion to the Security Committee, Oct. 23, 1947, BGA; Rabin 1979, p. 37.

12. Ben-Gurion, Diary, April 16, 1947; Ben-Gurion to the Security Committee, Oct. 23, June 8, 1947; Ben-Gurion 1969b, pp. 69, 271.

13. Ben-Gurion, Diary, June 27, 1947, BGA.

14. Ben-Gurion to the Mapai secretariat, March 25, Oct. 30, 1947, BGA; Ben-Gurion, Diary, May 6, 1947, BGA; Ben-Gurion at a gathering of Palmach commanders, Sept. 14, 1948, in Ben-Gurion 1951, p. 241.

15. Ben-Gurion to the Zionist Congress, Dec. 18, 1946, and to the Zionist General Council, April 6, 1948, in Ben-Gurion 1969b, pp. 68ff, 78; Ben-Gurion to a meeting of Palmach commanders, in Ben-Gurion 1951, p. 242.

16. Meir, June 13, 1978, p. 20, interview transcript, BGA.

17. Ben-Gurion to the Security Committee, June 8, 1947, BGA.

18. Stern 1974, p. 263ff.

19. Ben-Gurion to the Security Committee, Dec. 4, 1947, BGA.

20. Avizohar 1993b, p. 32; Ben-Gurion, Diary, April 17, 1947, BGA.

21. Ben-Gurion to the Mapai secretariat, Oct. 30, 1947, to the Mapai Council, Aug. 9,

1947, to the Zionist General Council, Aug. 26, 1947, to the Histadrut Executive, Aug. 6, 1947, in Ben-Gurion 1993b, pp. 445, 332, 341, 317.

22. Stern 1974, pp. 268, 263, 271; Avizohar 1993b, pp. 27, 81.
23. Ben-Gurion to the Mapai secretariat, April 21, Aug. 2, 1947, BGA; Ben-Gurion to the Histadrut Executive, Aug. 6, 1947, and to the Mapai Council, Aug. 8, 1947, in Ben-Gurion 1993b, pp. 316ff., 277.
24. Ben-Gurion to the Histadrut Executive, Aug. 6, 1947, and to the Mapai Council, Aug. 8, 1947, in Ben-Gurion 1993b, pp. 316ff., 277; Stern 1974, p. 271; Halamish 1990, p. 302ff.
25. Ben-Gurion to the Histadrut Executive, March 26, 1947, and to the Mapai Council, Aug. 9, 1947, Ben-Gurion 1993b, pp. 66, 328.
26. Ben-Gurion 1993b, p. 126, editor's note 13, and p. 417, editor's note 3.
27. Zemach 1947; Zemach 1983, p. 182.
28. Ben-Gurion to the Mapai secretariat, April 21, 1947, BGA.
29. Replies to questions from the public, April 18, 1947, and Ben-Gurion to the Mapai secretariat, April 24, 1947, BGA; Ben-Gurion, Diary, April 18, 1948, BGA; Naor 1988, p. 182ff.; Bein 1982, p. 271ff.
30. Ben-Gurion, Diary, March 6, 1938, BGA; Ben-Gurion to UNSCOP, July 7, 1947, in Ben-Gurion 1993b, p. 256.
31. Halamish 1990, p. 302.
32. Eban 1997, pp. 92–93; Ben-Gurion to Paula, Sept. 2, 1947, Ben-Gurion to a public meeting, Nov. 25, 1947, Ben-Gurion to the Assembly of Representatives, Oct. 2, 1947, and Ben-Gurion statement, Nov. 30, 1947, in Ben-Gurion 1993, pp. 349, and editor's note there, 493, 382, 502; Ben-Gurion to the Jewish Agency Executive, Nov. 30, 1947, BGA; Ben-Gurion to the Histadrut Executive and Mapai Central Committee, Dec. 3, 1947, in Ben-Gurion 1982a, p. 20; Ben-Gurion to the Mapai Central Committee, Dec. 13, 1947, and to the Mapai secretariat, Dec. 30, 1947, in Ben-Gurion 1949, 5, p. 255; Sheffer 2015, p. 345.
33. Ben-Gurion to the Jewish Agency Executive, May 22, 1947, BGA.
34. Ben-Gurion to the Mapai secretariat, Dec. 3, 1947, in Ben-Gurion 1949, 5, p. 259.
35. Ben-Gurion to the Mapai Council, Aug. 9, 1947, in Ben-Gurion 1993b, p. 284.
36. Ben-Gurion to the Mapai Central Committee, Oct. 11, 1947, and the Jewish Agency Executive, Oct. 26, 1947, in Ben-Gurion 1993b, pp. 394, 428; Ben-Gurion to the Histadrut Executive, Dec. 3, 1947, in Ben-Gurion 1982a, p. 21.
37. Ben-Gurion to the Mapai Central Committee, Dec. 3, 1947, in Ben-Gurion 1982a, p. 22; Ben-Gurion to the Zionist General Council, March 10, 1948, in Ben-Gurion 1982e, p. 132.
38. "Tokhnit Likrat Pelishah," Oct. 6, 1947, in Ben-Gurion 1993b, p. 390, also Shabtai Teveth collection, people, BGA; *Davar*, Jan. 24, 1946; Ben-Artzi, interview transcript, BGA; Ben-Gurion, Diary, Nov. 13, 1947, BGA.
39. "Hatkafah al Shnei Ha'otobusim," Dec. 4, 1947, BGA; Segev 2007.
40. Ben-Gurion, Diary, Dec. 22, 1947, BGA.
41. Ben-Gurion, Diary, Dec. 23, 1947, BGA; Moshe Kol, interview transcript, BGA.
42. Ben-Gurion to the Cabinet, Oct. 19, 1953, BGA.
43. Ben-Gurion 1993b, p. 147, editor's note 2, p. 440, editor's note 5; Slutsky 1973, 3, pp. 1325, 1372.
44. *Davar*, Dec. 12, 1947.

45. Ben-Gurion, Diary, Dec. 1, April 3, 1947.

46. Ben-Gurion, Diary, Dec. 11, 1947, BGA.

47. Galili to the Security Committee, Dec. 11, 1947, BGA; Amarami and Maletzky 1981, p. 154ff.; Operations Branch report, Dec. 19, 1947, in Ben-Gurion 1982a, Dec. 20, 1947, Jan. 1, 1948, pp. 61, 97.

48. Golda Meir with the high commissioner, Dec. 17, 1947, in Yogev 1979, p. 79ff.

49. Ben-Gurion, Diary, Sept. 19, 1947, BGA.

50. Ben-Gurion, Diary, Dec. 25, 27, 1947, BGA.

51. Ben-Gurion to the Council of the International Union of Zionist Labor Parties, Aug. 18, 1936, in Ben-Gurion 1973b, p. 381; *Davar*, Dec. 12–28, 1947; Slutsky 1973, 3, p. 1383.

52. Ben-Gurion to the Council of the International Union of Zionist Labor Parties, Aug. 18, 1936, in Ben-Gurion 1973c, p. 381; Ben-Gurion to the Security Committee, Jan. 1, 1947, in Ben-Gurion, Diary, BGA; Ben-Gurion to the Mapai Central Committee, Jan. 8, 1948, in Ben-Gurion 1951, p. 29.

53. Ben-Gurion, Diary, Feb. 23, 1948, BGA.

54. Ben-Gurion, Diary, March 11, 1948; Segev 2000, pp. 515–16.

55. Ben-Gurion to the Mapai Council, Feb. 7, 1948, in Ben-Gurion 1951, p. 62.

56. Ben-Gurion to the Zionist General Council, April 6, 1948, in Ben-Gurion 1949, 3, p. 288.

57. Ben-Gurion, Diary, March 20, 1948, BGA; press release, in Ben-Gurion 1982a, p. 313; Joseph Heller 2010, p. 61ff.

58. Ben-Gurion 1969b, p. 79.

59. Ben-Gurion, Diary, April 23, May 24, 1948, BGA; Morris 2008, p. 140ff.

60. Sapir and Ben-Gurion at the Security Committee, Oct. 23, 1947, March 30, April 4, 1948, BGA.

61. Ben-Gurion, Diary, May 2, 1947, BGA; Avizohar 1993b, p. 13.

62. Avizohar 1993b, pp. 12, 41; Ben-Gurion to the Security Committee, Oct. 23, 1947, BGA; Ben-Gurion, Diary, Oct. 22, 30, 1947, March 7, April 20, 1947, BGA.

63. Ben-Gurion 1969b, p. 86; Generals' revolt, Israel Galili's version, July 1948, BGA, general chronological material; Ben-Gurion, Diary, May 3, 5, 1948, BGA.

64. Ben-Gurion, Diary, May 1, 1948, BGA.

65. Ben-Gurion, Diary, Dec. 11, 1947, BGA.

66. Ben-Gurion, Diary, Dec. 10, 1947, March 10, 1948, BGA.

67. Ezra Danin, interview transcript, BGA.

68. Ben-Gurion, Diary, May 1, 1948, BGA; Ben-Gurion to the Cabinet, Nov. 7, 1948, ISA; Morris 2008, p. 140ff.

69. Ben-Gurion, Diary, Dec. 11, 1947, Feb. 10, April 30, May 21, 1948, BGA.

70. Ben-Gurion with invited guests, Jan. 21, 1948, and Ben-Gurion to the Zionist General Council, April 6, 1948, in Ben-Gurion 1951, pp. 41ff., 86ff.

71. Ben-Gurion to the Mapai Council, Feb. 7, 1948, and to the Zionist General Council, April 6, 1948, in Ben-Gurion 1951, pp. 68ff., 92.

72. Ben-Gurion to the Zionist General Council, April 6, 1948, in Ben-Gurion 1951, p. 92.

73. Gouri 1982, p. 11ff.

74. Ben-Gurion to the Security Committee, Feb. 3, 1948, BGA.

75. Ben-Gurion to UNSCOP, July 7, 1947, and Ben-Gurion to the Mapai secretariat, June 11, 1947, in Ben-Gurion 1993b, pp. 264, 213; Ben-Gurion to the Zionist General

Council, April 6, 1947, in Ben-Gurion 1982a, p. 345; Ben-Gurion to S.E., Feb. 5, 1954, in Ostfeld 1988, p. 241.

76. Shtiftel 2008, pp. 291, 298, 318ff., 330.
77. Summary of meeting, May 6, 1948, BGA, Shabtai Teveth collection, concepts, Plan Dalet; Slutsky 1973, 3, p. 447.
78. Ben-Gurion, Diary, Jan. 2, 1948, BGA; Messer 1996, pp. 118, 121; Shtiftel 2008, pp. 375, 299, 217; Morris 2008, p. 146.
79. Shtiftel 2008, pp. 275, 299; Ben-Gurion to the Jewish Agency Executive, April 11, 1948, BGA; Jewish Agency to Abdullah, April 12, 1948, in Yogev 1979, p. 625ff; Ben-Gurion, Diary, May 1, 1948, BGA; Morris 2005, p. 79ff.
80. Morris 1991, p. 405.
81. Sharett and Ben-Gurion to the People's Administration, May 12, 1948, in People's Administration (Minhelet Ha'am) 1978, p. 47ff; Ben-Gurion, Diary, March 16, 1948; Sheffer 2015, p. 367; Ben-Gurion to the Histadrut Executive, May 10, 1945, BGA.
82. Ben-Gurion, Diary, May 11, 1948, BGA; Nakdimon 2011, p. 33ff; Ben-Gurion to the Cabinet, Sept. 26, 1948, ISA.
83. Ben-Gurion 1993b, p. 5, editor's note 1.
84. Ben-Gurion to the Security Committee, Feb. 10, 1948, BGA; Ben-Gurion, Diary, Oct. 6, 1947, July 20, 29, 1948, BGA; Ehud Avriel, Golda Meir, interview transcripts, Aug. 7, 1977, p. 11, BGA.
85. Ben-Gurion, Diary, April 24, May 11, 24, 1948, BGA.
86. Ben-Gurion to the Mapai Central Committee, May 11, 1948, BGA; Ben-Gurion, Diary, May 7, 1948, BGA.
87. Ben-Gurion, Diary, May 11, 1948, BGA; Shlaim 2007, p. 25ff.
88. Avizohar and Bareli 1989, p. 480ff.
89. Tzachor 1994, p. 183ff.
90. Yigael Yadin, Ben-Gurion, and Pinchas Rosen at the People's Administration, May 12, 1948, in Minhelet Ha'am 1978, pp. 6, 28; Elam 201, p. 150ff; Ben-Gurion, Diary, April 25, 1948, BGA.
91. Ben-Gurion, Diary, May 14, 1948, BGA.
92. *Davar*, May 14, 1948; Lavi 1968, p. 167.

17. WAR

1. Mann 2012, p. 69.
2. *Davar*, Sept. 9, 1948; Gurari, interview transcript, BGA; Ben-Gurion, Diary, March 8, 1948, BGA; Levy 1986, p. 77ff.; Reuven Grossman dedication to Ben-Gurion, courtesy of the Ben-Gurion House Library; Ben-Gurion to Hannah and Reuven Grossman, Aug. 1, 1948, BGA.
3. Yigael Yadin, interview transcript, BGA.
4. Ben-Gurion, Diary, March 20, 1948, BGA.
5. Ben-Gurion to the Mapai Central Committee, Jan. 6, 1948, Ben-Gurion 1949, 5, p. 275.
6. Yigael Yadin, interview transcript, BGA.
7. Ben-Gurion, Diary, March 28, Oct. 16–18, 20, Nov. 17, 1948, inter alia, BGA; Ben-Gurion 1982a, p. 331, editor's note 6; Moshe Carmel, interview transcript, BGA.
8. Moshe Carmel, interview transcript, BGA.

9. Ben-Gurion to the Cabinet, May 26, June 20, Dec. 19, 1948, BGA; Yigael Yadin, interview transcript, BGA; Yigael Yadin interview with Dov Goldstein, *Ma'ariv*, May 6, 1973; Rabin 1979, p. 55.

10. Moshe Sharett, Ben-Gurion, and Ze'ev Haklai at the Mapai Council, June 19, 1948, BGA.

11. Ben-Gurion, Diary, May 16, 1948, BGA.

12. Ben-Gurion et al. in the Cabinet, June 20, 1948, ISA.

13. Ben-Gurion et al. in the Cabinet, June 22, 1948, ISA; Nakdimon 1978, p. 257.

14. Ben-Gurion, Diary, June 22, 1948, BGA; Yigael Yadin, interview transcript, BGA; Rabin 1979, p. 566ff.

15. Ben-Gurion to the Committee of Five, July 3, 1948, in Anita Shapira 1985, p. 128.

16. Ben-Gurion to the Committee of Five, July 6, 1948, in Anita Shapira 1985, p. 239ff.; Oren 1985, p. 50ff.

17. Anita Shapira 1985, p. 240; Yigael Yadin, interview transcript, BGA.

18. Ben-Gurion to the Provisional State Council, June 23, 1948, courtesy of Shlomo Nakdimon; Ben-Gurion to the Knesset, Jan. 4, 1949, *Divrei Haknesset*, 1949, p. 434; *Davar*, Jan. 5, 1950.

19. Moshe Shapira, Aharon Zisling, and Mordechai Bentov in the Cabinet, July 7, 1948, ISA.

20. Ben-Gurion et al. in the Cabinet, July 11, 1948, ISA.

21. Ben-Gurion to Moshe Dadashov, Oct. 17, 1948, BGA; Ben-Gurion, Diary, Sept. 14, 16, 1948, BGA; Ben-Gurion to Aharon Zisling in the Cabinet, Oct. 18, Dec. 12, 1948, ISA.

22. Ben-Gurion, Diary, March 21, May 28, May 14, 1948, Oct. 30, 1947, BGA.

23. Jaffe 2015, p. 50ff.; Ben-Gurion, Diary, July 16, 17, 1948, BGA.

24. Ben-Gurion, Diary, May 11, 24, 30, 1948, BGA; Ben-Gurion to the Cabinet, May 30, June 16, 1948, ISA.

25. Ben-Gurion, Diary, May 17, 24, 27, 31, June 1, 6, 1948, BGA; Ben-Gurion to the Cabinet, May 20, 1948, ISA; Arieh Levontin to *Ha'aretz*, Dec. 13, 2000; Mula Cohen 2000, p. 142ff.

26. Ben-Gurion, Diary, June 4, 1948, BGA; Ben-Gurion to the Cabinet, July 14, 1948, ISA.

27. Yitzhak Rabin interview with Shabtai Teveth, Jan. 8, 1989, and Yigal Allon interview with Elhanan Oren, Sept. 10, 1970, BGA, Teveth collection, concepts, Lod and Ramla, BGA; "Allon: The Arabs of Lod and Ramla Were Not Expelled," *Davar*, Oct. 25, 1979.

28. Zvi Ayalon to brigade commanders, July 6, 1948, YTA, Zisling archive, division 9, container 9, file 1.

29. Allon and Rabin to the Yiftach and 8th Brigades, July 12, 1948, BGA, Shabtai Teveth collection, concepts, Lod and Ramla.

30. Ben-Gurion, Diary, July 12, 1948, BGA; Ben-Gurion to the Cabinet, July 14, 1948, ISA.

31. Ben-Gurion 1982a, p. 513, editorial comments, and p. 589, editorial note 2.

32. Ben-Gurion 1982a, p. 589, editorial note 2; Ben-Gurion to the Cabinet, July 14, 1948, ISA.

33. Segev 1986, p. 27; Aharon Zisling to the Political Committee of Mapam, July 14, 1948, BGA, Teveth collection, concepts, Lod and Ramla; Oren 1976, p. 123ff.

34. Avi-Yiftah (Shmaryahu Gutman) 1948, p. 452ff.
35. Ben-Gurion, Diary, Sept. 26, 1948, BGA.
36. Ben-Gurion, Diary, Sept. 17, 22, 1948, BGA; Ben-Gurion et al. in the Cabinet, Sept. 18, 19, 20, 1948, ISA.
37. Ben-Gurion to the Cabinet, Sept. 29, 1948, BGA.
38. Ben-Gurion to the Security Committee, July 20, 1948, BGA; Ben-Gurion in the Cabinet, Sept. 20, 21, 1948, ISA.
39. Ben-Gurion et al. in the Cabinet, Sept. 26, 1948, ISA; Lavid 2012, p. 68ff.; Ben-Gurion, Diary, Sept. 26, 1948, BGA. For a later plan to expel Christian Arabs from the Galilee, see Walter Eitan to Moshe Sharett, December 4, 1948; *Ha'aretz*, December 21, 2018.
40. Ben-Gurion to the Cabinet, Sept. 20, 1948, ISA.
41. Ben-Gurion to the Cabinet, June 16, 1948, ISA; Ben-Gurion, Diary, May 19, July 12, June 9, 17, 18, 1948, BGA.
42. Ben-Gurion to the Security Committee, July 20, 1948, BGA; Ben-Gurion to the Cabinet, Aug. 1, 1948, ISA; Ben-Gurion, Diary, Sept. 8, 1948, BGA.
43. Ben-Gurion to the Cabinet, Oct. 6, 1948, ISA.
44. Ben-Gurion et al. in the Cabinet, Oct. 6, 1948, ISA.
45. Ben-Gurion, Diary, July 16, 17, 1948, BGA; Levy 1986, p. 313ff.
46. Ben-Gurion to the Mapai secretariat, Oct. 11, 1947, and to the Jewish Agency Executive, Oct. 26, 1947, in Ben-Gurion 1993b, pp. 394, 428.
47. Ben-Gurion to the Cabinet, Jan. 3, 1950, ISA.
48. Ben-Gurion to the People's Administration, May 12, 1978, and to the Cabinet, Dec. 19, 1948, ISA.
49. Ben-Gurion to the Cabinet, June 16, Sept. 12, 26, 1948, ISA; Ben-Gurion, Diary, Oct. 2, 1948, BGA.
50. Ben-Gurion to the Cabinet, Oct. 26, 31, 1948, ISA.
51. Ben-Gurion, Diary, Nov. 11, 29, 1948, BGA; Yigael Yadin et al. in the Cabinet, Nov. 18, 1948, ISA.
52. Ben-Gurion to the Cabinet, Oct. 4, 18, 1949, ISA.
53. Ben-Gurion, Diary, Oct. 22, 1948, BGA; Baruch Rabinov, interview transcript, BGA; Gilad 1953, p. 935.
54. Ben-Gurion, Diary, July 3, 1937, June 16, 1948, BGA; Ben-Gurion to the Security Committee, Feb. 3, 1948, ISA.
55. Ben-Gurion, Diary, Oct. 6, 8, 1948, in Ben-Gurion 1982a, p. 739, editorial note 6; Ben-Gurion to the Cabinet, June 16, Oct. 31, 1948, ISA.
56. Mann 2012, p. 229, note 2.
57. Ben-Gurion to the Cabinet, June 16, Dec. 30, 1948, ISA; Ben-Gurion conversation with an unidentified member of Mapam, 1969, BGA, division of minutes and meetings, p. 31; Anita Shapira 2004, p. 425ff.
58. Ben-Gurion, Diary, March 11, June 9, 12, 28, 1949, BGA.
59. Ben-Gurion, Diary, May 24, 1948, BGA; Ben-Gurion 1982a, p. 824, editorial note 6; Haim Gvati, interview transcript, BGA.
60. Gershon Zak, interview transcript, BGA.
61. Baruch Azanya, interview transcript, cassette 173, p. 29, BGA.
62. Ben-Gurion, Diary, Dec. 3, 1948, Jan. 8, 1949, BGA.
63. Ben-Gurion, Diary, Dec. 25, 1948, BGA.

64. Ben-Gurion lecture, Jan. 21, 1948, in Ben-Gurion 1951, p. 50; Ben-Gurion, Diary, Nov. 27, 1948, BGA; Ben-Gurion to the Security Committee, June 8, 1947, BGA; Ben-Gurion to the Cabinet, Sept. 26, 1948, ISA; Ben-Gurion to the Mapai Central Committee, Jan. 6, 1948, in Ben-Gurion 1949, p. 275; Ben-Gurion to the Mapai Central Committee with the Knesset faction, July 22–23, 1949, BGA; Ben-Gurion to the Cabinet, June 22, 1948, ISA; Ben-Gurion, Diary, July 15, 1948, BGA.

65. Baruch Rabinov, interview transcript, BGA; Ben-Gurion to the Cabinet, Sept. 20, 1948, ISA.

66. Ben-Gurion, Diary, July 14, 1948, BGA; Ben-Gurion to the Cabinet, July 14, 1947, ISA.

67. Ben-Gurion, Diary, June 2, 7, 18, July 20, 1948, BGA; Segev 1986, p. 68ff.; Sheetrit and Gruenbaum in the Cabinet, June 19, 1948, ISA; Ben-Gurion to the Cabinet, Nov. 11, 1956, ISA.

68. Aharon Zisling to the Cabinet, May 10, 1949, BGA; Segev 1986, p. 27ff., Ben-Gurion 1969b, p. 165; Ben-Gurion to the Mapai Council, Feb. 7, 1948, in Ben-Gurion 1951, p. 65.

69. Aharon Zisling to the Cabinet, June 27, 1948; Aharon Zisling and Mordechai Bentov to the Cabinet, July 14, 1948; Ben-Gurion, Aharon Zisling, et al. in the Cabinet, Nov. 14, 17, 1948; Ben-Gurion to the Cabinet, May 6, 1949, ISA; Ben-Gurion to Moshe Shapira, Nov. 19, 1948, BGA; Riftin report, YTA, Israel Galili collection, 116488; Ben-Gurion 1982a, p. 812.

70. Ben-Gurion, Diary, May 1, Nov. 11, 1948, BGA.

71. Ben-Gurion, Diary, Aug. 22, 1949, BGA.

72. Ben-Gurion, Diary, July 15, 1948, BGA; Ben-Gurion 1982a, p. 835ff.

73. Allon to Ben-Gurion, March 24, 1949, in Anita Shapira 2004, p. 445ff.

74. Ben-Gurion to the Cabinet, March 16, 1949, ISA.

75. Ben-Gurion to the Cabinet, Nov. 7, 1948, ISA.

76. Ben-Gurion, Diary, Jan. 31, 1950; Kroyanker 2002, p. 92ff; David Kroyanker to the author; *Davar*, Feb. 12, 17, 1948; Ben-Gurion, Diary, June 25, 1948.

77. Ben-Gurion to the Cabinet, Oct. 17, 1951, ISA; Ben-Gurion, Diary, June 16, 1948, Jan. 14, 1952, BGA; Morris 2008, p. 406.

78. Segev 1986, p. 45; Lavi to the Mapai Central Committee, July 24, 1948, BGA; Ben-Gurion to the Cabinet, June 16, 1948, ISA.

79. Ben-Gurion 1979, p. 22; Ben-Gurion to the Cabinet, Oct. 11, 1949, BGA; Morris 1991, p. 179ff.

80. Ben-Gurion, Diary, May 18, 1948; and Jan. 1, 1949, BGA; Shraga Netzer, interview transcript, cassette 14, p. 6, BGA.

81. Ben-Gurion to the Cabinet, May 19, 1948, ISA; Ben-Gurion to the Cabinet, July 21, 1948, Dov Yosef, Diary, notebook 2, photocopy in possession of the author.

82. Ben-Gurion to the Security Committee, July 20, 1948, BGA; Ben-Gurion to the Provisional State Council, May 4, 1948, in Ben-Gurion 1982a, p. 387; Ben-Gurion to the Cabinet, June 16, 1948, ISA.

83. Segev 2000, p. 514ff.

84. Yitzhak Ben-Zvi to the Mapai Central Committee, April 15, 1937, in Ben-Gurion 1974a, p. 158.

85. Ben-Gurion, Diary, Jan. 20, June 25, 1948, BGA; Ben-Gurion to the Cabinet, June 14, 1948, ISA; Dov Yosef to the Cabinet, April 26, 1953, ISA.

86. Ben-Gurion, Diary, May 19, 21, 1948, BGA; Ben-Gurion to the Cabinet, May 19, 23, 1948, ISA.
87. Cohen-Levinovsky 2014, p. 231.
88. Ben-Gurion to the Cabinet, June 16, 1948, Oct. 17, 1951, ISA.
89. Segev 1986, p. 31; Aharon Zisling to the Cabinet, June 16, 1948, ISA.
90. Ben-Gurion to the Cabinet, Sept. 12, June 16, 1948, Aug. 5, 1956, Jan. 5, 1949, ISA; Ben-Gurion interview with Avraham Avi-hai, Dec. 25, 1969, HICJ-OHA, p. 21; Segev 1986, p. 30; Ben-Gurion, Diary, July 18, 1948, Jan. 4, 11, 1949, BGA.
91. Ben-Gurion 1969b, p. 264; Ben-Gurion to the Cabinet, March 15, 1949, ISA; Ben-Gurion, Diary, Jan. 4, 1949, BGA.
92. Ben-Gurion to the Cabinet, June 16, 1948, ISA.
93. Ben-Gurion, Diary, Jan. 6, 1948, BGA; Yehudit Simhoni, interview transcript, p. 11, BGA.
94. Press release, Jan. 1, 1948, in Ben-Gurion 1951, p. 20; Ben-Gurion to the Zionist General Council and to the Mapai Council, Aug. 15, Aug. 8, 1947, in Ben-Gurion 1993b, pp. 338, 324.
95. Ben-Gurion, Diary, May 18, June 3, 1948, BGA; Ben-Gurion to the Cabinet, Oct. 20, 1953, ISA.
96. Ben-Gurion to the Cabinet, June 2, July 28, 1948, ISA; Shraga Netzer, Aharon Beker, interview transcripts, BGA.
97. Mordechai Bentov to the Cabinet, July 9, 1948, ISA.
98. Ben-Gurion, Diary, Feb. 8, 29, 1948, BGA.
99. Ben-Gurion, Diary, Nov. 27, 1947, BGA; Ben-Gurion to the Cabinet, June 16, 1948, and to the Mapai Council, June 19, 1947, in Ben-Gurion 1982a, pp. 526, 534.
100. Ben-Gurion, Diary, Jan. 3, 1949, BGA.
101. Ben-Gurion to the Cabinet, Dec. 19, 1948, ISA; Bar-On 2015, p. 79ff.; Kadish and Kedar 2005, p. 74; Ben-Gurion 1959, p. 3; Ben-Gurion to Shimon Shershevsky, Sept. 16, 1969, BGA.
102. Ben-Gurion to Yehoshua Manoah, July 30, 1961, BGA.
103. Directive to the Haganah Command, June 18, 1947, in Ben-Gurion 1993b, p. 304; Ben-Gurion to the Cabinet, Aug. 1, 1948, ISA.
104. Ben-Gurion to UNSCOP, in Ben-Gurion 1993b, p. 264; Ben-Gurion to the Cabinet, Oct. 17, 1951, ISA.
105. Directive to the Haganah Command, June 18, 1947, in Ben-Gurion 1993b, p. 304; Ben-Gurion to the Cabinet, Oct. 21, 1948, June 12, 1949, ISA.
106. Ben-Gurion to the Cabinet, Aug. 1, 1948, ISA; Ben-Gurion, Diary, June 19, 1948, BGA; Ben-Gurion 1982a, p. 814, editors' introduction; Golda Meir, interview transcript, Aug. 7, 1977, p. 11, BGA.
107. Ben-Gurion to the Cabinet, March 20, 1949, ISA.
108. Ben-Gurion, Diary, Jan. 18, 1949, BGA.
109. Ben-Gurion, Diary, April 27, 1953, BGA; Sivan 1991.
110. Ben-Gurion to the Cabinet, Nov. 14, 1948, ISA; Ben-Gurion, Diary, April 7, 1950, BGA.
111. Ben-Gurion to Meir in the Cabinet, March 20, 1949, BGA.

18. NEW ISRAELIS

1. Alterman 1949; "Hagigat Siyum Hamilyon Harishon," *Davar*, Dec. 16, 1949; BGA, Shabtai Teveth collection, concepts, "Avak Adam"; Ben-Gurion to the Cabinet, July 20, 1952, ISA.

2. Ben-Gurion, Diary, Dec. 23, 1950, July 2, 1951, BGA: Segev 1986, p. 95; Ben-Gurion to the Knesset, March 8, 1949, in *Divrei Haknesset*, 1, p. 54; Ben-Gurion to the Knesset, April 26, 1949, *Divrei Haknesset*, 1, p. 399.

3. Ben-Gurion, Diary, Jan. 1, 1948, BGA; Ben-Gurion to the Cabinet, April 26, July 12, Dec. 13, 1949, ISA; Ben-Gurion, "Netzah Yisra'el," "Yisra'el Vehatefutzah," in Ben-Gurion 1964a, p. 133ff.; Ben-Gurion, Diary, Aug. 17, 1948, BGA; Segev 1986, p. 96ff.

4. Ben-Gurion, Diary, Aug. 9, 1953, BGA.

5. Ben-Gurion to the Cabinet, July 20, 1952, ISA.

6. Ben-Gurion, "Netzah Yisra'el," in Ben-Gurion 1964a, p. 177.

7. Ben-Gurion to the Cabinet, June 16, 1948, ISA.

8. Duach al Matzavam shel Yehudei Iraq," Feb. 3, 1943, BGA; Ben-Gurion to the Mapai Central Committee, Feb. 24, 1943, BGA; Ben-Gurion to the Jewish Agency Executive, March 7, 1943, BGA; Ben-Gurion, "Al Mediniyutenu Hatziyonit," in Ben-Gurion 1949, 3, p. 133ff.; Ben-Gurion, Diary, Oct. 18, 1943, BGA: Anita Shapira 1980, p. 685; Slutsky 1973, 3, p. 163ff.; Ben-Gurion to the Jewish Agency Executive, Feb. 11, 1945, BGA; Ben-Gurion, Diary, Nov. 10, 1945, BGA.

9. Ben-Gurion to the Jewish Agency Executive, Feb. 11, 1946, BGA; "Netzah Yisra'el," in Ben-Gurion 1964a, pp. 143, 148.

10. Segev 2000, p. 150ff.

11. Jabotinsky 1981, p. 91.

12. Ben-Gurion to the Mapai Central Committee, July 22–23, 1949, BGA; Segev 1993, p. 153ff.; Ben-Gurion to the Cabinet, Jan. 10, 1950, ISA; Dvora Hacohen 1994a, p. 301ff.; Segev 1986, pp. 116, 139; Ben-Gurion 1954a, p. 37.

13. Ben-Gurion, "Netzah Yisra'el," in Ben-Gurion 1964a, p. 157; Ben-Gurion to the Knesset, Feb. 14, 1951, *Divrei Haknesset*, 8, p. 1102; Ben-Gurion, "Otonomiyah Leumit Veyahasei Shechenim," in Ben-Gurion 1931, p. 130; Ben-Gurion with the IDF high command, April 6, 1950, BGA.

14. Segev 1986, p. 156ff.

15. Ben-Gurion, Diary, July 30, 1945, BGA; Ben-Gurion to Yigael Yadin, Nov. 27, 1950, BGA; Ben-Gurion to the Cabinet, Aug. 5, 1956, March 6, 1955, ISA.

16. Ben-Gurion, Diary, Sept. 9, Nov. 23, 1951, BGA; Ben-Gurion and Golda Meir to the Cabinet, May 24, 1949, ISA; Ben-Gurion with the IDF high command, April 6, 1950, BGA; Ben-Gurion to Yigael Yadin, Nov. 27, 1950, BGA; Ben-Gurion to the Knesset, Aug. 18, 1952, in Ben-Gurion 1962a, 4, p. 90.

17. Ben-Gurion to the Cabinet, March 3, 1949, ISA; Ben-Gurion and Yigael Yadin to the Cabinet, July 20, 1952, ISA; Ben-Gurion to the IDF high command, April 6, 1950, BGA.

18. Ben-Gurion to the Cabinet, Jan. 27, July 20, 1952, ISA.

19. Ben-Gurion, Diary, Aug. 6, 1948, BGA.

20. Yadin to the Cabinet, April 26, 1950, Feb. 15, 1951, ISA.

21. Ben-Gurion to the IDF high command, April 6, 1950, BGA; Yigael Yadin and Ben-

Gurion to the Cabinet, April 26, 1950, and Ben-Gurion to the Cabinet, Aug. 3, 1952, ISA.

22. Ben-Gurion to the Cabinet, Dec. 2, 1951, ISA; Segev 1986, p. 155ff.

23. Ben-Gurion to the Cabinet, April 26, Oct. 18, 1953, ISA; Moshe Shapira, Yosef Serlin, and Israel Rokach to the Cabinet, Feb. 4, Nov. 15, 1953, ISA.

24. Morris 1993, p. 54ff.

25. Ben-Gurion, "Netzah Yisra'el," in Ben-Gurion 1964a, p. 148.

26. Ben-Gurion at the Sejera celebrations, Sept. 25, 1962, BGA; Ben-Gurion, "Beyehuda Uvegalil," in Ben-Gurion 1931, p. 271; Ben-Gurion to the Histadrut Convention, Feb. 7, 1923, in Ben-Gurion 1971a, pp. 216; Ben-Gurion, Diary, June 6, 12, 1939, BGA; Shabbetai Pinhas to Ben-Gurion, March 17, 1941, BGA; "Metzukat Hakurdim Yotzei Sejera," BGA, subject files, Sejera; Ben-Gurion to the Mapai Council, June 19, 1948.

27. Ben-Gurion to the Cabinet, Aug. 1, 1948, ISA.

28. Ben-Gurion, Diary, Sept. 14, 1949, Jan. 9, May 28, 1950, March 4, 1951, BGA.

29. Ben-Gurion to the Mapai Central Committee, July 22, 1949, BGA.

30. Ben-Gurion to the Knesset, Jan. 16, 1950, *Divrei Haknesset*, 3, p. 536; Ben-Gurion, Diary, April 8, 1950, ISA.

31. Ben-Gurion, Diary, March 28, 1950, BGA.

32. Ben-Gurion to the Cabinet, July 12, 1950, ISA.

33. Ben-Gurion to the Knesset, Aug. 15, 1949, *Divrei Haknesset*, 2, p. 1339.

34. Ben-Gurion 1971b, p. 135; Ben-Gurion at the Sejera celebrations, Sept. 25, 1962, BGA; Ben-Gurion, Diary, Aug. 29, 1950, BGA.

35. Segev 1986, p. 155ff.; Lissak 1986, p. 109ff.

36. *Davar*, May 23, 1950; Ben-Gurion, Diary, Dec. 29, 1950, June 29, Sept. 9, Nov. 23, 1951, April 22, Oct. 15, 1952, April 24, July 11, 1953, BGA.

37. Segev 1986, p. 190ff.; "Din Vaheshbon Va'adat Hahakirah Hamamlachtit be'inyan Parshat Hi'almutam shel Yeladim Mivein Olei Teman Bashanim 1948–1954," p. 27, ISA.

38. Ben-Gurion, Diary, Sept. 28, 1949, BGA.

39. Ben-Gurion to the Cabinet, Feb. 9, 1953, BGA.

40. Ben-Gurion, Diary, Dec. 3, 27, 1949, BGA; Segev 1986, p. 128ff.; Ben-Gurion to the Mapai secretariat, April 22, 1949, BGA.

41. Ben-Gurion to the Cabinet, Feb. 1, 1951, ISA.

42. Immigration emissaries to the Jewish Agency, Feb. 25, 1950, in possession of the author.

43. Segev 1986, p. 296ff.

44. Ben-Gurion to the Cabinet, Aug. 31, Sept. 7, 1950, Jan. 20, Feb. 7, 10, 1952, July 19, 1953, ISA.

45. Ben-Gurion to the Cabinet, June 7, 1950, Oct. 11, 1951, ISA; Eliezer Kaplan to the Cabinet, Aug. 31, 1950, ISA.

46. Ben-Gurion to the Knesset, Aug. 8, 1950, *Divrei Haknesset*, 6, p. 2499; Ben-Gurion to the Knesset, Oct. 8, 1951, *Divrei Haknesset*, 10, p. 251.

47. Ben-Gurion to the Cabinet, Sept. 24, Oct. 5, 1950, Sept. 26, 1951, ISA; Segev 1986, p. 310ff.

48. Yosef 1975, p. 228ff.; Segev 1986, p. 145ff.

49. Ben-Gurion to Yoel Hanohi, Aug. 27, 1965, BGA.

50. *Dvar Hashavua*, Nov. 10, 1949; Ben-Gurion, Diary, Sept 28, 1949, BGA; Ben-Gurion to the Knesset, Feb. 14, 1951, *Divrei Haknesset*, 8, p. 1102; Segev 1986, p. 185ff.

51. Ben-Gurion to Yisrael Yeshayahu, Sept. 21, 1954, BGA; Ben-Gurion to the Cabinet, March 18, 1953, ISA; Gershon Zak, interview transcript, BGA.

52. Ben-Gurion to Yigael Yadin, Nov. 27, 1950, BGA; Ben-Gurion to the Cabinet, Jan. 18, March 29, 1951, ISA; Ben-Gurion, Diary, March 28, June 29, 1950; Ben-Gurion to Yigael Yadin, June 29, 1951, BGA.

53. Ben-Gurion to Yigael Yadin, Nov. 27, 1950, BGA.

54. D. Ben Dov to the executive of the Jewish Agency's Absorption Department, Nov. 20, 1949, BGA; Ben-Gurion to the Knesset, Feb. 14, 1951, *Divrei Haknesset*, 8, p. 1102; Ben-Gurion et al. to the Cabinet, Jan. 10, May 10, June 14, Dec. 6, 1950, Jan. 3, 1951, ISA; Aryeh Dayan 2002.

55. Ben-Gurion to Yehuda Leib Maimon, Jan. 12, and to Yitzhak-Meir Levin and Yehuda Leib Maimon, Feb. 20, 1950, BGA; Ben-Gurion to the Cabinet, Jan. 17, 1950, ISA.

56. Moshe Shapira and Ben-Gurion to the Cabinet, Jan. 18, 1951, ISA.

57. Ben-Gurion to the Cabinet, Jan. 18, 1951, ISA; Zameret 1997, p. 141ff.

58. Ben-Gurion to the Cabinet, Jan. 18, 1951, June 7, 1953, July 8, 1962, ISA; Brown 2011, p. 267.

59. Ben-Gurion, Diary, Oct. 20, 1952, BGA; Navon 2015, p. 113ff.

60. Yitzhak-Meir Levin to the Cabinet, July 12, 1950, April 17, 1953, ISA; Ben-Gurion to Yitzhak-Meir Levin, April 10, 1949, BGA.

61. Ben-Gurion to Dov Tzvi Rothstein, Jan. 29, 1954, BGA; Golda Meir to the Cabinet, July 12, 1950, ISA.

62. Ben-Gurion to the Cabinet, Jan. 17, 1950, ISA.

63. Yeshayahu Leibowitz, interview transcript, BGA, p. 19ff.; Ostfeld 1988, p. 209ff.

64. Ben-Gurion, Moshe Shapira, Yehuda Leib Maimon, and Golda Meir to the Cabinet, July 12, 1950; Yitzhak-Meir Levin to the Cabinet, Nov. 28, 1948; Ben-Gurion to the Cabinet, Jan. 17, 1950, March 1, 1951, ISA.

65. "Dat Vemedinah Bamemshalah" 1953, ISA, including: Dec. 8, 15, 1948, May 24, 1949 (stores), March 23, 1952, July 5, 1953 (pork); Feb. 6, 1949 (prayer at the opening of Knesset sessions); July 12, 19, 1950 (public transportation and work on the Sabbath), Oct. 24, 1950 (special army units for religious soldiers), Jan. 25, 1951 (autopsies), May 16, 1948 (IDF swearing-in ceremony); June 1, 1952 (death penalty).

66. Ben-Gurion et al. to the Cabinet, Aug. 9, 1949, Jan. 17, Feb. 2, 1950, ISA; Ben-Gurion, Diary, Jan. 9, May 31, 1950, ISA.

67. Ben-Gurion, Diary, Nov. 3, 1948, BGA.

68. Ben-Gurion to the Cabinet, Feb. 21, 1950, ISA.

69. Elon 1951.

70. Ben-Gurion, Diary, June 15, July 2, 3, 10, 13, Jan. 26, 1951, BGA; Ziv 1958, p. 120.

71. Ben-Gurion, Diary, July 31, 1951, ISA.

72. Ben-Gurion to the Cabinet, July 12, 1950, ISA.

73. Dvora Hacohen 1994a, p. 314.

74. Ben-Gurion, Diary, June 25, 1953, BGA.

75. Ben-Gurion, Diary, March 11, Sept. 28, 1949; Ben-Gurion to Roni Baron, Sept. 28, 1949, BGA.

76. Ostfeld 1988, p. 9; Navon 2015, p. 95.

77. Ben-Gurion to the Cabinet, Nov. 8, 1953, ISA.
78. Ben-Gurion to the Cabinet, Dec. 20, 1948, ISA.
79. Ben-Gurion and Pinchas Rosen to the People's Administration, May 12, 1948, in Minhelet Ha'am 1978, p. 28; Ben-Gurion, "Hadegel," in Ben-Gurion 1951, p. 198; Ben-Gurion to the Cabinet, May 18, 1949, Jan. 10, 1950, ISA.
80. Ben-Gurion to the Cabinet, June 16, 14, July 12, 1949, Nov. 30, 1958, ISA.
81. Zerach Warhaftig, interview transcript, BGA.
82. Ben-Gurion to Ehud Sprinzak, Feb. 10, 1965, BGA.
83. Ben-Gurion, Diary, Dec. 14, 16, 17, 1949, BGA; Segev 1986, p. 40ff.
84. Dorit Rosen, Ruth Segal-Havilio, Sarah Meltzer, Malka Leef, Ehud Avriel, interview transcripts, BGA.
85. Dorit Rosen, Ruth Segal-Havilio, Sarah Meltzer, interview transcripts, BGA; Navon 2015, p. 111.
86. Navon 2015, pp. 110ff., 220.
87. Yitzhak Tunik, Yehuda Erez, interview transcripts, BGA.
88. Dorit Rozin, Ruth Sigal-Havilio, Sarah Meltzer, Malka Leef, interview transcripts, BGA.
89. Mazal Jibli, interview transcript, BGA.
90. Mazal Jibli, interview transcript, BGA; Yariv Ben-Eliezer, interview transcript, BGA.
91. Rivka Katznelson to Ben-Gurion, May 7, 1961, BGA.
92. Rivka Katznelson diary, Jan. 10, July 23, 1931, Feb. 8, 1949, Gnazim.
93. Rivka Katznelson Archive, Gnazim; Rivka Katznelson interview with Sarit Fuchs, Ma'ariv, July 22, 1988.
94. Rivka Katznelson to Simon Halkin, Nov. 25, 1974, Gnazim 175, 23484; Teveth 1987b, p. 27.
95. Rivka Katznelson interview with Shabtai Teveth, Oct. 2, 1977, BGA, Shabtai Teveth collection, subjects, Ben-Gurion and women.
96. Rivka Katznelson interview with Shabtai Teveth, Oct. 2, 1977, BGA, Shabtai Teveth collection, subjects, Ben-Gurion and women; Rivka Katznelson interview with Sarit Fuchs, Ma'ariv, July 22, 1988.
97. Rivka Katznelson interview with Sarit Fuchs, Ma'ariv, July 22, 1988; Rivka Katznelson to Simon Halkin, Nov. 25, 1974, Gnazim, 175, 23484 1; Ben-Gurion to Rivka Katznelson, Jan. 7, Feb. 17, March 1, June 1, 1963, Rivka Katznelson Archive, Gnazim, 894/15ff.; Rivka Katznelson diary, date unclear, and "Al Ben-Gurion," Gnazim kaf-24972, kaf-25644; Ben-Gurion, Diary, June 7, 1963, BGA.

19. ANXIETIES

1. Ben-Gurion, Diary, Sept. 23, 1951, BGA; Yigael Yadin, interview transcript, p. 37, BGA; Ben-Gurion to the Cabinet, Sept. 23, 1952, ISA.
2. Ben-Gurion, Diary, Aug. 30, 1950, BGA.
3. Ben-Gurion, Diary, Sept. 1, 1954, BGA.
4. Ben-Gurion interview with Ya'akov Ashman, Nov. 25, 1963, BGA; Bar-Zohar 1978, p. 1153; Dr. Moshe Rachmilevich to Batya Even-Shoshan, Feb. 4, 1970, BGA.
5. Ben-Gurion to the Zionist General Council, May 5, 1949, in Ben-Gurion 1962a, 1, p. 127; Ben-Gurion to the Cabinet, Aug. 30, 1949, ISA.
6. Ben-Gurion to the Cabinet, June 28, 1950, Jan. 20, 1952, ISA.

7. Ben-Gurion to the Zionist General Council, May 5, 1949, in Ben-Gurion 1962a, p. 127; Ben-Gurion to the Cabinet, Aug. 30, 1949, ISA.

8. Segev 1986, p. 294; Ze'ev Sherf, interview transcript, BGA.

9. Ben-Gurion to the Cabinet, Jan. 3, 1950, May 6, July 12, 1949, ISA; Ben-Gurion, Diary, Feb. 9, 20, 28, June 25, 1950, BGA; Ben-Gurion 1951, p. 7ff.

10. Ben-Gurion to the Cabinet, Jan. 3, 1950, ISA; Ben-Gurion to Yigael Yadin, Nov. 27, 1950, BGA.

11. Ben-Gurion, Diary, Nov. 25, Dec. 19, 1950, BGA; Ehud Avriel, interview transcript, BGA; Ben-Gurion's trip in the Israeli press, BGA, press clippings division, Nov.–Dec. 1950; Ben-Gurion to the Cabinet, Dec. 20, 1950, ISA; Doris May to Ben-Gurion, Nov. 5, 1950, BGA; Sir Knox Helm to the Foreign Office, Nov. 27, 28, 1950, NA (UK), FO 371/82530.

12. Ben-Gurion to the Cabinet, Feb. 15, 1951, ISA.

13. Ben-Gurion to the Cabinet, Oct. 12, 25, 1951, ISA.

14. Ben-Gurion to the Cabinet, Feb. 10, 1952, ISA.

15. Ben-Gurion to Moshe Sharett, Sept. 15, 1949, and to the Cabinet, Jan. 20, 1953, BGA; Ben-Gurion to the Cabinet, Oct. 25, 1951, ISA.

16. Goschler 2005.

17. Ben-Gurion et al. in the Cabinet, Dec. 27, 1950; Bechor-Shalom Sheetrit to the Cabinet, March 2, 1949, ISA.

18. Moshe Shapira, David Remez, et al. to the Cabinet, March 2, 1949, ISA; Ya'akov Sharett 2007, p. 105ff.

19. Ben-Gurion to the Cabinet, Jan. 3, 1951, ISA.

20. Ben-Gurion et al. to the Cabinet, Nov. 1, 1949, Feb. 15, Dec. 27, 1950, Jan. 3, Feb. 2, 8, Nov. 4, 1951, ISA; Ben-Gurion, Diary, April 21, 29, 1950, BGA; Weitz 2007, p. 11ff.

21. Ben-Gurion, Diary, April 29, 1950, BGA.

22. Ben-Gurion, Diary, Sept. 25, 1951, July 21, 1952, BGA; Segev 1993, p. 200ff.

23. Carlebach 1951; Ben-Gurion, Golda Meir, and Mark Dvorzhetski to the Mapai Central Committee, Dec. 13, 1951; Ya'akov Sharett 2007, pp. 253, 221ff., 237ff.

24. *Herut*, Jan. 8, 1952.

25. Ben-Gurion to the Cabinet, Jan. 13, 1952, June 28, 1953, ISA; Ben-Gurion to Haim Gouri, June 16, 1961, BGA; Ya'akov Sharett 2007, p. 328; Segev 1993, p. 211ff.

26. Ya'akov Sharett 2007, p. 448ff.

27. Ben-Gurion, Diary, April 12, 1953; *Davar*, April 19, 1953.

28. Ben-Gurion to the Cabinet, March 23, 1952; Segev 1993, p. 230ff.

29. Moshe Sharett to the Cabinet, March 2, 1949; Golda Meir and Ben-Gurion to the Cabinet, March 22, 1953; Ben-Gurion to the Cabinet, Sept. 7, 23, 1953, ISA.

30. Ben-Gurion to the Cabinet, Feb. 22, 1953, ISA.

31. Ben-Gurion to the Cabinet, Feb. 22, 1953, ISA.

32. Ben-Gurion to the Cabinet, July 6, 1952, ISA.

33. Yitzhak Navon, Diary, Nov. 10, 1952, YNA.

34. Ben-Gurion, Diary, Oct. 6, 1950, July 1, 2, Sept. 16, 1949, BGA.

35. Ben-Gurion, Diary, Oct. 6, 1950, July 1, 2, Sept. 16, 1949, BGA; Ben-Gurion to the Mapai Central Committee, March 10, 1951, Feb. 6, 1953, BGA; Zameret 1997, p. 190ff.; Reshef 1987, p. 114ff.

36. Ben-Gurion to the Cabinet, Jan. 13, 1952, Feb. 10, May 31, June 21, 1953, ISA.

37. Ben-Gurion to the Cabinet, May 31, 1953, ISA.
38. Ben-Gurion to the Mapai Political Committee, Nov. 23, 1952, Jan. 16, 1953, BGA.
39. Ben-Gurion to Moshe Shapira, Oct. 16, 1949, BGA; Lahav 1999, p. 154ff.; Ben-Gurion to members of the Cabinet, Jan. 20, 1953, BGA.
40. Navon 2015, p. 137ff.
41. Yehoshua Cohen to Haim Israeli, June 17, 1984, BGA; Oded Bauman to Haim Israeli, April 18, 1984, BGA, Shabtai Teveth collection, people, Ben-Gurion and Sde Boker; Ben-Gurion to Baruch Zuckerman, Dec. 19, 1953, BGA.
42. Grisaru 1971; *Davar*, May 29, 1952; *Ma'ariv*, June 25, 1962; Ben-Gurion, Diary, Oct. 13, 1952; Ben-Gurion to Zuckerman, Nov. 18, 1953, BGA.
43. Ben-Gurion to Ehud Avriel, Sept. 11, 1952; Ben-Gurion to the Histadrut, Sept. 12, 1952, BGA; Ben-Gurion to the Jewish Agency, Sept. 14, 1952, BGA.
44. Ben-Gurion, Diary, Oct. 5, 12, 23, 1952, BGA.
45. Ben-Gurion, Diary, Oct. 30, 1952, BGA.
46. Ben-Gurion, Diary, May 14, 1953, BGA; Ben-Gurion to the Cabinet, April 26, May 24, July 5, 1953, ISA; Ben-Gurion to the members of the Cabinet, Jan. 20, 1953, BGA.
47. Ben-Gurion to the Knesset, *Divrei Haknesset*, 4, Jan. 1950, 3, p. 434ff.; Ben-Gurion to the Foreign Affairs and Defense Committee, June 20, 1950, BGA; Ben-Gurion to the Cabinet, May 24, 1953, ISA.
48. Yitzhak Navon, Diary, Nov. 9, 1952, YNA.
49. Golda Meir, interview transcript, cassette 392, p. 25, BGA.
50. Ben-Gurion to Leo Cohen, Nov. 16, 1948, BGA; Ben-Gurion to the Cabinet, Feb. 2, 1949, ISA.
51. Weisgal 1971, p. 260ff.
52. Ben-Gurion, Diary, Nov. 15, 1952, BGA; Eban 1977, p. 166.
53. Ben-Gurion, Diary, Nov. 23, 1952; Golda Meir, interview transcript, cassette 269, p. 1, BGA.
54. Ben-Gurion to the members of Sde Boker, May 28, 1953, BGA; Ben-Gurion to the Cabinet, May 24, 1953, ISA.
55. Ben-Gurion, Diary, May 14, 1949, BGA.
56. Yitzhak-Meir Levin and Ben-Gurion to the Cabinet, Jan. 20, 1952; Ben-Gurion to the Cabinet, Feb. 1, May 24, 1953, ISA; Ben-Gurion, Oct. 19, 1952, in Freundlich 1981–92, p. 578; Ben-Gurion to the founding congress of Mapai, Jan. 6, 1930, in Ben-Gurion 1931, p. 226.
57. Moshe Sharett to the Cabinet, July 12, 1949, ISA; Segev 1986, p. 32.
58. Shlaim 2007, p. 47ff.
59. Shlaim 2000, p. 52ff.; Segev 1986, p. 18; Rabinovich 1991, p. 59ff.
60. Ben-Gurion to the Cabinet, Jan. 20, 1952, April 26, June 7, 1953, ISA.
61. *Davar*, Feb. 7, 1951; Ben-Gurion, Diary, Feb. 6, 1952, BGA; Bar-On 2014, p. 90; Morris 1996, p. 221; Ziv 1958, p. 108.
62. Ben-Gurion to Moshe Shapira, April 10, 1949, BGA; Morris 1993, p. 143ff.
63. Morris 1993, pp. 40, 137ff.; Lt. Col. Yitzhak Shani to the Cabinet, Nov. 15, 1953, ISA.
64. Ben-Gurion to the Cabinet, Dec. 3, 22, 1952, ISA; Ben-Gurion, Diary, Dec. 17, 1952, Jan. 4, 1953, BGA.
65. Ben-Gurion, Diary, Jan. 4, 5, 1953, BGA.
66. Ben-Gurion to the Cabinet, Feb. 4, 1953, ISA; *Davar*, Feb. 4, 1953.

67. Ben-Gurion to the Cabinet, Feb. 4, Pinhas Rosen to the Cabinet, Feb. 24, Ben-Gurion et al. to the Cabinet, Feb. 9, 1953, ISA; Ben-Gurion, Diary, March 9, 1953, BGA.

68. Ben-Gurion, Diary, July 8, 19, 1953, BGA.

69. Ben-Gurion, Diary, Oct. 4, 1953, April 6, 1954, BGA; Sheleg 1998, p. 128.

70. Yehoshua Cohen, interview transcript, BGA.

71. Elron 2016, pp. 106, 129ff.

72. Moshe Dayan to the Cabinet, Jan. 25, 1953, ISA; Turgan 2015, p. 350; Drori 2006, p. 243ff.; Nevo study, July 1954, IDFA, 694/60/20.

73. Elron 2016, p. 37ff.; Ben-Gurion to the Cabinet, March 1, 8, 1953, ISA; Ben-Gurion to the Knesset Foreign Affairs and Defense Committee, March 10, 1953, ISA; Ben-Gurion to the Cabinet, Oct. 17, 1960, ISA.

74. Ben-Gurion to the Cabinet, May 24, 1953, ISA.

75. Ben-Gurion, Diary, June 23, 1953, BGA.

76. Ben-Gurion to the Cabinet, May 24, 1953, ISA; Ben-Gurion, Diary, Aug. 11, 1953, BGA.

77. Ben-Gurion to the Cabinet, May 24, April 26, May 7, 1953, ISA.

78. Ben-Gurion, Diary, Nov. 16, 1948, BGA; Ben-Gurion to the Cabinet, Jan. 20, 1952, ISA; Ben-Gurion, Diary, July 6, 1953, BGA.

79. Ben-Gurion to the Cabinet, Feb. 9, May 24, June 11, 1953, ISA.

80. Ben-Gurion to Moshe Sharett in the Cabinet, June 11, 1953, ISA.

81. Morris 1993, p. 256ff.

82. *Davar*, Oct. 14, 1953; Morris 1993, p. 227ff.

83. Ben-Gurion et al. in the Cabinet, Oct. 18, 1953, ISA; Moshe Sharett, Diary, Oct. 13, 1953 in Sharett 1978, 1, p. 49; Ben-Gurion 1965, p. 13.

84. Ben-Gurion et al. in the Cabinet, Oct. 18, Nov. 22, 1953, ISA; Morris 1993, p. 256ff.

85. Ben-Gurion to the Cabinet, June 11, 1953, ISA; Morris 1993, pp. 108, 124ff., 179ff.

86. Ben-Gurion, Diary, Oct. 22, 1953, BGA; Sharon at Ben-Gurion House, Oct. 20, 1997, BGA, item 242452.

87. Uri Even 1974, p. 75.

88. Ariel Sharon at a gathering of officers from Brigade 202, April 25, 1957, courtesy of the Sharon family; Ben-Gurion, Diary, April 25, 1957, BGA.

89. Moshe Dayan 1976, p. 115.

90. Moshe Sharett, Diary, Oct. 14, 1953, in Sharett 1978, 1, p. 34ff.; Moshe Sharett to the Cabinet, Oct. 18, 1953, ISA.

91. Moshe Sharett to Nahum Goldmann, June 15, 1948, in Freundlich 1992, p. 163.

92. Ben-Gurion to Mapai's Political Committee, Nov. 2, 1953, BGA; Ben-Gurion 1972, p. 410; Ben-Gurion to Paula, Oct. 7, 1937, BGA.

93. Ben-Gurion, Diary, Nov. 19, 1951, BGA; Yechiam Weitz 2014a, p. 332ff.; Navon 2015, p. 144ff.; Elhanan Yishai, Shaul Avigur, interview transcripts, BGA.

94. Moshe Sharett, Diary, Nov. 17, 25, 1953, in Sharett 1978, 1, pp. 155ff., 193ff.; Ben-Gurion, Diary, Aug. 19, 1953, Oct. 4, 1951, BGA; Pinhas Rosen and Moshe Shapira to the Cabinet, Nov. 29, 1953, ISA.

95. Ben-Gurion to the Cabinet, Oct. 19, 20, 1953, ISA; Ben-Gurion, Diary, Oct. 19, 1948, BGA; Elron 2016, p. 410.

96. Ben-Gurion to Elimelech Avner, March 24, 1949, BGA; Ben-Gurion to the Cabinet, Nov. 8, 15, 1953, ISA; Kafkafi 1998, p. 168ff.

97. Ben-Gurion to the Cabinet, Nov. 15, 1953, ISA.

98. Ben-Gurion to Yitzhak Ben-Zvi, Nov. 2, 1953, BGA; Ben-Gurion to the Cabinet, Oct. 17, 1960, ISA.

99. Navon 2015, p. 99; Ben-Gurion interview with Malcolm Stuart, April 1968, p. 86, BGA; Golda Meir, interview transcript, p. 8, BGA.

100. Moshe Sharett, Diary, Nov 19, 1953, in Sharett 1978, 1, p. 164.

101. Moshe Sharett, Diary, Nov. 11, 1953, in Sharett 1978, 1, p. 140.

102. Ben-Gurion and Yosef Serlin to the Cabinet, Dec. 6, 1953, ISA.

103. Ben-Gurion, Diary, Dec. 17, 1953, BGA.

20. THE NASTY BUSINESS

1. Navon 2015, p. 139; Ben-Gurion, Diary, Dec. 14, 1953, BGA.

2. Berl Repetur, interview transcript, BGA; Rivka Hoz to Dov Hoz, April 19, 1940, BGA, Shabtai Teveth collection, people; Ben-Gurion to the Knesset, Jan. 16, 1950, *Divrei Haknesset*, 3, p. 536; Ben-Gurion to the Cabinet, July 12, 1950, ISA; Ben-Gurion to Baruch Zuckerman, Dec. 19, 1953, BGA; Ben-Gurion, Diary, Jan. 8, 1951, BGA.

3. Ben-Gurion, Diary, Feb. 5, 1952; *Davar*, Dec. 11, 1951; Kafkafi 1993, p. 427ff.; Tzachor 1994, p. 211ff.; *Davar*, Dec. 11, 1951.

4. Ben-Gurion to Shlomo Lavi, Jan. 11, 1954, BGA.

5. Shlomo Lavi to the Knesset, July 11, 1950, *Divrei Haknesset*, 6, p. 2173.

6. *Ma'ariv*, June 11, Nov. 23, 1954; Ben-Gurion to Yehuda Erez, June 29, 1954, BGA.

7. *Davar*, May 29, 1952; Grisaru 1971, p. 7.

8. Minutes of Sde Boker members' assembly, Oct. 17, 1953, *Dvar Hashavua*, Oct. 17, 1986.

9. *Davar*, Oct. 19, Nov. 11, 1953; *Ma'ariv*, Dec. 15, 1953; Yehoshua Cohen, interview transcript, BGA: Ben-Gurion, Diary, Dec. 17, 18, 1953, Jan. 4, 7, 1954; Ben-Gurion to Amos, Dec. 22, 1953, BGA.

10. Ben-Gurion, Diary, Sept. 1, 1954, BGA; Ben-Gurion to Marcus Winter, Dec. 23, 1954; Ben-Gurion to Moshe Sharett, Dec. 14, 1953, BGA: Ben-Gurion to Zalman Aran, Dec. 26, 1953, BGA.

11. Ben-Gurion to Yitzhak Ben-Zvi, Nov. 2, 7, 1953, BGA; Nehemiah Argov to the Mapai Central Committee, Nov. 4, 1953, BGA: Ben-Gurion on the radio and in a farewell letter to the IDF, Dec. 7, 1953, in Ben-Gurion 1958, pp. 14, 21; Shaul Avigur, interview transcript, BGA, p. 30.

12. Gordon (no date), *Sefer Iyov*.

13. Ben-Gurion to Dov Yosef, March 4, 1954, BGA.

14. Ben-Gurion, Diary, and Ben-Gurion to the Knesset secretariat, Dec. 26, 1953, BGA.

15. Ben-Gurion, Diary, Dec. 19, 1953, Jan. 18, 1954, BGA; Ben-Gurion to Dov Yosef, Jan. 23, 1954, BGA; Ben-Gurion to Teddy Kollek, Aug. 15, 1954, BGA.

16. Ben-Gurion, Diary, March 10, Sept. 19, 1954, BGA.

17. Ben-Gurion, Diary, March 6, 1954, BGA; Ben-Gurion 1954c; *Dvar Hashavua*, Jan. 21, 1954.

18. Dorit Rosen, interview transcript, BGA; Ben-Gurion to Amos, Dec. 22, 1953, BGA.

19. Ben-Gurion, Diary, Dec. 14, 1953, BGA; Navon 2015, p. 139; Yeshoshua Cohen, Dorit Rosen, Baruch Zuckerman, Mazal Jibli, interview transcripts, BGA; Ben-Gurion to Amos, Dec. 22, 1953, BGA; Paula to Renana, Jan. 20, 1954, BGA; Moshe Sharett, Diary, Jan. 29, 1954, in Sharett 1978, p. 329.

20. Ben-Gurion to Paula, Jan. 13, 18, 1954, BGA; Navon 2015, p. 111.

21. Ben-Gurion, Diary, Oct. 5, 1954, BGA.

22. Ben-Gurion, Diary, Dec. 18, 1953, Feb. 23, 24, 1954, BGA.

23. Moshe Sharett, Diary, Jan. 29, Feb. 1, 1954, in Sharett 1978, pp. 329, 333.

24. Ben-Gurion, Diary, Jan. 9, 16, 18, 27, Feb. 6, 27, 1954, BGA; Moshe Dayan 1976, p. 120ff.; Moshe Sharett, Diary, Jan. 29, 1954, in Sharett 1978, p. 329.

25. Amos Oz to Ben-Gurion, April 23, and Ben-Gurion's reply, March 28, 1954, BGA (one of them apparently recorded the month incorrectly).

26. Navon 2015, p. 142.

27. Ben-Gurion to Ben-Zion Dinur, March 20, 1954, BGA; Ben-Gurion, Diary, March 10, April 1, May 5, 1954, BGA.

28. Kafkafi 1998, p. 200; Moshe Sharett, Diary, June 9, 1954, in Sharett 1978, p. 539.

29. Ben-Gurion, Diary, June 22, 1954, BGA.

30. *Dvar Hashavua*, June 17, 1954.

31. Moshe Sharett, Diary, Jan. 4, 7, 1955, in Sharett 1978, pp. 624, 632.

32. Ben-Gurion, Diary, Feb. 27, Sept. 4, 17, 1954, BGA.

33. Ben-Gurion, "Pahot Miflagot Ufahot Miflagtiyut," in Ben-Gurion 1958e, p. 135ff; Ben-Gurion to the Mapai Central Committee, Sept. 16, 1954, in Ben-Gurion 1958, p. 140ff.; Moshe Sharett, Diary, May 17, 25, 1954, in Sharett 1978, pp. 488, 516; Ben-Gurion with Mapai leaders, Dec. 16, 1954; Ehud Avriel, interview transcript, BGA; Goldberg 1992, p. 51ff.; Kedar 2015, p. 198ff.

34. Aryeh Nehemkin, interview transcript, BGA.

35. Ben-Gurion, Diary, Dec. 29, 1947, June 19, 22, 1951, BGA.

36. Ben-Gurion, Diary, Aug. 7, 1954, BGA; Ben-Gurion to A. S. Stein, Aug. 17, 1955, BGA.

37. Moshe Sharett, Diary, Jan. 31, Feb. 15, June 8, 1954, in Sharett 1978, pp. 331, 358, 535.

38. Ben-Gurion, Diary, Aug. 24, 1954, BGA.

39. Moshe Sharett, Golda Meir, and Pinhas Lavon to the Ministerial Defense Committee, July 19, 1954, ISA gimmel-4/1269.

40. Mordechai Bentzur to the acting IDF intelligence chief, Oct. 5, 1954; IDF General Staff meeting, Nov. 1, 1954; copies of orders handed down without dates, quoted on the IDF Archives website, http://www.archives.mod.gov.il, May 2015; Eshed 1979, p. 17ff.

41. Israel Rokach, Peretz Bernstein, and Pinchas Rosen to the Cabinet, Feb. 6, 1955, ISA.

42. Nehemiah Argov, Diary, Oct. 18, 1954, quoted on the IDF Archives website, http://www.archives.mod.gov.il, May 2015.

43. Rabin 1979, p. 95.

44. Yehoshafat Harkabi to Binyamin Gibli, Dec. 3, 1954, *Davar*, Oct. 16, 1994.

45. Kafkafi 1998, p. 128ff.; "Mah Ha'emet al Parshat Baghdad," *Yediot Aharonot*, June 17, 1966; Israel Galili, "Haruei-Baghdad Venidoni Kahir," *Lamerhav*, Dec. 17, 1954; Ben-Gurion, Diary, July 19, 1963, BGA; Hillel 1985, p. 329ff.; Segev 2006; Moshe Dayan to the Cabinet, Jan. 1, 1960, ISA; Ben-Gurion 1965, p. 40.

46. Copies of documents in Eshed 1979, p. 260ff., on Dayan's trip, p. 63.

47. Moshe Sharett, Diary, Jan. 12, 1954, in Sharett 1978, p. 666.

48. Moshe Sharett, Diary, Jan. 12, 1954, in Sharett 1978, p. 666.

49. Moshe Sharett, Diary, Jan. 25, 1955, quoted from the online edition of the Moshe Sharett Heritage Society, http://www.sharett.org.il/cgi-webaxy/sal/sal.pl?ID=880900 _sharett_new&dbid=bookfiles&act=show&dataid=734, Ben-Gurion, Diary, Nov. 9, 1964, BGA.

50. Moshe Sharett, Diary, Jan. 25, 18, Feb. 12, 1953, in Sharett 1978, pp. 683, 671, 722.
51. Moshe Sharett, Diary, Feb. 10, 1955, Dec. 8, 1954, in Sharett 1978, p. 718.
52. Moshe Sharett, Diary, Jan. 10, 13, Feb. 7, 1955, and Moshe Sharett to Pinhas Lavon, Dec. 22, 1954, in Sharett 1978, pp. 638, 649, 709, 606; Moshe Sharett, Pinhas Lavon, Moshe Dayan, et al. to the Cabinet, Jan. 16, 1955, Jan. 1, 1961, ISA; "Lo Bagadeti: Parashat Uri Ilan, Helek Rishon—Sipur Hama'aseh," ISA website, http://israelidocuments .blogspot.co.il/2014/01/blog-post_13.html.
53. Moshe Sharett, Diary, March 29, May 23, Aug. 26, 1954, in Sharett 1978, pp. 419, 511, 570; Ben-Gurion, Diary, Aug. 7, 1954, BGA; Nehemiah Argov, Diary, Aug. 7, 1954, BGA, Shabtai Teveth collection, people.
54. Ben-Gurion to Shmuel Fox, Jan. 29, May 14, 1955; Shmuel Fox to Ben-Gurion, April 19, 1954, BGA.
55. Dayan at a meeting of the General Staff, Nov. 1, 1954, quoted on the IDF Archives website, http://www.archives.mod.gov.il, May 2015.
56. Gaon 2008.
57. Moshe Sharett, Diary, Jan. 8, 1955, in Sharett 1978, p. 634ff.
58. Ben-Gurion, Diary, Feb. 17, 18, 1955, BGA.
59. Moshe Sharett, Diary, Feb. 21, 1955, in Sharett 1978, p. 748ff.
60. Ben-Gurion et al. to the Cabinet, May 3, 1949, ISA; Toubi 2003, p. 139ff.
61. Ben-Gurion, Diary, Feb. 27, 1954, BGA; Moshe Sharett, Diary, April 23, Sept. 26, 1954, in Sharett 1978, pp. 477, 582; Pinhas Lavon, Moshe Dayan, et al. to the Cabinet, April 11, May 2, 30, 1954, ISA; Pinhas Lavon to the Ministerial Committee on Defense, July 19, 1954, ISA, gimmel-4/1269.
62. Moshe Sharett, Diary, Feb. 27, March 1, 1955, in Sharett 1978, p. 748ff.
63. Ben-Gurion with Ariel Sharon, March 1, 1955, courtesy of the Sharon family.
64. Ben-Gurion to the Cabinet, March 6, 1955; Ben-Gurion to the chief of staff, March 8, 1955, BGA.
65. Ben-Gurion to the Cabinet, March 6, 1955, ISA.
66. Sharon to a gathering of officers, April 25, 1957, courtesy of the Sharon family.
67. Moshe Sharett, Diary, March 13, 1955, in Sharett 1978, p. 840.
68. Moshe Sharett, Diary, March 5, 11ff., in Sharett 1974, p. 816ff.; Moshe Dayan to the General Staff, March 7, 1954, BGA; Seckbach 2013, p. 37ff.; Blum and Hefetz 2005, p. 117ff.
69. Moshe Sharett, Diary, March 8, 13, 1953, in Sharett 1978, pp. 832, 840.
70. Ben-Gurion to the Cabinet, March 6, 13, 1955, ISA: Ben-Gurion to the General Staff, March 7, 1954, BGA.
71. Tamir 2002, p. 1129; Moshe Sharett, Diary, March 16, 1955, in Sharett 1978, p. 847.
72. Ben-Gurion and Pinchas Rosen to the Cabinet, July 10, 1955, ISA; Moshe Sharett, Diary, March 16, July 10, 1955, in Sharett 1978, pp. 847, 1087.
73. Ben-Gurion, Diary, Feb. 21, 1955, BGA; Binyamin Gibli, interview transcript, BGA; Teveth 1992, p. 217.

21. THE SECOND ROUND

1. Ben-Gurion to the Cabinet, March 29, 1955, ISA; Ben-Gurion to the chief of staff, March 31, 1955, in Bar-On 1992, p. 428; Meir Rabinowitz, interview transcript, BGA; *Davar*, March 27, 28, 19, 1955.
2. Moshe Dayan 1976, pp. 185, 190ff.

3. Ben-Gurion, Diary, Oct. 18, 1956, BGA; Procopius p. 179.
4. Ben-Gurion Diary, April 6, 1955, BGA; Ben-Gurion to the Cabinet, March 29, 1955, ISA; Moshe Dayan 1976, p. 143.
5. Moshe Sharett, Diary, March 27, 29, April 3, 1955, in Sharett 1978, pp. 865, 874, 894; Pinchas Rosen to the Cabinet, Nov. 25, 1956, ISA; Ben-Gurion et al. to the Cabinet, March 29, April 4, 1955, ISA; Moshe Dayan 1976, p. 143; Weitz 2015, 20, 3, p. 131ff.
6. Ben-Gurion, Diary, Jan. 6, 1955, BGA; Moshe Sharett, Diary, Jan. 6, 1966, in Sharett 1978, p. 631.
7. Ma'ariv, July 5, 1955; Ben-Gurion, Diary, May 7, 23, 1955, BGA.
8. Ziv 1958, p. 274; Ma'ariv, May 30, July 17, 1955; Moshe Sharett, Diary, July 10, 1955, in Sharett 1978, p. 1086; Davar, July 18, 24, 25, 1955; New York Herald Tribune, July 18, 1955.
9. Davar, July 18, 1955; Ma'ariv, July 17, 22, 24, 25, 1955.
10. Ben-Gurion to Israel Levin, Aug. 14, 1955, BGA.
11. Moshe Sharett, Diary, Oct. 19, 1955, in Sharett 1978, p. 1211.
12. Burns 1962, p. 69ff.
13. Tzipora Sharett to her children, Aug. 24, 1955, in Moshe Sharett 1978, p. 1149.
14. "Elmore Jackson, 78, Quaker Mideast Envoy," New York Times, Jan. 19, 1989.
15. Moshe Dayan 1976, p. 151; Morris 1993, p. 349; BGA, subject file, Elmore Jackson; Golani 1997, p. 57ff.
16. Ben-Gurion et al. to the Cabinet, Aug. 28, Sept. 24, 1955, ISA; Moshe Dayan 1976, p. 143; Toubi 2003, p. 157; Morris 1993, p. 358ff.
17. Golani 1997, p. 63ff.; Bar-On 1992, p. 83; Sharett and Ben-Gurion to the Cabinet, Oct. 3, 1955, ISA; Moshe Sharett, Diary, Oct. 3, 1955, in Sharett 1978, p. 1185.
18. Moshe Sharett, Diary, Oct. 13–15, 21, 1955, in Sharett 1978, pp. 1208ff., 1235.
19. Moshe Dayan 1976, p. 162; Moshe Sharett, Diary, June 10, 1956, in Sharett 1978, p. 1423; Golani 1997, p. 63ff.
20. Elron 2016, p. 146ff.; Golani 1997, p. 84ff.
21. "Nevo," July 1954, IDFA, 20/694/1960.
22. Dov Tamari to the author, Aug. 26, 2016.
23. Moshe Dayan 1976, pp. 169, 174ff.
24. Moshe Dayan in the journal of the Bureau of the Chief of Staff, Oct. 23, 1955, in Bar-On 1992, p. 64; Shalom 1991, p. 141ff.
25. Moshe Sharett, Diary, Oct. 19, 1955, in Sharett 1978, p. 1211.
26. Moshe Sharett, Diary, Nov. 2, 3, 1955, in Sharett 1978, pp. 1281, 1284; Davar, Nov. 3, 1955; Morris 1993, p. 360ff.
27. Bar-On 1992, p. 429; Bar-On 2012, p. 69; Moshe Dayan 1976, pp. 153, 162ff.
28. Moshe Sharett, Diary, Oct. 22, 1955, in Sharett 1978, p. 1239.
29. Burns 1962, p. 69ff.; Moshe Sharett to the Cabinet, Aug. 21, 1955; Ben-Gurion et al. to the Cabinet, Sept. 9, 1955, ISA.
30. Ben-Gurion to the Cabinet, July 22, 1956, ISA; NA (UK) FO 371/115884; Bar-On 1992, p. 107ff.; Ben-Gurion 1979, p. 11ff.
31. Ben-Gurion, Diary, Jan. 15, 17, 1956, BGA.
32. Ben-Gurion to the Cabinet, Feb. 26, Oct. 7, 1956, ISA; Ben-Gurion, Diary, Aug. 2, 1956ff., BGA.

33. Bar-On 2007, p. 87ff.; Moshe Sharett, Diary, Dec. 25, 27, 1955, Jan. 8, 1956, in Sharett 1978, pp. 1314, 1316ff., 1328; *Ha'aretz*, Dec. 16, 1955; Tzipora Sharett to her children, Dec. 25, 1955, Jan. 5, 1956, in Moshe Sharett 1978, pp. 1315, 1327; Eban 1978, p. 187.
34. Ben-Gurion, Golda Meir, Moshe Shapira, et al. to the Cabinet, April 8, 1956, ISA; Bar-On 1991, p. 87ff.; Morris 1993, pp. 371ff., 628.
35. Israel National Insurance Institute, Atar Hantzahah Lezecher Ha'exrahim Halelei Pe'ulot Ha'evah, http://www.laad.btl.gov.il; *Ma'ariv*, April 12, 13, 1956.
36. Ben-Gurion to the Cabinet, April 13, 1956, ISA.
37. Ben-Gurion et al. to the Cabinet, April 13, 1956, ISA; Moshe Sharett, Diary, April 13, 1956, in Sharett 1978, p. 1392ff.
38. Moshe Sharett, Diary, April 13, 1956, in Sharett 1978, pp. 1392ff, 1405.
39. Moshe Sharett, Diary, June 14, 10, 28, 1956, in Sharett 1978, pp. 1436, 1423, 1504.
40. Moshe Sharett, Diary, June 28, 1956, in Sharett 1978, p. 1505, 1517 in the Ideological Circle, June 10, 16, 1956, in Sharett 1978, pp. 1423, 1496.
41. *Ma'ariv*, July 27, 1956.
42. Moshe Dayan 1976, p. 217; Ben-Gurion, Diary, Aug. 18, 1956, BGA; Ben-Gurion to the Cabinet, Aug. 19, 1956, ISA.
43. Moshe Dayan to the Cabinet, Aug. 22, 1954, ISA; Moshe Dayan to a gathering of Northern Command officers, April 8, 1956, Eyal Kafkafi papers, Kibbutz Ravid Archive.
44. Ben-Gurion 1969b, p. 518.
45. Ben-Gurion to the Cabinet, April 29, 1956, ISA.
46. Ben-Gurion, Diary, April 29, 1956, BGA; Isser Harel, interview for the LMA (Golda Meir Archive).
47. Bar-Zohar 2006, p. 174.
48. Ben-Gurion, Diary, July 31, 1956, BGA.
49. Ben-Gurion, Diary, July 25, 28, 29, Aug. 4, 1956, BGA.
50. Moshe Dayan 1976, p. 217; IDF Operations Branch planning, Jan. 1955, Eyal Kafkafi papers, Kibbutz Ravid Archive.
51. Ben-Gurion with representatives of the Working Intelligentsia, Dec. 12, 1955, BGA; Ben-Gurion to Israel Shohat, Jan. 15, 1956, BGA.
52. Ben-Gurion, Diary, Aug. 4, 1956ff., BGA; Ben-Gurion to the Cabinet, Aug. 5, 1956, ISA; Doris May to Ben-Gurion, March 27, 1953, BGA.
53. Ben-Gurion, Diary, Aug. 4, 13, Sept. 19, 1956, BGA.
54. Ben-Gurion, Diary, Sept. 3, 1956, BGA; Moshe Dayan 1976, p. 223.
55. Golani 1994, p. 117ff.
56. Ben-Gurion, Diary, Aug. 3, 1956ff., BGA.
57. Ben-Gurion, Diary, Sept. 22, 25, 1956, BGA.
58. Ben-Gurion, Diary, Oct. 17, 19, 22, BGA.
59. Ben-Gurion, Diary, Oct. 3, 1956, BGA.
60. Ben-Gurion, Diary, Oct. 22, 1956, BGA; Golani 1994, p. 117ff.; Bar-Zohar 2006, p. 210ff.; Bar-On 1992, p. 276ff.; Ben-Gurion to the Cabinet, Oct. 28, 1956, ISA; Gazit 2016, p. 94.
61. Ben-Gurion et al. to the Cabinet, Oct. 28, 1956, ISA; Navon 2015, p. 178ff.
62. Moshe Dayan 1965, p. 84; Ben-Gurion, Diary, Nov. 7, 1956, BGA; Ben-Gurion to the victory ceremony, Nov. 6, 1956, BGA; Navon 2015, p. 180; Gazit 2016, p. 98ff.

63. *Davar*, Nov. 6, 1956; Ben-Gurion to the Cabinet, Nov. 11, 1956, ISA; Ben-Gurion to the Knesset, Nov. 12, 1956, *Divrei Haknesset*, 21, p. 462; Navon 2015, p. 180; Reuven Rubik Rosenthal 2000, p. 11ff.

64. Ben-Gurion to the Knesset, Dec. 7, 1956, *Divrei Haknesset*, 21, p. 197ff.; Shaltiel 1996, p. 348; Ben-Gurion, Diary, Nov. 8, 1956, BGA; Moshe Dayan 1976–82, p. 317.

22. YES TO THE OLD MAN

1. Ben-Gurion to the Cabinet, April 13, 1958, ISA; Ben-Gurion, Diary, Feb. 24, April 24, 1958, BGA; *Davar*, April 24, 1958.

2. Ben-Gurion, introduction to Harman and Yadin 1948, no page numbers; Ben-Gurion, Diary, Jan. 18, 1953, BGA; Ziv, Statistical Appendix, no page numbers; Ben-Gurion to the Cabinet, June 16, 1957, ISA.

3. Ben-Gurion to the Cabinet, June 16, 1967, ISA.

4. Ben-Gurion et al. to the Cabinet, Nov. 25, Dec. 23, 1956, ISA.

5. Ben-Gurion, Diary, Nov. 12–13, 1956, BGA; Ben-Gurion to the Cabinet, Jan. 13, Feb. 25, 27, March 1, 1957, ISA; Lavi, open letter to BGA, Nov. 28, 1956, BGA; Ziv 1958, p. 430.

6. Flexer 1980, p. 192ff.; Ben-Gurion, Diary, Oct. 5, 1954, BGA.

7. Nehemiah Argov to Ben-Gurion, Nov. 2, 1957, BGA; Nehemiah Argov to his acquaintances, Nov. 2, 1957, and Nehemiah Argov, Diary, Oct. 16, 1954, in Argov 1959, pp. 182, 206.

8. Nehemiah Argov, Diary, May 26, 30, June 7, 9, July 7 (?), Aug. 10, 7, 23, Sept. 6, Oct. 18, 1954, Feb. 12, 1955, IDFA 383/1976/2208, 2181-890/1973.

9. Navon 2015, p. 93; Kollek 1979, p. 161; Yehuda Erez, Yigael Yadin, Yariv Ben-Eliezer, interview transcripts, BGA.

10. Rivka Katznelson, interview with Shabtai Teveth, Oct. 2, 1977, BGA, Shabtai Teveth collection, subjects, Ben-Gurion and women.

11. Navon 2015, p. 192ff.; *Davar*, Nov. 5, 1957; Ben-Gurion to the Knesset, Nov. 18, 1957, *Divrei Haknesset*, 23, p. 177.

12. Moshé Feldenkrais, interview transcript, BGA.

13. Yitzhak Navon, Diary, Nov. 18, 1957, YNA.

14. Alterman 1957; Navon 2015, p. 120; Ben-Gurion, Diary, Oct. 22, 1958, BGA.

15. Ben-Gurion to his friends, Nov. 5, 1957, in Yisraeli 2005, pp. 40, 49.

16. Ben-Gurion, Diary, May 9, 1958, BGA.

17. Ben-Gurion to the Cabinet, May 5, June 8, 1958, ISA.

18. Ben-Gurion to the Cabinet, Oct. 20, 1953, ISA.

19. Ben-Gurion to a Keren Hayesod gathering, Oct. 29, 1947, in Ben-Gurion 1993b, p. 436; Ben-Gurion to the Cabinet, June 16, 1948, ISA.

20. Israel Barzilai to the Cabinet, March 11, 1956, and Ben-Gurion to the Cabinet, June 10, 1956, ISA; Yozgof-Orbach and Soffer 2016, p. 30ff.

21. Benziman and Monsour 1992, p. 101ff.; Segev 1986, p. 43ff.; Azriel Carlebach 1953; Bar-Yosef 2014, 2016.

22. Ben-Gurion to the Cabinet, May 27, 1962, ISA; Ben-Gurion to the Knesset, Feb. 20, 1963, *Divrei Haknesset*, 36, p. 1212ff.

23. Ben-Gurion to the Cabinet, Feb. 26, 1956, ISA.

24. Ben-Gurion, Diary, Dec. 16, 17, 20, 1956, Nov. 2, 1958, BGA; Moshe Sharett, Diary, Dec. 19, 1956, in Sharett 1978, p. 1925.
25. Segev 1993, p. 299ff.
26. Ben-Gurion to the Cabinet, Nov. 11, 1956, ISA.
27. Pinchas Rosen to the Cabinet, Nov. 23, 1958, ISA; Ben-Gurion, Diary, Oct. 30, 1958, BGA.
28. Friedmann 2015, p. 243ff.; Ben-Gurion to the Cabinet, Nov. 16, 1958, ISA.
29. Ben-Gurion, Diary, Nov. 24, 1958, April 25, June 6, 1959, Jan. 29, Feb. 5, 1960, BGA; Ariel Sharon at Ben-Gurion House, Oct. 20, 1997, BGA, item 242452.
30. Arie Lova Eliav 1983, 2, p. 99ff.
31. Ben-Gurion, Diary, Nov. 15, 1956, BGA; Ben-Gurion to the Cabinet, Jan. 13, 1957, ISA.
32. Navon 2015, p. 103; Shlomo Zeira 1960, p. 147; Ben-Gurion to Shlomo Zeira, Oct. 15, 1961, BGA.
33. Ben-Gurion to Paula, Nov. 27, 1933, BGA.
34. Ben-Gurion to Ehud Avriel, March 4, 1948, BGA.
35. Ben-Gurion, Diary, June 1, July 16, Nov. 16, 1948, Sept. 28, 1949, BGA; Bachrach 2009.
36. Ben-Gurion, Diary, Aug. 15, 1945, BGA; Ben-Gurion to the Cabinet, Sept. 14, 1950, ISA.
37. Ben-Gurion with members of Hakibbutz Hameuchad, Sept. 11, 1948, in Ben-Gurion 1951, p. 236; Ben-Gurion, Diary, Nov. 16, Dec. 12, 25, 1948, March 16, 1949, BGA.
38. Ben-Gurion, Diary, Nov. 14, 1948, BGA.
39. Ben-Gurion, Diary, Nov. 24, 1958, BGA.
40. Ben-Gurion to Yosef Schechter, June 20, 1957, BGA; Ratner 1978, p. 338; Keren 1988, p. 28ff.
41. Ben-Gurion to the Cabinet, June 14, 16, 1948, July 12, 1949, Nov. 30, 1958, ISA.
42. Ben-Gurion, Diary, June 16, 1949, Sept. 5, Dec. 13, 1951, BGA.
43. *Ma'ariv*, Nov. 16–17, 1954; *Ha'aretz*, Nov. 21, 1954.
44. *Bamahaneh*, Nov. 25, 1954; Avner Cohen 1998, p. 44ff.; Moshe Sharett to the Cabinet, May 22, 1955, ISA.
45. Ben-Gurion to Shlomo Fuchs, May 14, 1955, BGA.
46. Ben-Gurion, "Daroma," Jan. 17, 1955, in Ben-Gurion 1958, p. 297.
47. Moshe Sharett, Diary, May 9, 23, 1954, in Sharett 1978, pp. 483, 508.
48. Ben-Gurion to the Cabinet, Dec. 24, 1956, ISA.
49. Ben-Gurion, Diary, May 20, 31, June 2, 3, 1958, BGA; Ben-Gurion et al. to the Cabinet, June 16, 1957, Feb. 2, June 1, 1958, ISA; Yitzhak Navon, Diary, May 3, June 1, 1958, YNA.
50. Ben-Gurion, Diary, Dec. 19, 1958, BGA.
51. Ben-Gurion, Diary, March 5, 1962, BGA.
52. Ben-Gurion to the Cabinet, Dec. 1, 1957, ISA; Ernst David Bergmann to Meir Yaari, July 6, 1966, YY, 6 19.7-95.
53. Ben-Gurion, Diary, May 19, 4, 3, 6, 23, Oct. 24, 1958, BGA; *Davar*, June 6, 1958.
54. Ben-Gurion, Diary, Nov. 26, 4, 1958, BGA.
55. Ben-Gurion, Diary, Jan. 27, 1959, BGA; Yitzhak Navon, Diary, Nov. 18, 1957, YNA.

56. Ben-Gurion to Dov Yermia, Sept. 14, 1959, IDFA, quoted from *Ha'olam Hazeh*, Jan. 5, 1972; Ben-Gurion to Dov Yermia, Oct. 2, Dec. 22, 1959, BGA.
57. Yitzhak Navon, Diary, July 20, 1958, YNA.

23. THE LAVON AFFAIR

1. Ben-Gurion, Diary, June 16, 9, 1959; Navon 2015, p. 11; Yitzhak Navon, Diary, Aug. 23, 1960, YNA.
2. Ben-Gurion to the Cabinet, March 27, 1960.
3. Ben-Gurion, Diary, June 16, Nov. 12, 1959, Feb. 26, July 26, 1960, BGA; Yitzhak Navon interview with Shabtai Teveth, Sept. 19, 1980, and Malka Leef, interview transcript, BGA, Shabtai Teveth collection, people; Nevo 1993.
4. Ben-Gurion to the Cabinet, April 24, 1955, ISA; Israel Kargman, interview transcript, BGA, p. 15; Ben-Gurion to the Cabinet, June 18, 1961, ISA.
5. Ben-Gurion to the Cabinet, Jan. 8, 1956, June 6, 16, Dec. 1, 22, 1957, ISA.
6. Ben-Gurion et al. to the Cabinet, Dec. 8, 15, 22, 24, 30, 1957, ISA.
7. Ben-Gurion et al. to the Cabinet, June 26, 1959, ISA; Ben-Gurion et al. to the Knesset, July 1, 1959, *Divrei Haknesset*, 27, p. 2403ff.; Shihor, 1958, p. 40ff.
8. Ben-Gurion, Diary, Dec. 29, 1957, April 4, 1958, BGA; Siebenmorgen 2015, p. 163ff.; Ben-Gurion to the Cabinet, Dec. 15, 1957, ISA; Maurice Fischer to Golda Meir, July 18, 1958, ISA 130.02/2457/10.
9. Ben-Gurion to the Cabinet, March 27, 1960, ISA; Shalom 1996, p. 604ff.
10. Ben-Gurion, Diary, Dec. 6, 1959, BGA.
11. Ben-Gurion, Diary, May 15, 1960, Dec. 6, 1959, BGA; Ben-Gurion and Isser Harel to the Cabinet, May 29, 1960, ISA; Mossad report on the pursuit of Nazi criminals, 2007, Yad Vashem Archive.
12. Levi Eshkol et al. to the Cabinet, July 12, 19, 27, Aug. 23, 1959, ISA.
13. Ben-Gurion to Moshe Etzioni, Aug. 3, 1959, BGA.
14. Ben-Gurion to the Cabinet, June 5, 1960, ISA.
15. Ben-Gurion to the Cabinet, July 3, 1960, ISA; Bar-Zohar 1978, p. 1371ff.; Raz 2015, p. 226.
16. Ben-Gurion, Diary, Jan. 3, 1960, BGA.
17. Ben-Gurion to Moshe Sharett, Oct. 26, 1960, in Sharett 1978, p. 764.
18. Ben-Gurion, Diary, May 5, Sept. 26, 28, Oct. 10, 1960, BGA; *Ma'ariv*, Sept. 26–28, 1960; Teveth 1992, pp. 228, 373.
19. Ben-Gurion, Diary, Sept. 26, 28, Oct. 20, 1960, BGA; *Davar*, Oct. 21, 1960; *Ma'ariv*, June 20–26, 1960; Ben-Gurion to Levi Eshkol et al., Nov. 12, 1960, BGA, LEA, container 2, file 9.
20. Kafkafi 1998, p. 128ff.; "Mah Ha'emet al Parshat Baghdad," *Yediot Aharonot*, June 17, 1966; Israel Galili, "Harugei-Baghdad Venidonei Kahir," *Lamerhav*, Dec. 17, 1954; Ben-Gurion, Diary, July 19, 1963, BGA; Hillel 1985, p. 329ff.; Segev 2006; Moshe Dayan to the Cabinet, Jan. 1, 1960, ISA.
21. Ben-Gurion to the Cabinet, Oct. 30, 1960, ISA.
22. Ben-Gurion et al. to the Cabinet, Oct. 30, 31, 1960, ISA.
23. Ben-Gurion to the Knesset, Dec. 21, 1960, *Divrei Haknesset*, 30, p. 545; Sharett to his son Ya'akov, Jan. 5, 1961, courtesy of the Moshe Sharett Heritage Society; Raz 2015, p. 55ff.; Avner Cohen 1998, p. 76ff.; *Ma'ariv*, Feb. 17, 1961.

24. Ben-Gurion, Diary, May 13, 1961, BGA.
25. Sharett to his son Ya'akov, Jan. 5, 1961, courtesy of the Moshe Sharett Heritage Society.
26. Yitzhak Navon, Diary, Oct. 20, Dec. 25, 1960, YNA; Raz 2013, p. 114ff.
27. Pinchas Rosen, Ben-Gurion, et al. to the Cabinet, Dec. 25, 1960, ISA.
28. Yitzhak Navon, Diary, Nov. 13, 15, 23, Dec. 3, 1960, YNA.
29. "Carrot and Stick," *New York Times*, Dec. 25, 1960.
30. Ben-Gurion, Diary, Jan. 30, March 29, 1961, BGA.
31. Ben-Gurion to Konrad Adenauer, Jan. 1, 1961, ISA, div. 43, gimmel-7229/11; Ben-Gurion to Felix Shinnar, May 16, 1961, ISA, Foreign Ministry, div. 130.09 2355/3; Felix Shinnar to Ben-Gurion, May 19, 1961, ISA, Foreign Ministry, div. 130.09 2355/6.
32. Carstens memorandum, June 12, 1961, AAPD 1965, Bd. 1 Dok 2; Bar-Zohar 2006, p. 239.
33. Ben-Gurion to the Cabinet, June 11, 1961, and to the Knesset Foreign Affairs and Defense Committee, June 11, 29, 1961, ISA; Avraham Harman interview with Reudor Manor, Feb. 3, 1975, Hebrew University, Institute of International Relations, quoted courtesy of David Harman; Memorandum of Conversation, May 30, 1961, FRUS, 1961–1963, 17, doc. 57; Avner Cohen 1998, p. 79ff.
34. Ben-Gurion et al. to the Cabinet, July 9, 1961, ISA; Raz 2015, p. 117.
35. Ben-Gurion to the Cabinet, July 9, 1961, ISA; Ben-Gurion to the Knesset Foreign Affairs and Defense Committee, Aug. 1, 1961, ISA.
36. Ben-Gurion et al. to the Cabinet, July 9, 16, 1961, ISA.
37. Ben-Gurion, Diary, Aug. 16, 1961, BGA.
38. David Hacohen to the Cabinet, March 11, 1956, ISA; Bar-Zohar 2006, p. 242.
39. Ben-Gurion to the Cabinet, Dec. 31, 1961, ISA; "Ben-Gurion Examines the Buddhist Faith," *New York Times Magazine*, April 29, 1962b.
40. *Dvar Hashavua*, Oct. 20, 1950; Cohen-Gil 2013, p. 21ff.; Ben-Gurion to A. Kalev, Oct. 11, 1957, BGA; Ben-Gurion to Eli Friedman, Feb. 8, 1967, BGA.
41. Moshé Feldenkrais, interview transcript, BGA.
42. Ben-Gurion to Dr. Chaim Sheba, May 16, 1962, BGA; Ohry and Tsafrir 2000.
43. Ben-Gurion, Diary, Feb. 16, March 2, 1966, BGA.
44. Ben-Gurion, Diary, May 11, Oct. 26, 1957, May 20, Aug. 20, 21, Oct. 30, 1958, March 12, 1959, BGA; Yitzhak Navon to Ben-Gurion, Nov. 25, 1958, BGA; Teachers Seminar to Feldenkrais, March 17, 1958, BGA.
45. Ben-Gurion, Diary, July 4, 1957; Ben-Gurion to Renana, Sept. 15, 1957, BGA; *Yediot Aharonot*, Sept. 15, 1957; *Ma'ariv*, Sept. 17, 19, 1957.
46. Ben-Gurion, Diary, May 23, July 23, 1958, BGA.
47. Lourie, interview transcript, Aug. 7, 1976, p. 8ff., and Aug. 25, 1977, p. 8ff., cassette 276, BGA.
48. Ben-Gurion to the Cabinet, June 11, 1961, ISA; Churchill 2009.
49. Ben-Gurion, "Ne'urei Be-Płońsk," in Zemach 1963c, p. 35; Ben-Gurion 1971a, p. 12; Zemach 1983, p. 32.
50. Ben-Gurion to Shlomo Zemach, Sept. 21, and Shlomo Zemach to Ben-Gurion, Sept. 28, 1961, BGA, Shabtai Teveth collection, people, Zemach.

24. TWILIGHT

1. Daniel M. Mich to Ben-Gurion, June 21, 1961, and Ben-Gurion to Daniel M. Mich, Aug. 4, 1961; Ben-Gurion to Zalman Shragai, Sept. 18, 1968, BGA.
2. Ben-Gurion to the Cabinet, Dec. 23, 1962, ISA.
3. Ben-Gurion to the Cabinet, March 23, 1958, ISA.
4. Ben-Gurion to the high commissioner, Feb. 12, 1935, in Ben-Gurion 1972, p. 282; Ben-Gurion et al. to the Cabinet, June 7, 1949, June 28, 1950, Jan. 20, 1952, ISA.
5. Ben-Gurion to the Cabinet, Nov. 30, 1952, ISA; Ben-Gurion, "Yetziyat Mitzra'im," lecture to the Israel Press Association, May 12, 1960, in Ben-Gurion 1969a, p. 243ff.
6. Ben-Gurion, Diary, March 6, 26, Aug. 12, 1959, BGA; Golda Meir, interview transcript, Aug. 7, 1977, cassette 269, BGA, p. 12; Bar-Zohar 2006, p. 236ff.
7. Yitzhak Navon, Diary, March 27, 31, April 14, 17, 26, 1963, YNA.
8. Yitzhak Navon, Diary, April 19, May 13, 1963, YNA.
9. Ben-Gurion, Diary, Jan. 1, Feb. 24, June 5, 1963, BGA; Bar-Zohar 2006, p. 268.
10. Avner Cohen 1998, p. 115ff.
11. Ben-Gurion, Diary, July 14, 28, Aug. 1, 16, 1958, BGA; Yitzhak Navon, Diary, July 13, 24, 1958, YNA.
12. Gideon Rafael in a consultation on the dispatch of the prime minister's letter to Kennedy, May 8, 1963, ISA, Foreign Ministry, 3377/9.
13. Goldstein 2012, p. 436; undated draft and Ben-Gurion to John F. Kennedy, April 12, May 12, 1963, ISA, Foreign Ministry, 4317/8.
14. Ben-Gurion to Mapai's founding convention, March 6, 1930, in Ben-Gurion 1931, p. 219; Ben-Gurion to the Cabinet, April 3, 1955, ISA.
15. Ben-Gurion, Diary, May 12, 1955, BGA; Ben-Gurion et al. to the Cabinet, April 30, 1963, BGA; Bialer 1998, p. 241ff.
16. Ben-Gurion et al. to the Cabinet, May 5, 1963, ISA.
17. Secretary of state to the ambassador of Israel, May 6, 1963, ISA, Foreign Ministry, 4317/8.
18. Ben-Gurion to Kennedy, May 12, 1963, ISA, Foreign Ministry, 4317/8.
19. Rafael 1981, p. 117; Avner Cohen 1998, p. 115ff.; Foreign Ministry to the embassy, April 25, 1963, ISA, Foreign Ministry, 4317/8; Yitzhak Navon, Diary, April 26, 1963, YNA.
20. Haim Yahil to Golda Meir, May 21, 1963, ISA, Foreign Ministry, 4317/8.
21. Gideon Rafael to Haim Yahil, May 8, 1963; Haim Yahil to Golda Meir, May 13, 1963; Discussion of Israel-American relations, headed by the foreign minister, June 13, 1963; Avraham Harmon and Mordechai Gazit to Golda Meir, June 25, 1963, ISA, Foreign Ministry, 4317/8; Avner Cohen and William Burr 2019.
22. Consultation on the exchange of letters with the president of the United States, Sept. 6, 1963, ISA, Foreign Ministry, 101177/10.
23. Ben-Gurion to Konrad Adenauer, May 15, 1963, BGA; Ben-Gurion, Diary, May 16, 1963, BGA; Ben-Gurion et al. to the Knesset, May 13, 1963, *Divrei Haknesset*, 17, p. 1821ff.; *Ma'ariv*, May 14, 1963; Segev 1993, pp. 374–75; Navon 2015, p. 254ff., Yitzhak Navon, Diary, May 13, 1963, YNA; *Ha'aretz*, May 14, 1963; Ben-Gurion, Diary, Sept. 28, 1964, BGA.

24. Gouri 1963; Ben-Gurion to Haim Gouri, May 15, 1963, BGA; Haim Gouri in conversation with the author.

25. *Ma'ariv*, June 16, 1963.

26. Goldstein 2012, p. 436ff.

27. Golda Meir et al. to the Mapai secretariat, Aug. 17, 1963, BGA; Medzini 2008, p. 394; Ben-Gurion to the Cabinet, June 16, 1963, ISA; Mapai secretariat, June 17, 1963, LPA 2-24-1963-73; Navon 2015, p. 267; Ben-Gurion, Diary, June 16, 1963, BGA; Isser Harel interview with Drora Beit-Or, Feb. 7, 1986, cassette 14, LMA; Moshé Feldenkrais, interview transcript, BGA.

28. Ben-Gurion, Diary, May 18, June 18, 1963, BGA.

29. Zemach 1996, Jan. 8, 20, June 24, 1963, pp. 57ff. 81ff.; July 21–Aug. 9, 1963, p. 91ff.

30. Ben-Gurion, Diary, July 25, 1963, BGA; *Davar*, July 24, 26, 1963.

31. Ben-Gurion, Diary, May 13, 1965, BGA.

32. Ben-Gurion, Diary, Nov. 1, 1965, BGA.

33. Ben-Gurion, Diary, Nov. 1, 1965, BGA.

34. Ben-Gurion, Diary, Nov. 1, 1965, BGA; Ben-Gurion 1965, p. 142; Ben-Gurion to Shaul Avigur, Jan. 7, 1967; Ben-Gurion to *Davar*, March 26, 1967, BGA; Ben-Gurion, Diary, May 22, 1967, quoted in Bar-Zohar 2006, p. 393.

35. Ben-Gurion, Diary, Oct. 17, 24, 1966, BGA; Segev 2007, pp. 90ff., 109; *Ma'ariv*, Oct. 3, 1966.

36. Ben-Gurion, interview with Geula Cohen, *Ma'ariv*, May 12, 1957; Ben-Gurion to Tzvi Ben-Arav, May 4, 1967, BGA; Segev 2007, p. 182ff.

37. Ben-Gurion, Diary, May 21, 26, 1967, BGA.

38. Ben-Gurion to the Cabinet, Oct. 19, 1953, Oct. 29, 1961, BGA.

39. Ben-Gurion, Diary, May 21, 1967, BGA; Segev 2007, p. 247ff.

40. Ben-Gurion, Diary, May 30, 1967.

41. Ben-Gurion, Diary, May 28, 1967.

42. Ben-Gurion, Diary, June 1, 1967, BGA; Ben-Gurion to the Cabinet, July 2, 1961, BGA.

43. Ben-Gurion, Diary, May 31, 1967; Bar-Zohar 2006, p. 399.

44. Yitzhak Navon, Diary, May 2, 1959, YNA.

45. Ben-Gurion, Diary, May 6, 1967, BGA; Ben-Gurion to Yosef Givoli, June 6, 1967, BGA.

46. Levi Eshkol et al. to the Cabinet and the Ministerial Defense Committee, June 6–16, 1967, ISA; Segev 2007, p. 419ff.

47. Press release, June 18, 1967, BGA.

48. Ben-Gurion to the Cabinet, Dec. 19, 1949, ISA.

49. Ben-Gurion, Diary, June 19, 1967, BGA.

50. Ben-Gurion to Yosef Weitz, June 12, 1967, BGA.

51. Ben-Gurion, Diary, June 17, 1967, BGA; Yitzhak Navon, Diary, Aug. 10, 1958, YNA.

52. Zemach 1996, Sept. 16, 1967, p. 230ff.

53. Segev 2007, p. 523ff.; Eshkol et al. to the Cabinet, June 14, 1967, ISA.

54. Ben-Gurion, Diary, Aug. 27, 1967, BGA; Ben-Gurion interviewed by Yosef Avner, Avraham Kushnir, and Tom Segev, *Nitzotz*, April 28, 1968; Ben-Gurion to Yehuda Ben-Azar, July 17, 1967, BGA.

55. Aharon Tamir, Yehoshua Cohen, interview transcripts, BGA.

56. Ben-Gurion, Diary, May 5, 1966, BGA; Ben-Gurion to Meir, Jan. 21, 1969, BGA.

57. Ben-Gurion interviewed by Yosef Avner, Avraham Kushnir, and Tom Segev, *Nitzotz*, April 28, 1968; Ben-Gurion, Diary, Feb. 29, 1969, BGA; *Ma'ariv*, May 3, 1968; Amos Elon 1981, p. 21.
58. Evening on Paula at Ben-Gurion House, May 15, 1968; Avrech 1965; Nina and Naomi Zuckerman, Ralph Goldman, Emmanuel and Yariv Ben-Eliezer, interview transcripts, BGA; Yehuda Erez, Diary, Jan. 3, 1973, BGA; Navon 2015, p. 265; Ben-Gurion, Diary, Jan. 6, 1970, BGA; Mary Ben-Gurion interview with Shabtai Teveth, BGA, Shabtai Teveth collection, file 361.

25. ANOTHER KIND OF JEW

1. Ben-Gurion to the Cabinet, July 6, 1958, ISA.
2. Ben-Gurion, Diary, June 8, 1963, BGA.
3. Ben-Gurion, Diary, June 8, 1963, BGA; Shmuel Fox to Ben-Gurion, April 19, 1954, BGA.
4. Ben-Gurion, Diary, Nov. 26, 1938, BGA.
5. Ben-Gurion to the Cabinet, May 3, 1949, ISA.
6. Ben-Gurion to the Cabinet, May 10, 1950, ISA; Ben-Gurion to the Knesset, July 3, 1950, *Divrei Haknesset*, 6, p. 2037.
7. Ben-Gurion to the Cabinet, Dec. 8, 1957, ISA.
8. Ben-Gurion to the Cabinet, July 6, 13, 1958, ISA; Ben-Gurion to Nisan Metzger, Oct. 3, 1964, BGA; Friedmann, 2015, p. 351ff.
9. Ben-Gurion to the Cabinet, Dec. 8, 1957, July 12, 1958, ISA; Ben-Gurion to Yitzhak Malaka, Nov. 6, 1968, BGA.
10. Ben-Gurion et al. to the Cabinet, July 15, 1958, ISA; Ben-Refael 2001.
11. Ben-Gurion to the Jewish Agency Executive, Nov. 21, 1945, BGA.
12. Ben-Gurion to the Cabinet, May 3, 1949, ISA.
13. Ben-Gurion to Paula, Feb. 10, 1946, BGA.
14. Zemach 1983, p. 9; Ben-Gurion to Shmuel Fuchs, June 2, 1904, in Erez 1971, p. 35; Ben-Gurion to the Cabinet, March 5, 1949, Dec. 8, 1957, ISA; Ben-Gurion, Diary, Feb. 13, 1936, BGA; Ben-Gurion to the Committee for the Investigation of the Arab Problem, Feb. 6, 1940, in Ben-Gurion 1997, p. 406; Wolfensohn 2014, p. 80.
15. Ben-Gurion to Paula, Feb. 10, May 1, 1946, BGA; Amos Ben-Gurion interview with Dov Goldstein, *Ma'ariv*, Oct. 17, 1986.
16. Ben-Gurion to Rabbi Isser Yehuda Unterman, Jan. 28, 1946, BGA.
17. Prinz 2008, p. 237ff.
18. Ben-Gurion 1968, p. 235.
19. Anita Shapira 1980, pp. 529, 548; Yitzhak Navon, Diary, Sept. 29, 1952, YNA.
20. Ben-Gurion to the Cabinet, March 16, 1958, ISA; Yehuda Erez, interview transcript, p. 8, BGA; Ben-Gurion, Diary, Feb. 4, 1949, Oct. 7, 1954, Jan. 28, 1955, BGA; Ben-Gurion to Y. Yerushalmi, Nov. 3, 1954, BGA.
21. Ben-Gurion 1954a, p. 43.
22. Ben-Gurion to the Mapai Council, Jan. 19, 1933, p. 42, BGA; Ben-Gurion to the Mapai Council, March 5–8, 1941, in Ben-Gurion 1949, 3, p. 60ff.
23. Ben-Gurion to the Cabinet, March 9, 1952, ISA.
24. Ben-Gurion to the Cabinet, Feb. 2, 1950, ISA.

25. Ben-Gurion to Amos Frisch, May 4, 1967, BGA; Ben-Gurion 1953c; Ben-Gurion to Moshe Zilberg, Dec. 7, 1970, BGA.

26. Ben-Gurion, Diary, Jan. 28, 1955, BGA.

27. Ben-Gurion to Nisan Metzger, Oct. 3, 1964, BGA.

28. Ben-Gurion to Moshe Bernstein, Dec. 16, 1967.

29. Ben-Gurion interviewed by Yosef Avner, Avraham Kushnir, and Tom Segev, *Nitzotz*, April 28, 1968.

30. Ben-Gurion to Moshe Zilberg, Dec. 7, 1970, BGA.

31. Ben-Gurion interview with George Hall, June 20, 1946, BGA; Teveth 2004, p. 661ff.

32. Ben-Gurion interviewed by Yosef Avner, Avraham Kushnir, and Tom Segev, *Nitzotz*, April 28, 1968; Ben-Gurion oral history interview, JFK 1, 7/16/1965.

33. Ben-Gurion et al. to the Cabinet, Feb. 25, July 1, 8, 15, 22, 1962, ISA; Harel 1982a, p. 108ff.; Harel 1989, p. 412ff.

34. Moshe Shapira et al. to the Cabinet, Feb. 20, Nov. 26, 1950; Ben-Gurion et al. to the Cabinet, Feb. 2, 1958, ISA.

35. Ben-Gurion to Paula, Oct. 7, 1938, in Ben-Gurion 1968, p. 243; Ben-Gurion 1971a, p. 280.

36. Ben-Gurion to the Mapai Knesset faction, Jan. 15, 1950, LPA 2-011-1950-10.

37. Letter to the Mapai Central Committee, July 1, 1937, in Ben-Gurion 1974a, p. 260; Heller 2017, p. 17ff.

38. Segev 2000, p. 47; Ben-Gurion, "Hamediniyut Hatziyonit," July 5, 1943, in Ben-Gurion 1949–50, p. 272; Ben-Gurion to the Palestine Council, Dec. 21, 1918, CZA J1/8766/2; Ben-Gurion to Ernest Bevin, Feb. 14, 1947, NA (UK), CO 537/2405.

39. Ben-Gurion to Baruch Zuckerman, July 26, 1923, in Erez 1972, p. 142.

40. Ben-Gurion to the Mapai Central Committee, July 1, 1937, in Ben-Gurion 1974a, p. 265.

41. Ben-Gurion to a Po'alei Zion Smol delegation, March 17, 1941, in Ben-Gurion 2008, p. 293.

42. Ben-Gurion to the Cabinet, Dec. 19, 1948, ISA; Ben-Gurion to the Jewish Agency Executive, Oct. 22, 1939, in Ben-Gurion 1997, p. 144; Ben-Gurion in a broadcast, Oct. 26, 1946, in Ben-Gurion 1993a, p. 221; Ben-Gurion at a gathering of Magbit Hahitgayesut, Feb. 17, 1948, in Ben-Gurion 1949, 5, p. 283; Raz 2015, p. 115.

43. Adolf Robison, interview transcript, BGA.

44. Liebman 1974, p. 271ff.

45. Rose Halprin, interview transcript, cassette 236, p. 2, BGA; Ben-Gurion to the Cabinet, May 26, 1960, ISA; Ben-Gurion interview with Avraham Avi-hai, Aug. 23, 1972, HICJ-OHA 13513, p. 11: Ben-Gurion at the jubilee celebration of *Ha'ahdut*, July 10, 1960, BGA.

46. Elam 1990, p. 561; Ben-Gurion, Diary, Jan. 22, 1939, ISA.

47. Theodor Herzl, Diary, June 13, 1895, in Herzl 1960, 1, p. 83.

48. Ben-Gurion to the Cabinet, July 20, 1961, ISA.

49. Berl Repetur, interview transcript, BGA.

50. Ben-Gurion, "Darkeinu Hamedinit La'ahar Hame'ura'ot," Ben-Gurion 1931, p. 213.

51. Ben-Gurion to Yehoshua Bertonov, Aug. 28, 1950, BGA.

52. Ben-Gurion to his father, Nov. 26, 1924, in Erez 1972, p. 270; Baruch Azanya, interview transcript, BGA.

53. Ben-Gurion to the Cabinet, June 16, 1948, April 26, 1949, July 18, 25, 1951, ISA.

54. Ben-Gurion to the Zionist General Council, March 14, 1940, in Ben-Gurion 1997, p. 468.
55. Ben-Gurion to the Jewish Agency Executive, May 16, 1941, in Ben-Gurion 2008, p. 405; Ben-Gurion to the Zionist General Council, March 14, 1940, in Ben-Gurion 1997, p. 468.
56. Ben-Gurion to the Cabinet, Nov. 10, 1948, ISA; Ben-Gurion, Diary, Jan. 22, 1950, BGA; Ben-Gurion at a party for the remaining members of the First Zionist Congress, Aug. 17, 1947, in Ben-Gurion 1949, 5, p. 214; Ben-Gurion to the Political Committee of the UN General Assembly, May 12, 1947, in Ben-Gurion 1993b, p. 114; Ben-Gurion to Dov Ben-Meir, Dec. 16, 1967, BGA; Holtzman 1993, p. 191ff.
57. Ben-Gurion agenda, Jan. 24–31, 1970, BGA.
58. Ben-Gurion interview with Mordechai Barkay, *Davar*, July 24, 1970.
59. Zemach 1996, Oct. 6, 1968, p. 249ff., March 17, 1969, p. 257, March 15, 1971, p. 290.
60. Yehuda Erez, Diary, Jan. 10, 1972, Feb. 13, 1973, BGA.
61. Aharon Tamir, interview transcript, BGA.
62. Yehuda Erez, Diary, Oct. 22, 1973, BGA.
63. Yehuda Erez, Diary, May 7, 1973, BGA; Aharon Tamir, interview transcript, BGA.
64. Ben-Gurion, Diary, Sept. 4, 1956, BGA; Ben-Gurion to Dr. Chaim Sheba, Nov. 11, 1969, and Dr. Chaim Sheba to Ben-Gurion, Nov. 19, 1969, BGA; Shilon 2013, p. 223; Yehuda Erez, Diary, Oct. 26, 1973, BGA; Israeli 2005, p. 225; Ben-Gurion interview with Mordechai Barkay, *Davar*, July 24, 1970; Mary Ben-Gurion interview with Shabtai Teveth, BGA, Shabtai Teveth collection, file 361; Golda Meir, interview transcript, BGA; Ben-Gurion to Golda Meir, Jan. 21, 1969, BGA; Ben-Gurion to Miriam Cohen, June 27, 1973, BGA, Shabtai Teveth collection, file 1205.
65. Yizhar Smilansky 1993, p. 2.
66. Quoted from the pages of a diary provided to the author.
67. Ben-Gurion to Hannah and Elhanan Yishai, Oct. 30, 1973, BGA.
68. Malka Leef, Ya'akov Grauman, Matilda Gez, Mordechai Surkis, interview transcripts, BGA.
69. Moshe Dayan 1982, p. 688.
70. *Ma'ariv*, Dec. 2, 1973; Ohana and Feige 2010; Mary Ben-Gurion interview with Shabtai Teveth, BGA, Shabtai Teveth collection, file 361; Ben-Gurion will, BGA, Shabtai Teveth collection, people, will.
71. Zemach 1996, Dec. 15, 1971, p. 290.

BIBLIOGRAPHY

Adams, Frank, et al. 1928. *Reports of the Experts, Submitted to the Joint Palestine Survey Commission*. Boston: Daniels Printing Co.

Aderet, Ofer. 2015. "Haprotokolim Hosfim: HaShabak Yada al Kavanat Harotze'ah Lehitnakesh BiIsrael Kastner." *Ha'aretz*, Jan. 11.

Ahad Ha'am. 1949. *Kol Kitvei Ahad Ha'am*. Dvir.

Alfasi, Yitzhak, ed. 1994. *Ha'irgun Hatzeva'i Hale'umi Be'eretz Yisra'el*. Jabotinsky Institute.

Almogi, Yosef. 1980. *Ba'ovi Hakorah*. Idanim.

Alroey, Gur. 2002. "Haherkev Hademografi shel 'Ha'aliyah Hasheniyah.'" *Israel* 2, p. 33ff.

Alroey, Gur. 2004. *Immigrantim*. Yad Ben-Zvi.

Alroey, Gur. 2008. *Hamahapechah Hasheketah*. Merkaz Zalman Shazar.

Alroey, Gur. 2009. "Meshartei Hamoshavah o Rodanim Gasei Ruah?" *Cathedra* 133 (Sept.), p. 77ff.

Alroey, Gur. 2011. *Mehapseit Moledet*. Ben-Gurion Institute.

Alterman, Natan. 1949. "Yom Hamilyon." *Davar*, Dec. 16.

Alterman, Natan. 1957. "Moto shel Nehemiah." *Davar*, Nov. 8.

Alterman, Natan. 1963. *Pundak Haruhot*. Amikam.

Amarami, Ya'akov, and Menachem Maletzky. 1981. *Divrei Hayamim Lemilhemet Hashihrur*. Ministry of Defense.

Amichal Yeivin, Ada. 1995. *Sambatyon*. Sifriyat Beit El.

Amit, Meir. 2002. *Ken, Adoni Hamifaked!* Sifriyat Ma'ariv.

Anglo-American Committee of Inquiry. 1946. *A Survey of Palestine*. Jerusalem: Government Printer (Palestine).

Argov, Nehemiah. 1959. *Pirkei Yoman*. Yedidim.

Ascher, Abraham. 1994. *The Revolution of 1905: Russia in Disarray*. Palo Alto, Calif.: Stanford University Press.

Avi-Yiftah (Gutman), Shmaryahu. 1948. "Lod Yotzet Legalut." *Mibifnim* 13:3 (Nov.), p. 452ff.

Avizohar, Meir, and Avi Bareli, eds. 1989. *Achshav o Le'olam Lo*. Ayanot.

Avizohar, Meir, and Isaiah Friedman, eds. 1984. *Iyunim Batochnit Hahalukah 1937–1947*. Ben-Gurion University.

Avizohar, Meir. 1987. "Hatziyonut Halohemet." P. 17ff. in David Ben-Gurion. *Zichronot 6*. Am Oved.

Avizohar, Meir. 1990. *Bere'i Saduk*. Am Oved.

Avizohar, Meir. 1993a. "Hiluf Mishmarot." P. 1ff. in David Ben-Gurion. *Likrat Ketz Hamandat*. Am Oved.

Avizohar, Meir. 1993b. "She'on Hahol." P. 5ff. in David Ben-Gurion. *Pa'amei Medinah*. Am Oved, p. 5ff.

Avizohar, Meir. 1997. "Ma'arachah betoch Ma'arachah." P. 1ff. in David Ben-Gurion. *Nilahem Ka'umah*. Am Oved.

Avneri, Uri. 2014. *Optimi*. Yediot Aharonot.

Avneri, Yitzhak. 1987. "Mered Aliyah." *Cathedra* 44 (June), p. 126ff.

Avnion, Eitan. 2000. *Milah Bemilah*. Eitav.

Avrech, Mira. 1965. *Paula*. Am Hasefer.

Bachrach, Uriel. 2009. *Beko'ah Hayeda*. N.N.D. Media.

Bacon, Gershon. 2001. "Hahevrah Hamasortit Batemurot Ha'etim." P. 453ff. in Israel Bartal and Israel Gutman, eds. *Kiyum Veshever*. Merkaz Zalman Shazar. Vol. 2.

Barel, Ari. 2012. "Epistemologiyah Tziyonit." *Iyunim Bitkumat Yisra'el* 22, p. 91ff.

Barel, Ari. 2014. *Melech Mehandes*. Ben-Gurion Institute.

Barnea, Nahum. 1981. *Yorim Uvochim*. Zemora Bitan Modan.

Bar-On, Mordechai. 1991. *Etgar Betigrah*. Ben-Gurion Heritage Center.

Bar-On, Mordechai. 1992. *Sha'arei Azah*. Am Oved.

Bar-On, Mordechai. 2007. "Alei Zait." In Mordechai Bar-On, ed. *Et Milhamah Va'et Shalom*. Keter.

Bar-On, Mordechai. 2012. *Moshe Dayan: Israel's Controversial Hero*. New Haven, Conn.: Yale University Press.

Bar-On, Mordechai. 2015. *El Mul Pnei Hamilhamah*. Efi Meltzer.

Baron, Natan. 2008. *Shoftim Umishpetantim Be'eretz Yisra'el*. Magnes.

Bartal, Israel. 2010. "Al Harishoniyut: Zeman Umakom Ba'aliyah Harishonah. P. 15ff. in Yaffa Berlowitz and Yosef Lang, eds. *Lesohe'ah Tarbut*. Hakibbutz Hameuhad.

Bartal, Israel, and Israel Gutman, eds. 2001. *Kiyum Vashever*. Merkaz Zalman Shazar.

Bar-Yosef, Dror. 2014. *Herut Ha'adam Behashkafato shel Menachem Begin*. Merkaz Moreshet Begin.

Bar-Yosef, Dror. 2016. *Ma'avakah shel Tenu'at Herut Levitul Hamimshal Hatzeva'i*. Merkaz Moreshet Begin.

Barzilay, Amnon. "Mi Natan et Hahora'ah?" *Ha'aretz*, March 15, 1985.

Bar-Zohar, Michael. 1970. *Hamemuneh*. Weidenfeld and Nicolson.

Bar-Zohar, Michael. 1977–78. *Ben-Gurion*. Am Oved.

Bar-Zohar, Michael. 2006. *Ka'of Hahol*. Yediot Aharonot.

Basok, Moshe, ed. 1940. *Sefer Hehalutz*. Jewish Agency.

Bauer, Yehuda. 1974. *Habrihah*. Moreshet and Sifriat Poalim.

Bauer, Yehuda. 1987. *Hasho'ah: Hebetim Histori'im*. Moreshet and Sifriat Poalim.

Bauer, Yehuda. 1994. *Jews for Sale: Nazi-Jewish Negotiations, 1933–1945*. New Haven, Conn.: Yale University Press.

Bauer, Yehuda. 2001. *Yehudim Lemechirah: Masa Umatan bein Yehudim LeNazim, 1933– 1945*. Yad Vashem.

Bauer, Yehuda. 2015. "Hasemel Halo Nachon: Madua Ha'amerikanim Lo Hayu Yecholim Lehaftzitz et Auschwitz." *Musaf Ha'aretz*, Oct. 4.

Bechor, David, et al. 1985. *Va'adat Hakirah Lehakirat Retzah Dr. Haim Arlororoff*. No publisher.

Beer, Israel. 1955. "Kravot Latrun." *Ma'arachot* 96 (Oct.), p. 7ff.

Bein, Alex. 1982. *Aliyah Vehityashvut Bimdinat Yisra'el*. Am Oved. Hasifriyah Hatziyonit.

Beit Halahmi, Rachel. 1963. "Bein Płońsk Le'eretz Yisra'el." P. 363ff. in Shlomo Zemach, ed. *Sefer Płońsk Uvnoteha*. Irgun Yotzei Płońsk.

Beit Halahmi, Rachel. 2006. *Halomot she'einam Supurei Agadah*. Gan Shmuel.

Beit Halahmi, Yehezkel. 1963. "Zichronot." P. 396ff. in Shlomo Zemach, ed. *Sefer Płońsk Uvnoteha*. Irgun Yotzei Płońsk.

Ben-Aharon, Yitzhak. 1977. *Be'ein Hase'arah*. Hakibbutz Hameuhad.

Ben-Arieh, Yeshoshua. 1977. *Ir Bere'i Tekufah*. Yad Ben-Zvi.

Ben-Arieh, Yeshoshua. 1999. "Hanof Hayishuvi." P. 75ff. in Israel Kolatt, ed. *Toldot Hayishuv*. Vol. 1. Israel Academy of Sciences.

Ben-Artzi, Yossi. 2002. "Hahityashvut Hayehudit Be'eretz-Yisra'el. P. 345ff. in Israel Kolatt, ed. *Toldot Hayishuv* 2. Israel Academy of Sciences.

Ben-Avram, Baruch, and Henri Nir. 1995. *Iyunim Ba'aliyah Hashelishit*. Yad Ben-Zvi.

Ben-Bassat, Yuval. 2014. "Mivrakim Othomani'im." *Zemanim* 126 (Spring), p. 52ff.

Ben-Gurion, David. 1905. "Mah Helkenu." *Hatzefirah* 4 (May).

Ben-Gurion, David. 1910a. "Leverur Matzavenu Hamedini." *Ha'ahdut* 3 (Sept.–Oct.).

Ben-Gurion, David. 1910b. "Leshe'elat Hayishuv Hayashan." *Ha'ahdut* 2 (Sept. 10).

Ben-Gurion, David. 1910c. "Midvarna De'umtei o Pakid Dati?" *Ha'ahdut* (July–Aug.).

Ben-Gurion, David. 1910d. "Ma'aseh Kalon." *Ha'ahdut* (July–Aug.).

Ben-Gurion, David. 1911a. "Even Mikir Tizak." *Ha'ahdut* (Jan. 20).

Ben-Gurion, David. 1911b. "Bamidron." *Ha'ahdut* (Sept. 17).

Ben-Gurion, David. 1911c. "Hapkidut Vehapo'alim." *Ha'ahdut* (March 22, 24).

Ben-Gurion, David. 1911d. "Hag Ha'avodah." *Ha'ahdut* (Jan.).

Ben-Gurion, David. 1911e. "Mihabamah Ha'ivrit Birushalayim. *Ha'ahdut* (March 15).

Ben-Gurion, David. 1912. "Hukah Ahat." *Ha'ahdut* (April 1).

Ben-Gurion, David. 1914. "Im Bitul Hakapitulatziyon." *Ha'ahdut* (Sept. 20).

Ben-Gurion, David. 1916a. "Bihudah Uvagalil." *Luah Ahi'ezer* 2 (1921).

Ben-Gurion, David. 1916b. "Di Farnikhtung fun der Armenisher Oytanami in Terkey." *Yiddisher Kempfer* (Aug. 27).

Ben-Gurion, David. 1917. "Unter Tsiens Fon." *Yiddisher Kempfer* (Nov. 30).

Ben-Gurion, David. 1919. "Le'asefat Hanivharim." *Kuntres* 24 (Oct.).

Ben-Gurion, David. 1920. "Anu Ma'ashimim." *Kuntres* 8 (April).

Ben-Gurion, David. 1925. "Irgun, Avodah, Chinuch." *Kuntres* (Nov. 27).

Ben-Gurion, David. 1931. *Anachnu Veshcheneinu*. Davar.

Ben-Gurion, David. 1932. *Avodah Ivrit*. Histadrut Ha'ovdim.

Ben-Gurion, David. 1933. *Legende un Virklekhkayt*. Lige farn Arbetenden Erets-Yisroel in Poyln.

Ben-Gurion, David. 1943. *Teshuvah Lidvar Hashalit*. Mapai.

Ben-Gurion, David. 1944. "Beshelihut Hahistadrut Lemoskvah." *Mibifnim* (June).

Ben-Gurion, David. 1949–50. *Bama'arachah* 1–5. Mapai.

Ben-Gurion, David. 1951. *Behilahem Yisra'el*. Mapai.

Ben-Gurion, David. 1953a. *Al Hakomunism Vehatziyonut*. Mapai. (Also in installments in *Davar*, beginning Jan. 23.)

Ben-Gurion, David. 1953b. "Bli Et." *Davar*, Aug. 14.

Ben-Gurion, David. 1953c. "Netaken Hame'uvat." *Davar*, Dec. 25.

Ben-Gurion, David. 1954a. "Netzah Yisra'el." P. 7ff. in *Shenaton Hamemshalah*. Hamadpis Hamemshalti.

Ben-Gurion, David. 1954b. "Ha'avdut Bechitvei Aplaton." *Eshkolot* 2, p. 1ff.

Ben-Gurion, David. 1954c. "Why I Retired to the Desert." *New York Times*, March 28.

Ben-Gurion, David. 1955a. *Mima'amad Le'am*. Ayanot.

Ben-Gurion, David. 1955b. "Avodah Ushemirah Bagalil." P. 309ff. in Efraim and Menachem Talmi, eds. *Sefer Hagalil*. Amihai.

Ben-Gurion, David. 1957. *Hazon Vaderech* 3. Am Oved.

Ben-Gurion, David. 1958. *Hazon Vaderech* 5. Am Oved.

Ben-Gurion, David. 1959. *Ha'am Utzeva'o*. IDF.

Ben-Gurion, David. 1961. "Autobiografiyah." *Davar*, Oct. 1.

Ben-Gurion, David. 1962a. *Hazon Vaderech* 1, 2, 4. Am Oved.

Ben-Gurion, David. 1962b. "Ben-Gurion Examines the Buddhist Faith." *New York Times Magazine*, April 29.

Ben-Gurion, David. 1963a. "Ne'urei BePłońsk. P. 31ff. in Shlomo Zemach, ed. *Sefer Płońsk Uvnoteha*. Irgun Yotzei Płońsk.

Ben-Gurion, David. 1963b. "Baderech Letzava Ulemedinat Yisra'el." Series of articles. *Davar*, Aug. 2, 1963–Feb. 5, 1965.

Ben-Gurion, David. 1964a. *Netzah Yisra'el*. Ayanot.

Ben-Gurion, David. 1964b. *Hapo'el Ha'ivri Vehahistadrut*. Tarbut Vesifrut.

Ben-Gurion, David. 1964c. "Havikuah Vehanigud Nimshach." *Davar*, April 10, 14.

Ben-Gurion, David. 1965. *Devarim Kahavayatam*. Am Hasefer.

Ben-Gurion, David. 1967. *Pegishot im Manhigim Arvi'im*. Am Oved.

Ben-Gurion, David. 1968. *Michtavim el Paula ve'el Hayeladim*. Am Oved.

Ben-Gurion, David. 1969a. *Iyunim Batanach*. Am Oved.

Ben-Gurion, David. 1969b. *Medinat Yisra'el Hamehudeshet*. Am Oved.

Ben-Gurion, David. 1971a. *Zichronot* 1. Am Oved.

Ben-Gurion, David. 1971b. *Yihud Veyi'ud*. Ma'arachot.

Ben-Gurion, David. 1971c. "Kesharai im Yitzhak Tabenkin." *Davar*, July 16.

Ben-Gurion, David. 1972. *Zichronot* 2. Am Oved.

Ben-Gurion, David. 1973. *Zichronot* 3. Am Oved.

Ben-Gurion, David. 1974a. *Zichronot* 4. Am Oved.

Ben-Gurion, David. 1974b. *Beit Avi*. Hakibbutz Hameuhad.

Ben-Gurion, David. 1979. *Sihot im Manhigim Aravi'im: Tosefet*. Ben-Gurion Heritage Institute.

Ben-Gurion, David. 1982a. *Yoman Hamilhamah*. Ministry of Defense.

Ben-Gurion, David. 1982b. *Zichronot* 5. Am Oved.

Ben-Gurion, David. 1987. *Zichronot* 6. Am Oved.

Ben-Gurion, David. 1993a. *Likrat Ketz Hamandat*. Am Oved.

Ben-Gurion, David. 1993b. *Pa'amei Medinah*. Am Oved.

Ben-Gurion, David. 1997. *Nilahem Ka'umah*. Am Oved.

Ben-Gurion, David. 2008. *Matif Tziyoni*. Ben-Gurion Institute.

Ben-Gurion, David. 2012. *Biltmore: Tochnit Medinit*. Ben-Gurion University.

Ben-Gurion, David. 2014. *Bikurim Begei Haharigah*. Ben-Gurion University.

Ben-Gurion, David, and Yitzhak Ben-Zvi. 1918. *Erets Yisroel in Fargangenheit un Gegenvart*. Poaley Tsien Palestine Komitet.

Ben-Gurion, David, and Yitzhak Ben-Zvi. 1980. *Eretz-Yisra'el Ba'avar Uvahoveh*. Yad Ben-Zvi.

Ben-Meir, Dov. 1978. *Hahistadrut*. Carta.

Ben-Refael, Eliezer. 2001. *Zehuyot Yehudiyot*. Ben-Gurion Heritage Institute.

Benziman, Uzi. 1985. *Sharon: Lo Otzer Be'adom*. Adam.

Benziman, Uzi, and Atallah Mansour. 1992. *Dayarei Mishneh*. Keter.

Ben-Zvi, Yitzhak. 1945. "Lereshit Darkah shel Ha'aliyah Hasheniyah." *Davar*, March 28.

Ben-Zvi, Yitzhak. 1967. *Zichronot Verashumot*. Yad Ben-Zvi.

Ben-Zvi, Yitzhak, et al., eds. 1962. *Sefer Hashomer*. Dvir.

Berdichevsky (Berdyczewski), Micha Josef. 1897. "Al Parshat Derachim: Michtav Galui el 'Ahad Ha'am.'" *Hashiloah* (March).

Berdichevsky (Berdyczewski), Micha Josef. 1967. *Tzefunot Ve'agadot*. Am Oved.

Berlin, Isaiah. 2004. *Letters 1927–1946*. Cambridge, U.K.: Cambridge University Press.

Berlowitz, Yaffa. 2010. "Hamoshavah Ha'ivrit." P. 70ff. in Yaffa Berlowitz and Yosef Lang, eds. *Lesohe'ah Tarbut*. Hakibbutz Hameuhad.

Bialer, Uri. 1998. "Ben-Gurion Veshe'elat Ha'orientatziyah." P. 217ff. in Anita Shapira, ed. *Atzma'ut*. Merkaz Zalman Shazar.

Bialik, Hayim Nahman. 1942. *Kol Kitvei Hayim Nahman Bialik*. Dvir.

Bilski Ben-Hur, Raphaella. 1988. *Kol Yahid Hu Melech*. Dvir.

Blatman, Daniel. 2001. "Habund." P. 493ff. in Israel Bartal and Israel Gutman, eds. *Kiyum Veshever* 2. Merkaz Zalman Shazar.

Bloom, Etan. 2008. *Arthur Ruppin and the Production of Modern Hebrew Culture*. Ph.D. diss. Tel Aviv University.

Blum, Gadi, and Nir Hefetz. 2005. *Haro'eh*. Yediot Aharonot.

Bodenheimer, Arieh (Buda). 2010. *Bizchut Hehaver MiPłońsk*. Hakibbutz Hameuhad.

Brenner, Uri, ed. 1984. *Nochah Iyum Hapelishah*. Yad Tabenkin.

Brown, Benjamin. 2011. *HeHazon Ish*. Magnes.

Burkhardt, John Lewis. 1822. *Travels in Syria and the Holy Land*. London: John Murray.

Burns, E.I.M. 1962. *Between Arab and Israeli*. London: George Harp.

Cahan, Abraham. 1925. "The Palestine Labor Movement." *Forward*, Dec. 10.

Cała, Alina. 2001. "Tenu'at Hahitbolelut BePolin." P. 337ff. in Israel Bartal and Israel Gutman, eds. *Kiyum Vashever* 1. Merkaz Shalman Shazar.

Carlebach, Azriel. 1951. "Amalek." *Ma'aiv*, Oct. 5.

Carlebach, Azriel. 1953. "Za'aki Eretz Ahuvah." *Ma'ariv*, Dec. 25.

Carmel, Alex. 1973. *Hityashvut Hagermanim*. Hahevrah Hamizrahit Hayisra'elit.

Carmel, Alex. 1999. "Pe'ilut Hama'atzamot Be'eretz Yisra'el." P. 143ff. in Israel Kolatt, ed. *Toldot Hayishuv* 1. Israel Academy of Sciences.

Chashin, Alexander, and David Ben-Gurion, eds. 1916. *Yizkor*. Poaley Tsien Palestine Komitet.

Churchill, Winston. 2009. P. 299ff. in Winston Churchill. *Thoughts and Adventures*. Wilmington, Del.: ISI.

Cohen, Avner. 1996. "Kennedy, Ben-Gurion, Vehakrav al Dimona." *Iyunim Bitkumat Yisra'el* 6: 110.

Cohen, Avner. 1998. *Israel and the Bomb*. New York: Columbia University Press.

Cohen, Avner, and William Burr, eds. 2015. *The U.S. Discovery of Israel's Secret Nuclear Project*. National Security Archive, George Washington University. http://nsarchive.gwu.edu/nukevault/ebb510.

Cohen, Avner, and William Burr. 2019. "How a Standoff with the U.S. Almost Blew Up Israel's Nuclear Program." *Ha'aretz*, May 3.

Cohen, Berl. 1986. *Leksikon fun der Yidish Shraybers*. New York: Ilman-Kohen.

Cohen, Geula. 1995. *Sipurah shel Lohemet*. Hamidrashah Hale'umit a.sh. Renee Mor.

Cohen, Hillel. 2013. *Tarpat*. Keter.

Cohen, Michael, ed. 1979. *The Letters and Papers of Chaim Weizmann*. Series A—Letters 20. Jerusalem: Transaction Books, Rutgers University, Israel Universities Press.

Cohen, Mula. 2000. *Latet Ulekabel*. Hakibbutz Hameuhad.

Cohen-Friedheim, Rachel. 2011. "Hayah o Lo Hayah? Hakibutzim Lo Ratzu Liklot Olim Mi'artzot Ha'islam." *Iyunim Bitkumat Yisra'el* 21: 317ff.

Cohen-Gil, Moshe. 2013. *Hayisra'elim Shebikshu Lerape et Ha'olam*. Keter.

Cohen-Levinovsky, Nurit. 2014. *Pelitim Yehudim Bemilhemet Ha'atzma'ut*. Am Oved.

Crossman, Richard. 1946. *Palestine Mission: A Personal Record*. London: Hamish Hamilton.

Danin, Ezra. 1987. *Tziyoni Bechol Tnai*. Kidum.

Dayan, Aryeh. 2002. "Gerush Amka." *Ha'aretz*, April 2.

Dayan, Dudu. 1991. *Osim Medinah*. Ministry of Defense.

Dayan, Moshe. 1965. *Yoman Ma'arechet Sinai*. Am Oved.

Dayan, Moshe. 1976–82. *Avnei Derech*. Idanim.

Dinur, Ben-Zion, ed. 1954–64. *Sefer Toldot Hahaganah*. Hasifriyah Hatziyonit and Ma'arachot.

Dotan, Shmuel. 1979. *Pulmus Hahalukah*. Yad Ben-Zvi.

Dror, Yuval. 1979. "Hagerim Harusi'im." *Cathedra* 10 (Jan.): 34ff.

Drori, Ze'ev. 2006. "Tzava Vehevrah Bemedinat Yisra'el." *Iyunim Bitkumat Yisra'el* 16: 243ff.

Druyanov, Alter. 1909. *Ketavim*. Hava'ad Leyishuv Eretz-Yisra'el.

Eban, Abba. 1977. *An Autobiography*. New York: Random House.

Eban, Abba. 1997. *Abba Eban: An Autobiography*. Random House.

Eilon, Avraham. 1959. *Hativat Givati Bemilhemet Hakomemiyut*. Ma'arachot.

Elam, Yigal. 1979. *Hahaganah*. Bitan Modan.

Elam, Yigal. 1984. *HaGedudim Ha'ivri'im*. Ma'arachot.

Elam, Yigal. 1990. *Hasochnut Hayehudit*. Hasifriyah Hatziyonit.

Elam, Yigal. 2012. *Mah Hitrahesh Kan*. Am Oved.

Elath, Eliahu. 1958. "Sihot im Musa Alami." *Yahadut Zemanenu* 3: 1ff.

Eliav, Arie Lova, 1983. *Taba'ot Edut*. Am Oved.

Eliav, Binyamin. 1990. *Zichronot Mehayamim*. Am Oved.

Eliav, Mordechai. 1978. "Hevlei Habereshit shel Petah Tikvah." *Cathedra* 9 (Oct.): 3ff.

Eliav, Mordechai. 1980. "Letoldot Hasefer." In David Ben-Gurion and Yitzhak Ben-Zvi, *Eretz Yisra'el Be'avar Uvahoveh*. Yad Ben-Zvi and Ben-Gurion Heritage Institute, p. 11ff.

Elon, Amos. 1951. "Hamashiah Ba." *Ha'aretz*, Jan. 13.

Elon, Amos. 1981. *Hayisra'elim*. Adam.

Elron, Ze'ev. 2016. *Likrat Hasivuv Hasheni*. Modan and IDF-Ma'arachot.

Epstein, Yitzhak. 1907. "She'elah Na'a'amah." *Hashiloah* 17: 193ff.

Erez, Yehuda, ed. 1953. *David Ben-Gurion: Album*. Ayanot.

Erez, Yehuda, ed. 1971. *Igrot David Ben-Gurion*, vol. 1. Am Oved.

Erez, Yehuda, ed. 1972. *Igrot David Ben-Gurion*, vol. 2. Am Oved.

Erez, Yehuda, ed. 1974. *Igrot David Ben-Gurion*, vol. 3. Am Oved.

Eshed, Haggai. 1979. *Mi Natan et Hahora'ah*. Idanim.

Eshel, Nimrod. 1994. *Shevitat Hayama'im*. Am Oved.

Even, Uri. 1974. *Arik: Darko shel Lohem*. Bustan.

Ever Hadani. 1955. *Hityashvut Bagalil Hatahton*. Masada.

Falk, Aner. 1987. *David Melech Yisra'el*. Tammuz–Bar.

Feldstein, Ariel. 1998. "Shlosha Yamim Behodesh Iyar." *Iyunim Bitkumat Yisra'el* 8: 354ff.

Fichman, Jacob. 1974. "Megilat Ha'esh." P. 314 in Gershon Shaked, ed. *Bialik: Yetzirato Lesugeha Bere'i Habikoret*. Bialik Institute.

Fisher, Louise, ed. 1994. *Chaim Weizmann*. Israel State Archives.

Fisher, Louise, ed. 2007. *Moshe Sharett: The Second Prime Minister*. Israel State Archives.

Flatau, Israel. 1963. "R. Avraham Gruen." P. 272 in Shlomo Zemach, ed. *Sefer Płońsk Uvnoteha*. Irgun Yotzei Płońsk.

Flexer, Yechiel. 1980. *Mar'ot Haknesset*. Self-published.

Foreign Relations of the United States, 1946: The Near East and Africa 7, 17 (1969). Washington, D.C.: U.S. Department of State.

Frankel, Jonathan. 1958. "Sefer 'Yizkor' Mishnat 1911." *Yahadut Zemaneinu* 4: 88ff.

Frankel, Jonathan. 1990. "Hitnagedut Hasotzialism Letziyonut." P. 147ff. in Haim Avni and Gideon Shimoni. *Hatziyonut Umitnagdeha Ba'am Hayehudi*. Hasifriyah Hatziyonit.

Freundlich, Yehoshua, ed. 1992. *Te'udot Lamediniyut Hahutz*. Israel State Archives.

Friedman, Isaiah. 1991. "Hitarvutan Shel Germaniyah Ve'Artzot Habrit." P. 168ff. in Mordechai Eliav, ed. *Bamatzor Uvamatzuk*. Yad Ben-Zvi.

Friedman, Isaiah. 1994. "Herzl Ufulmus Uganda." *Iyunim Bitkumat Yisra'el* 4: 175ff.

Friedmann, Daniel. 2015. *Lifnei Hama'hapechah*. Yediot Aharonot.

Friling, Tuvia. 1994. "Istanbul 1944." *Iyunim Bitkumat Yisra'el* 4: 299ff.

Friling, Tuvia. 1998. *Hetz Ba'arafel*. Ben-Gurion Heritage Center.

Frister, Roman. 1987. *Lelo Pesharah*. Zmora Bitan.

Furlonge, Geoffrey. 1969. *Palestine Is My Country*. London: John Murray.

Gali, Elkana. 1962. "Petek Shehishir Ahad Hasarim Hevi et Habchiah Ledorot." *Yediot Aharonot*, March 16.

Galili, Elazar. 1988. *Zichronotav*. Afikim.

Galili, Israel. 1990. *El Ve'al*. Hakibbutz Hameuhad.

Ganin, Zvi. 1978. "Tochnit Hahalukah Vashelihut Dr. Nahum Goldmann." *Hatziyonut*: 227.

Gaon, Boaz. 2008. "Dayan Natan et Hahora'ah." *Ma'ariv*, Oct. 8.

Gazit, Shlomo. 2016. *Bitzematim Machri'im*. Yediot Aharonot.

Gelber, N(athan) M(ichael). 1963. "Toldot Yehudei Płońsk Uvnoteha." P. 9ff. in Shlomo Zemach, ed. *Sefer Płońsk Uvnoteha*. Irgun Yotzei Płońsk.

Gelber, Yoav. 1990a. "'Masada': Haganah al Eretz-Yisra'el Bemilhemet Ha'olam Hasheni-yah." Bar-Ilan.

Gelber, Yoav. 1990b. *Moledet Hadashah*. Yad Ben-Zvi.

Genichovsky, Dov. 1993. "Hamilhamah neged Haprutzot." P. 417ff. in Ya'akov Gross, ed. *Yerushalayim 1917–1918*. Koresh.

Giere, Jacqueline, and Rachel Salamander. 1995. *Ein Leben aufs neu*. Vienna: Christian Brndstaetter.

Gilad, Zrubavel, ed. 1953. *Sefer Hapalmach*. Irgun Havrei Hapalmach.

Giladi, Dan. 1971. "Hamashber Hakalkali." *Hatziyonunt* 2: 119ff.

Giladi, Dan. 1973. *Hayishuv Bitkupfat Ha'aliyah Harivi'it*. Am Oved.

Giladi, Dan. 1999. "Hamoshavot Shelo Behasut Habaron." P. 503ff. in Israel Kolatt, ed. *Toldot Hayishuv*, vol. 1. Israel Academy of Sciences.

Giladi, Dan, and Mordecai Naor. 2002. "Hayishuv Bamilhemet Ha'olam." P. 457ff. in Israel Kolatt, ed. *Toldot Hayishuv*, vol. 1. Israel Academy of Sciences.

Gilbert, Martin. 2007. *Churchill and the Jews*. New York: Simon & Schuster.

Glass, Joseph B. 2002. *From New Zion to Old Zion: American Jewish Immigration and Settlement in Palestine, 1917–1939*. Detroit, Mich.: Wayne State University Press.

Golan, Haim, ed. 1989. *Mishlahat Po'alei Zion*. Yad Tabenkin.

Golan, Matti. 1989. *Rofe*. Zmora-Bitan.

Golani, Motti. 1994. "Dayan Movil Lemilhamah." *Iyunim Bitkumat Yisra'el* 4: 117ff.

Golani, Motti. 1997. *Tehiyeh Milhamah Bakayitz*. Ma'arachot.

Golani, Motti. 2008. "Hameina'i shel 'Homah Umigdal.'" P. 340 in Ya'akov and Rena Sharett, eds. *Shoher Shalom*. Moshe Sharett Heritage Society.

Goldberg, Giora. 1992. "Ben-Gurion ve-'Hazit Ha'am.'" *Medinah, Mimshal, Veyehasim Beinle'umi'im* 35: 51ff.

Goldstein, Yossi. 1996. "Ussishkin U'farashat Uganda.'" *Hatziyonut* 20: 9ff.

Goldstein, Yossi. 2003. *Eshkol*. Keter.

Goldstein, Yossi. 2012. *Golda*. Ben-Gurion University.

Goldstein, Yossi. 2016. *Anu Hayinu Harishonim*. Bialik Institute.

Goldstein, Yossi. In progress. *Ben-Gurion: Biografiyah*. Bar-Ilan University.

Gordon, Shmuel Leib. Undated. *Sefer Iyov*. Masada.

Gorny, Yosef. 1971. *Hitahdut Tziyonit Sotzialistit*. Tel Aviv University.

Gorny, Yosef. 1973. *Ahdut Ha'avodah*. Tel Aviv University.

Gorny, Yosef. 1975. "Shorasheha shel Toda'at Ha'imut." *Hatziyonut*: 72ff.

Gorny, Yosef. 1988. "Mima'amad Le'am." P. 73ff. in Shlomo Avineri, ed. *David Ben-Gurion*. Am Oved.

Gorny, Yosef. 2002. "Hayishuv Hehadash." P. 415 in Israel Kolatt, ed. *Toldot Hayishuv*, vol. 2. Israel Academy of Sciences.

Goschler, Constantin. 2005. *Schuld und Schulden, Die Politik der Wiedergutmachung fuer NS Verfolgte seit 1945*. Goettingen: Wallstein.

Gouri, Haim. 1963. "Al Habushah." *Lamerhav*, May 14.

Gouri, Haim. 1982. "Otzmah." *Ma'arachot* 285 (Dec.): 11ff.

Govrin, Nurit. 1989. *Dvash Misela*. Ministry of Defense.

Govrin, Nurit. 2006. "Shetei Predot: David Ben-Gurion UShlomo Zemach." *Ha'aretz*, May 29.

Govrin, Nurit. 2008. *Kriyat Hadorot*. Carmel.

Greenberg, Yitzhak. 1989. *Ra'ayon Hevrat Ha'ovdim*. Am Oved.

Gris, Ze'ev. 2009. "Manhigut Ruhanit Vecho'ah Politi." P. 20ff. in Israel Rozenson and Oded Yisraeli, eds. *Heyil Baru'ah*. Ministry of Defense.

Grisaru, Nimrod. 1971. "Reshito shel Kibbutz Sde Boker." Photocopy of final course paper in the National Library of Israel.

Grodzensky, Shlomo. 1965. "Mitoch Hirhurim Ba'ishiyut shel D. Ben-Gurion." *Davar*, Aug. 27.

Gruen, Avraham. 1963. "Sihot im Admorim." P. 272ff. in Shlomo Zemach, ed. *Sefer Płońsk Uvnoteha*. Irgun Yotzei Płońsk.

Gruenbaum, Yitzhak. 1963. "Yalduti." P. 86ff. in Shlomo Zemach, ed. *Sefer Płońsk Uvnoteha*. Irgun Yotzei Płońsk.

Habas, Bracha. 1950. "Ehad Vedoro." *Dvar Hashavua* (weekly series in forty-seven installments).

Habas, Bracha. 1952. *David Ben-Gurion Vedoro*. Masada.

Hacohen, David. 1974. *Et Lesaper*. Am Oved.

Hacohen, Dvora. 1994a. *Olim Bisa'arah*. Yad Ben-Zvi.

Hacohen, Dvora. 1994b. *Tochnit Hamilyon*. Ministry of Defense.

Hagani, Amira. 2010. *Beguf Rishon Rabim*. Hakibbutz Hameuhad.

Halamish, Aviva. 1990. "Hakrav al 'Exodus.'" P. 302ff. in Anita Shapira, ed. *Haha'apalah*. Tel Aviv University and Am Oved.

Halamish, Aviva. 1993. "Ha'im Haytah Shenat 1933 Nekudat Mifneh?" *Iyunim Bitkumat Yisra'el* 3: 98ff.

Harel, Isser. 1982a. *Mivtza Yossele*. Idanim.

Harel, Isser. 1982b. *Mashber Hamad'anim*. Sifriyat Ma'ariv.

Harel, Isser. 1989. *Bitahon Vedemokratiyah*. Idanim.

Hareuveni, Imanuel. 1999. *Leksikon Eretz-Yisra'el*. Yediot Aharonot.

Harman, Avraham, and Yigael Yadin, eds. 1948. *Be'asor Leyisra'el*. Masada.

Haver, Yosef. 1910. "Al Hizayon Hashmad." *Hapo'el Hatza'ir* (Nov.–Dec.).

Hayo'etz Hamishpati Lamemshalah neged Adolf Eichmann: Pesak Hadin. Merkaz Hahasbara.

Hazkani, Shay. 2015. "Sipuro shel Hadoh Hahatrani al 'Be'ayat Hamizrahim' BeTzahal." *Ha'aretz*, Aug. 12.

Heller, Daniel. 2017. *Jabotinsky's Children: Polish Jews and the Rise of Right-Wing Zionism*. Princeton, N.J.: Princeton University Press.

Heller, Joseph. 1981. "Hamediniyut Hatziyonit Bazirah Habeinleumit." *Shalem* 3: 213ff.

Heller, Joseph. 2010. *Yisra'el Vehamilhamah Hakarah*. Ben-Gurion Research Institute for the Study of Israel and Zionism.

Herzl, Theodor. 1960. *Kitvei Herzl*. Neuman.

Herzl, Theodor. 1960. *The Complete Diaries of Theodor Herzl*. Raphael Patai, ed. New York: Herzl Press and Thomas Yoseloff.

Herzl, Theodor. 1989. *The Jewish State*. New York: Herzl Press.

Heschel Yeivin, Yehoshua. 1937. *Pesha Hadamim shel Hasochnut*. No publisher.

Hestermann, Jenny. 2016. *Inszenierte Versoehnung*. Frankfurt: Campus.

Hillel, Shlomo. 1985. *Ruah Kadim*. Yediot Aharonot.

Hoffman, Bruce. 2015. *Anonymous Soldiers: The Struggle for Israel, 1917–1947*. New York: Knopf.

Holtzman, Avner. 1993. "Bein Micha Yosef Berdichevsky LeDavid Ben-Gurion." *Iyunim Bitkumat Yisra'el* 3: 191ff.

Horowitz, David. 1951. *Bishlihut Medinah Noledet*. Schocken.

Horwitz, Dalia. 1981. "Rashei Hamosdot Hatziyoni'im." *Hatziyonut* 7: 95.

Jabotinsky, Ze'ev. 1932. "Ken Lishbor." *Hazit Ha'am*. Dec. 2.

Jabotinsky, Ze'ev. 1949. "Mah Aleinu La'asot: Ha'avodah Be'eretz Yisra'el." P. 21 in Ze'ev Jabotinsky. *Ketavim Tzionim*. E. Jabotinsky.

Jabotinsky, Ze'ev. 1953. "Al Kir Habarzel." P. 260ff. in Ze'ev Jabotinsky. *Ketavim*. E. Jabotinsky. Vol. 11.

Jabotinsky, Ze'ev. 1981. *Ekronot Manhim Live'ayot Hasha'ah*. Jabotinsky Institute.

Jaffe, Aharon. 2015. "Baderech LeYisra'el Maftzitzim et Kahir." *Ma'arachot* 450 (April): 50ff.

The Jewish Case Before the Anglo-American Committee of Inquiry on Palestine. 1947. Jerusalem: The Jewish Agency for Palestine.

Josephus with an English Translation by Ht. St. J. Thackeray. 1956. Cambridge, Mass., and London: Harvard University Press and William Heinemann.

Kabalo, Paula. 2003. "Ezrahim Mitbagrim: Kinus Hatalmidim BeSheikh Munis." *Yisra'el* 4: 123ff.

Kabalo, Paula. 2007. *Shurat Hamitnadvim*. Am Oved.

Kadish, Alon, and Benjamin Z. Kedar, eds. 2005. *Me'atim mul Rabim?* Magnes.

Kafkafi, Eyal. 1993. "Hakera Be'Ein Harod." *Iyunim Bitkumat Yisra'el* 3: 437ff.

Kafkafi, Eyal. 1998. *Anti-Mahiah*. Am Oved.

Kagan, Berl. 1986. *Lexicon of Yiddish Writers*. New York: Ilman-Kohen.

Kanaan, Haviv. 1974. *200 Yemei Haradah*. Mul-Art.

Kanari, Baruch. 2009. "Yitzhak Tabenkin, Hasho'ah, Umilhemet Ha'olam Ha'sheniyah." P. 420ff. in Dina Porat, ed. *Sho'ah Mimerhak Tavo: Ishim Bayishuv Ha'eretz-Yisra'eli Vayahasam Lanatzism Velasho'ah, 1933–1948*. Yad Ben-Zvi.

Kantrovitz, Nati. 2007. "Lahatzot et Hashichehah." *Yisra'el* 12: 217ff.

Karlinsky, Nahum. 2000. *Prihat Hehadar*. Magnes.

Katz, Shmuel. 1993. *Jabo*. Dvir.

Katz, Yossi. 1998. "Eitan Beda'ato." *Iyunim Bitkumat Yisra'el* 8: 347ff.

Katz, Yossi. 2000. *Medinah Baderech*. Magnes.

Katzman, Avi. 1985. "Hayav Umoto shel Haterorist Ha'ivri Harishon." *Koteret Rashit* 10 (July).

Katznelson, Berl. 1949. *Ketavim*. Mifleget Po'alei Eretz-Yisra'el.

Kedar, Nir. 2004. "Hamamlachtiyut Harepublikanit." *Iyunim Bitkumat Yisra'el* 14: 131ff.

Kedar, Nir. 2015. *Ben-Gurion Vehahukah*. Dvir.

Kenan, Irit. 1991. "She'erit Hapleitah." *Iyunim Bitkumat Yisra'el* 1: 343ff.

Keren, Michael. 1988. *Ben-Gurion Veha'intelektu'alim*. Ben-Gurion University.

Kettaneh, Francis A. 1942. "From Chariots to Tanks." *The Rotarian* (May): 16.

Kettaneh, Francis A. 1949. *A Proposed Solution of the Palestine Refugee Problem 1949*. Council on Foreign Relations.

Klinitz-Vigdor, Tova. 1963. "Reshit Hasafah Ha'ivrit Be'irenu." P. 228 in Shlomo Zemach, ed. *Sefer Płońsk Uvnoteha*. Irgun Yotzei Płońsk.

Knesset Yisra'el. 1949. *Hava'ad Hale'umi: Sefer Te'udot.*

Kolatt, Israel. 1988. "Ha'im Haya Ben-Gurion Sotziyalist?" P. 118 in Shlomo Avineri, ed. *David Ben-Gurion.* Am Oved.

Kollek, Teddy. 1979. *Yerushalayim Ahat.* Ma'ariv.

Kressel, Getzel. 1953. *Em Hamoshavot Petah Tikvah.* Petah Tikvah Municipality.

Kroyanker, David. 2002. *Shechunot Yerushalayim.* Jerusalem Institute for Israel Studies and Keter.

Kroyanker, David. 2005. *Rehov Yafo.* Jerusalem Institute for Israel Studies and Keter.

Lahav, Pnina. 1999. *Yisra'el Bamishpat.* Am Oved.

Lam, Vered. 1990. "Me'ahevet David." *Monitin,* Sept.

Lamdan, Yitzhak. 1955. *Yizkor.* Ministry of Defense.

Lamdan, Yosef. 1999. "Ha'aravim Vehatziyonut, 1882–1914." P. 215ff. in Israel Kolatt, ed. *Toldot Hayishuv,* vol. 1. Israel Academy of Sciences.

Laor, Dan. 2013. *Alterman.* Am Oved.

Lapidot, Yehuda. 1994. *Hasaizon.* Jabotinsky Institute.

Laqueur, Walter. 1972. *A History of Zionism.* New York: Holt, Rinehart and Winston.

Laskov, Shulamit, ed. 1982. *Ketavim Letoldot Hibat Tziyon.* Tel Aviv University.

Laskov, Shulamit. 1979. *Habilu'im.* Hasifriyah Hatziyonit.

Laskov, Shulamit. 1999. "Hamoshavot shebli Temichah." P. 351ff. in Israel Kolatt, ed. *Toldot Hayishuv,* vol. 1. Israel Academy of Sciences.

Lavi, Shlomo. 1936. "Lezichro shel Simcha Isaac." *Davar,* April 20.

Lavi, Shlomo. 1947. *Megilati BeEin-Harod: Ra'ayonot, Zichronot, Uma'asim.* Am Oved.

Lavi, Shlomo. 1948. "El Hano'ar Hameshuseh." *Davar,* July 29.

Lavi, Shlomo. 1957. *Aliyato Shel Shalom Lish.* Am Oved.

Lavi, Shlomo. 1968. *Ma'arachot.* Ayanot.

Lavid, Lior. 2012. "Bechiyah Ledorot." *Yisra'el* 4: 68ff.

Lavie, Aviv. 2005. "Huhlat Vekuyam." *Ha'aretz,* Oct. 8.

Lazar, Hadara. 2012. *Shisha Yehidim.* Hakibbutz Hameuhad.

Lev, Uziel. 1983. "MiBar-Giora LeHashomer." P. 135ff. in Shmuel Stempler, ed. *Hayishuv Ba'et Hahadashah.* Ministry of Defense.

Levy, Yitzhak. 1986. *Tish'a Kabin.* Ma'arachot.

Liebman, Charles S. 1974. "Diaspora Influence on Israel: The Ben-Gurion–Blaustein 'Exchange' and Its Aftermath." *Jewish Social Studies* 36: 271ff.

Lissak, Moshe. 1986. "Binyan Mosdot Betefisat Ben-Gurion." P. 109ff. in Shlomo Avineri, ed. *David Ben-Gurion.* Am Oved.

Lissak, Moshe. 1994. "Aliyah, Kelitah, Uvinyan Hevrah." P. 173ff. in Moshe Lissak, ed. *Toldot Hayishuv,* vol. 2. Israel Academy of Sciences.

Litvinoff, Barnet, ed. 1978. *The Letters and Papers of Chaim Weizmann.* Jerusalem: Israel Universities Press, 1978.

Louis, Roger. 1984. *The British Empire in the Middle East 1945–1951.* Oxford, U.K.: Clarendon.

Ludvipol, Avraham. 1901. "Be'eretz Ha'avot." *Hatzefirah,* Feb. 27.

Lufban, Yitzhak. 1933. "Betzilo Shel Tzlav Hakeres." *Hapo'el Hatza'ir,* March 21.

Man, Rafi. 2012. *Hamanhig Vehatikshoret.* Am Oved.

Mann, Nir. 2012. *Hakiryah Bishnot Kinunah.* Carmel.

Mansour, Atallah. 2004. *Hofen Adamah.* Ministry of Education.

McDonald, James G. 2015. *To the Gates of Jerusalem*. Bloomington: Indiana University Press.

Medzini, Meron. 2008. *Golda*. Yediot Aharonot.

Meir, Golda. 1975. *My Life*. Weidenfeld and Nicolson.

Meiri, Shmuel. 1971. *Kehilat Płońsk*. Ministry of Education and Culture.

Meltzer, Emanuel. 2001. "Hama'arach Hapoliti shel Yahadut Polin." P. 427 in Israel Bartal and Israel Gutman, eds. *Kiyum Vashever*. Merkaz Zalman Shazar. Vol. 1.

Messer, Oded. 1996. *Tochniyot Operativiyot shel Hahaganah*. Hamerkaz Letoldot Ko'ach Hamagen.

Michaeli, Ben-Zion. 1991. *Ben-Gurion BeSejera*. Ministry of Defense.

Michelson, Mottel. 1963. "Magefat Haholira Vehupah Beveit Ha'almin." P. 125ff. in Shlomo Zemach, ed. *Sefer Płońsk Uvnoteha*. Irgun Yotzei Płońsk.

Minhelet Ha'am. 1978. *Protokolim*. Israel State Archives.

Mintz, Matityahu. 1983. "Yozmat Pinhas Rutenberg." *Hatziyonut* 8: 181ff.

Mintz, Matityahu. 1986a. *Haver Veyariv*. Yad Tabenkin.

Mintz, Matityahu. 1986b. "Bein David Ben-Gurion LeYitzhak Ben-Zvi." *Cathedra* 44: 81ff.

Mintz, Matityahu. 1988. "Hakontzeptziyah Hahistorit." *Hatziyonut* 13: 69ff.

Moked, Gabriel. 1971. "Va'ad Hahatzalah." *Yalkut Moreshet* 13 (June): 60ff.

Moked, Gabriel. 1982. "Tefisot Meshihiyot." *Cathedra* 24 (July): 52ff.

Moked, Gabriel. 2014. *Tefisot Hayahadut shel Hayim Nahman Bialik*. Emda Hadashah— Achshav.

Morris, Benny. 1987. *The Birth of the Palestinian Refugee Problem*. Cambridge, U.K.: Cambridge University Press.

Morris, Benny. 1991. *Ledatah shel Be'ayat Haplitim Hafalastinim*. Am Oved.

Morris, Benny. 1993. *Israel's Border Wars 1949–1956*. Oxford: Claredon.

Morris, Benny. 2000. "He'arot al Hahistoriografiyah Hatziyonit." P. 23 in Benny Morris. *Tikun Ta'ut*. Am Oved.

Morris, Benny. 2005. "The Historiography of Deir Yassin." *Journal of Israeli History* 24, no. 1 (March), 79 ff.

Morris, Benny. 2008. *1948: A History of the First Arab-Israeli War*. New Haven, Conn.: Yale University Press.

Mortimer, Gavin. 2010. *The Blitz*. Oxford, U.K.: Osprey.

Nachmani, Amikam. 1987. *Great Power Discord in Palestine*. London: Frank Cass.

Nakdimon, Shlomo. 1978. *Altalena*. Idanim.

Nakdimon, Shlomo. 2011. "May 1948." P. 33ff. in Avraham Diskin, ed. *Mi'Altalena ad Henah*. Carmel and Begin Heritage Center.

Nakdimon, Shlomo, and Shaul Mayzlish. 1985. *De Haan*. Modan.

Naor, Mordechai, and Dan Giladi, eds. 1993. *Eretz Yisra'el Bame'ah Ha'esrim*. Ministry of Defense.

Naor, Mordechai, ed. 1988. *Aliya Bet*. Yad Ben-Zvi.

Navon, Yitzhak. 2015. *Kol Haderech*. Keter.

Ne'eman, Yuval. 1995. "Yisra'el Be'idan Haneshek Hagar'ini." *Nativ* 5: 35ff.

Neumann, Boaz. 2009. *Teshukat Hahalutzim*. Am Oved.

Nevo, Amos. 1983. "Kach Tichnen Ben-Gurion Legayer et HaBedu'im." *Yediot Aharonot, Shivah Yamim*, Nov. 25.

Nevo, Amos. 1993. "Sali Shel Haruhot." *Yediot Aharonot, Shivah Yamim*, Jan. 15.

Nini, Yehuda. 1996. *Hahayit o Halamti Halom*. Am Oved.

Nordheimer, Nur Ofer. 2014. *Eros and Tragedy: Jewish Male Fantasies and the Masculine Revolution of Zionism*. Boston: Academic Cultural Press.

Ofer, Dalia. 1988. *Derech Hayam*. Yad Ben-Zvi.

Ohana, David. 2003. *Meshihiyut Vemamlachtiyut*. Ben-Gurion Research Institute for the Study of Israel and Zionism.

Ohana, David, and Michael Feige. 2010. "Halvayah al Saf Matzok." *Israel* 17: 25ff.

Ohry, Avi, and Jenny Tsafrir. 2000. "David Ben-Gurion, Moshé Felden Kreis, and Raymond Dart." *Israel Medical Association Journal* 2:1 (Jan.): 66ff.

Oren, Elhanan. 1976. *Baderech el Ha'ir*. Ma'arachot.

Oren, Elhanan. 1985. "Mashber Hapikud Ha'elyon." *Ma'arachot* 298 (March–April): 50ff.

Orian, Noah. 2012. *Hameyased Hanishkah*. Hasifriyah Hatziyonit.

Ostfeld, Zehava, ed. 1988. *Hazaken Veha'am*. IDF Archive.

Padeh, Benny. 1993. "Eilat Bahazon Hatziyoni." *Ariel* (June): 203.

Palestine Royal Commission. *Report*. London: HM Stationery Office. 1937.

Peled, Ammatzia. 2007. *Madrich Harehovot*. University of Haifa.

Penslar, Derek J. 1991. *Zionism and Technocracy: The Engineering of Jewish Settlement in Palestine, 1870–1918*. Bloomington: Indiana University Press.

Penslar, Derek Jonathan. 2004. "Herzl Veha'aravim Hafalastini'im." *Yisra'el* 6: 149ff.

Peres, Shimon, in conversation with David Landau. 2011. *Ben-Gurion: A Political Life*. New York: Nextbook–Schocken.

Picard, Avi. 2013. *Olim Bimsorah*. Ben-Gurion Institute for the Study of Israel and Zionism.

Poles. 1962. "Habchiyah Ledorot o Hinuh Lekalut Hada'at." *Ha'aretz*, March 23.

Porat, Dina. 1986. *Hanhagah Bemilkud*. Am Oved.

Porat, Dina. 2009. "Aseh Hakol Leamet Mivrakecha." P. 449 in Dina Porat, ed. *Sho'ah Mimerhak Tavo: Ishim Bayishuv Ha'eretz-Yisra'eli Vayehesam Lanatzism Ulesho'ah, 1933–1948*. Yad Ben-Zvi.

Porat, Dina. 2011. *Kafeh Haboker Bere'ah He'ashan*. Am Oved and Yad Vashem.

Porat, Dina, and Yechiam Weitz, eds. 2002. *Bein Magen David Letelai Tzahov*. Yad Vashem and Yad Ben-Zvi.

Prinz, Joachim. 2008. *Rebellious Rabbi*. Bloomington: Indiana University Press, 2008.

Procopius. 1914. *History of the Wars*. Cambridge, Mass.: Harvard University Press.

Rabin, Yitzhak. 1979. *Pinkas Sherut*. Ma'ariv.

Rabinovich, Itamar. 1991. *Hashalom Shehamak*. Keter.

Rabinowitz, A.Z., ed. 1911. *Yizkor*. No publisher.

Rafael, Gideon. 1981. *Besod Le'umim*. Idanim.

Raider, Mark A. 1998. *The Emergence of American Zionism*. New York: New York University Press.

Ram, Hannah. 1977. "Hathalot Shel Avodat Adamah Biydei Yehudim Be'eizor Yafo." *Cathedra* 6 (Dec.): 20ff.

Ratner, Yohanan. 1978. *Hayai Ve'ani*. Schocken.

Ratosh, Yonatan. 1974. "Shirat Ha'ahavah Hazarah etzel Bialik." P. 309 in Gershon Shaked, ed. *Bialik: Yetzirato Lesugeha Bere'i Habikoret*. Bialik Institute.

Raz, Adam. 2013. "Baderech LeDimona: Reshitah Shel Hamahloket al Mediniyut Hagar'in HaYisra'elit." *Politika* 25: 107ff.

Raz, Adam. 2015. *Hama'avak al Hapetzazah*. Carmel.

Reinharz, Jehuda, ed. 1978. *The Letters and Papers of Chaim Weizmann. Series A—Letters.* Vol. IX. Jerusalem: Transaction Books, Rutgers University, Israel Universities Press.

Reinharz, Jehuda. 1993. *Chaim Weizmann: The Making of a Statesman.* New York: Oxford University Press.

Reinharz, Jehuda, et al., eds. 2005. *Im Hazerem Venegdo.* Yad Ben-Zvi.

Reshef, Shimon. 1987. "Ben-Gurion Vehachinuch Ha'ivri." *Cathedra* 43 (March): 114ff.

Reuveni, Aharon. 1932. *Bereshit Hamevuchah.* Omanut.

Rogel, Nakdimon. 1993. "Mi Harag et Avraham Yosef Berl." *Cathedra* 69 (Sept.): 165ff.

Rogel, Nakdimon. 1999. "Mah Yada Ben-Gurion al Tel Hai?" *Iyunim Bitkumat Yisra'el* 1: 28ff.

Ronen, Avihu. 1986. "Shelihutah Shel Helinkah." *Yalkut Moreshet* 42: 55ff.

Ronen, Moshe. 2013. *Tehomot Ushehakim.* Yediot Aharonot.

Rose, Norman. 1990. *Chaim Weizmann.* Domino.

Rosenfeld, Aharon. 1982. *Hayai.* No publisher.

Rosenfeld, Shalom. "Bizchut Hahistoriyah Uvignut Hahastakah." *Ma'ariv*, April 12, 1963.

Rosenman, Avraham. 1992. *Hashamashim Ruppin Ve'Eshkol.* World Zionist Organization.

Rosenthal, Reuven Rubik. 2000. *Kafr Qasim.* Hakibbutz Hameuhad.

Rosenthal, Yemima, ed. 1994. *Chaim Weizmann.* Israel State Archives.

Rosenthal, Yemima. 1979. *Khronologiyah Letoldot Hayishuv.* Yad Ben-Zvi.

Salmon, Yosef. 1990. "Teguvat Haharedim." P. 51ff. in Haim Avni and Gideon Shimoni. *Hatziyonut Umitnagdeha Ba'am Hayehudi.* Hasifriyah Hatziyonit.

Salomon, Ya'akov. 1980. *Bedarki Sheli.* Idanim.

Schulman, Samuel. 1917. "Jewish Nation Not Wanted in Palestine." *New York Times*, Nov. 25.

Scott, Ury Y. 2012. *Barricades and Banners: The Revolution of 1905 and the Transformation of Warsaw Jewry.* Palo Alto, Calif.: Stanford University Press.

Seckbach, Efrat. 2013. "Pe'ulat Hanakam shel Meir Har-Zion." *Yisra'el* 21: 37ff.

Segev, Tom. 1986. *1949: The First Israelis.* New York: Free Press.

Segev, Tom. 1993. *The Seventh Million: The Israelis and the Holocaust.* New York: Hill & Wang.

Segev, Tom. 2000. *One Palestine, Complete: Jews and Arabs Under the British Mandate.* New York: Metropolitan Books.

Segev, Tom. 2006. "Pezatzot Be'Iraq." *Ha'aretz*, April 7.

Segev, Tom. 2007. "Hehalal Harishon." *Ha'aretz*, Dec. 4.

Segev, Tom. 2007. *1967: Israel, the War, and the Year that Transformed the Middle East.* New York: Metropolitan Books.

Segev, Tom. 2010. *Simon Wiesenthal: The Life and Legend.* New York: Doubleday.

Shachar, Yoram. 2002. "Hatiyutot Hamukdamot." *Iyunei Mispat* 26:2 (Nov.): 523ff.

Shaked, Gershon, ed. 1974. *Bialik: Yetzirato Lesugeha Bere'i Habikoret.* Bialik Institute.

Shaked, Gershon. 1977. *Hasiporet Ha'ivrit.* Keter and Hakibbutz Hameuhad.

Shalom, Zaki. 1991. "Mediniyut Habitahon." *Iyunim Bitkumat Yisra'el* 1: 141ff.

Shalom, Zaki. 1996. "Pegishat Ben-Gurion–Adenauer, March 14, 1960, Malon Waldorf Astoria." *Iyunim Bitkumat Yisra'el* 6: 604ff.

Shaltiel, Eli, ed. 1996. *David Ben-Gurion: Mivhar Te'udot.* Israel State Archives.

Shaltiel, Eli. 1990. *Pinhas Rutenberg.* Am Oved.

Shaltiel, Eli. 2000. *Tamid Bemeri*. Am Oved.

Shamir, Shlomo. 1994. *Bechol Mechir LeYerushayim*. Ma'arachot.

Shapira, Anita. 1977. *Hama'avak Hanichzav*. Hakibbutz Hameuhad.

Shapira, Anita. 1980. *Berl*. Am Oved.

Shapira, Anita. 1985. *Mipiturei Harama ad Peruk HaPalmach*. Hakibbutz Hameuhad.

Shapira, Anita. 1988. "Ben-Gurion VeBerl: Shnei Tipusei Manhigut." P. 45ff. in Shlomo Avineri, ed. *David Ben-Gurion*. Am Oved.

Shapira, Anita. 1989. *Hahalichah el Kav Ha'ofek*. Am Oved.

Shapira, Anita. 1992. *Herev Hayonah*. Am Oved.

Shapira, Anita. 2004. *Yigal Allon*. Hakibbutz Hameuhad.

Shapira, Anita. 2009. "Berl, Ha'antishemiyut Vehashoah." P. 237ff. in Dina Porat, ed. *Sho'ah Mimerhak Tavo: Ishim Bayishuv Ha'eretz-Yisra'eli Vayehesam Lanatzism Ulesho'ah, 1933– 1948*. Yad Ben-Zvi.

Shapira, Anita. 2014. *Ben-Gurion: Father of Modern Israel*. New Haven, Conn.: Yale University Press.

Shapira, Anita, ed. 1990. *Ha'apalah*. Tel Aviv University and Am Oved.

Shapira, Anita, ed. 2001. *Medinah Baderech*. Merkaz Zalman Shazar.

Shapiro, David H. 1994. *La'alot Bechol Haderachim*. Am Oved.

Shapiro, Jonathan. 1971. "Hamahloket Bayahadut Artzot Habrit." *Hatziyonut* 2: 90ff.

Sharett, Moshe. 1968–1974. *Yoman Medini*. Am Oved.

Sharett, Moshe. 1978. *Yoman Ishi*. Ma'aiv.

Sharett, Moshe. 2003. *Yemei London*. Moshe Sharett Heritage Institute.

Sharett, Moshe. 2013. *Davar Davur*. Moshe Sharett Heritage Institute.

Sharett, Ya'akov, ed. 2007. *Pulmus Hashilumim*. Moshe Sharett Heritage Society.

Shavit, Ya'akov, ed. 1983. *Havlagah o Teguvah*. Bar-Ilan.

Shchori, Ilan. 1990. *Halom Shehafach Lekrach*. Avivim.

Sheffer, Gabriel. 2015. *Moshe Sharett*. Carmel.

Sheleg, Yair. 1998. *Ruah Hamidbar*. Ministry of Defense.

Shepard, Richard F., and Vicky Gold Levi. 2000. *Live and Be Well: A Celebration of Yiddish Culture in America*. New Brunswick, N.J.: Rutgers University Press.

Sherf, Ze'ev. 1959. *Sheloshah Yamim*. Am Oved.

Shihor, Shmuel. 1958. *1958–1961. Eser Hashanim Harishonot*. Ha'aretz.

Shilon, Avi. 2013. *Ben-Gurion: Epilog*. Am Oved.

Shiloni, Zvi. 1985. "Temurot Bahanhaga." *Cathedra* 35 (April): 58ff.

Shlaim, Avi. 2000. *The Iron Wall: Israel and the Arab World*. New York: Norton.

Shlaim, Avi. 2007. *Lion of Jordan: The Life of King Hussein in War and Peace*. Allen Lane.

Shohat, Israel. 1962. "Shelihut Vaderech." In Yitzhak Ben-Zvi et al. *Sefer Hashomer*. Dvir.

Shtiftel, Shoshana, ed. 2008. *Tochnit Dalet*. Ministry of Defense.

Siebenmorgen, Peter. 2015. *Franz Josef Strauss: Ein Leben im Uebermass*. Munich: Siedler.

Sinai, Smadar. 2013. *Hashomrot Shelo Shamru*. Hakibbutz Hameuhad.

Sivan, Emmanuel. 1991. *Dor Tashah*. Ma'arachot.

Slater, Leonard. 1970. *The Pledge*. New York: Simon & Schuster.

Slutsky, Yehuda. 1973. *Sefer Toldot Hahaganah*, vol. 3. Am Oved.

Smilansky, Moshe. 1921. "Hame'ora'ot Birushalayim." *Ha'aretz*, Feb. 24.

Smilansky, Moshe. 1936a. "Leshe'elot Eretz Yisra'el." P. 1ff. in Moshe Smilansky. *Kitvei Smilansky*, vol. 11. Hitahdut Ha'ikarim.

Smilansky, Moshe. 1936b. "Hatziyonut Hama'asit." P. 36ff. in Moshe Smilansky. *Kitvei Smilansky*, vol. 11. Hitahdut Ha'ikarim.

Smilansky, Yizhar. 1993. "Hu Hayah Savur Shehasofrim Ya'aniku La'am et Hamabat Hahistori." *Iyunim Bitkumat Yisra'el* 3: 1ff.

Soker, Y., and Yitzhak Ivri. 1933. "Im Aliyato Shel Hitler." *Hapo'el Hatza'ir*, May 26.

Stein, Kenneth W. 1984. *The Land Question in Palestine, 1917–1939*. Chapel Hill: University of North Carolina Press.

Stern, Eliahu. 1974. *Khronologiyah Letoldot Hayishuv*. Yad Ben-Zvi.

Sternhell, Ze'ev. 1986. *Binyan Umah o Tikun Hevrah*. Am Oved.

Tamir, Shmuel. 2002. *Ben Ha'aretz Hazot*. Zmora-Bitan.

Tarle, Eugene. 1942. *Napoleon's Invasion of Russia*. New York: Oxford University Press.

Teveth, Shabtai. 1977. *Kinat David*, vol. 1. Schocken.

Teveth, Shabtai. 1980. *Kinat David*, vol. 2. Schocken.

Teveth, Shabtai. 1982. *Retzah Arlosoroff*. Schocken.

Teveth, Shabtai. 1985. *Ben-Gurion Ve'arviyei Yisra'el*. Schocken.

Teveth, Shabtai. 1987a. *Ben-Gurion: The Burning Ground, 1886–1948*. Boston: Houghton Mifflin.

Teveth, Shabtai. 1987b. *Kinat David*, vol. 3. Schocken.

Teveth, Shabtai. 1992. *Onat Hagez Vekalban*. Ish Dor.

Teveth, Shabtai. 1999. *Hashanim Hane'elamot*. Dvir.

Teveth, Shabtai. 2004. *Kinat David*, vol. 4. Schocken.

Toeplitz, Uri. 1992. *Sipurah shel Hatizmoret Hafilharmonit*. Sifriyat Poalim.

Tohn, Yehoshua. 1911. "Mesirut Nefesh." P. 17ff. in *Yizkor*. No publisher.

Tomaszewski, Jerzy. 2001. "Hayehudim Bemeshek Polin." P. 415ff. in Israel Bartal and Israel Gutman, eds. *Kiyum Veshever*. Merkaz Shalman Shazar. Vol. 1.

Toubi, Ya'akov. 2001. "Mediniyut Yisra'el klapei Retzu'at Azah." *Jama'ah* 7: 9ff.

Toubi, Ya'akov. 2003. "David Ben-Gurion, Moshe Sharett, Vesugiyat Ma'amadah shel Retzu'at Azah." *Iyunim Bitkumat Yisra'el* 13: 139ff.

Tsoref, Haggai, ed. 1998. *Yitzhak Ben-Zvi*. Israel State Archives.

Tsur, Muki, ed. 1998. *Im Einech Bodedah*. Hakibbutz Hameuhad.

Tsur, Ya'akov. 1968. *Yoman Paris*. Am Oved.

Tuchman, Barbara W. 1981. "The Assimilationist Dilemma: Ambassador Morgenthau's Story." P. 208ff. in Barbara Tuchman. *Practicing History*. New York: Knopf.

Turel, Sarah. 2006. *Gilguleha shel Utopia*. Eretz Israel Museum.

Turgan, Sagi. 2015. "Kur Hahituh." P. 332 in Alon Kadish, ed. *Tashah Ve'eilah*. Modan.

Twenty-Second Zionist Congress. 1947. *Din Veheshbon Stenografi*. Zionist Organization Executive.

Tzachor, Ze'ev. 1981. *Baderech Lehanagat Hayishuv*. Yad Ben-Zvi.

Tzachor, Ze'ev. 1990. "Va'adat Habirur Livdikat Hakibbutz Hahasha'i." *Cathedra* 58 (Dec.): 128ff.

Tzachor, Ze'ev. 1994. *Hehazon Vehaheshbon*. Yediot Aharonot.

Ury, Scott. 2012. "Yehudim Tze'irim, Arim Gedolot." *Zemanim* 119 (Summer): 58ff.

Ussishkin, Menachem. 1934. *Sefer Ussishkin*. Hava'ad Lehotza'at Hasfer.

Verses, Shmuel. 2001. "Hasifrut Ha'ivrit BePolin." P. 151ff. in Israel Bartal and Israel Gutman, eds. *Kiyum Vashever*. Merkaz Zalman Shazar. Vol. 1.

Vester, Valentine, ed. 2008. *The American Family Album*. Jerusalem: The American Colony.

Watts, Lawrence D. 1942. "A District Governor in Palestine." *The Rotarian* (Dec.): 41ff.

Weisgal, Meyer. 1971. *So Far*. New York: Random House.

Weitz, Yechiam. 1980. "She'erit Hapletah." *Yalkut Moreshet* 19 (May): 53ff.

Weitz, Yechiam. 2001. "Hapredah Meha'av Hameyased." P. 73ff. in Anita Shapira, ed. *Medinah Baderech*. Merkaz Zalman Shazar.

Weitz, Yechiam. 2007. "Moshe Sharett Vaheskem Hashilumim." P. 11 in Ya'akov Sharett, ed. *Pulmus Hashilumim*. Ha'amutah Lemoreshet Moshe Sharett.

Weitz, Yechiam. 2012. *Bein Jabotinsky LiMenachem Begin*. Magnes.

Weitz, Yechiam. 2014a. "Pinhas Lavon Bazirah Hapolitit." *Iyunim Bitkumat Yisra'el* 24: 332ff.

Weitz, Yechiam. 2014b. "Shnei Turim, Shnei Panim." *Cathedra* 152 (July): 111ff.

Weitz, Yechiam. 2015. "Why Was Moshe Sharett Deposed?" *Israel Studies* 20(3): 131ff.

Weizmann, Chaim. 1937. *Devarim*. Mitzpeh.

Weizmann, Chaim. 1942. "Palestine's Role in the Solution of the Jewish Problem." *Foreign Affairs* 20(2) (Jan.): 324ff.

Weizmann, Chaim. 1949. *Trial and Error*. Philadelphia: Jewish Publication Society of America. Vol. 2.

Whartman, Eliezer. 1961. *Ra'ayonot im Hotmei Megilat Ha'atzma'ut*. Self-published.

Witztum, Eliezer, and Moshe Kalian. 2013. *Yerushalayim shel Kedushah*. Henry Near.

Wolfensohn, Avraham. 2014. *Ben-Gurion Ba'asor Ha'aharon Lehayav*. Self-published.

Yaari, Avraham, ed. 1974. *Zichronot Eretz-Yisra'el*. Masada.

Yanait Ben-Zvi, Rachel. 1962. *Anu Olim*. Am Oved.

Yanait Ben-Zvi, Rachel. 1976. *Manya Shochat*. Yad Ben-Zvi.

Yankelevitch, Esti. 2001. "David Hayim: Hapakid she-'Ne'elam,' Vehakamat Havat Hahachsharah BeSejera." *Cathedra* 98 (Jan.): 97ff.

Yatziv, Y. 1963. "Avigdor Gruen." P. 235 in Shlomo Zemach, ed. *Sefer Płońsk Uvnoteha*. Irgun Yotzei Płońsk.

Yegar, Moshe. 2011. *Toldot Hamahlakah Hamedinit*. Hasifriyah Hatziyonit.

Yehoshua, Ya'akov. 1971. *Yaldut Birushalayim Hayeshanah*. Reuven Mas.

Yisraeli, Haim. 2005. *Megilat Haim*. Yediot Aharonot.

Yogev, Gedalia, and Yehoshua Freundlich, eds. 1984. *Haprotokolim shel Hava'ad Hapo'el Hatziyoni*. Hasifriyah Hatziyonit.

Yogev, Gedalia, ed. 1979. *Te'udot Mediniyot Vediplomatiyot*. Israel State Archives and Central Zionist Archives.

Yosef, Dov. 1975. *Yonah Vaherev*. Masada.

Yosifon, Yechezkel. 1963. "Hashevitah Harishonah BeWarsaw." P. 197ff. in Shlomo Zemach, ed. *Sefer Płońsk Uvnoteha*. Irgun Yotzei Płońsk.

Yozgof-Orbach, Nicola, and Arnon Soffer. 2016. *Bein Yihud Le'ibud Hagalil*. Chaikin Cathedra for Geostrategy, University of Haifa.

Yustus, H. 1963. "Hashtikah Hamahridah." *Ma'ariv*, March 22.

Zalkin, Mordechai. 2001. "Hahaskalah Hayehudit BePolin." P. 391ff. in Israel Bartal and Israel Gutman, eds. *Kiyum Vashever*. Merkaz Shalman Shazar. Vol. 2.

Zameret, Zvi. 1997. *Al Gesher Tzar*. Ben-Gurion Heritage Center.

Zariz, Ruth. 1990. "Berthold Storfer." P. 124ff. in Anita Shapira, ed. *Haha'apalah*. Tel Aviv University and Am Oved.

Zeira, Shlomo. 1960. *Ha'atom Besherut Ha'adam*. Amihai.

Zeira, Yosef. In process. *Kakalat Yisra'el.*

Zemach, Shlomo, ed. 1963c. *Sefer Płońsk Uvnoteha.* Irgun Yotzei Płońsk.

Zemach, Shlomo. 1947. "Kishlono Shel Mi?" *Ha'aretz*, March 14.

Zemach, Shlomo. 1963a. "Hahasidut BePłońsk." P. 24ff. in Shlomo Zemach, ed. *Sefer Płońsk Uvnoteha.* Irgun Yotzei Płońsk.

Zemach, Shlomo. 1963b. "Ha'arachah Lehevrat Dorshei Hatorah Vehahochma, May 1867." P. 228 in Shlomo Zemach, ed. *Sefer Płońsk Uvnoteha.* Irgun Yotzei Płońsk.

Zemach, Shlomo. 1965. *Shanah Rishonah.* Am Oved.

Zemach, Shlomo. 1983. *Sipur Hayai.* Dvir.

Zemach, Shlomo. 1996. *Pinkasei Reshimot.* Am Oved.

Zertal, Idith. 1990. "Bein Musar Lepolitikah." P. 87ff. in Anita Shapira, ed. *Haha'apalah.* Tel Aviv University and Am Oved.

Zerubavel, Ya'akov. 1953. "Miyemei Habereshit shel Ha'itonut Hasotziyalistit Be'eretz-Yisra'el." *Al Hamishmar*, July 31.

Zerubavel, Ya'akov, Yitzhak Ben-Zvi, and Alexander Chashin, eds. 1916. *Yizkor.* Poaley Tsien Palestine Komitet.

Ziv, Aryeh. 1961. *1958–1961: Yoman Iruei Shalosh Hashanim.* Ha'aretz.

Zoref, Efraim. 1964–65. *Gal-ed: Memorial Book to the Community of Racionz.* Ha-Irgun shel Ole Ratsyonz.

Zweig, Ronald, ed. 1991. *David Ben-Gurion: Politics and Leadership in Israel.* London: F. Cass.

Zweig, Stefan. 2012. *Ha'olam Shel Etmol.* Mahbarot Lesifrut.

ACKNOWLEDGMENTS

None of my previous books gave me the privilege of benefiting from the assistance of as many people as this one has; my gratitude is unbounded. Several biographers have taken up the task of diving into the sea of written material that David Ben-Gurion produced; I am indebted, first of all, to my predecessors. Neither could I have written this book without the hundreds of books and articles produced by scholars, which together constitute an admirable historiographical enterprise.

I owe thanks to a long list of historical archives, most of them in Israel. Unfortunately, Israel's official archives still operate under regulations that prevent them from opening for research a large part of the material they possess. In many cases, this material contains nothing detrimental to national security; at the very worst it might cast the country's history in a somewhat unfavorable light. Some of the material is forbidden for publication on order of the military censor and some is ostensibly confidential for reasons of privacy.

Nevertheless, the staff at every one of the archives I approached was willing and eager to assist and offered courteous service. First and foremost, I want to thank the Ben-Gurion Archives at Sde Boker. Aside from preserving his papers, the staff has also interviewed a long list of people who knew him. The result is a collection of vast importance, produced by, among others, Yigal Donyetz and Gershon Rivlin. Furthermore, the valuable material that served Ben-Gurion's biographer Shabtai Teveth is also available there. I also wish to express my appreciation for the Israel State Archives, the Central Zionist Archives, the Labor Movement Archives at the Pinhas Lavon Institute, the Moshe Sharett Israel Labor Party Archives, the Moshe Sharett Heritage Institute Archive, the Yitzhak Navon Archive, the Yad Yaari Research and Documentation Center, the Yad Tabenkin Archives, the Jabotinsky Institute Archives, the Menachem Begin Heritage Center Archives, the Ariel Sharon Archive, the Knesset Archives, the Israel Defense Forces Archives, the Haganah Historical Archives, the Central Archives for the History of the Jewish People, the Yad Vashem Archives, the Weizmann Archives, the Beit Hashomer Archives, the Haifa Municipal Archives, the Gan Shmuel Archive, the Degania Alef Archive, the Kfar Giladi Archive, the Kibbutz Ravid Archive, the Gnazim Archive of Hebrew Writers, the Felicja Blumental Archive, the Israel Museum of Comics, Ben-Gurion House, and the University of Haifa's Younes and Soraya Nazarian Library. I also received assistance at the Israel National Library's Manuscript Department and the interview collection of the Hebrew University of Jerusalem's Leonard Davis Institute of International Relations and Avraham Harman Institute of Contemporary Jewry. The Israel National Library and Tel Aviv University's Sourasky Central Library also maintain the Historical Jewish Press website. Other Internet sites were of great assistance as well, Wikipedia included.

I also owe thanks to the National Archives of the United Kingdom, the United States, and Germany. In New York, I benefited from the JDC Archives, the archive of the *Forverts* newspaper, and the New York Public Library. The John F. Kennedy Presidential Library and Museum in Boston and the Institute of Contemporary History in Munich were of assistance too. It was a special pleasure to visit the municipal archives of Płońsk, the city where Ben-Gurion was born, where his memory is preserved with touching care.

❖

During the course of my research, I discovered, to my surprise, that private individuals still possess letters and photographs from Ben-Gurion's life that are not in the possession of the archives. Neta Sivan of Kibbutz Gan Shmuel showed me a postcard that Ben-Gurion sent to her grandmother Rachel Beit Halahmi. It was sent from Istanbul more than a hundred years ago, and the stamps and postmarks of the Austrian Imperial Post, which conveyed it to its destination, are whole and clear. When she allowed me to take it into my hands, I felt a shiver of emotion. I want to thank Erez Navon, the son of Israel's fifth president, Yitzhak Navon, who was so good as to make parts of his father's diary available to me, and to Gilad Sharon, Ariel Sharon's son, who provided me with documents from the period of his father's service in the Israel Defense Forces. Yoram Verete allowed me to quote from previously unknown letters written by his grandfather Shlomo Zemach. David Harman provided me with a series of interviews with his father, who served as Israel's ambassador to the United States; Goni Rivlin-Tsur made available the papers of her father, who among other things edited Ben-Gurion's diaries. Nava Eisen allowed me to examine the papers of her aunt, Rivka Katznelson.

Beyond documentation, I was also fortunate to receive the assistance of countless people who responded to questions, and in some cases took part in my detective work, helping me puzzle out mysterious parts of Ben-Gurion's life. Many of them are university faculty members and researchers in Israel and other countries. I am most appreciative of their expertise, generosity, and, in particular, patience: Gur Alroey, Avraham Avi-hai, Uri Avneri, Uriel Bachrach, Yitzhak Clinton Bailey, Oren Baratz, Mordechai Bar-On, Yossi Ben-Artzi, Yuval Ben-Bassat, Yariv Ben-Eliezer, Daniel Blatman, Avner Cohen, Rachel Elior, Eben Fox, Osnat Gavrieli, Shlomo Gazit, Ralph Goldman, Haim Gouri, Ze'ev Gris, Eliyahu Hacohen, Michael Keren, David Kroyanker, Dan Laor, Werner Lott, Uri Lubrani, Hannah Meisel, Gabriel Moked, Shlomo Nakdimon, Shimon Peres, Yoel Peretz, Hannah Pollak, Adam Raz, Edna and Dorit Raz, Jehuda Reinharz, Rubik Rosenthal, Dov

Tamari, Naly Thaler, Shoshana and Dan Vardinon, Ruth Wisse, Avraham Wolfensohn, and Yosef Zeira.

Aryeh Dayan took part in my archival research; in addition to locating documents, he helped me understand them. Haim Watzman, who translated the book into English, and Ruth Achlama, who translated it into German, saved me from falling into a number of potholes.

As I finalized the manuscript, I benefited from hearing the opinions of dear friends who helped me understand, finally, what I in fact wanted to say: Nahum Barnea, Yechiam Weitz, and Avraham Kushnir. Avi Katzman edited the book with wisdom, care, and inspiration.

As with all my books, it is my pleasure to thank Deborah Harris, agent and friend.

TOM SEGEV
segevtom2@gmail.com

INDEX

A NOTE ABOUT THE AUTHOR

Tom Segev is one of Israel's leading journalists and historians. His works include *The Seventh Million*; *1967: Israel, the War, and the Year That Transformed the Middle East*; *Simon Wiesenthal*; and *One Palestine, Complete* (chosen as one of the ten best books of 2000 by *The New York Times*).

A NOTE ABOUT THE TRANSLATOR

Haim Watzman is a Jerusalem-based writer, journalist, and translator. He is the author, most recently, of *Necessary Stories*, a collection of short fiction. His previous books are *Company C: An American's Life as a Citizen-Soldier in Israel* and *A Crack in the Earth: A Journey up Israel's Rift Valley*.